Tolley's

Manual of Accounting

Published by
Tolley Publishing Company Limited
Tolley House
2 Addiscombe Road
Croydon Surrey CR9 5AF England
081-6869141

Typeset by Tek-Art (Typesetting) Ltd, Kent

Printed and bound in Great Britain by
Mackays of Chatham PLC, Chatham, Kent

ISBN 0 85459 474-4

FOREWORD

By Peter Morgan
Director General of the Institute of Directors

These is no doubt that the majority of businesses in the UK carry on trade as limited companies, but there are a substantial number of other ways of doing businesses both for gain and for charitable purposes. Such undertakings can have great significance to our economy. The Bank of England and the Church Commissioners are two good examples of this.

Ascertaining which provisions of the Law apply to such undertakings can be a problem. The position becomes more complex when you try to find out what accounting requirements and recommendations apply. Barry Johnson and Matthew Patient must again be congratulated on detailing the applicable accounting and legal requirements for over 26 different types of entity. Their clear explanations of the relevant legislation and of the innumerable other accounting principles and practices adopted by such businesses show their breadth of experience and knowledge in these diverse areas.

The accounting and legal world is becoming more regulated each year and it is difficult for the best of finance directors and accountants to keep abreast of the changes for companies let alone for other legal entities. Consequently, a major work like this is to be commended and the authors informed comment and examples taken from published accounts make what is invariably a dry subject come alive.

Volume III of 'Manual of Accounting' completes the major reference work which encompasses the detailed legal and accounting requirements of companies as well as for other legal entities. The three volumes are an extremely useful comprehensive explanatory text, exploring all aspects of UK GAAP. I am therefore only too pleased to commend it to its readers, as I know they will find it invaluable.

Peter Morgan

April 1991

Acknowledgments

We are gratefull to the following bodies for their pemission to reproduce previously published material:

Institute of Chartered Accountants in England and Wales - annex 1 to chapter 8 - SORP 1 'Pension scheme accounts' and annex 1 to chapter 25 - SORP 2 'Accounting by charities'.

Investment Management Regulatory Organisation - annex 3 to chapter 7 - IMRO SORP 'Authorised Unit Trust Schemes'

British Bankers' Association - annex 2 to chapter 15 - BBA SORP 'Securities'.

Association of British Insurers - annex 2 to chapter 16 - ABI SORP 'Accounting for insurance business'.

The Housing Corporation - annex 2 to chapter 24 - Recommended form of published accounts for housing associations - Association B.

The Law Society - annexes 1 - 4 to chapter 27 - Solicitors' accounts rules 1986, Solicitors' trust account rules 1986, Solicitors' accounts (deposit interest) rules 1988 and Accountant's report rules 1986 (incorporating amendments to 29th April 1988).

PREFACE

'Manual of Accounting' is the second (much revised) edition of our very successful book on accounting disclosure and measurement, which was previously entitled 'Accounting Provisions of the Companies Act 1985'. This time, we have published in three volumes. The first two volumes cover similar material to that dealt with in our previous edition, but much expanded. Volume I looks primarily at individual companies, whereas volume II deals with groups (and includes many of the provisions that stem from the Companies Act 1989). Volume III considers the varied accounting and disclosure requirements that apply to a number of specialised businesses.

Both volumes I and II detail explanations of the accounting provisions of the Companies Acts 1985 and 1989. They also refer throughout to the additional reporting requirements that limited companies have to comply with and that are set out in Statements of Standard Accounting Practice (including exposure drafts) and The International Stock Exchange's Continuing Obligations for listed companies and its General Undertaking for USM companies. The text of volumes I and II includes worked examples and extracts from published financial statements. The financial reporting provisions and Schedules to the Companies Act 1985 (as amended by the Companies Act 1989) are reproduced in the two volumes. The appendices include detailed checklists to those disclosure requirements that apply to company's and to group's financial statements and volume I includes a model set of financial statements.

Volume III is an introduction to the accounting requirements of a number of specialised businesses such as friendly societies, unlimited companies and banking companies. It considers how such entities are incorporated, the different statutes and regulations that apply to them, their filing responsibilities, the accounting requirements that apply to their financial statements and any requirements for audit. The annexes to each chapter also reproduce accounting regulations included in, for example, Statutory Instruments and Statements of Recommended Practice. Model sets of financial statements and extracts from published financial statements are also given.

The three volumes of 'Manual of Accounting' also include practical advice and comment we have gained through our work for the Technical Support Section of Coopers & Lybrand Deloitte in advising the Firm's clients, partners and staff.

We hope that finance directors, accountants, legal practitioners company administrators, financial advisers and auditors will find this manual useful.

We wish to thank a number of people for their contributions to volume III of the 'Manual of Accounting'. We thank Rex de Saram for his work in editing the text, Stephen Copp for much of the original work on the book and Gan Fan Choo for her work in checking some of the text. We also thank the following people for their efforts on particular chapters: Elizabeth Cathro and Christine Hayward - Unit Trusts; Hans Nailor and David Pimm - Pension schemes; Jyoti Ghosh - Banking companies and Investment companies and approved investment trusts; Jyoti Ghosh, Nicola Gale and her team - Insurance companies; Harry Venet - Building Societies; Geoff Swales - Housing Associations; David Wylie - Charities; Peter Milroy - Investment businesses; and Geoff Ashcroft - Solicitors.

Barry Johnson & Matthew Patient

Coopers & Lybrand Deloitte
London
April 1991

CONTENTS

Paragraph

6. Trusts

7. Unit trusts

Paragraph

Paragraph

ABBREVIATIONS AND TERMS USED

Statutes

AEA 1925	Administration of Estates Act 1925
BNA 1985	Business Names Act 1985
BA 1987	Banking Act 1987
BSA 1986	Building Societies Act 1986
CA 1985	Companies Act 1985 (as amended by the Companies Act 1989)
CA 1989	Companies Act 1989
CCA 1837	Chartered Companies Act 1837
CCCA 1845 & 1888	Companies Clauses Consolidation Act 1845 & 1888
ChA 1960	Charities Act 1960
CUA 1979	Credit Unions Act 1979
EA 1988	Employment Act 1988
EPA 1975	Employment Protection Act 1975
FA 1889	Factors Act 1889
FIPSA 1968	Friendly and Industrial and Provident Societies Act 1968
FSA 1974	Friendly Societies Act 1974
FSA 1986	Financial Services Act 1986
HA 1988	Housing Act 1988
HAA 1985	Housing Associations Act 1985 (as amended by the Housing Act 1988)
IAA 1923	Industrial Assurance Act 1923
ICA 1982	Insurance Companies Act 1982
IPSA 1965	Industrial and Provident Societies Act 1965
IPSA 1975	Industrial and Provident Societies Act 1975
IPSA 1978	Industrial and Provident Societies Act 1978
Ltd PA 1907	Limited Partnerships Act 1907
LPA 1925	Law of Property Act 1925
NAA 1948	National Assistance Act 1948
PA 1890	Partnership Act 1890
PTA 1906	Public Trustee Act 1906
SSPA 1975	Social Security Pensions Act 1975
TA 1925	Trustee Act 1925
TIA 1961	Trustee Investments Act 1961
TUA 1913	Trade Union Act 1913
TUA 1984	Trade Union Act 1984
TULRA 1974	Trade Union and Labour Relations Act 1974
WA 1837	Wills Act 1837
WCA 1940	War Charities Act 1940

Statutory Instruments

1940/1533	War Charities Regulations 1940
1960/2425	The Charities (Statements of Account) Regulations 1960
1968/1222	The Partnership (Unrestricted Size) No. 1 Regulations 1968
1969/1037	Industrial and Provident Societies (Group Accounts) Regulations 1969
1970/835	The Partnership (Unrestricted Size) No. 2 Regulations 1970
1970/992	The Partnership (Unrestricted Size) No. 3 Regulations 1970
1970/1319	The Partnership (Unrestricted Size) No. 4 Regulations 1970
1981/394	Industrial and Provident Societies (Increases in Deposit Taking Limits) Order 1981
1981/395	Industrial and Provident Societies (Increase in Shareholding Limits) Order 1981
1981/1654	Insurance Companies Regulations 1981
1982/530	The Partnership (Unrestricted Size) No. 5 Regulations 1982
1983/1811	Insurance Companies (Accounts and Statements) Regulations 1983
1985/680	Companies (Unregistered Companies) Regulations 1985 (as amended by SIs 1990/438,1990/1394 and 1990/2571)
1986/1046	Occupational Pension Schemes (Disclosure of Information) Regulations 1986
1987/1102	Occupational Pension Schemes (Auditors) Regulations 1987
1987/1105	The Occupational Pension Schemes (Disclosure of Information) (Amendment) Regulations 1987
1987/2072	Building Societies (Accounts and Related Provisions) Regulations 1987
1988/280	Authorised Unit Trust Scheme (Pricing of Units and Dealings by Trustees and Managers) Regulations 1988
1988/395	Registered Housing Associations (Accounting Requirements) Order 1988 (as amended by SI 1989/327)
1990/440	The Oversea Companies (Accounts) (Modifications and other Exemptions) Order 1990
1990/1580	The Limited Partnership (Unrestricted Size) No 2 Regulations 1990
1990/1581	The Partnership (Unrestricted Size) No. 6 Regulations 1990
1990/1969	The Partnership (Unrestricted Size) No. 7 Regulations 1990

Other abbreviations

ABI	Association of British Insurers
AC	Law Reports, Appeal Cases
ACAS	Advisory, Conciliation and Arbitration Service
accounts	Financial statements
AFBD	Association of Future Brokers and Dealers
AG	Auditing Guidelines (section of ICAEW members' handbook)
ALL ER	All England Law Reports
APC	Auditing Practices Committee
AR	Accounting recommendation (section of ICAEW members' handbook)
ARR	Accountants' Report Rules 1986 (issued by the Law Society)
AR(A)R	Accountants' Report Amendment Rules 1988 (issued by the Law Society)
ASB	Accounting Standards Board
ASC	Accounting Standards Committee
AVC	Additional Voluntary Contributions
BBA	British Bankers' Association
BCLC	Butterworth's Company Law Cases
BSC	Building Societies Commission
CCAB	Consultative Committee of Accountancy Bodies Limited
Ch	Law Reports, Chancery Division
chapter (1)	'Manual of accounting - specialised businesses volume III, chapter (1)
CIU	Clubs and Institute Union
CIUTS	Collective Investment Undertakings for Transferable Securities
CIS	Collective Investment Scheme
CO	Continuing Obligations, Section 5 of The International Stock Exchange's 'Admission of Securities to Listing'
DSS	Department of Social Security
DTI	Department of Trade and Industry
EC	European Community
ED	Exposure draft
ed	Edition
EEC	European Economic Community
ER	English Reports
FIMBRA	Financial Intermediaries, Managers and Brokers Regulatory Association

GAAP	Generally accepted accounting principles
GB	Great Britain
GU	The International Stock Exchange's General Undertaking of the Unlisted Securities Market
HAG	Housing Association grants
HDG	Hostel deficit grants
IAS	International Accounting Standard
IASC	International Accounting Standards Committee
IBNR	Icurred but not reported
IBRC	Insurance Brokers Registration Council
ICAEW	Institute of Chartered Accountants in England and Wales
IMRO	Investment Management Regulatory Organisation
LAUTRO	Life Assurance and Unit Trust Regulatory Organisation
LUTIRO	Life and Unit Trust Intermediaries Regulatory Organisation
LT	The Law Times Reports
MH	ICAEW members' handbook
NASDAQ	National Association of Securities Dealers Automated Quotation System
NASDIM	National Association of Securities Dealers and Investment Managers
NCVO	National Council of Voluntary Organisations
NFHA	National Federation of Housing Associations
NI	National Insurance
OPB	Occupational Pensions Board
para(s)	Paragraph(s) of Schedules to Acts, or SSAPs, or SORPs, or EDs, or Regulations, or text
PAYE	Pay as you earn
pg	Page
QBD	Law Reports, Queens Bench Division
reg	Regulation
RDG	Revenue deficit grants
RPB	Recognised Professional Body
SA(DI)R	Solicitors' Accounts (Deposit Interest) Rules 1988 (issued by the Law Society)

SAR	Solicitors' Accounts Rules 1986 (issued by the Law Society)
SC	Session Cases
Sch	Schedule of the (for example, Companies Act 1985)
Sec(s)	Section(s)
SERPs	State Earnings Related Pension Scheme
SFO	Superannuation Funds Office of the Inland Revenue
SI	Statutory Instrument
SIB	The Securities and Investment Board
SIBR	Solicitors' Investment Business Rules 1990 (issued by the Law Society)
SICAV	Societe d'Investissement a Capitale Variable
SOGAT	Society of Graphical and Allied Trades
SORP	Statement of Recommended Accounting Practice
SRO	Self regulatory bodies
SSAP	Statement of Standard Accounting Practice
STAR	Solicitors' Trust Accounts Rules 1986 (issued by the Law Society)
Times	The Times Law Reports
TR	Technical release
TSA	The Securities Association
TUC	Trade Union Congress
UCITS	Undertakings for Collective Investments in Transferable Securities - EC directive (85/611/EEC)
UK	United Kingdom
US	United States of America
USM	Unlisted Securities Market
UTA	Unit Trust Association
VAT	Value Added Tax
WLR	Weekly Law Reports
Yellow book	The International Stock Exchange's 'Admission of Securities to Listing'

Chapter 1

INTRODUCTION

Chapter 1

INTRODUCTION

Chapter 1

INTRODUCTION

Manual of accounting

1.1 This volume of the 'Manual of Accounting' is the third of three volumes covering many aspects of accounting in the United Kingdom (UK). The books not only cover the accounting provisions included in company law, but also deal with other accounting principles and practices that concern each different entity considered. Each volume covers different aspects of accounting in the UK and their titles are as follows:

- Manual of Accounting - volume I - Companies.
- Manual of Accounting - volume II - Groups.
- Manual of Accounting - volume III - Specialised businesses.

1.2 This volume of the 'Manual of Accounting' deals with a considerable variety of undertakings that have evolved to carry on business. Many of these undertakings have been developed to meet the needs of the changing business world, whilst many others exist for non-profit making purposes.

1.3 Volume I of the 'Manual of Accounting' looks in depth at the accounting requirements with which limited companies (including both public and private companies) have to comply. It also explains the special rules that apply to small and medium-sized companies and to dormant companies.

1.4 Volume II of the 'Manual of Accounting' considers in detail the requirements for consolidated financial statements that are included in the *Companies Act 1989* and other generally accepted accounting practices.

Scope of this book

1.5 Many of the businesses considered in this book have evolved over a substantial number of years from legislation that in some cases dates back to the 1830s. This book brings together for many different types of specialised business basic details about their constitution and summarises the accounting and auditing requirements that apply to them. However, it is not possible to cover all aspects of these specialised businesses in this book and, consequently, reference is made also to other texts.

1.6 Although this volume considers the many different types of specialised businesses that exist to carry on trade, it does not consider (except by way of example) individual bodies that have been established by particular legislation (such as The International Stock Exchange, or the Church Commissioners).

1.7 The book is split into three parts. Part I considers a number of ways of doing business as an unincorporated undertaking. Part II looks at a number of specialised corporate businesses (some of which are incorporated under the *Companies Act 1985*) where the accounting regulations that apply to the business differ from those that apply normally to companies incorporated under the *Companies Act 1985*. Part III looks at certain entities which may be incorporated businesses or unincorporated businesses that have been formed for a special purpose and as such have additional obligations placed on them.

1.8 In most instances, for each particular business in the chapters of this Manual the following information is given:

- Its regulatory framework and legal background.
- Brief details of its formation and its constitution.
- The benefits and responsibilities of its particular legal form.
- Its duty to keep accounting records.
- Its duty to establish and maintain systems of control.
- Its duty to prepare financial statements including consolidated financial statements.
- Additional disclosure information that has to be given.
- Any special accounting requirements that apply.
- Its duty to submit an annual return.
- Any unusual requirements (for example, to obtain an actuarial valuation of its assets and liabilities).
- Appointment of auditors.
- Any special auditing requirements.
- A specimen unqualified audit report.

The regulatory framework

1.9 Reference is made throughout this book to the different sources of regulatory framework that govern particular businesses. Some of the requirements laid down by the regulatory framework are mandatory, whereas others constitute best practice only. Summarised in the rest of this chapter are the various pronouncements that regulate specialised businesses and have an impact on how they should be accounted for and audited. It should be remembered when reading this book that the regulatory framework and accounting practices for many of the entities discussed are still evolving and can change relatively quickly. We have endeavoured to ensure that the content is up to date at the date of publication and have indicated where possible any changes that are in progress. However, before relying on any of the information contained in the chapters it is advisable to ascertain whether regulations or accounting pronouncements concerning the entity have changed since publication.

European Community company law harmonisation

1.10 The European Community (EC) is becoming the main driving force in the development of regulations that govern many different types of businesses. The reason for this is the programme to harmonise legal requirements in member states. Where there are different legal requirements between member states, this can act as a barrier to establishing a true 'common market' for goods and services. The process of creating laws in the EC is complicated. There are various types of EC legislation such as regulations, decisions and recommendations. These different types of legislation affect member states in different ways. However, the most important rules come in the form of directives.

1.11 As soon as a directive is enacted and comes into force, it binds member states to introduce legislation to implement it. Directives are intended to achieve a particular result and, accordingly, the form and method of implementation is left to the member state concerned. Where a member state fails to pass appropriate legislation, it can be taken to the European Court of Justice for failure to fulfil its obligations under the Treaty of Rome. Where a member state has introduced legislation that, on close scrutiny, may not implement a particular directive precisely, it may be necessary to look to the directive to interpret the national law.

1.12 By 1991, the UK had included a substantial number of EC Directives on its statute books. The major directives included in UK company legislation are as follows:

- 1st Directive - Nullity.
- 2nd Directive - Formation of companies and dividend requirements.
- 3rd Directive - Mergers.
- 4th Directive - Company accounts.
- Directive on listing particulars.
- Directive on continuing disclosure of information.
- 6th Directive - 'Scissions'.
- 7th Directive - Group accounts.
- 8th Directive - Auditors.

1.13 A summary of EC company law directives and their status is given in 'Manual of Accounting - volume I' appendix III. That appendix also indicates where the directives mentioned above are enacted in UK company law.

1.14 The EC company law harmonisation programme is still far from complete and will continue for many years. For example, the directive on the annual accounts and consolidated accounts of banks and other financial institutions (86/635/EEC) was adopted in December 1986 and member states were required to introduce it into national law by 31st December 1990 (although it need only apply to financial statements beginning on or after 1st January 1993). This particular directive has been reproduced as an annex 3 to chapter 15 on banking companies. Other directives concerning specialised businesses exist or are still being drafted and, where applicable, these are referred to in the text of this book.

The Companies Act 1989

1.15 The *Companies Act 1989* received Royal Assent on 16th November 1989. A major proportion of that Act implements the 7th and 8th EC Directives. In addition, there were a number of changes made to accounting provision already dealt with in the *Companies Act 1985*. The *Companies Act 1989* also amended other statutes including, the *Fair Trading Act 1973* and the *Financial Services Act 1986*.

1.16 In order to make the changes to the accounting provisions required to comply with the 7th Directive, Parliament has in Part I of the *Companies Act 1989* effectively re-enacted Part VII of the *Companies Act 1985*. Most of the changes to the *Companies Act 1985* are of a minor nature and do not alter greatly existing law, but a few other amendments do introduce substantial changes. These changes and the new provisions are dealt with in depth in 'Manual of Accounting - volumes I and II'.

The accounting provisions of the Companies Act 1985

1.17 Many of the undertakings considered in this 'Manual of Accounting' are subject to certain provisions of the *Companies Acts 1985 and 1989*. Consequently, throughout this manual reference is made to the *Companies Act 1985*. As explained above, all of the accounting provisions included in the *Companies Act 1989* are substitutions and amendments to the *Companies Act 1985*. The *Companies Act 1985* is split into 27 parts. A summary of these together with the arrangements of sections found in that Act is given on pages 933 to 956. Pages 957 to 1097 reproduce the provisions of the *Companies Act 1985* that relate to the different undertakings that are considered in this volume. The reproduction is a consolidated version of the *Companies Act 1985* as amended by the *Companies Act 1989*. Volumes I and II of the 'Manual of Accounting' also reproduce parts of the *Companies Act 1985* that are relevant to the accounting provisions considered in those volumes. Reproduced as an annex to certain chapters is a listing of the sections of the *Companies Act 1985* that apply to the particular business entity.

Other relevant legislation

1.18 Although companies are primarily regulated by the *Companies Acts 1985 and 1989*, there is a whole host of other legislation that affects businesses that are set up to trade in other ways. Some of this legislation may be in the form of Acts of Parliament, but very often the accounting provisions for such businesses are detailed by regulations issued as Statutory Instruments (SIs). In addition, some of the ways such businesses trade have been shaped over many years by common law. Throughout the text, this book refers to relevant legal cases and SIs. Where a particular SI details the accounting rules that apply to such businesses it is reproduced as an annex to the particular chapter.

Other generally accepted accounting principles and practices

1.19 In addition to summarising the accounting provisions included in legislation that apply to specialised businesses, this volume of the 'Manual of Accounting' makes reference to particular accounting standards, exposure drafts and SORPs that might affect the business. Furthermore, mention is made where applicable to The International Stock Exchange's Continuing Obligations (which applies to listed companies) and its General Undertaking (which applies to companies traded on the Unlisted Securities Market (USM)).

1.20 The Accounting Standards Committee (ASC) was set up in January 1970 to develop definitive standards for financial reporting, but ceased this role in August 1990 when this role was taken over by the Accounting Standards Board (ASB). The ASC issued 25 Statements of Standard Accounting Practice (SSAPs), which have subsequently been formally adopted by the ASB. A full list of those SSAPs is given in appendix I.

1.21 The legal status of SSAPs has been subject to some discussion. The ASC obtained Counsel's opinion on the meaning of the term 'true and fair' and the opinion encompassed the interaction between SSAPs and the law. The opinion is reproduced as appendix V to 'Manual of Accounting - volume I'.

1.22 The applicability of certain SSAPs to particular types of specialised business is considered throughout the text. The explanatory foreword to the SSAPs lays down the following general principles:

- SSAPs are applicable to all financial statements whose purpose is to give a true and fair view of a businesses' financial position and profit and loss for the period.

- SSAPs are intended to be applied where financial statements of overseas businesses are incorporated into UK group financial statements (see further 'Manual of Accounting - volume II').

- SSAPs need not be applied to items where the effect of the item is judged to be immaterial to an understanding of the financial statements of the undertaking.

- SSAPs are not intended to be a comprehensive code of rigid rules. A justifiable reason may exist why a SSAP may not be applicable in a given situation (that is, when its application would conflict with giving a true and fair view). In such situations, modified or alternative treatments should be adopted, having regard to the spirit and the reasoning behind the relevant SSAP and to the overriding aim of giving a true and fair view.

- Where SSAPs prescribe specific information to be contained in financial statements, such requirements do not override exemptions from disclosure given by the law governing certain types of entity.

- Significant departures from accounting standards should be disclosed and explained in the financial statements. The financial effects of such departures should be estimated and disclosed, unless this would be impracticable or misleading in the context of giving a true and fair view. If the financial effects of any such departure are not disclosed, the reasons for such non-disclosure should be stated. This provision conforms with the requirement now made in paragraph 36A of Schedule 4 to the *Companies Act 1985*, which requires a statement to be made in a company's financial statements whether those financial statements have been prepared in accordance with applicable accounting standards.

1.23 Statements of Recommended Practice (SORPs) were issued by the ASC when the need was seen for an accounting pronouncement to be made on a specific topic where an accounting standard was not necessary. Although entities are encouraged to comply with SORPs compliance is, unlike with SSAPs, not mandatory.

1.24 Only two SORPs have been issued, which are as follows:

- SORP 1 - Pension scheme accounts (see chapter 8).

- SORP 2 - Accounting by charities (see chapter 25).

1.25 Compliance with the provisions of SORP 1 is, however, effectively required by law (see chapter 8 para 8.67). SORP 1 is reproduced as annex 1 to chapter 8 and SORP 2 is reproduced as annex 2 to chapter 25. The ASB has indicated that it will not issue SORPs.

1.26 Franked SORPs are a sub-category of SORPs. They are intended to relate to topics of limited application, for example, to specific businesses or industries such as the BBA SORP on securities (see chapter 15, the SORP is reproduced as annex 2 to that chapter). Such SORPs were franked (that is approved) by the ASC and published by the industry concerned. Under the ASB, industries will still be able to issue SORPs and these will be reviewed by the ASB to ensure that they do not conflict with standard accounting practice. A list of franked SORPs is given in appendix II.

1.27 Exposure drafts (EDs) are proposed SSAPs and SORPs and are not mandatory, although during exposure they do indicate best accounting practice on the matter concerned. A list of current EDs is given in appendix I and appendix II.

1.28 Certain other guidance referred to in this Manual is contained in the ICAEW's members handbook. The matters mentioned are two Accounting recommendations included in section 2.2 of the Handbook, as follows:

- Trust accounts (see chapter 6).

- Trustee Investments Act 1961 (see chapter 6).

Auditing Standards and Guidelines

1.29 The Auditing Practices Committee (APC) was formed in 1976 to:

- Complete a framework of Auditing Standards and Guidelines on operational and reporting matters applicable generally to audits.
- Develop audit guidelines on specific issues relating to the audit or associated review activities and on particular industry and service groups, as the need arises.

1.30 Auditing Standards are issued by the APC and prescribe the base principles that members of the APC's governing bodies are expected to follow in the conduct of an audit. Unless otherwise stated, they apply whenever an audit is carried out. A full list of Auditing Standards is given in appendix III.

1.31 Auditing Guidelines are also issued by the APC and are intended to amplify the requirements laid down in auditing standards. They give guidance on:

- Procedures by which auditing standards may be applied.
- The application of Auditing Standards to specific items appearing in the financial statements of enterprises.
- Audit problems relating to particular industries and service organisations.

1.32 A full list of Auditing Guidelines is given in appendix III. Auditing Guidelines are particularly relevant to some of the businesses considered in this book. Those that are mentioned in the text are as follows:

- Auditing Guidelines - Industries.
  - ☐ Charities (see chapter 25).
  - ☐ Building societies in the UK (see chapter 23).
  - ☐ Trade unions and employers' associations (see chapter 10).
  - ☐ Housing associations (see chapter 24).
  - ☐ Pension scheme accounts in the UK (see chapter 8).
  - ☐ Banks in the UK (see chapter 15).

- Auditing Guidelines - other statements.
    - Auditors' reports - registered friendly societies and industrial and provident societies (see chapters 11 and 21).
    - Reports on accounts of sole traders and partnerships (see chapters 2 and 4).
    - General business insurers in the UK (see chapter 16).

Chapter 2

SOLE PROPRIETORS

Chapter 2

SOLE PROPRIETORS

Background

2.1 The simplest method of establishing a business is almost invariably to set up as a sole proprietor. The vast majority of businesses commence life in this way, whether they are industrial, commercial or professional in nature. The reason for this is that the regulatory burden is far lighter on a sole proprietor than it is on a limited company. The following types of sole proprietor are, however, subject to additional regulation:

- Investment businesses (see chapter 26).
- Professional persons, such as solicitors (see chapter 27).

2.2 There are a number of disadvantages of trading as a sole proprietor; the main one being that a sole proprietor is always personally liable for the debts and obligations he incurs. A sole proprietor cannot limit this liability unless he conducts his business as a limited company. A sole proprietor is not as readily accepted by the other businesses he may wish to deal with as a limited company would be. There are not as many ways that a sole proprietor can raise finance as there are for a limited company.

2.3 For many people who start in business as a sole proprietor the main advantage is that their affairs are kept relatively private.

Duty to keep accounting records

2.4 Although there is no statutory obligation on a sole proprietor to keep accounting records, such records are necessary in order to record his trading activities. There are two principal reasons for keeping such records. First, where a sole proprietor's turnover is in excess of certain limits, he will have to register for VAT and keep records that support his VAT returns. Secondly, a sole proprietor will have to make returns of his profits and losses for tax purposes annually to the Inland Revenue.

2.5 A sole proprietor may also have to keep other accounting records, which are governed by other statutes. For example, if the sole proprietor employs staff, then he will have to keep adequate accounting records to satisfy the PAYE and NI regulations.

Duty to prepare financial statements

2.6 There is no general legal obligation on a sole proprietor to prepare financial statements. However, in order to satisfy the Inland Revenue concerning returns of profits and losses, it will be necessary for a sole proprietor to prepare some form of account of his trading.

2.7 Other obligations to prepare financial statements may be placed on sole proprietors by third parties. For example, in order to raise finance for the business a sole proprietor may obtain a loan from a bank. The bank may then make certain stipulations concerning the records that the business should keep and the financial statements that it should prepare. In addition, suppliers may wish to see the sole proprietor's financial statements before entering into business with him.

Audit requirements

2.8 There are no general statutory provisions that require a sole proprietor's financial statements to be audited or filed on public record with a Registrar other than in specific industries where regulations apply (for example, sole proprietors authorised to conduct business under the *Financial Services Act 1986*; see chapter 26). In certain situations third parties, such as banks, may require financial statements of a sole proprietor to be prepared and they may also require those financial statements to be audited. Where this is so, the scope of the audit will be detailed in the engagement letter the auditor agrees with the sole proprietor on accepting the engagement. Furthermore, accountants may be required to report on a proprietor's handling of client money (see for example chapter 27).

2.9 The ICAEW statement on auditing and reporting 'Report on accounts of sole traders and partnerships' (AG 3.917), which was issued in July 1973, provides general guidance relating to reports issued on the financial statements of such entities.

Accountants' report

2.10 Where no audit is necessary, a sole proprietor may still require, for the reasons discussed above, an accountant to prepare financial statements for his business. Where this is so, the ICAEW's Auditing Guideline (AG 3.917) instructs its members to head their report 'Accountants' report' rather than 'Auditors' report' and word it in such a way that the association of their name with the financial statements cannot be misunderstood. This is necessary because without an audit it is not possible for such a report to be given in true and fair terms. Consequently, the report should not include expressions of opinion or disclaim responsibility for particular items.

Where, however, specific checks are requested by the proprietor, it may be necessary to refer to them specifically in the report.

2.11 A suitable accountants' report on the unaudited financial statements of a sole proprietor is given below:

ACCOUNTANTS' REPORT

We have prepared the financial statements on pages [] to [] from the books and records of [name of sole proprietor's business] and from information and explanations supplied to us. We have not carried out an audit [and accordingly do not express an opinion or any other form of assurance on them]*.

*The words within the brackets may be added where it is considered desirable to emphasise that no opinion is being expressed.

2.12 It would also be appropriate for the sole proprietor to approve his financial statements before the accountants' report is signed. Suitable wording for such a declaration would be as follows:

I approve these financial statements and confirm that I have made available all relevant records and information for their preparation.

Audit report

2.13 As explained above, in certain situations it may be necessary for the sole proprietor's financial statements to be audited. An example of an unqualified audit report on the financial statements prepared for a sole proprietor is given below. Often, however, there may be restrictions placed on the work that an auditor carries out on a sole proprietor's books and records. Where this is so, these restrictions would have to be referred to in the audit opinion.

REPORT OF THE AUDITORS TO [NAME OF SOLE PROPRIETOR]

We have audited the financial statements on pages [] to [] in accordance with Auditing Standards.

In our opinion the financial statements give a true and fair view of the state of [name of business] affairs at [date] and of its profit and source and application of funds for the [period] then ended.

[Name of firm]

Chartered Accountants,

[Address].

[Date of report].

Chapter 3

AGENTS

Chapter 3

AGENTS

Introduction

3.1 Agency has been defined as:

> *"The fiduciary relationship which exists between two persons, one of whom expressly or impliedly consents that the other should act on his behalf, and the other of whom similarly consents so to act and so acts. The one on whose behalf the act or acts are to be done is called the principal. The one who is to act is called the agent. Any person other than the principal and the agent may be referred to as a third party."*
>
> [Bowstead 'Law of Agency' (15th ed.) (1985)].

3.2 It can be seen from this definition that agency is a relationship and not a form of business entity. However, agency is one of the more common commercial relationships that exists for carrying on business and carries with it its own accounting responsibilities.

Types of agency

3.3 There are a number of categories of agents that depend on the reason for the agency and whether the existence of the agency is disclosed to persons that deal with it.

General agent

3.4 A general agent is an agent who has the authority to act on behalf of his principal in all matters concerning a particular part of the principal's business, or to act on a specific matter that is in the ordinary course of the agent's business.

Special agent

3.5 A special agent, in contrast to a general agent, has authority only to carry out a specific act for his principal, where that act is not in the ordinary course of the agent's business.

Agent for a disclosed principal

3.6 An agent enters into a contract with a third party and discloses that he is acting for a principal. Consequently, depending upon the circumstances, the name of the principal may or may not be revealed to the third party by the agent.

Agent for an undisclosed principal

3.7 An agent acts for an undisclosed principal when he enters into a contract with a third party, in effect in his own name, without disclosing either the identity of the principal or the existence of the agency to the third party.

Mercantile agent

3.8 A mercantile agent is defined by the *Factors Act 1889* as an agent who has:

> *"...in the customary course of his business as such agent authority either to sell goods, or to consign goods for the purpose of sale, or to buy goods, or to raise money on the security of goods."* [FA 1989 Sec 1(1)].

Del credere agent

3.9 A *del credere* agent is an agent who is employed to sell goods and who promises to indemnify the principal if clients introduced by him to his principal fail to pay for the goods sold. *Del credere* agency has largely been superseded by documentary credits.

Factor

3.10 A factor is a mercantile agent who is employed to sell goods for a commission and will have possession of the goods concerned.

Broker

3.11 A broker is a mercantile agent employed to bring about contracts between other parties for a commission. In contrast to a factor, a broker does not have possession of the goods concerned.

3.12 In practice, the terms 'factor' or '*del credere* agent' are not heard of much nowadays. 'Factor' is still used in other senses, for example that of credit factoring and 'broker' has been applied to many more types of activity, for example insurance brokers, stock brokers, which are also regulated by particular legislation.

Distributors, concessionaires and franchisees

3.13 Distributors, concessionaires or franchisees are generally appointed to receive supplies of a manufacturer's goods in order to sell them to customers. If they buy the goods from the manufacturer, they will not be an agent for this purpose. In this circumstance, it is likely that the terms and conditions of sale will include a reservation of title clause. Distributors, concessionaires or franchisees may, however, be appointed agents for other purposes under the distribution agreement or other agreement with the manufacturer.

Formation of an agency

3.14 The procedure for appointing an agent is very simple. The principal and the agent must both consent to establish a relationship between them. In a commercial context, this consent will often be laid down in writing. However, except in certain specific circumstances, it need not be in writing and the law will imply the formation of an agency from the words and conduct of the parties. In addition, the law will treat one person as the agent of another in the following circumstances.

Agency by ratification

3.15 A principal may ratify the acts of a person who purported to act in his name and on his behalf, but who did not have the actual authority to do so. If ratification takes place, the relationship of agency will be regarded by law as having been 'credited' with the full extent of the ratification retrospectively. However, an undisclosed principal cannot ratify such an act if the agent did not have the appropriate authority at the time the contract was entered into.

Agency of necessity

3.16 The law may, on rare occasions, regard a person as the agent of another in order to empower the agent to take any necessary steps to protect the interest of the other person.

Agency by estoppel

3.17 Some of the consequences of the relationship of agency can arise under the doctrine of 'estoppel'. This may arise where a person, by his words or his conduct, represents (or allows it to be represented) that another person is his agent. In such circumstances, that person (that is, the principal) will not be permitted to deny that the relationship of agency exists where someone who, on the faith of such a representation, deals with the person held out to be the agent.

Legal capacity

3.18 A fundamental requirement for establishing an agency is that both the principal and the agent must have legal capacity to be a principal and to be an agent respectively. Where they are both limited companies, this will in general mean that they should have the capacity to act as such under their memorandum or articles of association.

Authority

3.19 A principal's capacity to contract or do any other act by means of a duly authorised agent is an extension of his own capacity to enter a contract or perform a certain act and he can sue and be sued under such a contract. An agent must act within the authority given to him by his principal. The acts the agent can do on his principal's behalf should be clearly defined in the agency agreement, as an agent will be personally liable on a contract he enters into which is outside the terms of his agency.

3.20 The following people will not generally be able to act as agents:

- Minors.
- Insane persons.

Duty to keep accounting records

3.21 An agent has a duty under common law to keep an accurate account of all transactions that he enters into on his principal's behalf. [*Chedworth (Lord) v Edwards (1802) 8 Ves 46*]. This account of transactions must be available at all times in order that it can be produced to the principal. [*Pearse v Green (1819) 1 Jac & W 135*]. An agent is not, however, under an obligation to produce to his principal records of transactions that do not concern the principal. [*Gerard v Penswick (1818) 1 Swan 553*].

3.22 In the event of a dispute between the agent and the principal where the agent fails to maintain adequate accounting records, the courts will presume the most unfavourable position possible consistent with the rest of the proven facts. [*Gray v Haig (1855) 20 Beav 219*]. In addition, an agent must maintain accounting records as dictated by the agency's legal form, which might be, for example, a limited company.

3.23 If taxable supplies of goods or services are made through agents, Customs & Excise require certain procedures to be followed in order to account for VAT.

Duty to prepare financial statements

3.24 As mentioned in paragraph 3.22, an agent who operates as a limited company will have to maintain accounting records and, prepare financial statements in accordance with the requirements of the *Companies Act 1985*. In contrast, an agent who is a sole proprietor will merely have to prepare financial statements to satisfy the Inland Revenue for tax purposes and to keep accounting records to satisfy the Customs & Excise for VAT purposes.

3.25 A problem that arises in practice is whether the turnover disclosed in an agent's financial statements should include the amount of the gross transactions or whether it should include only commission earned. In general, the answer to this problem will depend on how the agent invoices. For example, if the agent is invoiced by his principal for the goods he supplies and then invoices the customer for those goods plus his commission, the amount included in turnover should be based on the gross amount invoiced. However, where an agent merely invoices the commission to his principal, then only the commission element should be included in turnover. It may also be possible that at the agent's year end he has been invoiced by his principal for goods that have not yet been invoiced to the customer and such amounts may need to be recognised in the agent's financial statements.

Audit implications

3.26 It is common practice for a parent company to operate an agency through a subsidiary company. In certain situations, principally where the agent is 'disclosed' and the subsidiary has no other business, the subsidiary company may be treated as dormant for accounting purposes. This means that its financial statements will be significantly simplified and, subject to electing not to appoint auditors in accordance with section 250 of the *Companies Act 1985*, they will not require to be audited. The provisions concerning dormant companies are detailed in section 250 of the *Companies Act 1985*. This matter is explained fully in 'Manual of Accounting - volume I' chapter 7.

3.27 In most other circumstances where an agency is operated by a limited company the auditing requirements are the same as for other limited companies. For example, where an agency is 'undisclosed' the agent effectively contracts on its own behalf and, as a consequence, has accounting transactions that require to be recorded in its own books of account, even where any liabilities it incurs are settled by (say) its parent immediately they become due. Technically, such subsidiaries cannot be dormant in accordance with section 250 of the *Companies Act 1985*.

Audit report

3.28 The audit report given on an agency business will depend on the type of vehicle used for the agency. For example, if the agency is conducted via a limited company and that company is not dormant (see para 3.24 above), then the audit report will follow that of a normal company.

Chapter 4

PARTNERSHIPS

Annex

Chapter 4

PARTNERSHIPS

Background

4.1 Partnerships have been used to conduct business for centuries and they are used extensively by certain professions (for example, the accounting and legal professions). The DTI recently indicated that there are as many as 500,000 partnerships in existence in the UK. The concept of partnership derives largely from common law, although partnerships were not actually regulated by statute until the *Partnership Act 1890*. This Act, however, does not provide a complete codification of partnership law and, consequently, it made no great changes to the law governing partnerships. The *Partnership Act 1890* covers the following matters:

- The nature of partnerships.
- The relationship of partners to third parties dealing with them.
- The relationship of partners to one another.
- The dissolution of partnerships and its consequences.
- Supplementary provisions which include the provision that the rules of equity and common law continue in force except where they are inconsistent with the *Partnership Act 1890*.

4.2 The *Partnership Act 1890* itself does not deal with the question of partnerships' legal status. However, one feature of partnership law is that a partnership is not a separate legal entity. This fact is peculiar to English law and is not found in Scotland or the rest of Europe. Consequently, a partnership cannot be sued, but its individual partners can be sued personally. Furthermore, a limited partnership is not an incorporated alternative to a normal partnership (see chapter 5) as one member of the partnership has unlimited liability.

4.3 A partnership is not restricted to being a business vehicle for individuals, it can also apply to agreements between any legal persons, including companies.

Definition of a partnership

4.4 Section 1(1) of the *Partnership Act 1890* defines 'partnership' as:

> *"... the relation which subsists between persons carrying on a business in common with a view to profit."*

4.5 The parties to a partnership agreement cannot override the legal definition of partnership. The courts have not hesitated to find a partnership where an agreement has said that no partnership exists. Conversely, the courts may find that a partnership does not exist even if, for example, there is a document headed 'Partnership Deed'.

4.6 The principles in the paragraphs that follow can be used as a general guide in determining whether or not a partnership exists.

Business

4.7 There must be a 'business'. For this purpose 'business' includes *"every trade, occupation or profession"*. [PA 1890 Sec 45]. Most commercial activities will fall within this definition. In addition, the two judicial decisions that follow are relevant:

- A 'business' can exist where an association is agreed for one deal only. [*Mann v D'Arcy (1968) 2 All ER 172*].
- A 'business' will not exist, however, where the persons concerned are merely preparing to carry on business as soon as they can. [*Keith Spicer Ltd. v Mansell (1970) 1 All ER 462*].

4.8 The business must be carried on by two or more persons in common.

View to profit

4.9 The business must be 'with a view to profit'. Joint ownership of property does not by itself create a partnership. The *Partnership Act 1890* provides that:

> *"Joint tenancy, tenancy in common, joint property, common property, or part ownership does not of itself create a partnership as to anything so held or owned...."*

4.10 This is so regardless of whether the parties who have an interest in the property share any profits. [PA 1890 Sec 2(1)].

Sharing gross returns

4.11 A partnership will exist where persons receive a share of profits, but not where they receive gross returns.

4.12 The *Partnership Act 1890* provides that sharing gross returns does not of itself create a partnership, even where the persons jointly own the source of the returns. [PA 1890 Sec 2(2)]. However, it does state that where a person receives a share of the profits of a business, this is *"prima facie evidence that he is a partner"*. [PA 1890 Sec 2(3)]. However, this situation will not necessarily give rise to a partnership automatically. In particular, a partnership is not created in the following situations where the receipt of profits:

- Represents the payment of a debt by instalments.
- Arises under a contract for the remuneration of an employee or agent.
- Derives from a loan to a partnership.
- Derives from the sale of the business's goodwill.

No sharing of losses

4.13 Certain agreements provide for sharing profits, but do not provide for sharing losses.

4.14 This type of situation is becoming more common, although it is not covered by the *Partnership Act 1890*. Depending upon whether the agreement includes a provision for certain parties to the agreement to indemnify others for losses, a partnership may or may not exist. For example, where there is a joint venture or corporate finance arrangement that includes provision for the party providing the finance to receive a share of the profits without being liable for losses, care should be taken in deciding whether the lender is also a partner. The principles that need to be considered to ensure that a partnership relationship has not been established are summarised in Underhill's 'Principles of the Law of Partnership' (12th ed.) as follows:

- The advance must really be a loan.
- The lender should not take a share of the capital.
- The loan should not be used as part of the capital.
- Reference should not be made to words used in the partnership agreement.
- Clauses should not be taken from partnership precedents.

Formation of partnerships

4.15 To be able to create a partnership the proposed partners must have the legal capacity to enter into a contract with each other. Difficulties may arise in respect of minors and those suffering from mental incapacity. These difficulties are not considered further here, as they are outside the scope of this book.

4.16 No partnership consisting of more than 20 partners may be formed to carry on any business with the object of the acquisition of gain by its members unless it is incorporated. [CA 1985 Sec 716]. However, certain partnerships have been exempted from this provision, as follows:

- Solicitors' partnerships (where each partner is a solicitor). [CA 1985 Sec 716(2)(a)].
- Accountants' partnerships (where each partner is qualified to be an auditor of a company). [CA 1985 Sec 716(2)(b)].
- Stockbrokers' partnerships (where each partner is a member of a recognised stock exchange). [CA 1985 Sec 716(2)(c)].
- Partnerships of patent agents (where each partner is a registered patent agent). [SI 1968/1222].
- Partnerships of surveyors, auctioneers, valuers, estate agents, land agents and estate managers (where no less than three-quarters of the total number of partners are members of one or more specified bodies). [SI 1968/1222].
- Actuaries' partnerships (where all the partners are either Fellows of the Institute of Actuaries or of the Faculty of Actuaries). [SI 1970/835].
- Partnerships between consulting engineers (where the majority of the partners are recognised by the Council of Engineering Institutions as Chartered Engineers). [SI 1970/992].
- Partnerships practising as building designers (where no less than three-quarters of the total number of partners are either registered under the *Architects (Registration) Act 1931* or are recognised by the Council of Engineering Institutions as Chartered Engineers or by the Royal Institution of Chartered Surveyors as Chartered Surveyors). [SI 1970/1319].
- Partnerships of loss adjusters (where no less than three-quarters of the total number of partners are members of the Chartered Institute of Loss Adjusters). [SI 1982/530].
- Partnerships between insurance brokers (where each partner is either a registered insurance broker or an enroled body corporate under the *Insurance Brokers Registration Act 1977*). [SI 1990/1581].

- Partnerships practising as town planners (where no less than three-quarters of the total number of partners are members of the Royal Town Planning Institute). [SI 1990/1969].

Constitution of a partnership

4.17 There is no legal requirement that a partnership agreement has to be in writing. Even where the partnership property includes land or where the partnership's object is to buy and sell land, a written partnership agreement is not necessary. In practice, however, most partnerships are formed by a properly drafted partnership agreement (sometimes this may be in the form of a partnership deed or articles of partnership). Where no partnership agreement exists all the terms of the *Partnership Act 1890* apply.

4.18 Typical terms of a partnership agreement include the following:

- The partnership's objects.
- The proposed place of business.
- The partnership's name.
- The partnership's commencement and duration.
- What is to be considered partnership property and the partners' interest in it.
- The proportion of capital to be subscribed by each partner and whether any interest is payable on it.
- The partnership's bankers.
- A requirement for partnership monies to be paid into the partnership bank account.
- The names of cheque signatories.
- A requirement to keep accounting records and prepare financial statements.
- Custody of the partnership's books.
- Ascertaining and dividing profits and losses. Typical terms will also include whether any partners are to be salaried.
- An express covenant by each partner to be 'just and faithful' in all his dealings with the other partners.

- The powers and duties of partners, such as:
  - □ The amount of attention to be given to partnership affairs.
  - □ Power to hire and dismiss employees.
  - □ Restrictive covenants on competition.
  - □ Decision-making powers.
  - □ Negative covenants, for example, not to lend partnership property.
- What will happen on a partner's death or retirement.
- The power to expel a partner.
- The entitlement and indemnity of an outgoing partner.
- The introduction of a new partner.
- How goodwill will be dealt with.
- The partnership's dissolution.
- Arbitration.

4.19 A partnership agreement will normally be interpreted in the same way as any other contract.

Business Names Act 1985

4.20 The *Business Names Act 1985* controls the use of business names. It applies to firms that carry out business under a business name that does not consist of the true surnames or corporate names of all the partners (with certain permitted additions). Such firms must in most situations disclose the names and addresses of all partners on business letters, invoices and other business documents. [BNA 1985 Sec 4(1)]. However, there is an exemption from this requirement for documents issued by partnerships that have more than 20 partners. This exemption applies where the partnership maintains at its principal place of business a list of names of all partners and it complies with the following:

- None of the names of the partners appears in the document apart from in the text or as a signatory.

- The document states the partnership's principal place of business and a list of the partners is open for inspection at that place.

[BNA 1985 Sec 4(3)].

Financial Services Act 1986

4.21 Partnerships that carry on 'investment business' have to comply with the *Financial Services Act 1986* (see further chapter 26). In this respect, professional partnerships are generally regulated by their professional bodies. For example, solicitor partnerships (see chapter 27) are regulated by the Law Society, which is a Recognised Professional Body under the *Financial Services Act 1986*.

Accounting and auditing background

4.22 As mentioned in chapter 2, the ICAEW issued a statement on auditing and reporting called 'Reports on accounts of sole traders and partnerships' (AG 3.917) in July 1973. This provides general guidance relating to the reports auditors make on financial statements of such entities. In addition, often professional bodies issue specific guidance for their particular professions, (for example, solicitors, surveyors, estate agents etc).

4.23 As mentioned above, the partnership is the usual vehicle for professions to carry on business. However, most professions, especially solicitors (see chapter 27), are subject to additional legal requirements.

4.24 In February 1990, the EC discussed proposals to extend the scope of the 4th and 7th EC Company Law Directives to certain partnerships and unlimited companies. These proposals would be made to apply to partnerships where all the members are either public or private limited companies, or other partnerships. So far, this directive has not been adopted.

Duty to keep accounting records

4.25 Every partner must, because of his personal liability for debts of the partnership, have the right to have accurate records kept of the partnership's transactions and to have free access to all its books and accounts. This right has been recognised by statute, which provides that:

> *"The partnership books are to be kept at the place of business of the partnership (or the principal place, if there is more than one), and every partner may, when he thinks fit, have access to and inspect and copy any of them."* [PA 1890 Sec 24(9)].

4.26 Any partner is entitled to exercise his right to examine the books and accounts of the partnership by using an agent, subject to reasonable objections made by the other partners. [*Bevan v Webb (1901) 2 Ch 59*]. However, partners and agents may not make use of any information obtained for an improper purpose. [*Trego v Hunt (1896) AC 7*].

4.27 No partner can deprive other partners of this right by, for example, keeping partnership records in a private book of his own containing matters that the others are not entitled to see. [*Freeman v Fairlie (1812) 3 Mer 43*]. However, an assignee of a partner's share has no right of inspection. [PA 1890 Sec 31].

4.28 The effect of failing to keep books of accounting records is that, on an application for an account of the partnership, a court will make every presumption against the parties who were responsible for keeping the accounting records. [*Walmsley v Walmsley (1846) 3 Jo & La. T. 556*].

Duty to prepare financial statements

4.29 There is no general legal duty for a partnership to prepare financial statements. However, in practice, financial statements will be necessary:

- To show the financial position of the partnership for use by third parties, such as the Inland Revenue or the partnership's bankers.
- To show the financial position of partners in the firm.

4.30 Normally partnership agreements also provide that a general account is made up each year. This account should show the assets and liabilities of the partnership and what is due to each partner in respect of his capital and share of the profit or what is due from him to the partnership.

4.31 It is also recommended that the partnership agreement should provide that the financial statements are to be treated as conclusive when they are signed by all partners. However, litigation has frequently resulted from such clauses in partnership agreements in the following circumstances where, for example:

- A partner claims that he has been induced to sign the financial statements by fraud.
- There are errors in the financial statements that could not have been discovered at the time of signing.
- A clause renders signed financial statements conclusive in certain respects only, but not for all purposes.

■ Partners refuse to sign the financial statements (although the courts tend to ignore this, unless there is a proper reason for them not to sign).

Special accounting requirements

4.32 In preparing the financial statements of a partnership due regard must be taken of the partnership agreement and any applicable provisions of the *Partnership Act 1890*. Areas that should be specifically considered are as follows.

Partnership's property

4.33 The partnership agreement will usually specify what is to be considered partnership property. Only partnership property can be included in the financial statements.

Contributions of capital

4.34 The proportions of capital contributed by the partners and their entitlement to it should be specified in the partnership agreement. They will not necessarily be the same. However, in the absence of an express or implied agreement between the partners, all partners will be entitled to share in the capital and profits equally, regardless of whether they have contributed to it equally. [PA 1890 Sec 24(1)].

Division of profits and losses

4.35 The partnership agreement will usually provide how to calculate the partner's profit share. It may also make provision for salaried partners. If there is no express or implied reference, then profits and losses (including capital losses) should be shared and borne by the partners in equal shares. [PA 1890 Sec 24(1)].

4.36 Provision will also usually be made in the partnership agreement concerning drawings by partners in anticipation of profits.

Interest on capital

4.37 In the absence of provision in the partnership agreement concerning interest on capital, no partner is entitled to interest on his capital account. [PA 1890 Sec 24(4)].

Change of partners

4.38 If the composition of a partnership changes, whether by admission, death expulsion of a partner, the partnership may be dissolved. Special provisions will usually be laid down in the partnership agreement enabling a partner to retire or be expelled without a general dissolution and for determining the following:

- Value of goodwill.
- Entitlement of incoming or outgoing partners.

The provisions of the Companies Act 1989

4.39 Under the provisions of the *Companies Act 1989* partnerships that are subsidiary undertakings of a holding company have to be consolidated into the consolidated financial statements of the ultimate holding company (and into any consolidated financial statements prepared by an intermediate holding company). However, where a partnership has investments in subsidiary undertakings, it is not required to prepare consolidated financial statements as it is not a parent company. See further 'Manual of Accounting – volume II' chapter 2.

4.40 Power is given to the Secretary of State under section 258D of the *Companies Act 1985* to apply to 'banking partnerships' the provisions of the *Companies Act 1985* that relate to preparing financial statements of banking companies. A 'banking partnership' is a partnership that is an authorised institution under the *Banking Act 1987* (see chapter 15).

Audit implications

4.41 It is usual for a partnership agreement to provide for the audit of partnership financial statements, although there is no statutory requirement to this effect. Where such an audit is made then its scope and nature must be ascertained from the terms of the engagement. Where no audit is required, but an accountant prepares the partnership's financial statements he should follow the guidance given in the ICAEW's statement 3.917 (see chapter 2 para 2.10).

4.42 As mentioned in paragraph 4.39 above, where a partnership is a subsidiary undertaking of a limited company it will have its financial statements included in the consolidated financial statements of the group. In this situation, the partnership's parent may impose certain accounting or audit requirements on the partnership. This may be necessary because, although the partnership's financial statements may not otherwise have to be audited, they may have to be audited for consolidation purposes. The scope of the audit will vary depending on the materiality of the partnership's results or assets and liabilities to the group's results and financial position.

Audit report

4.43 An example of an unqualified audit report for a partnership is as follows:

REPORT OF THE AUDITORS TO [NAME OF PARTNERSHIP]

We have audited the financial statements on pages [] to [] in accordance with Auditing Standards.

In our opinion the financial statements give a true and fair view of the state of the partnership's affairs at [date] and of its profit and source and application of funds for the [period] then ended.

[Name of firm]

Chartered Accountants,

[Address].

[Date of report].

SECTIONS OF THE COMPANIES ACT 1985 THAT APPLY TO PARTNERSHIPS

Section	Description
8A	Table G, articles of association for a partnership company
255D	Power to apply provisions to banking partnerships
259(1)	Meaning of undertaking and related expressions
390(3)	Right to attend company meetings
716	Prohibition of partnerships with more than 20 members
734	Criminal proceedings against unincorporated bodies.

Chapter 5

LIMITED PARTNERSHIPS

Annex

Chapter 5

LIMITED PARTNERSHIPS

Background

5.1 The limited partnership has not been a very popular business vehicle in the UK. The DTI recently indicated that there are only approximately 1,400 limited partnerships registered in the UK. This unpopularity may be because limited partnerships suffer from the disadvantages of normal partnerships, and, although limited, do not have the advantages of limited liability. In comparison, in the US limited partnerships are very popular.

5.2 In recent years, however, the limited partnership has become more popular in the UK, especially in the film industry, the oil and gas industry and with venture capitalists because of certain tax advantages. In essence, a limited partnership is a normal partnership, but some of its partners enjoy limited liability. As with normal partnerships (see chapter 4 para 4.2), a limited partnership is not considered a separate legal entity, as it cannot be separated legally from its members.

5.3 The statutory framework for limited partnerships was established by the *Limited Partnerships Act 1907*, which covers the following:

- Definition and constitution of limited partnerships.
- Registration of limited partnerships.
- Modification of general partnership law.
- Registration of changes in limited partnerships.

Legal status of limited partnerships

5.4 The limited partnership differs from a normal partnership in that a person may participate financially up to a fixed limit without actively taking part in the limited partnership's management. All the matters considered in chapter 4 above apply equally to limited partnerships although the matters considered below also apply to such partnerships.

General partner

5.5 There must be one or more general partners. The general partners are liable for all the debts and obligations of the limited partnership. [Ltd PA 1907 Sec 4(2)].

Limited partner

5.6 There must be one or more limited partners. Each limited partner must contribute an amount of capital or property (valued at a stated amount) on entering the partnership. The limited partner will not be liable for the debts or obligations of the limited partnership beyond that contribution. [Ltd PA 1907 Sec 4(2)]. Furthermore, such a partner cannot draw out, or receive back, any part of his contribution. Where a partner does, he will still be liable to the extent of his original contributions. [Ltd PA 1907 Sec 4(3)]. In addition, a limited partner may also be a corporate body. [Ltd PA 1907 Sec 4(4)].

5.7 A limited partner must not take part in the management of the partnership business. If he does, he will be liable for all the limited partnership's debts and obligations as if he were a general partner. [Ltd PA 1907 Sec 6(1)].

Formation of limited partnerships

5.8 Unless a limited partnership is registered under the *Limited Partnerships Act 1907*, it will be treated as an ordinary partnership. A limited partnership, therefore, must register with the Registrar of Companies by sending him a statement (on Form LP5) containing the following details:

- The limited partnership's name.
- The general nature of its business.
- The principal place of business.
- The full name of each partner.
- The date of its commencement (and duration, if specified in the partnership agreement).
- A statement that it is limited.
- A description of every limited partner.
- Details of the sum contributed by each limited partner.

[Ltd PA 1907 Sec 8].

5.9 A limited partnership must not consist of more than 20 partners. [Ltd PA 1907 Sec 4(2)]. Certain limited partnerships are exempted from this by the *Companies Act 1985*, as follows:

- Solicitors' partnerships (where each partner is a solicitor). [CA 1985 Sec 717(1)(a)].
- Accountant's partnerships (where each partner is qualified to be an auditor of a company). [CA 1985 Sec 717(1)(b)].
- Stockbrokers' partnerships (where each partner is a member of a recognised stock exchange). [CA 1985 Sec 717(1)(c)].
- Insurance brokers' partnerships (where each partner is either a registered insurance broker or an enroled body corporate under the *Insurance Brokers (Registration) Act 1977*). [SI 1990/1580].

The provisions of the Companies Act 1989

5.10 A limited partnership may now be a subsidiary of another undertaking under the provisions of the *Companies Act 1989*. This will normally arise where that other undertaking is the general partner. The general partner constitutes the board of the limited partnership and, consequently, the other undertaking will be in a position to *"appoint or remove a majority of its board of directors"*. The relevant provisions of the *Companies Act 1989* are considered further in 'Manual of Accounting - volume II' chapter 3.

Accounting and audit requirements

5.11 The accounting and auditing requirements for limited partnerships are identical to the requirements for ordinary partnerships outlined in chapter 4 paragraphs 4.21 to 4.41. A specific right is, however, given to limited partners to inspect the books of the limited partnership (personally or by using an agent) and to examine the state and the prospects of the partnership's business. The limited partner may then advise the partners on the business activities of the partnership, which is normally prohibited because the limited partner must not take part in the management of the partnership business (see para 5.4). [Ltd PA 1907 Sec 6(1)].

Audit report

5.12 The audit report of a limited partnership would be similar to that for a normal partnership as outlined in chapter 4 paragraph 4.43.

SECTIONS OF THE COMPANIES ACT 1985 THAT APPLY TO LIMITED PARTNERSHIPS

Section	Description
8A	Table G
259	Meaning of undertaking and related expressions
390	Right to attend company meetings
714	Registrar's index of company and corporate names
717	Limited partnerships: limit on number of members
734	Criminal proceedings against unincorporated bodies.

Chapter 6

TRUSTS

Chapter 6

TRUSTS

Introduction

6.1 Trusts do not fit logically into a book on legal entities. This is because a trust is essentially a legal means of placing obligations on people and is not, for example, a vehicle for carrying on a particular kind of business. However, many of the organisations discussed in this book depend upon trusts for their existence. Unincorporated associations, such as clubs, friendly societies and most trade unions, would not have developed were it not possible for their property to be held on their behalf by trustees. The more common uses of trusts are:

- Unit trusts (see chapter 7).
- Pension schemes (see chapter 8).
- Charitable trusts (see chapter 25).
- Various private trusts such as accumulation and maintenance trusts (which are considered in this chapter).

6.2 The concept of the trust derives from the obligations that are enforced by the Court of Chancery. In the main, however, the regulation of trusts has developed through case law. In addition, the legal regulation of certain trusts, such as pension schemes and charities, is now largely governed by statute and are dealt with in the chapters mentioned above. The principal legislation applying to trusts is contained in the statutes summarised below.

The Trustee Act 1925

6.3 This is the main legislation concerning the administration of trusts. It covers:

- Trust investment.
- Trustees' powers, particularly with regard to the administration of trust property.
- Trustees' appointment and discharge.
- The court's powers in relation to trusts.

The Variation of Trusts Act 1958

6.4 This is a complex piece of legislation enabling the courts to approve the following arrangements to:

- Vary or revoke any trust.

- Enlarge the management and administrative powers of trustees.

6.5 However, the circumstances to which this Act applies are very restricted.

The Trustee Investments Act 1961

6.6 Trust law permits trustees to invest only as expressly allowed by the trust instrument or by statute. Those investments allowed by statute were very restricted before this Act came into force. The *Trustee Investment Act 1961* permits trustees to invest in a wider range of investments, in particular, UK equity securities. However, special rules apply when trusts do invest in such securities (see para 6.30).

The Perpetuities and Accumulations Act 1964

6.7 The *Perpetuities and Accumulations Act 1964* was enacted to prevent property being held in trust in perpetuity by limiting the period before which property must rest in a beneficiary. The maximum period is a life in being plus twenty one years after that person's death or a period not exceeding in total 80 years. This Act also limits the period during which income can be accumulated.

The Recognition of Trusts Act 1987

6.8 The *Recognition of Trusts Act 1987* was enacted to give effect to the 1984 Hague Convention on the law applicable to trusts and their recognition. The purpose of the Convention was to achieve international recognition of the trust concept, so that trusts created in common law jurisdictions would be recognised in other jurisdictions. The British government has been prompt in ratifying the Convention and introducing legislation in order to encourage other states to do so.

Definition

6.9 A trust has been defined as:

> *"...an equitable obligation binding a person (who is called a trustee) to deal with property over which he has control (which is called trust property) for the benefit of persons (who are called beneficiaries...) of whom he may himself be one and any*

one of whom may enforce the obligation." [Underhill's 'Law of Trusts and Trustees' (12th ed. 1970)].

6.10 The nature of a trust becomes clear when it is compared and contrasted with other legal concepts, for example:

- Contractual obligations.

A trust can be enforced by a beneficiary who is not, in general, party to the instrument creating the trust. In contrast, a contract is enforceable only by a person who is party to the contract. However, a person may contract as trustee with a third party who may be entitled, as a consequence, to the benefit of that contract.

- Agency.

There is some similarity between the relationship of trustee and beneficiary in trust law and that of principal and agent. Agencies are considered in chapter 3. In particular, trustees are liable to their beneficiary in the same way as agents are liable to a principal for any profits made out of the property entrusted to him. The relationship between a principal and his agent is basically one of creditor and debtor, and is based on their agreement. An agent is subject to the control of his principal. In contrast, however, neither of these latter two rules apply to the relationship of trustee and beneficiary. Furthermore, a trustee has full legal title to property vested in him, whereas an agent does not. However, both a trustee and an agent are liable for negligence and fraud and breach of contract and both have to act *ubrimae fidei*.

Types of trusts

6.11 There are four ways in which a trust may be created:

- Statutory trusts.
- Express trusts.
- Implied trusts.
- Constructive trusts.

Statutory trusts

6.12 As mentioned above, a trust is an important device for holding property. In this respect, there are three situations where a statute expressly creates a trust:

■ Whenever land is conveyed to persons in undivided shares, it will vest in the first four people that are named on the trust deed. This is a trust for sale and all the grantees are beneficiaries as tenants in common. [LPA 1925 Sec 34].

■ Where land is conveyed to joint tenants, it vests in the first four people named on the trust deed. This is a trust for sale and all the grantees are beneficiaries as joint tenants. [LPA 1925 Sec 36].

■ Where a person dies intestate, his personal representatives hold his property on trust. This is a trust for sale and division between the surviving spouse and the issue of the intestate or other specified relatives. [AEA 1925 Sec 33].

Express trusts

6.13 An express trust is one that has been created intentionally by a settlor. The formation of express trusts is considered below in paragraph 6.18. It is essentially the same process as that used to establish unit trusts (see chapter 7), pension schemes (see chapter 8) and charitable trusts (see chapter 25). However, it is worth mentioning here that the courts have regarded a trust as being expressly created even where the settlor has, for example, expressed himself ambiguously, provided that the document concerned shows an intention to establish a trust.

6.14 With regard to express trusts, a further common distinction encountered in practice is that between 'fixed' and 'discretionary' trusts. Each beneficiary under a fixed trust is entitled in equity to a fixed share of the trust property and can enforce this against the trustees. In contrast, a beneficiary of a discretionary trust has no interest in any part of the trust property unless, and until, the trustees exercise their discretion in his favour.

Implied trusts

6.15 An implied trust is one where the courts consider that it arises from the unexpressed, but presumed, intention of the settlor. Such a trust commonly arises in one or other of the following two situations:

■ Where a person purchases property in another person's name, where that other person provided the money, subject to various exceptions, a trust may be implied in favour of the person who provided the purchase money. [*Dyer v Dyer (1788) 2 Cox Eq. 92 at 93*]. This situation is often encountered in matrimonial matters.

■ Where a person establishes a trust, but fails to deal effectively with the whole of the beneficial interest, a trust may be implied to the effect that any amount of the beneficial interest left over will be held on trust for that person. An example of the application of this rule is where a loan is made for a particular purpose and that purpose fails. In this situation, the money will be held on an implied trust for the lender. [*Barclays Bank Ltd. v Quistclose Investments Ltd. (1970) AC 567*].

6.16 Because an implied trust often gives rise to the return of money to a settlor of a trust, it is frequently referred to as a 'resulting trust'.

Constructive trusts

6.17 A well known definition of a 'constructive trust' is *"a trust which is imposed by equity in order to satisfy the demands of justice and good conscience"*. [Snell's 'Principles of Equity' (28th ed.)]. A common example used of the imposition of such a trust is the case of *Keech v Sandford (1726) Cas. temp King 61*. In this case a person held a leasehold property as trustee and used his position to obtain a renewal of the lease. This was held to be in bad faith and so the trustee was directed to hold the new lease on the same terms as the old lease.

Formation

6.18 To be able to create a trust the proposed settlor must have the legal capacity to do so. What this means in general terms is that anyone who has the power to own and dispose of a particular type of property may create a trust in respect of it (for example, persons over the age of eighteen). Difficulties may arise, however, in respect of minors or those suffering from mental incapacity wishing to form a trust, but these aspects are outside the scope of this book.

6.19 There are three ways in which an express trust may be created:

- Declaration of trust.

  A person may simply declare that he holds certain property on trust or for a specific permitted object or purpose.

- Conveyance to a trustee.

  A person may transfer property to another person in order for him to hold it on trust.

- Direction to a third party to hold on trust.

  A person may create a trust by directing a third party to hold his property on trust for another person. In this context, 'property' includes any form of property, including interests in property.

6.20 Whatever means of establishing a trust is used, the transfer of property to trustees must comply with the legal formalities for the transfer of that particular form of property. Common examples are noted below:

- Registered land.

  The settlor must execute the prescribed transfer form appropriately and register the transfer at the Land Registry.

- Unregistered land.

  The settlor must execute a deed of transfer and deliver the deed to the trustee.

- Personal property.

  The settlor must either deliver the property (or the means of obtaining it, such as a key) to the trustee or execute a deed of gift and deliver that to the trustee.

- Shares.

  The settlor must execute the appropriate share transfer form, register the transfer in the company's register and the company would then deliver the certificate, in the name of the trustee, to him.

6.21 Furthermore, there are certain circumstances where the trust itself must be created or evidenced in writing. In general terms these circumstances are as follows:

- A declaration of trust in respect of land (or an interest in land) must be evidenced in writing and signed. [LPA 1925 Sec 53(1)(b)].

- A disposition of an equitable interest or trust subsisting at the time must be in writing and signed. [LPA 1925 Sec 53(1)(c)].

- A will must be in writing and signed by the testator or some other person in his presence and under his direction. There must be two witnesses present at the same time. [WA 1837 Sec 9].

6.22 Finally, a trust will not take effect unless its provisions are certain. The areas where the courts are particularly concerned are:

- The settlor's intention to create a trust.

- The property that is to be the subject of the trust.

- The clear identification of the trust's beneficiaries.

Constitution

6.23 In practice, most express trusts are now established by a professionally drafted trust deed. The terms of the trust deed will obviously depend on the trust's purpose. A trust deed will normally include details of the following matters:

- The first trustees and their addresses.
- The trust fund.
- The trust's duration.
- The vesting of the trust fund in the trustees.
- Rules for the trustees' appointment and removal.
- An indemnity for the trustees.
- Rules for trustees' meetings.
- The number of trustees.
- Powers of trustees to:
  - Invest trust property.
  - Delegate or use agents.
  - Take advice.
  - Open bank accounts.
  - Make rules.
  - Vary the trust deed.
  - Borrow funds.
- Duties of trustees to:
  - Keep accounting records.
  - Prepare financial statements.
  - Submit the financial statements for audit.
  - Register investments promptly.

■ Rules to interpret the trust deed and the resolution of disputes.

Accounting background

6.24 The ICAEW has issued two accounting recommendations to its members in respect of trust accounts. 'Trust Accounts' (AR 2.203) was issued in October 1986 and deals with the financial statements of deceased persons' estates and the more general types of trusts (excluding special trusts, such as pension funds and unit trusts). This statement sets out the best practice to be applied in connection with the records and the preparation of trust financial statements. The second statement entitled 'Trustee Investments Act 1961' (AR 2.204) sets out notes for the assistance of those concerned with trusts. However, in relation to the types of trust normally encountered, it gives a broad appreciation of the accounting implications of the *Trustee Investments Act 1961*.

Duty to keep accounting records

6.25 There is no statutory duty upon trustees to keep accounting records. However, case law makes it clear that a trustee must be prepared, at any time, to give a beneficiary information about:

■ The state of trust property.

■ Dealings with trust property.

6.26 Although the duty to keep accounting records is personal to the trustee, in practice trustees may wish to appoint others to do it. Statute permits a trustee to employ an agent to do any act that has to be done in executing the trust, including the receipt and payment of money. [TA 1925 Sec 23(1)]. An agent appointed for this purpose may be paid out of the trust fund. [TA 1925 Sec 23(1)].

6.27 The extent of the accounting records necessary is not made clear from the law. Where the power of investment under the *Trustee Investments Act 1961* is exercised, then the accounting records will need to be such as to show that the requirements of that Act have been met (see para 6.31). A beneficiary is entitled to see all trust documents except those where the trustees record the reasons for their decisions. The accounting records will include all trust documents. Trust documents will include all vouchers supporting the information the beneficiary is entitled to and, in particular, extend to details of investments, such as stock or share certificates.

6.28 The accounting recommendation 'Trust Accounts' suggests:

> *'Trustees should maintain records from which, in the light of the trust instrument(s) and legal considerations, periodical*

statements of account and tax returns can be prepared. The records and/or trust accounts should preserve all the information that may be required at future dates (possibly long deferred) for any review of the trustees' transactions and for capital gains tax and inheritance purposes. Although traditionally it has been recommended that this should be achieved by keeping books on complete double-entry principles, less formal methods are now acceptable provided that those principles govern the preparation of the trust accounts..." [AR 2.203 para 16].

"Income and capital transactions should be segregated clearly. This may be assisted by the use of separate columns in accounting records..." [AR 2.203 para 19].

6.29 Trustees who do not keep proper accounting records may be ordered to do so by the court, and may be forced to bear the costs personally of the application to the court.

Accounting for investments

6.30 Many older trust deeds gave a power of investment that was restrictively worded or was left to be determined by general law. In practice, this meant that trustees could invest in little more than Government or local authority stock and similar investments. In the context of 1925 legislation, this was no doubt prudent. However, by the 1950's trustees were placed in the difficult position of seeing the value of trust funds decline in real terms. If, for example, they were to invest in equity securities they ran the risk of being in breach of trust. The *Variation of Trusts Act 1958* (see para 6.4) permitted trustees to apply to the court for an extension of their investment powers, but the procedure was expensive and cumbersome. The law was reformed by the *Trustee Investments Act 1961*. It applies to all trust instruments, even those executed before 3rd August 1961, to extend the powers of trustees.

6.31 Where a trust instrument already gives a wider power of investment, the *Trustee Investments Act 1961* does not restrict this. There is a tendency for trust deeds drafted since that Act's implementation to give trustees wider powers of investment than those of *Trustee Investments Act 1961*, and, as a consequence, such trust deeds would expressly exclude the operation of that Act.

6.32 The *Trustee Investments Act 1961* divides investments into three categories:

- ■ Narrower-range.

  Part I (investments not requiring advice) include:

  - □ Defence Bonds.
  - □ National Savings Certificates.
  - □ Savings Bank deposits.

  Part II (investments requiring advice) include:

  - □ Various fixed-interest securities.
  - □ UK registered debentures of UK companies.
  - □ Deposits in certain building societies.
  - □ Mortgages of certain freehold and leasehold property.

- ■ Wider-range.

  These include:

  - □ Securities issued by certain UK companies.
  - □ Shares of certain building societies.
  - □ Units of authorised unit trusts.

- ■ Special range.

  These are investments made under 'special powers', that is powers conferred by the trust instruments to hold or acquire investments other than narrower range investments.

6.33 In all situations investments in debentures, shares and stock are restricted to certain UK companies that satisfy the following conditions:

- ■ The company must be listed on a recognised stock exchange. [TIA 1961 1 Sch Part IV para 2(a)].
- ■ The shares or debentures must be fully paid up or issued on terms that they are to be fully paid up within nine months of the issue date. [TIA 1961 1 Sch Part IV para 2(b)].
- ■ The company must have a total issued or paid up capital of at least £1 million. [TIA 1961 1 Sch Part IV para 3(a)].

- The company must have paid a dividend on all its shares in each of the immediately preceding five years. [TIA 1961 1 Sch Part IV para 3(b)].

6.34 The *Trustee Investments Act 1961* gives trustees power to invest in, or to retain wider range securities, provided that they divide the trust fund into two parts, a narrower-range part and a wider-range part. A division into three parts may be necessary where there is a special range part. Only the wider-range part can be used for investment in wider-range investments. The division must be made in two equal parts. Once made, it is permanent and the two parts must be kept separate. However, the trustees are still free to invest the wider-range fund in narrower-range investments if they choose to. [TIA 1961 Sec 2]. There are complex accounting provisions for compensating transfers, accruals and withdrawals. These provisions are not, however, considered further in this book.

6.35 Case law also gives rise to further accounting rules for trust investments governing the rights between different categories of beneficiary (for example, a life-tenant and a remainderman). Similarly these are outside the scope of this book.

Duty to establish and maintain a system of control

6.36 Frequently, trusts will not be large entities and so the need for a detailed system of control may not arise. However, where trustees appoint an agent to maintain the trust's accounting records or investment activities, the trustees should ensure that there are adequate systems of control to enable them to discharge their responsibilities.

Duty to prepare financial statements

6.37 The purpose of maintaining accounting records is so that financial statements may be available for inspection by a beneficiary when called for. There is no statutory obligation on trustees to prepare financial statements at regular intervals, although this will usually be necessary for taxation purposes and will also normally be provided for in the trust deed.

6.38 The accounting recommendation 'Trust Accounts' suggests that periodical financial statements should normally consist of the following accounts:

- Balance sheet of the whole of the trust estate.
- Capital account, summarising capital transactions either from the commencement of the trust or since the last account.

- Income account, where appropriate.
- Schedules and subsidiary accounts explaining in greater detail the major items appearing in the balance sheet, capital account and income account, showing separately the figures for any special funds.

[AR 2.203 para 20].

Accounting period

6.39 It will be unusual for the accounting period of a trust to be specified in the trust deed and it is not subject to legal regulation. The accounting recommendation 'Trust Accounts' suggests:

> *"The date to which accounts are made up should be decided according to the circumstances and will not necessarily be the anniversary of the creation of the trust. Having regard to the taxation liabilities of the trust and of the beneficiaries, it may frequently be convenient for accounting periods to correspond with fiscal years; but in some cases it may be necessary for accounts to be made up to the anniversary of the trust's creation if the rules of law relating to equitable apportionments are applicable or if there are other special circumstances. The nature of the trust assets, the date on which income is receivable, the due dates of annuities, are all factors that may affect the selection of the most convenient accounting date."* [AR 2.203 para 18].

Audit requirements

6.40 Any trustee or beneficiary can apply to the Public Trustee for the *"condition and accounts"* of any trust to be *"investigated and audited"* by a solicitor or *"public accountant"* as may be agreed on by the applicant and the trustee. Where there is no agreement the Public Trustee, or someone appointed by him, may decide who the auditor shall be. Such an investigation or audit cannot be required within 12 months of a previous audit, except with the permission of the court. [PTA 1906 Sec 13(1)].

6.41 The costs of an investigation and audit will normally be paid for out of trust funds, but the Public Trustee has the power to order them to be paid by the trustees or by both the trustees and the applicant.

6.42 The scope of the term 'investigation and audit' is not clear. Any auditor accepting appointment for such work should ensure that the terms of his engagement are carefully considered and documented in the engagement letter.

6.43 However, it is unusual for an audit to be instigated under the statutory power mentioned above. In practice, the audit of trust accounts is generally carried out voluntarily. Trustees are empowered to have the trust accounts *"examined or audited"* by an *"independent accountant"*, once in every three years. [TA 1925 Sec 22(4)]. The decision to have an audit is, therefore, at the trustee's discretion. However, where the nature of the trust or any special dealings with the trust property make a more frequent exercise of this power reasonable, the trustees may do so more than once in every three years. [TA 1925 Sec 22(4)].

Rights of auditors

6.44 An auditor appointed under the *Public Trustee Act 1906* does not have any express rights. Any auditor accepting such an appointment should, therefore, ensure that the terms of this engagement cover those rights necessary for him to perform his duties. In addition, an auditor appointed under the *Trustee Act 1925* is not given any rights as such. However, the *Trustee Act 1925* does provide that trustees must produce such vouchers and give such information to the auditor as he may require.

Audit report

6.45 There will normally be restrictions placed by trustees on the scope of the audit work carried out by an auditor, in addition to any restrictions as to its scope contained in statutes. Occasionally, the restrictions may be such that an auditor is unable to express an opinion on the trust's financial statements. However, where it is possible to express an opinion, the audit report should set out any restrictions on the scope of the audit that have been agreed with the trustees.

6.46 An example of the suggested wording for an unqualified trust audit report, where restrictions on the scope of the audit have been agreed to is given below:

REPORT OF THE AUDITORS TO THE TRUSTEES OF [NAME] TRUST

We have audited the financial statements on pages [] to [] in accordance with Auditing Standards, except that in accordance with your instructions the scope of our work was limited by the matters referred to below:

(a) We have accepted the trust's stockbrokers' written confirmation that they were holding in safe custody, on the trust's behalf, overseas investments in their name having a book value of [].

(b) Our examination of the receipts and payments in respect of properties has not extended beyond agreeing them with the accounting records and with the return signed by your agents.

Subject to the foregoing, in our opinion the financial statements give a true and fair view of the state of affairs of the trust at [date] and of its excess of [income over expenditure/expenditure over income] and source and application of funds for the [period] then ended.

[Name of firm]

Chartered Accountants,

[Address].

[Date of report].

Chapter 7

UNIT TRUSTS

Annexes

Chapter 7

UNIT TRUSTS

Introduction

7.1 Unit trusts are a specialised type of private trust. Authorised unit trust schemes are constituted under UK trust law by a trust deed (see further chapter 6) and must have a depository (referred to below as the 'trustee') separate from the management company (referred to below as the 'manager'). The basic concept of a unit trust is simple, a large number of investors pool their money in order to build up a portfolio of professionally managed investments. The investors are the beneficiaries of the trust and in exchange for money invested receive units in the trust. Unitholders are entitled to share in the dividends, interest or other income arising from the securities held. Unit trusts are open-ended funds, that is, they have a variable capital and the price of the units is determined by the underlying value of the net assets of the trust. In comparison, the price of the shares or other participations in closed-ended funds (for example, investment companies - see chapter 17) is determined by supply and demand.

7.2 In the UK at the end of February 1991, there were 1,404 authorised unit trusts with a total of £52.3 billion of funds under management and 4,595,000 unit trust account holders.

7.3 Unit trusts were brought within the regulation of the Board of Trade (now the DTI) under the *Prevention of Fraud (Investments) Acts*. Those Acts empowered the Board to authorise unit trust schemes that complied with certain criteria. During 1988, new regulations were enacted that now govern the activities of UK authorised unit trust schemes. The statutory provisions that relate to authorised unit trusts and other Collective Investment Schemes (CIS) are now contained in Chapter VIII of the *Financial Services Act 1986*. As explained in chapter 26, one aspect of the *Financial Services Act 1986* was to introduce a higher standard of investor protection for those investing through the medium of authorised unit trust schemes.

EC legislation

7.4 EC member states were required by the directive on 'Undertakings for Collective Investment in Transferable Securities' (UCITS) to have incorporated the directive's provisions in their national legislation by 1st October 1989 (Greece and Portugal by 1st April 1992). Implementation of this directive allows certain types of CIS, authorised in any one member state, to be freely marketed throughout the EC. The basic purpose of the directive is to ensure protection for investors and to harmonise competitive conditions between UCITS from different member states. Although individual member states are solely responsible for the authorisation of all UCITS in their countries, approval in one member state automatically gives the right for the UCITS to operate throughout the EC in the countries where the appropriate legislation has been enacted. UCITS are then subject only to formal notification to the host state's authority and to any local regulations that would apply in the case of a comparable investment vehicle established in that particular country.

Schemes covered by the UCITS directive

7.5 The directive permits UCITS to be constituted in different ways in accordance with local law. Therefore, UCITS may be established in the following ways:

- Under the law of contract (as common funds managed by management companies). For example, a German public fund.
- Under trust law (as unit trusts). For example, a UK authorised unit trust scheme.
- Under statute (as investment companies). For example a French SICAV.

7.6 Consequently, UCITS are essentially of two types. They may take the form of mutual or pooled funds managed by a manager under contractual arrangements or trust law (as for UK unit trusts), or open-ended investment companies which are considered in chapter 16 and are common in Europe outside the UK.

7.7 The main types of CIS operated in the UK are authorised unit trust schemes, which include:

- Authorised securities schemes, investing solely in transferable securities (these include Government and other public securities funds).
- Fund of funds, which invest in units in other authorised or recognised schemes.
- Money market funds, investing in deposits, loans, instruments of indebtedness (even if not transferable) and transferable securities.
- Feeder funds, set up to invest in units of a single authorised unit trust scheme or recognised scheme and intended for personal pension schemes.

- Umbrella funds, which comprise classes of units representing other permitted forms of authorised scheme.

7.8 At present, authorised unit trusts can only invest in futures and options for hedging purposes. However, a revision (see para 7.19) to the 1988 regulations has been proposed whereby futures and options schemes will be able to become authorised in their own right, thereby, enabling investment in futures and options for other than hedging purposes. Proposals for the authorisation of property unit trusts and equity warrant funds are also being considered.

Authorisation

Authorisation and registration of a unit trust as UCITS

7.9 For a UK unit trust to achieve authorised status, the manager and the trustee of the trust must make an application to SIB under section 78 of the *Financial Services Act 1986*. The trust will only become authorised once SIB approves the scheme's trust deed, and has satisfied itself that the manager and the trustee are independent, incorporated in the UK and authorised to carry out investment business. Only authorised unit trust schemes may qualify as a UCITS. (Umbrella funds (see para 7.7) will qualify if all classes of unit qualify in their own right.)

7.10 To register as a UCITS the fund manager or the manager's professional adviser should notify SIB of his proposals, specifying the member state in which he intends to market the scheme as a UCITS. SIB, after consulting its trust records, will then issue a certificate of registration.

Authorisation of the manager and trustee

7.11 The manager and trustee of an authorised unit trust constituted in the UK both, by definition, carry on investment business and must, therefore, obtain authorisation under the *Financial Services Act 1986* (see chapter 26). The manager who manages the day to day operations of the scheme (in return for a management charge) and the trustee who performs a depository role and ensures that the operations are conducted in accordance with the law (in return for a fee), would normally apply to IMRO for authorisation (see chapter 26). Once they are admitted to membership they are subject to IMRO's rules. IMRO must be satisfied that applicants are 'fit and proper persons' to obtain authorisation.

7.12 Managers and trustees must have sufficient financial resources at their disposal to enable them to conduct their business effectively and meet their liabilities. The capital requirement levels for members are set out in the IMRO rules. [IMRO rule book Chapter V para 4.01].

7.13 In order to market units in a trust the manager must apply for membership of the Life Assurance and Unit Trust Regulatory Organisation (LAUTRO).

7.14 As an alternative to membership of IMRO and LAUTRO, it is possible, although not common, to obtain direct authorisation from SIB, in which case the manager will be subject to SIB's own marketing rules.

Promotion and advertising

7.15 The following categories of CIS may be promoted and sold to the general public in the UK:

- Authorised unit trust schemes.

  As explained, these may include funds that would not at present qualify as UCITS.

- Recognised unit trust schemes.

  Section 86 of the *Financial Services Act 1986* sets out the process whereby schemes constituted in other member states may become 'recognised' in the UK. An operator of a recognised scheme must be authorised to carry on investment business connected with that scheme and will be subject to SIB's conduct of business regulations, for example on marketing. [FSA 1986 Sec 24]. This, in essence, implements the requirements of the EC UCITS directive.

  Schemes constituted outside the EC may become 'recognised' and, therefore, be allowed to be marketed in the UK if the territory from which they operate has been 'designated' under section 87 of the *Financial Services Act 1986*. There is also a procedure whereby individual schemes constituted outside the UK may become 'recognised'. [FSA 1986 Sec 88].

7.16 Unregulated schemes (that is, forms of CIS not recognised under the above two categories) may be promoted only to certain limited classes of investor, such as charities and pension schemes.

7.17 Advertising of overseas schemes is restricted by section 90(2) of the *Financial Services Act 1986*, but exceptions are permitted for advertisements issued by a person in another EC country provided they conform with the rules laid down as to their form and content. [FSA 1986 Sec 58(1)(c)].

Regulations

7.18 UK authorised unit trust schemes are subject to the regulations made by the Secretary of State and SIB under the *Financial Services Act 1986* chapter VIII. The principal regulations, currently in force are:

- *The Financial Services (Authorised Unit Trust Schemes) Regulations 1988* (issued by SIB).

- *The Financial Services (Scheme Particulars) Regulations 1988* (issued by SIB).

- *The Authorised Unit Trust Scheme (Investment and Borrowing Powers) Regulations 1988* (SI 1988/284) (as amended by SI 1989/1437).

- *The Authorised Unit Trust Scheme (Pricing of Units and Dealings by Trustee and Manager) Regulations 1988* (SI 1988/280).

7.19 SIB is in the process of revising the regulations governing authorised unit trust schemes. The proposed regulations, to be known as *The Financial Services (Regulated Schemes) Regulations 1991*, bring together in one document all of the regulations relating to the constitution and management of authorised unit trust schemes. The draft regulations also incorporate the provisions of the SORP 'Authorised Unit Trust Schemes', which is reproduced as annex 3 to this chapter. The impact of the SORP on unit trust financial statements is outlined in paragraphs 7.29 to 7.46.

Accounting records

7.20 The accounting records that a unit trust must keep will be specified in its trust deed. The general principles relating to accounting records are considered in chapter 6. The accounting records must additionally be adequate to demonstrate compliance with the regulations mentioned in paragraphs 7.18 and 7.19.

Systems of control

7.21 A unit trust's systems of control cover a number of related functions. There are four accounting areas for which unit trusts are required to have adequate accounting systems to enable compliance with the current regulatory requirements. These areas of accounting are as follows:

- Trust accounting.

- Manager's accounting.

- Trustee's accounting.

- Registrar's accounting.

7.22 These systems quite often overlap and the distinction between them may be blurred.

7.23 The main functions that a unit trust's systems should address are as follows:

- Box management.

  The manager's accounting system must be capable of providing up-to-date box management information (that is, information on the number of units the manager is holding for sale at any point in time). The system should monitor the sale and repurchase by the manager of units and the resulting position. This is necessary to ensure the manager can make sound commercial decisions and to ensure that a negative box (whereby the manager has sold more units than there are units in issue) does not arise, particularly at a valuation point. [SI 1988/280 para 11.2].

- Pricing.

  The bid and offer prices for a unit trust should be based on the respective bid and offer prices for the trust's underlying investments. The system must, accordingly, be capable of valuing the underlying assets of the trust and calculating unit prices. [SI 1988/280 para 3].

- Registration.

  The trust's registrar (generally, the manager or a bank) is required to maintain up-to-date records of unitholders and issue accurate certificates on a timely basis.

7.24 The accounting system must give trustees and managers sufficient information to provide the following functions:

- Treasury management (that is, trust cash flow and cash management).

- Income collection.

- Custodianship of the trust's property.

- Settlement of broker accounts.

Manager's report and accounts

Current regulations

7.25 Current best practice for the form and content of the manager's report and accounts is determined by the *Financial Services (Authorised Unit Trust Schemes) Regulations 1988*. The regulations became applicable for unit trusts with accounting periods commencing on or after 1st January 1989.

7.26 Under the regulations, the manager is required to prepare a report in relation to each annual and half-yearly accounting period. However, a report need not be prepared in relation to the first half-yearly accounting period if the first annual accounting period is less than 12 months.

7.27 The structure under the 1988 regulations for unit trust annual financial statements is as follows:

- ■ Manager's report:
  - □ Management commentary.
  - □ Comparative table of prices, net income distributable and net asset values.
  - □ Portfolio changes statement.
- ■ Financial statements:
  - □ Statement of assets and liabilities.
  - □ Capital account.
  - □ Income and distribution statement.
  - □ Notes to the financial statements.
- ■ Signature of two directors of the manager.
- ■ Trustee's report.
- ■ Auditors' report.

7.28 A pro-forma manager's report and accounts fully cross-referenced to the regulations is illustrated in annex 1.

Proposed regulations

7.29 The form and content of future unit trust financial statements is set out in the draft *Financial Services (Regulated Schemes) Regulations 1991*. Part 10 of the regulations incorporates the provisions of the SORP 'Authorised Unit Trust Schemes' (issued in April 1991). The regulations are expected to be issued in the Summer of 1991 and the SORP's recommendations apply to accounting periods beginning on or after 1st September 1991 with comparatives required for accounting periods beginning on or after 1st September 1992.

7.30 Under the new regulations the frequency of reporting remains unchanged. In addition, the manager's report is broadly similar.

7.31 The major changes relate to the form of the financial statements. The accounting and disclosure issues that relate to such financial statements are addressed in detail in the SORP.

7.32 The proposed structure of the annual financial statements is as follows:

- Manager's report:
  - Management commentary.
  - Comparative table of prices, net income distributable and net asset values.
  - Statement of commissions on dealings in the property of the scheme.
- Financial statements:
  - Balance sheet.
  - Income account.
  - Statement of movement in net assets.
  - Portfolio statement.
  - Portfolio changes statement.
  - Notes to the financial statements.
- Signature of two directors of the manager.

■ Trustee's report.

■ Auditors' report.

7.33 A suggested format for the manager's report and accounts under the draft regulations and the SORP is given in annex 2.

7.34 The principal differences in the format of the financial statements are that the draft regulations propose that:

■ A full unit trust balance sheet should be included in the financial statements comprising both the capital and the income accounts. The current regulations require a statement of net assets which does not reflect the income balances. Inclusion of these income balances will provide an indication of the fund manager's efficiency in cash collection and also act as a measure of the fund's liquidity.

■ The detail underlying the value of the fund's investments should be disclosed in a separate portfolio statement.

■ The present statement of movement in the capital account is to be replaced by a statement of movement in net assets of the trust. The movement in net assets will include the movement in both capital and income balances.

■ Items in the income account will be given both in absolute terms by way of figures and as a percentage of the average net assets of the scheme.

■ Comparatives will have to be given for all major categories on the face of the balance sheet and the income account in terms of the percentage of the value of the fund, but the previous year's comparatives in monetary terms are still not required.

Accounting policies

7.35 The SORP not only deals with the presentation of the financial statements, but also details the accounting policies that should be adopted in preparing the financial statements. These policies are considered in paragraphs 7.36 to 7.46.

Valuation of investments

7.36 The general principle is that investments should be valued at market value at the balance sheet date. This valuation should be made either on a mid-market basis or on a bid basis and should be applied consistently. [IMRO SORP paras 84,85].

7.37 Investments that bear interest should be valued at market value net of any accrued interest. Such accrued interest should be included in the balance sheet as an income related item. [IMRO SORP para 87].

7.38 Investments that are neither approved investments (within the meaning of the *Financial Services (Regulated Schemes) Regulations 1991* (issued by SIB), nor investments in a CIS, should be identified in the portfolio statement and valued at a judgemental valuation. The basis of this valuation should be disclosed in the notes to the financial statements. [IMRO SORP para 85].

7.39 Purchases and sales of investments should be recorded in the investment portfolio on the date of trade. Amounts due to and from the same broker in respect of purchases and sales of investments should be shown separately (and not netted off) unless there is a legal right of set off. [IMRO SORP para 88].

Property valuation

7.40 The SORP acknowledges that property valuations are costly to obtain. It states, however, that an annual valuation is necessary together with a monthly review of the valuation in order to provide unitholders with an up-to-date estimate of the value of the portfolio. The disclosure and accounting treatment of such properties should accord with the provisions of SSAP 19, 'Accounting for investment properties'. [IMRO SORP paras 30,89].

Currency hedging

7.41 Hedging transactions are usually entered into to minimise the risks arising from exchange rate movements. Currency hedging transactions include:

- Back-to-back loans.

  This involves borrowing in one currency and matching that borrowing by a deposit in another currency. Any currency loss or gain on the deposit is then matched by a currency gain or loss on the borrowing. In such transactions there is often an interest gain or loss where the loan interest paid differs from the deposit interest earned. Currency and interest gains or losses on back-to-back loans should be taken to the capital account, with the interest income and interest expense separately disclosed. This is considered to be the correct treatment when loans are entered into to hedge the capital value of a portfolio and the interest gain and loss is an integral part of the hedging transaction. Where the manager believes that the net interest paid or earned should be taken to the income account, the reasons for this treatment should be explained. [IMRO SORP paras 18,91].

■ Forward exchange contracts.

An unrealised gain or loss on a forward exchange contract outstanding at the balance sheet date will arise where there is a difference between the contracted rate and the relevant market rate prevailing at the balance sheet date. This gain or loss should be taken to the capital account where it is designed as a hedge. Where the gain or loss relates to specific items of income it should be recognised in the income account. [IMRO SORP paras 20,92].

■ Currency options or futures.

Where a gain or loss on a currency option or futures contract offsets the currency movement in the value of the portfolio, it should be taken to the capital account. [IMRO SORP paras 21,92].

Other futures and options

7.42 The value of an asset in the portfolio may be hedged by, for example, purchasing a put option which entitles the manager to dispose of the security at an agreed price. In this situation, the cost of the hedging instrument should be treated as a capital item. Open positions in both options and futures should be marked to market. Short positions should be treated as liabilities of the scheme and deducted from the value of the capital asset it is hedging. Realised and unrealised gains or losses (including those on option writing) should be taken to the capital account. [IMRO SORP paras 22,23,93].

7.43 Full details of all open option positions at the balance sheet date, including their strike price, their final exercise date and whether or not the position is covered should be shown in the financial statements. [IMRO SORP para 94].

Fund of funds

7.44 Where a trust invests in units of another trust those units should be valued at market value. Where the units in that other trust are accumulation units, the income accumulated in the underlying trust should be shown in the income account of the investing trust. [IMRO SORP paras 27,28,95].

Income recognition

7.45 Dividend and interest income should be accounted for on the accruals basis. A dividend should be accounted for when the underlying investment becomes ex-dividend. Shares received in lieu of cash dividends should be taken to the capital account with a corresponding transfer made to the income account representing the net amount of deemed income (except where this treatment would result in an additional tax charge arising). [IMRO SORP para 101,102].

Treatment of expenses

7.46 Expenses that are not included in the costs of purchasing or selling an investment should be charged to the income account. If permitted by the general law of trust, transfers may be made from the income account to the capital account in respect of items of expense that are considered to be capital in nature. Where such transfers are made, full details should be disclosed in the notes to the financial statements and the basis of the transfers should be consistent from year to year. [IMRO SORP para 106].

Audit requirements

7.47 *The Financial Services (Authorised Unit Trust Schemes) Regulations 1988* and the draft *Financial Services (Regulated Schemes) Regulations 1991* require the manager, with the approval of the trustee, to appoint auditors for a unit trust scheme. The auditors' duty is to report on the annual financial statements prepared by the manager.

Audit report

7.48 The standard audit report on the annual financial statements must be addressed to the members, that is the unitholders of the unit trust scheme. The report should include the following statements (the items marked with an asterisk are additional requirements included in the draft *Financial Services (Regulated Schemes) Regulations 1991*):

- Whether the audit has been conducted in accordance with Auditing Standards.

- Whether in the auditors' opinion the financial statements have been properly prepared in accordance with generally accepted accounting principles and in accordance with the regulations in force, the SORP* and the trust deed.

- Whether in the auditors' opinion a true and fair view is given of the financial position of the scheme at the end of the period.

7.49 The auditors shall report by exception that:

- In the auditors' opinion, proper accounting records have not been kept by the manager and that the financial statements are not in agreement with the manager's accounting records.

- The auditors have not received all information and explanations, to the best of their knowledge and belief, necessary for the purposes of their audit.

- In the auditors' opinion, the information given in the report of the manager is not consistent with the financial statements.

7.50 An unqualified audit report under the current regulations is given below:

REPORT OF THE AUDITORS TO THE UNITHOLDERS OF [NAME OF TRUST]

We have audited the financial statements on pages [] to [] in accordance with Auditing Standards.

In our opinion the financial statements give a true and fair view of the financial position of the scheme as at [date], and of its [income/deficit] and source and application of funds for the [period] then ended, and have been properly prepared in accordance with generally accepted accounting principles, with the Financial Services (Authorised Unit Trust Schemes) Regulations 1988 and with the Trust Deed.

[Name of firm]

Chartered Accountants,

[Address].

[Date of report].

7.51 An unqualified audit report drawn up in accordance with the proposed new regulations and the SORP is given below:

REPORT OF THE AUDITORS TO THE UNITHOLDERS OF [NAME OF TRUST]

We have audited the financial statements on pages [] to [] in accordance with Auditing Standards.

In our opinion the financial statements give a true and fair view of the financial position of the scheme as at [date], and of its [income/deficit] and source and application of funds for the [period] then ended, and have been properly prepared in accordance with generally accepted accounting principles, with the Financial Services (Regulated Schemes) Regulations 1991, with the Statement of Recommended Practice for Authorised Unit Trust Schemes and with the Trust Deed.

[Name of firm]

Chartered Accountants,

[Address].

[Date of report].

PRO-FORMA MANAGER'S REPORT AND ACCOUNTS – CURRENT REGULATIONS

This annex provides in concise form the information that should be disclosed in the report and accounts of authorised unit trusts schemes to comply with the current disclosure requirements of the *Financial Services Act 1986* and the related SIB regulations, '*Financial Services (Authorised Unit Trust Schemes) Regulations 1988*'. This pro-forma cannot serve as a substitute for reference to the regulations. Its purpose, however, is to provide guidance on the content of unit trust financial statements.

The references relate to the *Financial Services (Authorised Unit Trust Schemes) Regulations 1988.*

The pro-forma does not extend to the recommendations of the draft SORP 'Authorised Unit Trust schemes' or to the proposed new regulations, which are both illustrated in annex 2.

XYZ Trust
Manager's Report and Accounts
for the period ended [date]

Contents

FACTS

The Aim — *This is dependent upon the type of trust in question, but would typically include whether the trust aims to provide:*
1) Secure long-term capital growth.
2) An above average and increasing yield.
3) High income combined with capital growth, through investment in a specified geographical area or sector of market.
The policy for achieving the aim of the scheme must also be set out.
6.01 (1); Sch 2 Part I, Notes 2,3

Minimum Investment

Launch Date

Actual Gross Annual Yield

Period End Dates

Distribution Dates

Management Charges Initial [ ]% Annual [ ]% (plus VAT)
The Trust Deed allows for these charges to be increased up to a maximum of [ ]% and [ ]% respectively after written notice to unitholders.

Investment Manager

Notes — *Significant information, for example:*
— Changes in scheme particulars
— Sub-division of units
6.01 (1); 2 Sch Part I, Notes 7, 11, 12

Constitution — 6.01 (1); 2 Sch Part I Notes 4, 5

This Trust is an authorised unit trust scheme within the meaning of the Financial Services Act 1986 and is an authorised securities scheme as defined in the regulations made under Section 81 of that Act.

1

PERFORMANCE: PRICES AND DIVIDENDS

6.01 (2)(b); 2 Sch Part III
Note 2

6.01 (1); 2 Sch Part I
Note 10
At beginning and end of current period

Trust Size to....

Year	Net Asset Value (£)	Per Unit (Pence) Net Asset Value	Mid-market Price	No. of Units in Issue
1989				.... (income)
				.... (accumulation)
1990				.... (income)
				.... (accumulation)
1991				.... (income)
				.... (accumulation)

6.01 (2)(b); 2 Sch Part III
Note 1

Unit Price Range to....

Year	Income Units		Accumulation Units	
	Highest Offer (Pence)	Lowest Bid (Pence)	Highest Offer (Pence)	Lowest Bid (Pence)
1982				
1983				
1984				
1985				
1986				
1987				
1988				
1989				
1990				
1991				

6.01 (2)(b); 2 Sch Part III
Note 1

Net Income Distribution/Accumulation to....

Year	Income Units		Accumulation Units	
	Pence per Unit	Per £1000 invested at beginning of the 10 year period (£)	Pence per Unit	Per £1000 invested at beginning of the 10 year period (£)
1982				
1983				
1984				
1985				
1986				
1987				
1988				
1989				
1990				
1991				

Past performance is not necessarily a guide to future performance. Investors are reminded that the price of units and the income from them is not guaranteed and may go down as well as up.

2

MANAGER'S REPORT

6.01 (1); 2 Sch Part I Note 6

Review

This section typically includes a review of the economic conditions prevailing in the market place during the accounting period.

Activity

This section typically includes a description of the structure of the portfolio together with details of changes in the geographical/sector weightings within the portfolio during the accounting period.

Outlook

This section typically includes an outlook for the trust.

(Date)

3

6.01 (3)(a); 3 Sch Part I

STATEMENT OF ASSETS AND LIABILITIES as at. . .

Investments
All investments are in common or ordinary stocks and shares except where otherwise stated. See note 1(d)

Holding	Investment	Value £	% of Trust

Note a — Holding, Investment, Value £
Note b — % of Trust

Total Value of Investments

Net Liquid Assets

Note d — Sterling current and deposit bank balances

Currency deposits

6.01 (3)(c)(ii); 3 Sch Part IV Note 5(a) — Settlement due for sale of securities

Note f — Total Value of Assets

Note d — Bank overdrafts

Loans

6.01 (3)(c)(ii); 3 Sch Part IV Note 5(b) — Settlement owing for purchase of securities

Note h — Total Value of the Trust

(Net Liquid Assets: The analysis may be given in the notes to the accounts 6.01 (3)(c)(ii); 3 Sch Part IV Note 5)

(The investments shown in the above statement may be categorised by geographical area or by industrial sector.)

4

PORTFOLIO CHANGES

6.01 (2)(a); 2 Sch Part II

During the period [ ] to [ ] the following changes have been made to the portfolio.

Quantity/Nominal Value | Description — Note 1

New Holdings

Increase in Existing Holdings

Partial Disposals

Total Disposals

Bonuses Received

Capital Changes

Total cost of purchases — Note 2

Total proceeds of sales — Note 3

5

6.01 (3)(c)(i); 3 Sch Part III

CAPITAL ACCOUNT

For the accounting period [ ] to [ ]
(Incorporating a Statement of the Source and Application of Funds)

		Investments £	Net Liquid Assets £	Total £
Note 1	Value of Trust at *(Beginning of Period)*			
	Cash Movement			
Note 2	Cash received for units created			
Note 3	Cash paid for units liquidated *(Where applicable include: Capital/Revenue shortfall transferred from/to Income and Distribution Statement)*			
	Net cash movement from units			
	Investment Movement			
	Proceeds of investments sold			
	Cost of investments purchased			
Note 4	Net cash movement from investment			
	Realised Profits/(Losses)			
	Realised profits/(losses) on investments			
	Less: Appreciation/(depreciation) thereon brought into account at *(End of previous period)*			
Note 8	Net realised profits/(losses) for the period			
	Unrealised Profits/(Losses)			
	Unrealised appreciation/(depreciation) at *(End of current period)*			
	Less: Unrealised appreciation/(depreciation) at *(End of previous period)*			
Note 4	Unrealised appreciation/(depreciation) movement in the period			
Note 5	Charges			
Note 6	Value of Trust at *(End of period)*			

6

INCOME AND DISTRIBUTION STATEMENT — 6.01 (3)(b); 3 Sch Part II

For the accounting period [ ] to [ ]

	£	£	Pence per unit Income	Accumulation
Income Receivable Notes 1(a)(b)(c) — Note a *(The analysis may be given in the notes to the accounts 6.01 (3)(c)(ii); 3 Sch Part IV Note 2)*				
Dividends from UK investments (franked)				
Other income (unfranked)				
Interest on bank and short-term deposits				
Interest on deposits and loans in foreign currencies				
Interest on fixed interest stocks				
Underwriting commission				
Dividends on overseas investments				
Less Trust Expenses Note 7				
Manager's service charge — Note c				
Trustee's fees — Note h				
Custody charges — Note h				
Auditor's remuneration — Note i				
Other charges — Note j				
Net income before taxation				
Less Taxation Note 3 — Note e				
Net income after taxation				
Add				
Income received on units created — Note b				
Less				
Income paid on units liquidated — Note b				
Add				
Amount brought forward from previous period — Note f				
Less				
Amount carried forward to next period — Note f				
Less				
Interim distribution/ accumulation paid on — Note k				
(Where applicable include: Capital/Revenue shortfall transferred to/from Capital Account) — Notes m,n				
Final distribution/accumulation no [ ] payable on [ ] — Notes g,l				

7

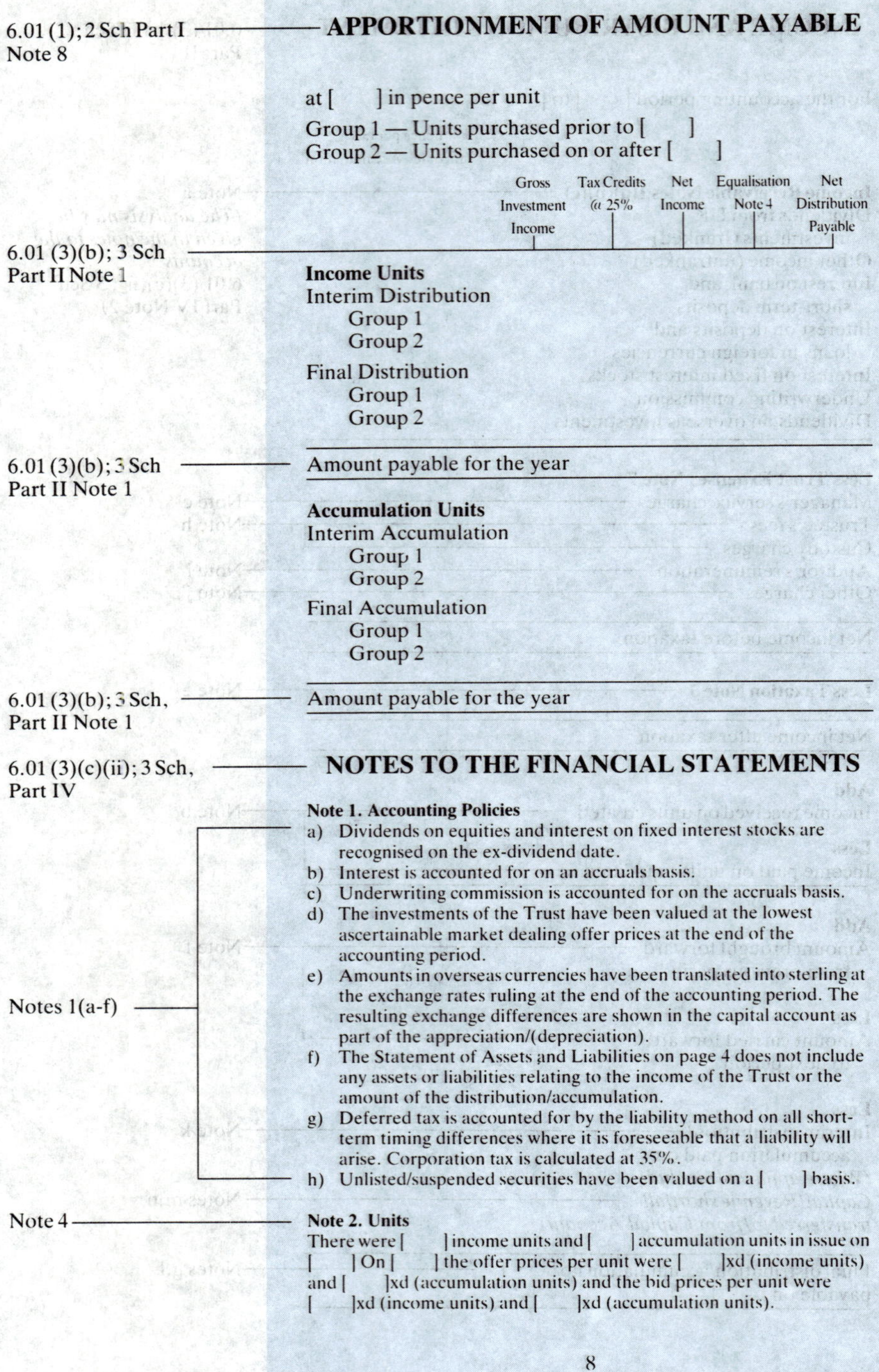

6.01 (1); 2 Sch Part I Note 8

APPORTIONMENT OF AMOUNT PAYABLE

at [ ] in pence per unit

Group 1 — Units purchased prior to [ ]
Group 2 — Units purchased on or after [ ]

6.01 (3)(b); 3 Sch Part II Note 1

	Gross Investment Income	Tax Credits @ 25%	Net Income	Equalisation Note 4	Net Distribution Payable
Income Units					
Interim Distribution					
Group 1					
Group 2					
Final Distribution					
Group 1					
Group 2					
Amount payable for the year					
Accumulation Units					
Interim Accumulation					
Group 1					
Group 2					
Final Accumulation					
Group 1					
Group 2					
Amount payable for the year					

6.01 (3)(b); 3 Sch Part II Note 1 — Amount payable for the year (Income Units)

6.01 (3)(b); 3 Sch, Part II Note 1 — Amount payable for the year (Accumulation Units)

6.01 (3)(c)(ii); 3 Sch, Part IV

NOTES TO THE FINANCIAL STATEMENTS

Notes 1(a-f)

Note 1. Accounting Policies

a) Dividends on equities and interest on fixed interest stocks are recognised on the ex-dividend date.
b) Interest is accounted for on an accruals basis.
c) Underwriting commission is accounted for on the accruals basis.
d) The investments of the Trust have been valued at the lowest ascertainable market dealing offer prices at the end of the accounting period.
e) Amounts in overseas currencies have been translated into sterling at the exchange rates ruling at the end of the accounting period. The resulting exchange differences are shown in the capital account as part of the appreciation/(depreciation).
f) The Statement of Assets and Liabilities on page 4 does not include any assets or liabilities relating to the income of the Trust or the amount of the distribution/accumulation.
g) Deferred tax is accounted for by the liability method on all short-term timing differences where it is foreseeable that a liability will arise. Corporation tax is calculated at 35%.
h) Unlisted/suspended securities have been valued on a [ ] basis.

Note 4

Note 2. Units

There were [ ] income units and [ ] accumulation units in issue on [ ] On [ ] the offer prices per unit were [ ]xd (income units) and [ ]xd (accumulation units) and the bid prices per unit were [ ]xd (income units) and [ ]xd (accumulation units).

8

NOTES TO THE FINANCIAL STATEMENTS

Note 3. Taxation — 6.01 (3)(c)(ii); 3 Sch Part IV Note 1(e)

	£
Tax on UK dividends	
Corporation tax	
Foreign withholding tax	
Double tax relief	
Deferred tax	
Provision for advance corporation tax on proposed distribution	

Corporation tax is calculated at [ ]% on unfranked income received during the accounting period after taking into account the accrued income scheme and other adjustments. — *Trusts certified as complying with the provisions of the UCITS Directive are subject to a different tax regime.*

The provision for advance corporation tax represents that part of the amounts paid during the year and the amounts payable in respect of the proposed distribution which cannot be recovered against the tax liabilities of the current or previous periods.

The deferred tax charge/credit represents the movement in the deferred tax provision in the year which takes account of the fact that income and expenditure are recognised in different periods for accounting and tax purposes.

Note 4. Equalisation — 6.01 (3)(c)(ii); 3 Sch Part IV Note 3

This applies only to units purchased during the distribution period (Group 2 units). It is the average amount of income included in the purchase price of Group 2 units and is refunded to the holders of these units as a return of capital. Being capital it is not liable to income tax but must be deducted from the cost of units for capital gains tax purposes.

Note 5. Commission — 6.01 (3)(c)(i); 3 Sch Part III Note 7 a,c,d

The amount of commission paid in the period totalled £[ ]. The mark-up/down incurred in dealing in the scheme property was [ ] and the average rate of commission [ ]%.

(Broker) acted for the Trust in respect of more than 10% of the aggregate value of transactions. The proportion of the aggregate value of transactions done with or through each associate of the Manager (or Trustee) was £[ ].

Note 6. Loans — 6.01 (3)(c)(ii); 3 Sch Part IV Note 6

During the year under review loans of US$ [ ] and HK$ [ ] were repaid. A further loan of US$ [ ] was drawn down. This loan was converted to sterling to provide currency cover against fluctuations in the value of the portfolio. Interest rates on borrowing ranged from [ ] % to [ ] % and interest earned on the sterling deposits were at rates between [ ] % and [ ] %.

Note 7. Trust Expenses — 6.01 (3)(b); 3 Sch Part II Note d

Auditors' and Trustee's fees, including registration fees, are charged to the Trust through the Income and Distribution Account. The Manager has paid fees or expenses of the Trustee of £[ ] from his own resources for the period. Trust expenses are inclusive of VAT where applicable.

Note 8. Yield

The actual gross yield was [ ] on [ ] and is based on the gross dividends paid or declared for the last full year divided by the offered price at the period end.

Note 9. Contingent Liabilities — 6.01 (3)(c)(ii); 3 Sch Part IV Note 7, 6.01 (3)(a); 3 Sch Part I Note g

There are contingent liabilities in respect of nil paid shares amounting to £[ ] and partly paid shares amounting to £[ ] Contingent liabilities not provided for relate to [ ]

Note 10. Forward Exchange — 6.01 (3)(c)(ii); 3 Sch Part IV Note 8

The open forward exchange position is [ ]

9

6.01 (4)

DIRECTORS' STATEMENT

In accordance with the requirements of the Financial Services (Authorised Unit Trust Schemes) Regulations 1988, we hereby certify the report on behalf of the Directors of XYZ Unit Trust Managers Ltd.

[Director]

[Director]

[Date]

6.01 (2)(d); 2 Sch Part V

TRUSTEE'S REPORT TO THE UNITHOLDERS OF XYZ

In our opinion the Manager managed the scheme during the annual accounting period ended [date], in accordance with the limitations imposed on the investment and borrowing powers of the Manager and the Trustee by the Trust Deed, by the scheme particulars and by all regulations, for the time being, in force under section 81 of the Financial Services Act 1986, and otherwise in accordance with the provisions of the Trust Deed and those regulations.

[TRUSTEE]
[Address]
[Date]

6.01 (2)(c); 2 Sch Part IV

AUDITORS' REPORT TO THE UNITHOLDERS OF XYZ

We have audited the financial statements on page 4 and pages 6 to 9 in accordance with Auditing Standards.

In our opinion the financial statements give a true and fair view of the financial position of the scheme at [date], of the [income/deficit] and the source and application of funds and have been properly prepared in accordance with generally accepted accounting principles, with the Financial Services (Authorised Unit Trust Schemes) Regulations 1988 and with the Trust Deed.

[Name of Firm]
Chartered Accountants

[Address]

[Date]

10

MANAGEMENT/PROFESSIONAL SERVICES — 6.01 (1); 2 Sch Part I
DETAILS

Manager — Note 1(a)
[Name and address]

Trustee — Note 1(b)
[Name and address]

Investment Adviser — Note 1(c)
[Name and address]

Registrar — Note 1(d)
[Name and address]

Auditor — Note 1(e)
[Name and address]

11

PRO-FORMA MANAGER'S REPORT AND ACCOUNTS – PROPOSED REGULATIONS

This annex provides in concise form the proposed information that should be disclosed in the report and accounts of authorised unit trust schemes to comply with the disclosure requirements of the *Financial Services Act 1986* and the related draft SIB regulations to be named the *Financial Services (Regulated Schemes) Regulations 1991*, which incorporate the provisions of the IMRO SORP, 'Authorised Unit Trust Schemes'. This pro-forma cannot serve as a substitute for reference to the new regulations. Its purpose, however, is to provide guidance on the proposed content of unit trust financial statements.

The references relate to the draft *Financial Services (Regulated Schemes) Regulations 1991* and the IMRO SORP 'Authorised Unit Trust Schemes'.

The pro-forma does not cover the current regulations contained in the *Financial Services (Authorised Unit Trust Schemes) Regulations 1988*, which are illustrated in annex 1.

XYZ Trust
Manager's Report and Accounts
for the period ended [ ]

Contents

MANAGER'S REPORT

10.02.1; 3 Sch Part I

The objective

This is dependent upon the type of trust in question but would typically include whether the trust aims to provide:

1) secure long-term capital growth,
2) an above average and increasing yield, or
3) high income combined with capital growth, through investment in a specified geographical area or sector of the market.

The manager's policy for achieving the objective of the scheme must also be set out.

Notes 2, 3

Review of investment activities

This section typically includes a review of the economic conditions prevailing in the market place and of the manager's investment activities during the accounting period to which the report relates.

Note 6

[Date]

1

10.02.2(b); 3 Sch, Part III

PERFORMANCE RECORD

Note 2

Trust Size

Year	Net asset Value (£)	Net Asset Value per Unit (pence)	No. of Units in Issue
1989			
1990			
1991			

Note 1

Unit Price Range

	Income Units		Accumulation Units	
Year	Highest Offer (Pence)	Lowest Offer (Pence)	Highest Offer (Pence)	Lowest Bid (Pence)
1982				
1983				
1984				
1985				
1986				
1987				
1988				
1989				
1990				
1991				

Note 1

Net Income distribution/Accumulation

	Income Units		Accumulation Units	
Year	Pence per Unit	Per £1000 invested at beginning of the 10 year period (£)	Pence per Unit	Per £1000 invested at beginning of the 10 year period (£)
1982				
1983				
1984				
1985				
1986				
1987				
1988				
1989				
1990				
1991				

Note 3(a)(b) – Where the scheme has been the subject of an amalgamation, reconstruction or unitisation which has an effect on the size of the scheme or where the objectives of the scheme have changed, this should be stated.

Past performance is not necessarily a guide to future performance. Investors are reminded that the price of units and the income from them is not guaranteed and may go down as well as up.

2

STATEMENT OF COMMISSIONS — 10.02.2(a); 3 Sch Part II

Transactions effected directly with a market maker — Note 1

The proportion of the aggregate value of the transactions effected with associates of the manager and trustee was £[ ] and £[ ] respectively. — (a), (b)

More than 10% of the transactions in the property of the scheme were effected through [name of market-maker(s)] — (c)

Transactions effected through the agency of an intermediary — Note 2

The average rate of commission on such transactions was [ ]% — (a)

The aggregate amount of commission paid to associates of the manager and the trustee was £[ ] and £[ ] respectively. — (b), (c)

[Name of broker(s)] received more than 10% of the aggregate amount of the commissions paid. — (d)

Soft commission — Note 3

Soft commission arrangements entered into by the manager or any affected person operating in relation to the manager were [ ] — (a), (b)

3

10.02.3; SORP Appendix 1

BALANCE SHEET

Reference		1991 £'000	Percentage of net assets 1991	Percentage of net assets 1990
Paras 8, 83				
Para 12	Investments at market value			
	Debtors			
	Amounts receivable for creations			
Paras 33, 88	Sales awaiting settlement			
	Loans to income property			
	Other debtors			
Para 26	Amounts held at futures clearing houses and brokers			
Para 82	Cash and bank balances			
Paras 34, 91	Back-to-back deposits			
Para 93	Creditors – amounts falling due within one year			
	Amounts payable for liquidations			
Paras 33, 88	Purchases awaiting settlement			
Paras 34, 91	Back-to-back loans			
	Net current capital assets			
	Net capital property			
	Net income property (Note 7)			
			100.00%	100.00%
	Capital account			
	Income account			
			100.00%	100.00%

4

INCOME ACCOUNT

10.02.3; SORP Appendix 2

	Note	1991	% value of the fund for the period to	
		£'000	1991 †	1990 †
Gross income	8			
Expenses	9			
Net income before taxation				
Taxation	10			
Transfer (to)/from capital account				
Equalisation				
Received on units created				
Deducted on units cancelled				
Distribution				
Interim				
Final				
Income retained for the year				
Undistributed income brought forward				
Undistributed income carried forward				

Para 39, 99

Paras 29, 44, 102

Distribution

Para 100

Group 1: Units purchased prior to [ ] 1991
Group 2: Units purchased on or after [ ] 1991

Appendix 4 Note 11

	Gross income	Tax credit	Net income	Equalisation	Distribution Payable	Distribution Paid
	1991 pence per unit	1991 pence per unit	1991 pence per unit	1991 pence per unit	1991 pence per unit	1990 pence per unit
Income units						
Group 1						
Group 2						
Accumulation units						
Group 1						
Group 2						

Paras 39, 100

Notes:
† See Note 2

A statement may also be presented showing the interim distribution

5

10.02.3; SORP Appendix 3 —

STATEMENT OF MOVEMENT IN NET ASSETS

	Investments £'000	Other net assets £'000	Total £'000
Net assets at start of period			
Para 110 — Movements due to sales and repurchases of units			
Cash or value received on creation of units			
Cash or value given on cancellation of units			
Para 110 — Cash movements due to purchases and sales of investments †			
Proceeds of investments sold			
Cost of investments purchased			
Net realised gains/(losses for the period)			
Paras 17, 22, 93, 111 — Gains/(losses) realised on sale of investments †			
Net appreciation/(depreciation) thereon brought forward			
Paras 22, 24, 93, 110, 111 — Net unrealised appreciation/ (depreciation) for the period			
Paras 18, 112 loans * — Net gains/(losses) on back-to-back			
Paras 20, 92 — Gains/(losses) on forward foreign exchange contracts			
Para 21 — Other currency movements			
Paras 61, 62, 113 — Transfers (to)/from income account			
Para 113 — Net movement in income account			
Net assets at end of period			

Notes:

* *Further details of gross interest income and expense, currency gains and losses and tax effect on back-to-back loans to be given in note 5 to the financial statements.*

† *Including derivatives*

6

PORTFOLIO STATEMENT

10.02.3; SORP Appendix 5

	Holding 1991	Market Value	Percentage of total net assets
		£	%
Japan ([ ]%; 1990 [ ]%)			
**Japan A			
*Japan B			
Options:			
*Japan B [date] [ ] put			
			%
United States ([ ]%; 1990 [ ]%)			
* USA A			
† USA B			
Options:			
* USA A [date] [ ] call			
			%
United Kingdom			
Options:			
A plc [date] [ ] call			
Unrealised profit on open futures contracts			
Investments as shown in the balance sheet			%
Net current assets			%
Total net assets			%

Para 7

Paras 25, 94

† Not approved securities within the meaning of the Financial Services (Regulated Schemes) Regulations 1991 (issued by SIB). — Paras 15, 64, 85

* Matched security and option positions

** Recently issued securities within the meaning of the Financial Services (Regulated Schemes) Regulations 1991 (issued by SIB). — Para 64

An equivalent standard of disclosure is required for other types of scheme

7

10.02.3; SORP Appendix 6

PORTFOLIO CHANGES

Para 63

Major purchases	Cost £'000	Major sales	Proceeds £'000
Japan A		Japan D	
USA A		USA F	
USA B		Hong Kong A	
Japan C		Spain B	
UK A		Hong Kong B	
UK B		Australia A	
Germany A		Australia C	
Netherlands A		Japan G	
Germany B		Hong Kong D	
UK D		Australia F	
Japan X		USA H	
UK C		Hong Kong J	
Japan J		USA G	
Spain R		Germany K	
USA N		USA M	
Japan P		UK E	
Australia K		Japan Y	
USA K		France S	
UK L		Germany S	
Japan Y		USA T	

Disclose material purchases and sales. (Materiality level – 1% of total value of purchases and sales as disclosed in statement of movement in net assets or, as a minimum, the 20 largest purchases and sales.)

8

NOTES TO THE FINANCIAL STATEMENTS — 10.02.3; SORP Appendix 4

1. Accounting policies — Para 81

Income

Dividends on equities and interest on fixed interest stocks are recognised when the security is quoted ex-dividend. — Paras 10, 42, 45, 101

Interest, underwriting commission and other income are accounted for on the acruals basis. — Paras 46, 47, 103, 104

Valuation

Quoted investments have been valued at mid-market value net of any accrued interest which is included in the balance sheet as an income related item. Unlisted securities and unapproved securities have been valued at the manager's valuation. — Paras 12, 13, 84, 85, 87 (Para 13 – a bid valuation basis consistently applied from one year to the next would be acceptable.)

Suspended securities have been valued at nil. — Paras 15, 85

Properties have been valued at the open market value. — Paras 30, 89

(Para 14 – the precise valuation point should be disclosed where it is not that of the balance sheet date.)

Foreign currencies — Paras 12, 86

Assets and liabilities have been translated into sterling at the exchange rates prevailing at the balance sheet date. The resulting exchange differences are disclosed in the statement of movement in net assets.

Deferred tax — Para 56

Deferred tax is provided for in respect of all material timing differences where it is foreseeable that a liability or asset will crystallise.

Fund of funds — Para 28

Income from accumulation units in the underlying trusts is recognised gross in the income account. The net income is then accumulated from the income account into the balance sheet.

2. Units in issue and the average net assets

There were [ ] income units and [ ] accumulation units in issue at the balance sheet date.

The average net assets of the scheme are based on an average of the daily net assets. — Paras 40, 99 (As a minimum standard standard of accuracy the calculation of net assets should be based on monthly figures for net assets.)

9

Paras 30, 89 — **3. Properties**

Interests in property were valued on [ ] 1991 by [ ] independent valuers.

Paras 25, 94 — **4. Forward foreign exchange transactions**

Open option positions at the balance sheet date which are all covered are shown in the portfolio statement. Unrealised gains/(losses) on forward foreign exchange transactions are taken to capital. Details of the gains/(losses) are given in the statement of movement in net assets.

Paras 18, 19, 31, 91 (Para 19 – where net interest is included in the income account the reasons for this treatment and the value of the gain/loss should be disclosed.) — **5. Back-to-back loans and deposits**

Back to back loans at the balance sheet date include a loan of US$[ ] which was converted into sterling to provide currency cover against fluctuations in the value of the portfolio. Interest rates on borrowing ranged from [ ]% to [ ]% and interest earned on the sterling deposits was at rates between [ ]% and [ ]%.
Gross interest income on back-to-back loans of [ ] together with the associated tax effect of [ ] and, currency gains/(losses) of [ ] are taken to capital and are disclosed in the statement of movement in net assets.

Paras 31, 90 — **6. Stock lending activities**

The aggregate value of securities on loans at the balance sheet date was [ ] and the value of the collateral held by the scheme in respect of these securities was [ ].

7. Net income property

		£
	Debtors	
Paras 11, 35, 82	Accrued income	
	Other debtors	
Para 82	Cash at bank	
	Creditors	
	Loans from capital property	
	Accrued expenses	
Para 82	Distribution payable	
Para 82	Corporation tax payable	
Paras 53, 96	Advance corporation tax	
	Deferred taxation	
	Net income property	

These items may be shown on the face of the balance sheet.

10

8. Gross income —————— £ —————— Appendix 2, Note 2

UK dividends
Overseas dividends
Bank interest
Interest on securities
Underwriting commission
Other income

Gross income

Gross interest income on back-to-back loans was [ ] and expenses were [ ]. The aggregate amount of income written off during the year was [ ] and provisions of [ ] were made.

9. Expenses —————— Para 106 Appendix 2 Note 3

	£	£
Payable to the manager or associate of the manager:		
Manager's periodic charge		
Registration fees		
Other (*specify*)		
Payable to the trustee or associate of the trustee:		
Trustee's fee		
Handling charges		
Safe custody charges		
Other (*specify*)		
Other expenses:		
SIB fees		
Audit fees		
Safe custody		
Other (*specify*)		
Total expenses		

Transaction related handling charges of [ ] have been transferred to the capital account, as they are considered to be capital in nature. —————— Paras 51, 106

A transfer of [ ] was made from the capital account to income to cover the shortfall in income during the period. —————— Para 106

11

Paras 9, 52, 54, 108

(These items may be shown on the face of the income account.)

(Trusts certified as complying with the provisions of the UCITs Directive are subject to a different tax regime.)

10. Taxation

	£
Tax attributable to franked investment income	
Corporation tax	
Irrecoverable ACT	
Overseas tax	
Deferred tax	

Corporation tax is calculated at [ ] % on unfranked income received during the accounting period after taking into account the accrued income scheme and other adjustments.

Para 53

The deferred tax charge/credit represents the movement in the deferred tax provision in the year as a result of income and expenditure being recognised in different periods for accounting and tax purposes.

11. Equalisation

This applies only to units purchased during the distribution period (Group 2 units). It is the average amount of income included in the purchase price of Group 2 units and is refunded to the holders of these units as a return of capital. Being capital it is not liable to income tax but must be deducted from the cost of units for capital gains tax purposes.

12. Distributions

Paras 48, 105

During the year securities were purchased cum dividend and sold ex dividend. This resulted in an increased distribution payable. This income is at the expense of the capital account and is not guaranteed to be sustained in future periods.

12

13. Contingent liabilities

The aggregates of contingent liabilities not provided for at the balance sheet date are as follows: — Paras 37, 38, 97 (Where results of issues underwritten are known or securities sold prior to the signing of the financial statements, the value of contingent liabilities should be adjusted accordingly.)

	£
Underwriting commission	
Placing arrangements	
Partly paid shares	
Nil paid rights	

14. Post balance sheet events

The following material post balance sheet events have a bearing on the understanding of the financial statements. — Appendix 4, Note 10

[ ]

15. Additional notes required by regulators

(Any additional disclosures as required from time to time by the SIB or other regulators.) — Appendix 4, Note 13

The financial statements on pages 4 to 13 were approved by the manager and signed on its behalf by: — 10.02.4 (If the manager has only one director then by that director.)

[ ] *Director*

[ ] *Director*

13

10.02.2(d); 3 Sch
Part V
10.06

TRUSTEE'S REPORT TO THE UNITHOLDERS OF XYZ TRUST

In our opinion the Manager managed the scheme during the annual accounting period ended [date], in accordance with the limitations imposed on the investment and borrowing powers of the Manager and the Trustee by the Trust Deed, by the scheme particulars and by all the regulations, for the time being, in force under section 81 of the Financial Services Act 1986, and otherwise in accordance with the provisions of the Trust Deed and those regulations.

[Trustee]

[Address]

[Date]

10.02.2(c); 3 Sch
Part IV

AUDITORS' REPORT TO THE UNITHOLDERS OF XYZ TRUST

We have audited the financial statements on pages 4 to 13 in accordance with Auditing Standards.

In our opinion the financial statements give a true and fair view of the financial position of the scheme as at [date], and of its [income/deficit] and source and application of funds for the [period] then ended and have been properly prepared in accordance with generally accepted accounting principles, with the Financial Services (Regulated Schemes) Regulations 1991, with the Statement of Recommended Practice for Authorised Unit Trust Schemes and with the Trust Deed.

[Name of Firm]
Chartered Accountants

[Address]
[Date]

14

GENERAL INFORMATION

Constitution

This trust is an authorised unit trust scheme within the meaning of the Financial Services Act 1986 and is an authorised (name of category of scheme) scheme as defined in the Regulations made under section 81 of that Act. — 10.02.1; 3 Sch Part I Notes 4, 5

Launch date

Accounting end dates

Distribution dates

Minimum investment

Management charges

Initial [ ]%
Annual [ ]%
The Trust Deed allows for these charges to be increased up to a maximum of [ ]% and [ ] respectively after written notice to unitholders.

Investment Manager

Notes — 10.02.1: 3 Sch Part I, Notes 7, 8, 9 (Significant information, for example:

- Changes in scheme particulars.
- Sub-division or consolidation of units.)

15

PRICING AND DEALING

The buying (offer) price and the selling (bid) price of units are determined by reference to the underlying market value of the net assets of the trust at the valuation point, (time). Unit prices are normally calculated daily, however, if the markets are exceptionally volatile they may be recalculated more frequently to reflect any major changes in the value of the trust's underlying assets.

The prices and the initial charge are published daily in the Financial Times and other leading newspapers on the day following the valuation. The difference between the quoted offer and bid prices is called the spread and takes account of the manager's initial charges and expenses. Whilst the maximum spread is laid down by statutory regulations, the Manager has the discretion, and will endeavour to quote a narrower spread between these prices.

Dealing in units takes place from [ ] am to [ ] pm daily, on an historic price basis. However, exceptions to this when the Manager will deal on a foward price basis are:

- If the investor so requests.
- If the market and currency movements indicate that the value of units would have changed by more than 2% of the value calculated at the last valuation point.
- Where the Manager has agreed to deal without the investor knowing the price at which units will be issued or redeemed (for example, postal applications).
- Where the Manager considers it appropriate (for example, large deals).
- If new prices have not been notified to the Trustee within two hours of the valuation point.

BUYING UNITS

Units may be bought on any business day (subject to an initial minimum investment) from the Manager or through a financial adviser by telephoning or completing an application form. The units will be allocated at the offer price ruling on receipt of the order. A contract note will be issued by the next business day after the valuation point and payment is due within four business days of the date of the contract. A certificate of ownership will be issued within 21 days of receipt by the Manager of the payment and full registration details.

16

SELLING UNITS

Units may be sold back to the Manager on any business day at the bid price ruling on receipt of instructions to sell. Payment will be made not later than the close of business on the fourth business day following the later of the next valuation point occurring after receipt of the request to redeem the units and, the time when the Manager is in possession of the renounced certificate.

CANCELLATION RIGHTS

Investors entering into a contract to purchase units following advice from an authorised representative of XYZ Unit Trust Managers Ltd or an independent intermediary will under the Financial Services (Cancellation) Rules 1989 have the right to cancel their purchase of units within 14 days of receipt of the cancellation notice. However, investors purchasing units without first receiving advice will have **no** rights of cancellation.

DISTRIBUTIONS AND ACCUMULATIONS

On the distribution date net income is paid to unitholders in possession of income units on the basis of their holding at the accounting date. However, investors may choose to automatically reinvest their income by opting for accumulation units. In this event, the net income is incorporated in the price of the units so that the price of accumulation units increases more rapidly than the price of income units.

Investors are reminded that past performance is not necessarily a guide to future performance and that the price of units and the income from them is not guaranteed and may go down as well as up.

REINVESTMENT OF INCOME

Unitholders may build up their Trust holding by having all the net income earned by the units reinvested to purchase additional units. Income will be reinvested at the offer price ruling 14 days prior to the distribution date, or the preceding business day. Unitholders electing for this option will receive a statement on each distribution date showing the number of units purchased and the price paid.

TAXATION

Income Tax

Income is distributed/accumulated net of basic rate tax. Tax vouchers are sent to unitholders with each distribution/ accumulation and investors will be taxed on the net income together with the credit shown on the voucher. Investors not liable to income tax can reclaim the tax credit from the Inland Revenue, whilst investors paying higher rate tax will be subject to an additional tax liability.

Capital Gains Tax

The trust is not liable to capital gains tax arising on the disposal of its investments.

An investor disposing of units in the trust will only be liable to capital gains tax where the investor's total of taxable gains from all sources (net of losses and after indexation relief) in any tax year exceeds the annual exemption limit. Gains in excess of the exemption will be taxed at the top slice of the unitholder's taxable income.

Investors should note that no indexation relief is available on capital gains arising on the disposal of units in gilt funds.

SCHEME PARTICULARS AND MANAGER'S REPORTS

The Manager will send to all unitholders annual and half-yearly report and accounts.

Copies of the scheme particulars and the most recent annual or half-yearly report and accounts are available to all persons free of charge from XYZ Unit Managers Ltd upon request.

(The General Information section should be amended so as to fall in line with an individual trust's pricing and dealing policy.)

18

OTHER FUNDS AND SERVICES

PERSONAL EQUITY PLANS

XYZ Unit Managers Ltd (a member of IMRO) offers a range of personal equity plans (PEPs).

PEPs are an attractive and tax efficient means of building up a long term investment portfolio. The range of options allows investors to choose between risk and return by investing in unit trusts and equities. Income and capital gains arising from investment in a PEP are free from tax. Investors in a PEP should, however, remember that the value of investments within a PEP can go down as well as up.

SHARE EXCHANGE SCHEMES

XYZ Unit Managers Ltd operates a share exchange scheme whereby potential investors may exchange all or part of their investment in equities or unit trusts (minimum of £[ ]) for units in XYZ unit trusts.

Investors are advised that disposals by means of a share exchange scheme are subject to capital gains tax.

MONTHLY SAVINGS PLAN

The monthly savings plan provides investors with an investment programme based on regular contributions. Investments are subject to a minimum of £[ ] per month but this may be topped up by additional contributions. Accumulation units will normally be issued at the offer price ruling on the [ ] day of the month or on the following business day.

Once the investment plan has reached £[ ] investors may stop saving and resume investment whenever they wish. However, where investment stops before this minimum, XYZ Unit Managers Ltd reserves the right to sell units at the ruling bid price.

Further details and Terms and Conditions of the above services may be obtained by completing the enclosed information request or by contacting the Manager.

19

10.02.1; 3 Sch Part I —— **MANAGEMENT AND PROFESSIONAL SERVICES**

Note 1(a) —— Manager
[Name and address]

Note 1(b) —— Trustee
[Name and address]

Note 1(c) —— Investment Adviser
[Name and address]

Note 1(d) —— Registrar
[Name and address]

Note 1(e) —— Auditor
[Name and address]

Note 1(f) —— Independent Property Valuer
[Name and address]

20

IMRO SORP-AUTHORISED UNIT TRUST SCHEMES

FOREWORD

This Statement of Recommended Practice ("SORP") sets out recommendations on the manner in which the manager of an authorised unit trust scheme should present the scheme's financial statements to the unitholders.

It is issued by the Investment Management Regulatory Organisation Limited ("IMRO"), a recognised Self Regulatory Organisation under the Financial Services Act 1986. The members regulated by IMRO include most managers and trustees of authorised unit trust schemes.

The Accounting Standards Board ("ASB") has approved IMRO for the purposes of issuing recognised SORPs for unit trusts. This arrangement requires IMRO to follow the ASB's code of practice for the production and issuing of SORPs.

The code of practice provides the framework to be followed by IMRO for the development of SORPs, but does not entail a detailed examination of the proposed SORP by the ASB. However, a review of limited scope is performed.

On the basis of its review, the ASB has concluded that the SORP has been developed in accordance with the ASB's code of practice and does not appear to contain any fundamental points of principle which are unacceptable in the context of current accounting practice or to conflict with any existing or currently contemplated accounting standard.

Managers of authorised unit trust schemes are required to comply with statutory regulations issued by the Securities and Investments Board ("SIB"), including regulations on reports to unitholders. The SIB has indicated that it will, through such regulations, require managers of authorised unit trusts to follow the recommendations contained in this SORP.

April 1991

Authorised Unit Trust Schemes

Contents

Paragraphs

Authorised Unit Trust Schemes

This Statement of Recommended Practice (SORP) sets out recommendations on the manner in which the managers of an authorised unit trust scheme should present the scheme's financial statements to the unitholders. The recommendations do not address the content of the report of the managers of a unit trust scheme: this is covered in other rules and regulations relating to authorised unit trust schemes.

The recommendations in this statement should be read in conjunction with the Explanatory Foreword *to SORPs, and any rules and regulations relating to Authorised Unit Trust Schemes and other collective investment schemes which are in force and the law relating to these matters. Although the recommendations are not mandatory, managers of unit trust schemes are encouraged to follow them and state in the financial statements that they have done so. They are also encouraged to disclose any departure from the recommendations and the reason for it. The recommendations should be applied within the concept of materiality.*

Part 1 - Explanatory note

Background

1. The primary purpose of the annual and semi-annual report or indeed more frequent reports to a holder of units in a unit trust is to provide appropriate details of the disposition of the trust's assets at the relevant accounting date and their performance during the period, together with information regarding the distribution or accumulation of net income accruing to the unitholder. The publication of these reports and the financial statements contained therein will also assist an investor or financial intermediary in reaching an informed opinion as to the relative merits of one investment product as compared with another. It is therefore desirable for financial statements to contain sufficient information, presented where applicable in a uniform manner, to enable meaningful comparisons to be performed.

2. In 1981, the Department of Trade in conjunction with the Unit Trust Association published a report setting out a recommended format of the financial statements. In general, the recommendations of the report have been adopted by unit trust management groups, and this structure was broadly incorporated into the rulebook of the Securities and Investments Board ("SIB") relating to Collective Investment Schemes after the implementation of the Financial Services Act 1986 ("FSA"), and were thus given statutory force. However, while the FSA and the related SIB rules and regulations prescribe the minimum content of such reports, they give only limited guidance on the format of the financial statements and on the accounting policies to be adopted in their preparation. Consideration of these issues has been left to the unit trust industry, managers and trustees, and the accounting profession. In addressing this task, and in the light of some variation in the practices adopted, it is considered desirable to set out a statement of recommended practice.

3. The purpose of setting out the recommendations in this statement is to help further improve the quality of financial reporting by authorised unit trusts. The aim is also to provide assistance to those who are responsible for the preparation of unit trusts' annual reports and financial statements. It is hoped that the recommendations will reduce diversity in accounting practice and presentation although the intention is not to try to create total uniformity. This SORP only addresses accounting and disclosure issues insofar as they affect the truth and fairness of the financial statements.

4. Various accounting and disclosure issues which face the manager and trustee of an authorised unit trust scheme are considered below. Part 3 of this document sets out the recommended practice in relation to these issues.

Balance Sheet

Disclosure

5. Under the SIB regulations dated April 1988 the financial statements of authorised unit trust schemes must contain a statement of assets and liabilities. The specific regulations regarding the content of this statement have been interpreted hitherto as requiring only items relating to the capital property of the scheme to be disclosed. Whilst the items incorporated in the capital account generally comprise by far the most significant portion of the total property of the scheme, there may also be income-related items which are significant and of interest to the unitholders. Such items might include the following:

- accrued income receivable
- tax recoverable
- expenses payable
- other liabilities and provisions

6. A fundamental concept in the preparation of financial statements is that all the accounting balances at the period end will be incorporated in the accounts drawn up. It is therefore felt that there should be a balance sheet which incorporates items relating to the income account as well as those relating to capital, to ensure completeness of accounting and disclosure. Having regard to the distinction between capital property and income property, which is still fundamental to the nature and taxation of an authorised unit trust scheme, it is recommended that the balance sheet should show clearly the division of the net assets of the scheme between those held on capital account and those held on income account. It is recognised that undue detail on the face of the balance sheet may confuse the reader and accordingly, where appropriate, full disclosure should be made in the notes to the financial statements. A recommended format for the balance sheet is given in Appendix 1.

Comparatives

7. It is a current SIB requirement to disclose for each holding in the portfolio the percentage of the value of the property of the scheme that the holding represents. It has become common practice for the financial statements to show this statistic for each category of holding in the property of the scheme in addition to the individual holdings. Thus percentages by geographical area or industrial sector are shown, depending on the nature of the portfolio. It is

considered that to give comparative percentages for these statistics would give the reader of the financial statements a concise indication of how the disposition of the assets of the scheme has changed over the accounting period, in a more helpful manner than listing individual purchases and sales of securities. Accordingly, it is recommended that such comparative figures should be presented in the portfolio statement. A suggested format for the portfolio statement is set out in Appendix 5.

8. The above recommendation in relation to comparative figures for categories of assets within the portfolio is also applicable to all other assets and liabilities of the scheme, whether of a capital or income nature. It is therefore recommended that on the face of the balance sheet, current and prior period percentages should be given for current capital assets and net income property, as well as for the total value of the portfolio of investments, as shown in Appendix 1.

Fundamental accounting policies

9. One of the four fundamental accounting concepts as set out in Statement of Standard Accounting Practice number 2 ("Disclosure of accounting policies") is that of accruals, whereby revenue and costs are recognised when they are earned or incurred. By the nature of accruals, precise values may not be attributable to the amounts in question, particularly where provisions are required. In these circumstances, adjustments will be made in the next accounting period. It is particularly important to apply the accruals concept to unit trusts where a potentially changing body of investors in a trust must receive reasonable equity in entitlements between accounting periods. Accounting for transactions on a cash basis increases the possibility that the most equitable treatment between periods is not achieved.

10. In the case of a security, the income can normally be regarded as earned when the security is quoted *ex-dividend*, when the price quoted falls to reflect the value of the impending dividend. Even if the dividend is not expected to be received within a very short period after the balance sheet date it would still in most cases be appropriate to accrue the dividend since to exclude the income would be inconsistent with valuing the investment at market value, because the market value will have fallen through lack of entitlement to the impending dividend. For the purposes of the financial statements, therefore, the balance sheet should state the investments at market value and the income account should recognise the income, including accruals.

11. Following the accruals concept, interest on debt securities should also be recognised as it is earned. To achieve this, accrued interest purchased and sold on interest bearing securities should be excluded from the capital cost of these securities and dealt with as part of the income assets of the scheme. In the case of recently acquired securities held at the balance sheet date, the difference between accrued interest receivable at the balance sheet date and the interest purchased should be taken to revenue as a distributable item; if there has been an interest payment date between the date of purchase and the balance sheet date then only that amount of interest accrued since the payment date should be included in the balance sheet. In the case of investments sold prior to the balance sheet date, the difference between accrued interest sold and accrued

interest purchased should be taken to revenue. The desired result will be that in the balance sheet at the accounting period end there will be a balance representing total coupon interest receivable on securities held at that date, and the income account will recognise that amount of interest which has been earned whilst a security has been held. Taxation provisions, including deferred tax, are considered in paragraphs 52 to 57 below.

Accounting for Investments

Valuation

12. The general principle regarding the valuation of the investments of the scheme is that they should be stated at market value at the balance sheet date. Where applicable, investments should always be valued at clean prices, excluding any element of accrued income, which will be included in the income property of the scheme. The value of overseas securities should be translated into the base currency at exchange rates prevailing at the balance sheet date.

13. The accounting system used for valuing the investments for financial statements purposes at the period end will normally be the same as that used for unit valuation purposes. The international accounting convention for valuing securities in financial statements is mid market valuation; indeed in other countries "single pricing" of units or shares is the accepted method. The current convention in the unit trust industry for accounts purposes is to adopt "lowest ascertainable market dealing offer price" in valuing investments. However, whilst this basis is ascertainable for UK stocks, a mid market price is often the price available in overseas markets. It is therefore recommended that, to achieve greater consistency, a mid-market valuation basis is used, whilst recognising that since not all accounting systems readily allow mid market valuations a policy of conservatively valuing the portfolio on a bid basis consistently from one year to the next is acceptable. The policy adopted for valuing the investments should be stated in a note to the financial statements.

14. As part of the normal operation of the scheme, the scheme's managers produce regular valuations, usually daily, the effective time of which is known as the "valuation point". It would be appropriate to use the closest normal valuation of the property of the scheme for the purposes of the financial statements rather than performing an additional valuation. This would be acceptable where there is little market volatility, provided that the valuation point is sufficiently near to the close of business on the balance sheet date, such that any distortion in price is clearly immaterial. Where this approach is adopted, the precise valuation point should be disclosed in the notes to the financial statements. In the case where valuations are less frequent than daily, however, an additional valuation as at the close of business on the balance sheet date (practically interpreted as the last business day of the accounting period) would be required if no valuation occurred on that date.

15. In the majority of schemes the determination of the market value of the portfolio should be reasonably straightforward, since the values are readily available through published sources. However, in certain situations the value of a security may not be readily determinable, as will often be the case where

the investment is not an approved security within the meaning of the Authorised Unit Trust Schemes (Investment and Borrowing Powers) Regulations 1988 (or equivalent subsequent rules). In such circumstances the securities may be stated at a judgemental valuation, provided that adequate details are disclosed by way of notes to the financial statements of the basis for the valuation and any provisions made against the original cost. Managers should keep these specific valuations under review to ensure that the balance sheet always fairly represents the current value of the assets in the portfolio. Any securities within the portfolio which are not approved should be clearly identified in the portfolio statement.

Efficient portfolio management ("EPM")

16. Under current regulations, there is a variety of techniques which a scheme may use to control the risk of market movements and also to seek to generate additional gains for the scheme at limited risk. Many of these techniques involve the use of derivative products. It is recognised that to address all potential situations and transactions arising from EPM would be to extend the current document to unmanageable proportions. Examples of such techniques and the accounting principles involved are discussed in outline below.

Currency hedging

17. Hedging transactions may be entered into with a view to minimising the risks arising from exchange rate movements. Such transactions are generally designed to preserve the capital value of the portfolio and accordingly any gains or losses resulting from these hedging activities should also be treated as capital in nature. Occasionally a hedging transaction may be designed to protect future income receipts, in which case it would be appropriate to deal with the effects of the transaction in the income account.

18. One traditional method which may be used to hedge the currency risk is to enter into a back-to-back loan, i.e. a borrowing in one currency matched by a deposit in another currency. Any currency loss on a security is then matched by a currency gain on the borrowing or *vice versa*, and this currency gain or loss on the borrowing is conventionally included in the capital account. This is considered to be the correct accounting treatment since such loans are typically entered into to hedge the capital value of the portfolio.

19. As well as a currency gain or loss on the back-to-back loan there is often an interest gain or loss, where the loan interest paid is different from the deposit interest earned. It is considered that this interest gain or loss is an integral part of the hedging transaction, not least because there is often a direct relationship between interest rate differentials and currency movements. Further, it is considered that to recognise the amount in the income account could lead to uneven distributions. Accordingly in these circumstances it is considered that the interest gain or loss on back-to-back loans should be taken to the capital account. The related tax charge or credit should also be shown in the capital account: there is provision in the Taxes Act to allow specifically a deduction for interest paid to a bank carrying on a *bona fide* banking business in the UK, even where that interest is charged to capital account. Where the managers of the scheme believe that the net interest earned or paid should be included in the income account, the reasons for this treatment should be explained in the notes

to the financial statements, quantifying any associated capital gain or loss, whether realised or unrealised.

20. Forward foreign exchange contracts may also be used to control the risk of exchange rate movements. There may be an unrealised gain or loss on a contract outstanding at the balance sheet date, representing the difference between the contracted rate and the relevant market rate prevailing at the period end. This gain or loss should normally be to taken to capital, since the contract will usually be associated with a specific security transaction or will be designed to hedge the currency value of a group of investments. Where a forward contract is used to cover a future income receipt accrued at the balance sheet date, the accrual may be translated at the contracted rate; the effect of this contract will therefore be on the income account rather than the capital account.

21. The exposure to exchange rate risk can also be managed by the use of currency options and futures where the gain or loss on the derivative instrument offsets the currency movements in the value of the portfolio. Since the intention in entering into a currency option or futures transaction is to preserve the value of the capital property of the scheme, the gain or loss on the transaction should be taken to capital account and should not therefore be distributable.

Other techniques

22. When using EPM, the manager of the scheme may protect the value of an asset or category of assets by, for example, purchasing a put option entitling him to dispose of the related security in the portfolio at an agreed price. The cost of the relevant derivative instrument should not be treated as an item of expenditure but rather as a capital item since it relates to the capital property of the scheme. The treatment of the derivative should be consistent with that of the item hedged. The most appropriate treatment is therefore to mark the derivative product to market and to take to capital both the unrealised gains and losses on positions existing at the period end and the realised gains or losses crystallised on closing out any positions held during the period. If, in the example of a put option purchased, the manager decided to exercise the option, the profit to be taken to capital would normally be the net sale proceeds of the security less its original cost and less the cost of the option.

23. Whether the scheme's derivatives activities are undertaken for EPM or for other purposes, the resulting positions, both long and short, can be regarded as no different from any other investment, and hence the positions should be marked to market. Realised and unrealised gains and losses on these investments should be taken to the capital account.

24. The manager may also write an option or a contract for difference on a security in the scheme's portfolio entitling the buyer of the option to buy or sell the security at an agreed price, in exchange for which right a premium is paid to the scheme. The purpose of such a transaction from the manager's viewpoint would be to increase the return from the assets of the scheme. In the example of a written call option, it could be argued that the resulting short option position need not be recognised in the balance sheet because in the case where

the writer of the option already owned the underlying security there would be no contingent liability: the premium is already earned and the price of the potential sale is fixed. Acceptance of this argument could lead to recognition of the option writing premium in the income account when the option is written, and recognition of a capital profit or loss when the option is exercised. This treatment would allow income to be generated to the detriment of capital simply by writing call options with a low strike price. Therefore the premium income should be treated as deferred sale proceeds, and the increase in cash from writing the option should be balanced not by income but by the deferred sales proceeds of a short position which is recognised in the capital account. This short position should be valued at market value, and any unrealised profits or losses taken to capital account. When the position is closed, whether through lapse, exercise or by buying an equal and opposite call option in the market, the profit or loss should again be taken to the capital account. The same principles would apply to the writing of put options and contracts for differences.

25. Given the volatility of the market value of option positions, where there are open option positions at the balance sheet date, the unitholder should be given sufficient information to assess the nature and risk relating to items contained in the portfolio. This information should include the strike price and final exercise date of the option, together with an indication of whether the position is covered or not.

26. When futures and options transactions constitute a material part of the activities of the scheme, the amounts held at clearing houses or brokers should be separately disclosed as debtors within the capital assets on the balance sheet. The balance to be disclosed should be the ledger balance arising from cash movements and realised profits and losses. Any unrealised profits arising from contracts remaining open at the balance sheet date should have their marked to market value reflected in the portfolio statement.

Fund of funds

27. Where a scheme invests in units of another scheme, the units held should be valued at market value like any other investment. Where the units held are those of schemes managed by the same management group as the one managing the fund of funds, the cost of the units will generally be free of the initial charge, whereas funds investing in the schemes of a variety of management groups may suffer the full spread. The valuation of units held at the balance sheet date should in both cases observe the same principles as for other investments, namely the mid of the purchase price and sale price available to the fund.

28. Where the units held by the fund of funds are accumulation units the question arises of how the investing scheme should recognise the accumulation of income in its own accounts. In order to represent fairly the performance of the scheme for the period, it is considered that the accumulation of income relating to the units held should be recognised gross in the income account, and any tax credit included in the scheme's tax charge disclosed in the income statement. If the fund of funds is itself an accumulation trust, the net income taken to the income account should then be accumulated into the capital

account, although because of the fund of funds' own expenses the amount accumulated may differ from the net income arising in the underlying unit trusts.

29. If the fund of funds investing in the accumulation units is a distributing fund then the distribution of the net accumulation recognised in the income account emphasises the anomaly of investment objectives between the two funds. However, it is considered acceptable to distribute the income recognised in the income account should the managers and the trustees agree that such a policy is in accordance with the scheme particulars. Alternatively, the amount recognised in the income account may be accumulated and added back to the value of units in the capital account, notwithstanding the fact that the fund is a distributing fund; this should be achieved by means of disclosure of the transfer from the income account. The agreed policy should be consistently applied from one accounting period to the next, and should be in accordance with the scheme particulars.

Properties

30. The valuation of properties in a property unit trust or other scheme is more difficult and more costly than that of securities because quotations are not readily available. Valuations for each "immovable" in the fund must be commissioned by the standing independent valuer ("SIV") of the fund in order to provide the support for the balance sheet carrying values. Whilst it is acknowledged that this cost may be significant, a full annual valuation is necessary together with a monthly review of the valuation, in order to give unitholders an up-to-date estimate of the value of the portfolio. The disclosures and accounting treatment for properties should be in accordance with Statement of Standard Accounting Practice number 19 ("Accounting for investment properties") and accordingly the name and qualifications of the valuer should be given by way of note to the financial statements, together with details of the basis of valuation of the properties and the date of the most recent full valuation. The expenses and fees of the SIV will be met by the property of the scheme and in accordance with paragraph 50 should be taken in the first instance to the income account.

Stock lending activities

31. Stock lending is a common practice in developed securities markets, providing increased liquidity to market makers. Under a stock lending agreement, a scheme enters into an agreement whereby it disposes of securities to a counterparty, in return for which it is agreed that securities of the same kind and amount should be transferred back at a later date. Until the subsequent transfer takes place, the scheme generally receives collateral in the form of cash or liquid securities marginally in excess of the market value of the securities transferred. Although legal title to the securities passes from the scheme during the transaction, taken as a whole, the arrangement has the substance of a loan of the scheme's securities in return for collateral. During the life of the transaction, the scheme retains the risks and rewards of ownership, since it is exposed to fluctuations in the market, and in addition is compensated for any income payable on the securities while they are on loan. Furthermore, the scheme is not exposed to any market risks attaching to the collateral. In view of the above considerations and the economic substance of

the transaction, it is recommended that the securities transferred (or "lent") should be included in the financial statements as if they were registered in the name of the scheme, and no account should be taken of any collateral held. In order that the unitholder is aware of the extent to which the scheme's securities are the subject of stock lending arrangements, disclosure should be given in a note to the financial statements of the aggregate value of securities on loan at the balance sheet date, together with the value of collateral held by the scheme in respect of these securities.

Net current assets

Securities awaiting settlement

32. The usual method of accounting for purchases and sales of investments is to include the investments in the portfolio from trade date. This is appropriate since from the date of the trade the purchaser has incurred the risks and rewards of ownership: specifically, he is exposed to market movements both adverse and favourable. Similarly, the seller is no longer exposed to the market once he has entered into an agreement to sell.

33. When purchases and sales are accounted for on a trade date basis, there will at any time be balances owing to and due from brokers in respect of these trades. These amounts should be separately disclosed in the balance sheet under debtors and creditors falling due within one year. Where purchases and sales have been effected through the same broker, the question arises of whether it is permissible to net off purchases and sales effected through that broker. To show the trades gross gives a fairer indication of the volume of transactions outstanding at the period end, and accordingly balances due to and from the same broker should not be netted off except where there is a legal right of set-off.

Back-to-back loans

34. Under present legislation, authorised unit trust schemes are not permitted to borrow, except as permitted under the Authorised Unit Trust Schemes (Investment and Borrowing Powers) Regulations 1988. Normally, any foreign currency borrowing entered into to hedge the value of an investment denominated in that currency is matched by a deposit. As for sales and purchases of securities, the question arises of whether balances with the same bank may be shown net in the balance sheet, particularly when a right of offset exists. It is considered that the loans should be shown gross in order to give an indication of the total value of the portfolio for which the currency risk has been hedged. The deposits against which the loans were made should not be included with other cash and deposit balances because the former deposits are not available for investment, and it is appropriate that liquid assets available for investment should be clearly segregated from those which are not so available.

Accrued income

35. As discussed above, the amount of income receivable under the accruals basis should be incorporated in the balance sheet. This item should include both dividends receivable, interest on bank deposits and accrued interest receivable on debt securities. In occasional circumstances a dividend accrued in a prior period may still be outstanding at the balance sheet date. Where it is still

considered to be recoverable and that therefore no provision is necessary, it will continue to be carried forward as an asset in the balance sheet. The aggregate of any income written off or provisions required should be disclosed in the notes to the financial statements.

36. As noted in paragraph 11 above, the accrued interest purchased on debt securities should be excluded from the capital cost of those securities, but the amount purchased should be included in the income property balance sheet, together with interest earned since the date of purchase. In accordance with Statement of Standard Accounting Practice number 20 ("Foreign currency translation"), the balance sheet accrual of any accrued income denominated in a foreign currency should be translated into sterling at the rate ruling on the balance sheet date, unless a forward foreign exchange contract has been entered into, in which case the contractual rate may be used.

Notes to the accounts

Contingent liabilities

37. Statement of Standard Accounting Practice number 18 ("Accounting for contingencies") requires the disclosure of contingent liabilities which have not been provided for in the financial statements. The Statement defines a contingency as "a condition which exists at the balance sheet date, where the outcome will be confirmed only in the occurrence or non-occurrence of one or more uncertain future events". One of the main contingencies which faces a scheme is the liability to subscribe for shares pursuant to an underwriting, placing or similar agreement. The treatment of underwriting income is discussed below in paragraph 46. The contingent liability is often material in the context of the financial statements and accordingly it is recommended that disclosure be made of underwriting commitments outstanding at the balance sheet date. Where there are several underwriting agreements outstanding at the balance sheet date it is not considered necessary to disclose each individual commitment, but simply to disclose the aggregate commitment. A scheme might also enter into a placing arrangement which may be contingent on certain resolutions being passed by the issuing company. Where such resolutions have not been passed at the balance sheet date the arrangement is a contingent liability and should be disclosed as such in aggregate. Where the results of the placings or issues underwritten at the balance sheet date are known prior to finalising the financial statements, the revised figure should be disclosed together with the total contingent liability still outstanding at the latest practical date before the finalisation of the financial statements where this does not prejudice the prescribed timetable for publication.

38. Contingent liabilities may also exist on partly paid shares. Even though these securities might be sold before the calls become due, the aggregate contingent liability should be disclosed. Where the securities have actually been sold prior to signing the financial statements and no further liability exists, then no disclosure is required, and accordingly the contingent liability should be adjusted to reflect this fact, without prejudicing the prescribed timetable for publication of the financial statements.

Income account

Comparatives - use of pence per unit

39. It is the current practice to express certain items in the income account in terms of pence per unit. This is a useful statistic in comparing the performance of a portfolio from one period to the next, but is of limited use in comparing the performance of different funds because the units of different funds will represent different net asset values. In evaluating the performance of individual investments and portfolios in the investment management industry, much use is made of percentages; thus income yields are expressed as a percentage of the value of an investment; similarly, management and other fees are usually based on the net assets of a portfolio. It is therefore recommended that subtotals of income and expenditure should be expressed as a percentage of the net assets of the scheme. This will enable the unitholder to determine the return generated by the manager from the scheme's assets, and also the amount of income which has been absorbed by expenses. Prior period comparatives should also be shown, expressed in terms of the net assets of the prior accounting period. The amount of the distribution should however be expressed in pence per unit terms to enable comparison with the dividend warrants.

40. If the size of the scheme has altered substantially during the course of the year, using opening or closing net assets as the basis for these percentage figures would give a misleading impression, and compromise the ability of the investor to compare one trust with another or compare the performance of the fund from one year to the next. It is therefore considered that the percentage figures should be based on average net assets of the scheme for the accounting period. It is desirable that this average should be calculated as accurately as possible, using the average of the daily net assets; it is recognised, however, that this may not be possible in all cases and therefore, as a minimum standard of accuracy, the figures should be based on an average of the month end net assets. The basis of calculation should be disclosed in a note to the financial statements. It is recognised that there are certain problems associated with expressing income in terms of a percentage of average net assets of an open ended scheme, but this statistic is considered to be more useful than pence per unit inasmuch as it allows for more meaningful comparisons to be made between schemes.

Income recognition

41. As discussed above, the accruals concept should be applied to all items of income and expenditure. This not only ensures that best accounting practice is followed but also permits greater comparability in the financial statements of different unit trust schemes.

42. The application of the accruals concept to dividends requires that the income should be recognised on *ex-dividend* date. This practice is straightforward to apply for UK dividends, where the information on dividend declarations is readily available and there is seldom any significant delay in payment beyond the due date. The manager therefore knows with reasonable certainty at the balance sheet date the amount of UK income receivable and the date it will be received, and prudent distributions can be made on the basis of this knowledge. For overseas dividends, however, information may not be so readily available,

and it is recognised that there is often some difficulty in obtaining the cash dividend on the date it is payable. It is nevertheless recommended that, subject to the practicalities imposed by publication deadlines, wherever it is known at the balance sheet date or within the distribution period that a dividend is receivable on a particular security at the balance sheet date, that dividend should be recognised as earned in the financial statements. If a dividend is not expected to be received for a significant period after the income allocation date of the scheme, it may be excluded from the calculation of the amount of income available for allocation. For the purposes of determining the amount available for income allocation, a "significant period" may be taken to be twelve months.

43. In cases where income is received after the deduction of withholding tax, whether UK or overseas, the income should be shown gross of taxation, and the tax consequences should be shown within the tax charge.

44. For certain securities the holder may elect to receive a dividend in the form of additional shares rather than cash. Even though no cash is received the implied dividend is nevertheless part of the income of the fund and should therefore be recognised in the income account. The additional shares acquired for capital account will be matched by an equal and opposite transfer of cash to the income account; in the capital account the securities received should be added to the portfolio at the amount transferred. The only exception to this approach might be where, because of the treatment of stock dividends for taxation purposes, an ACT charge would arise on the distribution or accumulation of the notional dividend which could not be relieved against other taxation amounts such that a cost to the trust would result. In these circumstances, no transfer between capital and income need be made.

45. Interest on bank deposits and on debt securities should be recognised, as for dividends, as it is earned. In the case of debt securities, the amount of interest which has accrued since the last payment date will be recognised. Again, interest should be shown gross of taxation.

46. A scheme may have income from other sources, such as underwriting commission and fees from stock lending. Underwriting commission should in general be taken to the income account; the commission is earned in exchange for assuming a contingent liability and in most cases is received whether or not the scheme is required to take up any shares. However, in certain rare circumstances the issue underwritten might not proceed and hence the commission might not be earned; it is therefore recommended on the grounds of prudence that the income be recognised when the issue takes place. In the circumstances when the scheme is required to take up all of the shares underwritten, there are grounds for regarding the commission received in respect of the underwriting commitment as an item which offsets the cost of the shares taken up. The scheme may therefore take the commission received to capital. Where the scheme is required to take up a proportion of the amount underwritten, the same proportion of commission received may be taken to capital and the balance taken to income. The treatment adopted should be consistent from one year to the next. As discussed in paragraph 24 above, the premium received in respect of written put options or relevant contracts for

differences (which could be regarded as similar in economic substance to the practice of underwriting) should always be taken to capital.

47. Any income arising from stock lending should be recognised on an accruals basis; income is normally in the form of a fee based on interest calculated on the market value of securities on loan, and the amount of accrued interest should in most cases be readily determinable since recognised moneybrokers send frequent statements of the value outstanding. It is further considered that the fees earned should be recognised in the income account rather than the capital account.

48. It is occasionally the practice to purchase securities *cum dividend* when a large income payment is expected, and immediately to sell the security *ex dividend* (or less frequently, *vice versa).* Where such a practice has affected the distribution payable by 5% or more, appropriate disclosure should be made in the notes to the financial statements to enable investors to be aware that this income is at the expense of the capital account and may not be sustainable.

49. Circumstances may arise where the trust is distributing an amount which, although distributable, may give rise to cash flow difficulties. Appropriate steps will therefore be needed to fund the distribution, if necessary, through a temporary loan from capital account.

Expenses

50. At present there is some diversity in the treatment of expenses. In some schemes, certain expenses are part of the manager's fee, whilst in others they are shown separately. This difference is not overly significant in view of the requirements in the SIB regulations to give full disclosure of certain specified expenses of the scheme, whether borne by the manager or by the scheme directly. In some cases, however, certain expenses have been charged directly to the capital account where this has been permitted by the trust deeds. There may be some arguments for the distinction between "capital" and "income" expenses. However, lack of consistency in the treatment of expenses throughout the unit trust industry has adverse consequences for the comparability of the financial statements. Therefore all expenses should be charged in the first instance to the income account, regardless of any alternative treatment which may be permitted in the trust deed. This will ensure that all income accounts are comparable in respect of expenses.

51. If and so far as the general law of trust permits, a transfer may be made from the income account to the capital account of items of expense which are considered to be capital in nature. Whilst dealing commissions are included by the broker in the cost of the security and hence are automatically included in the capital account, there are other transaction–related incidental charges such as telex and bank charges incurred in making the investments or disposing of holdings. These charges may be considered capital in nature and therefore there may be an argument for allowing the expenses to be taken ultimately to the capital account. Conversely, auditors' fees are a general cost of operating the scheme and are typically borne by the income property of the scheme rather than the capital property. The determination of which expenses may be regarded as capital is fundamentally a matter for agreement between the

manager and the trustee in the light of general principles of the law of trust as to what is proper in the circumstances; clearly this allocation will be considered by the auditors. Full disclosure of the reasons for the transfer and details for the basis of the amount transferred should be given in the notes to the financial statements. The treatment should be consistent from one period to the next, and should where appropriate be net of any tax relief which may be available.

Taxation

52. It is considered that the following items will normally be the significant components of the tax charge and should therefore be separately identified:

- tax attributable to franked investment income
- UK corporation tax
- irrecoverable ACT
- overseas taxation
- deferred tax

These items may be shown in the notes to the financial statements if it is considered that investors may be confused by excessive detail on the face of the income account.

Advance Corporation Tax payable

53. The accounting treatment of advance corporation tax ("ACT") for an authorised unit trust should be in compliance with Statement of Standard Accounting Practice number 8 ("The treatment of taxation under the imputation system in the accounts of companies"). Thus full provision should be made for ACT on distributions proposed at the balance sheet date. In some cases, particularly in a scheme invested wholly in UK equities, some or all of the ACT liability may not in fact be payable because of franked investment income. In such circumstances, only that amount of ACT which is actually payable should be shown as a liability in the balance sheet. In determining the amount of ACT which is expected to be payable the manager should take a prudent view of available franked investment income. In most cases this will be done by reference to the franked investment income position at the trust's *ex-dividend* date.

Irrecoverable Advance Corporation Tax

54. Even though in practice ACT paid can be carried forward indefinitely to be offset against future corporation tax liabilities, for accounting purposes it is necessary to decide whether recovery of the ACT is reasonably certain. Any ACT in excess of this amount should be written off. In the case of ACT on the proposed distribution at the balance sheet date, this provision should strictly be made on the basis of the estimated corporation tax liability for the following accounting period; normally, however, the liability for the current accounting period should be used as a best estimate. In effect this discontinuance basis seeks to ensure equity between different groups of unitholders in separate accounting periods. ACT not expected to be recovered in accordance with prevailing tax legislation should be written off and shown as part of the tax charge.

Overseas taxation

55. For schemes invested mainly overseas, owing to the treatment of double tax relief there is likely to be irrecoverable ACT as well as irrecoverable withholding tax. In addition, there may be a large amount of overseas taxation recoverable under double tax treaties. There may often be a significant time lag between the receipt of the overseas dividend net of taxation and the receipt of the tax refund. Whether the distribution should assume that all tax claims will be recovered in full will depend on the circumstances and recovery experience in respect of the investments and territories involved. If provision is considered necessary owing to significant uncertainty as to receipt, this should be deducted from the amount receivable and disclosed; further, the estimated expense of recovering the taxation should also be provided for and included within expenses.

Deferred Taxation

56. With the adoption of the accruals concept for income items there will be timing differences between the accounting treatment of certain items and their taxation. It is considered that the accounting treatment of the taxation effect of these timing differences should be consistent with that of the timing differences themselves, and that deferred taxation should be provided on these timing differences to the extent that any tax liability or asset is likely to crystallise. The provisions of Statement of Standard Accounting Practice number 15 ("Accounting for deferred tax") should be applied, and the related disclosures made in the notes to the financial statements.

Value Added Tax

57. The VAT recovery position will vary from scheme to scheme, depending in part on the geographical specialisation. As for all other items in the income account and balance sheet, the recovery of VAT should be treated on an accruals basis. Thus if the percentage recovery of VAT is reasonably certain based on the manager's past experience, the relevant amount should be accrued in the quarter to which it relates. Any irrecoverable VAT should be included with the item of expenditure to which it relates in accordance with Statement of Standard Accounting Practice number 5 ("Accounting for value added tax").

Statement of movement in net assets

58. The statement of movement in the capital account, which is a requirement of the 1988 SIB regulations, is a useful reconciliation of the opening and closing capital assets of the scheme. For the sake of consistency with the recommendation outlined in paragraph 6 above, it is recommended that this statement should incorporate income balances as well, thus reconciling the opening and closing total net assets, both capital and income. Clearly the income account, as set out in Appendix 2, gives the unitholder information regarding the income, expenditure and distribution of the scheme, thus explaining the movement in the net income assets for the period, and the statement of movement in net assets need not duplicate this detailed information. A suggested format for the statement of movement in net assets is given in Appendix 3.

59. In a scheme that is invested in overseas securities, a significant proportion of both realised and unrealised gains will be attributable to currency movements. A useful additional disclosure in the statement of movement in net assets would therefore be to show the amount of gains or losses in the accounting period, both realised and unrealised, which are attributable to currency movements. However because at present not all accounting systems in the unit trust industry are able to provide such analysis cost effectively no recommendation is made in this regard at this time.

60. In paragraph 34 above, it was recommended that there should be no netting off of back-to-back loans with their related sterling deposits. The same practice should be adopted with respect to interest income and expense on these transactions. As discussed above, the interest gain or loss should normally be shown in the capital account; the foreign currency interest expense and the sterling interest income should be disclosed individually in order to give the unitholder information of the cost of hedging the overseas element of the portfolio.

61. As discussed in paragraph 51 above, there may in certain circumstances be a transfer of expenses from the income account to the capital account. This transfer should be shown prominently in the statement of movement in net assets, together with any tax effect, so that it is immediately evident precisely what expenses are being charged to capital. Full explanation should be given in the notes to the financial statements of why the expenses are considered to be capital in nature.

62. There may be circumstances in which there is insufficient income to cover the expenses of the scheme. In this situation a cash transfer will need to be made from capital to cover this deficit of income.

Changes in the composition of the portfolio

63. A statement of portfolio changes is required by the UCITS directive and the SIB rules. The purpose of this statement is to identify the significant changes in the disposition of the assets of the scheme, and in complying with this requirement it is recommended that the concept of materiality is applied in determining those changes which require disclosure. It is not suggested that EPM transactions need to be disclosed in the statement of portfolio changes. By way of guidance as to what changes are considered material, it is recommended that aggregate purchases of a security exceeding 1% by value of the total value of purchases for the period as shown in the statement of movements in net assets should be disclosed, together with aggregate disposals greater than 1% of the total value of sales. There may be occasions where in a portfolio with a high turnover there may be no transactions in a security which satisfy this test. It is therefore recommended that as a minimum level of disclosure the largest 20 purchases and 20 sales are given where such an extent of disclosure would not be required under the above guidelines. A suggested format for the statement of material portfolio changes is set out in Appendix 6.

Other requirements

64. It is a requirement of the UCITS directive to distinguish in the portfolio statement between those securities admitted to an official stock exchange listing, those dealt on another regulated market, and those securities which are unapproved. It is the SIB's interpretation that a geographical analysis of the portfolio gives an adequate indication of the official stock exchange on which the securities are listed and is sufficient for meet the UCITS requirement. As discussed in paragraph 15 above, unapproved securities should however be identified in the portfolio statement by means of a suitable marker. Recently issued securities (as defined in the Authorised Unit Trust Schemes (Investment and Borrowing Powers) Regulations 1988) should be identified in a similar manner.

Part 2 - Definition of terms

65. The definitions which follow are of those terms which are relevant in the context of this SORP. A comprehensive list of definitions relating to collective investment schemes is given in the relevant SIB regulations.

66. *Scheme.* An authorised unit trust scheme.

67. *Property of the scheme.* The capital property and the income property.

68. *Capital property.* All the property for the time being held on trust in accordance with the trust deed other than the income property.

69. *Income property.* All sums, including income equalisation, deemed by the manager, to be in the nature of income received or receivable by the trustee in respect of the property of the scheme after making provision for expenses and distribution payable.

70. *Market value.* In relation to the value of investments for the purposes of the financial statements, the mid-market or bid valuation, where such valuation is consistently applied from one accounting period to the next .

71. *Income equalisation.* The manager's best estimate of the amount of income included in the creation or cancellation price of a unit by reference to which the price of that unit was determined.

72. *Creation price.* The amount for each unit payable by the manager to the trustee on the creation of units.

73. *Issue price.* The price per unit at which the manager sells units as a principal.

74. *Cancellation price.* The price per unit payable by the trustee on the cancellation of units.

Part 3 - Recommended practice

The scope of the recommendations

75. These recommendations are intended to be applicable to all authorised unit trust schemes. The recommendations apply to the financial statements which are included in the annual report of the manager to the unitholders and are intended to be applied in conjunction with the requirements of the SIB collective investment schemes rules and regulations. The recommendations are not intended to extend to the contents of the manager's report to unitholders, which is addressed by the SIB rules.

76. The SORP should be read in conjunction with any rules and regulations relating to Authorised Unit Trust Schemes and other collective investment schemes which are in force and the law relating to these matters.

77. The recommendations are applicable for all accounting periods beginning on or after 1st September, 1991. It is recognised that managers may have insufficient information to provide the recommended comparative figures, and accordingly the recommendations relating to the provision of comparatives are applicable to accounting periods beginning on or after 1st September, 1992, although their adoption for earlier accounting periods is encouraged.

78. Any departure from the recommendations should be disclosed and explained in the notes to the financial statements. For the sake of consistency the same accounting policies recommended herein should be applied in the half-yearly financial statements.

Contents of the financial statements

Annual financial statements

79. The annual financial statements of a unit trust should contain appropriate information on the transactions in the portfolio during the year, the investment performance over the period, the income and distributions for the period and the value of the portfolio at the period end. The following items should be included:

- a balance sheet setting out the details specified in Appendix 1;
- an income account setting out the details specified in Appendix 2;
- a statement of movements in net assets showing the items specified in Appendix 3;
- a statement of the material accounting policies used in preparing the financial statements;
- further details in the notes to the financial statements as set out in Appendix 4;
- a portfolio statement in the format suggested in Appendix 5; and
- a summary of material portfolio changes in the format suggested in Appendix 6.

Half-yearly financial statements

80. The half-yearly financial statements should include the following items:

- a portfolio statement together with a statement of assets and liabilities;
- an income account setting out the details specified in Appendix 2, if a distribution or accumulation of income is to be made in respect of the period; and
- notes to the financial statements as required.

The statement of assets and liabilities is a requirement of the EC UCITS Directive. The manager may wish to present this statement in the same format as the balance sheet to be included in the annual financial statements. The half-yearly financial statements are not required to be audited, and this fact should be displayed prominently in the financial statements.

Accounting policies

81. Accounting policies should comply with the Statements of Standard Accounting Practice. Appropriate disclosure of the policies should be made in the notes to the financial statements. Specific recommended accounting policies are set out below.

Balance Sheet

82. The balance sheet should contain not only those assets and liabilities relating to the capital account but also those relating to income. Such assets and liabilities include cash, accrued income, and the distribution and taxation payable. A suggested format for the balance sheet is set out in Appendix 1; the required disclosures may be made by way of note to the financial statements rather than on the face of the balance sheet.

Comparative figures

83. Comparative figures should be given for the percentage of the value of the property of the scheme represented by each category of asset at the prior period end date.

Valuation of investments

84. Investments should be valued consistently on a mid-market basis or bid basis.

85. Quoted investments should be valued at market value, as defined. Securities which are neither approved (within the meaning of the Authorised Unit Trust Schemes (Investment and Borrowing Powers) Regulations 1988) nor investments in a collective investment scheme should be clearly identified in the portfolio statement and valued at a judgemental valuation, and the basis of the valuation should be set out in the notes to the financial statements. The valuation of these securities should be kept under review.

86. Investments and other assets and liabilities denominated in foreign currencies should be translated using exchange rates prevailing at the balance sheet date or, where appropriate, the rates of exchange fixed under the terms of any related forward foreign exchange contract.

87. Interest bearing securities should be valued at market value net of any accrued interest, which should be included in the balance sheet as an income related item.

88. Purchases and sales of investments should be reflected in the balance sheet on trade date. Amounts due to and from the same broker in respect of purchases and sales should be shown separately and not netted off except where there is a legal right of set off.

89. Properties owned by the trust should be valued at open market value in accordance with Statement of Standard Accounting Practice number 19. The name and qualifications of the person valuing the properties should be disclosed in a note to the financial statements.

90. Securities on loan to third parties at the balance sheet date should be included within the portfolio as if they were registered in the name of the scheme. The aggregate value of securities on loan at the balance sheet date should be disclosed in a note to the financial statements together with the aggregate value of collateral held in respect of those loans.

Efficient portfolio management

91. Currency and interest gains or losses on back-to-back loans should be taken to the capital account, with interest income and interest expense separately disclosed. Where the manager believes that net interest earned or paid should be taken to income account, the reasons for this treatment should be explained in a note to the financial statements quantifying any related capital gain or loss, realised or unrealised. Loans should be shown separately from their related deposits in the balance sheet. The related deposits should be disclosed separately from other cash balances.

92. Gains and losses on currency futures and options should be taken to the capital account. Gains and losses on forward foreign exchange contracts should be taken to the capital account except where they relate to specific items of income, when they should be recognised in the income account.

93. Open positions in options and futures should be marked to market. Short option positions, including covered call options, should be treated as liabilities of the scheme and accordingly deducted from the value of the capital property. Realised and unrealised gains or losses, including gains or losses from option writing, should be taken to the capital account.

94. Where there are open option positions at the balance sheet date, the unitholder should be given sufficient information to assess the nature and risk relating to items contained in the portfolio. This information should include the strike price and final exercise date of the option, together with an indication of whether the position is covered or not.

Fund of funds

95. A fund of funds investing in accumulation units should show in its income account the income accumulated in the underlying trusts. The income should

then be accounted for as dictated by the objectives of the fund of funds as stipulated in the scheme particulars.

Advance corporation tax

96. ACT provisions on distributions proposed or payable at the balance sheet date should be disclosed in the balance sheet or in a note to the financial statements.

Contingent liabilities

97. Contingent liabilities outstanding at the balance sheet date should be disclosed in the notes to the financial statements, after adjustment where practical for those liabilities which have not subsequently crystallised.

Income account

98. The income account should show all items of income and expenditure, including management expenses. A suggested format for the income account is given in Appendix 2.

Comparatives

99. Income and expenditure should be shown not only in monetary terms but also as a percentage of the average net assets of the scheme for the period. Comparative figures should be given as a percentage of prior period average net assets. The basis for calculating average net assets should be given in the notes to the financial statements; as a minimum standard of accuracy the calculation should be based on monthly figures for net assets.

100. The distribution or accumulation of income for the accounting period should be shown in pence per unit, together with comparative figures in terms of pence per unit. This may be disclosed in a separate distribution statement.

Income recognition

101. Dividend and interest income should be accounted for on an accruals basis. Dividends should be recognised when the underlying securities become *ex dividend*, or the overseas equivalent. Interest on interest bearing securities should be included in the income account on an accruals basis, with only the amount earned since the date of acquisition recognised. Income should be shown gross, with any taxation deducted at source dealt with in the tax charge.

102. Stock received in lieu of cash dividends should be taken to the capital account, and a cash transfer made to income account representing the net amount of deemed income, except where this treatment would result in an additional tax cost to the scheme.

103. Underwriting commission received should be taken to income when the securities issue proceeds. Commission received in respect of securities taken up by the scheme pursuant to the underwriting agreement may be netted off against the capital cost of those securities.

104. Income receivable on stock lending activities should be recognised in the income account on an accruals basis.

105. Where the practice of buying securities *cum dividend* and selling *ex dividend* (or *vice versa*) has affected the distribution by 5% or more this fact and the reasons therefor should be disclosed in the notes to the financial statements.

Treatment of management and other expenses

106. All expenses which are not included in the costs of purchasing or selling an investment should be charged in the first instance to the income account. If and so far as the general law of trust permits, a transfer may be made from the income account to the capital account of items of expense which are considered to be capital in nature. Full explanations should be given in the notes to the financial statements of the basis for the transfer, and an analysis provided of the expenses in respect of which the transfer is made. The basis of the transfer should be consistent from one accounting period to the next. Any transfers from capital to income to cover any deficit of income should also be fully disclosed.

Distributions

107. Distributions should only be made on the basis of income received or accrued at the accounting date, including undistributed income from prior periods.

Taxation

108. Deferred taxation should be provided where material on timing differences which are likely to reverse in the foreseeable future, at the rate at which taxation is likely to become payable. ACT should be written off to the extent that it is not considered to be recoverable. Overseas tax suffered should be shown as part of the tax charge to the extent to which it is not expected to be recovered.

109. Irrecoverable value added tax should be recognised in the category of expense to which it relates.

Statement of movement in net assets

110. The statement should show cash movements from the sale and purchase of investments and the creation and cancellation of units. It should also show any movement in net assets which does not involve the movement of funds.

111. Realised and unrealised gains or losses on investments should be separately shown in the statement of movement in net assets.

112. The statement should contain details of currency and interest gains and losses on back-to-back loans, with the minimum of netting off.

113. Any transfer between capital and income should be shown prominently together with its tax effect. The net movement in the income account should also be shown. A suggested format of the statement is set out in Appendix 3.

Appendix 1

Balance sheet

The following information should be included in the balance sheet or in a note thereto; details of specific note disclosures are given in Appendix 4.

(a) the number or quantity, description and market value of each asset, showing separately in respect of each asset or group of assets in relation to which a hedging transaction has been effected any right or obligation under that hedging transaction;

(b) the percentage of the value of the property of the scheme that each holding and each category represents;

(c) other capital assets and liabilities of the scheme, showing separately:

- (i) amounts receivable from brokers for sales of securities;
- (ii) amounts payable to brokers for purchases of securities;
- (iii) amounts receivable from the trustees in respect of cancellations;
- (iv) amounts payable to the trustees in respect of creations;
- (v) amounts held at futures clearing houses and brokers;
- (vi) cash and bank balances;
- (vii) bank overdrafts;
- (viii) loans to the income account;
- (ix) back-to-back loans, showing separately the loans and related deposits;
- (x) other debtors;
- (xi) other creditors.

(d) the net assets of the income property of the scheme, showing separately:

- (i) cash and bank deposits;
- (ii) accrued income receivable;
- (iii) accrued interest receivable and payable;
- (iv) accrued expenses;
- (v) taxation payable/recoverable, including Advance Corporation Tax;
- (vi) distribution payable;
- (vii) deferred taxation;
- (viii) loans from the capital account;
- (ix) other debtors;
- (x) other creditors.

(e) the balance on the capital account and the undistributed balance on the income account;

(f) the total net value of all assets of the scheme less the net value of the liabilities of the scheme;

(g) comparative figures expressed in terms of the percentage of the net assets of the scheme at the period end dates.

A recommended format of the balance sheet is set out overleaf. It is suggested that there should be a separate portfolio statement setting out all the investments of the scheme (excluding net liquid assets relating to the capital property of the scheme), the total of which should be shown as the first item in the balance sheet. In addition, material portfolio changes must be summarised; a suggested format for this disclosure is included as Appendix 6.

BALANCE SHEET

	£'000	£'000	Percentage of net assets 19X2	19X1
Investments at market value (appendix 5)		38,880	95.65%	91.83%
Debtors				
Amounts receivable for creations	98			
Sales awaiting settlement	52			
Loans to income property	-			
Other debtors	6			
Amounts held at futures clearing houses and brokers	50			
Cash and bank balances	2,375			
Back-to-back deposits	750			
	3,331			
Creditors - amounts falling due within one year				
Amounts payable for liquidations	(32)			
Purchases awaiting settlement	(762)			
Back-to-back loans	(770)			
Net current capital assets		1,767	4.34%	8.17%
Net capital property		40,647	99.99%	100.00%
Net income property (note 1)		3	0.01%	0.00%
		40,650	100.00%	100.00%
Capital account		40,647	99.99%	100.00%
Income account		3	0.01%	0.00%
		40,650	100.00%	100.00%

£'000 is an optional presentational matter

NOTES TO THE BALANCE SHEET

Note 1 - Net Income property

	£
Debtors	
Accrued income	71,000
Other debtors	3,000
Cash at bank	113,000
	187,000
Creditors	
Loans from capital property	-
Accrued expenses	(12,000)
Distribution payable	(156,000)
Corporation tax payable	-
Advance corporation tax	(5,000)
Deferred taxation	(11,000)
Net income property	3,000

Appendix 2

Income account

The following information should be included in the income account or in a note thereto:

(a) the total income of the scheme, specifying the descriptions;

(b) any amounts payable to the manager or associate of the manager out of the property of the scheme, giving an analysis of the amount payable;

(c) any amounts payable to the trustee or associate of the trustee out of the property of the scheme, giving an analysis of the amount payable and distinguishing fees for custody of documents and assets from other fees;

(d) any amounts payable in respect of other expenses, giving an analysis of the amount payable and disclosing separately the auditors' remuneration. Where the auditors' remuneration is borne by the manager or trustee, this should be disclosed under (b) or (c) above;

(e) the total amount deducted for taxation before distribution to the unitholders, analysed into the following categories:

- tax attributable to franked investment income
- UK corporation tax
- irrecoverable ACT
- overseas taxation
- deferred tax

(f) the amount of any transfers to or from the capital account, showing by way of note to the financial statements the basis for any such transfer;

(g) the effect on the income account of equalisation on units cancelled and created;

(h) the amount of income available for allocation to the unitholders in respect of the period;

(i) the amount of any interim allocation of income and the amount of the final allocation or accumulation of income in respect of the accounting period;

(j) the balance of income brought forward from the last accounting period and the balance carried forward to the next accounting period;

(k) amounts expressed as a percentage of the average net assets of the fund for the period for subtotals of the items listed above in (a) to (f), together with comparatives expressed in terms of a percentage of the average net assets of the scheme for the prior period;

(l) summarised information in respect of the distribution payable for the period together with the previous period's comparative figure in terms of pence per unit.

A suggested format for the income account is set out overleaf.

INCOME ACCOUNT

	Note	19X2	% value of the fund † for the period to	
		£'000	31/12/X2	31/12/X1
Gross income	2	990	2.68%	2.59%
Expenses	3	(588)	(1.59%)	(1.30%)
Net income before taxation		402	1.09%	1.29%
Taxation	4	(153)	(0.41%)	(0.33%)
		249	0.68%	0.96%
Transfer (to)/from capital account (note x)		5	0.01%	0.03%
		254	0.69%	0.99%
Equalisation				
Received on units created		8		
Deducted on units cancelled		(10)		
		(2)		
		252		
Distribution				
Interim		94		
Final		156		
		250		
Income retained for the year		2		
Undistributed income brought forward		1		
Undistributed income carried forward		3		

Distribution *

Group 1: - Units purchased prior to 1st July, 19X2
Group 2: - Units purchased on or after 1st July, 19X2

	Net income 19X2 pence per unit	Equalisation 19X2 pence per unit	Distribution payable 19X2 pence per unit	Distribution payable 19X1 pence per unit
Income units				
Group 1	0.28		0.28	0.26
Group 2	0.15	0.13	0.28	0.26
Accumulation units				
Group 1	0.35		0.35	0.32
Group 2	0.19	0.16	0.35	0.32

Notes: † Based on average net assets for the relevant accounting period
* A statement may also be presented showing the interim distribution

£'000 is an optional presentational matter

NOTES TO THE INCOME ACCOUNT

Note 2 - Gross income

	19X2 £
UK Dividends	311,000
Overseas dividends	441,000
Bank interest	124,000
Interest on securities	76,000
Underwriting commission	30,000
Other income	8,000
Gross income	990,000

Note 3 - Expenses

	£	£
Payable to the manager or associate of the manager		
Manager's periodic charge	525,000	
Registration fees	13,000	
Other (specify)	3,000	541,000
Payable to the trustee or associate of the trustee		
Trustee's fee	24,000	
Handling charges	5,000	
Safe custody charges	4,000	
Other (specify)	3,000	36,000
Other expenses		
SIB fees	1,000	
Audit fees	5,000	
Safe custody	3,000	
Other (specify)	2,000	11,000
Total expenses		588,000

Note 4 - Taxation

	£
Tax attributable to franked investment income	78,000
Corporation tax	23,000
Irrecoverable ACT	5,000
Overseas tax	43,000
Deferred tax	4,000
	153,000

Appendix 3

Statement of movement in net assets

The following matters should be set out in the statement of movement in net assets or in a note thereto:

(a) the value of the net assets of the scheme at the beginning of the period;

(b) the amount of cash or the value of assets received or paid on the creation or cancellation of units;

(c) the total cost of investments purchased and the total proceeds of investments sold during the accounting period;

(d) an analysis of the total gains or losses attributable to the capital account for the accounting period, showing separately:

   (i) the net realised profits or losses on sales of investments during the period, including profits or losses on futures and options activities; where material, profits or losses on futures and options should be disclosed separately; where practicable, separate disclosure may be made identifying the profits or losses attributable to movements in foreign exchange rates, although this is not a required disclosure;

   (ii) the net increase or decrease in the unrealised appreciation or depreciation in the value of the capital property during the period; where practicable, separate disclosure may be made identifying the amount of this movement attributable to currency movements, although this is not a required disclosure;

   (iii) the effect of currency hedging transactions, showing separately the currency gains and losses and, where appropriate, interest income and expense on back-to-back loans, and any tax effect thereof.

(e) any transfers to or from the income account, together with the reasons and basis for any such transfers;

(f) the net movement in the income account;

(g) the value of the net assets of the scheme at the end of the period.

A suggested format for the statement of movement in net assets is set out below.

	Investments	Other net assets	Total
	£'000	£'000	£'000
Net assets at start of period	30,400	2,706	33,106
Movements due to sales and repurchases of units			
Cash or value received on creation of units	55	1,496	1,551
Cash or value given on cancellation of units	-	(2,729)	(2,729)
	55	(1,233)	(1,178)
Cash movements due to purchases and sales of investments †			
Proceeds of investments sold	(17,301)	17,301	-
Cost of investments purchased	16,910	(16,910)	-
	(391)	391	-
Net realised gains / (losses for the period)			
Gains / (losses) realised on sale of investments †	2,664	(45)	2,619
Net appreciation / (depreciation) thereon brought forward	(830)	-	(830)
	1,834	(45)	1,789
Net unrealised appreciation / (depreciation) for the period	6,982	60	7,042
Net gains / (losses) on back-to-back loans *	-	50	50
Gains / (losses) on forward foreign exchange contracts	-	(34)	(34)
Other currency movements	-	(122)	(122)
Transfers (to) / from income account	-	(5)	(5)
Net movement in income account	-	2	2
Net assets at end of period	38,880	1,770	40,650

Notes £'000 is an optional presentational matter

* Further details of gross interest income and expense, currency gains and losses and tax effect to be given in further note.

† Including derivatives

Appendix 4

Notes to the financial statements

The following matters should be set out in the notes to the financial statements, in addition to any matters required by Appendices 1 to 3 above, and any further disclosures required to give a true and fair view:

1. Accounting policies

(a) the policy regarding the recognition of dividends and other income receivable;

(b) the basis of valuation of the property of the scheme;

(c) if applicable, an explanation of the basis for valuing unquoted, illiquid or suspended securities;

(d) if applicable, a statement of the basis for translating amounts denominated in foreign currencies into sterling;

(e) the accounting policy in respect of deferred tax;

(f) for a fund of funds investing in accumulation units, the policy regarding treatment of accumulation of income relating to units purchased.

2. Units in issue and average net assets

The number of units in existence at the end of the period to which the financial statements relate, and a statement of the basis of calculating average net assets in issue during the year

3. Properties

The name and qualifications of the person valuing the properties, together with the basis of valuation.

4. Forward foreign exchange transactions

A statement of open foreign exchange positions and the unrealised profit or loss thereon.

5. Back-to-back loans and deposits

Details of any back-to-back loans outstanding at the year end, including the terms and interest margins. Details of gross interest and expense and currency gains and losses, together with the tax effect, where these are not given within the statement of movement in net assets.

6. Stock lending activities

Details of the aggregate value of securities on loan to third parties at the balance sheet date, together with the value of collateral held by the scheme in respect of these securities.

7. Taxation

A statement of the rate of corporation tax with an explanation of any other tax charge or refund appearing in the income account.

8. Contingent liabilities

Details of contingent liabilities outstanding at the balance sheet date including aggregate commitments in the following categories:

- underwriting commitments
- placing arrangements
- partly paid shares
- nil paid rights.

9. Equalisation

A definition of equalisation and its effect upon the unitholder's potential capital gains tax liability.

10. Post balance sheet events

An indication of any material post balance sheet events which have a bearing on the understanding of the financial statements.

11. Distribution

An analysis of the final distribution, taking account of tax and any income equalisation adjustment if not given elsewhere in the financial statements.

12. Income

The effect on the distribution of buying cum dividend and selling ex dividend (or vice versa).

13. Additional notes required by Regulators

Any additional disclosures as required from time to time by the SIB or other regulators.

Appendix 5

Portfolio statement

		Holding 31/12/X2	Market Value	Percentage of total net assets
Japan (31.95%; 19X1 25.76%)			£	%
	Japan A	17,000	371,609	0.91%
*	Japan B	25,000	102,739	0.25%
	etc			
	Options:			
*	Japan B Feb 19X3 390 put	25,000	4,522	0.00%
			12,987,510	31.95%
United States (50.55%; 19X1 56.43%)				
*	USA A	3,000	345,972	0.85%
†	USA B	6,000	298,250	0.73%
	etc			
	Options:			
*	USA A March 19X3 120 call	(3,000)	(15,775)	0.00%
			20,549,804	50.55%
etc				
United Kingdom				
	Options:			
	A plc Jan 19X3 340 call	5,000	9,842	0.00%
Unrealised profit on open futures contracts			23,468	0.00%
Investments as shown in the balance sheet			38,880,000	95.65%
Net current assets			1,770,000	4.35%
Total net assets			40,650,000	100.00%

† Not approved securities within the meaning of the Authorised Unit Trust Schemes (Investment and Borrowing Powers) Regulations 1988.

* Matched security and option positions

An equivalent standard of disclosure is required for other types of scheme.

Appendix 6

Portfolio changes

Major purchases	Cost £'000	Major sales	Proceeds £'000
Japan A	371	Japan D	468
USA A	346	USA F	355
USA B	298	Hong Kong A	350
Japan C	250	Spain B	305
UK A	249	Hong Kong B	256
UK B	235	Australia A	254
Germany A	222	Australia C	246
Netherlands A	211	Japan G	235
Germany B	209	Hong Hong D	220
UK D	195	Australia F	215
Japan X	185	USA H	201
UK C	164	Hong Kong J	194
Japan J	162	USA G	187
Spain R	158	Germany K	174
USA N	149	USA M	167
Japan P	147	UK E	164
Australia K	138	Japan Y	155
USA K	128	France S	148
UK L	127	Germany S	147
Japan Y	125	USA T	120

Chapter 8

PENSION SCHEMES

Annexes

Chapter 8

PENSION SCHEMES

Background

8.1 Pension schemes are one of the most important forms of trust. More than 11 million people, over half the country's work force, are members of the 90,000 or more pension schemes. Many more people have rights to preserved benefits of some form under other schemes, or are already retired and draw pensions from pension schemes. The funds established from employers' and employees' contributions towards pension funds have grown to enormous proportions, well over £100 billion. A large proportion of these funds is invested in company securities, giving the schemes ownership of a considerable portion of UK industry. In addition, pension schemes hold large property portfolios and other assets (including valuable paintings). However, despite their importance, pension schemes were, until 1986, only regulated by trust law (see chapter 6). Although, in addition, certain tax legislation also exists to prevent pension schemes from abusing the tax advantages that they enjoy.

8.2 This general lack of regulation led, in practice, to wide discrepancies in the nature and quality of the information disclosed in different pension schemes' financial statements.

8.3 A new regulatory framework was introduced by the *Social Security Act 1985* and *The Occupational Pension Schemes (Disclosure of Information) Regulations 1986* (SI 1986/1046) (as amended by *The Occupational Pension Schemes (Disclosure of Information) (Amendment) Regulations 1986* (SI 1986/1717) and *The Occupational Pension Schemes (Disclosure of Information) (Amendment) Regulations 1987* (SI 1987/1105)). These regulations are referred to in this chapter as the 'Disclosure Regulations' and are reproduced as annex 2 to this chapter. The Disclosure Regulations cover a variety of matters including the following:

- The disclosure of information concerning the scheme's constitution, administration and finance.
- The audit of pension scheme financial statements.
- Actuarial valuations.
- The submission of an annual report to pension scheme members and others.

Accounting and auditing background

8.4 In May 1986, shortly before the Disclosure Regulations were made, the ASC issued SORP 1, 'Pension scheme accounts'. This statement covers:

- The basis of preparing financial statements.
- The financial statements' content and format.
- Accounting policies.
- Relationship to actuarial statement.
- Valuation of investments.
- Accounting for:
  - Associated and subsidiary companies.
  - Long-term insurance policies.
  - Additional voluntary contributions.
- The preparation of an investment report.

8.5 The origin and authority of SORPs is explained in chapter 1. This SORP, which was the first to be issued, has been given a measure of legal recognition, because the Disclosure Regulations require pension scheme trustees to state whether their financial statements have been prepared in accordance with parts 2 to 4 of SORP 1. In addition, where pension scheme financial statements are not prepared in accordance with SORP 1, the pension scheme trustees have to indicate where there are any material departures from it in their financial statements. [SI 1986/1046 3 Sch 9]. SORP 1 is reproduced as annex 1 to this chapter.

8.6 The APC also issued an auditing guideline, 'Pension schemes in the United Kingdom' (AG 3.306), in November 1988. This auditing guideline gives guidance on the special factors to be considered in applying auditing standards and guidelines to the audit of pension schemes in the light of the new legislation and SORP 1.

8.7 Annex 3 to this chapter includes an example of a pension scheme's financial statements and annex 4 includes a compliance checklist covering the provisions of both the Disclosure Regulations and the SORP.

Legal status

8.8 The legal status of pension schemes was summarised in the DSS consultation document dated 29th February 1984 entitled 'Greater security for the rights and expectations of members of occupational pension schemes' in the following terms:

> *"The decision to set up a pension scheme is taken by the employer, usually after consultation with his employees and their representatives. The decision to wind it up can also be taken by the employer. The rules are generally drawn up to reflect the employer's wishes. As between employer and trustee, pension schemes are set up and administered under trust law. The purpose is to alienate in a legally unassailable and irrevocable trust the funds set aside for pension provision, so that they are held separate from other assets (e.g. of the company) and cannot be diverted for other purposes. One or more trustees, usually appointed by the employer, administer the scheme in accordance with the provisions of trust law and of the terms of the trust deed governing the particular scheme. The terms of the trust generally give the trustee wider powers, particularly in the matter of investment and investment management, than they would otherwise have under the provisions of the Trustee Act 1925 and the Trustee Investments Act 1961."*
>
> *"As between employee and trustees, once an employee has become a member of a pension scheme, his rights and obligations lie as a matter of law between the trustees and himself, because the trustees are legally obliged to administer the trust in the interests of all members. In practice, however, matters are not as simple as that. As the employer normally accepts at least a moral obligation to meet any emerging deficits in the scheme, and as it is largely considered to be up to the employer whether he makes any other additional contributions which might be considered appropriate (e.g. to finance post-retirement increases), he expects to be consulted, if not already closely involved, in certain decisions of the trustees, e.g. on investment. There is in fact nothing to debar the employer from being one of the trustees or even the sole trustee; and the trustees can be and often are his nominees or under his control, though this does not affect their legal duties. In the larger schemes, trustees are assisted by professional advisors and may employ professional managers (e.g. to handle investments)."*

8.9 Since this was written, the legal and accounting regulation of pension schemes has increased considerably. However, the basic legal framework of trust law still applies and has not been affected.

8.10 It is sometimes the case that company pension schemes outperform the companies that set them up. Not surprisingly, where massive surpluses have built up in a scheme, corporate purchasers have attempted to liberate pension scheme assets by acquisition. An example that made the headlines was *Re: Courage Pension Schemes (1986), Financial Times, 16th December 1986*. In that case, the Chancery Division of the High Court disallowed proposals by Hanson Trust plc to remove, for its own benefit, or for the benefits of other employees of companies in the Hanson Group, all but £10 million of the surplus of £80 million in three pension schemes intended for the benefit of Imperial Brewing & Leisure Ltd's employees.

Constitution

8.11 A pension scheme's constitution is contained in the trust deed that establishes it. Depending upon the trust deed's terms, the rules of the scheme issued to its members may, or may not, be part of the constitution of the scheme. It is common for a separate rulebook to be issued to members, stating that the rules do not form part of the trust deed.

8.12 The trust deed of a pension scheme is usually a lengthy and complex document. Its terms will normally be drafted in such a way as to gain Inland Revenue approval (see para 8.43 and 8.45). The terms of the trust deed will be the same as for any formally drafted trust although the level of detail for pension trust schemes may be greater. In addition, the following matters will usually be dealt with in a pension scheme's trust deed:

- Details of any interim trust deed necessary in order to obtain Inland Revenue approval.
- Covenants for the scheme's administration by the employer concerned.
- Provisions concerning the status of the scheme's rules.
- The trustees' duty to keep records of members.
- Rules for terminating the scheme.

Types of pension scheme

8.13 Providing pensions to satisfy employers' and employees' requirements has given rise to considerable ingenuity in forming pension schemes. The principal variations on the type of schemes likely to be encountered in practice are summarised in the paragraphs that follow.

Public service pension schemes

8.14 Public service pension schemes are occupational pension schemes that are established by statute, or Royal Prerogative or Royal Charter. The particulars of the scheme are set out in the relevant legislation, or Royal Warrant or Royal Charter (or delegated legislation). (See further chapter 19). In addition, the scheme will require the approval of a minister or a government department before it can come into force, or be amended.

8.15 Public service pension schemes also include occupational pension schemes that are provided by regulations made by the Secretary of State and the Minister for the Civil Service jointly. [SSPA 1975 Sec 66(1)].

Unfunded pension schemes

8.16 Unfunded pension schemes are occupational pension schemes where benefits are paid directly by the employer. Before the introduction of SSAP 24, 'Accounting for pension costs', the employer was not required to provide, by setting aside assets under trusts, for future liabilities under the scheme. Now, however, companies do have to provide for benefits under such schemes, by providing for them over the average service lives of employees in the scheme. The assets are, however, part of the general business assets and may be eroded by trading losses.

Funded schemes

8.17 These are schemes where the future liabilities for benefits are provided for by the accumulation of assets held externally to the employing company's business.

Contracted-out employment and contracted-out schemes

8.18 The rates of contributions payable by members to the state scheme and, consequently, receivable from the state scheme, are reduced where an occupational pension scheme provides for its members to be contracted-out. The rules regarding contracting-out are exceedingly complex and any disputes should be referred for their determination to the Occupational Pensions Board (see para 8.39). [SSPA 1975 Sec 60(2)]. The broad intention of the rules is to ensure that pension rights available from a contracted-out scheme will be at least as good as those available from the State Earnings Related Pension scheme (SERPs). It is not possible to contract out of the basic state pension.

8.19 In general terms a scheme will be contracted-out, in relation to a person's employment, if it is specified as such in a contracting-out certificate. A contracting-out certificate will only be issued if the scheme complies with certain conditions concerning the benefits of the employee and his widow and certain other matters. Furthermore, the rules of the scheme must be framed to comply with various requirements. Even then, the certificate may be withheld or cancelled. In addition, any amendments to the rules must also be approved. In most other respects, the legal nature of contracted-out pension schemes is essentially similar to that of other pension schemes.

Defined benefit schemes

8.20 Defined benefit schemes are pension schemes where the rules specify the benefits to be paid, typically by reference to final salary levels, and the scheme is financed accordingly.

Defined contribution schemes

8.21 Defined contribution schemes are pension schemes where the benefits are determined directly by the value of contributions paid in respect of each member and the investment performance achieved on those contributions. Normally, the rate of contribution will be specified in the scheme's rules. An alternative term for this is a 'money purchase scheme' (see para 8.24).

Fully-insured schemes

8.22 Fully-insured schemes are pension schemes where the trustees have effected an insurance contract in respect of each member that guarantees benefits corresponding at all times to those promised under the scheme's rules.

8.23 This classification, however, has no legal significance. SORP 1 applies to fully-insured schemes, even though they may not have any assets (see para 8.76).

Money purchase schemes

8.24 Money purchase schemes are pension schemes where the benefits are directly determined by the value of contributions paid in respect of each member. An alternative term for this is a 'defined contribution scheme' (see para 8.21).

8.25 Again, the classification 'money purchase scheme' has no legal significance. SORP 1 applies to money purchase schemes even though they may have no need for an actuarial valuation of the scheme's assets (see para 8.84).

Self-administered schemes

8.26 As the title suggests, a self-administered scheme is one that is administered by the company itself for the benefit of its employees. This contrasts with a fully-insured scheme, which would be administered solely by an insurance company. Nowadays, it is common for insurance companies to offer self-administered facilities on top of an insured scheme. These are known as 'hybrid' plans. They avoid the high set-up costs of an ordinary self-administered scheme.

Pension funds and the Financial Services Act

8.27 No person may carry on an investment business in the UK unless he is an authorised person under the *Financial Services Act 1986* (see further chapter 26). The question of authorisation is complex and trustees who are in doubt as to their position should seek specialist guidance. The following guidance is based on guidelines issued by the SIB and covers three pensions-related activities that may constitute an 'investment business' and may require trustees and managers to be authorised under the *Financial Services Act 1986*:

- Advising on investments (see para 8.28).
- Managing investments (see paras 8.29 and 8.30).
- Arranging deals in investments (see paras 8.31 and 8.32).

In each situation, 'investments' includes stocks, shares, financial futures, traded options, currency options, insurance contracts having an investment element in them and unit trusts.

8.28 'Advising on investments' would include recommending to a member the purchase of a particular 'buy-out' pension policy from an insurance company or a transfer to a scheme of such a policy or advice concerning AVCs. 'Investment', however, does not include a member's rights under an occupational pension scheme and trustees or managers providing information in respect of the benefits from a scheme would not appear to need to be authorised. In addition, where trustees or managers describe the benefits from schemes and the pros and cons of policies in general terms, so long as the information does not constitute a recommendation or advice on particular policies, it would normally fall outside the scope of the legislation.

8.29 Parties managing pension fund assets are required to be authorised unless all (or all day-to-day) investment management decisions are taken on their behalf by an authorised person. Day-to-day decisions include the following:

- Recommendations with a force amounting to direction relating to individual investments if done habitually and frequently.
- Frequent interventions outside regular scheduled review meetings in the decision-making of external fund managers.

8.30 Consequently, trustees or managers will not need to be authorised if their involvement extends no further than strategic decisions on allocation of funds between sectors or decisions on specific issues (for example, how to respond in a takeover situation) and the investment is dealt with by independent investment managers. For example, trustees or managers would not require authorisation if their decisions related only to the choice of particular managed funds underlying an insurance or pension contract.

8.31 Trustees and managers may require authorisation if they arrange deals in investments by way of business (for example, negotiating special terms for a leaver's buy-out policy). Criteria such as the receipt of commissions and the frequency with which deals are arranged will also be relevant to the requirement to be authorised.

8.32 If independent intermediaries are retained to advise members then, so long as execution is in the hands of the members and not the intermediary, the trustees and managers would not themselves need authorisation.

Pension funds and the Data Protection Act

8.33 Pension funds who have computerised systems, and are, therefore, 'data users' must register the following information under the *Data Protection Act 1984*:

- Personal data held.
- The purpose for which such data is used.
- The sources from which the data is obtained.
- The people the data may be disclosed to.
- The countries or territories outside the UK to which the data may be transferred.

8.34 Data that is held only for the purpose of calculating amounts payable by way of remuneration or pensions, or of sums deducted therefrom, is exempt from the requirements of the *Data Protection Act 1984*. Where the trustees directly maintain computerised records containing personal data that is held for other purposes, then the need to register is clear. However, where records are maintained by others, it may be difficult to determine whether registration is necessary. For example:

- Where a scheme employer and the scheme trustees arrange for day-to-day administration of the scheme to be conducted by another party ('the administrator') and records are maintained by the administrator containing information on employees supplied by the trustees or the employer at the trustees' request, the trustees are the data users and should register.

- Where the administrator uses the personal data for its own purposes (for example, an insurance company insuring benefits under a policy issued) then both the administrator and the trustees are data users and should register.

- Where the trustees delegate management of residential properties to an estate agent and the agent keeps details of tenants on a computer, mainly for the purpose of collecting rent, as well as the details (say, of the state of repair of the properties) the agent is the data user because the trustees' interest is in the income received from the properties, rather than in the contents of individual computer records. In this situation the trustee would not be required to register this information.

Scope of the Disclosure Regulations and SORP 1

8.35 The Disclosure Regulations apply to all occupational pension schemes except:

- Those with only one member.

- Those that only provide death-in-service benefits.

[SI 1986/1046 para 3].

Separate disclosure regulations apply to personal pension schemes.

8.36 Furthermore, the accounting requirements set out in the Disclosure Regulations do not apply to:

- Unfunded schemes.

- Public service pension schemes.

[SI 1986/1046 para 7].

8.37 SORP 1, in contrast, applies to all pension schemes except:

- Those with only one member.

- Unfunded schemes.

[SORP 1 para 29].

8.38 There is, therefore, a difference in the scope of the Disclosure Regulations and SORP 1. In particular, SORP 1 applies to public service pension schemes and those that only provide death-in-service benefits.

The Occupational Pensions Board

8.39 The Occupational Pensions Board (OPB) is the principal regulatory body for occupational pension schemes. It consists of a chairman, a deputy chairman, and between eight and twelve other members, all appointed by the Secretary of State. One of these members is appointed in consultation with appropriate employers' organisations and another in consultation with other organisations' representatives of employed earners. The OPB comes under the general supervision of the Council on Tribunals.

8.40 The principal functions of the OPB are to:

- Determine whether a contracting-out certificate (see para 8.18) should be issued, varied or revoked. The latter course is the ultimate sanction used to enforce the limited supervision function explained below.

- Determine questions on whether an employment is contracted-out.

- Determine questions concerning conformity with the equal access requirements (that is, where membership of the scheme must be open to both men and women on the same terms).

- Perform a limited supervisory function over contracted-out schemes.

  Contracted-out schemes relate to nearly 90 per cent of all occupational pension scheme members and, consequently, this limited supervision applies to most pension scheme members. The OPB's responsibilities in relation to the financial supervision of contracted-out schemes are not designed to ensure their overall solvency or the competence of those managing the scheme funds. The OPB's sole concern is to ensure that in the event of a scheme being wound up, its resources would be sufficient to safeguard the guaranteed minimum pension and other benefits. The OPB monitors the solvency of pension schemes by requiring them to:

  - ☐ Submit periodic actuarial certificates.

- ☐ Submit annual statements confirming the contribution payments or, for insured schemes, the premium payments.

- ☐ Confirm, for self-administered schemes, that annual financial statements have been prepared and audited and that statements are made by the scheme concerning the degree of self-investment or concentration of investments.

Procedures are laid down to review the OPB's determinations and for the OPB to refer questions of law to the courts.

8.41 *The Occupational Pension Schemes (Modification) Regulations 1990* (SI 1990/2021) allow the OPB to make orders to enable schemes to reduce the amount of their surplus assets in accordance with Schedule 22 to the *Income and Corporation Taxes Act 1988* and the regulations made under that Schedule. There are certain requirements which must be satisfied before the OPB can make such an order. These are set out in paragraph 3 of SI 1990/2021.

The Superannuation Funds Office

8.42 The Superannuation Funds Office of the Inland Revenue (SFO) is the arm of the Inland Revenue that monitors the approval and compliance of pension schemes. It also monitors claims for relief in respect of the income of pension funds for overseas employees and monitors applications for the approval of retirement benefits schemes.

8.43 Inland Revenue approval of a pension scheme and its trust deed is vital as it exempts members from any charge to tax on the employer's contributions.

8.44 The tax legislation with regard to pension schemes is relatively brief. The legislation has been amplified substantially, however, by more than 100 pages of practice notes issued by the Inland Revenue.

The Joint Office

8.45 The SFO and the OPB established a 'Joint Office' to consider jointly the conditions for approving pension schemes.

Duty to keep accounting records

8.46 Pension schemes are under no specific duty to keep accounting records, beyond that applying generally to trusts (see chapter 6). This means that they must:

> *"...maintain adequate accounting records to enable them to carry out their duties, including discharging their responsibilities*

for investment decisions and safeguarding the scheme's assets." [AG 3.306 para 38].

8.47 Pension schemes are now required to prepare financial statements that give a true and fair view and contain certain specified information (see para 8.50) and these financial statements have to be audited (see para 8.51). Although this does not place any specific duty on trustees to keep accounting records, clearly such records must be kept to enable financial statements to be prepared and audited.

Duty to establish and maintain systems of control

8.48 There is no duty to establish and maintain systems of control laid down by law. However, the auditing guideline points out that because the trustees' responsibilities in respect of accounting records cannot be delegated, the trustees will need to ensure that they operate adequate accounting systems and controls, even where certain administrative or investment activities are undertaken by agents. [AG 3.306 para 38]. The extent and nature of the accounting systems, procedures and internal controls will depend mainly upon:

- The size of the scheme.
- The extent to which the trustees delegate the scheme's administration.
- The types of investment involved.

[AG 3.306 para 39].

8.49 Important procedures and controls are, however, specifically identified in the auditing guideline, in respect of:

- Contributions receivable and benefits payable.
- Transfers in and out.
- Additional voluntary contributions.
- Administration expenses.
- Investment transactions.
- Assets.
- Membership records.

[AG 3.306 paras 42 - 52].

Duty to prepare financial statements

8.50 Until 1986, pension scheme trustees were under no greater duty to prepare financial statements than other trustees (see chapter 6). A duty to prepare financial statements would frequently be included in the trust deed. In practice, however, most schemes have been required by the OPB to confirm that annual financial statements have been prepared and audited.

8.51 In addition, pension scheme trustees are now placed under a legal duty to obtain audited financial statements as soon as is reasonably practicable after the end of each scheme year. Where the pension scheme has been in operation for only part of a scheme year, this duty is in respect of that part only. [SI 1986/1046 para 7(1)]. The effect of this is that the first financial statements of a new scheme will be for a year *or less* than a year.

Accounting period

8.52 As mentioned above, the scheme's trustees must obtain audited financial statements for the 'scheme year'. [SI 1986/1046 para 1(2)]. 'Scheme year' is defined as whichever out of the following four periods the scheme's trustees select:

- A year specified in any of the documents that comprise the scheme or in the scheme rules.
- A calendar year.
- 12 months ending 31st March.
- 12 months ending 5th April.

[SI 1986/1046 para 1(2)].

8.53 'Scheme year' also includes a period of between 12 and 24 months where the trustees select that period to replace a previously selected period. [SI 1986/1046 para 1(2)].

The annual report

8.54 For each scheme year, the Disclosure Regulations require pension scheme trustees to make available copies of a document that includes the following information:

- Audited financial statements.
- The latest actuarial statement (see for example Table 8.1).

■ Other information (specified in Schedule 5 to the Disclosure Regulations).

[SI 1986/1046 para 9(1)].

Table 8.1: Illustration of an actuarial statement on the pension scheme

Extract from the Rolls-Royce Pension Fund Annual Report for the year ended 31 March 1990.

Actuarial Statement.

An Actuarial assessment of the Fund took place as at 30 November 1989 and the actuaries' formal statement, complying with statutory requirements, is show below.

Acturial Statement made for the purposes of Regulation 8 of the Occupational Pension Schemes (Disclosure of Information) Regulations 1986

Name of Scheme: The Rolls-Royce Pension Fund

1. Security of Accrued Rights
   In our opinion, the scheme's assets existing on 30 November 1989 fully cover its liabilities as at that date.
2. Security of Prospective Rights
   In our opinion, the resources of the scheme are likely in the normal course of events to meet in full the liabilities of the scheme as they fall due. In giving this opinion, we have assumed that the following amounts will be paid to the scheme:

From Employees:	6 per cent of Scheme Earnings (as defined in the Rules)
From Employers:	10 per cent of Scheme Earnings, plus the cost of lump sum disability benefits

3. Summary of Methods and Assumptions used
   The Employers' contribution rate shown above has been derived in the following way:
   (i) A normal contribution rate has been calculated by dividing the present value of all benefits which will accrue in the year following the valuation as at 31 March 1988 (with reference to service in that year and projected final earnings) by the capital value of 1 per cent of members' Scheme Earnings during that year; there is an implicit assumption that there will be a continuing flow of new entrants such that the contribution rate required in successive years will be at the same rate.
   (ii) From this rate was deducted the rate of contributions payable by employees.
   (iii) The rate was then adjusted to take account of the excess of the amount needed to provide the benefits which have already accrued by 30 November 1989 (allowing, in the case of Contributors, for future increases in earnings) over the value of the scheme's assets; the adjustment has been designed to reduce the excess to zero over the working lifetimes of the existing Contributors.

   The technical name for this method of obtaining the contribution rate is the "Projected Unit Method".
   The main assumptions used in applying these methods were:

Investment return:	9 per cent per annum
Earnings increases:	7 per cent per annum (plus an allowance for promotional increases)
Increases to pensions in payment:	5 per cent per annum

Table 8.1 continued

Rate of increase in the lower earnings limit:	5.5 per cent per annum
Turnover of staff:	Allowance for a proportion of members to leave service each year. Members leaving service before age 50 are assumed to take a transfer value in lieu of their deferred pension entitlement. Members leaving service after age 50 are assumed to retire with an immediate pension.
Mortality	
– in retirement:	PA(90) rated down 1 year for both current and prospective pensioners
– before retirement:	A1967/70 ultimate rated down 3 years for men FA 1975/78 ultimate rated down 3 years for women

The assets were valued by assuming that their market value was reinvested in the FT Actuaries All-Share Index. The dividends on this notional investment were assumed to grow in perpetuity at 4.5 per cent per annum and then discounted at 9 per cent per annum.

Mrs L.S. Parsonage FIA
Bacon & Woodrow
St Olaf House
London Bridge City
London
SE1 2PE
30 March 1990

Mr B.C. Coote FIA
Noble Lowndes Actuarial Services Limited
PO Box 144
Wellesley Road
Croydon
Surrey
CR9 3EB
30 March 1990

8.55 Although SORP 1 is mainly concerned with the annual financial statements of pension schemes, it additionally recommends that the annual report of such schemes should include:

- A trustees' report.
- An investment report.

[SORP 1 para 2].

8.56 The combination of these various reports and the accounts is commonly referred to as the 'annual report'.

The trustees' report

8.57 SORP 1 recommends that the trustees' report should comment on:

- Membership statistics and any major changes in benefits, constitution or legal requirements.

- The scheme's financial development as disclosed in the financial statements.

- The actuarial position of the scheme as disclosed by the actuary's statement. This section should include precise information as to the employer's legal commitment to make good any deficiencies that may arise so that a reader may understand fully the significance of the actuarial position of the fund.

- The investment policy of the fund and its performance. These are both important aspects of the stewardship function and it is desirable for a description of the long-term investment objectives to be given, together with the long-term investment strategy, its implementation in the current year and the level of performance achieved. Details of any delegation of investment management responsibilities by the trustees are also to be given.

[SORP 1 para 2(a)].

The financial statements

8.58 The pension scheme's financial statements should include:

- A revenue account.

- A net assets statement.

- A reconciliation of the revenue account to the net assets statement.

- Notes to the financial statements.

8.59 The financial statements must give a true and fair view of the scheme's financial transactions during the scheme year and of the disposition of the scheme's assets and liabilities at the end of the scheme year. In this context:

- 'Assets' do not include insurance policies that are specifically allocated to the provision of benefits for, and that provide all the benefits payable under the scheme to, particular members or other persons.

- 'Liabilities' do not include liabilities to pay pensions and benefits after the end of the scheme year (see Table 8.2).

[SI 1986/1046 para 8(4)(b)(ii)].

Table 8.2: Illustration of a note explaining the actuarial valuation of the fund of a pension scheme

Extract from the Rolls-Royce Pension Fund Annual Report for the year ended 31 March 1990.

Notes to the accounts (extract)

1. Principal Accounting Policies (extract)

2 Actuarial

These accounts summarise the transactions and net assets of the Fund. They do not take account of liabilities to pay pensions and other benefits in the future. The actuarial position of the Fund, which does take account of such liabilities, is dealt with in the Actuarial Statement on page 17, and these accounts should be read in conjunction therewith.

8.60 The Disclosure Regulations and SORP 1 do not make any specific recommendations concerning the format the financial statements should take. However, the Pensions Research Accountants Group has recommended certain formats that may be adopted. An example of a pension scheme's financial statements has been reproduced as annex 3 to this chapter.

The revenue account

8.61 The Disclosure Regulations require the financial statements to contain:

> *"an account of the financial additions to and withdrawals from the fund of the scheme during the scheme year to which the accountsrelate."* [SI 1986/1046 3 Sch 1].

8.62 SORP 1 lists those items that the revenue account should contain, but states that this is not to be regarded as a recommendation either on the layout or the order of the items. [SORP 1 Part 4]. An illustration is given in Table 8.3 and note information in Table 8.4.

8.63 Where the administrative expenses of a scheme are borne directly by the participating employer, that fact should be disclosed. The trustees may, if they so wish, disclose the amount of such expenses in the scheme's financial statements as well. [SORP 1 Part 4 para 6].

Table 8.3: Illustration of the fund accounts of a pension scheme

Extract from the Rolls-Royce Pension Fund Annual Report for the year ended 31 March 1990.

Fund Accounts for the year to 31 March 1990.

	Notes	1990 £m	1989 £m
Opening Fund Account		1,216.7	1,006.5
Employers' Contributions	3	47.5	43.6
Employees' Contributions	4	23.3	21.1
		70.8	64.7
Benefits	5	(68.7)	(73.7)
		2.1	(9.0)
Income	6	54.6	46.6
Surplus for Investment		56.7	37.6
Change in Market Value	7	32.5	172.6
		89.2	210.2
Closing Fund Account		1,305.9	1,216.7
Represented by:	8		
Fixed Interest Securities		108.5	112.9
Ordinary Stocks		1,030.7	928.1
Property		129.5	125.6
Cash and Deposits		29.5	46.6
		1,298.2	1,213.2
Net Current Assets	9	7.7	3.5
		1,305.9	1,216.7

The Notes on pages 16 to 19 form part of these Accounts. The Auditors' Report is on page 19.

H. G. MOURGUE
Chairman

A. R. HUGHES
Secretary

The net assets statement and reconciliation

8.64 The Disclosure Regulations require a statement as at the end of the scheme year of the scheme's assets at market value, or a trustees' estimate thereof where market value is not readily ascertainable, and liabilities of the scheme, other than liabilities to pay pensions and benefits after the end of that scheme year. This statement must show the distribution of the scheme's investments over each of the following categories:

- Insurance policies.
- Public sector fixed interest investments.

- Other fixed interest investments.
- Index-linked securities.
- Equities (including convertible shares).
- Property, meaning any right or interest in land or buildings.
- Unit trusts invested in property.
- Other unit trusts.
- Managed funds (other than unit trusts) invested in property.
- Other managed funds.
- Loans.
- Cash deposits and cash in hand.
- Other investments.

See for example Tables 8.3, 8.4 and 8.5

8.65 In each situation, investments must be shown separately between those made in, or outside, the UK, or in companies registered in, or outside, the UK. [SI 1986/1046 7 Sch 3].

8.66 The net assets statement must be reconciled to the revenue account above. The main reconciling item will be the change in market value of investments (see Table 8.5).

Notes to the financial statements

8.67 The Disclosure Regulations require the financial statements to include certain specified information, unless the information is not material for the purpose of giving a true and fair view. [SI 1986/1046 para 7(4)(a)(i)]. These matters include:

- Currency translation details.
- Particulars of any investments exceeding five per cent of the scheme's net assets.
- Particulars of self-investment exceeding five per cent of the scheme's net assets. Self-investment is investment in the business of the scheme employer and any connected companies and persons. Investment in this context includes shares and securities of a company, mortgages on real property of a company, loans

Table 8.4: Illustration of a note to the accounts on investment income and change in market value of investment of a pension scheme

Extract from the Rolls-Royce Pension Fund Annual Report for the year ended 31 March 1990.

Notes to the accounts (extract)

6 Income from Investments

		1990 £000	1989 £000
(i)	Investment Income		
	Fixed Interest Securities		
	British Government	1,391	3,475
	Index Linked Stocks	2,559	1,221
	Industrial Loan Stock	688	1,477
	Sterling bonds	567	1,685
	Local Authority Bonds	335	435
	Preference Stocks	19	6
	Overseas Bonds	10	3
		5,569	8,302
	Ordinary Stocks		
	United Kingdom		
	Convertibles	306	310
	Listed	34,597	25,893
	Overseas	4,753	3,829
		39,656	30,032
	Property		
	Direct	4,118	3,522
	Overseas	2,604	2,606
		6,722	6,128
	Cash and Deposits	5,973	4,667
		57,920	49,129
(ii)	Investment Management Fees	(3,296)	(2,599)
		54,624	46,530

7 Change in Market Value

	1990 £000	1989 £000
Change in valuations of investments held at 31 March		
Fixed Interest	(3,571)	1,279
Ordinary Stocks	(43,440)	113,334
Property	1,514	20,642
Short Term Deposits	(378)	1,273
	(45,875)	136,528
Realised surpluses on sales of investments during the year representing excess of sales proceeds over cost		
Fixed Interest	(81)	1,843
Ordinary Stocks	74,372	33,238
Property	4,082	1,023
	78,373	36,104
	32,498	172,632

Table 8.5: Illustration of an investment report in the annual report of a pension scheme

Extract from the Rolls-Royce Pension Fund Annual Report for the year ended 31 March 1990.

Analysis of Movement of Investments in the Fund over 1989/90.

	Market Value at 1.4.89 £m	Purchases £M	Sales £m	Net Investment £m	Change in Market Value £m	Market Value at 31.3.90 £m
Fixed Interest Securities						
British Government	23.8	60.3	82.5	(22.2)	(1.6)	–
Index Linked Stocks	52.2	103.6	46.1	57.5	(1.2)	108.5
Industrial Loan Stocks	13.8	16.6	29.8	(13.2)	(0.6)	–
Sterling Bonds	16.3	16.1	32.2	(16.1)	(0.2)	–
Local Authority Bonds	6.5	4.6	11.1	(6.5)	–	–
Preference Stocks	0.3	–	0.3	(0.3)	–	–
	112.9	201.2	202.0	(0.8)	(3.6)	108.5
Ordinary Stocks						
United Kingdom						
Convertibles	2.4	2.1	3.6	(1.5)	0.6	1.5
Listed	664.7	192.7	193.6	(0.9)	11.8	675.6
Unlisted	4.3	7.5	3.5	4.0	(1.2)	7.1
Europe	38.7	62.6	43.5	19.1	12.4	70.2
North America	106.9	132.0	105.6	26.4	13.7	147.0
Japan	88.1	158.4	143.9	14.5	(11.4)	91.2
Other	23.0	30.3	20.2	10.1	5.0	38.1
	928.1	585.6	513.9	71.7	30.9	1,030.7
Property						
UK Direct	81.1	9.3	10.0	(0.7)	3.6	84.0
Forestry	9.8	–	2.8	(2.8)	1.3	8.3
Unlisted Investments UK	0.1	0.4	–	0.4	(0.1)	0.4
Unlisted Investments Overseas	34.6	1.7	0.3	1.4	0.8	36.8
	125.6	11.4	13.1	(1.7)	5.6	129.5
	1,166.6	798.2	729.0	69.2	32.9	1,268.7
Cash and Deposits	46.6			(16.7)	(0.4)	29.5
	1,213.2			52.5	32.5	1,298.2
Net Current Assets	3.5			4.2	–	7.7
	1,216.7			56.7	32.5	1,305.9

made to a company and freeholds or leaseholds owned by the scheme's trustees but effectively leased directly to a company.

- Prior year comparatives.
- The total purchases and sales of investments during the scheme year.
- A statement whether the financial statements have been prepared in accordance with SORP 1 and, if not, an indication of any material departures from the SORP.

Significant accounting policies

8.68 The significant accounting policies should be clearly, fairly and briefly disclosed. The SORP gives the following examples:

- The extent of the application of the accruals concept to income and expense items.
- The valuation bases for assets (see Table 8.6).
- The basis of foreign currency translation.
- The treatment of interest on property developments.
- The basis of accounting for subsidiary and associated companies and joint ventures (see for example Table 8.7).

Table 8.6: Illustration of the accounting policy on valuation of investments in the accounts of a pension scheme

Extract from the Rolls-Royce Pension Fund Annual Report for the year ended 31 March 1990.

Notes to the Accounts (extract)

1 Principal Accounting Policies (extract)

(d) Valuation of Investments

Investments are stated at market value at the balance sheet date which is determined as follows:

(i) Listed investments and unit trusts at mid-market price.

(ii) Unlisted investments, which include indirect overseas property investments, at the Trustees' valuation.

(iii) Direct investments in properties and forestry are professionally valued at least every three years at an open market value. In the intervening years the valuation of existing properties and forestry is reviewed by the investment managers. Properties in course of construction are stated at the Trustees' valuation.

(iv) The change in market value is the difference between the opening and closing balances of market value and the respective cost figures added to or reduced by the realised surplus or deficit on sale of investments.

Valuation of investments

8.69 The SORP recommends and the Disclosure Regulations require that investments should be included in the net assets statement at:

- Market value at the accounting date.

- The trustees' estimate of market value (but only if the market value is readily ascertainable).

[SORP 1 para 46; SI 1986/1046 3 Sch 2].

Table 8.7: Illustration of an accounting policy on associated companies in the accounts of a pension scheme

Extract from the Rolls-Royce Pension Fund Annual Report for the year ended 31 March 1990.

Notes to the accounts (extract)

1. Principal Accounting Policies (extract)

(f) Shareholdings

The shareholdings of the Fund are held as investments but in some cases Trustees or Officers of the Fund may be appointed directors of the investee company. Despite their participation on the boards of these companies, the trustees do not regard the entities concerned as associated companies within the meaning of the Statement of Standard Accounting Practice dealing with accounting for associated companies.

8.70 The SORP contains the following specific guidance on the valuation of assets:

- UK quoted securities should be included at the mid-market price quoted in the Stock Exchange Daily Official List for the day following the accounting date (see Table 8.6).

- Overseas quoted securities should be included on a basis similar to UK quoted securities using mid-market prices from overseas stock exchanges translated at closing rates of exchange.

- All unquoted securities should be included at the trustees' valuation (see Table 8.6).

- Investments in units should be included at the average of the bid and offer prices at the accounting date. If the bid price is not quoted, the offer price should be reduced by an appropriate amount.

- Financial futures, options and forward currency positions should be included at market value if available, failing that, at trustees' valuation.

8.71 The inclusion, in the balance sheet, of investments at market value gives rise to an extra item in the movement between opening and closing fund values. The SORP indicates in paragraph 70.11 the way in which this type of movement should be disclosed. It should not be included in the revenue account, but should be part of the reconciliation of the movement in the net assets of the scheme.

Subsidiary and associated companies

8.72 Pension schemes may own investments in subsidiary or associated companies. Subsidiaries may include investment holding companies or trading subsidiaries. Associated companies may include joint ventures, such as managed funds or pooled investments.

8.73 There is no legal requirement for consolidated financial statements to be prepared for a pension scheme. SORP 1, however, recommends consolidation of the results, assets and liabilities of investment-holding subsidiaries and associated companies that are joint ventures. Other subsidiaries should be equity accounted (see 'Manual of Accounting - volume II' chapter 11). [SORP 1 paras 56(a)(b)]. Investments in other associated companies should be treated as ordinary investments. [SORP 1 para 56(c)].

Property valuations

8.74 Property should be included at open market valuation, giving the name and qualification of the valuer. Where applicable, it should be stated that the valuer is an employee of the scheme or of the participating employers.

8.75 Appendix 1 to the SORP recognises that it would lead to costs disproportionate to the benefit gained to require an annual revaluation by a qualified independent valuer of all properties held. Consequently, the SORP allows for the trustees to reassess the revaluation each year and to adjust it if they think it appropriate. The frequency of the independent revaluation depends on the proportion of investments held as property (that is, the more significant the proportion, the more frequent the valuation). However, the SORP suggests that the minimum frequency should be at least once every five years. In order to make the effect of this as even as possible, the appendix suggests that a proportion of the total property portfolio should be valued by a qualified valuer each year.

Accounting for fully-insured schemes

8.76 Although fully-insured schemes may not have any assets to disclose in their net assets statement, SORP 1 says, in its scope paragraph, that its provisions apply to such schemes. A pension scheme is said to be 'fully-insured' when the trustees have effected an insurance contract in respect of each member, which guarantees benefits corresponding at all times to those promised under the scheme's rules. How such insurance policies are to be accounted for will depend on the type of insurance contract that the trustees enter into.

8.77 Where the long-term insurance policy is purchased to match and fully guarantee the pension obligations of the scheme in respect of specific individuals, the acquisition cost of the policy should be treated as the cost of discharging the obligations at the time of purchase. Consequently, the revenue account will show contributions receivable from the employer and members and premiums paid to the insurance company. In this situation, a valuation of the policy should not be included in the scheme's net assets statement. It will also not be necessary in the scheme's financial statements to show benefits paid by the insurance company.

8.78 However, many fully-insured schemes fully guarantee the pension obligations of a number of employees collectively and do not match them individually. As far as the revenue account is concerned, the scheme should show the contributions received from the employer and members and also the benefit payments made by the insurance company. The premium paid to the insurance company would not be included, because it reflects the cost of purchasing an investment and not a discharge of the trustees' obligations. The insurance policy or investments would, therefore, be included in the statement of net assets, on a basis equivalent to market value. In accordance with paragraph 8 of Schedule 3 to the Disclosure Regulations the premium paid and the benefits paid should be disclosed in the notes to the pension scheme financial statements as purchases and sales, respectively, of investments during the scheme year.

8.79 Appendix 2 to the SORP discusses seven main methods of valuing long-term insurance policies. Each method is likely to produce a different value. The aim is to arrive at the method that most nearly coincides with middle market value (thereby being consistent with other asset valuation methods). The conclusion reached is that schemes should use the premium value or modified premium value, or, if these are impracticable, the valuation for actuarial assessment of the discontinuance position. Premium value is an estimate of a single premium required to purchase the payments at present secured under the policies.

Additional voluntary contributions (AVCs)

8.80 The method of accounting for AVCs depends on whether or not they are invested separately from the rest of the scheme's assets. Where they are invested separately in such a way that the proceeds from the investment determine the benefit to the members, they should be dealt with in either of the following ways:

- Accounted for within the financial statements, with the transactions and assets separately disclosed.

- Mentioned in the notes, and reported on separately to the individual concerned.

8.81 Where they are used to secure benefits within the provisions for benefits under the principal scheme (for example, by way of added years), they should be included as contribution income and the assets acquired should be included in the net assets statement along with the other assets of the scheme.

The investment report

8.82 SORP 1 assumes that the annual report will include a statement containing a more detailed analysis of the investment portfolio and income than disclosed in the financial statements. This statement will often form part of the trustees' report. Its contents are not prescribed by SORP 1 but the SORP suggests that such a statement will usually include:

- Investments analysed by industrial sector.

- Investments analysed by geographical sector.

- Details of the ten or twenty largest investments.

- Details of investments that represent five per cent or more of any class of shares of any company being invested in.

- Details of the extent to which properties are subject to rent reviews.

See for example Table 8.8.

8.83 The totals shown in the investment report must be reconciled to those shown in the financial statements. [SORP 1 paras 68, 69].

Actuarial valuation

8.84 Until 1986, pension schemes were under no general duty to obtain an actuarial valuation, although those regulated by the OPB, in practice, have had to obtain a three-yearly valuation report.

8.85 Now, an actuarial valuation, signed and made by a qualified actuary must be obtained by all pension schemes except:

- Schemes with one member only.

Table 8.8: Illustration of a note to the accounts of a pension scheme on the investment portfolio

Extract from the Rolls-Royce Pension Fund Annual Report for the year ending 31 March 1990.

Notes to the accounts extract

8 Investments at Market Value

An analysis of the portfolio of investments by investment manager at market value at 31 March 1990 is shown below:

	Investments £000	Cash £000	Total £000
Hill Samual – Index Linked	108,504	1,572	110,076
Philips and Drew – FT All-Share Index Fund	410,545	330	410,875
Fleming – United Kingdom equities	116,280	5,152	121,432
GMO Woolley – United Kingdom equities	90,174	5,733	95,907
Throgmorton – United Kingdom equities	59,264	779	60,043
Mercury – Unlisted equities	3,846	–	3,846
Mellon-Pictet – European equities	37,346	859	38,205
Columbia – North American equities	49,302	839	50,141
Provident – North American equities	18,012	299	18,311
Jundt/Capen – North American equities	33,769	1,059	34,828
Jardine Fleming – Pacific Basin equities	73,377	3,812	77,189
New Japan – Japanese equities	7,889	677	8,566
Fidelity – International equities	50,728	4,144	54,872
Philips and Drew – FTA World-ex-UK Index Fund	61,411	–	61,411
Baring, Houston & Saunders – Property	84,853	765	85,618
Bidwells – Forestry	8,255	1	8,256
Grosvenor – Overseas Property	36,809	–	36,809
Rolls-Royce Pensions Trust – Miscellaneous	18,336	3,488	21,824
	1,268,700	29,509	1,298,209

Investments include transactions due for settlement, see Note 9, which will be settled from Cash.

An analysis of the portfolio of investments at market value at 31 March 1990 is shown below:

	1990 £000	%	1989 £000	%
Fixed Interest Securities				
British Government	–	–	23,762	2.0
Index Linked Stocks	108,504	8.3	52,161	4.3
Industrial Loan Stocks	40	–	13,794	1.1
Sterling Bonds	–	–	16,360	1.4
Local Authority Bonds	–	–	6,544	0.5
Preference Stocks	–	–	305	–
	108,544	8.3	112,926	9.3
Ordinary Stocks				
United Kingdom				
Convertible	1,509	0.1	2,397	0.2
Capital Goods	139,847	10.8	167,093	13.7
Consumer Group	206,586	15.9	200,124	16.5
Other Groups	109,761	8.5	117,265	9.7
Oils	87,688	6.8	66,619	5.5
Financial	104,646	8.1	89,449	7.4
Investment Trusts	16,170	1.2	15,014	1.2
Overseas Traders	10,889	0.8	9,136	0.7
Unlisted	7,101	0.6	4,313	0.4
	684,197	52.8	671,410	55.3
Europe	70,202	5.4	38,671	3.2
North America	146,994	11.3	106,923	8.8
Japan	91,194	7.0	88,102	7.3
Other	38,093	2.9	22,989	1.9
	1,030,680	79.4	928,095	76.5

Table 8.8 continued

Property				
Direct Freehold and Long Leasehold				
Offices	39,745	3.1	35,980	3.0
Shops	34,120	2.6	35,316	2.9
Retail Warehouses	–	–	1,450	0.1
Industrial	10,100	0.8	8,415	0.7
Forestry	8,255	0.6	9,752	0.8
	92,220	7.1	90,913	7.5
Unlisted Property Investments				
United Kingdom	447	–	73	–
Overseas	36,809	2.9	34,585	2.9
	129,476	10.0	125,571	10.4
Cash and Deposits	29,509	2.3	46,556	3.8
	1,298,209	100.0	1,213,148	100.0

The ten largest equity holdings of the Fund, by market value and as a percentage of the total investments of the Fund at 31 March 1990, were:

	£000	%
The British Petroleum Company plc	28,371	2.2
Glaxo Holdings plc	26,884	2.1
The Shell Transport and Trading Company plc	20,084	1.5
British Gas plc	19,066	1.5
British Telecommunications plc	16,189	1.2
The RTZ Corporation PLC	14,009	1.1
Hanson PLC	13,973	1.1
BAT Industriesplc	13,789	1.1
BTR plc	11,303	0.9
Imperial Chemical Industries PLC	11,281	0.9

The Fund does not hold any shares in Rolls-Royce plc.

- Death benefit only schemes.
- Public service pension schemes.
- Unfunded benefits or money purchase benefits.

[SI 1986/1046 paras 3, 8(2)].

8.86 Valuations must be made at least every three and a half years. [SI 1986/1046 para 8(4)]. Recognising the delays common in obtaining actuarial reports, the duty to obtain a valuation report is only expressed in the Disclosure Regulations as being as soon as is reasonably practicable after the due valuation date. [SI 1986/1046 para 8(5)].

8.87 There is no requirement that the actuary should be independent of the pension scheme.

8.88 The actuarial valuation should:

- Be so framed as to enable the expected future course of the scheme's contribution rates and funding level to be understood.
- State whether it has been prepared in accordance with the current guidelines concerning 'Retirement benefit schemes - actuarial reports' published by the Institute of Actuaries and Faculty of Actuaries.
- Indicate where there are any material departures from those guidelines.

[SI 1986/1046 para 8(1)].

Duty to submit an annual return

8.89 There is no equivalent duty to that placed on companies to submit an annual return, although the Government has power under the Disclosure Regulations to set up such a register. The documents required by the OPB are very similar to those of an annual return.

Duty to make information available to scheme members

8.90 There is a widely expressed duty to make financial statements, valuations and other information available to members of the pension scheme and other interested parties. However, this requirement does not apply to the following:

- Schemes with one member only.
- Death benefit only schemes.
- Public service pension schemes (see para 8.14).

[SI 1986/1046 paras 3, 9(1)(2)].

8.91 The people who are entitled to this information on request are:

- The scheme's members and prospective members.
- Beneficiaries under the scheme.
- Independent recognised trade unions (see chapter 10).

8.92 The 'other information' referred to in paragraph 8.90 relates to the detailed information concerning the administration of the scheme. [SI 1986/1046 para 9(1), Sch 5]. In addition, members or prospective members are generally entitled to certain basic information. [SI 1986/1046 para 5(1), Sch 1].

Appointment, resignation and removal of auditors

8.93 The *Occupational Pension Schemes (Auditors) Regulations 1987* (SI 1987/1102) regulates the appointment, resignation and removal of auditors of those pension schemes to which paragraph 7 of the Disclosure Regulations apply. The Appointing Body of a scheme (designated in the scheme's constitution to appoint auditors), usually the trustees, shall appoint one or more persons who satisfy the requirements of paragraph 7(3) of the Disclosure Regulations, to audit the scheme's financial statements. [SI 1987/1102 para 3(1)].

8.94 An auditor of a scheme may be removed at any time by the Appointing Body serving notice in writing. This notice must state the date with effect from which the auditor's appointment is terminated. [SI 1987/1102 para 3(2)].

8.95 The auditor shall within 14 days of his removal serve on the Appointing Body and the trustees of the scheme either of the following:

- A statement specifying any circumstances connected with his removal which, in his opinion, significantly effect the interests of the members or prospective members of, or beneficiaries under, the scheme.
- A statement that he knows of no such circumstances.

[SI 1987/1102 para 3(5)].

8.96 An auditor may resign by serving notice in writing to the Appointing Body and the trustees of the scheme. Such a resignation is not effective unless the notice contains a statement similar to that outlined in paragraph 8.95 above. [SI 1987/1102 para 3(3)(4)].

8.97 A copy of the statement mentioned in paragraphs 8.95 and 8.46 above must be given by the trustees to the next appointed auditor as well as members of the scheme. [SI 1987/1105 para 2(10].

8.98 The *Occupational Pension Scheme (Auditors) Regulations 1987* also prescribes the duty of the employers and trustees to provide the auditor of the scheme with such information and explanations as may reasonably be required for him to perform his duties as auditor. [SI 1987/1102 para 4, 5].

Audit report

8.99 The audit report should include:

- A statement of whether or not, in the auditor's opinion, the financial statements:

- ☐ Contain the information specified in Schedule 3 to the Disclosure Regulations (see para 8.58).

- ☐ Give a true and fair view of the scheme's financial transactions during the scheme year and of the disposition, at the end of the scheme year, of the scheme's assets and liabilities other than liabilities to pay pensions and benefits after the end of the scheme year.

- ■ A statement whether or not, in the auditor's opinion, contributions payable to the scheme during the scheme year have been paid in accordance with the scheme's rules or contracts under which they were payable, and with the recommendation of the actuary, if appropriate.

- ■ If either of the two statements above is negative or qualified, a statement of the reasons for the negative or qualified statement.

[SI 1986/1046 para 7(5)].

8.100 The wording for an unqualified pension scheme audit report is as follows:

REPORT OF THE AUDITORS TO THE TRUSTEES AND MEMBERS OF [NAME] PENSION SCHEME

We have audited the financial statements on pages [] to [] in accordance with Auditing Standards.

In our opinion the financial statements give a true and fair view of the financial transactions of the scheme during the year ended [date] and of the disposition at that date of its assets and liabilities, other than liabilities to pay pensions and benefits after the end of the year, and contain the information specified in Regulation 7 of, and Schedule 3, to the Occupational Pension Schemes (Disclosure of Information) Regulations 1986.

In our opinion the contributions payable to the scheme during the year ended [date] have been paid in accordance with the scheme rules [and with the recommendation of the actuary]*.

[Name of firm]

Chartered Accountants,

[Address].

[Date of report].

*Omit for money purchase schemes, if there is no actuarial recommendation.

SORP 1 – PENSION SCHEME ACCOUNTS

Contents

Paragraphs

Pension Scheme Accounts

(Issued by the Accounting Standards Committee in May 1986)

This Statement of Recommended Practice ('SORP') sets out recommendations, intended to represent current best practice, on the form and contents of the accounts of pension schemes. It also explains the context in which it has been assumed the accounts will be placed.

The provisions of this statement should be read in conjunction with the Explanatory Foreword *to SORPs. Although SORPs are not mandatory, entities falling within their scope are encouraged to follow them and to state in their accounts that they have done so. They are also encouraged to disclose any departure from the recommendations and the reason for it. The provisions need* ***not be applied to immaterial items.***

Part 1 – Explanatory note

Introduction

1 The objectives of a pension scheme's annual report are to inform members and other users as to:

(a) the general activity, history and development of the scheme;
(b) the transactions of the scheme and the size of its fund;
(c) the progress of the scheme towards meeting its potential liabilities and obligations to members; and
(d) the investment policy and performance of the scheme.

To be of value to the users, this information should be provided on a timely basis.

2 In order to achieve these objectives and to present a balanced report on the pension scheme as a whole, the annual report should be made available as soon as possible after the accounting date and should comprise:

(a) A trustees' report. This is primarily a review of, or comment on:

(i) membership statistics and major changes in benefits, constitution or legal requirements;
(ii) the financial development of the scheme as disclosed in the accounts;
(iii) the actuarial position of the scheme as disclosed in the actuary's statement; and
(iv) the investment policy and performance of the scheme, including details of any delegation of investment management responsibilities by the trustees.

(b) Accounts. These are a stewardship report, designed to give a true and fair view of the financial transactions of the scheme during the accounting period and of the disposition of its net assets at the period end. An auditors' report on the accounts should be attached if the accounts have been audited.

(c) An actuary's statement. This is a statement by an actuary based on his investigation into, and report on, the ability of the current fund of the pension scheme to meet accrued benefits and the adequacy of the fund and future contribution levels to meet promised benefits when due.

(d) An investment report. Investment policy and performance are important aspects of the stewardship function and accordingly the trustees' report in amplification of the accounts should contain or have appended additional information on investments held and investment income earned and comment on investment policy and performance.

3 As explained in paragraph 2, the information required of the investment report may instead be included in the trustees' report. The accounts and the actuary's statement are, however, two separate expert reports, having fundamentally different objectives. The former is a record of the origin and current size and disposition of the fund and the latter is a statement based on an investigation into, and report on, the present and future ability of the scheme to meet the accrued and prospective obligations to its members. These two reports require to be read in conjuction with each other, but neither should form a part of, or be subsumed into, the other.

Form and context in which the accounts appear

4 The form and context in which the accounts appear can have a significant effect on the overall message conveyed to the reader. It is therefore important that the separate components of the annual report are consistent with each other and do not omit any information which could affect the view given by the annual report as a whole. For example, the trustees' report's review of the financial development of the scheme should be both a fair review and consistent with the accounts. Similarly, the accounts should be presented in conjunction with an actuary's statement which comments comprehensively on the adequacy of the current fund and funding policy.

5 It is suggested, therefore, that when preparing pension scheme accounts one must consider the contents of the remainder of the annual report in order to ensure that the accounts are not submitted to members and employers in a misleading form or context.

Fundamental accounting concepts and materiality

6 The recommendations contained in this statement should be considered in conjunction with the fundamental accounting concepts

described in SSAP 2 'Disclosure of accounting policies' and should be applied only after taking into account the materiality of the item or matter involved.

Legislation

7 Legislation designed to regulate certain aspects of pension schemes is being enacted in Great Britain and Northern Ireland. This legislation will impose on most schemes constituted in Great Britain or Northern Ireland a requirement that they prepare annual reports which include a set of accounts. The legislation will also set out in some detail requirements on the form and contents of the accounts and the principles to be applied in preparing them. As a consequence, some of the recommendations contained in this statement are also expected to be embodied in legislation. This is dealt with further in Part 5.

Terminology

8 Although this statement adopts the terms 'revenue account', 'net assets statement' and 'movement of funds statement', alternative terminology may be equally acceptable. The word 'company' is used in this statement to represent any incorporated or unincorporated entity. The statement is intended to be applied to schemes in the United Kingdom and the Republic of Ireland. However, for simplicity, it adopts terms such as 'UK investments' and 'sterling' rather than using phrases such as 'investments in assets domiciled at home' and 'local currency'.

Part 2 – Definition of terms

9 The *accruals concept* is a concept of accounting whereby revenues and costs are recognised as they are earned or incurred (not as money is received or paid) and matched with one another so far as their relationship can be established or justifiably assumed.

10 *Added years* is a form of provision of additional benefits whereby a member is promised benefit for a period in excess of that which would otherwise be taken into account in calculating the pension benefit.

11 *Additional voluntary contributions* are the contributions (over and above the regular contributions, if any, required from a member by the scheme rules) which a member elects to pay in order to secure additional benefits.

12 An *associated company* is a company, not being a subsidiary of the investing group or company, in which:

(a) the interest of the investing group or company is effectively that of a partner in a joint venture or consortium and the investing group or company is in a position to exercise a significant influence over the company in which the investment is made; or

(b) the interest of the investing group or company is for the long term and is substantial and, having regard to the disposition of the other shareholdings, the investing group or company is in a position to exercise a significant influence over the company in which the investment is made.

13 The *closing rate of exchange* is the exchange rate for spot transactions ruling at the accounting date and is the mean of the buying and selling rates at the close of business on that day.

14 *Concentration of investment* arises when a significant proportion of the assets of the scheme is invested in one company and any connected companies and persons, or in one property. For the purpose of this definition, an investment includes:

(a) an interest in shares and securities of a company;
(b) mortgages on real property owned by a company or person;
(c) freeholds and leaseholds owned by the scheme's trustees and effectively leased directly to a company or person; and
(d) loans made to a company or person.

15 *A pension scheme is a *fully insured scheme* when the trustees have effected an insurance contract in respect of each member which guarantees benefits corresponding at all times to those promised under the rules.

16 A *fund* of a pension scheme is the net assets held on behalf of the scheme by the trustees for the purpose of meeting benefits when they become due.

17 *The *members* of a pension scheme are all employees and former employees entitled to a benefit from the scheme.

18 *A *money purchase scheme* is a pension scheme in which the benefits are directly determined by the value of contributions paid in respect of each member.

19 *Movement of funds statement* is the term used in this statement of recommended practice to describe the reconciliation of the movement in the net assets of the scheme during the accounting period when it is presented as a separate statement within the accounts.

20 The *net assets* of the scheme are its assets and its liabilities other than those for pensions and other benefits falling due after the date of the accounts.

21 *Net assets statement* is the term used in this statement of recommended

---

*Definition taken from 'Pensions Terminology – A Glossary for Pension Schemes' published by PMI/PRAG in 1984.

practice to describe a summary of the net assets of a pension scheme presented as part of the accounts.

22 A *pension scheme* is an arrangement (other than for accident insurance) to provide pension and/or other benefits for members on leaving service or retiring and, possibly, after a member's death, for his or her dependants.

23 *Quoted securities* are, for the purposes of this statement, securities for which an established market exists and market prices are readily available. Any other security is an unquoted security.

24 *Revenue account* is the term used in this statement of recommended practice to describe a summary of the financial additions to, and withdrawals from, the fund of a pension scheme presented as part of the accounts.

25 *Self-investment* is investment of all or part of a scheme's assets in the business of the scheme employer and any connected companies and persons. For the purpose of this definition, investment includes all investment set out in (a) to (d) of paragraph 14 and, in addition, includes money currently due to the scheme but held by the employer or any connected companies or persons, such as employer and employee contributions.

26 *A *state scheme premium* is a payment which may be made when either the pension scheme or a member of it ceases to be contracted out, in return for which the state scheme will provide the equivalent of the whole or a part of the guaranteed minimum pension, i.e. the statutory minimum pension which a pension scheme must provide as one of the conditions of contracting out under the Social Security Pensions Act 1975.

27 *Subsidiary company*. A company is a subsidiary of another if, but only if,

(a) that other either:
  (i) is a member of it and controls the composition of its board of directors; or
  (ii) holds more than half in nominal value of its equity share capital; or
(b) the first mentioned company is a subsidiary of any company which is that other's subsidiary.

28 *Term insurance* is a form of life insurance which provides a lump sum on death before a fixed future date.

---

*Definition taken from 'Pensions Terminology – A Glossary for Pension Schemes' published by PMI/PRAG in 1984.

Part 3 – Recommended practice

Scope

29 The recommendations contained in this statement are intended to be applicable to all pension schemes constituted in the United Kingdom or the Republic of Ireland other than:

(a) those which have only one member at the accounting date; and
(b) those which are unfunded, i.e. those under which benefits are paid directly by the employer and no provision is made for future liabilities by setting aside assets under trusts.

30 As such, the scope of this statement is intended to include, *inter alia:*

(a) schemes which are fully insured and which may not, therefore, have any assets to disclose in the net assets statement; and
(b) schemes which are money purchase schemes and which may, therefore, have no need for an actuary's statement.

Primary addressees

31 The primary addressees of the accounts of a pension scheme are the members, the dependants of deceased former members and the participating employers.

Basis of accounting

32 The accounts should normally be prepared on the basis of the accruals concept.

33 All the assets and liabilities of the scheme at the period end should be included in the net assets statement in order to show the current size and disposition of the fund. The only exceptions to this are:

(a) the liabilities to pay pensions and other benefits in the future, which will be reported upon separately in the actuary's statement (see paragraphs 43 to 45);
(b) insurance policies purchased to match the pension obligations of specific individual members (see paragraphs 61 and 62); and
(c) additional voluntary contributions separately invested from the assets of the principal scheme (see paragraphs 63 and 64).

34 The carrying amount of investments should be the market value at the date of the net assets statement, where such a value is available, or else at the trustees' estimate thereof. This is dealt with further in paragraphs 46 to 54.

35 The carrying amount of all other assets and liabilities recognised in the net assets statement should be based on normal accounting conventions.

Content of accounts

36 The accounts and notes thereto should comprise:

(a) a revenue account which discloses the magnitude and character of the financial additions to, and withdrawals from, the fund during the accounting period;
(b) a net assets statement which discloses the size and disposition of the net assets of the scheme at the period end; and
(c) a reconciliation of the movement in the net assets of the scheme to the revenue account. This reconciliation may be shown as a separate statement (i.e. a 'movement of funds statement') or alternatively it may be incorporated into the revenue account or the net assets statement.

37 The revenue account, net assets statement, movement of funds statement (if any), and notes to the accounts should contain as a minimum the items set out in Part 4 of this statement.

38 Corresponding amounts should be disclosed. The accounting period will usually be one year in duration. If this is not the case for both the current and corresponding periods, this fact should be clearly stated.

39 The accounts should contain such additional information as is necessary to give a true and fair view of the financial transactions of the scehem for the accounting period and of the disposition of its net assets at the period end. This will include, for example, information about capital commitments, post balance sheet events and contingencies (other than future liabilities to pay pensions and related outgoings).

Accounting policies

40 The accounting policies followed in dealing with items which are judged material or critical in accounting for or reporting on the transactions and net assets of the scheme should be explained in the notes to the accounts. The explanations should be clear, fair and as brief as possible.

41 The following are examples of some areas where it will be appropriate to disclose the accounting policies adopted:

(a) the policies adopted in applying the accruals concept to significant categories of income and expenditure, such as contributions, investment income, transfer values and benefits;
(b) the bases adopted for the valuation of assets;
(c) the basis of foreign currency translation;
(d) the treatment of interest on property developments; and
(e) the bases adopted for accounting for investments in subsidiary and associated companies.

42 It is a fundamental accounting concept that there is consistency of

accounting treatment within each accounting period and from one period to the next. A change in accounting policy should not be made unless it can be justified on the ground that the new policy is preferable to the one it replaces because it will give a fairer presentation of the transactions and of the disposition of the net assets of the scheme. When changes are made they should be disclosed, along with the reasons for making the change. If the effect is material it should be accounted for as a prior year adjustment by restating the opening balance of the fund and the corresponding amounts.

Actuarial position

43 The responsibility for reviewing the adequacy of the funding arrangements made to meet expected pensions and other benefits from the fund lies with the actuary to the scheme. This responsibility will normally be discharged by the preparation of an actuary's report which, although usually addressed to the trustees, is also made available to the members. A statement by the actuary based on this report forms a separate component of the annual report.

44 An actuary's report will often not be prepared annually, and, when it is prepared, it will not necessarily coincide with the date of the annual report and accounts. Accordingly, the actuary will often provide an interim or supplementary statement explaining whether he is aware of any changes in circumstances or necessary changes in assumptions which would indicate that his previous statement could not, if prepared at the current date, be made.

45 The accounts should refer to the actuary's statement by way of a note. This note might take the following form:

'The accounts summarise the transactions and net assets of the scheme. They do not take account of liabilities to pay pensions and other benefits in the future. The actuarial position of the fund, which does take account of such liabilities, is dealt with in the statement by the actuary on pages 00 to 00 of the annual report and these accounts should be read in conjunction therewith.'

If the actuary's report is not recent and the actuary's statement has not been updated by an interim or supplementary statement, the above wording may need to be amended.

Valuation of investments

46 Investments should be included in the net assets statement at their market value at the date of the net assets statement, where such a value is available, or else at the trustees' estimate thereof. The carrying amount of the principal categories of investment should be arrived at by applying the valuation bases set out below in paragraphs 48 to 54. The bases adopted should be disclosed in the notes to the accounts.

47 Any significant restrictions affecting the ability of the scheme to realise its investments at the accounting date at all or at the value at which they are included in the accounts should be disclosed in a note to the accounts. This will include, for example, legal or contractual restrictions on the surrender of units (e.g. managed funds) or material penalties which would have been suffered if they had been surrendered at the accounting date. It will not include the inherent difficulties in disposing of a large investment.

48 Securities quoted in the UK should be valued at the mid-point of the quotations in the Stock Exchange Daily Official List or at similar recognised market values.

49 Other securities quoted overseas should similarly be valued at middle market prices from overseas stock exchanges translated at closing rates of exchange.

50 Unquoted securities (including venture capital funds where appropriate) should be valued by the trustees.

51 Investments which are held in units should be valued at the average of the unit bid and offer prices at the accounting date. For some unitised funds, offer prices are regularly quoted but bid prices are not. In such circumstances, a basis such as reducing the offer price by an amount which takes account of the specific circumstances is likely to give a suitable valuation. Where unit bid and offer prices are both not available or have otherwise not been used, the basis adopted in arriving at an estimate of market value should be disclosed.

52 Financial futures, options, and forward currency positions should be included or provided for at market value, where such market value is available. If it is not available, a trustees' valuation should be used.

53 Freehold and leasehold property should be included in the net assets statement at open market value. Guidance on this matter is given in Appendix 1 to this statement. The name, or employing firm, and qualification of the valuer should be stated. If the valuer is an employee of the scheme or the participating employers this fact should be stated.

54 If practicable, long-term insurance policies should be valued using a premium valuation method. Where there are difficulties in obtaining this value, however, the latest value established by the actuary for the assessment of the discontinuance position, adjusted by subsequent additions to and withdrawals from the policy, will usually be satisfactory. Guidance on this matter is given in Appendix 2 to this statement.

Accounting for associated and subsidiary companies

55 Pension schemes may have investments in associated or subsidiary

companies. These companies will be either investment-holding companies or trading companies. The associated companies may include joint ventures such as managed funds or pooled investments.

56 In principle, such investments should be accounted for as follows:

(a) the results, assets and liabilities of subsidiary companies should be consolidated with the transactions, assets and liabilities of the scheme. For investment-holding subsidiaries the basis of this consolidation will usually be a proportional consolidation on a line-by-line basis; for other subsidiaries it will be a single-line equity method of accounting;
(b) investments in associated companies which are joint ventures should be treated in the same way as investments in subsidiary companies; and
(c) investments in associated companies which are not joint ventures should be treated in the same way as ordinary investments by including them in the net assets statement at market value and including only dividends received and receivable in the revenue account.

Where consolidated accounts are prepared, they may be the only accounts of the scheme; there is no need to produce separate 'entity' accounts. The consolidation bases to be used are explained more fully in paragraphs 57 to 60 below.

57 It will usually be appropriate to include in the scheme's accounts, on a line-by-line basis, a proportion of the results, assets and liabilities of subsidiary investment-holding companies based on the percentage equity shareholding of the scheme in the companies.

58 However, if the pension scheme in effect has an interest or obligation in respect of the whole of the results, assets or liabilities of a subsidiary company, for example because it has agreed to acquire or indemnify the minority interests, it will be appropriate to consolidate the whole of the company's results, assets and liabilities and include the minority shareholders' interest in the net assets statement.

59 Uniform group accounting policies should be followed by a pension scheme in preparing its consolidated accounts. For example, investments held by investment-holding subsidiary companies should be included in the consolidated accounts at market value. Where such group accounting policies are not adopted by a subsidiary, adjustments should be made in preparing the consolidated accounts.

60 The scheme's investment in trading subsidiary companies should be included in the net assets statement at market value. Although the same principles as in paragraphs 57 and 58 should be applied in determining the proportion of the net result of such companies which

should be included in the scheme's revenue account, this proportion should be included on a single line rather than line-by-line as for investment-holding companies. The unrealised gains arising from the revaluation to market value of investments in trading subsidiaries should be treated in exactly the same way as those on other investments.

Accounting for long-term insurance policies

61 If long-term insurance policies are purchased which match, and fully guarantee, the pension obligations of the scheme in respect of specific individual members, the acquisition costs of the policy should be treated as the cost of discharging the obligations at the time of purchase. Such a policy should not be included in the net assets statement of the scheme.

62 All other long-term insurance policies should be included in the net assets statement.

Accounting for additional voluntary contributions ('AVCs')

63 Where AVCs are made to purchase added years or additional defined benefits within the provisions for benefits under the principal scheme, they should be included as contributions receivable from members in the scheme's revenue account and the assets acquired with them should be included in the net assets statement.

64 Where AVCs are separately invested in such a way that the proceeds from the investment determine the benefit to the members, they should be disclosed separately from the transactions and net assets of the fund but accounted for within the accounts of the scheme or the notes thereto.

Disclosure items

65 If there is any self-investment in excess of 5% of the value of the net assets of the scheme, then this should be disclosed in a note to the accounts, together with details of the nature and value of the investment involved.

66 Where there is a concentration of investment (other than in UK Government securities) which exceeds 5% of the value of the net assets of the scheme, then this should be disclosed in a note to the accounts, together with details of the amount and nature of the investment and the company involved.

67 Where insurance policies form a material part of the net assets of the scheme, the main characteristics relevant to the overall investment policy, for instance whether the policies are with or without profits, should be disclosed.

Investment report

68 This statement assumes that the annual report includes a report which

contains a greater analysis of the investment portfolio and income than is disclosed in the accounts. This analysis will often include:

(a) analysis of investments by industrial sector;
(b) analysis of investments by geographical sector;
(c) details of the ten or twenty largest investments;
(d) details of investments which represent 5% or more of any class of shares of any company; and
(e) details of the extent to which properties are subject to rent reviews.

69 The totals shown in any such report should be reconciled to the amounts shown in the accounts.

Part 4 – Format of accounts

70 The accounts of a pension scheme, and the notes thereto, should contain the items listed below where they are material. These are not intended to be recommendations on either the layout or the order of these items.

Revenue account

1. Contributions receivable:
   - 1.1 from employers:
     - 1.1.1 normal;
     - 1.1.2 additional;
   - 1.2 from members:
     - 1.2.1 normal;
     - 1.2.2 additional voluntary (see paragraphs 63 and 64);
   - 1.3 transfers in:
     - 1.3.1 group transfers in from other schemes;
     - 1.3.2 individual transfers in from other schemes.

2. Investment income:
   - 2.1 income from fixed interest securities;
   - 2.2 dividends from equities;
   - 2.3 income from index-linked securities;
   - 2.4 income from managed or unitized funds;
   - 2.5 net rents from properties. Any material netting-off should be separately disclosed;
   - 2.6 interest on cash deposits;
   - 2.7 share of profits/losses of trading subsidiary companies and joint ventures.

3. Other income:
   - 3.1 claims on term insurance policies;
   - 3.2 any other category of income which does not naturally fall into the above classification, suitably described and analysed where material.

4. Benefits payable:
   - 4.1 pensions;
   - 4.2 commutation of pensions and lump sum retirement benefits;
   - 4.3 death benefits;
   - 4.4 payments to and on account of leavers:
     - 4.4.1 refunds of contributions;
     - 4.4.2 state scheme premiums;
     - 4.4.3 purchase of annuities to match preserved benefits,
     - 4.4.4 group transfers out to other schemes;
     - 4.4.5 individual transfers out to other schemes.

5. Other payments:
   - 5.1 premiums on term insurance policies;
   - 5.2 any other category of expenditure which does not naturally fall into the above classification, suitably described and analysed where material.

6. Administrative and other expenses borne by the scheme, with suitable analysis where material.

   Where the administrative expenses are borne directly by a participating employer, that fact should be disclosed.

Net assets statement

7. Investment assets:
   - 7.1 fixed interest securities (analysed between public sector and other);
   - 7.2 equities;
   - 7.3 index-linked securities;
   - 7.4 managed funds (analysed between property and other);
   - 7.5 unit trusts (analysed between property and other);
   - 7.6 trading subsidiary companies and joint ventures;
   - 7.7 freehold and leasehold property;
   - 7.8 cash deposits;
   - 7.9 insurance policies;
   - 7.10 other investments, such as works of art;
   - 7.11 debtors and creditors in respect of investment transactions where these form part of the net assets available for investment within the investment portfolio;
   - 7.12 other assets and liabilities directly connected with investment transactions (e.g. financial futures, options and forward dealings in currencies and, where appropriate, tax recoverable).

   Investments should be further analysed between 'UK' and 'foreign' and between 'quoted' and 'unquoted', and freehold and leasehold property should be further analysed between 'short leasehold' and 'other'.

8. Fixed assets held primarily for reasons other than investment potential.

9. Long-term borrowings:
   9.1 sterling; and
   9.2 foreign currency.

10. Current assets and liabilities:
   10.1 contributions due from employer;
   10.2 unpaid benefits; and
   10.3 other current assets and liabilities (other than liabilities to pay pensions and other benefits in the future).

Reconciliation of the movement in the net assets of the scheme

11. The reconciliation of the movement in the net assets of the scheme may be incorporated into the revenue account or net assets statement, or alternatively be shown as a separate statement. Whichever method of presentation is adopted it should clearly disclose:
   11.1 opening net assets of the scheme;
   11.2 net new money invested, per revenue account;
   11.3 change in market value of investments (realised and unrealised); and
   11.4 closing net assets of the scheme.

71 The amount of sales of purchases of investments should be disclosed either within one of the accounting statements referred to in paragraph 70 or elsewhere in the notes.

Part 5 – Note on legal requirements in Great Britain, Northern Ireland and the Republic of Ireland

Great Britain and Northern Ireland

72 Legislation designed to regulate certain aspects of pension schemes, including the periodic preparation of annual reports, is being enacted in Great Britain, and is contained within the Social Security Act 1985 and the Regulations being made under the Act. Corresponding legislation for Northern Ireland is expected to be contained in the Social Security (Northern Ireland) Order 1985 and the Regulations being made under that Order.

73 As well as imposing on the trustees the requirement to prepare annual reports, the legislation will include detailed requirements on the form and content of the annual report, including the accounts. These requirements will provide a framework for the accounting for, and reporting on, the transactions, assets and liabilities of pension schemes. The legislation is expected to require the accounts of pension

schemes to give a true and fair view of the financial transactions of the scheme during the period and of the disposition of its net assets at the period end.

74 The legislation is also expected to require the inclusion as a note to the accounts of a statement explaining whether or not the accounts have been prepared in accordance with Parts 2 to 4 of this Statement of Recommended Practice and, if not, giving particulars of material differences.

75 The recommendations contained in this Statement of Recommended Practice, which are expected to be consistent with the forthcoming legislation in all respects, provide guidance on best practice in complying with the legislation. However, the recommendations deal with some aspects of pension scheme accounting not expected to be dealt with in the legislation (for example, accounting for associated and subsidiary companies) and they go further than the legislation is expected to go in some respects. Examples of respects in which they go further include:

(a) the scope of the recommendations. As explained in paragraph 29, the recommendations are intended to be applicable to all pension schemes other than one-member schemes and unfunded schemes. The accounting requirements of the legislation are expected to apply to all occupational pension schemes other than one-member schemes, unfunded schemes, and public service schemes. 'Occupational pension scheme' is expected to be more narrowly defined than this statement's 'pension scheme'; and

(b) the disclosure required in respect of self-investment and concentration of investment. The definitions and terminology which are expected to be adopted in respect of these disclosures are not the same as those adopted in this statement. Consequently, whilst the minimum disclosure recommended in respect of these disclosures is (with the exception of the treatment of UK Government securities in paragraph 66 of this statement) expected to be sufficient to comply with legislation, the reverse will not necessarily be the case.

Republic of Ireland

76 There is no equivalent legislation to the Social Security Act 1985 or the Social Security (Northern Ireland) Order 1985 enacted in, or planned for, the Republic of Ireland.

77 Nevertheless, as this statement is complete in itself and does not rely on legislation in any way, its provisions are suitable for application to schemes operating in the Republic of Ireland.

78 Paragraph 26 of this statement refers to the Social Security Pensions

Act 1975. This is Great Britain legislation and, whilst there is equivalent legislation in Northern Ireland (the Social Security Pensions (Northern Ireland) Order 1975), there is no equivalent in the Republic of Ireland. Consequently, the term defined ('state scheme premium') is not relevant in the context of schemes constituted in the Republic of Ireland.

79 Paragraph 27 of this statement adopts a definition of subsidiary company based on the statutory definitions given in the Companies Act 1985 and the Companies Act (Northern Ireland), 1960, as inserted by Article 3 of The Companies (Northern Ireland) Order 1982. However, the Companies Act 1963 (Republic of Ireland) gives a slightly different definition, in that a company in which the holding company holds more than half of the shares carrying voting rights, as distinct from more than half of the equity share capital, is also included. Such companies will normally come within the definition of paragraph 27 because holding more than half of the shares with voting rights will be equivalent to controlling the composition of the board of directors.

Appendix 1

This appendix does not form part of the statement of recommended practice.

Valuation of freehold and leasehold properties held as investments

Paragraph 53 of the statement recommends that freehold and leasehold property should be valued annually at open market value for inclusion in the accounts. The annual valuation of all such properties by external, qualified valuers may be expensive and time-consuming with no commensurate benefit. This appendix is intended to provide guidance on the matter.

1 Although a valuation of properties should be undertaken annually, it need not necessarily be by a qualified or independent valuer. It will usually be acceptable to have a valuation carried out by a qualified valuer at regular intervals, with an appraisal and, if necessary, update of this valuation carried out by the trustees during the intervening years.

2 The regularity with which the valuation should be carried out by a qualified valuer, and the possible involvement of independent valuers, depends, to some extent, on the proportion of the assets held in the form of properties. In the absence of unusual circumstances a valuation by a qualified valuer should be undertaken every five years.

3 In order to ensure that the trend of the movement in market values is not distorted unnecessarily by carrying out such valuations every five years it may be appropriate to undertake them on a rolling basis, with a proportion of the total property portfolio being valued by a qualified valuer each year.

Appendix 2

This appendix does not form part of the statement of recommended practice.

Valuation of long-term insurance policies

The statement recommends that all investments of the pension scheme, including long-term insurance policies (other than policies referred to in paragraph 61), should be included in the net assets statement at market value. The market value of long-term insurance policies is not readily ascertainable, hence a basis of valuation which is consistent with that adopted for other assets (i.e. a middle-market price) and which is practicable should be used.

1 The main methods of valuing long-term insurance policies are as follows:

(i) surrender value;
(ii) assignment value;
(iii) value determined for an insurance company's own actuarial valuation;
(iv) premium value. This is an estimate of a single premium to purchase the payments at present secured under the policies;
(v) modified premium value. Although the premium value does not represent a middle-market price, it can be made similar by excluding the loadings made by the insurer in premium rating for initial expenses, such as issue expenses, brokerage and stamp duty. This 'modified premium value' is lower than the premium value;
(vi) valuation for actuarial assessment of the discontinuance position; and
(vii) valuation for actuarial assessment of the future contribution rate.

2 Surrender value is the value at which the insurer is prepared to buy back the policy and is consequently a realisable value. The surrender value quoted by the insurance company will depend on many factors unrelated to the policy's worth in normal circumstances, such as the willingness of the insurance company to buy the policy and the need to realise assets. Surrender value will therefore be the relevant valuation basis only if it is likely that the policy will be surrendered.

3 An assignment value is also a realisable value. Assignment of pension policies is unusual and the assignment value involved will be a matter of negotiation on each occasion. As such, it will be neither appropriate nor practicable to use such values for accounting purposes unless the policy is to be assigned.

4 The value determined by an insurance company for its own internal

purposes will have been calculated on different assumptions and for different purposes than a valuation for use in pension scheme accounts. It will not, therefore, reflect the market value of the policy.

5 Premium value and the modified premium value are replacement costs. There may be practical problems in trying to determine these values when certain policy benefits could not be purchased in their existing form, for example those under long established with-profits policies. When premiums are continuing under annual premium contracts the estimated single premium should be such as would, together with the contractual future premiums, purchase the same policy benefits.

6 A valuation for the actuarial assessment of the discontinuance position should be directly comparable to the market values attributed to other assets.

7 A valuation for the actuarial assessment of the future contribution rate will, like the value referred to in 4, have been based on different assumptions from those usually adopted in determining market value.

8 All of these methods are likely to produce different values. Surrender value, assignment value, the value determined by an insurance company for its own internal purposes and the value established by the actuary for the assessment of the future contribution rate will generally not be consistent with middle-market values. Premium value or modified premium value is most closely akin to middle market value and should, therefore, be used. Where this is impracticable, the carrying amount should be based on the value established by the actuary for the assessment of the discontinuance position.

9 Such actuarial valuations should be undertaken at least every three years. In the interim years the value determined by the latest actuarial valuation should be adjusted to take account of additions to and withdrawals from the policy.

10 These actuarial values are based on different principles from those on which premium values and modified premium values are based. Consequently they will not necessarily give comparable results. Although arguments can be advanced in favour of the use of actuarial values rather than premium values or vice versa, either of these bases will, as long as it is consistently applied, provide a satisfactory valuation for use in the accounts.

THE OCCUPATIONAL PENSION SCHEMES (DISCLOSURE OF INFORMATION) REGULATIONS 1986 (SI 1986/1046) AS AMENDED BY SI 1986/1717 AND SI 1987/1105

Made – – – – – – – –	18th June 1986
Laid before Parliament	25th June 1986
Coming into Operation	1st November 1986

The Secretary of State for Social Services, in exercise of the powers conferred upon him by section 168(1) of, and Schedule 20 to, the Social Security Act 1975(**a**) and sections 56A(1), (3) and (4), 56E(1), (3) and (4), 62(4) and 66(4) of, and paragraph 14(3) of Schedule 1A to, the Social Security Pensions Act 1975(**b**) and of all other powers enabling him in that behalf, by this instrument, which contains only regulations made under sections 56A and 56E of, and paragraph 14(3) of Schedule 1A to, the Social Security Pensions Act 1975, makes the following regulations:-

Citation, commencement and interpretation

(1) These regulations may be cited as the Occupational Pension Schemes (Disclosure of Information) Regulations 1986 and shall come into operation on 1st November 1986.

(2) In these regulations, unless the context otherwise requires:

"the Act" means the Social Security Pensions Act 1975;

"beneficiary", in relation to a scheme, means a person, other than a member of the scheme, who is entitled to payment of benefits under the scheme;

"connected company", in relation to a company, means another company where one of the companies is a subsidiary (within the meaning of section 736 of the Companies Act 1985(**c**) of the other, or where both companies are subsidiaries of a third company;

(**a**) 1975 c.14. *See* definitions of "prescribe" and "regulations" in Schedule 20. Section 168(1) applies, by virtue of section 66(2) of the Social Security Pensions Act 1975 (c.60), to the exercise of certain powers conferred by that Act.

(**b**) 1975 c.60; sections 56A and 56E were added by section 3 of and Schedule 2 to the Social Security Act 1985 (c.53) and Schedule 1A was added by section 2 of and Schedule 1 to that Act.

(**c**) 1985 c.6.

"employer", in relation to a member or prospective member of a scheme, has the meaning assigned to it by regulation 2(4) and (5) of the Occupational Pension Schemes (Preservation of Benefit) Regulations 1984(**a**);

"funded", in relation to benefits under a scheme, means provided by setting aside resources (other than assets at the disposal of the employer of any person who is employed in relevant employment) in advance which are related to the intended rate or amount of the benefits;

"independent trade union" has the meaning assigned to it by section 153 of the Employment Protection (Consolidation) Act 1978(**b**);

"money purchase benefit" means any benefit which is calculated by reference to a payment or payments made by the member, or by any other person in respect of him, not being a benefit the rate or amount of which is calculated by reference to the member's average salary over the period of service on which that benefit is based;

"normal pension age", "pensionable service" and "relevant employment" are to be construed in accordance with Schedule 16 to the Social Security Act 1973(**c**);

"request" means request in writing;

"scheme" means an occupational pension scheme;

"scheme year", in relation to a scheme, means whichever of the following periods the trustees of the scheme select –

(a) a year specified for the purposes of the scheme –
   (i) in any document comprising the scheme or which is included among the documents comprising it: or
   (ii) in the rules of the scheme;

(b) a calendar year;

(c) the 12 months ending with 31st March;

(d) the 12 months ending with 5th April,

and also includes, in a case where the trustees have selected a period ("new scheme year") to replace a previously selected period ("old scheme year"), a period exceeding 12 months but not exceeding 24 months between the last old scheme year and the first new scheme year;

"self-investment", in relation to a scheme, means investment of all or part of its fund in the business of –

(a) the employer of any person who is emplolyed in relevant employment; or

(b) if that employer is a company, a connected company;

(**a**) S.I. 1984/614, to which there are amendments not relevant to these regulations.
(**b**) 1978 c.44.
(**c**) 1973 c.38.

"tax-approved scheme" means a scheme which is –

(a) approved by the Commissioners of Inland Revenue for the purposes of Chapter II of Part II of the Finance Act 1970(**a**);

(b) a statutory scheme as defined in section 26(1) of the Finance Act 1970; or

(c) a scheme to which section 36 of the Finance Act 1980(**b**) applies;

"trustees", in relation to a scheme which is not set up or established under a trust, means the managers of the scheme;

"unfunded scheme" means a scheme whose benefits are not funded;

and other expressions have the same meaning as in the Act.

(3) Except so far as the context otherwise requires, any reference –

(a) in these regulations to a numbered section is to the section of the Act bearing that number;

(b) in these regulations to Schedule 1A is to Schedule 1A to the Act;

(c) in these regulations to a numbered regulation or Schedule (other than Schedule 1A) is to the regulation in, or, as the case may be, Schedule to, these regulations bearing that number;

(d) in a regulation or Schedule to a numbered paragraph is to the paragraph of that regulation or Schedule bearing that number;

(e) in a paragraph to a lettered sub-paragraph is to the sub-paragraph of that paragraph bearing that letter.

Meaning of expressions "members" and "prospective member" in relation to a scheme

2 (1) The following provisions of this regulation shall apply for the purposes of section 56A(2) and of these regulations.

(2) Any person is to be regarded as a member of a scheme during, or at any time after, a period when his service in relevant employment is or was such that at the time when it is or was given it either –

(a) qualifies or qualified him for benefits (in the form of a pension or otherwise, payable on the termination of his service otherwise than by his death, or on his retirement or his death thereafter) under the scheme which in the opinion of the Occupational Pensions Board are or were referable to that period; or

(b) is or was certain so to qualify him subsequently if it continues or continued for a sufficiently long time and the rules of the scheme and the terms of his contract of service remain or remained unaltered during that time.

(**a**) 1970 c.24.
(**b**) 1980 c.48.

(3) There are to be regarded as prospective members of a scheme any persons in relevant employment who are not members but –

(a) who, by virtue of the terms of their contracts of service, are able to become members at their own option or the option of any other person; or
(b) who, by virtue of the terms of their contracts of service, will become so able, if their service in relevant employment continues for a sufficiently long time and the terms of their contracts of service remain unaltered during that time; or
(c) who, by virtue of the rules of the scheme or the terms of their contracts of service, will become members in any event, if their service in relevant employment continues for a sufficiently long time and the rules of the scheme or, as the case may be, the terms of their contracts of service remain unaltered during that time.

Schemes to which, persons in relation to whom and trade unions in relation to which regulations 4 to 9 do not apply

3 (1) None of the requirements of regulations 4 to 9 shall apply to a scheme –

(a) whose members (excluding persons whose entitlement to benefits under the scheme has been extinguished) are fewer than 2, or
(b) which provides benefits only in the event of the death of a person who is, immediately before his death, employed in relevant employment.

(2) None of the requirements of regulations 4 to 9 shall impose on the trustees of a scheme any duty in relation to –

(a) any person if his entitlement to benefits under the scheme has been extinguished;
(b) any member or prospective member if no person who employs him in relevant employment has in formed the trustees that he is a member or prospective member; or
(c) any independent trade union recognised to any extent for the purposes of collective bargaining in relation to members and prospective members of the scheme if no person who employs any such member or prospective member in relevant employment has informed the trustees that that trade union is so recognised.

Constitution of scheme

4 (1) Subject to the provisions of regulation 3, the trustees of any scheme shall make provision, in the manner specified in paragraphs (2) and (3), for the disclosure, to persons and trade unions in the categories specified in paragraph (4), of –

(a) the contents –
  (i) of the trust deed constituting the scheme, if it is constituted by such a deed; and

(ii) of any document constituting the scheme, if it is not constituted by a trust deed;

and, if the rules of the scheme are not set out in any trust deed or other document the contents of which fall to be disclosed under head (i) or (ii) above, the contents of the rules;

(b) the contents of any document which amends or supplements or wholly or partly supersedes a document the contents of which fall to be disclosed under sub-paragraph (a) or this sub-paragraph; and

(c) if the name and address of every person who employs any member of the scheme in relevant employment is not set out in any trust deed or other document the contents of which fall to be disclosed under sub-pargraph (a) or (b), the contents of a document setting out the name and address of every such person.

(2) A copy of the contents of any of the documents of which disclosure is required by paragraph (1) shall be made available free of charge for inspection on request (not being a request made by a person or trade union within 12 months of the last occasion on which a copy of the contents of the same document was made available for inspection by the same person or the same trade union) by any person or trade union in the categories specificied in paragraph (4), within a reasonable time after the request is made, at a place which is reasonable having regard to the circumstances of the request and of the person who or trade union which made it.

(3) A copy of any of the documents of which disclosure is required by paragraph (1) shall be furnished, on request, on payment of a reasonable charge, to any person or trade union in the categories specified in paragraph (4), within a reasonable time after the request is made, so however that in the case of document which is publicly available the trustees may, instead of furnishing a copy, advise the person who or trade union which has requested it where copies may be obtained.

(4) The categories of persons and trade unions mentioned in paragraphs (1) to (3) are the following, namely –

(a) members and prospective members of the scheme;
(b) spouses of members and prospective members;
(c) beneficiaries under the scheme;
(d) independent trade unions recognised to any extent for the purposes of collective bargaining in relation to members and prospective members of the scheme.

Basic information about the scheme

5 (1) Subject to the provisions of regulation 3 and paragraph (4), the trustees of any scheme shall furnish in writing the information specified in Schedule 1 to persons and trade unions in the categories specified in paragraphs (2) and (3).

(2) The information specified in Schedule 1 shall be given as of course to every person who becomes a member of the scheme on or after 1st November 1987, within 13 weeks of his becoming a member.

(3) The information specified in Schedule 1 shall be given to –

(a) any member or prospective member of or beneficiary under the scheme; or
(b) the spouse of any member or prospective member; or
(c) [any independent trade union, in so far as that information is relevant to the rights of members or prospective members of the scheme who are of a class of employee in relation to which that trade union is recognised, to any extent, for the purposes of collective bargaining.]

on request (not being a request made by a person or trade union within 3 years of the last occasion on which the same person or the same trade union was given information in accordance with paragraph (2) or this paragraph) as soon as practicable after he or, as the case may be, that trade union requests it.

(4) Where different information is applicable to different members, prospective members and beneficiaries, nothing in this regulation shall be construed as requiring the trustees to disclose information in relation to a member, prospective member or beneficiary that is not relevant to his rights under the scheme.

(5) All members of and beneficiaries under the scheme shall be notified by the trustees of any material alteration in the information specified in paragraph 17 of schedule 1 within one month of the occurrence of the alteration.

(6) The trustees shall take reasonable steps to draw to the attention of all members of the scheme who are employed in relevant employment any material alteration in the information specified in paragraphs 1 to 16 of Schedule 1.

(7) When any information specified in Schedule 1 is provided, it shall be accompanied by a written statement that further information about the scheme is available, giving the address to which enquiries about it should be sent.

Information to be made available to individuals

6 (1) Subject to the provisions of regulation 3, the trustees of any scheme shall furnish in writing the information specified in Schedule 2 to the persons, and in the circumstances, specified in paragraphs (2) to (11).

(2) Where benefit under the scheme has become, on or after 1st November 1986, or is about to become, payable to a person, the information mentioned in paragraphs 1 to 3 of Schedule 2 shall be furnished to him as of course before or as soon as practicable after the benefit becomes payable.

(3) Where the amount of benefit payable to a person is or is about to be altered otherwise than in accordance with a provision such as is mentioned in paragraph 3 of Schedule 2, the information (as altered) that is mentioned paragraph 1 of Schedule 2 shall be furnished to him as of course before or as soon as practicable after the alteration takes place.

(4) Except in relation to money purchase benefits, the information mentioned in paragraph 4 of Schedule 2 shall be furnished to any member [whose pensionable service has not terminated before normal pension age, on request (not being a request made within a year of the last occasion on which such information as is mentioned in that paragraph was furnished to him) as soon as practicable after he requests it.]

[(4A) In the case of a scheme which provides only –

(a) money purchase benefits; or

(b) (i) money purchase benefits, and

(ii) salary-related benefits which are payable only in the event of the death of a member who is, immediately before his death, employed in relevant employment.

the information mentioned in paragraphs 4B and 4C of Schedule 2 shall be furnished, as of course, to each member of the scheme, at least once in every period of 12 months after the date of his becoming a member of it.

(4B) Except in the case of a scheme to which paragraph (4A) applies, in relation to money purchase benefits the information in paragraph 4C of Schedule 2 shall be furnished to any member on request (not being a request made within a year of the last occasion on which any such information as is mentioned in that paragraph was furnished to him) as soon as practicable after he requests it.

(4C) Where a scheme is, or has been, a money purchase contracted-out scheme in relation to one or more members' employments, and that member has or those members have protected rights under it, the information mentioned in paragraph 4D of Schedule 2 shall be sent, as of course, to each member with such rights –

(a) not less than 4 months, but not more than 6 months, before he attains pensionable age, and

(b) not less than 4 months before the member attains the age of 75 years if effect has not been given to his protected rights by the beginning of the sixth month before the member attains the age of 75 years.]

[(4D) Where a scheme which has been a money purchase contracted-out scheme in relation to one or more members' employments ceases to be such a scheme in relation to any of them, the trustees of the scheme shall inform each member ("the affected member"),in relation to whose employment the scheme has ceased to be such a scheme, as soon as practicable and in any event not more than 4 weeks after the date on which it ceased to be such a scheme that the scheme has so ceased, and furnish the affected member, as soon as practicable and in any event not more than 4 months after the date on which it ceased to be such a scheme with –

(a) the information mentioned in paragraphs 4B, 4C, 4E, 4F and 4G of Schedule 2, and
(b) except where the scheme is able to meet in full its liabilities to the affected member, the information mentioned in paragraph 4H of Schedule 2."]

(5) Where a member of or a beneficiary under a scheme has died and rights or options are available to a person in consequence, the information mentioned in paragraphs 5 and 6 of Schedule 2 shall be furnished –

(a) as of course to that person, if he is at least 18 years old and his address is known to the trustees, as soon as practicable after the trustees receive notification of the death; and
(b) on request (not being a request made within 3 years of the last occasion on which information was furnished under this paragraph to the same person in the same capacity) to any person who is a personal representative of the deceased person or who is authorised to act on behalf of the person to whom rights or options under the scheme are available in consequence of the death, as soon as practicable after he requests it.

["(6) The information mentioned in paragraph 7 of Schedule 2 shall be furnished –

(a) as of course to any person as soon as practicable after he or his employer has notified the trustees that his pensionable service has terminated or is about to terminate; and
(b) to any member on request (not being a request made less than 12 months after the last occasion on which such information was furnished to him) as soon as practicable after he requests it."]

(7) The information mentioned in paragraphs 8 and 9 of Schedule 2 shall be furnished on request (not being a request made less than 12 months after the last occasion on which such information was furnished to the same member) to any member as soon as practicable after he requests it.

(8) The information mentioned in paragraphs 10 and 11 of Schedule 2 shall be furnished on request (not being a request made less than 12 months after the last occasion on which such information was furnished to the same person) to any member or prospective member as soon as practicable after he requests it.

(9) The information mentioned paragraph 12 of Schedule 2 shall be furnished on request (not being a request made –

(a) after such information has already been furnished to the same person, in a case where –
   (i) all the contributions in question were in respect of a period of service before 6th April 1975, or
   (ii) the information was that no refund of contributions is available or would be available in any circumstances;

or

(b) less than 12 months after the last occasion on which such information was furnished to the same person, in any other case)

to any person who has paid contributions to the scheme which have not been refunded, as soon as practicable after he requests it.

(10) When the trustees have started to take steps to wind up the scheme, they shall as of course, and as soon as practicable, inform all members of and beneficiaries under the scheme that they have done so.

(11) When the trustees are taking steps to wind up the scheme, they shall, as of course, as soon as practicable after the [proceeds of the realisation of the assets of the scheme] are applied in accordance with the winding up rules –

(a) furnish the information mentioned in paragraphs 1 to 3 of Schedule 2 to every beneficiary and to every member who is entitled to payment of benefits, and (except in relation to money purchase benefits) the information mentioned in paragraph 4[A] of Schedule 2 to all other members; and

(b) inform each person who is entitled to information under sub-paragraph (a) –
   (i) whether, and if so by how much, the ebnefits in question are reduced because the scheme's resources are not sufficient to meet its liabilities as they fall due; and
   (ii) who will be liable to pay those benefits after the scheme is would up.

(12) When any information specified in Schedule 2 is provided, it shall be accompanied by a written statement that further information about the scheme is available, giving the address to which enquiries about it should be sent.

Audited accounts

7 (1) Subject to the provisions of regulation 3 and paragraph (2), the trustees of any scheme shall obtain as soon as reasonably practicable after the end of each scheme year [which commences on or after 1st November 1986] audited accounts for that scheme year, or, if the scheme has been in operation for only part of that scheme year, for that part of that scheme year.

(2) This regulation shall not apply to unfunded schemes or to public service pension schemes.

(3) An auditor for the purpose of auditing the accounts shall be a person qualified to act as an auditor of a company under section 389 of the Companies Act 1985(**a**), or a person approved by the Secretary of state, not being –

(a) a member of the scheme;
(b) a trustee of the scheme;
(c) a person who is employed under a contract of service by the trustees of the scheme;
(d) the employer of any member of the scheme who is in relevant employment; or
(e) where such an employer as is mentioned in sub-paragraph (d) is a company, a director or employee of that company or any connected compay.

(4) The audited accounts shall consist of –

(a) accounts which –
  (i) contain the information specified in Schedule 3 (so however that any such information which is immaterial for the purposes of head (ii) below may be omitted), and
  (ii) show a true and fair view of the financial transactions of the scheme during the scheme year and of the disposition, at the end of the scheme year, of the assets, not including [insurance policies which are specifically allocated to the provision of benefits for, and which provide all the benefits payable under the scheme to particular members or other persons in respect of particular members or both] and liabilities, other than liabilities to pay pensions and benefits after the end of the scheme year; and
(b) report by the auditor more particularly described in paragraph (5).

(5) The auditor's report mentioned in paragraph (4)(b) shall include –

(a) a statement whether or not in his opinion the requirements of paragraph (4)(a) are satisfied;
(b) a statement whether or not in his opinion contributions payable to the scheme during the scheme year have been paid in accordance with the scheme rules or contracts under which they were payable, and with the recommendation of the actuary, if appropriate; and

---

(**a**) 1985 c.6.

(c) if the statement under sub-paragraph (a) or (b) or both is negative or qualified, a statement of the reasons.

Actuarial valuation and statement

8 (1) Subject to the provisions of regulation 3 and paragraph (2), the trustees of any scheme shall obtain from time to time, in accordance with paragraphs (4) and (5), a signed actuarial valuation, as at a date which is called in this regulation its "effective date", of the scheme's assets in relation to its liabilities, which shall –

(a) be so framed as to enable the expected future course of the scheme's contribution rates and funding level to be understood;
(b) state whether it has been prepared in accordance with the guidelines "Retirement Benefit Schemes – Actuarial Reports (GN9)" published by the Institute of Actuaries and Faculty of Actuaries and current on the date of signature of the actuarial valuation; and
(c) indicate where there are any material departures from those guidelines if it has not been so prepared.

(2) This regulation shall not apply –

(a) to public service pension schemes; or
(b) in relation to –
   (i) benefits which are not funded and
   (ii) money purchase benefits.

(3) The effective date of the first actuarial valuation to be obtained under this regulation in relation to any scheme shall be not later than whichever is the latest of –

(a) 1st November 1987;
(b) the date which is 3 years and 6 months later than that on which the scheme first had effect; and
(c) the date which is 3 years and 6 months later than the effective date of an actuarial valuation obtained by the trustees before 1st November 1986.

(4) The effective date of any subsequent actuarial valuation shall be not later than 3 years and 6 months after the previous one.

(5) Each actuarial valuation shall be obtained as soon as reasonably practicable after its effective date.

(6) The actuarial valuation shall be made by –

(a) a Fellow of the Institute of Actuaries; or
(b) a Fellow of the Faculty of Actuaries; or
(c) a person with other actuarial qualifications who is approved by the Secretary of State, at the request of the trustees of the scheme in question, as being a proper person to act for the purposes of this regulation in connection with that scheme.

(7) Each actuarial valuation shall be accompanied by an actuarial statement made by the actuary who signed the valuation, so however that at any time after a valuation is made but before the next valuation is made an actuary may issue a revised statement.

(8) Any statement made in accordance with paragraph (7) (whether or not a revised statement) shall be in the form set out in Schedule 4, so however that –

(a) the words from "with the following exceptions" to the end of paragraph 1 of the statement may be deleted or omitted in a case where, in the actuary's opinion, there are no exceptions;
(b) [in relation to members whose pensionable service was continuing on the effective date] the accrued rights and the liabilities referred to in paragraph 1 of the statement shall mean respectively the rights to, and the liabilities to provide, benefits for each member himself and his survivors which would have been payable from normal pension age or from his death if his service in relevant employment had terminated on the effective date, and shall be valued accordingly;
(c) liabilities which in the actuary's opinion are not fully covered and which have different priorities in the event of a winding-up shall be described separately, in descending order of priority, and a separate percentage given for each;
(d) if paragraph 2 of the statement does not correctly set out the actuary's opinion, he shall substitute a negative or qualified opinion, giving reasons; [and
(e) where the statement is a revised statement, the line which begins with the words 'Effective date of valuation' may be omitted and in paragraph 1 of the statement a specific date may be substituted for the words 'the effective date', and if this is done the references to the effective date in sub-paragraph (b) above shall be construed as references to the substituted date.]

(9) The trustees shall make available copies of any actuarial valuation which they obtain in accordance with this regulation to the persons and trade unions, and in the circumstances, specified in paragraphs (10) to (12).

(10) A copy of the latest actuarial valuation shall be made available free of charge for inspection on request (not being a request made by a person or trade union within 3 years of the last occasion on which a copy of the same actuarial valuation was made available for inspection by the same person or the same trade union) by any person or trade union in the categories specified in paragraph (12), within a reasonable time after the request is made, at a place which is reasonable having regard to the circumstances of the request and of the person who, [or trade union which,] made it.

(11) A copy of the latest actuarial valuation shall be furnished on request and on payment of a reasonable charge to any person or trade union in the categories specified in paragraph (12) as soon as practicable after he or, as the case may be, that trade union requests it.

(12) The categories of persons and trade unions mentioned in paragraphs (9) to (11) are the following, namely –

(a) members and prospective members of the scheme;
(b) beneficiaries under the scheme;
(c) independent trade unions recognised to any extent for the purposes of collective bargaining in relation to members and prospective members of the scheme.

Availability of audited accounts, actuarial statements and other information.

9 (1) Subject to the provisions of regulation 3 and paragraph (2), the trustees of any scheme shall, in relation to, and not more than one year after the end of, each scheme year which commences on or after 1st November 1986, make available copies of a document which contains –

(a) a copy of the audited accounts (if any) for the scheme year to which the document relates;
(b) a copy of the latest actuarial statement (if any, and whether or not a revised statement) made in accordance with regulation 8(7); and
(c) other information, consisting of or including the information specified in paragraphs 1 to 8 (so far as it applies to the scheme) and (except in the case of unfunded schemes) 9 to [15] of Schedule 5,

to the persons and in the circumstances mentioned in paragraphs (4) to (6).

(2) The requirements of this regulation do not apply to public service pension schemes.

(3) The trustees shall take reasonable steps to draw to the attention of the persons and trade unions specified in paragraph (6) the availability of any such document as is mentioned in paragraph (1).

(4) A copy of any such document as is mentioned in paragraph (1), being neither the latest nor one which relates to a scheme year which ended more than 5 years previously, shall be made available free of charge for inspection on request (not being a request made by a person or trade union within 3 years of the last occasion on which a copy of the same document was made available for inspection by the same person or the same trade union) by any person or trade union in the categories specified in paragraph (6), within a reasonable time after the request is made, at a place which is reasonable having regard to the circumstances of the request and of the person who made it.

(5) A copy of the latest such document as is mentioned in paragraph (1) shall be furnished free of charge on request (not being a second or subsequent request by the same person or, as the case may be, trade union for a copy of the same document) to any person or trade union in the categories specified in paragraph (6) as soon as practicable after he, or, as the case may be, that trade union, requests it.

(6) The categories of persons and trade unions mentioned in paragraphs (3) to (5) are the following, namely –

(a) members and prospective members of the scheme;
(b) beneficiaries under the scheme;
(c) independent trade unions recognised to any extent for the purposes of collective bargaining in relation to members and prospective members of the scheme.

(7) When a copy of a document is furnished in accordance with paragraph (5), it shall be accompanied by a written statement that further information about the scheme is available, giving the address to which enquiries about it should be sent.

Recognised trade unions

10 Any question whether an organisation is an independent trade union recognised to any extent for the purposes of collective bargaining in relation to members and prospective members of a scheme shall be referred to an industrial tribunal.

Service of documents by post

11 (1) Any –

(a) information or document which these regulations require the trustees of a scheme to furnish;
(b) request for information or a document to be furnished in pursuance of these regulations; or
(c) information given to the trustees of a scheme for the purpose of these regulations,

may be furnished, made or given by post.

(2) Any notification or document which these regulations require the trustees of a scheme to furnish as of course to a beneficiary or a member who is not employed in relevant employment shall be deemed to have been furnished if it was sent to him by post to his last address known to the trustees.

Amendment of regulation

12 In regulation 4 of the Occupational Pension Schemes (Transfer

Values) Regulations 1985(**a**) (increases and reductions of cash equivalents), for paragraph (3) there shall be substituted the following paragraphs:

"(3) Where –

(a) the latest actuarial statement issued to the scheme in accordance with the provisions of regulation 8(7) of the Occupational Pension Schemes (Disclosure of Information) Regulations 1986 shows that on the date of that statement,

or

(b) in a case to which paragraph (3A) of this regulation applies, an actuary certifies that,

the scheme does not have sufficient assets to meet its liability in respect of the whole or any specified part of the accrued rights to benefit of members, the cash equivalent, or, as the case may be, the part of that cash equivalent which corresponds with that specified part of those accrued rights, may be reduced by the percentage by which the scheme is so shown to be deficient.

(3A) This paragraph applies to a case where the trustees of the scheme receive an application made under paragraph 16 before whichever is the earlier of –

(a) the effective date of the first actuarial valuation obtained by the scheme in accordance with the provisions of regulation 8 of the Occupational Pension Schemes (Disclosure of Information) Regulations 1986, and

(b) the latest date which the effective date of an actuarial valuation otherwise complying with that regulation may be if that actuarial valuation is to satisfy the requirements of paragraph (3) of that regulation."

Signed by authority of the Secretary of State for Social Services.

John Major,
Parliamentary Under-Secretary of State,
Department of Health and Social Security.

18th June 1986

(**a**) S.I. 1985/1931, to which there are amendments not relevant to these regulations.

[ ] Text within square brackets inserted by SI 1986/1717 and SI 1987/1105.

SCHEDULE 1

Regulation 5

BASIC INFORMATION ABOUT THE SCHEME

1. The categories of persons who are eligible to be members of the scheme.

2. The categories of persons who are required, as a condition of their employment, to be members of the scheme.

3. The conditions of membership.

[3A. The period of notice (if any) which a member of the scheme must give to terminate his pensionable service.

3B. Whether, and if so upon what conditions (if any), a member of the scheme, whose pensionable service has terminated before normal pension age, may re-enter pensionable service.]

4. How members' contributions are calculated.

5. How employers' contributions are calculated.

6. Whether the scheme is a tax-approved scheme, and if not whether an application for the scheme to become a tax-approved scheme is under consideration by the Commissioners of Inland Revenue.

7. Which of the relevant employments are, and which are not, contracted-out employments within the meaning of section 30 of the Act.

8. What benefits are payable under the scheme, and how they are calculated.

9. The conditions on which the benefits are paid.

10. Which benefits, if any, are payable only at some person's discretion.

11. Which of the benefits are, and which are not, funded.

12. Which of the benefits, if any, are such that the [fulfilment of the obligation to pay them] to or in respect of particular members is guaranteed by means of one or more insurance policies which are specifically allocated to the provision of benefits payable to or in respect of those members.

13. The short title of the statute (if any) which provides for both –

    (a) the setting up of the scheme, and
    (b) the determination of the rate or amount of the benefits under the scheme.

14. Whether, and if so to what extent, the employer of any person who is entitled to benefits under the scheme has entered into an obligation to pay the benefits if the scheme's resources are insufficient to do so.

15. Whether there is power under the scheme rules to increase pensions after they have become payable, and if so what it is, who may exercise it, and whether and to what extent it is discretionary.

16. What arrangements are made, and in what circumstances, for the refund of contributions to, and the preservation or transfer of the accrued rights of, a member whose relevant employment or pensionable service in relevant employment terminates before he reaches normal pension age.

17. The address to which enquiries about the scheme generally or about an individual's entitlement to benefit should be sent.

SCHEDULE 2

Regulation 6

INFORMATION TO BE MADE AVAILABLE TO INDIVIDUALS

1. The amount of benefit which is payable to the person.

2. If a benefit is payable periodically, the conditions (if any) subject to which payment will be continued.

3. If a benefit is payable periodically, the provisions (if any) under which the amount payable will be altered.

4. The information specified in any one (the trustees having the option to choose which one) of the following sub-paragraphs, namely –
   (a) the amounts of the member's own benefits and of his survivors' benefits which would be payable from normal pension age or death thereafter if his pensionable service were to terminate on the date on which the information is furnished to him, calculated without regard to possible increases in his salary;
   (b) the amounts of the member's own benefits and of his survivors' benefits which would be payable from normal pension age or death thereafter if his pensionable service were to terminate on his attaining normal pension age, calculated without regard to possible increases in his salary; and
   (c) the method by which the amounts mentioned in one of sub-paragraphs (a) and (b) may be calculated, together with sufficient information about the member's past salaries and service to enable the calculation to be made.

[4A. The amounts of the member's own benefits and of his survivors' benefits which are expected to be payable from normal pension age or death thereafter.

4B. The amount of contributions (before the making of any deductions), credited to the member under the scheme during the 12 months preceding a specified date, and, where the scheme was for the whole or any part of that period, a contracted-out scheme, the amount of those contributions which is attributable to –
   (a) the minimum payments to the scheme made in respect of the member by his employer; and
   (b) the payments (if any) made to the trustees of the scheme by the Secretary of State in accordance with section 7(1) of the Social Security Act 1986 in respect of the member.

4C. (a) As at a specified date –
      (i) the value of the member's protected rights under the scheme, and
      (ii) the value of the member's accrued rights (other than his protected rights) under the scheme.
   (b) Where the cash equivalent (calculated, as at the date specified for the purposes of sub-paragraph (a), in accordance with paragraph 14 of Schedule 1A to the Act, and regulations made thereunder), in respect of the transfer of the member's rights mentioned in sub-paragraph (a)(i) or (ii) or both would be different from the values to be specified under that sub-paragraph, that cash equivalent.

4D. The options available to the member, including those in respect of any accrued rights which are not protected rights.]

[4E. The date on which the scheme ceased to be a money purchase contracted-out scheme in relation to the member's employment.

4F. Whether arrangements for the preservation or transfer of the member's protected rights have been, or are to be, proposed to the Occupational Pensions Board and an explanation of the intended effects of any such proposed arrangements.

4G. The options available to the member in respect of his protected rights.

4H. An account of the amount by which the member's –

(a) protected rights; and
(b) accrued rights other than his protected rights,

have been reduced, and of the arrangements which have been made by the scheme, or are open to the member, to restore the value of his accrued rights under the scheme.]

5. The rights and options (if any) available on the death of a member or beneficiary, and the procedures for exercising them.

6. The provisions (or, as the case may be, a statement that there are no provisions) under which any pension payable to a survivor of a member or beneficiary may or will be increased, and the extent to which such increases are dependent on the exercise of a discretion.

7. The rights and options (if any) available to a member whose pensionable service terminates before he attains normal pension age.

8. Whether any cash equivalent (within the meaning of Part II of Scheduel 1A) is available to the member or would be available to him if his pensionable service were to terminate, and if so –

(a) an estimate of its amount, calculated on the basis that the member's pensionable service terminated or will terminate on one particular date;
(b) the accrued rights to which it relates;
(c) whether any part of the estimated amount of the cash equivalent is attributable to additional benefits –
    (i) which have been awarded at the discretion of the trustees, or
    (ii) which will be awarded at their discretion if their established custom continues unaltered,
    and in either case whether that part is attributable to the whole or only to part of those benefits; and
(d) if, by virtue of regulations made under paragraph 14 of Schedule 1A, the estimated amount of the cash equivalent is less than the amount for which paragraph 12(1) of Schedule 1A provides –
    (i) a statement to that effect and an explanation,
    (ii) an estimate of the date (if any) by which it will be possible to make available a cash equivalent which is not less than the amount for which paragraph 12(1) of Schedule 1A provides, and
    (iii) a statement of the member's rights to obtain further estimates.

9. Whether any transfer value (not being a cash equivalent within the meaning of Part II of Schedule 1A) is available to the member or would be available to him if his pensionable service were to terminate, and if so –

(a) an estimate of its amount, calculated on the basis that the member's pensionable service terminated or will terminate on one particular date;
(b) the accrued rights to which it relates;
(c) whether any part of the estimated amount of the transfer value is attributable to additional benefits –
    (i) which have been awarded at the discretion of the trustees, or

(ii) which will be awarded at their discretion if their established custom continues unaltered,

and in either case whether that part is attributable to the whole or only to part of those benefits; and

(d) if the estimated amount of the transfer value has been reduced to an amount which is less than it otherwise would be because of an actuary's opinion that the scheme's assets are insufficient to meet its liabilities in full –
   (i) a statement of that fact and explanation,
   (ii) an estimate of the date (if any) by which it will be possible to make available a transfer value the amount of which is not so reduced, and
   (iii) a statement of the member's rights to obtain further estimates.

10. Whether the member or prospective member is entitled to acquire transfer credits in exchange for a specificied cash equivalent (within the meaning of Part II of Schedule 1A), provided by another scheme, and if so, a statement of those transfer credits.

11. Whether the member or prospective member is entitled to acquire transfer credits in exchange for any transfer payment provided by another scheme (not being a cash equivalent within the meaning of Part II of Schedule 1A), and if so, a statement of those transfer credits.

12. Whether a refund of contributions is available, or would be available in any circumstances, and in the latter case, a statement of the circumstances, and in either case, an estimate of the amount of the refund and an explanation of the method of calculating it.

SCHEDULE 3

Regulation 7

CONTENTS OF ACCOUNTS

1. An account of the financial additions to and withdrawals from the fund of the scheme during the scheme year to which the accounts relate.

2. A statement, as at the end of the scheme year to which the accounts relate, of the assets (which expression in this Schedule does not include [insurance policies which are specifically allocated to the provision of benefits for, and which provide all the benefits payable under the scheme to particular members or other persons in respect of particular members or both]) at market value, or a trustees' estimate thereof where market value is not readily ascertainable, and liabilities of the scheme, other than liabilities to pay pensions and benefits after the end of that scheme year –

(a) giving, in the case of any assets which are stated at an estimate of their market value, the reasons why;

(b) showing the distribution of the investments of the scheme between each of the following categories (so however that where none of the investments falls within a particular category, that fact is not required to be stated), namely –
   (i) insurance policies;
   (ii) public sector fixed interest investments;
   (iii) other fixed interest investments;
   (iv) index-linked securities;
   (v) equities (including convertible shares);
   (vi) property (which in this paragraph means any right or interest in freehold or leasehold land or buildings);

(vii) unit trusts invested in property;
(viii) other unit trusts;
(ix) managed funds (other than unit trusts) invested in property;
(x) other managed funds (not being unit trusts);
(xi) loans (whether or not secured by mortgages);
(xii) cash deposits and cash in hand;
(xiii) investments not included in heads (i) to (xii) above; and

(c) showing separately, in the case of investments in each category, investments in the United Kingdom and investments outside the United Kingdom, and in the case of investments mentioned in heads (vii) to (x) of sub-paragraph (b) investments where the company operating the unit trust or managed fund is, and investments where it is not, a company registered in the United Kingdom.

3. A reconciliation of the account mentioned in paragraph 1 with the statement mentioned in paragraph 2.

4. Where any assets or liabilities are denominated in currencies other than sterling, a translation of those assets into sterling and an explanation of the basis on which they have been translated.

5. Particulars of any investment in which more than 5 per cent of the total value of the net assets of the scheme is invested, and if any such investment is an insurance policy, a statement of its main characteristics.

6. Particulars of any self-investment in excess of 5 per cent of the total value of the net assets of the scheme.

7. In respect of every amount shown in the accounts, a statement of the corresponding amount for the scheme year previous to the one to which the accounts relate, except in a case where regulation 7 is complied with by trustees of a scheme for the first time.

8. The total amount of the purchases, and the total amount of the sales, of investments during the scheme year to which the accounts relate.

9. A statement whether the accounts have been prepared in accordance with parts 2 to 4 of the Statement of Recommended Practice No.1, the guidelines published by the Accounting Standards Committee, current at the end of the scheme year to which the accounts relate, and if not, an indication of where there are any material departures from those guidelines.

SCHEDULE 4

Regulation 8

FORM OF ACTUARY'S STATEMENT

ACTUARIAL STATEMENT MADE FOR THE PURPOSES OF REGULATION 8 OF THE OCCUPATIONAL PENSION SCHEMES (DISCLOSURE OF INFORMATION) REGULATIONS 1986

Name of scheme ....
Effective date of valuation ....

1. *Security of accrued rights*

In my opinion, the scheme's assets existing on the effective date fully cover its liabilities as at that date with the following exceptions:

Description of liability	*Percentage covered*
....	....
....	....

The measure(s) to be taken to bring these to 100% and the date by which it is expected that this will be achieved are as follows:

....
....
....
....

2. *Security of prospective rights*

In my opinion, the resources of the scheme are likely in the normal course of events to meet in full the liabilities of the scheme as they fall due. In giving this opinion, I have assumed that the following amounts will be paid to the scheme:

Description of contributions

....
....

3. Summary of methods and assumptions used

Signature .... Date ....
Name .... Qualification ....
Address .... Name of employer (if applicable)

SCHEDULE 5

Regulation 9

INFORMATION TO ACCOMPANY AUDITED ACCOUNTS AND ACTUARIAL STATEMENT

1. The names of the persons who were trustees of the scheme during the scheme year to which the information relates (in this Schedule called "the year").

2. The provisions of the scheme for appointing trustees and removing them from office.

3. The names of any actuaries, auditors, solicitors, banks and other persons and organisations acting for or retained by the trustees during the year, with an indication (except in a case where regulation 9 is complied with by trustees of a scheme for the first time) of any change since the previous year.

4. The address to which enquiries about the scheme generally or about an individual's entitlement to benefit should be sent.

5. Any changes since the previous year in the information specified in Schedule 1.

6. The number of members and beneficiaries as at any one date during the year.

7. The percentage increases made (otherwise than in accordance with a legislative requirement) during the year (or, if there have been different increases for different individuals or groups of individuals, the maximum, minimum and average percentage increases) to –

   (a) pensions which were payable; and
   (b) deferred pensions,

   with a statement whether the increases were to any extent discretionary, and if so to what extent.

8. A statement –

   (a) whether any cash equivalents (within the meaning of Part II of Schedule 1A) paid during the year were calculated and verified in the manner prescribed by regulations under paragraph 14 of Schedule 1A;
   (b) whether any of the cash equivalents paid during the year were less than the amount for which paragraph 12(1) of Schedule 1A provides, and if so –
      (i) why they were less, and
      (ii) when full values became, or are estimated to be likely to become, available.

9. If the auditor's statement mentioned in regulation 7(5)(b) shows that in his opinion contributions payable to the scheme during the year have not been paid in accordance with the scheme rules or contracts under which they were payable, or with the recommendation of the actuary, if appropriate, an account of the reasons for the discrepancy and a statement how it has been or is likely to be resolved.

10. If any such discrepancy was left unresolved in a previous year, a statement how it has been or is likely to be resolved.

11. A review by the trustees of the financial development of the scheme during the year, as shown by the audited accounts, and its financial prospects, having regard to the actuarial valuation and statement (if any).

12. Who has managed the investment of the scheme during the year and the extent of any delegation of this function by the trustees.

13. The basis on which any investment manager is paid, and on which any fee or commission payable to him is calculated, if these costs are borne by the scheme.

14. An investment report containing –
(a) a statement by the trustees, or the investment manager, of the investment policies pursued during the year on behalf of the scheme, and any material changes in these policies during the year;
(b) a review of the investment performance of the scheme's fund during the year, and the nature, disposition, marketability, security and valuation of the scheme's assets.

[15. A copy of any statement which any auditor of the scheme has made in the year, in accordance with the provisions of regulation 3(4) or (5) of the Occupational Pension Schemes (Auditors) Regulations 1987.]

EXPLANATORY NOTE

(This Note is not part of the Regulations.)

These regulations are either made under section 56A or 56E of the Social Security Pensions Act 1975 or made under paragraph 14(3) of Schedule 1A to that Act, and are made before the expiry of the period of 6 months beginning with the commencement (on 1st January 1986) of sections 2 and 3 of the Social Security Act 1985. Consequently, by virtue of section 26(1)(a) and (c) of the Social Security Act 1985, the provisions of section 61(2) and (3) of the Social Security Pensions Act 1975 (which require reference to the Occupational Pensions Board of, and a report by the Board on, proposals to make regulations for certain purposes of that Act) do not apply to them.

These regulations specify the information that is to be made available to certain persons, in certain circumstances, by the trustees of occupational pension schemes.

Regulation 2 defines the persons who are to be regarded as members or prospective members of an occupational pension scheme.

Regulation 3 provides for the conditions on which an occupational pension scheme is excepted from these regulations.

Regulation 4 provides for the trustees to make available documents containing information about the constitution of the scheme for inspection by specified persons, and for copies to be furnished on request on payment of a reasonable charge.

Regulation 5 and Schedule 1 provide for certain basic information about the scheme to be given by the trustees to every member on joining the scheme and to members and other specified persons on request, and for material alterations to be drawn to the attention of members.

Regulation 6 and Schedule 2 provide for the trustees to make information about individual benefit entitlement available to specified persons in specified circumstances.

Regulation 7 and Schedule 3 provide for the trustees to obtain audited accounts, including the auditor's report, and containing specified information, prepared by an auditor who fulfils certain requirements.

Regulation 8 and Schedule 4 provide for the trustees to obtain an actuarial statement and valuation in a certain form and at specified intervals, for the actuarial valuation to be made available for inspection and for copies to be furnished to specified persons on request on payment of a reasonable charge.

Regulation 9 and Schedule 5 provide for the trustees to make available copies of documents which contain the audited accounts, the actuarial statement and certain other information when requested by specified persons.

Regulation 10 provides that any question as to the recognition of a trade union for the purposes of collective bargaining in relation to the members of a scheme shall be referred to an industrial tribunal.

Regulation 11 relates to the service of documents by post.

Regulation 12 amends the Occupational Pension Schemes (Transfer Values) Regulations 1985.

The publication "Retirement Benefit Schemes – Actuarial Reports (GN9)", referred to in regulation 8(1)(b), may be obtained from the Institute of Actuaries, Staple Inn Hall, High Holborn, London WC1V 7QJ, and from the Faculty of Actuaries, 23 St Andrew Square, Edinburgh EH2 1AQ.

The publication "Statement of Recommended Practice No. 1" (ISBN 085921 7457), referred to in paragraph 9 of Schedule 3, may be obtained from the Accounting Standards Committee, PO Box 433, Moorgate Place, London EC4P 2BJ.

[ ] Text in Schedules within square brackets inserted by SI 1986/1717 and SI 1987/1105

ANNUAL REPORT OF SORPCO PENSION SCHEME

The financial statements that follow are for the Sorpco pension scheme, a fictitious scheme.

These financial statements have been prepared to comply with the provisions of SORP 1, 'Pension scheme accounts'. The suggested disclosure throughout is intended for guidance only and would not necessarily be applicable to all pension schemes.

Sorpco Pension Scheme Annual Report for the year ended 31st March 1991

Contents **Page**

Sorpco Pension Scheme
Trustee and advisors to the scheme

TRUSTEE:
Sorpco Pension Trustees Limited

DIRECTORS:
A. Palmer (Chairman)
B. Barnes FCA (Finance Director)
S. Lyle
J. Nicklaus

The directors are also directors of Sorpco Plc.

PENSIONS MANAGER
G. Player

SECRETARY OF TRUSTEE COMPANY
L. Trevino

ACTUARIES
T. Weiskopf & Co.

AUDITORS
Coopers & Lybrand Deloitte

INVESTMENT MANAGERS
Eagle and Sons

PROPERTY ADVISERS
Ballesteros and Sons

SOLICITORS
Writ and Co.

BANKERS
Barcland Bank Plc.

2

Trustee's Report

The report and financial statements for the year ended 31 March 1991 are presented in compliance with Schedule 2 to the Social Security Act 1985 (which inserted a new section 56 into the Social Security Pensions Act 1975) and the Occupational Pension Schemes (Disclosure of Information) Regulations 1986 (the Regulations) issued under that Act in June 1986.

The financial statements, therefore, have been prepared in accordance with Parts 2-4 of Statement of Recommended Practice 1 (SORP 1) and Schedule 3 to the Regulations.

1. Constitution of the Scheme

The Scheme is a defined benefits scheme and provides benefits for the staff of Sorpco Plc and its subsidiary companies in the United Kingdom. It is an exempt approved scheme under Chapter 1 of Part 14 of the Income and Corporation Taxes Act 1988 and is established under and governed by a trust deed and rules which have been approved by the Occupational Pensions Board and the Superannuation Funds Office. It is contracted out of the State Earnings Related Pension Scheme under the provisions of the Social Security Pensions Act 1975.

2. Membership

(a) Total members

	31st March 1991	1st April 1990
Contributing members	1000	1074
Deferred pensioners	156	134
Pensioners	468	450
	1624	1658

(b) Contributing members

At 1 April 1990		1074
New members		118
		1192
Less:		
Leavers	154	
Retired with pension	36	
Died in service	2	192
At 31 March 1991		1000

(c) Deferred pensioners

These are members who have left service but have elected to have their benefits retained within the Scheme until they become payable.

At 1st April 1990		134
Leavers		28
		162
Less:		
subsequently transferred	2	
pensions becoming payable	2	
deaths	2	6
At 31st March 1991		156

(d) Pensioners

At 1 April 1990	450
Contributing members who retired	36
Deferred pensions becoming payable	2
Widows' or widowers' pensions becoming payable	8
	496
Less: deaths	28
At 31st March 1991	468

3. Principal company and participating companies

The principal company is Sorpco Plc.

The following companies were participating companies during the year:

Sorpco UK Limited
Sorpco Manufacturing Limited
Sorpco Finance Limited
Sorpco Trading Limited.

4. Growth of the fund

The revenue account on page 9 shows that the surplus for the year was £7,906,000 (1990: £6,774,000). The change in the value of the Scheme due to the increase in current market values of investments during the year was £12,870,000 (1990: £10,992,000), making the total growth in the Scheme's assets for the same period £20,776,000 (1990: £17,766,000).

5. Contributions

Total contributions paid into the Scheme during the year amounted to £5,792,000 (1990: £5,492,000). Of this, members contributed £2,172,000 (1990: £2,192,000) at the rate of Y% of pensionable salary. The balance was provided by the participating companies.

6. Increases in pensions and deferred pensions

It is the current policy of the Scheme to carry out a review of pensions in payment at 1 January each year. The aim is to increase pensions above the Guaranteed Minimum Pension by X% each year. With effect from 1st January 1990, pensions in the course of payment were increased by X%.

Deferred pensions are required by current legislation to be increased each year by a minimum of the lower of the change in the RPI and five per cent. The extent of any increase above the statutory minimum is being considered by the Trustee.

7. Additional Voluntary Contributions

41 members were paying Additional Voluntary Contributions (AVC's) during the year to increase their pension entitlement at retirement. The contributions are separately invested at the Viewit and Buyit Life Association Limited. Statements are sent annually to members paying AVCs, in respect of their contributions and the accumulation of their funds.

8. Investment Report and Performance

Under the terms of their appointment, Eagle and Sons are responsible for the investment of available funds in securities. They are not responsible for investments in properties, which are separately managed by Ballesteros and Sons. Overall responsibility for investment and performance lies with the Trustee alone.

Classification by industrial sector

Sector	% of portfolio
Fixed interest	29.2
Consumer goods	22.0
Financial	19.8
Property	17.3
Oil and gas	7.4
Other	4.3

Classification by geographical sector

Market	% of portfolio
United Kingdom	65.2
United States of America	22.4
Far East	11.3
Other	1.1

The ten largest investments of the scheme

All classes of investment held in a company are treated as one investment.

	Market value £'000	% age of Portfolio
Equities		
1. Imperial Chemical Industries	2834	2.15
2. General Motors	2668	2.03
3. Treasury Stock 12½% 2003/05	2503	1.90
4. Hanson Trust	2284	1.74
5. Exchequer Stock 12% 2013/17	1545	1.17
6. Bell Atlantic	1325	1.01
7. BAT	1281	0.97
8. GEC	1280	0.97
9. Treasury Stock (index linked) 2% 2006	925	0.70
Properties		
10. 327 Queen Victoria Street, London EC2	1022	0.78

The total investment shown above is £17,667,000 and represents 13.6% of the scheme's investment portfolio.

Investments greater than 5% of any class of shares

At 31 March 1991 the Scheme held 7.2% of the ordinary share capital of XYZ Hardware Ltd. which is involved in the production of self-assembly units. The scheme also held 4.3% of the preferred ordinary share capital of XYZ Hardware Ltd.

Rent reviews

The scheme's freehold properties are let on both long and short term leases and are subject to regular rent reviews. All short term leases are subject to rent reviews every five years.

(The investment report may also contain a summary of the scheme's investment strategy and its performance, a greater analysis of investment income, a more detailed report on investments in securities and in properties and comparative information.)

10. Actuarial position

The last actuarial valuation of the Scheme was completed as at 31st March 1988.

The Actuary has since then confirmed that the present rates of contribution are adequate to enable the Trustee to provide the benefits set out in the Trust Deed and Rules.

The next valuation, due as at 31st March 1991, is currently in progress.

The Actuary's latest statement on the Scheme is set out on page 18.

11. Transfer values

The Trustee confirms that 'cash equivalents' (within the meaning of Part II of Schedule 1A of the Social Security Pensions Act 1975) paid during the year were calculated and verified in a manner prescribed by regulations under paragraph 14 of Schedule 1A.

12. Expenses

The Scheme bears the full cost of administration, including costs incurred in buying and selling investments, and the fees and expenses of Eagle and Sons (as approved by the Trustee).

L Trevino
Secretary
Sorpco Pension Trustees Limited

10 July 1991

Auditors' Report
To the Trustee and Members of Sorpco Pension Scheme

We have audited the financial statements on pages 9 to 17 in accordance with Auditing Standards.

In our opinion the financial statements give a true and fair view of the financial transactions of the scheme during the year ended 31 March 1991 and of the disposition at that date of its assets and liabilities, other than liabilities to pay pensions and benefits after the end of the year, and contain the information specified in Regulation 7 of and Schedule 3 to the Occupational Pension Schemes (Disclosure of Information) Regulations 1986.

In our opinion the contributions payable to the scheme during the year ended 31 March 1991 have been paid in accordance with the scheme rules and with the recommendation of the actuary.

Coopers & Lybrand Deloitte
Chartered Accountants
London

10 July 1991

Revenue Account
For the year ended 31st March 1991

		Notes	1991 £'000	1990 £'000
Income				
Contributions receivable	-employers	7(a)	3,620	3,300
	-members	7(b)	2,172	2,192
Transfers in			90	560
Investment income		8	8,186	7,118
Unrealised exchange gain			170	14
			14,238	13,184
Expenditure				
Pensions payable			3,578	3,228
Other benefits payable		9	1,624	2,398
Transfers out			384	212
Administrative expenses borne by the scheme		10	746	572
			6,332	6,410
New money available for investment			7,906	6,774
Net profit on sale of investments and property			1,648	856
Change in market value of investments			12,870	10,992
Increase in fund for the year			20,776	17,766
Opening balance of fund			109,384	91,618
Closing balance of fund			130,160	109,384

Net Assets Statement
At 31st March 1991

	Notes	**1991**	**1990**
		£'000	£'000
Accumulated fund		130,160	109,384
Represented by:			
Investments	11	129,940	109,096
Current assets	12	436	446
Less: Current liabilities	13	(216)	(158)
Net current assets		220	288
Total assets less current liabilities		130,160	109,384

The financial statements on pages 9 to 17 were approved by the Trustee on 7th July 1991 and are signed on its behalf by:

A. Palmer)
B. Barnes) Directors of Sorpco Pension Trustees Limited

Notes to the Financial Statements

1. Accounting policies

(a) Investments and Cash Deposits

(i) Freehold and leasehold properties are valued each year at the balance sheet date by professional valuers. No depreciation is provided on freehold properties. The existing valuation of leasehold properties is amortised over the remaining life of the lease concerned.

(ii) Listed investments are included at market value at the balance sheet date. Where appropriate, market values listed in overseas currencies are translated into sterling at the rates of exchange ruling at the balance sheet date.

(iii) Cash deposits in overseas currencies are translated into sterling at the relevant rates of exchange ruling at the balance sheet date.

The change in the market value of investments during the year including both realised and unrealised gains and losses, is shown as a movement in the Scheme's accumulated fund separately from other income and expenditure.

(b) Income from Investments

(i) Income from cash deposits is dealt with in these accounts on an accruals basis.

(ii) Dividends and other income from investments are accounted for on a due and received basis.

(iii) Rental income is accounted for on the dates on which it is due.

(c) Administrative expenses

It is the policy of the Trustee that the Scheme shall bear the full costs of administration. These are set out in Note 10.

(d) Contributions

Current service and other contributions are accounted for on an accruals basis.

(e) *Benefits*

Benefits are accounted for as they fall due for payment.

(f) *Transfer values*

Transfer values represent the capital sums either received in respect of newly-joined members from the pension schemes of their previous employers or paid to the pension schemes of new employers of members who have left service. Provision is made for asset transfers when the Scheme's actuary has advised the Trustee of the assets to be transferred to satisfy an agreed transfer value.

2. Pensions and benefits

The financial statements summarise the transactions and net assets of the scheme. They do not take account of liabilities to pay pensions and other benefits in the future. The actuarial position of the fund, which does take account of such liabilities, is dealt with in the statement by the actuary on page 18 of the annual report and these financial statements should be read in conjunction therewith. The financial statements do not include as assets insurance policies which are specifically allocated to the provision of benefits for, and which provide all the benefits under the Scheme, to particular members. *(Note: this sentence need only be included if it is applicable to the Scheme.)*

3. Members' additional voluntary contributions

Members are entitled to make additional voluntary contributions to the Scheme to secure extra benefits within certain permissible limits set out by the Inland Revenue. These additional voluntary contributions are included as contributions receivable in the revenue account and the assets acquired with them are included in the net assets statement.

4. Taxation status of the pension scheme

The SORPCO Pension Scheme has been approved by the Inland Revenue as exempt from United Kingdom taxation to the extent that it relates to members employed by group participating companies resident in the United Kingdom.

5. Capital commitments

At 31st March 1991 (and 31st March 1990) there were no capital commitments.

6. Contingent liabilities

Other than the liability to pay future pensions, there are no contingent liabilities of the scheme at 31st March 1991.

7. Contributions receivable

	1991	**1990**
	£'000	£'000
(a) From employers		
Normal	3,602	3,286
Additional	18	14
	3,620	3,300
(b) From members		
Normal	2,084	2,112
Members' Additional Voluntary Contributions	88	80
	2,172	2,192

8. Investment income

	1991	**1990**
	£'000	£'000
Dividends received	2,987	2,185
Interest receivable	3,831	3,625
Net rentals receivable	1,350	1,300
Underwriting commission	18	8
	8,186	7,118

9. Other benefits payable

	1991 £'000	1990 £'000
Payments on retirement of members		
– commutations	1,046	1,688
– Additional Voluntary Contributions	20	18
Payments on death of members		
– lump sum	184	198
Payments on withdrawal of members		
– refund of contributions	336	450
– interest thereon	38	44
	1,624	2,398

10. Administrative expenses borne by the scheme

	1991 £'000	1990 £'000
Legal, audit, and actuarial	188	132
Security, handling and other charges	20	24
Administration expenses, wages and other staff costs	274	202
Property management costs	56	42
Amortisation of leasehold property	68	70
Investment managers' fees	122	82
Value added tax	18	20
	746	572

11. Investments

	1991			1990		
	UK	Foreign	Total	UK	Foreign	Total
	£'000	£'000	£'000	£'000	£'000	£'000
Fixed interest securities						
Government	34,494	–	34,494	32,962	–	32,962
Other	–	642	642	–	652	652
Index linked securities	2,818	–	2,818	–	–	–
Equities	45,180	22,874	68,054	36,248	16,922	53,170
	82,492	23,516		69,210	17,574	
		Note (a)	106,008			86,784
Property						
Freehold		Note (b)	22,280			20,796
Short leasehold		Note (c)	230			380
Insurance policies		Note (d)	12			12
			128,530			107,972
Cash deposits			1,740			1,238
Debtors for sale proceeds			1,046			–
Creditors for purchases			(1,376)			(114)
Total investment assets			129,940			109,096

	At cost	Revaluation	Market Value
	£'000	£'000	£'000
(a) Listed investments			
1st April 1989	62,310	24,474	86,784
Net additions - Note (e)	11,572	7,652	19,224
At 31st March 1991	73,882	32,126	106,008

	Market Value
	£'000
(b) Freehold property	
Valuation at 1st April 1990	20,796
Disposal - Note (e)	(266)
Revaluations during the year	1,750
Valuation at 31st March 1991	22,280

	Market Value
	£'000
(c) Leasehold property	
Valuation at 1st April 1990	380
Disposals	(110)
Amortisation	(68)
Revaluation during the year	28
Valuation at 31st March 1991	230

	At cost	Revaluation	Market Value
	£'000	£'000	£'000
(d) Insurance policies			
at 1st April 1990 and at 31st March 1991	8	4	12

Members can pay additional contributions, within the provisions for benefits under the principal scheme, to provide extra lump sum benefits on retirement. These contributions are paid to the Viewit and Buyit Life Assurance Limited.

(e) Net additions at cost or valuation comprise

	Listed Investments	Freehold Property	Leasehold Property	Total
	£'000	£'000	£'000	£'000
Additions	21,942	–	–	21,942
Disposals	(10,370)	(266)	(110)	(10,746)
	11,572	(266)	(110)	11,196

Proceeds from disposals of investments were £14,188,00 (1990: £8,342,000)

12. Current assets

	1991	1990
	£'000	£'000
Due from participating companies	122	–
Other debtors	220	232
Cash at bank	94	214
	436	446

13. Current liabilities

	1991	1990
	£'000	£'000
Accrued expenses	216	110
Due to participating companies	–	48
	216	158

14. Self - investment

The scheme does not hold any investment in Sorpco Plc or in any other company or person connected with that company.

15. Concentration of investments

The scheme does not hold over 5% of its net assets in any one form of investment.

18

Actuarial Statement

Effective date of valuation [date]

1. Security of accrued rights

In my opinion, the scheme's assets existing on the effective date fully cover its liabilities as at that date with the following exceptions:

Description of liability	Percentage covered

The measure(s) to be taken to bring these to 100% and the date by which it is expected that this will be achieved are as follows:

2. Security of prospective rights

In my opinion, the resources of the scheme are likely in the normal course of events to meet in full the liabilities of the scheme as they fall due. In giving this opinion, I have assumed that the following amounts will be paid to the scheme:

Description of contributions

3. Summary of methods and assumptions used

[Signature] [Date]
[Name] [Qualification]
[Address] [Name of Employer]

CHECK LIST TO THE RECOMMENDATIONS OF SORP 1 AND THE REQUIREMENTS OF SI 1986/1046 (AS AMENDED) FOR PREPARING ANNUAL REPORTS OF PENSION SCHEMES

Introduction

1. This checklist is directed at the accounts of pension schemes established in the UK and includes requirements in force at 31 March 1990.

2. The checklist embodies three sources of requirements:

(a) The Occupational Pension Schemes (Disclosure of Information) Regulations 1986 Statutory Instrument 1986 No. 1046 as amended (referred to as 'Regs').

(b) SORP 1 'Pension Scheme Accounts' (referred to as 'SORP 1').

(c) Requirements of the Occupational Pensions Board for contracted-out pension schemes (referred to as 'OPB').

3. The following should be noted in relation to the need for an individual pension fund to comply with these requirements:

(a) The Occupational Pension Schemes (Disclosure of Information) Regulations 1986 apply to pension schemes established in the UK except:

(i) schemes having fewer than 2 members or

(ii) schemes providing benefits only in the event of death.

> Note: These regulations are effective for scheme years beginning on or after 1 November 1986.

(b) SORP 1 is not mandatory although the regulations referred to in paragraph 3(a) above require any material departures from the SORP to be disclosed.

(c) The OPB requirements apply to schemes which have been granted 'contracted-out' status from the state scheme.

1. PENSION FUND ANNUAL REPORT – GENERAL

1.1	The annual report on a pension scheme should be made available as soon as possible after the accounting date and not more than one year after the end of the scheme year.	SORP 1 para 2 Regs para 9(a)
1.2	The annual report should contain:	
	(a) A copy of the accounts and an auditor's report thereon.	Regs para 9(a) SORP 1 para 2(b)
	(b) A copy of the latest actuarial statement.	Regs para 9(b) SORP 1 para 2(c)
	(c) Other information, which can conveniently be disclosed in:	Regs para 9(c), 5 Sch
	(i) A trustee report.	SORP 1 para 2(a)
	(ii) An investment report.	SORP 1 para 2(d)

Note: The detailed requirements in relation to each element of the annual report are dealt with in sections 2 to 8.

2. THE TRUSTEES' REPORT

2.1 The trustees have a responsibility to make certain information available to accompany the audited accounts and the actuarial statement. In practice the following information will normally be set out in a trustees' report. Regs para 9(1)(c), 5 Sch

2.2 So far as it applies, information on the following should be given: Regs 5 Sch

(a) The names of the persons who were trustees of the scheme during the year.

(b) The provisions of the scheme for appointing trustees and removing them from office.

(c) The names of the actuaries, auditors, solicitors, banks and other persons and organisations acting for or retained by the trustees during the year, with an indication (except in a case where the Regulations are complied with by trustees of a scheme for the first time i.e. the first scheme year beginning on or after 1 November 1986) of any change since the previous year.

(d) The address to which enquiries about the scheme generally or about an individual's entitlement to benefit should be sent.

(e) A general summary of the nature of the scheme and the benefits paid. CLD

(f) Any changes since the previous year in the following basic information about the scheme specified in the Regulations:

(i) The categories of persons who are eligible to be members of the scheme.

(ii) The categories of persons who are required, as a condition of their employment, to be members of the scheme.

(iii) The conditions of membership.

(iv) How members' contributions are calculated.

(v) How employers' contributions are calculated.

(vi) Whether the scheme is a tax-approved scheme and, if not, whether an application for the scheme to become a tax-approved scheme is under consideration by the Commissioners of Inland Revenue.

(vii) Which of the employments covered by the scheme are, and which are not, 'contracted-out' employments.

> Note: An employment is a contracted-out employment if covered by the benefits of an occupational pension scheme which has in force a certificate issued by the Occupational Pensions Board (known as the contracting-out certificate).

(viii) What benefits are payable under the scheme and how they are calculated.

(ix) The conditions on which the benefits are paid.

(x) Which benefits, if any, are payable only at some person's discretion.

(xi) Which of the benefits are, and which are not, funded.

(xii) Which of the benefits, if any, are such that fulfilment of the obligation to pay them to, or in respect of, particular members is guaranteed by means of one or more insurance policies which are specifically allocated to the provision of benefits payable to, or in respect of, those members.

(xiii) The short title of the statute (if any) which provides for both:
– the setting up of the scheme and
– the determination of the rate or amount of the benefits under the scheme.

(xiv) Whether, and if so to what extent, the employer of any person who is entitled to benefits under the scheme has entered into an obligation to pay the benefits if the scheme's resources are insufficient to do so.

(xv) Whether there is power under the scheme rules to increase pensions after they have become payable and, if so, what it is, who may exercise it, and whether and to what extent it is discretionary.

(xvi) What arrangements are made, and in what circumstances, for the refund of contributions to, and the preservation or transfer of the accrued rights of, a member whose relevant employment or pensionable service in relevant employment terminates before he reaches normal pension age.

(xvii) The address to which enquiries about the scheme generally or about an individual's entitlement to benefit should be sent.

(g) The number of members and beneficiaries as at any one date during the year.

(h) The percentage increases made (otherwise than in accordance with a legislative requirement) during the year (or, if there have been different increases for different individuals or groups of individuals, the maximum, minimum and average percentage increases) to:

(i) Pensions which were payable.
(ii) Deferred pensions.

A statement should disclose whether the increases were to any extent discretionary and if so to what extent.

(i) A statement:

(i) Whether the calculations of any cash equivalents paid during the year were certified by an actuary as prescribed by regulations under paragraph 14 of Schedule 1A of the Social Security Pensions Act 1975.

(ii) Whether any of the cash equivalents paid during the year to individual members whose pensionable service terminated were less than the benefits which had accrued under the scheme rules or the benefits which would have accrued to them if their relevant employment had terminated when their pensionable service terminated and, if so:
– why they were less and
– when full values became, or are estimated to be likely to become, available.

2.3 The following information should also be given:

(a) If the auditor's statement given in compliance with regulation 7(5)(b) shows that in his opinion contributions payable to the scheme during the year have not been paid in accordance with the scheme rules or contracts under which they were payable, or with the recommendation of the actuary, if appropriate, an account of the reasons for the discrepancy and a statement how it has been or is likely to be resolved. Regs 5 Sch 9

(b) If any such discrepancy was left unresolved in a previous year, a statement how it has been or is likely to be resolved. Regs 5 Sch 10

(c) A review by the trustees of the financial development of the scheme during the year, as shown by the audited accounts, and its financial prospects having regard to the actuarial valuation and statement (if any). Regs 5 Sch 11

(d) Who has managed the investment of the scheme during the year and the extent of any delegation of this function by the trustees.* Regs 5 Sch 12

(e) The basis on which any investment manager is paid and on which any fee or commission payable to him is calculated, if these costs are borne by the scheme.* Regs 5 Sch 13

> Note: The items marked with an asterisk could be dealt with alternatively in the investment report.

3. THE INVESTMENT REPORT

3.1 The investment report should contain:

(a) A statement by the trustees or the investment manager of the investment policies pursued during the year on behalf of the scheme and any material changes in these policies during the scheme year. Regs 5 Sch 14(a)

(b) A review of the investment performance of the scheme's fund during the year, and the nature, disposition, marketability, security and valuation of the scheme's assets. Regs 5 Sch 14(b)

3.2 Unless given elsewhere in the accounts, an analysis of the investment portfolio and income should be given including the following: SORP 1 para 68

(a) Analysis of investments by industrial sector.

(b) Analysis of investments by geographical sector.

(c) Details of the 10 or 20 largest investments.

(d) Details of investments which represent 5% or more of any class of shares of any company.

(e) Details of the extent to which properties are subject to rent reviews.

3.3 Totals shown in the report should be reconciled to the amounts shown in the accounts. SORP 1 para 69

3.4 The report should also contain: CLD

(a) A statement of the investment policy for the longer term and its objectives.

(b) The procedures in force for the review of investment policies and the factors likely to be taken account of during such reviews.

(c) Where investment management is delegated to an external manager, the monitoring process operated by the scheme.

4. AUDITED ACCOUNTS – GENERAL

4.1 Content of accounts

4.1.1 The annual accounts should comprise the following: Regs 3 Sch SORP 1 para 36

(a) A statement (a revenue account) disclosing the financial additions to, and withdrawals from, the fund during the scheme year.

(b) A statement of the assets and liabilities of the scheme as at the end of the scheme year (the assets should not include insurance policies which are specifically allocated to the provision of all the benefits of particular scheme members and the liabilities should not include the liabilities to pay pensions and benefits after the end of the scheme year).

(c) A reconciliation of the movement in net assets to the revenue account either as a part of the other two statements described above or as a separate statement.

4.1.2 Corresponding amounts for the previous scheme year should be disclosed for every amount shown in the accounts (relief is however available in respect of the first year in relation to which accounts are prepared under the Regulations). Regs 3 Sch 7 SORP 1 para 38

4.1.3 Where a pension scheme prepares consolidated accounts (for example where it has investments in investment-holding subsidiaries), these may be the only acounts of the scheme and it is not necessary to produce separate 'entity' accounts. SORP 1 para 56

4.2 True and fair view

4.2.1 The accounts should contain such additional information as is necessary to give a true and fair view of the financial transactions of the scheme for the accounting period and of the disposition of its net assets at the end of the scheme accounting period. Regs 7(4)(a)(ii) SORP 1 para 39

4.3 Basis of accounting

4.3.1 The accounts should normally be prepared on the basis of the accruals concept. SORP 1 para 32

> Note: In practice: CLD
>
> (a) Interest on fixed interest stocks and deposits should be accrued.
>
> (b) Dividends on equities should be accounted for when the investment goes ex-div.
>
> (c) Property income should be accounted for when it is due.
>
> (d) Contributions should be accounted for when they are due.
>
> (e) Benefits payable up to the accounting date which had not been paid over by that date should be accrued in the accounts.

4.3.2 The carrying amount of investments should be the market value at the date of the net assets statement where such a value is available or else at the trustees' estimate thereof. Regs 3 Sch 2 SORP 1 para 34

4.3.3 In the case of any assets which are stated at an estimate of their market value, the reasons why should be given in the statement of net assets or in a note thereto. Regs 3 Sch 2(a)

4.3.4 The carrying amount of all other assets and liabilities recognised in the statement of net assets should be based on normal accounting conventions. SORP 1 para 35

4.3.5 There should be a consistency of accounting treatment within each accounting period and from one period to the next. A change in accounting policy should not be made unless it can be justified on the ground that the new policy is preferable for the one it replaces because it will give a fairer presentation of the transactions and of the disposition of the net assets of the scheme. When changes are made they should be disclosed, along with the reasons for making the change. If the effect is material it should be accounted for as a prior year adjustment by restating the opening balance of the fund and the corresponding amounts. SORP 1 para 42

4.3.6 In preparing consolidated accounts, uniform group accounting policies should be followed. Where group accounting policies are not adopted by a subsidiary, adjustments should be made in preparing the consolidated accounts. SORP 1 para 56

4.4 Accounting policies

4.4.1 The accounting policies followed in dealing with items which are judged material or critical in accounting for, or reporting on, the transactions and net assets of the scheme should be explained in the notes to the accounts. The explanations should be clear, fair and as brief as possible. SORP 1 para 40

4.4.2 The following are some areas where it will be appropriate to disclose the accounting policies adopted: SORP 1 para 41

(a) The policies adopted in applying the accruals concept to significant categories of income and expenditure, such as contributions, investment income, transfer values and benefits.

(b) The bases adopted for the valuation of assets.

(c) Where any assets or liabilities are denominated in foreign currencies, the basis of the translation of these amounts into sterling. Regs 3 Sch 4

(d) The treatment of interest on property developments.

(e) The bases adopted for accounting for investments in subsidiary and associated companies.

4.5 Accounting for associated and subsidiary companies

4.5.1 The results, assets and liabilities of subsidiary companies should be consolidated with the transactions, assets and liabilities of the scheme. For investment-holding subsidiaries the basis of this consolidation will normally be a proportional consolidation on a line by line basis. For other subsidiaries it will be a single line equity method of accounting. SORP 1 para 56(a)

> Note: Investments in associated companies which are joint ventures should be treated in the same way as investments in subsidiary companies SORP 1 para 56(b)

4.5.2 Investments in associated companies which are not joint ventures should be treated in the same way as ordinary investments by including only dividends received and receivable in the revenue account. SORP 1 para 56(c)

4.6 Accounting for additional voluntary contributions ('AVCs')

4.6.1 Where AVCs are made to purchase added years or additional benefits within the provisions for benefits under the principal scheme, they should be included as contributions receivable from members and the assets acquired with them should be included in the net assets statement. SORP 1 para 63

4.6.2 Where AVCs are separately invested in such a way that the benefits paid to the members depend on the proceeds from the investment, members' contributions and the assets acquired with them should be disclosed within the accounts of the scheme or the notes thereto but separately from the transactions and assets of the fund. SORP 1 para 64

4.7 Actuarial position

4.7.1 The accounts should refer to the actuary's statement by way of note which might take the following form: SORP 1 para 45

'The accounts summarise the transactions and net assets of the scheme. They do not take account of liabilities to pay pensions and other benefits in the future. The actuarial position of the fund, which does take account of such liabilities, is dealt with in the statement by the actuary on pages 00 to 00 of the annual report and these accounts should be read in conjunction therewith.'

If the actuary's report is not recent and the actuary's statement has not been updated by an interim or supplementary statement, the above wording may need to be amended.

4.8 Compliance with SORP 1

4.8.1 The accounts should contain a statement whether they have been prepared in accordance with parts 2 to 4 (paras 9 to 71 inclusive) of SORP 1, and if not, an indication of where there are any material departures from those guidelines. Reg 3 Sch 9

4.9 Compliance with SSAPs

4.9.1 Pension fund accounts should comply with generally accepted accounting principles, including relevent SSAPs.

5. THE REVENUE ACCOUNT

5.1 Disclosures

5.1.1 The revenue account of pension scheme and the notes thereto should contain the items listed in 5.1.1 to 5.1.8 below where they are material. SORP 1 para 70

5.1.2 Contributions receivable:

(a) From employers – normal.
– additional.

(b) From members – normal.
– additional voluntary.

(c) Transfers in – group transfers from other schemes.
– individual transfers in from other schemes.

5.1.3 Investment income:

(a) From fixed interest securities.

(b) From equities (dividends).

(c) From index-linked securities.

(d) From managed or unitised funds.

(e) From properties (net rents).

Note: Any material netting off should be separately disclosed.

(f) From cash deposits (interest).

(g) Share of profits/losses of trading subsidiaries and joint ventures.

5.1.4 Other income:

(a) Claims on term insurance policies.

(b) Other categories of income not falling naturally into the categories listed above should be suitably described and analysed where material.

5.1.5 Benefits payable:

(a) Pensions.

(b) Commutation of pensions and lump sum retirement benefits.

(c) Death benefits.

(d) Payments to and on account of leavers:

(i) Refunds of contributions.

(ii) State scheme premiums.

(iii) Purchase of annuities to match preserved benefits.

(iv) Group transfers out to other schemes.

(v) Individual transfers out to other schemes.

5.1.6 Other payments:

(a) Premiums on term insurance policies

(b) Other categories of expenditure not falling into the categories listed above should be described and analysed where material.

5.1.7 Administrative and other expenses borne by the scheme should be suitably analysed where material.

5.1.8 Where the administrative expenses are borne directly by a participating employer, that fact should be disclosed.

5.2 Purchases of long-term insurance policies

5.2.1 The acquisition cost of long-term insurance policies which are purchased and match and fully guarantee all of the pension obligations of the scheme in respect of specific individuals should be treated as the cost of discharging the obligations at the time of purchase and therefore should not be carried as an asset in the accounts. Regs 3 Sch 2 SORP 1 para 61

6. THE NET ASSETS STATEMENT

6.1 Disclosure of investment assets

6.1.1 The net assets statement (or fund account) as at the end of the scheme year should show the distribution of the investments of the scheme stated at market value or a trustees' estimate thereof between each of the following categories: Regs 3 Sch 2(b) SORP 1 para 70

(a) Insurance policies, excluding those which are allocated to provide all the benefits payable under the scheme in respect of particular members.

(b) Public sector fixed interest investments.

(c) Other fixed interest investments.

(d) Index-linked securities.

(e) Equities including convertible shares.

(f) Rights or interests in freehold or leasehold land and buildings.

(g) Unit trusts invested in property.

(h) Other unit trusts.

(i) Managed funds (other than unit trusts) invested in property.

(j) Other managed funds not being unit trusts.

(k) Interests in trading subsidiary companies and joint ventures.

(l) Loans whether or not secured by mortgages.

(m) Cash deposits and cash in hand.

(n) Investments not falling under the above headings.

6.1.2 Investments within each category should be separately analysed between investments in the UK and investments outside the UK and between 'quoted' and 'unquoted'. In the case of investments in unit trusts or managed funds, this analysis should be based on whether or not the company operating the unit trust or managed fund is a company registered in the UK. Regs SORP 1 para 70

6.1.3 Investments in freehold and leasehold property should be further analysed between 'short leasehold' and 'other leasehold'. SORP 1 para 70

6.1.4 The accounts should contain disclosure of the total amount of the purchases, and the total amount of the sales, of investments during the scheme year. Regs 3 Sch 8 SORP 1 para 71

6.1.5 If there is any self-investment (investment in the business of the scheme employer(s) or any connected companies and persons, 'investment' including an interest in shares or securities, mortgages on real property, freeholds and leasehold properties owned by the scheme trustees and effectively leased to a company or person, loans made or money currently due to the scheme but held by the employer or connected parties) in excess of 5% of the total value of the net assets of the scheme, then particulars should be disclosed in the accounts including the nature and value of the investment(s) involved. Regs 3 Sch 6 SORP 1 para 65

6.1.6 Where there is a concentration of investment, i.e. a significant proportion of the scheme assets invested in one company and connected companies and persons or in one property (other than in UK Government Securities) which exceeds 5% of the total value of the net assets of the scheme, particulars should be disclosed in the accounts including details of the amount and nature of the investment, the company involved and, if the investment is an insurance policy, a statement of its main characteristics. 'Investment' includes shares or securities of a company, mortgages on real property owned by a company or person, freehold and leasehold property owned by the scheme trustees and effectively leased directly to a company or person and loans made to a company or person. Regs 3 Sch 5 SORP 1 para 66

6.1.7 Where insurance policies form a material part of the net assets of the scheme, the main characteristics relevant to the overall investment policy (for example whether the policies are with or without profits) should be disclosed. SORP 1 para 67

6.2 Disclosure of other assets and liabilities

6.2.1 Debtors and creditors in respect of investment transactions where these form part of the net assets available for investment within the investment portfolio should be included, but be separately disclosed in investment assets. SORP 1 para 70

6.2.2 Other assets and liabilities directly connected with investment transactions (for example financial futures, options, forward dealings and, where appropriate, tax recoverable) should be included, but be separately disclosed in investment assets. SORP 1, para 70

6.2.3 The following should be separately disclosed in the net assets statement: SORP 1 para 70

(a) Fixed assets held primarily for reasons other than investment potential.

(b) Long-term borrowings:
- Sterling.
- Foreign currency.

(c) Current assets and liabilities:
- Contributions due from the employer.
- Unpaid benefits.
- Other current assets and liabilities, other than liabilities to pay pensions and other benefits in the future.

6.3 Valuation of investments

6.3.1 Securities quoted in the UK should be valued at the mid-point of the quotations in the Stock Exchange Daily Official List or at similar recognised market values. SORP 1 para 48

6.3.2 Other securities quoted overseas should be valued at middle market price from overseas stock exchanges translated at closing rates of exchange. SORP 1 para 49

6.3.3 Unquoted securities, including venture capital funds where appropriate, should be valued by the trustees. SORP 1 para 50

6.3.4 Investments which are held in units should be valued at the average of unit bid and offer prices at the accounting date. For some unitised funds, offer prices are regularly quoted but bid prices are not. In such circumstances, a basis such as reducing the offer price by an amount which takes account of the specific circumstances is likely to give a suitable valuation. Where unit bid and offer prices are both not available or have otherwise not been used, the basis adopted in arriving at an estimate of market value should be disclosed. SORP 1 para 51

6.3.5 Financial futures, options and forward currency positions should be included or provided for at market value, where such market value is available. If it is not available, a trustees' valuation should be used. SORP 1 para 52

6.3.6 Freehold and leasehold property should be included in the net assets statement at open market value. The name, or employer firm, and qualification of the valuer should be stated. If the valuer is an employee of the scheme or the participating employers this fact should be stated. SORP 1 para 53

Note: For more detailed guidance refer to Appendix 1 to SORP 1.

6.3.7 If practicable, long-term insurance policies should be valued using a premium valuation method. Where there are difficulties in obtaining this value, however, the latest value established by the actuary for the assessment of the discontinuance position, adjusted by subsequent additions to and withdrawals from the policy, will usually be satisfactory. SORP 1 para 54

Note: For more detailed guidance refer to Appendix 2 to SORP 1.

6.3.8 Any significant restrictions affecting the ability of the scheme to realise its investments at the accounting date at all or at the value at which they are included in the accounts should be disclosed in a note to the accounts. This will include, for example, legal or contractual restrictions on the surrender of units (e.g. managed funds) or material penalties which would have been suffered if they had been surrendered at the accounting date. It will not include the inherent difficulties in disposing of a large investment. SORP 1 para 47

6.4 Other information

6.4.1 In order to give a true and fair view of the financial transactions of the scheme for the accounting period and of the disposition of its net assets at the period end, additional information may need to be given of capital commitments, post balance sheet events and contingencies other than liabilities to pay pensions and related outgoings in the future. SORP 1 para 39

7. RECONCILIATION OF REVENUE ACCOUNT WITH NET ASSETS STATEMENT

7.1 The accounts should contain a reconciliation of the revenue account with the statement of net assets. Regs 3 Sch 3 SORP 1 para 36(c)

7.2 This reconciliation may be shown as a separate statement (i.e. as a 'movement of funds statement') or alternatively it may be incorporated into the revenue account or the net assets statement. SORP 1 para 36(c)

7.3 Whichever method of presentation is adopted, the reconciliation should clearly disclose the following:

(a) Opening net assets of the scheme.

(b) Net new money invested per the revenue account.

(c) Total realised and unrealised change in the market value of investments.

(d) Closing net assets of the scheme.

8. THE ACTUARY'S STATEMENT

8.1 With the exception of public service pension schemes, benefits which are not funded or money purchase arrangements, the trustees of a scheme must obtain from time to time a signed actuarial valuation of the scheme's assets in relation to its liabilities. Regs para 8(1)(2) 8(2)

> Note: The date as at which the signed actuarial valuation is performed is its 'effective date'.

8.2 The effective date of the first actuarial valuation to be obtained is the latest of: Regs para 8(3)

(a) 1 November 1987.

(b) The date which is three years and six months later than that on which the scheme commenced.

(c) The date which is three years and six months later than the effective date of an actuarial valuation obtained by the trustees before 1 November 1986.

The effective date of any subsequent actuarial valuation is to be no later than three years and six months after the previous one. Each valuation is to be obtained as soon as reasonably practicable after its effective date. Regs para 8(4)(5)

8.3 The actuarial valuation must:

(a) Be made by a Fellow of the Institute of Actuaries or of the Faculty of Actuaries or a person with other actuarial qualifications who is approved by the Secretary of State at the request of the trustees of the scheme. Regs para 8(6)

(b) Be presented so as to enable the expected future contribution rates and funding levels to be understood. Regs para 8(1)(a)

(c) State whether it has been prepared in accordance with the guidelines 'Retirement Benefit Schemes – Actuarial Reports (GN9)' published by the Institute of Actuaries and Faculty of Actuaries current on the date of signature of the actuarial valuation. Regs para 8(1)(b)

(d) Indicate where there are any material departures from the guidelines. Regs para 8(1)(c)

8.4 Each actuarial valuation must be accompanied by an actuarial statement in the format prescribed in Schedule 4 of the regulations made by the actuary who signed the valuation. At any time after a valuation is made and before the next valuation is made an actuary may issue a revised statement. Regs para 8 (7)

8.5 A copy of the latest actuarial statement (if any) in the format prescribed in Schedule 4 of the regulations is required to accompany the audited accounts. Regs para 9

8.6 It should be stated whether or not the statement is a revised statement. Regs para 8 (8)

8.7 In the transition period there may be some accounts produced under the regulations where an actuarial statement is not required (see 8.2 above). In this case appropriate actuarial information should be made available, in whatever format is possible. CLD

8.8 In years between actuarial valuations, the actuary should be requested to provide an interim or supplementary statement of whether he is aware of any changes in circumstances or necessary changes in assumptions which would indicate that his previous statement could not, if prepared at the current date, be made. CLD

9. OPB REQUIREMENTS – CONTRACTED-OUT SCHEMES

> Note: The following additional requirements apply to schemes which have sought and obtained contracted-out status from the Occupational Pensions Board ('OPB').

9.1 Contracting-out certificate

9.1.1 Where the scheme provides guaranteed minimum pensions (GMPs) in respect of more than one employment, the scheme's contracting-out certificate should cover all of the relevant employers.

9.2 Certificate A

9.2.1 The scheme should hold a current certificate A from the scheme's actuary in relation to the normal current rate of contributions.

> Note:
>
> (a) Unless requested to do so by the OPB, the scheme is not required to submit actuarial reports to the OPB.
>
> (b) If the funding arrangements involve a planned change in contribution rates during the period covered by the certificate, each rate should be shown with the period to which it will apply.
>
> (c) It is normal practice for the certificate to show the contribution rates which relate to the funding of the scheme as a whole. However it is possible that the certificate will show contribution rates for funding only the liabilities shown on the certificate.

9.2.2 The actuary to the scheme should have obtained an 'undertaking from the principal employer', before he can issue the current certificate A. This informs the actuary if any of the events specified on the form occurs or if there is a proposal to wind up the scheme in the period covered by the certificate A.

> Note: The employer has a responsibility to inform the actuary whenever any event occurs which might, in his view, significantly affect the scheme's resources – whether or not this event falls within the terms of the undertaking.

9.3 Certificate B

9.3.1 Where the actuary issued the certificate A subject to a qualification regarding self-investment, he should have provided a certificate B to the OPB when self-investment needs to be taken into account in order to cover the prior liabilities of the scheme.

9.4 Insured schemes – life office certificate OP14

9.4.1 Insured schemes' life office insurers should send a completed form OP14 either to the employer to submit with his election to contract-out or direct to the OPB with a copy to the employer. This certificate states, *inter alia*, that the contract with the scheme provides for the payment of premiums at a rate not less than the rate of contributions considered by the actuary to be satisfactory for the scheme.

9.5 Self-administered schemes – annual statement OP21

9.5.1 Self-administered schemes should complete and submit to the OPB an OP21 within three months of the end of the scheme's year. The statement must normally be signed by a trustee, the scheme administrator or the scheme's auditor.

9.5.2 The statement must include the following:

(a) Confirmation that the accounts of the scheme for the scheme year most recently ended have been audited (or for the previous scheme year if the most recent accounts have not yet been prepared or audited).

(b) A statement that the auditor's report was not qualified in any way or, if it was qualified, a statement that a copy of the qualified report is attached.

(c) Confirmation that contributions at the appropriate rate were paid to the scheme for the scheme year just ended (this will normally be the rate entered by the actuary on certificate A). A statement of the latest position is required if appropriate contributions were not paid.

(d) A statement with regard to self-investment covering one of the following:

(i) There was no self-investment.

(ii) Aggregate self-investment did not exceed 10% of the scheme's total resources.

(iii) Self-investment exceeded 10% of the scheme's total resources, with an attached statement giving the type and value of self-investment.

(iv) It cannot be decided whether or not self-investment exceeded 10% of the scheme's total resources, with an attached statement giving full information about the self-investment.

Substantial changes in self-investment should be commented on.

Note: Self-investment means investment of part or all of the resources in the business of the employer or an associated company.

(e) A statement with regard to concentration of investment; either there was:

  (i) No concentration of investment.

  (ii) Concentration of investment with an attached statement giving details.

Substantial changes in concentration of investment should be commented on.

> Note: Concentration of investment means investment (other than in the employer's own undertaking) of more than 10% of the scheme's total resources in one undertaking and in any associate of it or in one property. However, concentrations of investment in British Government securities and possible concentrations arising out of investments in managed funds, deposit administration arrangements, unit trusts or investment trusts are disregarded.

(f) A statement that the appropriate actuary has been given the opportunity of considering any change which might affect the scheme's current actuarial certificate.

9.6 Insured schemes – life office annual return OP13

9.6.1 Where a scheme is insured, an annual return OP13 should be completed and returned to the OPB by the life office within three months of its issue (an OP13 is issued during the calendar month in which the insured scheme year starts).

Chapter 9

UNINCORPORATED ASSOCIATIONS

Chapter 9

UNINCORPORATED ASSOCIATIONS

Introduction

9.1 An unincorporated association is established whenever a group of people (which may include a company) join together for a common purpose, other than for business purposes. An unincorporated association is formed by the contractual obligations that exist between the association's members. The more common uses of an unincorporated association are as follows:

- Clubs.
- Trade associations.
- Trade unions and employers' associations (see chapter 10).
- Friendly societies (see chapter 11).

9.2 Unincorporated associations are regulated by the general law of contract and (with the exception of trade unions, employers' associations and friendly societies) are not regulated by any statutory framework. In practice, however, the laws applicable to gaming, lotteries and entertainment do apply to many clubs, and these laws may require, for example, an association to be registered in order to obtain a licence. In addition, in certain situations the *Financial Services Act 1986* may apply to associations that undertake investment business (see further chapter 26).

9.3 As a consequence, there are no specific statutory rules concerning the accounting requirements for unincorporated associations, or concerning how they should be audited.

Definition

9.4 An unincorporated association has been defined in case law in the following way:

> *"Two or more persons bound together for one or more common purposes, not being business purposes, by mutual undertakings, each having mutual duties and obligations, in an organisation which has rules which identify in whom control of it and its funds rests and upon what terms and which can be joined or left at will."* [*per Lawton L.J. in Conservative and Unionist Central Office v Burrell (1982) 1 WLR 522 at 525 CA*].

9.5 The reference above to 'business purposes' stems from section 716 of the *Companies Act 1985*, which prohibits any unincorporated association, consisting of more than 20 persons, from being formed to carry on any business that has the acquisition of gain as its object. This rule applies unless the unincorporated association is registered under the *Companies Act 1985*, or is formed under some other Act, or is formed by letters patent. The purpose of this rule is to ensure that large business associations are properly regulated to protect people that deal with them [see, for example, *Smith v Anderson (1880) 15 Ch D 247 at 273*]. The exceptions to this rule include solicitors, accountants and stockbrokers.

9.6 Clubs that carry out social, educational or recreational functions will not usually contravene the prohibition mentioned above, even where their members exceed 20 (see chapter 4).

9.7 However, the following types of association have been held, by the courts, to be prohibited from trading as unincorporated associations:

- Mutual assurance clubs. [*Re. Arthur Average, Association* etc. *(1875) 10 Ch App 542*].

- Building and loan societies. [*Shaw v Benson (1883) 11 QBD 563* CA].

9.8 In addition, where an unincorporated association has more than twenty members, but where its business is carried on by less than twenty trustees, it will be allowed to trade as an unincorporated association. Examples of these types of association are:

- Sickness benefit clubs. [*Re. One and All Sickness and Accident Assurance Association (1909) 25 TLR 674*].

- Investment trusts (see chapter 17). [*Smith v Anderson (1880) 15 Ch D 247*].

Types of unincorporated association

9.9 There are four main types of unincorporated association that come under the broad headings of clubs and trade associations (see para 9.1) and these are:

- Members' clubs.
- Proprietary clubs.
- Charitable associations.
- Trade associations.

Members' clubs

9.10 A members' club is the most common form of unincorporated association. The contractual obligation mentioned in paragraph 9.1 exists between the members of the association themselves, which contrasts with the contractual obligation for proprietary clubs considered in paragraph 9.12. In a members' club, in accordance with the rules adopted by the members as part of their contract with each other, the club property and income belongs to the members themselves.

9.11 There are, therefore, several legal consequences from this:

- The provision of drinks to members is regarded in law as a supply rather than a sale, and thus internal profits generated are exempt from taxation as it trades mutually with its own members.
- Upon dissolution of the club, the members share equally in the remaining free assets, divided in accordance with the rules.
- The club is run by an elected committee.
- Certain privileges under section 39 of the *Licensing Act 1964* are available to the club.

Examples of members' club include sports clubs, social clubs, religious clubs, political clubs, ex-servicemen's clubs and trades clubs.

Proprietary clubs

9.12 A proprietary club is a business where a person (or group of persons) provides the services of a club for the use by its members who are, in effect, its customers. In contrast to a members' club (see para 9.10) the members have a contractual relationship, not with each other, but with the proprietor. The proprietor owns the club property and income and lays down the rules that members must observe. His objective is usually to produce a profit at the end of the financial year, which is subject to taxation. Examples of proprietary clubs include night clubs and gaming clubs.

Charitable associations

9.13 Where an association is established for charitable purposes it must register as a charity with the Charity Commissioners. These types of association are considered in chapter 25.

Trade associations

9.14 A trade association is an association whose purpose relates to a particular occupation or business. Those establishing or advising trade associations should ensure that its objects do not infringe UK or EC competition law.

Formation

9.15 There are no formal requirements necessary to establish an unincorporated association. As mentioned above, such associations are in essence a contractual relationship between the members. For many purposes an oral contract may suffice. However, in practice, an association will often have a written constitution.

9.16 An unincorporated association is, by definition, not a corporate person and, therefore, cannot hold property. Where it is necessary for an association to hold property, trustees will need to be appointed in order to hold it (see chapter 6), and the constitution of the association should provide for their appointment.

Constitution

9.17 There are no legal requirements concerning the content that the rules of an unincorporated association should provide. However, the content of a typical set of rules for an unincorporated association would include the following:

- Its name and address.
- Its status and objects.
- Rules for the appointment, resignation and removal of:
  - □ A management committee.
  - □ A treasurer.
  - □ A secretary.
  - □ A chairman.
- Duties of officers.
- Rules for holding members' meetings, usually including a mandatory annual general meeting.
- Rules for the admittance, resignation, expulsion and conduct of members.

- Rules for subscription payments.
- Rules giving the committee power to make the association's bye-laws.
- Rules giving the committee power to borrow.
- Rules for trustees to hold property.
- Rules relating to the association's finances, including financial statements.
- Provision for the association's rules to be altered.
- Provision for the association's dissolution.

Club and Institute Union

9.18 The Club and Institute Union (CIU), was founded in 1862 with the purpose of helping working men to establish clubs or institutes where they could meet and socialise away from public houses. These clubs at the same time provided an avenue for mutual help in various ways. Today, it has a membership of over 3,500 clubs with members exceeding six million.

9.19 The CIU has special subcommittees for particular activities as follows:

- Parliamentary.

  This committee meets about six times a year and submits its views and ideas on matters of concern and interest, (in particular on future legislation or EC directives) to the parliamentary group.

- National accounting.

  This was set up to liaise with clubs on the following matters:

  - ☐ Brewery loans of up to £250,000 are made by brewers at interest rates of up to six per cent usually with a ten-year repayment period.
  - ☐ Brewery discounts are usually available when there is no borrowing.
  - ☐ National agreements on the purchase of supplies and equipment at discount prices.

Duty to keep accounting records

9.20 It is normal for the constitution of an unincorporated association to provide that the association's financial transactions must be recorded in a proper set of books by the treasurer of the association. Where the association has trustees the obligations upon them will be determined by the principles that apply generally to trusts (see chapter 6).

Duty to prepare financial statements

9.21 The constitution of an unincorporated association will rarely lay down any specific duties concerning the preparation of financial statements. However, it is usual to provide in the association's rules that at the annual general meeting the members should receive and consider the association's financial statements for the previous year together with a treasurer's report summarising the association's financial position.

Accounting period

9.22 An association's constitution usually provides for its financial statements to relate to the year previous to the annual general meeting. Whether this means the previous calendar year or the year actually prior to the annual general meeting will depend upon the association's constitution. However, because the rules of unincorporated associations are contractual, an accounting period other than that specified in the contract cannot be used, unless the rules are specifically amended to allow for a different period.

Appointment and removal of auditors

9.23 An association's constitution usually provides for the appointment and the removal of auditors at the annual general meeting. Consequently, unless specifically allowed under the rules, the treasurer and the managing committee will not generally have the power to remove an auditor between annual general meetings.

Qualification of auditors

9.24 There are rarely any rules specifying who can audit an unincorporated association. It is usual, however, for the appointment to be held by a member of the unincorporated association itself who has an accounting qualification.

Audit report

9.25 The rules of the unincorporated association will usually provide for the auditor's report on the financial statements to be considered at the association's annual general meeting. The restrictions on the scope of an association's audit will be similar to those in respect of a trust and these restrictions are considered in chapter 6 paragraphs 6.43 and 6.44.

9.26 An example of the suggested wording for an unqualified club's or association's audit report is as follows:

REPORT OF THE AUDITORS TO THE MEMBERS OF [NAME OF CLUB/SOCIETY/ASSOCIATION]

We have audited the financial statements on pages [] to [] in accordance with Auditing Standards.

In our opinion, the financial statements give a true and fair view of the state of the club's affairs at [date] and of its excess of income over expenditure [expenditure over income] and source and application of funds for the [period] then ended.

[Name of firm]

Chartered Accountants,

[Address].

[Date of report].

Chapter 10

TRADE UNIONS AND EMPLOYERS' ASSOCIATIONS

Chapter 10

TRADE UNIONS AND EMPLOYERS' ASSOCIATIONS

Background

10.1 Unlike the other entities considered in this book, the legal background of trade unions is distinctive in that for long periods they were regarded as illegal or potentially illegal. For example, for a time trade unions were viewed as a criminal conspiracy at common law. This treatment only ceased finally towards the end of the 19th century. However, political controversy over the regulation of trade unions has continued to the present time. Economically, trade unions are the most important form of unincorporated association, because of both their function and their size. At the end of 1988 there were 314 trade unions in the UK with a total membership in excess of 10 million people. Employers' associations are also considered in this chapter, because they are subject to very similar legal regulation as trade unions.

10.2 The principal legislation governing trade unions and employers' associations is now contained in the following statutes:

■ The *Trade Union Act 1913*.

The *Trade Union Act 1913* (TUA 1913) as amended by the *Trade Union and Labour Relations Act 1974* defines both trade unions and employers' associations. It also places restrictions on the application of trade union funds for political purposes (see para 10.42).

■ The *Trade Union (Amalgamation, etc) Act 1964*.

The *Trade Union (Amalgamation, etc) Act 1964* lays down rules for the amalgamation and transfer of engagements of trade unions.

■ The *Trade Union and Labour Relations Act 1974*.

The *Trade Union and Labour Relations Act 1974* (TULRA 1974) is the main source of the rules governing trade unions and employers' associations. It covers the following matters:

□ Their legal status (see paras 10.6 and 10.9).

□ Membership rights.

- ☐ Listing (see para 10.13).
- ☐ Duty to keep accounting records (see para 10.26).
- ☐ Auditors (see paras 10.52 to 10.62).
- ☐ Duty to submit an annual return (see para 10.44).
- ☐ Duty to have an actuarial valuation in respect of members' superannuation schemes (see para 10.45).
- ☐ Restrictions on legal liability and legal proceedings.
- ☐ The enforceability of collective agreements.

■ The *Employment Protection Act 1975*.

The *Employment Protection Act 1975* (EPA 1975) established much of the machinery for dealing with industrial relations, such as setting up the Advisory, Conciliation and Arbitration Service (ACAS). The *Employment Protection Act 1975* is also important for trade unions, because it sets out the procedure for the certification of 'independent' trade unions and the rights of such trade unions. These procedures and rights are considered further in paragraph 10.13.

■ The *Employment Protection (Consolidation) Act 1978*.

This Act deals with the rights of officials of trade unions that arise in the course of employment, for example, time off work for carrying out trade union duties and activities.

■ The *Employment Act 1980*.

The *Employment Act 1980* mainly covers the rights of individual trade union members, such as payments in respect of secret ballots. Important regulations made under this Act are *The Funds for Trade Union Ballots Regulations 1980* (SI 1980 No. 1252) which provide for the detailed implementation of payments for ballots. It imposes a duty on trade unions to compile and maintain a list of the names and addresses of their members.

■ The *Employment Act 1982*.

The *Employment Act 1982* contains important provisions aimed at removing legal immunity from trade union funds and controlling the closed shop.

- The *Trade Union Act 1984*.

  The *Trade Union Act 1984 (TUA 1984)* contains important and controversial rules in respect of holding secret ballots for both trade union elections and industrial action. It also lays down more precise requirements in respect of the political fund of trade unions. Some of these aspects are considered in paragraph 10.42 below.

- The *Employment Act 1988*.

  The *Employment Act 1988* created a new office of Commissioner for the Rights of Trade Union Members and establishes new rights for trade union members. It imposes a duty on trade unions to keep their accounting records available for inspection by members. It also makes unlawful, except in prescribed cases, for the property of a trade union to be applied unreasonably in or towards payment of a penalty for any individual or towards indemnifying any individual in respect of any penalty imposed by a court for a criminal offence or contempt of court. The union can, however, recover from the individual the amount of any payment made. Under another provision, if trustees of the union's property, in carrying out their functions, permit any unlawful application of union property, the court may, on the application of a member, make an order to protect or recover the property. It also further limits a trade union's immunity for action in connection with employing non-union labour.

- The *Employment Act 1989*.

  The *Employment Act 1989*, amending the *Employment Protection (Consolidation) Act 1978*, limits the duties in respect of which employers must allow union officials paid time off.

- The *Employment Act 1990*.

  The *Employment Act 1990* makes it unlawful to refuse access to employment on grounds related to trade union membership and amends the law relating to strikes and other industrial action. That Act received Royal Assent on 1st November 1990 and some provisions came into effect on that date.

10.3 The legislation that applies to trade unions and employers' associations is prone to rapid and fundamental change. Accordingly, professional advisors and auditors of trade unions and employers' associations must always ensure that they are aware of any developments in the law.

Definition of a trade union

10.4 Trade unions are defined in the following way:

"An organisation (whether permanent or temporary) which either:

(a) consists wholly or mainly of workers of one or more descriptions and is an organisation whose principal purposes include the regulation of relations between workers of that description or those descriptions and employers or employers' associations; or

(b) consists wholly or mainly of:

(i) constituent or affiliated organisations which fulfil the conditions specified in paragraph (a) above (or themselves consist wholly or mainly of constituent or affiliated organisations which fulfil those conditions), or

(ii) representatives of such constituent or affiliated organisations,

and in either case is an organisation whose principal purposes include the regulation of relations between workers and employers or between workers and employers' associations, or include the regulation of relations between its own constituent or affiliated organisations." [TUA 1913 Sec 2(1); TULRA 1974 Sec 28(1)].

10.5 Although this definition describes a trade union, it does not, however, define its legal status.

Legal status of trade unions

10.6 A trade union is in legal terms an 'unincorporated association'. As a consequence, a trade union is no more than a members' club (see chapter 9), except for special privileges given to it by statute. Although during the brief life of the *Industrial Relations Act 1971*, trade unions were permitted to incorporate, generally this has been prohibited. The present legislation provides that a trade union must not be, or be treated as, a corporate body and in particular may not:

- Register as a company.
- Register as a friendly society.
- Register as an industrial and provident society.

- Remain a body corporate under these or any other provisions.

[TULRA 1974 Sec 2(1) - (4)].

10.7 The practical importance of this restriction is diminished, however, because trade unions are given many attributes of a corporate body by statute. For example:

- A trade union is capable of making contracts.
- All property belonging to a trade union is vested in trustees for the 'union'.
- A trade union may sue and be sued in its own name.
- A trade union may be prosecuted in its own name.

- Legal judgements may be enforced against a trade union and property held in trust for it as if it were a body corporate.

[TULRA 1974 Sec 2(1)].

Definition of an employers' association

10.8 The definition of an employers' association is similarly phrased to that of a trade union. However, instead of referring to *"workers"* it refers to *"employers or individual proprietors"*. This reflects the fact that, whereas trade unions are organisations established by workers, employers' associations are established, not surprisingly, by employers.

Legal status of an employers' association

10.9 An employers' association, in contrast to a trade union, may be formed as either a corporate body or an unincorporated association. However, where an employers' association is merely an unincorporated association, it is given the same attributes of incorporation as a trade union by statute (see para 10.6). Furthermore, such an unincorporated employers' association is permitted to have in excess of 20 members and section 716 of the *Companies Act 1985* does not apply (see chapter 4 para 4.16).

Branches

10.10 It is very common for a trade union's activities to be divided up into various types of district and local area organisations, such as areas, regions, sections and chapels. These are referred to collectively as 'branches' in this chapter. The legal status of a branch will depend upon its constitution. Some will be administrative areas of a trade union, others will be separate organisations.

10.11 An example of the difficulties that may arise can be seen from the case of *News Group Newspapers Ltd. and Others v Society of Graphical and Allied Trades 1982 (1986)* IRLR 227, CA. In this case, the High Court granted News Group Newspapers an order of sequestration for all the property of SOGAT for contempt of a court order. A London branch of the union and a chapel of that branch claimed that their funds should not be subject to sequestration, because they were not the property of the union. The case was of considerable importance because the union had 94 branches and numerous chapels with very substantial funds. Each of the 200,000 members of the union belonged to a branch and in every place of employment where there were two or more members, they had to form and join a chapel.

10.12 The assets of the London branch were held by trustees of the branch. However, the chapel was only small and there were no trustees to hold its funds. The Court of Appeal considered the effect of the rules of the union and branch. Both sets of rules provided that the property and funds of the London branch were to be held for the benefit of that branch. It was accepted that each branch was an unincorporated association that could hold property for the benefit of its members and that the chapel was analogous to a social club whose members held its property on behalf of all other members. Consequently, the funds were not available for sequestration.

Listing of trade unions

10.13 A number of legal privileges are given by statute to 'independent' trade unions. A precondition of gaining a 'certificate of independence' is that an organisation must be listed by the Certification Officer (see para 10.23) as a trade union and not as an employers' association. The reason for this requirement, which has been supported by successive Parliaments, is that the legal privileges granted should be enjoyed only by 'genuine' trade unions. A genuine trade union, is one that is able *"to offer a vigorous challenge to the employers on behalf of their members, whether collectively or individually"*. [*per Kilner Brown J. in Association of HSD (Hatfield) Employers v Certification Officer (1978) ICR 21 EAT*].

10.14 The statutory definition is that a union will only be independent where it is both of the following:

- Not under the domination or control of an employer.

- Not liable to interference by an employer (arising out of the provision of financial or material support or by any other means tending towards such control).

[TULRA 1974 Sec 30(1)].

10.15 The criteria followed by the Certification Officer in assessing the independence of a trade union are as follows:

- Its history.
- Its membership base.
- Its finance.
- Employer provided facilities.
- Collective bargaining record.
- Organisation and structure.

Distinction between trade unions and employers' associations

10.16 The difference in legal status between trade unions and employers' associations is discussed above. The significance of this distinction is that the independent trade union, its members and officials are entitled to the following legal privileges that are not available to employers' associations:

- To take part in trade union activities.
- To make union membership agreements.
- To gain information for collective bargaining.
- To secure consultation over redundancies.
- To insist on reasonable time off for trade union duties and activities.
- To appoint health and safety representatives.

10.17 In addition, independent trade unions may gain some taxation advantages.

Special register bodies

10.18 The concept of the 'Special Register' derives from the repealed *Industrial Relations Act 1971*. The Special Register brought within the regulatory structure of that Act those bodies who were active in industrial relations, but whose principal objects were not employment relations. Examples of such bodies are the British Medical Association and the Royal College of Nursing.

10.19 There were no restrictions on the form that such bodies should take and they were usually incorporated. Following the repeal of the 1971 Act, the list is now closed. However, those that remain registered retain a limited immunity in respect of restraint of trade. There is no significance in accounting or auditing terms to a body being listed on the Special Register. Such bodies will be regulated in the manner appropriate to their legal form.

Constitution

10.20 The constitution of a trade union or an employers' association will be set out in its rules. In principle, these are usually similar to those of any unincorporated association (see chapter 9). However, the rules will usually contain:

- The objects of the body, which must satisfy the definition of a trade union or employers' association (see paras 10.4 and 10.8).
- Rules for administering any trust that holds the body's property. These rules are considered in detail in chapter 6 as they apply to trusts generally.
- Rules regarding establishing any branches.
- Provision for appointing and removing auditors. [TULRA 1974 2 Sch 11]. Although statute does not specify the rules that must be included, restrictions are, however, placed on what the rules may contain (see para 10.52).
- Where the union maintains a members' superannuation scheme, in general the constitution must provide for a separate fund for the payments (see para 10.46). [TULRA 1974 2 Sch 34, 35].
- Provisions for establishing and maintaining a political fund (see para 10.42).

10.21 There are, in addition, legal restrictions on a trade union's freedom to make its own rules. For example, the rules of a trade union cannot affect the trade union's duty to hold elections for certain positions.

10.22 The annual return (see para 10.44) of a trade union or employers' association must contain a copy of its rules in force at the end of the period to which the return relates. [TULRA 1974 2 Sch 2(d)].

The Certification Officer of ACAS

10.23 The Registrar of Friendly Societies prior to 1971 used to maintain a register of trade unions. This was in many ways a mere formality. However, the *Industrial Relations Act 1971* established a 'Registrar of Trade Unions' and made registration a key requirement for obtaining any benefits under that Act. Most trade unions refused to register because registration might lead to the possible intervention in trade union's internal affairs and judicial control of a trade union's constitution. The TUC, in fact, expelled any trade union that registered. The functions formerly performed by the Registrar are now performed by the Certification Officers appointed by the Secretary of State after consultation with ACAS. Following the *Employment Protection Act 1975*, the Certification Officer was given the responsibility of maintaining a voluntary list of trade unions and employers' associations. By 1988, 314 trade unions and 672 employers' associations were listed.

10.24 The Certification Officer is now responsible for:

- Maintaining lists of trade unions and employers' associations.
- Determining the independence of trade unions (see para 10.13).
- Supervising various aspects of the statutory rules governing secret ballots.
- Ensuring that trade unions and employers' associations keep accounting records, have their financial statements properly audited and submit annual returns.
- Ensuring the periodical examination of members' superannuation schemes.
- Securing the observance of statutory procedures for transferring engagements, for amalgamation and for changes of name.
- Supervising the establishment and operation of political funds and dealing with any complaints about political fund rules.

Accounting and auditing background

10.25 The APC issued a specific auditing guideline, 'Trade Unions and Employers' Associations' (AG 3.303) on 22nd August 1984. This gives guidance on the special factors to be considered in applying auditing standards to the audits of these organisations.

Duty to keep accounting records

10.26 Both trade unions and employers' associations must keep such proper accounting records relating to their transactions, assets and liabilities as necessary in order to give a true and fair view of the state of their affairs and to explain their transactions. [TULRA 1974 Secs 10(2)(a), (3)]. However, there are no requirements in the *Trade Union and Labour Relations Act 1974* concerning the format of accounting records.

10.27 Where the trade union or employers' association consists wholly or mainly of the representatives of constituent or affiliated organisations, there is no duty to keep accounting records. [TULRA 1974 Sec 10(1)]. In practice, however, the constitution of such an organisation is likely to impose a requirement to keep proper accounting records anyway.

10.28 The duty to keep accounting records falls on the trade union or employers' association. Where those include a branch or section, the branch or section may discharge that duty instead on behalf of the trade union or association, or vice-versa, where the branch or section itself is a trade union or employers' association. [TULRA 1974 Sec 10(4)]. What this means is that a trade union cannot avoid responsibility for the accounting records, solely because they are kept at branch level.

Duty to allow inspection of accounting records

10.29 The *Employment Act 1988* imposes a duty on trade unions to keep their accounting records available for inspection from their creation for six years beginning with the 1st January following the end of the period to which the records relate. [EA 1988 Sec 6]. That Act gives a member of a trade union right to inspect certain accounting records. The trade union must, on request by a member of the union, comply with the request by making arrangements for that member and any accountant (qualified to be an auditor of a trade union) who may accompany him to be allowed to inspect the records relating to the period of his membership within 28 days of the request.

10.30 The trade union has the right not to permit a person inspecting the records to be accompanied by an accountant if the accountant fails to enter into such agreement as the union may reasonably require for protecting the confidentiality of the records. The union must also supply the person with such copies of the extracts he has inspected as he may require and it is permitted to make a charge to cover the union's reasonable administrative expenses in complying with a request to inspect the records. 'Accounting records' are the documentary or non-documentary accounting records of a union, or of any branch or section of a union, kept under section 10 of TULRA 1974 and relating to a period beginning after 31st December 1987.

10.31 The Commissioner for the Rights of Trade Union Members may assist members contemplating legal proceedings against a union to enforce their rights and such assistance could be given regarding the above provisions.

Duty to establish and maintain systems of control

10.32 Trade unions must establish and maintain a satisfactory system of control over their records, cash holdings and all their receipts and remittances. [TULRA 1974 Sec 10(2)(b)].

10.33 The auditing guideline recommends that large trade unions should have those internal controls appropriate to any large enterprise. It gives some indication of the internal controls that most trade unions might implement, in respect of:

- Financial organisation.
- Contributions (including political fund contributions) and entrance fees.
- Fines and special levies receivable.
- Benefits payable.
- Travel, subsistence and attendance payments and allowances.
- Dispute payment and receipts.
- Separate funds.
- Cash and bank deposits.
- Investments.
- Properties.

[AG 3.303 paras 52 - 61].

10.34 The auditing guideline also draws attention to the problem that may arise where control is concentrated in a particular senior official, such as the general secretary or the branch secretary. [AG 3.303 para 63].

Duty to prepare financial statements

10.35 There is no express requirement for trade unions or employers' associations to prepare financial statements, but this can be deduced from the requirement to submit an annual return containing financial statements. [TULRA 1974 Sec 11(1), 2 Sch 2]. It is not clear, therefore, what requirements are placed specifically upon branches. For example, whether or not branches may prepare separate financial statements which may be prepared at branch or central level (see para 10.28 above).

Accounting period

10.36 The revenue account prepared by a trade union must be made up for the period to which its annual return relates and its balance sheet must be made up as at the end of the year. The annual return must relate to the last preceding calendar year. [TULRA 1974 2 Sch 1(1), 2].

The revenue account

10.37 Every trade union or employers' association must prepare a revenue account indicating its income and expenditure for the calendar year. This must give a true and fair view of the matters to which it relates. [TULRA 1974 Sec 11(1), 2 Sch 2(a), 3].

The balance sheet

10.38 Every trade union or employers' association must prepare a balance sheet as at the end of the period for which the revenue account has been prepared. This must also give a true and fair view. [TULRA 1974 Sec 11(6), 2 Sch 2(b), 3].

Other accounts

10.39 The Certification Officer may require a trade union or employers' association to prepare other accounts that must give a true and fair view. [TULRA 1974 Sec 11(6), 2 Sch 2(c), 3].

Fund accounts

10.40 A trade union or its branches may have funds under its management that have no direct connection with their rules or objects. Examples of these are moneys collected for recreational, charitable or social purposes, contributions to which are totally voluntary and not a condition of trade union membership. These should not be included in the annual return. Such funds are receipts in trusts and the regulation of such trusts is considered in chapter 6.

10.41 Where funds are established for specific purposes, in accordance with trade union rules or conference decisions, those funds should generally be separately identified in the annual return. It is important that income and expenditure relating to one fund account is only shown in the appropriate fund account, especially in the case of payments for political purposes.

Political funds

10.42 The funds of a trade union or employers' association must not be used directly or indirectly in furtherance of specified political objects unless:

- This has been approved by a resolution of the members.

- Rules approved by the Certification Officer are in force providing in general terms for:

  - A separate political fund.

  - Non-discrimination against those who do not contribute.

[TUA 1913 as amended by TUA 1984 Secs 3(1), 6A].

10.43 The political objects specified include the expenditure of money on:

- Contributing to the funds, or meeting the expenses, of a political party.

- Providing services or property for a political party.

- Candidature for political office.

- Maintenance of the holder of a political office.

- Holding of conferences or meetings by or on behalf of a political party.

- Providing, publishing or distributing any literature, document, film or advertisement, the main purpose of which is to persuade people to vote for, or against, a political party or candidate.

Duty to submit an annual return

10.44 Every trade union or employers' association must send to the Certification Officer (see para 10.23) a return relating to the last preceding calendar year before 1st June of each year. [TULRA 1974 Sec 11(6), 2 Sch 1]. This must be on Form AR 21 (for a trade union) or on Form AR 27 (for an employers' association), and must contain:

- A revenue account.

- A balance sheet.

- Any other accounts.

- A copy of the rules in force at the end of the period.

- A note of all changes in officers.

- A note of any change in address of the head or main office.

- A copy of the audit report (see paras 10.59 to 10.62 below).

- Any further particulars required by the Certification Officer, although with respect to financial statements, this requirement is subject to any modifications that may be necessary to secure a true and fair view.

[TULRA 1974 Sec 11(6), 2 Sch 2].

Actuarial valuation of member's superannuation schemes

10.45 A 'members' superannuation scheme' means any scheme or arrangement made by, or on behalf of, a trade union or employers' association to provide pension benefits either directly out of its own funds or by an insurance scheme maintained by its own funds to members, former members, their widows, children or dependants. [TULRA 1974 Sec 11(7), 2 Sch 36(a)].

Requirement for prior actuarial examination

10.46 A trade union or employers' association is not permitted to maintain a scheme unless the proposals for it have been examined by a properly qualified actuary. [TULRA 1974 Sec 11(7), 2 Sch 27(a)]. The actuary must make a signed report to the trade union or employers' association, stating whether in his opinion:

- The premium or contribution rates are adequate.

- The accounting or funding arrangements are suitable.

- The separate fund that must be maintained for the payment of benefits is adequate.

[TULRA 1974 Sec 11(7), 2 Sch 25, 27].

10.47 A copy of this report must be sent to the Certification Officer. [TULRA 1974 Sec 11(7), 2 Sch 27(b)].

Requirement for periodical actuarial valuation

10.48 Every trade union or employers' association that maintains a superannuation scheme must periodically arrange for it to be examined by a properly qualified actuary. [TULRA 1974 Sec 11(7), 2 Sch 32(1)]. The date of each successive examination may be decided by the trade union or employers' association. However, it must not be more than five years from the date of either the last examination, or the date on which the examination of the proposals for the scheme was carried out. In addition, the Certification Officer may direct that a shorter period should apply. [TULRA 1974 Sec 11(7), 2 Sch 32(2)]. The examination must include a valuation of the assets and liabilities in the separate funds. The report must express the actuary's opinion on the superannuation fund in the same way as stated under paragraph 10.46 above.

10.49 A copy of the report made and signed by the actuary must be sent to the Certification Officer within a year of the actuarial examination being carried out. [TULRA 1974 Sec 11(7), 2 Sch 26].

Exemption from actuarial examination

10.50 The Certification Officer may exempt a scheme from the requirement for prior or periodical examination where the trade union or employers' association concerned applies for this because it either has a small number of members or for any other special reason. [TULRA 1974 Sec 11(7), 2 Sch 39].

10.51 Such an exemption may, however, be revoked subsequently if the reasons for granting the exemption no longer apply. [TULRA 1974 Sec 11(7), 2 Sch 33B].

Appointment of auditors

10.52 The rules of every trade union and employers' association must provide for the appointment of auditors. [TULRA 1974 2 Sch 11]. The *Trade Union and Labour Relations Act 1974* prescribes the scope of the audit and the terms of the audit report. In addition, the rules adopted by a trade union may seek to extend or limit the auditor's responsibilities in some way. However, most limitations are rendered void by that Act. The auditing guideline draws attention to the following areas that should be clarified in the written contract between the auditor and trade union. In particular:

- It should exclude any requirements in the rules that the auditor cannot reasonably fulfil, such as to 'certify' financial statements.
- It should deal with the treatment of branch funds within the annual return and the annual financial statements and the extent to which branch funds are included within the auditor's responsibilities.

[AG 3.303 paras 31 to 34].

Qualification of auditors

10.53 To be qualified for appointment, a person must be one of the following:

- A member of a recognised Institute.
- Authorised by the Secretary of State on the basis of qualifications obtained outside the UK.
- Authorised by the Secretary of State where:
  - □ The trade union or employers' association was registered under the *Trade Union Acts 1871 to 1964* on 30th September 1971.
  - □ A person acted as the union's auditor in respect of the last period for which it had to make an annual return under section 16 of the *Trade Union Act 1871*.
  - □ He has acted as its auditor for every subsequent accounting period.

[TULRA 1974 2 Sch 8].

10.54 An auditor must be qualified in order to audit a trade union or an employers' association. However, in certain circumstances two or more unqualified persons may act as an auditor of a trade union or employers' association in respect of its last preceding accounting period, where the following apply:

- Its receipts and payments do not exceed £5,000.
- Its members at the end of the period do not exceed 500.
- Its assets at the end of the period do not exceed £5,000.

[TULRA 1974 Sec 11(6), 2 Sch 9].

10.55 The Certification Officer may direct at any time that a trade union or employers' association, that has an unqualified person acting as its auditor, should appoint a qualified person for an accounting period. [TULRA 1974 2 Sch 9(2)]. The auditing guideline considers what reliance an auditor may place on unqualified auditors who may audit branches of the trade union. [AG 3.303 paras 36 - 38].

10.56 The following people are prohibited from acting as an auditor of a trade union or an employers' association:

- An officer (which does not include an auditor for this purpose) or employee of the trade union or employers' association or any branch or section.

- A partner, employee or employer of a person falling within the first category above.

- A body corporate.

[TULRA 1974 2 Sch 10].

Removal of auditors

10.57 The rules of every trade union and employers' association must provide for the removal of auditors. [TULRA 1974 2 Sch 11]. However, they cannot provide for removal other than by a resolution passed at a general meeting of members or their delegates. [TULRA 1974 2 Sch 12].

Auditors' rights

10.58 The auditors of a trade union or employers' association have the following rights, regardless of the body's own rules:

- Access at all times to its accounting records and to all other documents relating to the trade union's or employers' association's affairs. [TULRA 1974 2 Sch 16(a)].

- To require from its officers, or the officers of any of its branches or sections, such information and explanations as the auditors think necessary to perform their duties. [TULRA 1974 2 Sch 16(b)].

- To attend any general meeting of the union's or association's members, or of delegates of its members, and to receive all notices of, and other communications relating to, any general meeting that any member or delegate is entitled to receive. [TULRA 1974 2 Sch 17(a)].

- To be heard at any meeting that the auditors attend on any part of the business of the meeting that concerns them as auditors. [TULRA 1974 2 Sch 17(b)].

Audit report

10.59 The auditors of a trade union or employers' association must make a report to it on the financial statements that they have audited, which are contained in its annual return. [TULRA 1974 2 Sch 18].

10.60 The audit report must state the following:

- Whether, in the auditors' opinion, those financial statements give a true and fair view. [TULRA 1974 2 Sch 19].

- If, in the auditors' opinion, the trade union or employers' association has failed to comply with the matters they are required to investigate. These matters concern whether the:

  - ☐ Union or association has kept proper accounting records (see paras 10.26 to 10.28 above).

  - ☐ Union or association has maintained a satisfactory system of control over its transactions (see paras 10.32 to 10.34 above).

  - ☐ Financial statements to which the report refers are in agreement with the accounting records.

  [TULRA 1974 2 Sch 20].

- If the auditors fail to obtain all the information and explanations that, to the best of their knowledge and belief, are necessary for the purposes of an audit they shall state that fact in their report. [TULRA 1974 2 Sch 21].

10.61 In addition, the auditing guideline makes it clear that an auditor should report his disagreement where income or expenditure relating to one fund account is shown in another fund account, or where a payment in furtherance of political objects is made out of a fund other than the political fund. In the latter situation, the auditor should make clear in his report reference to the fact that this is in contravention of the *Trade Union and Labour Relations Act 1913*.

10.62 An example of the suggested wording for an unqualified trade union or employers' association audit report on the financial statements contained in the annual return is as follows:

REPORT OF THE AUDITORS TO THE MEMBERS OF [NAME OF TRADE UNION OR EMPLOYERS' ASSOCIATION]

On the financial statements contained in the Annual Return for the year ended [date].

We have audited the financial statements set out on pages [] to [] of this return in accordance with Auditing Standards.

In our opinion the financial statements give a true and fair view of the state of the [name of trade union or employers' association] financial affairs at [date] and of its transactions and source and application of funds for the year then ended.

[Name of firm]

Chartered Accountants,

[Address].

[Date of report].

Chapter 11

FRIENDLY SOCIETIES

Chapter 11

FRIENDLY SOCIETIES

Background

11.1 Friendly societies have been in existence for several centuries. Their origins lie in associations whose members paid a subscription in return for being granted various benefits in certain circumstances (for example, on the birth of a child or on the death of a relative). These societies are termed in law 'unincorporated mutual insurance associations'. However, although in strict legal terms friendly societies are not corporate entities, societies that are registered share some of the benefits of a corporate entity. A distinctive feature of friendly societies is often the unusual names they possess, for example, the Sheffield Order of Druids Society. Since the end of the eighteenth century various legislation has been passed to encourage friendly societies to promote thrift, better management and protection of their funds.

11.2 It should not be assumed, however, that although friendly societies have existed for some time, that they are archaic or have fallen into disuse. For example, they are increasingly recommended as a vehicle for pension planning. Many professional partnerships used them as vehicles to invest their retirement funds.

Legislation

11.3 The current statutory framework for these societies is provided by the *Friendly Societies Act 1974*. In particular, the provisions of that Act cover the following matters:

- Registration of societies.
- Their rules.
- Their membership.
- Accounting and audit requirements.
- Actuarial valuations.
- Their investments, funds, and property.
- Benefits.
- The amalgamation and winding up of societies.

11.4 The *Friendly Societies Act 1974* requires the rules of a friendly society to limit its activities to some or all of those specified in Schedule 1 of that Act (see para 11.14). A society can only properly extend its activities beyond those in Schedule 1 by converting to an insurance company. Such a conversion, however, requires a radical change in the nature and objectives of the friendly society and few societies have done so in the past 20 years.

11.5 There were, in addition, numerous changes in legislation which affected the powers and regulation of friendly societies in the last five years, in particular the *Financial Services Act 1986* (see further chapter 26). That Act regulates most long-term insurance business undertaken by societies. When a society is registered with the Registrar of Friendly Societies (see para 11.9 below), the society is automatically authorised under the *Financial Services Act 1986* to carry on investment business, which includes long-term insurance business. However, in order to market long-term insurance business a society must generally also register with, and be regulated in that respect by, LAUTRO.

A new framework for friendly societies

11.6 The Treasury Green Paper entitled 'Friendly Societies: A New Framework' was published in January 1990. It proposes to provide friendly societies with wider powers (including the management of unit trusts and personal equity plans) while retaining their distinct characteristics as a friendly society. The adoption of these proposals will require a change in status of a friendly society from an unincorporated body of individuals to a body corporate under the *Industrial and Provident Fund Societies Acts* (see chapter 21).

11.7 The Green Paper also sets out proposals for a revised regulatory framework for friendly societies, which would bring the supervision of their extended activities into line with other regimes of investor protection.

11.8 It is unlikely that the proposals of the Green Paper will be passed into law before late 1991 at the earliest and a Bill is currently being drafted.

The Chief Registrar of Friendly Societies

11.9 The Central Office of the Registry of Friendly Societies consists of the Chief Registrar and one or more assistant registrars. The registrars are appointed by the Treasury. In addition, the Central Office has a staff of actuaries and accountants.

11.10 The Central Office collects statistics on life expectancy and sickness of friendly society members, together with particulars of societies' returns, asset valuations and other information that the Chief Registrar deems useful. This information also has to be published and circulated to societies.

11.11 The Registrar has a variety of functions such as the registration and supervision of friendly societies. These functions are not, however, just restricted to friendly societies, as Industrial and Provident societies and Credit Unions also come under the provisions of the Registrar of Friendly Societies (see chapter 21 and 22 respectively).

Formation of societies

11.12 Friendly societies can be formed without being registered. This can be achieved by setting up an unincorporated association (see chapter 9) for the purposes specified in paragraph 11.14 below otherwise than with a view to profit. In addition, the difficulties experienced by unregistered industrial and provident societies (see chapter 21), because members are restricted to 20 by section 716 of the *Companies Act 1985* do not apply to unregistered friendly societies. [*Re. One and all Sickness and Accident Assurance Association (1909) 25 TLR 674; Marrs v Thompson 86 LT 759*]. However, where, a society is not registered, there are a number of disadvantages (summarised below) and in addition the privileges awarded to registered societies are not available (see para 11.19):

- ■ An unregistered society cannot carry on insurance business without special authorisation. [ICA 1982 Sec 2(1)].

- ■ An unregistered society cannot carry on industrial assurance business. [IAA 1923 Sec 1(2)].

11.13 In practice, however, unregistered societies are rarely encountered.

Registration of societies

11.14 The following categories of society are eligible for registration:

- ■ Societies established for:

  - □ The relief or maintenance of members or their relatives in sickness, if orphaned or if unemployed.

  - □ Insuring money to be paid on birth, marriage, death or a specified period of life.

- ■ Cattle insurance societies, that is, those that insure against loss of any farm animals.

- ■ Benevolent societies, including some charities.

- Working mens' clubs.
- Old peoples' home societies.
- Societies specifically authorised by the Treasury, which now include:
  - ☐ Rest centres.
  - ☐ Loan societies.
  - ☐ Societies to encourage sport, science, literature, fine arts, music or cookery.

[FSA 1974 Sec 7].

11.15 An application to register a society must be made to the Chief Registrar of Friendly Societies (see para 11.9) on Form A. This form must be signed by seven members of the society and its secretary (who need not be a member) and must be sent with two printed copies of the rules and a list of names of the secretary, trustees and other officers. [FSA 1974 Sec 8(2)]. Model rules can be obtained from the Registrar free of charge.

11.16 A society will be accepted by the Registrar for registration if the following apply:

- It is eligible for registration. [FSA 1974 Sec 7(1)].
- Its rules contain provisions for certain specified matters (see para 11.21). [FSA 1974 Sec 7(2)(a)].
- Its rules provide for the society's registered office to be situated in England, Wales, the Channel Islands or the Isle of Man. [FSA 1974 Secs 7(2)(b), 4(1)].
- It has seven or more members. [FSA 1974 Sec 7(2)(c)].
- The Registrar considers that its name is neither identical to another society, nor resembles another society's name so closely that it would be likely to deceive the public concerning its identity nor is otherwise undesirable. [FSA 1974 Sec 8(3)].

11.17 There are special provisions in respect of dividing societies and societies assuring annuities (see para 11.25). [FSA 1974 Sec 9].

11.18 Where the Registrar is satisfied that a society has complied with all of the statutory requirements outlined above, he must issue the society with an acknowledgement of registration, which specifies the class of society. [FSA 1974 Sec 15(1)]. This certificate is conclusive evidence that the society is properly registered. [FSA 1974 Sec 15(2)].

Effects of registration

11.19 The principal effects of registering as a friendly society are as follows:

- The society gains some attributes of corporate status, although it remains an unincorporated association. For example:
  - Although a society's trustees can only hold property, there is a procedure for the devolution of title on a change of trustees. [FSA 1974 Sec 58]. Furthermore, the trustees are given a measure of protection if deficiencies in the society's funds are found. [FSA 1974 Sec 54(3)].
  - There is a procedure for the dissolution of societies. [FSA 1974 Sec 93].
  - A society's trustees can sue, or be sued, in their proper names without any description other than the title of their office. [FSA 1974 Sec 103(1)].
- Even if the society's purposes are charitable, it need not register under the *Charities Act 1960* (see chapter 25). [ChA 1960 Sec 4(4)(a), Sch. 2(g)].

11.20 A registered society has the power to convert into a company under the *Companies Act 1985*. [FSA 1974 Sec 84(1)]. Once it is registered as a company, registration under the *Friendly Societies Act 1974* is cancelled.

Constitution

11.21 The friendly society's constitution is found in its rules. Schedule 2 of the *Friendly Societies Act 1974* lays down in detail the matters societies' rules must provide for in their rules and specifies additional rules for friendly societies and cattle insurance societies.

11.22 The rules that a friendly society must specify include the following:

- Its name.
- Its registered office.
- Its objects.
- The purposes for which its funds must be applied.

- Its rules in respect of:
  - □ Members' admission.
  - □ Members' entitlement to any assured benefits.
  - □ Penalties that can be imposed on members.
  - □ Details regarding holding meetings, voting rights, and the alteration of the scheme's rules.
- Appointing and removing a management committee.
- Appointing and removing a treasurer, other officers, and trustees.
- The central body's composition and powers where there are branches.
- The conditions under which a branch may secede from the society.
- Investment of funds.
- Keeping accounts and their audit at least yearly.
- Annual returns.
- Inspection of the scheme's books.
- Settling disputes.

11.23 The rules of a friendly society or cattle insurance society must also contain rules dealing with the following matters:

- Keeping proper accounts and a separate account of management expenses, net of any contributions received.
- Its voluntary dissolution by the consent of three-quarters of its members.
- Minority rights to request investigations or winding-up by the Registrar.

11.24 The rules of a friendly society must provide for statutory actuarial valuations of its assets. Also, the rules of a society that may divide its activities in the future, must deal with how all the society's claims may be met before any division takes place.

Types of registered society

11.25 There are four principal types of registered society, that differ because of the way they hold their funds. These types of society are as follows:

- Accumulating societies.

  Accumulating societies accumulate income that is used solely for benefit payments.

- Dividing societies.

  Dividing societies periodically divide, between members, the balance of their funds remaining after the payment of any claims.

- Deposit societies.

  Members' contributions are credited in part to a common fund and in part to a personal account. Withdrawals can be made by the member from his personal account and benefits can be paid from both the common fund and the personal account.

- Collecting societies.

  Members' contributions are collected for death benefits, or life assurance. Such societies are subject to the provisions of the *Industrial Assurance Acts*.

Branches of societies

11.26 The *Friendly Societies Act 1974* only recognises 'branches' that fall within a special definition. Consequently, a branch will only be recognised where members of a society are controlled by a central body (to which they must contribute), but where they (or a committee) administer a separate branch fund. [FSA 1974 Sec 11(1)]. A society with branches may either register as a single society, or it may apply for registration itself and to register its branches separately. [FSA 1974 Sec 11(2)]. In both these circumstances, the application to register (see para 11.15) must be accompanied by the following information:

- A list of all branches and their registered offices.

- A list of all trustees and officers authorised to sue, or be sued, on behalf of particular branches only.

- Two copies of all branch rules.

[FSA 1974 Sec 11(1)].

11.27 An acknowledgement of registration (see para 11.18) is then given in respect of each branch. To register a new branch a similar procedure to that required to register a new society must be followed, except that the application need only be signed by three members, and must be signed by both the branch secretary and the society's secretary.

11.28 In practice, however, most branches will be separately registered and are autonomous with regard to their administration and investment. The effect of this is that contributions payable and benefits provided by separate branches in the same society frequently vary.

11.29 Societies may have branches that are not recognised under the *Friendly Societies Act 1974*. These are often referred to as 'business branches' and are, in effect, agencies. These types of branch cannot be separately registered. Their distinguishing feature is that their administration is centrally managed and, accordingly, their terms for contributions and for benefits are common to all members. Such branches may have local committees, but these are subject to a central committee and they must anyway account for monies receivable and payable to their head office.

Duty to keep accounting records

11.30 Registered societies and branches must keep books of account that relate to their transactions, assets and liabilities. [FSA 1974 Sec 29(1)(a)] . These records have to give a true and fair view of the society's or branch's state of affairs and explain their transactions. [FSA 1974 Sec 2.29(2)]. Books of account may be kept in either bound books or in another format. [FSA 1974 Sec 29(3)]. If the books of account are kept in some other format adequate precautions must be taken to guard against their falsification and to facilitate their discovery. [FSA 1974 Sec 29(4)].

Duty to establish and maintain a system of control

11.31 A satisfactory system of control must be established and maintained for books of account, cash holdings and all receipts and remittances. [FSA 1974 Sec 29(1)(b)].

Duty to prepare financial statements

<u>Revenue account</u>

11.32 Every registered society or branch must prepare a revenue account for each year. Two alternative forms of presentation are permitted:

- A revenue account dealing with the society's or branch's affairs as a whole (for example see Table 11.1 and 11.2). [FSA 1974 Sec 30(2)(a)]. The revenue account must give a true and fair view of the income and expenditure for the period. [FSA 1974 Sec 30(1)(a)].

- Two or more revenue accounts dealing separately with the particular businesses conducted by the society or branch. [FSA 1974 Sec 30(2)(b)]. However, each revenue account must give a true and fair view of the income and expenditure in respect of the business to which it relates. [FSA 1974 Sec 30(1)(b)]. Also, when the accounts are viewed together, they must give a true and fair view of the income and expenditure of the society or branch as a whole. [FSA 1974 Sec 30(3)].

Table 11.1: Illustration of a revenue account of a friendly society

Extract from Liverpool Victoria Friendly Society Report and Accounts for the year ended 31 December 1989.

Industrial Assurance Fund Account

1988 £,000	During the year ended 31st December	1989 £,000
	We received ...	
87,605	**Premiums**	87,210
100,552	**Investment Income (less sundry charges)**	114,961
	We transferred from ...	
	Investment Reserve	25,000
188,157		227,171
	We paid or provided ...	
23,725	**Claims on Death**	25,087
40,009	**Claims on Maturity**	47,692
18,690	**Surrenders and premiums returned**	16,722
35,817	**Expenses of Management charged against premium income**	35,599
—	**Taxation (note 3)**	5,215
	We transferred to ...	
4,500	**Management Fund Reserve (Industrial) (note 5)**	8,000
122,741		138,315
	Resulting in ...	
65,416	**An excess of Income over Expenditure of**	88,856
891,704	**Which, when added to the Fund at the beginning of the year**	957,120
957,120	**Brings the Fund at 31st December to**	1,045,976

Table 11.2: Illustration of accounting policies of a friendly society

Extract from Liverpool Victoria Friendly Society Report and Accounts for the year ended 31st December 1989.

Statement of Accounting Policies (extract)

a. **INVESTMENTS.** The assets are shown in the Balance Sheet as follows:—

Quotes Securities are stated at cost less amounts written off.

Land and Property. Properties are valued annually and the Board do not consider it necessary to provide for depreciation on any of the properties, those occupied by the Society not being material in the context of total assets. The Board has valued the land and property on an open market basis, after having received the advice of the Society's Estates Manager, Mr. R. K. Rolfe, F.R.I.C.S.

Leasehold properties with less than 20 years to redemption are written off from the rental income by annual instalments over the remaining periods of their leases.

Mortgages and Loans are stated at the amount repayable less provision for any anticipated loss.

c. **REVENUE FROM INVESTMENTS.** The Society maintains common assets for all funds. Investment Revenue is allocated on the following basis:
a sum is transferred to the Management Fund in accordance with Rule 25, certified by the Actuary as not exceeding the costs of investment administration.

The Revenue net of this sum is then allocated to the Industrial and Ordinary Assurance Funds and the Management Fund Pensions Reserve. Allocations are based on the respective proportions to the total of (i) all Industrial Funds and Reserves, (ii) all Ordinary Funds and Reserves and (iii) the Management Fund Pensions Reserve.

Profits and losses from realisations of investments and adjustments of book values are allocated to the Industrial and Ordinary Investment Reserves. Allocations are based on the respective proportions to the total of (i) all Industrial Funds and Reserves and (ii) all Ordinary Funds and Reserves.

Where necessary, provision for taxation is made in each fund.

11.33 In these circumstances 'year of account' means, in respect of the first year of registration, the period from the date of registration to 31st December, and in other cases, the 12 months ending on 31st December. [FSA 1974 Sec 111(4)].

Balance sheet

11.34 The following requirements for the balance sheet of a friendly society are laid down in the *Friendly Societies Act 1974*:

- Registered societies or branches and other societies required to carry out a valuation of assets and liabilities must prepare a balance sheet. The balance sheet must give a true and fair view of the society's assets, current liabilities and resulting balances of the society's funds at the balance sheet date (for example see Table 11.2 and 11.3). [FSA 1974 Sec 30(5)].

- Other registered societies or branches must prepare a balance sheet that must give a true and fair view of their state of affairs at the balance street date. [FSA 1974 Sec 30(4)].

Table 11.3: Illustration of a balance sheet of a friendly society

Extract from Liverpool Victoria Friendly Society Report and Accounts for the year ended 31st December 1989

Balance Sheet at 31st December, 1989

1988 £,000	£,000	At the end of the year	£,000	1989 £,000
		The Funds and Reserves of the Society were ...		
		Assurance Funds:		
	957,120	Industrial	1,045,976	
	215,742	Ordinary	257,152	
1,172,862				1,303,128
		Investment Reserves:		
	266,203	Industrial	310,705	
	50,996	Ordinary	46,269	
317,199				356,974
2,136		**Management Fund Pensions Reserve**		1,971
1,492,197		**Total Funds and Reserves**		1,662,073
		Which were represented by ...		
		Investments:		
		Quoted Investments (note 1)		
	480,767	Government Securities	490,636	
	52,540	Other Fixed Interest Stocks & Securities	58,819	
	400,411	Ordinary Stocks and Shares	462,679	
933,718				1,012,134
449,933		Land and Property		524,826
100,204		Mortgages and Loans		110,766
1,483,855				1,647,726
2,131		Furniture and Equipment (note 2)		2,027
		Current Assets:		
	767	Cash at bank or in hand	1,426	
	4,381	Arrears of Premiums	4,649	
	20,144	Investment Income accrued (less provision)	20,264	
	2,166	Other Debtors	6,103	
	27,458		32,442	
		Less Current Liabilities:		
	3,913	Claims admitted or intimated, but not paid	5,240	
	2,253	Premiums received in advance	2,402	
	15,081	Other Creditors	12,480	
	21,247		20,122	
6,211		**Net Current Assets**		12,320
1,492,197		**Total Assets**		1,662,073

Statement of affairs

11.35 Section 720 of the *Companies Act 1985* requires every company, being an insurance company, or a deposit, provident or benefit society to publish a statement of affairs in February and August of each year in the format laid down in Schedule 23 to that Act (see the extracts of that Act reproduced towards the end of this book).

Requirement for actuarial valuation

11.36 Registered societies and branches must have their assets and liabilities valued by a qualified actuary at least once every five years. [FSA 1974 Sec 41(1)(a)]. However, there are exemptions for those societies that fall into any of the categories set out below:

- Benevolent societies.
- Working mens' clubs.
- Old peoples' home societies.
- Cattle insurance societies.
- Those societies given dispensation by the Registrar of Friendly Societies.
- Branches of the above societies.

11.37 The following societies and branches must have their assets and liabilities valued by a qualified actuary at least once every three years:

- Societies and branches registered on or after 26th July 1968 that carry on long- term insurance business.
- Societies and branches registered before that date, if at their last valuation the annual return showed that their life or endowment funds exceeded £1,000,000, or that their contribution income in respect of such funds exceeded £150,000.
- Those societies directed to do so by the Registrar.

11.38 The actuarial report must be submitted to the Registrar of Friendly Societies by the actuary, who must sign it and state his address. [FSA 1974 Secs 41(1)(b), 41(3)(a). It must be made in such a form and contain such particulars as the Registrar of Friendly Societies prescribes. [FSA 1974 Sec 41(a)]. Furthermore, it must contain an abstract made by the actuary of the results of his valuation, together with a statement containing information of, for example, the benefits assured. [FSA 1974 Sec 41(3)(b)].

Duty to submit an annual return

11.39 Every registered society and branch must send to the Chief Registrar of Friendly Societies once a year (not later than the 31st May) a return relating to its affairs. The annual return must be made up for the year of account preceding the year in which the return is required to be sent. [FSA 1974 Sec 43(1)]. The annual return must contain the following information:

- The revenue accounts for the year. [FSA 1974 Sec 43(3)(b)].
- A balance sheet at the end of the year. [FSA 1974 Sec 43(3)(b)].
- A copy of the auditor's report on the revenue accounts and the balance sheet. [FSA 1974 Sec 43(4)].
- Where applicable, particulars of the most recent actuarial valuation report or the reason for exemption from the requirement to have such a report. [FSA 1974 Sec 43(5)].
- Any other particulars prescribed by the Registrar of Friendly Societies. [FSA 1974 Sec 43(6)].

11.40 The annual return must not contain any other accounts than those prescribed above, unless they have been examined and reported on by the auditors. [FSA 1974 Sec 43(3)(c)].

Appointment and removal of auditors

11.41 Subject to specific exemptions, every registered society and branch must in each year of account appoint one or more qualified auditors to audit its financial statements for that year. [FSA 1974 Secs 31, 32]. The *Friendly Societies Act 1974* contains detailed provisions that specify the procedures to appoint or remove an auditor and are, in general terms, similar to those for audits made under the *Companies Act 1985*. [FSA 1974 Secs 33 to 37]. An additional provision prohibits the appointment of an auditor that employs any person who is an auditor of the society.

Auditors' rights

11.42 Friendly society auditors have the following rights:

- Access at all times to the society's or branch's books, deeds and accounts and to all other documents relating to their affairs. [FSA 1974 Sec 39(1)(a)].
- To require from the society's officers such information and explanations as they think necessary to perform their duties. [FSA 1974 Sec 39(1)(b)].
- To attend any general meeting and to receive all notices of, and other communications relating to, general meetings that any member is entitled to receive. [FSA 1974 Sec 39(2)(a)].
- To be heard at any meeting that they attend, on any part of the business of the meeting that concerns them as auditors. [FSA 1974 Sec 39(2)(b)].

Audit report

11.43 The auditors of a registered friendly society or branch must make a report to the society or branch on the accounts they examine and on the revenue accounts and the balance sheet for the year. [FSA 1974 Sec 38(1)]. These matters are considered in the ICAEW's members handbook in a statement entitled 'Auditors' reports - registered friendly societies and industrial and provident societies' (MH 3.910).

11.44 The audit report must state the following:

- Whether the revenue accounts and the balance sheet for the year comply with the requirements of the *Friendly Societies Act 1974*. [FSA 1974 Sec 38(2)].
- Whether the revenue accounts give a true and fair view (in accordance with the *Friendly Societies Act 1974's* requirements) of the society's or branch's income and expenditure as a whole for the year. In addition, if any income and expenditure accounts are prepared separately in respect of a particular business, they must be reported on and must give a true and fair view. [FSA 1974 Sec 38(2)(a)].
- Whether the balance sheet gives a true and fair view (in accordance with the Act's requirements) either of the society's or branch's state of affairs, or, as the circumstance may require, of its assets and current liabilities and the resulting balances of its funds, as at its year end. [FSA 1974 Sec 38(2)(b)].

- Whether the auditors have not received satisfactory explanations on any of the matters they are required to investigate and form an opinion on. These matters concern whether:

  - ☐ The society or branch has kept proper books of account.
  - ☐ The society or branch has maintained a satisfactory system of control over its transactions.
  - ☐ The revenue accounts and any other accounts being reported on and the balance sheet are in agreement with the books of account.

  [FSA 1974 Sec 38(4)].

- Whether the auditors have failed to obtain all the information and explanations that, to the best of their knowledge and belief, are necessary for the purposes of their audit. [FSA 1974 Sec 38(5)].

11.45 The last two requirements differ in their scope despite appearing similar.

11.46 An example of the suggested wording for an unqualified friendly society audit report is set out below:

REPORT OF THE AUDITORS TO [NAME OF SOCIETY OR BRANCH]

We have audited the financial statements on pages [] to [] in accordance with Auditing Standards.

In our opinion the financial statements give a true and fair view of the state of affairs of the society [or branch] at [date] and of its excess of [income over expenditure/expenditure over income] and source and application of funds for the [period] then ended and comply with the requirements of the Friendly Societies Act 1974.

[Name of firm]

Chartered Accountants,

[Address].

[Date of report].

11.47 The audit report will differ if section 41(1) of the *Friendly Societies Act 1974* applies to the society. That section applies to societies that carry on insurance business. In this situation auditors are not required to report a long-term insurance liabilities that can only be determined actuarially (see para 11.35). The financial statements must, however, include a statement about the last valuation or where the Registrar dispenses with this requirement the reason for the exemption. An audit report for a friendly society that undertakes long-term insurance business is given below.

REPORT OF THE AUDITORS TO [NAME OF SOCIETY OR BRANCH]

We have audited the financial statements on pages [] to [] in accordance with Auditing Standards.

In our opinion the financial statements give a true and fair view of the assets and current liabilities of the society [or branch] and the resultant balance of its funds at [date] and of its excess of [income over expenditure/expenditure over income] and source and application of funds for the [period] then ended and comply with the requirements of the Friendly Societies Act 1974.

[Name of firm]
Chartered Accountants,

[Address],

[Date of report].

Chapter 12

CORPORATE BUSINESSES

Chapter 12

CORPORATE BUSINESSES

Paragraph

CORPORATE BUSINESSES

Introduction

12.1 Part II of this book concerns corporate businesses as opposed to unincorporated businesses, which are covered in Part I. The hall mark of a corporate business is the creation of an entity that is in legal terms a person itself. An early case concerning a limited company, *Salomon v Salomon & Co. Ltd (1897) AC 22*, illustrates this legal personality.

12.2 Mr. Salomon owned a leather business. He converted this business into a limited company formed by himself, his wife and five of his children as subscribers (then the legal minimum number). He sold his business to the company at an overvaluation, partly for debentures, partly for paid-up shares, and partly for cash. A year later the company went into liquidation and its assets were sufficient to pay the debentures (which Mr. Salomon had used as security for a business loan). However, the assets were insufficient to pay the unsecured creditors. Initially, and in the Court of Appeal, the company was viewed as an alias for, and agent of, Mr. Salomon. The company was not recognised as a corporate legal entity separate from Mr Salomon.

12.3 The House of Lords, however, overruled the decision and held that Mr. Salomon was not liable to indemnify the company against unsecured creditors' claims. This was explained in the following terms by two of their Lordships:

> *"The company is at law a different person altogether from the subscribers to the memorandum; and, though it may be said that after incorporation the business is precisely the same as it was before, and the same persons are managers, and the same hands receive the profits, the company is not in law the agent of the subscribers or trustee for them."* (Lord Macnaghten)
>
> *"... once the company is legally incorporated it must be treated like any other independent person with its rights and liabilities appropriate to itself, and that the motives of those who took part in the promotion of the company are absolutely irrelevant in discussing what those rights and liabilities are. ... Either the limited company was a legal entity or it was not. If it was, the business belonged to it and not to Mr. Salomon. If it was not, there was no person and no thing to be an agent at all; and it is impossible to say at the same time that there is a company and there is not."* (Lord Halsbury L.C.)

12.4 This rule has subsequently been applied generally to corporate businesses. A number of exceptions to it have, however, arisen. In particular, corporate status may be disregarded in the following situations:

- Where the formal legal requirements to establish a particular corporate business have not been complied with.

- Where incorporation is a vehicle for fraud, the equitable principles applied by the courts will not permit the statutory provisions for incorporation to be used.

12.5 The attributes of a corporate business are, generally, the same as those of an ordinary person, considered in Part I of this book. These principally include the capacity to:

- Make contracts.
- Own property in its own name.
- Sue and be sued in its own name.
- Prosecute or be prosecuted in its own name.

12.6 However, along with this separate legal identity and the benefits it brings, comes a substantial amount of statutory and non-statutory obligations that vary with the type of vehicle used for the corporate business. The chapters that follow and the paragraphs below summarise these varying responsibilities for a number of corporate businesses.

Unregistered companies

12.7 There are various forms of company that exist without being registered with the Registrar of Companies. Corporate status can only be granted by the Crown or by Parliament and, because of this, until the mid-nineteenth century it was regarded as a privilege. Consequently, it is not possible for individuals to create a company merely by using contracts or by other means. The provisions of the *Companies Act 1985* that apply to unregistered companies are set out in annex 1 to chapter 19.

12.8 There are only three types of business undertaking that the courts will recognise as a corporate entity where this has not been granted by the Crown or by Parliament. These entities are as follows:

- Foreign corporations.

- Bodies incorporated by prescription.
- Corporations sole.

Foreign corporations

12.9 Where a foreign legal system recognises an entity as having legal personality, the courts in England and Wales will also award it legal personality for trading purposes in the UK. [*Lazard Brothers & Co. v Midland Bank Ltd. (1933) AC 289 HL*]. In addition, if a foreign corporation established a 'place of business' in England or Wales it will be treated as an 'oversea company' (see para 12.23).

Bodies incorporated by prescription

12.10 A body of persons may, in theory, claim that they have become incorporated by prescription. This means that the body must prove, on a balance of probabilities, that it has been treated as a corporation since 'time immemorial', which for legal purposes is taken to be the reign of King Richard I. The relevant date is, therefore, 1189.

12.11 Not surprisingly, such corporations are not met frequently in practice. Furthermore, the legal provisions that regulate such corporations are unclear. Such bodies do, however, satisfy the definition of 'body corporate' in section 740 of the *Companies Act 1985*, but they do not satisfy the definition of 'company' in section 735.

Corporations sole

12.12 The courts have taken the view that certain public and ecclesiastical offices are corporations, such as the Crown, or a bishop, or a parson of the Church of England. Such corporations only have one member. Accordingly, they are referred to as 'corporations sole'. This term is used in contrast to 'corporations aggregate' which refers to a corporation with more than one member. However, this latter term has fallen into disuse.

12.13 The reason for the courts regarding these entities as corporations is less obscure than for bodies incorporated by prescription. It was, for example, to protect the ecclesiastical property of a bishopric from being seized to pay the incumbent bishop's personal debts.

12.14 It is unlikely that any significant provisions of the *Companies Act 1985* apply to corporations sole. This is because, corporations sole neither satisfy the definition of 'body corporate' in section 740, nor of 'company' in section 735 of the *Companies Act 1985*.

Special statutory provisions and Royal Charter

12.15 Corporate entities that have been created by special statutory provisions are considered in chapter 20, and those created by Royal Charter in chapter 19. Consequently, these entities do not have to register with the Registrar of Companies to acquire corporate status.

Companies registered under the Companies Act 1985

12.16 There are three fundamentally different types of company that must be incorporated under the *Companies Act 1985* before they can begin to trade. The distinction between these different types of company depends upon how their members' liability for the company's debts is limited. The three types of company are as follows:

- Companies limited by shares.
- Companies limited by guarantee.
- Unlimited companies.

Companies limited by shares

12.17 A company limited by shares is the most common form of incorporated entity. Usually such a company will be incorporated initially as a private company, although it may be incorporated, or re-register, at a later date as a public company. The distinction between a private company and a public company is explained in detail in 'Manual of Accounting - volume I'. Also explained in 'Manual of Accounting - volumes I and II' are the detailed accounting and reporting requirements that companies limited by shares have to comply with. In summary, a public company can offer its shares for sale to the public. In addition, it must have a minimum issued share capital of £50,000, of which £12,500 has to be paid up. In contrast, a private company cannot offer its shares to the public, but can be incorporated without a minimum requirement as to issued share capital.

12.18 The distinction between small companies, medium-sized companies, dormant companies and other companies does not relate to the legal status of those companies, but merely relates to the burden of disclosure and audit to which they are subject. These categories of company are considered in some detail in 'Manual of Accounting - volume I'.

Companies limited by guarantee

12.19 The members of a company (private only) limited by guarantee undertake to contribute a specified sum to the company towards its debts and expenses in the event of it being wound up. This sum is the members 'guarantee' and represents a contingent asset that only arises when the company goes into liquidation. The member is thus under no obligation to pay the sum guaranteed while the company is a going concern. Companies limited by guarantee are considered in detail chapter 14.

Unlimited companies

12.20 The members of an unlimited company can be made liable without limit for the debts and obligations of the company. This liability will only arise in practice when the company is wound up. Although the creditors of an unlimited company can petition for it to be wound up if debts remain unpaid, only the liquidator can claim against the members of an unlimited company to contribute to the company's assets. An unlimited company, in general, is not required to file financial statements with the Registrar of Companies. Other matters relating to unlimited companies are considered further in chapter 13.

Banking and insurance companies

12.21 Banking and insurance companies are classes of limited company that are permitted to prepare financial statements in a specified way. The rules that apply to these types of company are considered in chapter 15 and chapter 16 respectively.

Investment companies

12.22 Investment companies are a special type of public company that invest their funds in securities for their members' benefit. An approved investment trust is a particular type of investment company which has satisfied the Inland Revenue that it complies with certain conditions. These companies are considered in chapter 17.

Oversea companies

12.23 As mentioned above, an oversea company is any company incorporated outside Great Britain that has established a 'place of business' in Great Britain. Such companies are obliged to fulfil certain obligations under the *Companies Act 1985*. These companies are considered in chapter 18.

Industrial and provident societies

12.24 An industrial and provident society is a society that has been registered and as a result incorporated under the *Industrial and Provident Societies Acts 1965*. Briefly there are two categories of society which are eligible for registration:

- *Bona fide* co-operative societies which do not carry on, or intend to carry on, business with the object of making profits to pay interest, dividends or bonuses on money invested with the society.
- Societies whose business is, or intended to be, conducted for the community's benefit.

Industrial and provident societies are considered in chapter 21.

Credit unions

12.25 Essentially a credit union is a special form of co-operative society, which takes deposits from members in order to lend money back to some of its members at low rates of interest. Since the enactment of the *Credit Unions Act 1979*, any society that wishes to use the name 'credit union' must register as an industrial and provident society, provided it fulfils the conditions laid down in the *Credit Unions Act 1979.* Credit unions are dealt with in chapter 22.

Building societies

12.26 Building societies are mutual associations incorporated by various statutes and are made up of people who pooled their savings together to enable them or others to buy land and build houses or to enable houses to be bought and sold readily. Building societies were governed by the *Building Societies Act 1962* and the *Building Societies Act 1986* extended the powers available to building societies and strengthened the regulatory regime of building societies. Chapter 23 deals with building societies.

Chapter 13

UNLIMITED COMPANIES

Chapter 13

UNLIMITED COMPANIES

Background and legal status

13.1 An unlimited company is a corporate body, whose members' liability is not limited to the value of any shares held. It is the oldest form of company that can be formed by registration (as opposed to, for example, being formed by Royal Charter (see chapter 19)).

13.2 To understand the nature of unlimited companies it is useful to consider their historical origin. In the mid-nineteenth century to further commercial trading there was a need to create a business vehicle that would have corporate status and limit the liability of its members. At that time, however, large unincorporated associations (see chapter 9) were being established for this purpose with cumbersome constitutions. These unincorporated associations attempted to contract with third parties on the basis of limiting their members' liability and also had transferable ownership rules. The *Joint Stock Companies Act 1844* was enacted to curb the practices of these large unincorporated associations and enabled the creation and registration of joint stock companies. Joint stock company members were expressly made liable for the company's debts as if they were partners. Thus, the unlimited company was born.

13.3 The unlimited company proved to be of doubtful value and attempts to give it limited liability failed (see, for example, *Greenwood's case (1854) 3 De G.M. & G. 459*). Accordingly, the *Limited Liability Act 1855* was enacted, which enabled a company to limit its members' liability to the nominal amount of the shares they held. However, these companies were subject to additional conditions, including the disclosure of their limited liability status.

13.4 Following this legislation, the unlimited liability company became less useful for commercial trading purposes. It has, however, been retained in companies' legislation.

13.5 Unlimited companies can still, therefore, be incorporated under the *Companies Act 1985*. The DTI has recently indicated that 3,700 such companies are registered. Although they are less useful for most commercial undertakings, there are circumstances where they can be advantageous, as for example, in the following situations:

- An unlimited company may sometimes be used in preference to a small limited company. This is because with small limited companies the protection of limited liability is frequently lost, as directors, who are also the company's shareholders, often have to personally guarantee the company's debts.

- An unlimited company's financial affairs can be kept secret, as there is no requirement, in general, for such companies to file financial statements with the Registrar of Companies. This can be particularly useful where the primary activity of the company is the provision of a service. For example, financial institutions use unlimited companies expressly to avoid their financial statements being made available to competitors.

- Unlimited companies are not subject to capital duty on the allotment of their shares. Accordingly, they are useful for conducting investment activities within a group of otherwise limited liability companies.

13.6 Although an unlimited company's members can be made liable without limit for the debts and obligations of the company, this liability will only arise in practice when the company is being wound up. Whilst an unlimited company is a going concern, its members can only be called upon to contribute further any amounts unpaid on their shares. In addition, the creditors of an unlimited company have the ability to petition for its winding up only where their debts remain unpaid. Furthermore, only the liquidator, during winding up proceedings, can claim against an unlimited company's members to contribute to the company's assets in excess of their share capital.

Proposed EC legislation

13.7 The EC has proposed a directive to amend the fourth and seventh Company Law directives in order that they should apply to, *inter alia*, unlimited companies whose members are limited companies. However, this will not require any change in UK law, because the range of companies covered by existing UK legislation is more extensive than those covered by the proposals. The present UK law extends to unlimited companies where more than half of their members are limited companies. In contrast, the EC proposals extend to unlimited companies that have only limited companies as their members.

Formation

13.8 The procedure for forming an unlimited company is very similar to the procedure for forming a limited company. In practice, it is often simpler to create an unlimited company by purchasing an off-the-shelf limited company and re-registering it as an unlimited company. However, if an unlimited company is formed in this way it cannot then re-register as a limited company.

13.9 The principal differences in forming an unlimited company as opposed to a limited company are as follows:

- The company may or may not have a share capital. Even where it does, the Memorandum of Association is not required to state the amount of the share capital and the division of the share capital into shares of a fixed amount.
- The company's name should not end with 'limited'.
- The company must register its Articles of Association. These must state the amount of the company's share capital with which the company proposes to be registered if it has a share capital. [CA 1985 Secs 7(1), (2)].
- The Articles of Association must be in accordance with Table E. [CA 1985 Sec 8(4)].

Application of company law

13.10 The provisions of the *Companies Act 1985* apply to unlimited companies in the same way as they apply to other companies, unless that Act states otherwise (see generally 'Manual of Accounting - volumes I and II').

13.11 One difference between a limited company and an unlimited company concerns the reduction of the company's share capital. Provided that an unlimited company is permitted to do so by its Articles of Association, it can reduce its share capital without obtaining a court order. This is not possible with a limited company. This can have certain advantages where, for example, an unlimited company wishes to write goodwill off against its capital, as there is no necessity for it to go to the court to sanction the reduction in capital (see 'Manual of accounting - volume II' chapter 8).

13.12 Furthermore, there are no restrictions on an unlimited company purchasing its own shares. Accordingly, it may be advantageous, in some situations, to convert a company into an unlimited company if that company is otherwise unable to meet the requirements of Chapter VII of Part V of the *Companies Act 1985* (which relate to the restrictions placed on companies wishing to purchase their own shares).

Constitution

13.13 An unlimited company's constitution is found in its Memorandum and Articles of Association. Such an undertaking's Memorandum and Articles are very similar in content to the provisions of Table A, the table used for limited companies, and the standard provisions for unlimited companies can be found in Table E.

Share capital

13.14 An unlimited company must have a share capital (see para 13.9). Generally, the same considerations apply to the share capital of an unlimited company as apply to a private company limited by shares. However, an unlimited company has considerable flexibility in reducing or purchasing its share capital as mentioned above.

13.15 Chapter VII of Part V of the *Companies Act 1985* does not give any express statutory power to an unlimited company to issue redeemable shares. However, as an unlimited company is able to purchase any of its shares, there seems to be no legal bar to it issuing share capital that will, or may, be redeemed at some future date.

Accounting and audit requirements

13.16 The accounting and audit requirements for unlimited companies are the same as those applicable to companies generally. However, the directors of an unlimited company are not required to file a copy of the company's financial statements with the Registrar of Companies, if the company was not, at any time during the relevant accounting period, any one of the following:

- A subsidiary of a limited company (wherever incorporated).
- A parent company of a limited company (wherever incorporated).
- Subject to rights exercisable by or on behalf of two or more limited undertakings (wherever incorporated) which if exercised by one of them would have made the company a subsidiary undertaking of it.
- A company carrying on a business as the promoter of a trading stamp scheme (under the *Trading Stamp Act 1964*).

[CA 1985 Sec 241(1)(2)(3)].

13.17 Unlimited companies are still, however, required to prepare financial statements to be issued to their members. Furthermore, the duties in respect of preparing those financial statements and in respect of their audit are the same as for other limited companies. These requirements are covered in detail in 'Manual of Accounting - volumes I and II'.

Audit report

13.18 The audit report for an unlimited company is the same as that used generally for limited companies.

SECTIONS OF THE COMPANIES ACT 1985 THAT APPLY SPECIFICALLY TO UNLIMITED COMPANIES

Section	Description
1	Mode of forming incorporated company
2	Requirements with respect to memorandum
3	Forms of memorandum
7	Articles prescribing regulations for companies
8	Tables A, C, D and E
48	Modification for unlimited company re-registering
49	Re-registration of limited company as unlimited
51	Re-registration of unlimited company as limited
124	Reserve capital of unlimited company
254	Exemption from requirement to deliver accounts and reports
369	Length of notice for calling meetings
675	Companies formed and registered under former Companies Acts
677	Companies re-registered with altered status under former Companies Acts
678	Companies registered with Joint Stock Companies Acts
680	Companies capable of being registered under this Chapter
744A	Index of defined expressions
Sch 21	Effect of registration under section 680

Chapter 14

COMPANIES LIMITED BY GUARANTEE

Annex

COMPANIES LIMITED BY GUARANTEE

Background

14.1 The members of a private company limited by guarantee are not necessarily liable to the extent of any share capital that they provide. However, they do undertake to contribute a specified sum to the company towards its debts and expenses in the event of it being wound up. This specified sum is the member's 'guarantee' and in practice is usually expressed to be one pound.

14.2 Many companies limited by guarantee are formed for non-trading purposes, such as charitable activities or social events. Where certain conditions are complied with, companies limited by guarantee need not include 'limited' after their name (see para 14.10). They are, consequently, used to establish schools, trade associations and clubs.

Application of company law

14.3 The provisions of the *Companies Act 1985* apply to guarantee companies in the same way as they apply to other companies, unless that Act expressly provides otherwise. However, clearly the provisions of the *Companies Act 1985* that relate to a company's share capital will not normally apply to companies limited by guarantee.

Formation

14.4 The procedure for forming a guarantee company is similar to that for incorporating a private company limited by shares. There are, however, the following differences:

- The Memorandum of Association must state that each member undertakes to contribute a specified sum to the assets of the company if it should be wound up while he is a member, or within one year after he ceases to be a member (for payment of the debts and liabilities of the company contracted before he ceases to be a member). This amount would include any costs, charges and expenses of winding up. [CA 1985 Sec 2(4)].

- The Memorandum of Association must state that the company's liability is limited. [CA 1985 Sec 2(3)]. However, a guarantee company will usually be founded for a purpose that will entitle it to exemption from this requirement (see para 14.10).

- The company must register its Articles of Association. [CA 1985 Sec 7(1)].

- The Memorandum and Articles of Association must be in accordance with Table C or Table D. [CA 1985 Sec 8(4)].

Constitution

14.5 The constitution of a company limited by guarantee will be found in its Memorandum and Articles of Association. These are very similar to the Memorandum and Articles of Association that apply to normal limited companies set out in Table A. For a private company limited by guarantee its Memorandum and Articles of Association are detailed in Table C. In addition, the Memorandum and Articles of Association of a public company limited by guarantee is given in Table D (see para 14.7).

Share capital and guarantees

14.6 With a normal limited company, its members are limited to the extent of their shareholding. The members of a company limited by guarantee, however, act as the company's guarantors.

14.7 Prior to 22nd December 1980 a company limited by guarantee could be formed with both a share capital and guarantees, in which case its Memorandum and Articles of Association had to be in accordance with those now contained in Table D. The sole advantage of being registered with a share capital and guarantees is that such companies can be re-registered as a public company limited by guarantee. However, it is hard to envisage circumstances where such a company would be useful. In particular, there is a real disadvantage in that a member of such a company may incur a dual liability in respect of both his guarantee and his share capital.

14.8 The liability of the members for a company limited by guarantee is limited to the value at which the guarantee is stated and represents only a contingent asset that may arise if the company goes into liquidation. Consequently, there is no obligation on a member to pay the sum guaranteed while the company is a going concern. The value of the guarantee cannot be regarded as the company's asset until a call is made and that will arise only on liquidation. In addition, the guaranteed amount cannot be increased or reduced in the same way as a normal company's share capital (for example, by a reduction of capital).

Distributions

14.9 The legal provisions relating to distributions by a guarantee company are the same as those that apply to companies generally. These provisions are considered in detail in 'Manual of Accounting - volume I' chapter 19.

14.10 It is common for a company limited by guarantee to seek exemption from the requirement to include 'limited' after its name. Such a company can only use this exemption if the company's objects are for the promotion of commerce, art, science, education, religion, charity or any profession. [CA 1985 Sec 30(3)(a)]. In addition the Memorandum or Articles of Association must provide for the following:

- The company's profits or other income must be applied in promoting its objects.
- The payment of dividends to its members must be prohibited.
- On the company's winding up, the assets usually available to its members should be transferred either to a body with similar objects or to a charity.

[CA 1985 Sec 30(3)(b)].

14.11 A statutory declaration that the company has complied with the requirements of section 30(3) of the *Companies Act 1985* has to be made to the Registrar of Companies, before the word 'limited' can be dropped.

Accounting and audit requirements

14.12 The accounting and audit requirements that apply to companies limited by guarantee are the same as those that apply to companies generally. These requirements are dealt with in detail in 'Manual of Accounting - volume II'.

14.13 A question that is occasionally asked is whether or not a company limited by guarantee can be a subsidiary of another company. For example, a university may establish a company limited by guarantee for a particular purpose. The university might be one guarantor and the other guarantor might be the university's Vice-Chancellor. In this situation, is the company limited by guarantee a subsidiary of the university?

14.14 A person becomes a member of a guarantee company where he agrees to do so and his name is entered into the company's register of members. Consequently in this example, both the university and the Vice Chancellor are members of the company limited by guarantee.

14.15 A company is a subsidiary of another company if that company either holds a majority of the voting rights or is a member of it and has the right to appoint or remove a majority of the board of directors, or is a member of it and controls alone, pursuant to an agreement with other members, a majority of the voting rights. [CA 1985 Sec 736(1)].

14.16 In the example above, the university would most likely have the right to appoint or remove a majority of the board of directors. In that situation, the guarantee company will be a subsidiary of the university.

Audit report

14.17 The audit report for a company limited by guarantee will not differ from the audit reports that apply to normal limited companies generally.

SECTIONS OF THE COMPANIES ACT THAT APPLY SPECIFICALLY TO COMPANIES LIMITED BY GUARANTEE

Sections	Descriptions
1	Mode of forming incorporated company
2	Requirements with respect to memorandum
3	Forms of memorandum
8	Tables A, C, D and E
15	Memorandum and articles of company limited by guarantee
30	Exemption from requirement of 'limited' as part of the name
81	Restriction on public offers by private company
88	Return as the allotments etc.
121	Alteration of share capital (limited companies)
135	Special resolution for reduction of share capital
675	Companies formed and registered under former Companies Acts
680	Companies capable of being registered under this Chapter
681	Procedural requirements for registration
686	Other requirements for registration
Sch 21	Effect of registration under section 680

Chapter 15

BANKING COMPANIES

Annexes

BANKING COMPANIES

Introduction

15.1 The banking industry constitutes one of the most important sectors of any market economy. Its roles of credit intermediation and money transmission make it essential to the smooth functioning of such an economy. Maintaining confidence in its solvency and liquidity is, therefore, a primary concern of government and its banking supervisors. The UK is no exception.

15.2 The UK banking community is made up of a variety of institutions engaged in a wide range of financial activities and offering prospective customers every kind of banking service and facility. These institutions comprise, amongst others, clearing banks, merchant banks, discount houses, authorised deposit-takers and consortium and overseas banks. In addition, the National Savings Bank also provides banking services.

15.3 Many of the institutions that grant credit or provide banking services are also deposit-takers. However, in order to carry on a deposit-taking business the institution must be authorised by the Bank of England under the *Banking Act 1987*. The title 'bank' is reserved under that Act for those previously allowed to use it and those banking businesses with more than £5m of paid up capital and reserves. Overseas institutions can use the name under which they carry on their business in their country of origin. The term 'banking company' is referred to in the *Companies Act 1985* as a company which is authorised under the *Banking Act 1987*. [CA 1985 Sec 744]. Throughout this chapter, the term 'bank' is used to refer to any authorised institution unless the context clearly implies otherwise and the term 'The Bank' is used to refer to the Bank of England.

Legislation and regulation

The Banking Act 1987

15.4 The principal legislation relating to the regulation of banks in the UK is the *Banking Act 1987*. This Act came into force in October 1987 and strengthened the previous system of banking supervision under the *Banking Act 1979* following the collapse of the secondary market in the 1970s. The Act covers:

- The responsibilities of The Bank.

- Restrictions on the acceptance of deposits except by authorised institutions.

- The criteria for authorisation (see para 15.5).

- The powers of The Bank to restrict, revoke or refuse to grant authorisation and to give directions to institutions so affected.

- Its powers to object to controllers of banks and to changes in control. A controller means a managing director, a chief executive or a partner or a person in accordance with whose instructions the directors are accustomed to act or who exercises, or controls the exercise of, 15 per cent or more of the voting power.

- The establishment of a Board of Banking Supervision to advise The Bank (see para 15.7) .

- Its powers to require routine and *ad hoc* information and, where necessary, an accountant's report on that information from authorised institutions and related entities and persons (see para 15.137). The information is extended to cover the holding companies, subsidiaries, directors, controllers and significant shareholders of authorised institutions as well as the institutions themselves.

- The Bank's powers of investigation.

- The regulation of advertisements and other invitations to make deposits.

- The notification to The Bank when auditors are changed, resign, fail to seek reappointment or qualify the financial statements. In addition, the auditors themselves have to notify The Bank if they decide to resign or not to seek reappointment or to qualify the institution's financial statements (see para 15.136).

- The release of auditors from their duty of confidentiality where it is necessary to communicate information to The Bank relevant to the latter's functions (see para 15.141).

- The further development of the Deposit Protection Scheme set up by the *Banking Act 1979*.

- The restriction of the use of the name 'bank' to authorised institutions with a share capital of not less than £5m.

- The powers of the Treasury to object to controllers from overseas countries not offering reciprocal facilities.

- The creation of a criminal offence of knowingly or recklessly providing false or misleading information to a supervisor or of failing to provide relevant information.

Authorisation

15.5 In order to carry on a deposit-taking business, an institution must be authorised by The Bank under the *Banking Act 1987*, unless it is exempt or the deposit is an exempted transaction. [BA 1987 Secs 3, 4]. Institutions must submit with their applications for authorisation a business plan together with any other information or documents that The Bank may require. [BA 1987 Sec 8(2)]. The Bank may also require a report by an accountant or other qualified person on any aspect of the information provided. [BA 1987 Sec 8(5)].

15.6 The Bank may then grant or refuse the application once it has satisfied itself that the criteria in Schedule 3 to the *Banking Act 1987* are fulfilled. [BA 1987 Sec 9(2)]. These criteria can be summarised as follows:

- The directors, controllers and managers must be fit and proper persons.

- At least two individuals must effectively direct the business.

- The board of a UK incorporated institution must include as many non-executive directors as The Bank deems appropriate.

- The institution must conduct its business in a prudent manner. It will not be regarded as doing so unless it:

  - □ Maintains net assets (paid up capital and reserves), commensurate not only with the nature and scale of its operations, but also with the risks inherent in them. Maintaining commensurate net assets is currently taken by The Bank to mean meeting the risk asset ratio that it agrees with each institution. The risk asset ratio represents the ratio of a bank's capital to its weighted risk assets, with weights primarily reflecting credit risks. The method by which this ratio is to be calculated is defined in the own funds and solvency directives and its implementation in the UK described in The Bank's Notices 'Implementation in the United Kingdom of the directive on own funds of credit institutions' (BSD 1990/2) and 'Implementation in the United Kingdom of the solvency ratio directive' (BSD 1990/3).

  - □ Maintains adequate liquidity in the form of liquid and maturing assets to meet its actual and contingent liabilities as they fall due. Maintaining adequate liquidity is currently taken by The Bank to mean taking the three measures set out in its 1982 paper on 'The measurement of other liquidity' viz. holding sufficient immediately available cash or other liquid assets, ensuring an appropriately matching future profile of cash flows from maturing assets and liabilities, and maintaining an adequately diversified deposit base.

- ☐ Makes adequate provision for diminution in the value of its assets (including provision for bad and doubtful debts), for actual and contingent liabilities and for its actual and potential losses.
- ☐ Maintains adequate accounting and other records and systems of internal control (see para 15.15).
- ☐ Carries on its business with the integrity and professional skills appropriate to the nature and scale of its activities.
- ☐ Has at the time of its authorisation net assets of not less than £1m.

[BA 1987 Secs 8-18].

Supervision

15.7 The principal supervisory authority of banks operating in the UK is The Bank. The main purpose of banking supervision is to protect depositors and potential depositors of banks by ensuring that banks are financially sound. This is usually referred to as 'prudential' supervision.

15.8 To assist The Bank in the exercise of its functions, a Board of Banking Supervision was established by the *Banking Act 1987*. The Board consists of three *ex-officio* members, namely the Governor of The Bank, the Deputy Governor and the Director in charge of banking supervision, and six independent members appointed by the Governor and the Chancellor of the Exchequer. The function of the independent members is to receive reports from the Banking Supervision Division and to give advice on the exercise of The Bank's functions under the Act to the *ex-officio* members. If the latter do not take this advice, they must notify the Chancellor in writing. The Board is required to produce an annual report on its activities for inclusion in The Bank's own annual report.

15.9 In practice, The Bank rarely makes use of its extensive powers and its approach to supervision is reasonably flexible. The Bank requires institutions to submit a large volume of statistical reports, which form the basis of regular detailed discussions with the institutions' senior management.

The Financial Services Act 1986

15.10 In addition to their responsibilities under the *Banking Act 1987*, banks that provide financial advice, for example, in connection with takeovers and mergers, and investment management services and facilities are also subject to regulations under the *Financial Services Act 1986*, which was enacted for the purpose of controlling the conduct of investment business. Banks that are so involved require prior authorisation and are subject to regulation by the SIB or particular SROs in respect of such business.

EC directives

15.11 The EC has power to legislate or influence legislation that affects the business of banks. The first banking co-ordination directive dealing with a common system of bank authorisation throughout the EC was implemented in the UK by the *Banking Act 1979*. There are also a number of other EC directives, both proposed and adopted, which when enacted into UK law will affect banks. Chief amongst these are:

- The second banking co-ordination directive, which allows banks established in one member state to branch into, or provide services in, other member states.
- The own funds and solvency directives, which together define a method for calculating bank solvency and set out a minimum solvency ratio. (Both definition and ratio are essentially the same as those laid down by the Basle Committee and already adopted by The Bank.)
- The bank accounts directive, which sets out strict rules (along the lines of the company accounts directive) for the accounting treatment, valuation and disclosure of banking assets, liabilities and transactions (see para 15.22).

Most of the provisions of these directives are being or will be introduced by means of regulations or statutory instruments.

The Companies Act 1985

15.12 The basic legal regulation dealing with banks' financial statements, as for other companies, is contained in the *Companies Act 1985*. However, the accounting and disclosure rules that are contained in Schedule 4 to the *Companies Act 1985* apply to companies generally and do not reflect the special nature of a banking business. Therefore, banks are afforded special treatment under that Act. The special accounting and disclosure provisions that apply to the financial statements of banks are included in Schedule 9 to the *Companies Act 1985* and these provisions are discussed further in this chapter.

15.13 However, Schedule 9 to the *Companies Act 1985* also provides certain banks with significant disclosure exemptions, which are not available to other banks (for example, clearing banks). Many of the banks with these exemptions are discount houses, older merchant banks and branches of overseas bank that file financial statements under chapter II, Part XXIII of the *Companies Act 1985* (delivery of accounts and reports by oversea companies) and these banks are referred to in this chapter as 'exempt' banks. The disclosure provisions that apply to exempt banks are very wide in their application, and most exempt banks will be able to restrict the information that they are required to disclose under paragraphs 2 to 18 of Schedule 9. These exemptions are considered in paragraphs 15.107 to 15.109 below.

15.14 It should be noted, however, that the Schedule 9 rules that apply to banks generally and that are discussed in this chapter are intended to be temporary. As mentioned in paragraph 15.11 above, the EC has issued a directive on the annual accounts and consolidated accounts of banks and other financial institutions (86/635/EEC) which will shortly be incorporated into UK law (see further para 15.22). The new rules will supersede the rules currently set out in the *Companies Act 1985* that relate specifically to banks and effectively bring them into line, in a manner appropriate to banks, with those applicable to the generality of companies governed by that Act. In particular, the distinction between exempt banks and other banks will disappear.

Accounting and other records and internal control systems

15.15 In common with all companies incorporated under the *Companies Act 1985*, banks are subject to the requirements of section 221 of that Act, which requires that proper accounting records must be kept in sufficient detail so as to disclose with reasonable accuracy the financial position of the bank at any one point in time. Furthermore, the *Banking Act 1987* explicitly places a wider requirement on banks to maintain accounting and other records, and internal control systems, *"such as to enable the business of the institution to be prudently managed and the institution to comply with the duties imposed on it by or under this Act"*. [BA 1987 3 Sch 4(7)(8)].

15.16 It is the responsibility of a bank's directors and management to ensure that adequate records and systems are maintained. As supervisor, The Bank is concerned with obtaining evidence to enable it to form a view as to whether the requirements of the *Banking Act 1987* on accounting and other records and internal control systems are met. It does this *inter-alia* by considering any evidence provided by the reporting accountant (see further para 15.138).

Financial statements

General rules

15.17 As stated in paragraph 15.12 above, the *Companies Act 1985* currently permits banks to prepare their financial statements in accordance with the requirements of section 255 of, and Part I of Schedule 9 to that Act. In addition, the parent company of a banking group may prepare consolidated financial statements under section 255A of, and Schedule 4A as modified by Part II of Schedule 9 to the *Companies Act 1985*. This means that banking companies and groups have two choices as to the way in which they prepare their financial statements. They can decide to adopt the standard rules that apply to the majority of companies and groups set out respectively in sections 226 and 227, and Schedules 4 and 4A to the *Companies Act 1985*. Alternatively, they can prepare the financial statements in accordance with the rules specifically provided for banks in accordance with Schedule 9 to that Act.

15.18 A banking group is referred to in the *Companies Act 1985* as a group where the parent company is a bank or where at least one of the undertakings in the group is an authorised institution under the *Banking Act 1987* and the predominant activities of the group are such as to make it inappropriate to prepare consolidated financial statements in accordance with the formats in Part I of Schedule 4 to the *Companies Act 1985*. [CA 1985 Sec 255A(3)].

15.19 Where banking companies or groups prepare their financial statements in accordance with Schedule 9, those financial statements must contain a statement that they are prepared in accordance with the special provisions of Part VII of the Companies Act 1985 applicable to banking companies or groups. [CA 1985 Secs 255(2), 255A(2)].

15.20 Furthermore, both exempt and non-exempt banks must comply with provisions contained elsewhere in the *Companies Act 1985*. For example, Schedule 5 to the *Companies Act 1985* (additional disclosure: related undertakings) and Schedule 6 to that Act (disclosure: emoluments and other benefits of directors and others) apply to banks, subject to certain exemptions contained in Part III and Part IV respectively of Schedule 9 to that Act. These requirements are considered in paragraphs 15.87 to 15.91 and 15.127 respectively.

15.21 The Secretary of State may also modify any of the disclosure requirements that apply to banks and banking groups in order to adapt them to a particular bank's circumstances. This modification may be made either on the application of the bank's directors or with their consent. However, the Secretary of State cannot waive the overriding requirement of the *Companies Act 1985* that the financial statements must give a true and fair view. [CA 1985 Secs 255(4), 255A(6)].

EC directive on bank accounts

15.22 As stated in paragraph 15.11 above, the EC has issued a directive on the annual accounts and consolidated accounts of banks and other financial institutions. The directive adapts the provisions of the 4th and 7th Company Law Directives that apply to the financial statements of most companies to financial statements prepared by banks. The directive, which is reproduced as annex 3 to this chapter, deals specifically with the following matters:

- Comprehensive balance sheet and profit and loss account formats.
- Definition of items to be included under each statement heading.
- Additional disclosures to be made by way of notes to the financial statements.
- Special valuation rules for certain balance sheet and profit and loss account items.
- Requirements to prepare consolidated financial statements.
- Publication and auditing requirements.

15.23 The directive will be implemented into UK law and draft regulations have been prepared by the DTI. The Regulations to be known as the *Companies Act 1985 (Bank Accounts) Regulations* are expected to be issued as a statutory instrument during 1991. Banks will be required to comply with their provisions for accounting periods beginning on or after 1st January 1993.

Accounting policies and standards

15.24 Banks are required to adopt accounting policies that are applied consistently within the same financial statements and from one financial year to the next. [CA 1985 9 Sch Part I 18A(1)]. In addition, SSAP 2 requires any significant accounting policies a company has adopted in preparing its financial statements to be stated in the notes to the financial statements. Table 15.1 illustrates the accounting policies adopted by a major bank.

Table 15.1: Illustration of accounting policies adopted by a banking company

Extract from Midland Bank PLC Annual Report & Accounts 31st December 1989.

ACCOUNTING POLICIES (extract)

Accounting policies adopted by the Group are set out below and are consistent with those adopted in 1988 with the exception of the introduction of the policy on embedded value, the impact of which is not material.

(a) Accounting convention

The Accounts are prepared in accordance with the requirements of the UK Statements of Standard Accounting Practice under the historical cost convention modified by the revaluation of freehold and long leasehold properties and dealing assets.

(b) Basis of consolidation

The Group accounts are prepared in accordance with sections 258 and 259 of, and Schedule 9 to, the Companies Act 1985 and deal with the state of affairs and profits and losses of Midland Bank plc and all its subsidiaries and the attributable share of profits and reserves of its associated companies.

(c) Bad and doubtful debts

Specific and general provisions for bad and doubtful debts are based on the year-end appraisal of advances. The specific element relates to individual banking relationships; the general element relates to other positions not separately identified but known from experience to exist in any portfolio of banking relationships.

Interest on bad and doubtful loans continues to be charged to the customer's account and credited to interest income where insolvency law permits, although in most instances a corresponding specific provision is made. When it becomes apparent that recovery is unlikely, interest ceases to be accrued and the outstanding debt is written off.

(d) Instalment finance

Income from fixed rate instalment finance business, after making a deduction for certain initial expenses, is credited to profit and loss account in proportion to the reducing balance outstanding. These balances are stated in the balance sheet after deduction of unearned charges and interest.

(e) Equipment leased to customers

Income from leasing contracts, other than those with major recourse or similar agreements, is credited to profit and loss account in proportion to the funds invested. The great majority of such leases related to finance lease since substantially all the risks and rewards attaching to the assets leased are transferred to the lessee.

Where leasing contracts are covered by major recourse or other similar agreements, income is released to maintain the book amount of the asset at a value consistent with the contractual arrangements.

(f) Depreciation of premises and equipment

The directors consider that, except for certain specialised properties, residual values of freehold and long leasehold buildings (50 years and over unexpired) are such that a nil rate of depreciation should be currently applied. Specialised properties are depreciated on an individual basis having regard to their anticipated useful lives. Other leasehold land and buildings are written off on the straight-line basis over ten years, or the period of the lease whichever is the shorter. Obsolescence of buildings is charged to profit as it arises. Furniture, fittings and equipment are depreciated on the straight-line basis over their estimated useful lives at rates ranging from 5% to 50% per annum.

(g) Dealing assets

Where assets are acquired with the intention of reselling them in the short term at a profit, they are stated in the balance sheet as market value. Income from dealing assets arises in two ways, interest income and dealing income, and is analysed between 'interest receivable' and 'other operating income'.

(h) Fixed interest investments Where fixed interest investments with fixed redemption dates have been purchased for the long term at a premium or discount, these premiums and discounts are amortised through the profit and loss account over the period from date of purchase to date of maturity. If the date of maturity is at the borrower's option within a specified range of years, the maturity date which gives the more conservative result is adopted. These investments are included in the balance sheet at amortised cost. Profits and losses on the realisation of these investments are

Table 15.1 continued

dealt with in the profit and loss account as they arise.

(j) Retirement benefits

Annual contributions are made to UK pension schemes on the advice of actuaries for funding of retirement benefits in order to build up reserves for each full-time employee during the employee's working life to pay to the employee or dependant a pension after retirement. The costs of providing these benefits are charged to the profit and loss account on a regular basis. Overseas subsidiaries make provisions for pensions in accordance with local law and practice.

(k) Deferred taxation

Deferred taxation is calculated, using the liability method, on all timing differences to the extent that they are likely to crystallise in the future.

(l) Currency translation

Assets and liabilities of UK resident companies maintained in foreign currencies, including investments in associated companies and trade investments financed by loans in foreign currencies and commitments for future purchases or sales, are translated into sterling at the exchange rates ruling at the balance sheet dates of those companies and any difference is taken to profit and loss account.

On consolidation, the accounts of overseas subsidiaries and associated companies are translated into sterling at the exchange rates ruling at their balance sheet dates and the consequential adjustments to the opening balances are dealt with through reserves.

(m) Premium on acquisition of shares in associated and subsidiary companies

Premiums on acquisition of shares in associated and subsidiary companies are written off to reserves in the year of acquisition.

(n) Investments in associated and subsidiary companies

Midland Bank plc's investments in associated and subsidiary companies are stated at its share of their net tangible assets.

15.25 Where the figures concerned are material, Schedule 9 to the *Companies Act 1985* specifically requires the accounting policies for the following three areas to be explained:

- The method used to arrive at the amount of fixed assets under each heading.
- Stocks and work in progress.
- The translation of foreign currency amounts into sterling.

[CA 1985 9 Sch Part I 4(3), 13(15)(16)].

15.26 In addition, the notes to the financial statements should disclose the basis used to compute the UK corporation tax liability. [CA 1985 9 Sch Part I 13(17)].

15.27 The obligation to give a true and fair view means that a bank should follow applicable Accounting Standards unless there are good reasons not to do so. The *Companies Act 1989* introduced for the first time the requirement for banking companies to state whether the financial statements have been prepared in accordance with Accounting Standards that are applicable to them. If there are material departures from these standards, the particulars and the reasons for the departure must be given in a note to the financial statements. [CA 1985 9 Sch Part I 18B].

15.28 There is no accounting standard in the UK that deals specifically with the financial accounting and reporting requirements of banks. The absence of specific accounting standards has hindered convergence of accounting practices amongst UK banks. In order to narrow the areas of difference and variety in the accounting treatments of matters relevant to the business of banks, the British Bankers' Association (BBA) has issued a SORP on accounting for securities (see para 15.60). This SORP was franked by the ASC and is the first in what is planned to be a series of SORPs for the banking industry. An exposure draft of a second SORP on commitments and contingencies (see para 15.68) has also been issued and is to be followed by a third SORP on advances and a fourth SORP on segmental reporting. These SORPs are intended to be authoritative and persuasive, but not mandatory.

IAS 30

15.29 The IASC published IAS 30, 'Disclosures in the Financial Statements of Banks and Similar Financial Institutions', in August 1990. The statement applies to the separate financial statements and the consolidated financial statements of a bank, and is effective for accounting periods beginning on or after 1st January 1991. Whilst IASs are not required to be adopted by UK companies until incorporated into SSAPs, they are indicative of best practice to the extent they do not conflict with SSAPs or company law.

15.30 The statement deals only with matters of presentation and does not cover issues of measurement or valuation. The statement does not conflict with the EC directive on bank accounts although, in some areas, it requires disclosure of greater detail than the EC directive. The main implications for UK banks are as follows:

- The aggregate amount, and the basis of valuation, of loans on which interest is not being accrued should be disclosed.
- Assets and liabilities should be analysed into relevant maturity groupings, based on the remaining period from the balance sheet date to the contractual maturity date.
- Significant concentrations of assets, liabilities and off balance sheet risks should be disclosed according to the geographical areas, customer or industry groups or other concentrations of risk.
- The amounts of significant net foreign currency exposures should be disclosed.

Corresponding amounts

15.31 Corresponding amounts for the year immediately preceding the year in question must be shown in respect of every item in a bank's balance sheet or profit and loss account or in the notes to the financial statements. Where the amount for the previous year is not comparable with the amount shown in respect of the current year, the previous year's amount must be adjusted. Where this has been done, particulars of the adjustment and the reasons for it must be disclosed in the notes to the financial statements. [CA 1985 9 Sch Part I 18C(1)(2)].

15.32 However, corresponding amounts do not need to be given for:

- The amount of additions and disposals of fixed assets (see para 15.49).
- The movements on reserves and provisions (see para 15.82).
- Information required under paragraph 13 of Schedule 4A to the *Companies Act 1985* (information with respect to acquisitions taking place in the financial year).
- The information that must be disclosed in respect of the classes and proportion of the nominal value of shareholdings in other undertakings.
- The information that must be disclosed in respect of loans and other dealings in favour of directors and others under Parts II and III of Schedule 6 to the *Companies Act 1985*.

[CA 1985 9 Sch Part I 18C(3)].

True and fair view

15.33 Banks are bound by the overriding requirement that the balance sheet and the profit and loss account must give a true and fair view of the bank's state of affairs and profit or loss for the financial period (see also para 15.37). [CA 1985 Sec 226(2)].

15.34 In addition, where compliance with the disclosure provisions of the Act (including Part I of Schedule 9) would not be sufficient to give a true and fair view, then a bank should disclose the additional information required for this purpose in the notes to the financial statements. This additional information needs to be in sufficient detail to ensure that its disclosure enables the financial statements to give a true and fair view. [CA 1985 Secs 226(4), 255(3)].

15.35 Furthermore, if in 'special circumstances' compliance with any of the Act's provisions (including Part I of Schedule 9) would be inconsistent with the requirement to give a true and fair view, the directors of a bank must depart from that provision to the extent necessary to give a true and fair view. Where such a departure is necessary, the particulars of the departure, the reasons for it and its effect should be given in a note to the financial statements. [CA 1985 Secs 226(5), 255(3)].

15.36 Similar provisions to those discussed above apply to banking groups that prepare consolidated financial statements in accordance with Schedule 4A as modified by Part II of Schedule 9. [CA 1985 Secs 227(3)(5)(6), 255A(5)].

15.37 As stated in paragraph 15.13 above, certain banks are exempt from many of the disclosure requirements of Schedule 9 to the *Companies Act 1985*. Consequently, where these exemptions are adopted in the preparation of the financial statements, these financial statements will not be deemed to breach the requirement to give a true and fair view even though they do not give certain of the information that paragraphs 2 to 18 of Schedule 9 requires. [CA 1985 9 Sch Part I 27(4), Part II 5(2)]. However, the auditors will modify their opinion (see para 15.135).

The balance sheet

General rules

15.38 Schedule 9 to the *Companies Act 1985* does not currently specify formats that a bank's balance sheet must follow, although the new Bank Accounts Regulations to be introduced in 1991 will specify formats, which will apply from 1993 onwards (see para 15.22). However, Schedule 9 does require the financial statements to disclose certain information for balance sheet items. An illustration of a consolidated balance sheet of a banking group prepared in accordance with the existing Schedule 9 rules is given in Table 15.2.

15.39 The balance sheet should show amounts for share capital, reserves, provisions, assets and liabilities with such details as explain the general nature of the assets and liabilities. [CA 1985 9 Sch Part I 2]. These amounts should be classified under headings appropriate to the bank's business, except that:

- If the amount for a particular class is not material, it may be included with another class.

- If assets of one class are not separable from assets of another class, then both these classes may be included under the same heading.

[CA 1985 9 Sch Part I 4(1)].

Table 15.2: Illustration of the balance sheet of a bank prepared in accordance with Schedule 9

Extract from Barclays PLC Report and Accounts 31st December 1989.

CONSOLIDATED BALANCE SHEET

AS AT 31ST DECEMBER 1989

	Note	1989 £m		1988 £m	
Assets:					
Cash and short-term funds	*10*		20,192		17,150
Items in course of collection			708		761
Investments	*11*		1,938		1,770
Trading assets of securities business	*12*		7,837		4,644
Advances and other accounts	*13*		94,244		78,179
			124,919		102,504
Investments in associated companies and trade investments	*14*	435		348	
Property and equipment	*15*	2,262		1,793	
			2,697		2,141
			127,616		104,645
Liabilities:					
Deposits, current accounts and other borrowings	*18*		103,806		87,034
Trading liabilities of securities business	*12*		7,269		4,208
Other accounts	*19*		5,672		3,775
Current taxation			697		495
Deferred taxation	*20*		452		658
Dividend			180		145
			118,076		96,315
Capital Resources:					
Loan capital	*22*		1,547		1,507
Undated capital notes	*23*		1,320		996
Minority interests			448		116
Shareholders' funds:					
Called up share capital	*24*	1,124		1,114	
Reserves	*25*	5,101		4,597	
			6,225		5,711
			127,616		104,645

John Quinton, *Chairman*
Andrew Buxton, *Managing Director*
Brian Pearse, *Finance Director*

15.40 Assets should be split between fixed assets, current assets and assets that are neither fixed nor current. [CA 1985 9 Sch Part I 4(2)]. Schedule 9 does not define the terms 'fixed assets' and 'current assets', but it is reasonable that, in deciding which assets to include under each category, banks should look to the definition of fixed assets in Schedule 4 to the *Companies Act 1985*. However, banks do have the alternative of classifying assets as neither fixed nor current.

15.41 Unlike Schedule 4 companies, banks may capitalise and state under separate headings, the following items if they have not been written off:

- Preliminary expenses.
- Expenses incurred in connection with any issue of share capital or debentures.
- Any commission paid in respect of any shares or debentures.
- Any amount allowed by way of discount in respect of debentures.
- The amount of the discount allowed on any issue of shares at a discount.

[CA 1985 9 Sch Part I 3].

Fixed assets

15.42 The financial statements must state the method used to arrive at the amount included in the balance sheet for each category of fixed assets. [CA 1985 9 Sch Part I 4(3)]. This disclosure normally forms part of the bank's accounting policies. In addition, SSAP 12 requires that the method should be stated.

15.43 In general, any fixed asset should be included in the balance sheet at its original cost (or, if it has been revalued, at the amount of the valuation), less any amounts provided for depreciation or diminution in value. [CA 1985 9 Sch Part I 5(1)].

15.44 Certain fixed assets are exempted from the general principles outlined in the above paragraph. The assets that are exempted are:

- Assets acquired before 1st July 1948, where their cost cannot be obtained without unreasonable expense or delay.
- Assets whose replacement will be provided for either wholly or partly in one of the following ways:

- □ By setting up a provision for renewal and charging the cost of the replacement against that provision (see para 15.46).
- □ By charging the cost of the replacement direct to revenue.

- ■ Listed investments.
- ■ Unlisted investments, provided that the directors have estimated their value, and provided also that this estimated value is either included in the balance sheet or disclosed in the notes to the financial statements.
- ■ Goodwill, patents or trade marks.

[CA 1985 9 Sch Part I 5(2)].

15.45 If the assets were acquired before 1st July 1948, and their original cost cannot be determined without unreasonable expense or delay, then they should be treated as if they were revalued at 1st July 1948 to the net book value that was recorded in the company's accounting records at that date. Where any of these assets are sold, the proceeds from their disposal should be deducted from the net book value of the remaining assets that were acquired before 1st July 1948. Consequently, no profit on disposal will be recognised in the bank's profit and loss account until the remaining assets that were purchased before 1st July 1948 stand in the accounting records at nil value. [CA 1985 9 Sch Part I 5(1)].

15.46 As stated in paragraph 15.44 above, Schedule 9 to the *Companies Act 1985* permits an alternative to a depreciation charge in respect of an asset that has a limited useful economic life. This alternative is to set up a provision for the renewal of the asset by transferring an amount to this provision from the profit and loss account each year. Nevertheless, SSAP 12 requires that any asset that has a finite useful life must be depreciated and the depreciation charge in the profit and loss account must be based on the carrying value of the asset, whether historical cost or revalued amount. However, it does not preclude a bank from transferring an additional amount to reserve for the replacement of fixed assets by an appropriation from retained profits.

15.47 If a bank does set aside an amount for the replacement of fixed assets, then Schedule 9 requires that the financial statements must disclose both the aggregate amount set aside and the basis on which it has been provided. [CA 1985 9 Sch Part I 5(4)].

15.48 In respect of all fixed assets other than those that are exempted from complying with the general principle stated in paragraph 15.43 above, the financial statements must disclose:

- The aggregate cost (or the valuation) of the fixed assets.

- The aggregate accumulated amount that has been provided for depreciation or diminution in value.

[CA 1985 9 Sch Part I 5(3)].

15.49 In addition, the financial statements must show the amount of any additions and disposals during the year of each category of fixed assets (other than investments). [CA 1985 9 Sch Part I 13(10)].

15.50 Land must be subdivided between freehold, long leasehold and short leasehold. [CA 1985 9 Sch Part I 13(11)]. For this purpose, a lease includes an agreement for a lease, and a long lease is a lease in respect of which the unexpired portion exceeds 50 years at the end of the financial year. [CA 1985 9 Sch Part I 34].

15.51 If any fixed assets are included in the balance sheet at a valuation and not at their original cost, the notes to the financial statements must show:

- The year in which each valuation, was made (so far as the directors know them).

- The amount of the valuations, analysed according to the years when each valuation was made.

[CA 1985 9 Sch Part I 13(9)].

15.52 Furthermore, where any assets are valued during the financial year, then the notes to the financial statements should state the names of the valuers (or the valuers' qualifications) and the bases of valuation that they used. [CA 1985 9 Sch Part I 13(9)]. SSAP 19 requires similar disclosure where investment properties are revalued (see 'Manual of Accounting - volume I' chapter 8).

15.53 The balance sheet must include the aggregate amount of any goodwill, patents and trade marks that have not been written off. This figure should include any goodwill arising on consolidation. [CA 1985 9 Sch Part I 10(1)(b), (2)]. SSAP 22 applies also to the disclosure and the accounting treatment of goodwill. The rules contained in SSAP 22 are considered in 'Manual of Accounting - volume I' chapter 7.

15.54 The notes to the financial statements should state the amount of any proposed capital expenditure that has been:

- Contracted for, but not provided for, at the balance sheet date.

- Authorised by the directors, but not contracted for, at the balance sheet date.

[CA 1985 9 Sch Part I 13(8)].

Investments

15.55 The aggregate amount of investments should be split between listed investments and unlisted investments (defined in the same way as for other companies - see 'Manual of Accounting - volume I' chapter 9). [CA 1985 Part I 9 Sch 10(1)(a)]. In addition, listed investments should be subdivided between investments listed on a recognised investment exchange and other listed investments. [CA 1985 9 Sch Part I 10(3)].

15.56 If the bank is listed or traded on the USM, The International Stock Exchange's Continuing Obligations and the USM's General Undertaking respectively require certain additional information to be disclosed about the company's investments. These additional requirements are set out in detail in 'Manual of Accounting - volume I' chapter 9.

15.57 The notes to the financial statements must state the aggregate market value of listed investments (unless they are included at that value in the balance sheet). Where the market value of any investments is considered to be higher than the stock exchange value of those investments, their stock exchange value should also be stated. [CA 1985 9 Sch Part I 13(13)]. This disclosure is required because the market value and stock exchange value may differ according to the size of the investment and its marketability. For example, a controlling stake could be worth proportionately more than a minority interest in a company, because stock exchange prices traditionally reflect the values of small parcels of shares.

15.58 If a bank has investments in the form of equity share capital in unlisted companies, the directors should estimate the value of these investments (either individually or collectively). They should then include this value in the balance sheet, or, alternatively, disclose the value in the notes to the financial statements. [CA 1985 Sch Part I 6].

15.59 Where the directors have not valued these investments, the information set out below should be disclosed about the unlisted companies. It should be disclosed either in the notes to the financial statements or in a statement annexed to the financial statements:

- The aggregate amount of income the bank received from them during the year.

- The total of the bank's share of their profits less losses before and after taxation.

- The bank's share of their accumulated post-acquisition undistributed profits less losses.

- The manner in which any losses the unlisted companies have incurred have been dealt with in the company's financial statements.

[CA 1985 9 Sch Part I 6].

15.60 In addition to the above rules, banks should have regard to the accounting treatments and disclosures that are specified in the SORP on Securities. The SORP was issued by the BBA in July 1990 and franked by the ASC in September of that year. The scope of the SORP is confined to on-balance sheet transferable securities, whether equities, bonds or money market instruments including bills of exchange, and warrants and other instruments conferring a right to subscribe for securities. It does not cover interests in associated companies and other participating interests since these types of investments are no different for banks than for other entities.

15.61 The principal provisions of the BBA SORP on securities, which is reproduced as annex 2 to this chapter, are summarised below:

- The accounting treatment of securities should have regard to the purpose for which the securities are held, not the precise nature of the securities.

- Investment securities, that are intended for use on a continuing basis in the activities of the bank, should be valued at adjusted cost, provided the purpose for which the portfolio is held is properly documented and the securities held for the documented purpose are clearly identifiable. Cost is adjusted to reflect the amortisation of the premium or discount representing the difference between cost and the redemption proceeds, and to reflect any diminution in their value which is expected to be permanent. Premiums and discounts arising on redeemable securities should be amortised in such a way as to give a level gross redemption yield. In the case of index-linked securities, the book value and the amount of the amortisation should be updated at each balance sheet date to reflect the movement in the relevant index.

- All other securities held should be marked to market or held at directors' valuation. For the purposes of valuing all other securities, the following specific rules apply:

- □ Large holdings, which are unlikely to be realisable without affecting the market price to a significant extent, are to be subject to a further discount.
- □ Long positions are to be valued at bid price and short positions at offer price.

- ■ Where investments are held as hedges, they should be carried at a value which properly reflects the hedge, having regard to the accounting treatment of the items which are being hedged.
- ■ Where particular investment securities are the subject of temporary switching, possibly to obtain a temporary yield advantage without changing the long-term nature of the bank's exposure, then this should not be treated as affecting the original cost of the holding, so that the profit or loss as a result of the switch would be spread over the life of the security.
- ■ Securities transactions should be accounted for on the date on which the trade is made and not on the date on which the settlement takes place.
- ■ Securities lent or the subject of a repurchase agreement (Repo) should be retained in the balance sheet whenever substantially all the risks and rewards of ownership remain with the seller.
- ■ Income from debt securities should be recognised on an accruals basis except where there is an abnormal risk of default, when it is to be recognised on a paid basis.
- ■ Dividend income from quoted equity securities should be recognised when declared or when the security becomes 'ex-div'.
- ■ Exchange differences arising on securities denominated in foreign currencies should be taken to the profit and loss account as they arise.
- ■ Selling fees for the placement of a large number of securities, part of which are retained by the arranger, should be deducted from the cost of that part.

In addition to the above requirements, there are further requirements regarding disclosure of banks' securities holdings.

Current assets

15.62 The financial statements must disclose the aggregate amount of any outstanding loans a bank has given in respect of financial assistance for the acquisition of shares in it as a result of the following:

- Financial assistance the bank has provided under an employees' share scheme.

- Financial assistance provided by the bank or any subsidiary for the purpose of anything done by the bank (or another group company) to facilitate transactions in the bank's shares between, and acquisition of beneficial ownership of those shares by, employees (or former employees or their close relatives) of that or another group company.

- Loans the bank has made to employees (other than directors) to enable them to acquire, for their own benefit, fully-paid shares in the bank or its parent company.

- Financial assistance a private company has given to assist the acquisition of shares in either the bank or its parent company (if that parent company is a private company). (Financial assistance of this nature can be given only if the conditions in sections 155 to 158 of the *Companies Act 1985* are satisfied.)

[CA 1985 9 Sch Part I 10(1)(c)].

15.63 Where the directors consider that the value included in the balance sheet for any current asset is greater than the amount that it would realise in the ordinary course of the bank's business, they should state that fact in the notes. [CA 1985 9 Sch Part I 13(12)]. However, in this type of situation, best accounting practice, and in particular the concept of prudence outlined in SSAP 2, requires that the current asset should be written down to its realisable value.

Liabilities

15.64 The balance sheet or the notes to the financial statements must disclose the following in respect of a bank's liabilities:

- The aggregate amount of bank loans and overdrafts. [CA 1985 9 Sch Part I 10(1)(d)]. Overdrafts are not normally shown in the financial statements of banks, but are included in amounts due to other banks.

- The aggregate amount of loans (other than bank loans and overdrafts) that are repayable either wholly or partly in more than five years after the balance sheet date together with the terms on which each such loan is repayable and the rate of interest on each loan. [CA 1985 9 Sch Part I 10(1)(d)]. However, if the latter part of this requirement would require a statement of excessive length to be included in the notes to the financial statements, then the information may be given in general terms. [CA 1985 9 Sch Part I 10(4)]. (Loans or loan instalments are deemed to fall due for repayment or payment on the earliest date on which the lender can require repayment or payment if he exercises all options and rights available to him. [CA 1985 9 Sch Part I 35].)

- The amount of any proposed dividends. [CA 1985 9 Sch Part I 10(1)(e)].

15.65 Listed banks and banks that are traded on the USM have to comply also with the requirements that relate to loans that are outlined in The International Stock Exchange's Continuing Obligations and in the USM's General Undertaking respectively. These requirements are discussed in 'Manual of accounting - volume I' chapter 11.

15.66 If the bank has used any of its assets to secure a liability, its financial statements should indicate that the liability is secured. However, the bank does not need to indicate the assets that have been charged as security. [CA 1985 9 Sch Part I 11]. In addition, the notes to the financial statements must give details of any charge there is on the bank's assets to secure the liabilities of any other person. If it is practicable, the amount of the liability that is secured in this way should also be stated. [CA 1985 9 Sch Part I 13(6)].

15.67 Furthermore, the notes to the financial statements should disclose details of any other contingent liabilities that have not been provided for, together with (if this is practicable) the actual amount of, or an estimate of, the liabilities. [CA 1985 9 Sch Part I 13(7)]. In this respect, the financial statements should also comply with the requirements of SSAP 18.

15.68 The Schedule 9 rules lay down no particular valuation methods for commitments and contingent liabilities. Any method is, therefore, permissible so long as it provides a true and fair view. Furthermore, the significant growth in the number of on and off-balance sheet instruments during the last decade has brought about an associated increase in the level of commitments and contingencies inherent in a bank's business. In order to provide practical guidance in this area, the BBA issued in September 1990 an exposure draft of a SORP on off-balance instruments and other commitments and contingencies. The proposed SORP contains recommendations on the valuation of interest rate, exchange rate and market price related contracts. It also gives guidance on the timing and method of income recognition and on the information that needs to be disclosed in respect of all commitments and contingencies.

15.69 The principal proposals of the exposure draft are summarised below:

- Commitments and contingencies should be distinguished between hedging transactions and trading or speculative transactions. To be treated as hedges, transactions must match or eliminate a substantial part of the market rate risk attaching to the items hedged. There must also be adequate evidence of the intention to hedge, and proper procedures should be in place to identify hedges.

- Hedging transactions should be valued on an equivalent basis to the assets, liabilities or positions which they are hedging. Trading or speculative transactions should be marked to market.
- In determining the market value for the purposes of marking to market, the following rules would apply:
  - The costs of completing the transaction must be taken into account.
  - The more prudent of bid and offer price should be used, except for active market participants, which may use the mid market price.
  - Where no market price is available, but an active market exists for the component parts of that instrument, a price may be constructed on the basis of interest rates, exchange rates or other prices that provides a reasonable approximation to market price.
  - Where there is no liquid market or where a position in particular instruments is so significant as to affect the market price materially, then a discount to market price should be used.
- Where it is considered doubtful that the counterparty to an existing off-balance sheet transaction will meet its future obligations, adequate provision should be made for the cost of replacing that transaction.
- Where transactions are switched from trading/speculative portfolios to hedging portfolios, they should be marked to market on transfer. Where a hedging transaction is replaced by another transaction, the original transaction should immediately be marked to market before being transferred to a trading portfolio, the profit or loss that arises should be amortised over the remaining life of the transaction previously being hedged.
- In recognising income on transactions that are not treated as hedges, a distinction should be made between those instruments which are immediately realisable and those that are not. Profits and losses that result from marking to market realisable transactions (for example, traded options) should be recognised immediately in full. For those transactions that are not realisable in cash until maturity, such as

forward foreign exchange, an appropriate discount rate should be applied to the anticipated cash flows to arrive at the net present value of expected future profits. The net present value should then be spread over the life of the transaction. The amount deferred should be sufficient to cover all likely future costs, including the cost of maintaining capital and of any continuing credit and other risks.

- Fees for services rendered, the receipt of which are not in doubt, should be recognised in the accounting period in which the services are rendered. Fees in respect of credit or other risk borne should only be recognised as income over the period in which the risk is borne.

- Arrangement fees paid should normally be written off on payment, but where they represent the cost of arranging an instrument that is used for hedging purposes, they may be spread over the period of the hedge.

- Losses expected to be incurred on any discrete transaction or group of transactions should be recognised in full immediately.

15.70 In addition, the SORP strongly recommends detailed disclosure, in tabular form, of all forms of commitments and contingent liabilities. There is a further requirement to disclose in detail the principal accounting practices followed for valuation and income recognition.

Share capital

15.71 The authorised share capital and the issued share capital must be shown either on the face of the balance sheet or in the notes to the financial statements. [CA 1985 9 Sch Part I 2].

15.72 If any part of the issued share capital includes redeemable shares, the following information must be given:

- The identity of the part of the issued share capital that includes redeemable shares.

- The earliest and the latest dates on which the bank has power to redeem those shares.

- A statement of whether the shares must be redeemed in any event, or whether redemption is exercisable either at the bank's option or at the shareholder's option.

- The amount of any premium that is payable on redemption or, if none is payable, a statement to that effect.

[CA 1985 9 Sch Part I 2(a)].

15.73 Where a person has an option to subscribe for any of the bank's shares, the notes to the financial statements must show the number, the description and the amount of those shares. Also, the following information must be given in respect of options granted:

- The period during which the option is exercisable.
- The option price to be paid for the shares.

[CA 1985 9 Sch Part I 13(2)].

The requirement to disclose directors' share options is considered in 'Manual of Accounting - volume I' chapter 20.

15.74 Where a bank is in arrears in paying any fixed cumulative dividends on its shares, this fact should be noted in the financial statements, together with the period for which the dividends are in arrears. [CA 1985 9 Sch Part I 13(5)].

Reserves and provisions

15.75 The term 'provision' is defined in Schedule 9 to the *Companies Act 1985* for banks as:

> *"Any amount written off or retained by way of providing for depreciation, renewals or diminution in value of assets or retained by way of providing for any known liability of which the amount cannot be determined with substantial accuracy."*

15.76 The expression 'liability' includes in this context all liabilities in respect of expenditure contracted for, and all disputed or contingent liabilities. [CA 1985 9 Sch Part I 32(1)(a)].

15.77 Although the definition of a provision in Schedule 4 to the *Companies Act 1985* is expressed in different terms from those used in the definition given above that applies to banks, there is little if any difference in the meaning of the two definitions. However, the definition given in Schedule 9 to the *Companies Act 1985* does include provisions for renewals, whereas this item is not included in the definition of a provision given in Schedule 4 to that Act.

15.78 The term 'reserve' is not defined in Schedule 4 to the *Companies Act 1985*, but, in respect of banks, it is stated as *excluding:*

> *"Any amount written off or retained by way of providing for depreciation, renewals or diminution in value of an asset or*

retained by way of providing for any known liability or any sum set aside for the purpose of its being used to prevent undue fluctuations in charges for taxation." [CA 1985 9 Sch Part I 32(1)(b)].

15.79 Where an amount has been provided for depreciation of an asset (including provisions for renewals or the diminution in value), or an amount has been provided for a liability, and the directors consider that the amount provided is excessive, they must treat the excess as a reserve, rather than as a provision. [CA 1985 9 Sch Part I 32(2)].

15.80 Many banks make both specific and general provisions against bad and doubtful loans. The specific element relates to particular loans identified as bad or doubtful. The general element relates primarily to those risks associated with loans that may prove to be wholly or partly irrecoverable which have not been separately identified, but which can reasonably be expected to exist. In aggregate, the specific and general elements of a bank's provision for bad and doubtful loans should represent the aggregate amount by which management considers it necessary to write down its loan portfolio in order to state it at its net realisable value in the ordinary course of business. Determining an appropriate level of general provision requires careful assessment because if the provision is excessive, it would be treated as a reserve. There is no statutory requirements for UK banks to disclose in their financial statements information about their bad and doubtful debt provisions although some banks do provide voluntary disclosure.

15.81 The aggregate amount of reserves and provisions must be stated separately, unless the provisions are for depreciation, or renewals or the diminution in value of assets. If either of these amounts is immaterial, it may be combined with the other amount. In addition, a separate statement of provisions is not necessary if the Secretary of State is satisfied that the public interest does not require a separate statement, and that, if one were given, it would be disadvantageous to the company. Where this statement is omitted, the financial statements must identify any heading that includes a provision that has not been separately disclosed. [CA 1985 9 Sch Part I 7].

15.82 The financial statements must disclose the following movements on reserves and provisions during the year, unless they are provisions for depreciation, or renewals or the diminution in value of assets:

- The source of the increase or application of the decrease, where the amount of *reserves* shown in the financial statements has increased or decreased since the previous year end.

- The source of the increase, where the amount of *provisions* has increased since the previous financial year.

- The application of any amount that has not been used for the purposes for which the *provisions* were set up. This need only be disclosed where the amount of provisions at the previous year end exceeds the aggregate of the amounts applied during the year for the purposes of the provisions and the amounts still retained for the same purposes.

This information must be given separately for each sub-heading of reserves and provisions. [CA 1985 9 Sch Part I 8].

15.83 If the bank has a share premium account, this must be shown separately. [CA 1985 9 Sch 2(c)].

15.84 Any provision for deferred taxation must be disclosed to comply with both the *Companies Act 1985* and SSAP 15 (see further 'Manual of accounting - volume I' chapter 11). [CA 1985 9 Sch Part I 9]. If a provision for deferred taxation that has previously been set up is applied during the year to some other purpose, both this fact and the amount that has been applied must be stated. [CA 1985 9 Sch Part I 13(14)].

The profit and loss account

General disclosure

15.85 Schedule 9 to the *Companies Act 1985* does not detail formats that a bank's profit and loss account must follow (although the new Bank Accounts Regulation will do so). However, the profit and loss account (or the related notes) must disclose the information that is outlined below. An illustration of a consolidated profit and loss account prepared in accordance with the existing Schedule 9 is given in Table 15.3.

- The aggregate amount of provisions for depreciation, or renewals or the diminution in value of fixed assets that have been charged in the profit and loss account. [CA 1985 9 Sch Part I 14(1)(a)]. If provision has been made both for depreciation or diminution in value and for the renewal of a particular asset, the amount of the provision for renewal should be disclosed separately. [CA 1985 9 Sch Part I 14(3)]. Where the amount charged in the profit and loss account to provide for any fixed asset's depreciation or diminution in value is based on a value other than the value at which that asset is included in the balance sheet, this fact must be stated. [CA 1985 9 Sch Part I 14(4)]. This latter provision specifically allows a bank to use the method of 'split depreciation' whereby depreciation based on the historical cost is charged to the profit and loss account and that based on the revaluation is charged to the revaluation reserve. The practice of split depreciation, however, has been prohibited by SSAP 12.

Table 15.3: Illustration of the profit and loss account of a bank prepared in accordance with Schedule 9

Extract from Barclays PLC Report and Accounts 31st December 1989.

CONSOLIDATED PROFIT AND LOSS ACCOUNT

FOR THE YEAR ENDED 31ST DECEMBER 1989

	Note		1989 £m		1988 £m
Interest income	*1*		13,468		9,147
Interest expense	*2*		10,048		6,181
Net interest income			3,420		2,966
Other operating income	*3*		2,127		1,785
			5,547		4,751
Operating expenses:	*4*				
Staff		2,064		1,882	
Property and equipment		626		568	
Other		860		705	
		3,550		3,155	
Charge for bad and doubtful debts	*13*	1,397		301	
			4,947		3,456
Operating profit			600		1,295
Share of profit of associated companies			92		96
Profit before taxation			692		1,391
Taxation	5		215		498
Profit after taxation			477		893
Profit attributable to minority interests			25		6
Profit attributable to members of Barclays PLC	6		452		887
Dividends:	7				
First interim		128		111	
Second interim		180		145	
			308		256
Profit retained	8		144		631
Earnings per Ordinary Share	9		40.4p		87.8p

Movements in reserves are shown in note 25.

The Board of Directors approved the accounts set out on pages 29 to 46 on 28th February 1990.

- The amount of interest on bank loans, overdrafts and other loans that are wholly repayable within five years of the balance sheet date. [CA 1985 9 Sch Part I 14(1)(b)].

- The amount of interest on any other loans not included in the point directly above. [CA 1985 9 Sch Part I 14(1)(b)].

- The amount of the UK corporation tax charge and the basis used in computing it. Where the UK corporation tax charge would have been greater if double taxation relief had not been receivable, the gross amount must be disclosed. [CA 1985 9 Sch Part I 14(1)(c), 18(3)]. The disclosure requirements of SSAP 8 must also be complied with. These are considered in 'Manual of accounting - volume I' chapter 14.

- The amount of the UK income tax charge and the basis used in computing it. [CA 1985 9 Sch Part I 14(1)(c), 18(3)].

- The amount of the taxation charge that has been imposed outside the UK on profits, income and (to the extent to which it has been charged to income) capital gains. [CA 1985 9 Sch Part I 14(1)(c)].

- Details of any special circumstances that affect any liability to taxation (whether for the financial year in question or for future years, and, also, whether in respect of profits, or income or capital gains). [CA 1985 9 Sch Part I 18(4)].

- Any amount that has been set aside for the redemption of either share capital or loans. [CA 1985 9 Sch Part I 14(1)(d)].

- The amount that has been, or is proposed to be, set aside to, or withdrawn from, reserves. [CA 1985 9 Sch Part I 14(1)(e)].

- The amount that has been set aside to provisions, or withdrawn from provisions (and not applied for the purpose for which the provision was set up). This applies to provisions other than provisions for depreciation, or renewals, or the diminution in value of fixed assets. [CA 1985 9 Sch Part I 14(1)(f)]. The Secretary of State may waive this requirement if the disclosure of this information would be detrimental to the bank and the public interest does not require it to be disclosed. Where this requirement is waived, the financial statements must indicate any amount that is stated after taking account of any amount that has been set aside, but that because of this requirement has not been separately disclosed. [CA 1985 9 Sch Part I 14(2)].

- The amount of investment income. This must be split between income from listed investments and income from unlisted investments. [CA 1985 9 Sch Part I 14(1)(g)].

- The amount of rents from land, after deducting ground rents, rates and other outgoings. This information has to be disclosed only if a substantial part of the bank's income for the year consists of such rent. [CA 1985 9 Sch Part I 14(1)(h)]. However, it is unlikely that this information will be disclosed in the financial statements of banks.

- The amount that has been charged in respect of rentals, analysed between amounts payable in respect of the hire of plant and machinery and in respect of other operating leases. [CA 1985 9 Sch Part I 14(1)(j), SSAP 21 para 55].

- The aggregate amount of any dividends that either have been paid or are proposed. [CA 1985 9 Sch Part I 14(1)(k)].

- The amount of any charge or credit that has arisen because of an event that occurred in a preceding financial year. [CA 1985 9 Sch Part I 15].

- The amount of the auditors' remuneration paid in cash (including any expenses the auditors incurred and the bank reimbursed) and the nature and estimated money value of any benefits in kind paid to the auditors. [CA 1985 Sec 390A(3)(4)].

- The turnover for the year, and the method used to arrive at the figure for turnover. Disclosure of turnover is not required where the bank is neither a parent company nor a subsidiary undertaking, and the bank's turnover does not exceed £1m. However, where the amount of turnover attributable to the business of banking or discounting has been omitted, the fact that it has been omitted must be stated (for example, see Table 15.4). [CA 1985 9 Sch Part I 17]. Also a banking company or group need only disclose that part of the turnover that is attributable to non-banking business.

Table 15.4: Disclosure of non-banking turnover

Extract from Midland Bank PLC Annual Report & Accounts 31st December 1989.

Note extract

1 Turnover

The turnover of the Group as a whole is not shown as it results mainly from the business of banking. Non-banking turnover consists of commissions on travel arrangements and sales in respect of tour operations amounting to £370m (1988 £385m). Aggregate leasing rentals were £822m (1988 £644m) the majority of which related to finance leases. Aggregate hire purchase instalments were £367m (1988 £392m).

- Details of any exceptional or extraordinary items and of the effect of any changes in accounting policy. [CA 1985 9 Sch Part I 18(6)]. Compliance with SSAP 6 will ensure that the profit and loss account complies with this requirement of the *Companies Act 1985.*

Other information to be disclosed

15.86 The financial statements must disclose particulars of any redeemed debentures that the bank has power to reissue. [CA 1985 9 Sch Part I 2(d)]. Also, if any of the bank's debentures are held by a nominee of, or a trustee for, the bank, the financial statements must disclose both the nominal amount of those debentures and the amount at which they are stated in the bank's books. [CA 1985 9 Sch Part I 12].

15.87 Where a banking company or group at the end of its financial year has a 'significant holding' of shares in another undertaking, other than a subsidiary undertaking, the *Companies Act 1985* requires the bank to disclose certain information. For Schedule 4 companies, that Act defines a 'significant holding' as a holding of ten per cent or more of the nominal value of *any class of shares* in the undertaking, or a holding that exceeds one tenth of the amount of the company's assets, as disclosed in its balance sheet. [CA 1985 5 Sch 7(2), 23(2), 27(2)]. For banking companies or groups, however, the information to be disclosed in respect of significant holdings applies only to holding of shares comprised in the *equity share capital* of the undertaking. [CA 1985 9 Sch Part III (1)(a)].

15.88 The information to be disclosed, *viz,* name, country of incorporation, etc. is similar to Schedule 4 companies and is detailed in 'Manual of Accounting - volume I' chapter 9.

15.89 Furthermore, where a banking company or group has a 'significant holding' in an undertaking (which is not a subsidiary) amounting to 20 per cent or more of the nominal value of the equity shares in the undertaking, the following information should be given in addition to the information required by the above paragraph.

- The aggregate amount of the capital and reserves of the undertaking at the end of its relevant financial year.

- The profit or the loss of that undertaking as disclosed by those financial statements.

[CA 1985 5 Sch 9(1), 25(1), 28(1), 9 Sch Part III 1(b)].

15.90 The information required by paragraphs 15.88 and 15.89 above need not be disclosed with respect to an undertaking that is established outside the UK or carries on business outside the UK, and if it would, in the opinion of the directors, be seriously prejudicial to the business of the bank or any of its subsidiary undertakings. However, in this situation, the Secretary of State has to agree that the information need not be disclosed. Where advantage is taken of this exception, this fact must be stated in the notes to the financial statements. [CA 1985 Sec 231(3)(4)]. Also, the information may be disclosed for material undertakings only, if the directors believe that information of excessive length would be given if the relevant information is given for all such undertakings. [CA 1985 Sec 231(5)].

15.91 Moreover, the additional information in paragraph 15.89 above does not need to be given in either of the following two situations where:

- The bank is exempt by virtue of section 228 of the *Companies Act 1985* from the requirement to prepare consolidated financial statements, because the bank is itself included in the financial statements of a larger group. Where this exemption applies, the bank's investment in all such undertakings must be shown, in aggregate, in the notes to the bank's financial statements by way of the equity method of valuation. [CA 1985 5 Sch 9(2)].

- The bank's or the group's investment is in an undertaking that is not required by any of the Act's provisions to deliver a copy of its balance sheet to the Registrar of Companies and it does not otherwise publish that balance sheet in Great Britain or elsewhere. Where this situation exists, the information need not be given, provided the bank's holding is less than 50 per cent of the nominal value of the shares in the undertaking. [CA 1985 5 Sch 9(3), 25(2), 28(2)].

Consolidated financial statements

15.92 As stated earlier, a group that meets the definition of a banking group (see para 15.18 above) may, if it so wishes, prepare its consolidated financial statements in accordance with Schedule 4A as modified by Part II of Schedule 9 to the *Companies Act 1985*. However, if the parent company is not a bank, its own balance sheet and related notes must be prepared in accordance with Schedule 4 to the *Companies Act 1985*.

15.93 Consolidated financial statements are not required, however, where the bank is itself a subsidiary undertaking and its immediate parent is established under the law of an EC Member State and where the conditions specified in sections 228(1)(a)(b) of the *Companies Act 1985* are satisfied (see further 'Manual of Accounting - volume II' chapter 2).

15.94 Consolidated financial statements should cover the parent and all its subsidiary undertakings at home or overseas unless one, or more, of the subsidiary undertakings fall to be excluded from consolidation for any of the reasons specified in section 229 of the *Companies Act 1985* (see further 'Manual of Accounting - volume II' chapter 3). However, where the activities of a bank's subsidiary undertaking are a direct extension of or ancillary to banking business, that subsidiary undertaking cannot be excluded from consolidation under section 229(4) of the *Companies Act 1985* on the grounds that its activities are different from those of the undertakings consolidated. [CA 1985 9 Sch Part II 1(a)].

15.95 An Interim Statement on consolidated accounts issued by the ASB on 11th December 1990 addresses the issue of exclusion of subsidiaries from the consolidated financial statements where their activities are different from those of the rest of the group. The statement is effective for financial years commencing on or after 23rd December 1989, and has the force of an accounting standard. The ASB believes that the circumstances under which a subsidiary undertaking's activities are so different that its inclusion in the consolidated financial statements would be incompatible with the obligation to give a true and fair view, are so exceptional that it would be misleading to link them to any particular contrast of activities. Therefore, unless there are conclusive grounds for believing that their inclusion is incompatible with the obligation to give a true and fair view, a banking subsidiary of a non-banking parent company should be consolidated. In the event of exclusion, the grounds for considering that inclusion is not compatible with the obligation to give a true and fair view must be explained in a note to the financial statements.

15.96 A banking group's consolidated financial statements have to comply as far as practicable with the provisions of Part I of Schedule 9 to the *Companies Act 1985* as if the undertakings included in the consolidation were a single company. [CA 1985 9 Sch Part II 2(1)]. With certain exceptions, the requirement to prepare consolidated financial statements, the methods that should be used to produce them, and their form and the content are exactly the same for a banking group as for a normal group. Consequently, they should generally follow the requirements set out in 'Manual of Accounting - volume II'. However, the general application of the provisions of Part I of Schedule 9 is subject to the provisions in the paragraphs that follow.

15.97 The rules in paragraph 21 of Schedule 4 to the *Companies Act 1985* relating to the treatment of goodwill (disclosure of amortisation period and the reasons for choosing that period) and the rules in paragraph 17 to 19 of Schedule 4 to that Act (valuation of fixed assets) so far as they relate to goodwill, apply as well to any goodwill arising on consolidation. [CA 1985 9 Sch Part II 3(1)].

15.98 Goodwill must be shown as a separate item in the balance sheet under an appropriate heading. This applies even though the amount of goodwill, patents and trade marks are only required to be stated, to the extent that they are ascertainable and not written-off, as a single item in the bank's individual financial statements under paragraph 10(1)(b), 10(2) of Part I of Schedule 9. [CA 1985 9 Sch Part II 3(2)]. SSAP 22 also requires separate disclosure of goodwill. This requirement applies to both goodwill on consolidation and other goodwill (for example, goodwill arising on the purchase of an unincorporated business).

15.99 If the parent company is a bank, the aggregate amount of its assets that consist of shares in, or amounts owing from, its subsidiary undertakings should be shown separately from all other assets in its balance sheet. Shares should be shown separately from indebtedness. Similarly, the aggregate amount owing to the bank's subsidiary undertakings should be shown separately from all the bank's other liabilities. [CA 1985 9 Sch Part I 19(2)]. However, the parent company may show its investment in, and loans to and from, its subsidiary undertakings as one aggregate figure, provided that the aggregate figure is analysed in the notes to the financial statements in such a way as to give the information required above. This type of disclosure is not acceptable for a Schedule 4 parent company. The above requirements apply also where the subsidiary undertaking is excluded from consolidation. [CA 1985 9 Sch Part II 2(1), 4A Sch 1(2)].

15.100 A bank that is a subsidiary undertaking of another company must show separately, in its balance sheet, the aggregate amount that it owes to any parent company or any fellow subsidiary undertakings, and also the aggregate amount that such companies owe to it. Each of these two amounts should be split between indebtedness in respect of debentures and otherwise. The balance sheet should also disclose the aggregate amount of any shares in fellow subsidiary undertakings. [CA 1985 9 Sch Part I 20].

15.101 The amounts in respect of minority interests and associated undertakings including other participating interests that are shown under separate items in the formats set out in Part I of Schedule 4 to the *Companies Act 1985* must be shown separately in the balance sheet and the profit and loss account under appropriate headings. [CA 1985 9 Sch Part II 4]. The proposed Bank Accounts Regulations mentioned in paragraph 15.22 above will prescribe definitive positions for these items in the formats.

15.102 Where a parent bank holds shares in a subsidiary undertaking, that is also a credit institution, as a result of a financial assistance operation with a view to its reorganisation or rescue, and that subsidiary is excluded from consolidation because control is intended to be temporary (subsidiary acquired with a view to resale), certain information has to be disclosed. [CA 1985 9 Sch Part II 6(1)]. A credit institution is defined as an undertaking carrying on a deposit taking business within the meaning of the *Banking Act 1987*. The consolidated financial statements must disclose the following information:

- The nature and terms of the financial assistance operation.

- A statement that a copy of the excluded undertaking's latest financial statements and, if it is a parent, its latest consolidated financial statements have been appended to the copy of the consolidated financial statements delivered to the Registrar of Companies in accordance with section 242 of the *Companies Act 1985*. A copy of the auditors' report should also be appended if the financial statements are required by law to be audited. If any document required to be appended is in a language other than English, a certified translation of that document should accompany it.

[CA 1985 9 Sch Part II 6(2)(3)].

15.103 The above requirements are, however, subject to the following qualifications.

- No financial statements need be prepared specifically to satisfy the above requirements, and if no financial statements satisfying the above requirements are prepared none need to be appended.

- A document need not be appended if it is not otherwise required to be published, or made available for public inspection, anywhere in the world. The reason for not appending it should, however, be given in the notes to the consolidated financial statements.

[CA 1985 9 Sch Part II 6(4)].

Exempt banks

15.104 As stated in paragraph 15.13 above, exempt banks are permitted to prepare their financial statements according to the special rules in paragraph 27(2) of Schedule 9 to the *Companies Act 1985*, which allow the maintenance of undisclosed reserves and impose more limited disclosure requirements. However, an exempt bank must satisfy the Secretary of State that it ought to benefit from the special rules. [CA 1985 9 Sch Part I 27(1)]. The limited disclosure requirements extend to the consolidated financial statements of the group where the parent company heading the group is entitled to the exemptions. [CA 1985 9 Sch Part II 5(1)]. These special rules are expected to disappear, however, when the proposed Bank Accounts Regulations are issued, putting all banks on the same basis.

15.105 Although these exemptions are given in the *Companies Act 1985*, exempt banks may still have to comply with the accounting and measurement requirements of all SSAPs (such as, the requirement to provide depreciation on fixed assets that have a limited useful life). However, the explanatory foreword to SSAPs says that *"where accounting standards prescribe specific information to be contained in accounts, such disclosure requirements do not override exemptions from disclosure requirements given to and utilised by special classes of companies under Statute"*. Consequently, exempt banks may, without contravening any requirements of SSAPs, take advantage of those exemptions in paragraph 27(2) of Schedule 9 to the *Companies Act 1985* that relate to disclosure.

15.106 The exemptions conferred by paragraph 27 of Part I of Schedule 9 to the *Companies Act 1985* on exempt banks and groups are discussed in the paragraphs that follow. The references given in brackets are to the paragraph numbers in Schedule 9 to the *Companies Act 1985* with which exempt banks and groups need not comply.

Balance sheet exemptions

15.107 An exempt bank or group need not in respect of its balance sheet:

Fixed assets

- Include fixed assets in the balance sheet at cost (or valuation) less any provisions for depreciation or diminution in value, or disclose the cost and accumulated depreciation of fixed assets (see para 15.43 to 15.48). (CA 1985 9 Sch Part I 5).

- Give the information detailed in paragraph 15.51 that must normally be stated if any fixed assets are shown at a valuation. (CA 1985 9 Sch Part I 13(9)).

- Give details of additions and disposals of fixed assets (see para 15.49). (CA 1985 9 Sch Part I 13(10)).

- Analyse land between freehold, long leasehold and short leasehold (see para 15.50). (9 Sch 13(11)).

Investments

- Give the information regarding unlisted investments detailed in paragraph 15.59. (CA 1985 9 Sch Part I 6).

- Show the aggregate market value, and the stock exchange value (if applicable) of listed investments (see para 15.57). (CA 1985 9 Sch Part I 13(13)).

Reserves, provisions and liabilities

- Classify reserves, provisions and liabilities under suitable headings (see para 15.39). (CA 1985 9 Sch Part I 4 except in so far as they relate to assets).

- Show the aggregate amounts of reserves and provisions and the movements on such reserves and provisions during the year (see paras 15.81 and 15.82). (CA 1985 9 Sch Part I 7, 8).

- Give details of the aggregate amount of bank loans and overdrafts and the aggregate amount of other loans that are repayable (either wholly or partly) more than five years after the balance sheet date, and of the repayment terms and rates of interest applicable to such loans (see para 15.64). (CA 1985 9 Sch Part I 10(1)(d),(4)).

- Disclose the amount of any provision for deferred taxation or give details of any amount that has previously been provided for deferred tax but has been used for an alternative purpose during the year (see para 15.84). (CA 1985 9 Sch Part I 9, 13(14)).

[CA 1985 9 Sch Part I 27(2)(a)].

15.108 If an exempt bank takes advantage of the exemption that allows reserves and provisions not to be stated separately and described as such, then the financial statements must identify any heading in the balance sheet that contains such a reserve or provision. They must also explain how these reserves and provisions have been treated in the profit and loss account. [CA 1985 9 Sch Part I 27(3)].

Profit and loss account exemptions

15.109 In respect of its profit and loss account, an exempt bank or group need not disclose the following information discussed in paragraph 15.85 above:

- The amount of any depreciation charge and any amount provided for either renewals or the diminution in value of fixed assets. (CA 1985 9 Sch Part I 14(1)(a), (3)).

- The amount of interest on loans that are wholly repayable within five years of the balance sheet date. (CA 1985 9 Sch Part I 14(1)(b)).

- Details concerning the tax charge and how it is computed. (CA 1985 9 Sch Part I 14(1)(c), 18(3)(4)).

- Any amount set aside for the redemption of either share capital or loans. (CA 1985 9 Sch Part I 14(1)(d)).
- Details of the amount set aside to, or proposed to be set aside to, or withdrawn from, reserves or provisions. (CA 1985 9 Sch Part I 14(1)(e)(f), (2)).
- The amounts of income from both listed investments and unlisted investments. (CA 1985 9 Sch Part I 14(1)(g)).
- Any amount charged for the hire of plant and machinery. (CA 1985 9 Sch Part I 14(1)(j)).
- State, if this is so, that an amount charged for either depreciation or the diminution in value of any asset has been based on a value other than the value at which that asset is included in the balance sheet. (CA 1985 9 Sch Part I 14(4)).
- Show the turnover for the year or the method used to compute turnover. (CA 1985 9 Sch Part I 17).
- Give details of either any extraordinary items or any items that have been affected by a change in accounting policy. (CA 1985 9 Part I Sch 18(6)).

[CA 1985 9 Sch Part I 27(2)(b)].

The directors' report

15.110 The information to be included in the directors' report of a bank is essentially similar to that of a Schedule 4 company (see further 'Manual of Accounting - volume I' chapter 20). Therefore, all the requirements of Schedule 7 to the *Companies Act 1985* apply equally to banking companies and groups. However, there are some additional specific matters that apply to directors' reports of banking companies and groups and these are discussed below.

15.111 The directors' report is allowed to contain the following information that would otherwise be given elsewhere in the financial statements:

- Information required under paragraph 6 of Part I of Schedule 9 to the *Companies Act 1985* (directors' valuation of unlisted investments - see para 15.59).
- Information required under paragraph 8 of Part I of Schedule 9 to the *Companies Act 1985* (movements on reserves and provisions - see para 15.82).

- Information required under paragraph 13 of Part I of Schedule 9 to the *Companies Act 1985* (share options, dividend arrears, contingent liabilities, contracted capital expenditure, fixed assets, current assets, investments, stocks and work in progress, foreign exchange and taxation).

[CA 1985 Sec 255C(2)].

15.112 In addition, if an item is included in the directors' report that would normally have been included elsewhere in the financial statements, the directors' report must be treated as forming part of the financial statements. Consequently, it must be audited, but only to the extent that it gives information that would otherwise be shown elsewhere in the financial statements. [CA 1985 Sec 255C(2)].

15.113 As with any other companies, the directors must state, in their report, the amount that they propose to carry to reserves. In this context, the amount proposed to be carried to reserves should be construed within the meaning of Part I of Schedule 9. [CA 1985 Sec 255C(3)].

15.114 An exempt bank or group need not give details of the following:

- Significant changes in fixed assets of the bank or any of its subsidiary undertakings. [CA 1985 Sec 255C (4), 7 Sch 1(1)].

- Significant differences between the book value and the market value of interests in land. [CA 1985 Sec 255C(4), 7 Sch 1(2)].

15.115 In addition, Schedule 10 to the *Companies Act 1985* sets out certain information that the directors' reports of all banks must contain. This information is considered below:

Issues of shares or debentures

15.116 If the bank has issued any shares or debentures during the year, the directors' report must state:

- The reason for making the issue.

- The classes of shares or debentures issued, and, in respect of each class of shares or debentures issued:

  - □ The number of shares or the amount of debentures issued.

  - □ The consideration the bank received for the issue.

[CA 1985 10 Sch 1(1)(2)].

Disaggregated information

15.117 A banking group that prepares consolidated financial statements must disclose, in the directors' report, the information set out below. However, this requirement applies only if the bank carries on business of two or more classes that, in the directors' opinion, are substantially different. The information required is:

- A description of each class of business.
- The proportion of turnover for the year that is attributable to each class of business.
- The amount of profit or loss before taxation that is, in the directors' opinion, attributable to each class of business.

[CA 1985 10 Sch 2(1)(2)].

15.118 The disclosure required above excludes turnover and profit that is attributable to the classes of banking or discounting. [10 Sch 2]. Furthermore, if in the directors' opinion, two classes of business do not differ substantially from each other, they should be treated as one class. [CA 1985 10 Sch 2(4)].

15.119 If the bank is either listed on The International Stock Exchange or traded on the USM, it will have to comply also with The International Stock Exchange's Continuing Obligations or the USM's General Undertaking as appropriate as to the disclosure of disaggregated information for turnover and profit. This requirement is discussed in 'Manual of Accounting - volume I' chapter 13.

Employees and their remuneration

15.120 The directors' report of a bank that does not have subsidiaries must disclose:

- The average number of people the bank employed in the UK during each week of the year. This figure should be calculated by first adding up the total number of people employed under contracts of service for each week of the year. These weekly totals should then be added, and the total should be divided by the number of weeks in the year.
- The total remuneration paid or payable in respect of the year to these people. For this purpose, remuneration is the gross remuneration, including bonuses, that was paid or was payable.

[CA 1985 10 Sch 3(1)-(4), (6)].

15.121 If, at the end of the financial year, the bank has subsidiaries, the directors' report should give the same information as above. But the information it gives should relate to both the bank and its subsidiaries. [CA 1985 10 Sch 3(1)].

15.122 However, none of this information has to be given if either the bank is a wholly-owned subsidiary of another company incorporated in Great Britain or the bank (together with subsidiaries, if applicable) employs on average fewer than 100 people each week in the UK. [CA 1985 10 Sch 3(5), (7)].

Mixed groups

15.123 A situation may arise where a holding company prepares its financial statements in accordance with Schedule 4 to the *Companies Act 1985*, but the consolidated financial statements are prepared in accordance with Schedule 9 to that Act (because the group meets the definition of a banking group).

15.124 Because the directors' report is attached to the holding company's balance sheet, it should comply with the requirements of Schedule 7 to the *Companies Act 1985*. However, because the consolidated financial statements are prepared in accordance with Schedule 9 to the *Companies Act 1985*, the directors' report should contain also the information required by paragraphs 2 and 3 of Schedule 10 to that Act. These paragraphs require the disaggregation of turnover and profit or loss before tax by class of business, and also the disclosure of the average number of employees and their aggregate remuneration. [CA 1985 Sec 255C(5)]. The information to be disclosed is outlined in paragraphs 15.117 to 15.122 above.

Auditors' consideration of the directors' report

15.125 As with Schedule 4 companies, auditors are required to consider if, in their opinion, the directors' report is consistent with the financial statements. If there is an inconsistency, auditors are required to draw attention to that fact in their report. [CA 1985 Sec 235(3)]. The directors' report does not form part of the financial statements on which the auditors report. However, as stated in paragraph 15.112 above, where information that would normally be shown in the company's financial statements is included in the directors' report, the auditors' report should cover that information.

Loans to directors and officers

15.126 In general, banks may provide any amount of loans and quasi-loans and guarantees in respect of such loans to a director or his connected person, provided the bank makes the transaction in the ordinary course of business and on terms that are no different from that offered to persons unconnected with the bank. [CA 1985 Sec 338(1)(3)(4)]. Also banks may make loans on beneficial terms to directors for the purpose of house purchase or improvement up to a maximum amount of £100,000 provided the bank makes similar loans of that type available to its employees on no less favourable terms. The special rules that cover the legality of these transactions for banks are set out in 'Manual of Accounting - volume I', chapter 21.

15.127 Banks are also exempted from some of the disclosure requirements that apply to other companies. The provisions of Schedule 6 to the *Companies Act 1985* have effect subject to Part IV of Schedule 9 to that Act. [CA 1985 Sec 255B(2)]. Banks and their parent companies need only disclose the following information in respect of loans made by the banks to directors and officers (being a chief executive or manager within the meaning of the *Banking Act 1987*):

- The aggregate amounts outstanding at the end of the financial year, analysed under loans, quasi-loans and credit transactions.

- The number of persons for whom the bank made those transactions.

[CA 1985 6 Sch 29, 9 Sch Part IV 3(1)].

15.128 A bank, or its parent company must, however, maintain a register that contains a copy of every transaction whose particulars would have been disclosed in the financial statements had the company not been a bank. The register must contain this information for the current year and for the ten preceding years. [CA 1985 Sec 343(1)(2)]. Banks are also required to make available for inspections by their members at the bank's annual general meeting and, for a period of 15 days ending with the date of the annual general meeting, a statement containing particulars of those transactions for the financial year preceding its annual general meeting. [CA 1985 Sec 343(4)(5)]. The bank's auditors are required to examine the annual statement and to report to the members stating whether or not all the particulars the Act requires have been included in it (see further 'Manual of accounting - volume I' chapter 21). [CA 1985 Sec 343(6)(7)].

Banking partnerships

15.129 Section 18(2) of the *Companies Act 1989* inserted a new section 255D in the *Companies Act 1985* dealing with banking partnerships. A banking partnership means a partnership which is an authorised institution under the *Banking Act 1987*. [CA 1985 Sec 255D(2)]. It should be noted that there are currently no banking partnerships in the UK. However, for safe measure, section 255D gives the Secretary of State powers to bring banking partnerships within the scope of the company legislation that applies to accounts and audit of banks. Any

Regulations relating to banking partnerships will be made by statutory instruments.

Distributable profits

15.130 Distributable profits are determined by reference to a company's relevant accounts (see 'Manual of Accounting - volume I' chapter 19). However, a bank's relevant accounts will normally not be prepared in accordance with the rules in Schedule 4 to the *Companies Act 1985* (in particular, as regards the balance sheet formats).

15.131 Consequently, certain of the amounts that are normally used to determine distributable profits either may not appear in a bank's relevant accounts, or may not comply with the definitions given in Schedule 4 to the *Companies Act 1985*. For example, fixed assets are not defined in Schedule 9 to the *Companies Act 1985*, and the definition of provisions in Schedule 9 is different from that given in Schedule 4 to that Act.

15.132 Schedule 11 to the *Companies Act 1985* modifies the rules for determining distributable profits when the relevant accounts are those of a bank. [CA 1985 Sec 279]. The principal provisions of Schedule 11 are outlined below:

- If an asset is included in a bank's relevant accounts as neither a fixed asset nor a current asset, then it shall be treated as a fixed asset for the purpose of:
    - □ Determining the distributable profits of a investment company that is also a bank (see chapter 17). [CA 1985 11 Sch 2(b)].
    - □ Determining whether a provision for the diminution in the value of an asset is realised or unrealised (see 'Manual of Accounting - volume I' chapter 19). [CA 1985 11 Sch 7(b)].
- Development costs that have been capitalised and included as an asset in the balance sheet do not have to be treated as a realised revenue loss (see 'Manual of Accounting - volume I' chapter 19). [CA 1985 11 Sch 3].
- Provisions stated in accordance with the definition in Part I of Schedule 9 to the *Companies Act 1985* should be used to calculate the distributable profits of a bank (as opposed to provisions stated in accordance with the tighter definition in Schedule 4 - see pàra 15.77 and 'Manual of Accounting - volume I' chapter 11). [CA 1985 11 Sch 1, 2(a), 4(a), 7(a)].
- The requirement that the relevant accounts should be properly prepared (whether they be annual financial statements, or interim

accounts or initial accounts) does not prevent a bank from taking advantage of the exemptions in paragraph 27(2) of Part I of Schedule 9 to the *Companies Act 1985* in preparing those financial statements (see paras 15.104 to 15.109). [CA 1985 11 Sch 5(a), 6(b)].

15.133 The CCAB also issued a Technical Release 'Distributable profits of banks and deposit taking institution' (TR 556). The statement does not seek to deal with those problems relating to distributable profits which are common to all types of company and which are considered in detail in 'Manual of Accounting - volume I' chapter 19. The statement is limited to giving guidance on distributability in the context of the various accounting practices that are adopted by banks. The adoption of such accounting practices give rise to profits that may properly be regarded as realised and, consequently, distributable which would not, necessarily, be so identified in other types of company. The areas of particular significance to a bank's operations that are examined in the statement are dealing assets, foreign exchange, financial futures and additionally the particular problems posed to banks by operating through overseas branches and holding investments.

Audit report

Reporting under the Companies Act 1985

15.134 The auditors' report on the financial statements of a banking company or group that is not entitled to benefit from, or that has not taken advantage of, the exemptions conferred by paragraph 27(2) of Part I of Schedule 9 to the *Companies Act 1985*, is expressed in true and fair view terms. If the financial statements do not give a true and fair view, the auditors' report should be qualified in accordance with the Auditing Standard 'The Audit Report'.

15.135 In the case of an exempt bank that has prepared its financial statements under the more limited disclosure requirements of Schedule 9 (see para 15.104 above), the auditors are not required to report whether, in their opinion, the financial statements of the bank give a true and fair view. As a result, the auditors are only required to report whether, in their opinion, the financial statements have been properly prepared in accordance with the *Companies Act 1985*. [CA 1985 9 Sch Part I 28A]. Similar requirements apply to consolidated financial statements where the parent company heading the group has taken advantage of the exemptions from the disclosure requirements of paragraph 27(2) of Part I of Schedule 9 to the *Companies Act 1985*. [CA 1985 9 Sch Part II 5(2)]. If the auditors are unable to give an unqualified opinion on whether the financial statements have been properly prepared in accordance with the *Companies Act 1985*, they should state the reasons for their qualification. An example of an unqualified audit report of an exempt bank is given below.

REPORT OF THE AUDITORS TO [NAME OF BANKING COMPANY]

We have audited the financial statements on pages [] to [] in accordance with Auditing Standards.

In our opinion the financial statements have been prepared in accordance with the provisions of the Companies Act 1985 applicable to banking companies.

[Name of firm]

Chartered Accountants,

[Address].

[Date of report].

15.136 In addition, auditors are required to give written notice to The Bank if they decide to include in their report any qualification as to a matter mentioned in section 235 of the *Companies Act 1985* (true and fair view and compliance with the Act), or any statement about accounting records pursuant to section 237 of that Act. [BA 1987 Sec 46(2)(c)].

Reporting under the Banking Act 1987

15.137 As stated in paragraph 15.4 above, the *Banking Act 1987* gives The Bank power to obtain information from any bank and to require that this information be reported upon by a 'reporting accountant' (appointed by the bank and normally expected to be the auditor). The reporting accountant is required to report to the directors of the bank or to the senior manager of UK branches of banks incorporated overseas, on the following matters, for onward transmission to the Bank:

- Accounting and other records and internal control systems.
- Bank of England returns used for prudential purposes.

15.138 In order to express an opinion on a bank's records and systems of control for the purposes of the *Banking Act 1987*, the auditor should have regard to the Bank's Guidance Note on 'Accounting and other records and internal control systems and reporting accountants' reports thereon' (BSD 1987/2) and the Auditing Guideline, 'Banks in the United Kingdom' (AG 3.307). The Guidance Note sets out the Bank's interpretation of the statutory requirements and provides guidance to both the banks and their accountants as to how they are to be met. It includes the standard letter to be used for the purposes of reporting, the forms that it may take and procedures for its issue. It should be noted that an examination of a bank's records and internal control system to meet the requirements of the *Banking Act 1987* differs in purpose and scope from a study and evaluation of the records and systems undertaken in connection with the audit of statutory financial statements. It is, therefore, unlikely that the reporting accountants will be able to rely solely on work carried out for audit purposes and, consequently, they will almost certainly need to adopt additional procedures.

15.139 Accountants reporting on prudential returns should have regard to the Bank's Guidance Note on 'Reporting accountants' reports on the Bank of England returns used for prudential purposes' (BSD 1987/3). It provides guidance to accountants on the scope of their examination and the form of their report. It includes the standard letter to be used for reporting, the forms that it may take and procedures for its issue.

15.140 The scope of the above work will be determined at trilateral meetings between The Bank, the bank reported on and the reporting accountants or auditors.

15.141 Under the protection of section 47 of the *Banking Act 1987*, the auditors or the reporting accountants are able to communicate with The Bank information or opinions relating to the business or affairs of the banking company without contravening the duty of confidence owed to the banking company. These matters include those that are relevant to the reports made by reporting accountants, to the regular discussions with the Bank and to those exceptional circumstances where the auditors or reporting accountants feel that in the interests of protecting depositors, it is not appropriate or practical to discuss the matter with the management of the bank. The Bank's Guidance Note on 'The Bank of England's relationship with auditors and reporting accountants' (BSD 1987/4) sets out the circumstances under which it expects auditors and reporting accountants to take the initiative in reporting to it. It also sets out the way in which such *ad hoc* reports should be made as well as its proposed arrangements for trilateral meetings between itself, the banks and their auditors and reporting accountants.

SECTIONS OF THE COMPANIES ACT 1985 THAT APPLY SPECIFICALLY TO BANKING COMPANIES

Section	Description
246	Exemption for small and medium-sized companies
248	Exemption for small and medium-sized groups
255	Special provisions for banking and insurance companies
255A	Special provisions for banking and insurance groups
255B	Modification of disclosure requirements in relation to banking company or group
255C	Directors' report where accounts are prepared in accordance with special provisions
255D	Power to apply provisions to banking partnerships
262A	Index of defined expressions
279	Distributions by banking or insurance companies
330	General restrictions on loans etc. to directors and persons connected with them
338	Loans or quasi-loans by money lending company
343	Record of transactions not disclosed in company accounts
344	Exemptions from section 343
449	Provisions for security of information obtained
450	Punishment for destroying, mutilating etc. company documents
451A	Disclosure of information by Secretary of State or inspection
452	Privileged information
460	Order on application of Secretary of State

Section	Description
720	Certain companies to publish periodical statement
735	'Company', etc.
744	Expressions used generally in this Act
Sch 9	Special provision for banking and insurance companies and groups
Sch 10	Directors' report where accounts prepared in accordance with special provisions for banking or insurance companies or groups
Sch 11	Modification of Part VIII where company's accounts prepared in accordance with special provisions for banking or insurance companies

BBA SORP – SECURITIES

THE ASC FRANK

This Statement of Recommended Practice (SORP) on accounting for securities has been prepared by the British Bankers' Association and the Irish Bankers' Federation.

The Accounting Standards Committee has reviewed the SORP and the consutative procedures that have been followed in preparing it, and has approved and franked it as representing recommended accounting practice for the banking industry in the United Kingdom and Ireland.

Explanatory foreword

This Statement of Recommended Accounting Practice (SORP) issued jointly by the British Bankers' Association (BBA) and the Irish Bankers' Federation (IBF) on accounting for securities is the first in what is planned to be a series of SORPs for the banking industry. Like other industry SORPs, they are intended to supplement the Statements of Standard Accounting Practice (SSAPs) issued until recently by the Councils of the members of the Consultative Committee of Accountancy Bodies (CCAB). The SORP has been 'franked' by the Accounting Standards Committee in accordance with its report 'Review of the Standard Setting Process' published in 1983.

Differences of accounting treatment between one bank and another can sometimes make it difficult for users of accounts to interpret the information given. There is also growing pressure, both domestically and internationally, for the accounts of banks to be made more informative. The primary aim of drawing up SORPs is to narrow the areas of difference and to enhance the value of the accounts to those who use them.

The accounts of banks are prepared within the statutory framework laid down in the Companies Acts. Both in the United Kingdom and in the Republic of Ireland the legislation provides somewhat different rules for banks from those applying to the generality of companies. These rules will undergo substantial changes as a result of the implementation of the EC Bank Accounts Directive (86/635/EEC). Wherever possible, however, an attempt has been made to anticipate the effects the directive will have once it is implemented.

Banks' accounts must also be prepared with regard to relevant accounting standards. The SORPs may provide guidance on how the requirements of a SSAP can best be interpreted in the circumstances of a bank, but they cannot override those requirements. The international standard IAS 30 issued by the International Accounting Standards Committee on disclosures in the financial statements of banks and similar financial institutions is also relevant.

The recommendations in the SORP are, of course, also subject to the overriding requirement that the accounts must present a true and fair view.

The SORPs issued by the BBA and IBF are recommendations addressed by the two associations to their own members and, as such, are intended to apply to the entity accounts of banks incorporated in the United Kingdom or the Republic of Ireland and to the consolidated accounts of British and Irish banking groups. However, although they are intended to be authoritative and persuasive, it is recognised that it is not compulsory to disclose the fact or nature of any departure from recommended practice.

September 1990

STATEMENT OF RECOMMENDED ACCOUNTING PRACTICE – SECURITIES

Contents

STATEMENT OF RECOMMENDED ACCOUNTING PRACTICE – SECURITIES

Part 1 – Introduction

Why securities are held

1 Securities held by banks and their subsidiaries may perform a variety of functions. Leaving aside investments in subsidiary and associated companies and other participating interests, three main categories of holdings can be identified. These are dealing, market making and investment securities. In addition, securities positions may be maintained for the purpose of 'hedging' other transactions, whether on or off the balance sheet.

2 Dealing securities are holdings, or short positions, which are turned over relatively rapidly. They tend to be mainly, but not exclusively, short-term paper. The description 'dealing' is not really an apposite one, because such holdings may serve more than one purpose simultaneously, and the relative importance of the different factors can change over time.

3 A minimum stock of short-term paper is needed by a bank as part of its liquidity management: a bank needs both 'operational' liquidity to help smooth out day-to-day variations in its cash flow and 'prudential' liquidity available to meet unexpected outflows resulting from a possible disruption in its access to sources of funding. Such a stock is needed at all times. However, the extent of a bank's holdings beyond its basic liquidity needs are conditioned by its view of the market and the prospects for making short-term profits as the portfolio is turned over. Part of the stock of liquid assets may also be held to 'hedge' liabilities or commitments, either in a general sense or by specifically matching one transaction with another.

4 Those banks and their securities subsidiaries which quote a regular two-way price in particular securities, with the aim of profiting primarily from the bid/offer spread, need to maintain securities positions for that purpose. This is what is meant by market making securities. The size of the positions depends on the ebb and flow of the demand experienced, but obviously the size of the 'book' will be adjusted in the light of the market maker's view of the market. To that extent the distinction, in terms of the purpose for which they are held, between market making securities and other dealing securities is somewhat tenuous. Banks have engaged in market making for many years, for example in eurobonds, but the importance of market making activities to some banks has been greatly increased by their acquisition of securities firms following the relaxation in the rules for corporate membership of the Stock Exchange in 1986.

5 Banks' investment portfolios are comprised of securities bought for the longer term and they are turned over with far less frequency. Such portfolios often comprise gilt-edged securities held on a longer-term basis but equities may also be held, for example in the course of venture capital activities.

6 The holding period may be several years, and in some banks gilt-edged securities may be held until maturity, or close thereto. In others, gilt-edged securities are considered to be available for switching operations, in which case the holding period for individual securities may be shorter but the portfolio as a whole retains its essential character. The purpose of such portfolios is primarily prudential. They provide a second line of defence, behind the shorter-term paper held in the dealing portfolio, available to be pledged or sold in the unlikely event of crisis withdrawals of deposits. They are also available for repurchase transactions with the central bank in times of temporary liquidity shortages in the money markets. At first sight it might seem paradoxical that securities held for liquidity reasons can be regarded as held for the longer term. However, the need to raise cash from them arises only very rarely, if at all, and then mainly as a result of factors extraneous to the bank, while the need to maintain the portfolio in existence is a continuing one.

7 Investment securities are traditionally valued at cost, adjusted where necessary for the amortisation of premiums and discounts to redemption. The same treatment has often been applied to dealing securities, especially where they are held with liquidity motives to the fore; dealing securities held more for the purpose of taking a view have often been valued at the lower of cost and market value. In recent years, however, there has been a move towards valuing dealing securities at market value, which is also the normal treatment for market making positions.

The Scope of the SORP

8 It is appropriate that the accounting treatment for securities covered by this SORP should relate to the purpose for which securities positions are taken, rather than to the precise nature of the instruments. In today's complex markets, the interchangeability of different types of security makes this the only workable approach.

9 Distinctions based on types of instrument are, however, needed for the purpose of delineating the scope of the SORP. The interchangeability of many instruments and the close interrelationships between different types of assets and liabilities on a bank's balance sheet that are a feature of modern treasury management argue for a broad scope. In reality, a bank's securities positions interrelate not only with one another but also with the loan and deposit book; nevertheless, for accounting purposes, there is a clear distinction between tradeable

securities and deposit and loan instruments which, though capable of being bought and sold, are not in practice generally traded. Securities positions may also be closely interrelated with positions in off-balance sheet derivative products, such as swaps, options and futures. However, such instruments are to be covered in the separate SORP on commitments and contingencies.

10 The scope of this SORP is confined to on-balance sheet transferable securities, whether equities, bonds or money market paper. It covers not only certificates of deposit and commercial paper but also bills of exchange, which banks for the most part regard as money market instruments. (Cheques, however, are not included and nor are overdue bills; when a bill is unpaid, the holder acquires claims against the parties to the bill which, for accounting purposes, are included with loans and advances.) Securities held as associated companies or other participating interests are outside the scope of the SORP, since they are no different for banks than for other entities.

11 This SORP is concerned with assets and liabilities arising from contracts to purchase, sell or subscribe for securities. Assets arising out of agreements to lend money, whether or not supported by the issue of 'debentures', are to be covered by a separate SORP on advances. Some banking transactions take the legal form of an acquisition of securities (typically preference shares) but are in substance lending transactions; these should be accounted for as advances, as should securities acquired in substitution for an advance and held only with a view to its orderly realisation.

12 This SORP applies to outright forward transactions in securities as well as to transactions for immediate delivery. It also covers warrants and other instruments conferring a right to subscribe for securities, since these are commonly dealt with in the same way as the securities themselves.

Part 2 – Commentary

Valuation – dealing and market making securities

13 The prime objective of the SORP is to narrow areas of difference in bank accounting by reducing the number of different methods of valuation in use and specifying the circumstances in which different methods should be used. It is considered that the recommended accounting treatment for both dealing and market-making securities should be the same. Indeed, it is only tradition, dating back to before the restructuring of the financial services industry, when market making and banking were more clearly differentiated, that has given rise to different treatments. It is further considered that, of the various valuation methods in use, market value is the only basis of accounting which allows an institution properly to measure its operating results.

14 Market value accounting, or 'marking to market', as it is often known, offers a number of important advantages. The 'concept of prudence' implications are considered below, but it should be emphasised that, even though the price at which a security is subsequently sold may be lower than the market value at the accounting date, that market value is nevertheless the most realistic available measure of performance up to that date. It is a value which could, with reasonable certainty, have been realised in cash. It reflects the management decision not to sell the security at that date, a decision just as valid as a decision to sell. Such a basis of valuation is also more relevant for management purposes and, increasingly, it is market value that is required for regulatory reporting purposes.

15 Furthermore, there are significant disadvantages in adopting cost-based methods of accounting for dealing and market-making securities. The most serious is that reported profits can be seriously distorted by the timing of disposals. In addition, there are practical problems. Where securities are actively traded, perhaps involving short positions as well as long positions, it is not always clear what is meant by 'cost', which can be open to different interpretations depending upon the precise sequence in which a quick succession of purchases and sales are recorded when positions are booked.

16 One difficulty with market value accounting for securities is that it may cause the effects of market factors on the values of securities positions to be reflected in the accounts earlier than the effects of the same market factors on the associated funding. In principle, this problem can be overcome by valuing borrowings at their market value when they can be specifically identified as funding a securities trading book; however, the treatment of borrowings is outside the scope of this SORP. The worst effects are avoided by the use of hedge accounting, as described in paragraphs 36-38.

17 The legal position on market value accounting is discussed in Part 5. Other arguments against market value accounting have been put forward based on the apparent imprudence of taking credit for gains that have not been turned into cash. It is considered, however, that there is an important distinction between the position of purchases of goods and that of trades in securities. Unlike the stocks of goods contemplated by SSAP 9, securities dealing portfolios, at least where active dealers in liquid markets are concerned, can be sold at the prevailing market price without the need to search for customers. It is true that, in the case of market makers, part of the economic function is matching buyers and sellers, but the remuneration for this function is merely the bid/offer spread. The remainder of the price movement between cost and disposal value is the return resulting from position taking, not the return on market making as such. Accordingly, the bid/offer spread should not be regarded as earned until disposal has been accomplished, but the rest of the movement in market value can

be. These arguments lead to the conclusion that, for both dealing and market making securities, long positions should be valued at bid price and short positions at offer price.

18 The SORP does not attempt to spell out in detail how bid prices and offer prices should be arrived at; common practices include taking from dealing screens a sample of the prices quoted by recognised market makers and averaging them. The procedure adopted should, however, be consistent from one year to the next. In some overseas markets there may be no price directly analogous to the screen prices available from systems with competing market makers and, where this is the case, it will be necessary to use some other publicly ascertainable price such as, for example, an official stock exchange quotation.

19 Where market value accounting is adopted, it is necessary to ensure that there is no premature recognition of profit. Particular care is needed in the case of illiquid securities, or where holdings are of larger than normal market size, or in respect of certain exceptional dealing positions.

Unquoted securities

20 Paragraph 59 in Part 4 provides that securities for which there is no active market, and for which no publicly ascertainable price is regularly available, be carried at directors' estimate of market value. Such securities are described as 'unquoted'. They fall into two main categories. First, there are those for which a directors' valuation can be constructed by reference to the value of analogous quoted securities. In the case of non-convertible debt securities, for example, it will normally be possible to carry out a valuation by discounting the cash flows at suitable rates of interest. The interest rates chosen can be taken from those implicit in the market's valuation of similar debt, but they should reflect the risk inherent in the security and the valuation should adequately reflect the future costs of realising the security. It is not usually possible to construct an equally dependable valuation for equities and equity-type instruments, although occasionally it may be possible to base a valuation on the market's valuation of quoted equity in the same company. In these cases, although the security is unquoted it can nevertheless be regarded as readily realisable, because there is reasonable assurance as to the price at which a dealer would have been willing to assume the position.

21 Into the second category of unquoted securities fall those that cannot easily be valued by analogy. These often have the distinguishing feature that in order to dispose of them it may be necessary to undertake an active search for buyers. For example, a dealer may acquire a block of illiquid securities with a view to reselling them in smaller amounts. In such cases the position may be akin to that of a dealer in goods and it would not necessarily be appropriate to take full

immediate credit for a presumed uplift in market value. Careful consideration has been given to whether it would be prefereable to use cost-based accounting in such circumstances. However, the distinction between securities which are readily realisable and those which are not is not always clear cut and there is merit in treating them consistently. It should be appreciated that, by their nature, securities which are difficult to dispose of will anyway usually fall to be treated as investment securities. Consequently, it is considered preferable that there should be no departure from the principle that dealing portfolios should be carried at market value. However, it must be acknowledged that the approach to the assessment of 'market value' may sometimes need to be conservative. The cardinal principle is that there should be no premature recognition of profit. This means that the value at which a position in an unquoted security is carried must be one at which there is reasonable assurance that the position could have been liquidated at the balance sheet date, taking into account the costs of disposal.

Holdings larger than normal size

22 Somewhat similar considerations apply to holdings of securities which are actively traded, but where the holding is so large in relation to normal market turnover that it cannot necessarily be realised at the screen price. Such large lines of stock should normally be valued at a discount to the screen price which is sufficient to reflect the costs of disposing of them in the ordinary course of business: normally the bank will either sell the whole line all at once at an unfavourable price or it will incur additional costs in gradually releasing smaller parcels of stock on to the market over time. (Part 3 of the SORP defines 'market price' as the screen price for transactions of normal size. Paragraph 60 in Part 4 provides that holdings of abnormal size should in general be carried at a discount to market price.)

Exceptional dealing positions

23 In the particular circumstances where, in the view of the directors of a bank, the current market price of a holding of dealing securities is unrepresentative of its actual worth, because, for example, of extraneous factors which have exaggerated the volatility of the market price, a mechanistic application of market value accounting could impinge on the prudence concept alluded to in paragraph 19. Where such holdings have been identified they may be valued at an appropriate lower amount.

Practical problems

24 It is acknowledged that, for some dealing securities, strict adherence to market value accounting principles could pose practical difficulties. This is especially true where there is no proper market and a directors' estimate of market value needs to be undertaken. However, it is

believed that such problems can usually be overcome when regard is had to materiality. For example, one potential area of difficulty concerns bill portfolios, which typically comprise a large number of bills each of relatively small value. It should be sufficient to value such bills by maturity bands, using the quoted rates appropriate to each band. In some instances – for example, bill portfolios in overseas branches, where markets are poor and interest rate data difficult to obtain – the size of the portfolio is likely to be small and regard to materiality may justify valuation at cost plus accrual of discount or, equivalently, face value less unearned discount.

Valuation – investment securities

25 The arguments in favour of market value accounting do not apply with the same force where investment securities are concerned. Moreover, where securities are held for a purpose which involves them being held over a longer term, often with the intention of holding them until maturity, there is a strong case for bringing their treatment into line with that of loans and deposits by adopting a cost-based valuation. Nevertheless, the principal disadvantage of cost-based accounting – the arbitrary dependence of reported profits on the timing of disposals – still applies. Hence it is desirable to limit the use of cost-based accounting in such a way as to minimise this problem. It is therefore proposed to deal by exception: the SORP recommends the use of market value accounting unless securities can be identified as being held for the longer term. There should be sufficient documentary evidence of the purpose for which the securities are held to demonstrate that a cost-based valuation is appropriate.

26 It is arguable that the disadvantages of cost-based accounting are such that banks should be at liberty, if they so wish, to use market value accounting for all their securities portfolios. However, the EC Bank Accounts Directive, when implemented in the United Kingdom, will require that certain securities be valued on the basis of cost, namely debt securities held as 'financial fixed assets'. Article 35(2) of the Directive explains that this means "securities intended for use on a continuing basis in the normal course of an undertaking's activities". This form of words has been adopted in the definition of 'investment securities' in Part 3, and it is recommended that cost-based accounting be used only where securities are held for purposes meeting this criterion.

27 In the case of gilt-edged and other debt securities, the Bank Accounts Directive permits their cost to be adjusted for the amortisation over the period to redemption of the premium or discount at which they are purchased. This should always be done. (Similarly, where a security is subject to a put option, it may be appropriate for the premium of discount to the option price to be amortised.) Many banks calculate this amortisation on a straight-line basis. Where the use of such a basis

would materially distort reported profits, as, for example, would be the case with deep-discount bonds, amortisation should be calculated on an 'actuarial' basis which gives expression to a level yield over the period to redemption.

28 With index-linked securities, including those linked to a currency or a commodity price as well as those linked to inflation, the same principle should be applied. This is not straightforward, because the redemption value continually alters according to the movement of the index and the treatment of the accrual of discount (or depletion of premium) becomes more complicated. When the security is first acquired, the premium or discount at which the cost stands to the redemption value at the time of purchase should be amortised over the period to redemption in the usual way. At the first balance sheet date thereafter, the book value should be adjusted not only for the amortisation of this initial discount or premium but also by a further amount to reflect the movement in the relevant index since purchase. For the next accounting period, the amortisation should be recalculated so as to spread the difference between the new book value and the new redemption value over the remaining life. At subsequent balance sheet dates the same adjustments should be made. Since at each stage the book value and the redemption value are both altered by the same percentage amount, namely the movement in the index, the amortisation will be altered by that same amount. Where the difference is not material, it may be acceptable to adopt market value as a simpler approach to the valuation of index-linked securities.

29 Banks which hold venture capital investments usually regard them as held for the longer term and value them on the basis of cost. Such investments will generally fall within the SORP's definition of an investment security, and they should be treated as such unless an alternative classification can be justified. For these investments, as for all other investment securities, provision should be made for any diminution in value which is expected to be other than temporary. The Bank Accounts Directive requires such provisions to be made for each investment individually, not for the portfolio as a whole.

30 Occasionally securities will be acquired not by purchase but by way of fee, and then taken into an investment portfolio. Their 'cost' can then be taken to be the market price at the start of dealings. Where, however, there are restrictions on resale it may be appropriate to use a lower valuation. Investment securities may also occasionally be acquired by means of a paper for paper exchange. In these circumstances the new security should be recorded at the book value of the old one, and the difference between that value and the new redemption value should be amortised in the usual way. Where more than one class of paper is received in the exchange, it will be necessary to apportion the book value of the original security to each such class on the basis of a market valuation.

Sales of investment securities

31 It is necessary to consider how best to deal with the position that arises when securities intended to be held on a longer-term basis are sold prematurely. In many circumstances, such as where a strategic decision is taken to reduce the size of the investment portfolio, the profit or loss on disposal should be taken straight to profit and loss account. Such profits, if material, should be clearly identified so that users of accounts can make allowance for the distortion caused.

Transfers between portfolios

32 In rare circumstances, a bank may alter the purpose for which securities are held, reclassifying them from an investment portfolio to a dealing portfolio or vice versa. Transfers on reclassification should always be effected at market value. In the former case, the change from cost-based to market value accounting will in general give rise to a profit or loss, which should be taken to the profit and loss account; the amount concerned should be disclosed if it is material. When the transfer is in the opposite direction, the market value at the date of transfer becomes the 'cost' of the holding in the investment portfolio. It is appreciated that a cost-based accounting method for securities could be abused by the unjustifiable reclassification of holdings. Reclassifications should therefore take place only rarely and appropriate documentary evidence must exist to justify the treatment.

33 It is considered acceptable, for example, to recognise a profit on the reclassification of an investment security where a bank decides to sell an investment security and where the stock is taken up by a market maker which is a division of the bank or a company within the same banking group. Provided that the market maker holds the stock in the ordinary course of its market making business it is considered that the reclassification can be regarded as amounting in substance to a sale from the investment portfolio and be treated accordingly. In practice, such a reclassification will normally lead to an actual sale shortly afterwards.

Switching transactions

34 It is arguable that different considerations apply to switching transactions within an investment portfolio. Paragraph 63 in Part 4 makes provision for a restricted class of such transactions, described there as 'temporary switching transactions', where a security is switched into a similar one with the firm intention of reversing the switch at a later date. It is then not inappropriate to retain the security in the books at cost adjusted for amortisation. The economic substance of the transaction is that a specialist dealing activity is superimposed on to the investment portfolio in order to generate, by exploiting temporary market anomalies, a flow of cash profits which provide a

modest enhancement to the portfolio yield. Such profits can properly be brought into account as they arise, without disrupting the accounting basis for the securities held on what is, in effect, a continuing basis. Accordingly, paragraph 63 allows for the security sold to be retained on the balance sheet as though it were at all times held in the investment portfolio but combined, during the period while the switch is open, with a short position valued at market value. The long position in the security temporarily acquired should, of course, also be carried at market value. In the unlikely event that they are material, the amounts concerned should be disclosed. The switching transactions covered by this treatment seldom remain open for more than a few weeks and will therefore normally have been closed by the time the accounts are signed.

Stock lending and 'repos'

35 Both investment securities and dealing securities are sometimes lent, or they may be sold subject to a commitment to repurchase them. The securities lent or sold should be retained in the books whenever substantially all the risks and rewards of ownership remain with the seller, as, for example, where the repurchase commitment is at a predetermined price (paragraph 67). Similarly, securities purchased subject to a commitment to resell should be treated as lending transactions if the bank does not acquire the risks and rewards of ownership.

Hedging

36 A bank's securities positions cannot be viewed in isolation when they are held on an interrelated basis with other assets and liabilities or with off-balance sheet items. Where securities positions are maintained for the purpose of hedging other transactions, it is necessary for the accounting treatment applied to the securities to be consistent with that applied to the assets, liabilities or off-balance sheet items constituting the other side of the hedge.

37 Where all the assets and liabilities involved in hedging operations are valued at market value, the accounting basis reflects the economic effect of the transactions to a high degree of accuracy. Indeed, this strengthens the case for market value accounting. Separate provision, however, needs to be made for circumstances in which one side of a hedge is not valued at market value, for example where deposits and loans are concerned. When securities positions are taken for the express purpose of hedging borrowing and lending items, it is clearly inappropriate for the securities to be carried at market value. Instead, they should be accounted for so that the income from them and the changes in their value are recognised in the profit and loss account consistently with the income and expenditure flows from the items hedged.

38 Market value accounting should only be overridden, however, for securities positions held with the intention of fulfilling a hedging function and specifically identified as such. There should be appropriate documentary evidence of this intention, identifying the securities position concerned, the assets, liabilities or off-balance sheet positions which it hedges and the period for which the hedge is intended to operate. The hedge need not be perfect, but there must be a high degree of probability that it will eliminate a substantial part of the market risk that would otherwise be borne. It is not necessary for the transactions to be matched on a one-to-one basis: it is acceptable for a position or an identified part of such a position to be regarded as hedging a group of liabilities, assets and off-balance sheet transactions. Where a securities position already held is assigned to a hedging operation, the transfer should take place at market value. Where a securities position accounted for as a hedge is prematurely liquidated, or is deemed no longer to be part of the hedge and consequently is revalued to market value, the profit or loss arising should be treated so as to match the flow of income or expenditure from the remaining assets or liabilities which had been hedged.

Trade date or settlement date accounting

39 Some banks account for securities transactions as of the date of the settlement of the transaction rather than the date on which the trade is made. It is considered that only trade date accounting gives a true and fair view in the case of securities transactions, as during the period between the trade date and the settlement date of a purchase of a security the bank has all the risks and rewards of ownership of the security, just as it does after the transaction is settled. For this reason, it is increasingly trade date accounting that is required by regulatory bodies. In the case of gilt-edged securities, however, where settlement takes place only one business day after the trade date, the distinction may not be material and it may therefore be acceptable to use settlement date accounting. (Different considerations apply in the case of forward exchange transactions. The distinction between securities and foreign exchange is that with the latter the bank acquires offsetting claims on and liabilities to its counterparties, and because these are of the same type they can appropriately be netted against one another. In the case of securities transactions the outstanding claims and liabilities are not of the same type.)

Interest and dividends

40 It is considered that interest on debt securities should be brought into profit as it accrues. To accomplish this, it is necessary to separate out the accrued interest from the market value where the security is not one which is quoted 'clean' of accrued interest. However, where there is abnormal risk of default interest should be brought into profit only as it is paid. Preference dividends should be treated in the same way as

debt interest, although in some circumstances, such as market making in listed preference shares, a departure from this treatment may be justified on materiality grounds. It should be noted that the Bank Accounts Directive requires holdings of debt securities and preference shares to be recorded together on the balance sheet.

41 For debt securities carried at adjusted cost, the accretion of discount (or depletion of premium) should be treated as interest. In principle, the same applies to securities carried at market value. Strictly, the accretion of discount should be calculated and separated from the remainder of the movement in market value in order to make a proper distinction between interest earnings and trading profits (a distinction which the Bank Accounts Directive requires). However, in many cases the amounts concerned will not be material and the need for burdensome calculations and record keeping which strict adherence to the requirement would entail will be obviated. For example, where securities are turned over rapidly, it will normally be a sufficient approximation to accrue the interest at the coupon rate and treat the movement in the 'clean' market value as trading profit. However, where the circumstances are such that the amounts may be material – for example, where zero-coupon bonds or bills of exchange are concerned, or where the holding periods are of significant length in relation to the life of the security – it is considered that banks should be in a position to identify precisely the accretion of discount.

42 In the case of index-linked securities, adjustments to the book value to reflect movements in the relevant index are part of the accretion of the discount to redemption and so should be treated as interest.

43 Dividends receivable on equity securities should in theory be brought into account on the date of the announcement of the directors' recommendation, unless there is reason to suppose that payment will be countermanded by the shareholders in general meeting. The dividend would then be recorded as a debtor between the announcement date and the date of payment, and in the case of quoted securities carried at market value it would be necessary while the security is still quoted 'cum dividend' to make an adjustment to the market price in order to avoid double counting the dividend. In practice, it is usual in the case of quoted securities to bring the dividend into profit on the ex-dividend date. The difference between the two methods will not normally be material. It may also be acceptable on materiality grounds to recognise the dividend on the date of payment, or on the date when it is expressed to be payable, although in either case this will necessitate adding the dividend entitlement back to the quoted price during the ex-dividend period.

Fee earnings

44 Several different types of fee are receivable in respect of primary

market securities transactions. In euromarket transactions, there is normally a clear distinction between selling group fees on the one hand and underwriting and management fees on the other. Selling group fees are paid by reference to the amount of stock the bank takes on its book and are paid regardless of whether the bank sells the stock on or retains it for itself. Such fees are best regarded as an adjustment to the price at which the stock is purchased. They should therefore be deducted from the cost of the holding. This means that, where securities are retained and are valued at market value, the whole fee will be treated as earned immediately if trading opens at or above the issue price gross of the fee. Underwriting and management fees, which are often negotiated as a package, are paid to members of the syndicate for other services and are related to the commitment made, rather than to the amount of stock taken up. The distinction between them is that the management fee is payable regardless of the success or otherwise of the issue, whereas the underwriting fee is contingent on the outcome of the stabilisation operations and potential issue expense recoveries. Management fees should be brought into profit when they are receivable, which will normally be when the securities are allotted. Underwriting fees should also be recognised on allotment, subject to a provision being made to take account of possible retentions for the stabilisation costs and expenses. This provision should be a prudent estimate based on past experience and should be monitored until the fee is received.

45 Fees for UK-type underwriting activities are not fees for securities *transactions* but fees for assuming a contingent liability. They are therefore outside the scope of this SORP and are to be covered in the SORP on commitments and contingencies.

Foreign currency securities

46 So far as the balance sheet position is concerned, if a security is carried at market value it is immaterial in which currency it is booked. Where a security is traded in more than one currency, arbitrage activities should ensure that it makes little or no difference which country's price is taken. It does make a difference, however, so far as the profit and loss account is concerned.

47 In principle, debt securities should be booked in the currency in which the redemption value is expressed. (This is the 'relevant currency' as defined in Part 3.) This will automatically ensure that the trading profit recorded reflects only the price movement in that currency and that the effect of any exchange rate movement is excluded. As well as making for a more informative presentation in the statutory accounts, this approach has the merit of focusing management attention on the true extent of the bank's currency mismatching. The alternative approaches of booking securities in the currency used to pay for them or in the currency of the place where they are booked can have the

effect of disguising the true currency exposure; indeed, the place where a transaction is booked and currency used to settle it can on occasion be quite arbitrary. Nevertheless, it is recognised that when securities are actively traded it may not always be practicable to adopt the preferred treatment.

48 For equity securities, the position is less clear-cut, but it is considered that the same general principle should apply. Equities should therefore be booked in a currency appropriate to the nature of the security in question. In most cases, it will be obvious which is the relevant currency; for example, the relevant currency for shares in a company operating wholly or mainly in France and traded only on the Paris Bourse is the French franc. Where the choice is not obvious, banks should decide the question on the basis of which currency most accurately reflects the substance of the position from a management viewpoint. The currency selected should in any event be one in which the security is actually traded.

49 It is considered that investment securities as well as dealing securities should be booked in their 'relevant currencies'. Where an investment security is funded in a different currency, for example sterling, the profit and loss account will then reflect that part of the movements in its sterling value which is due to currency fluctuations, but not the rest of the market movement. However, this is not illogical because, whereas the security is being held for a longer-term purpose, the funding can be altered at any time and it is right that the consequences of the funding decision be reflected in profits as they arise. Where the funding is committed for the holding period of the security, however, the accounting treatment should reflect the substance of the related transactions in accordance with the principles applicable for hedging.

Disclosure issues

50 The Bank Accounts Directive requires that securities be recorded in the balance sheet under three separate headings covering respectively treasury bills and other bills eligible for central bank refinancing, debt securities and preference shares, and equities. These are required to be analysed in a variety of ways. It is recommended that the required analyses of the three balance sheet items be provided in the notes to the accounts rather than on the face of the balance sheet.

51 The Directive's required balance sheet captions distinguish securities by type rather than by the purpose for which they are held. It is considered that this should be redressed in the notes to the accounts so as to make a clear distinction between investment securities on the one hand and dealing and market-making securities on the other. Securities in each balance sheet category should therefore be analysed in the notes between investment securities and other securities.

52 The Directive requires a breakdown between listed and unlisted securities. It is recommended that this breakdown should be given for investment securities and other securities separately, as should the required breakdown between public sector and private sector debt securities. The latter breakdown should be amplified in order to distinguish between government securities and other public sector securities where such a distinction is practicable and material. Holdings of bank and building society certificates of deposit should also be separately identified. Short positions in securities should be shown separately on the liabilities side of the balance sheet and analysed in the same way as long positions.

53 The Directive requires the disclosure of the aggregate cost of securities carried at market value. Conversely, it is considered that the market value of investment securities should be shown and that this should be given separately for each category of investment securities which is identified in the breakdown in the notes to the accounts.

54 An illustration of how this information might be presented in the notes to the accounts is given in the appendix.

55 Under the description 'Accounting Policies' in the notes to the accounts there should be a clear explanation of the bases of valuation adopted and the circumstances in which each is applied. This should include the use of market value and cost-based accounting, the treatment of hedging transactions, the treatment of securities acquired by way of fee, the method of amortising premiums and discounts on debt securities and the treatment of sale and repurchase transactions.

Part 3 – Definition of terms used in Part 4

56 The terms listed below are used in Part 4 with the meanings indicated:

'Bank' includes banking group where the context so admits.

'Banking group' means a group whose predominant activity is banking.

'Cost', in relation to securities held, means the amount paid or payable under the contract which gives rise to the holding, including any charges, taxes and duties, but net of any selling fee received or receivable and excluding accrued interest in the case of securities quoted 'clean' of accrued interest. Where part of a holding is sold, the cost of the holding should be apportioned between the part sold and the part retained on a pro-rata basis.

'Interests in securities' means assets or liabilities arising from contracts to purchase, sell or subscribe for securities. It does not include liabilities arising from securities issued by a bank itself or another company in the banking group.

'Investment securities' means securities intended for use on a continuing basis in the activities of the bank, but securities should not be treated as investment securities unless:

(a) they are held for an identified purpose and there is documentary evidence of that purpose; and
(b) the securities held for the documented purpose are clearly identifiable.

'Market price', in relation to quoted securities, means:

(a) in the case of securities traded on exchanges with competing market makers,
– for long positions, bid price
– for short positions, offer price
based on quotations for transactions of normal market size by recognised market makers; and
(b) in other cases, the exchange's official quotation or – if there is no official quotation – some appropriate and publicly ascertainable quoted price.

'Quoted', in relation to securities, means either:

(a) that they are listed on a recognised investment exchange or other investment exchange of repute; or
(b) that a market in them exists and a publicly ascertainable price is regularly available.

'Relevant currency', in relation to interests in securities, means:

(a) in the case of securities redeemable at a fixed price, the currency in which the redemption proceeds are expressed to be payable;
(b) in the case of irredeemable debt securities, the currency in which interest is expressed to be payable; and
(c) in the case of equity securities, a currency in which the security is quoted and which can be associated with the pattern of the investee company's business.

'Relevant redemption date' means the latest possible redemption date in the case of a security purchased at a discount to its redemption value, and the earliest possible redemption date in the case of a security purchased at a premium.

'Securities' means: any units comprising a proportion of the share capital of a company, howsoever constituted; units in a collective investment scheme; debentures, debenture stock, loan stock, bonds and other instruments creating or acknowledging indebtedness (including bills of exchange not overdue, but excluding cheques) by whomsoever issued; instruments entitling the holder to subscribe for any of the foregoing, and all instruments having similar attributes to the foregoing.

'Selling fees' in relation to issues of securities, means fees calculated by reference to the quantity of securities taken on to the books.

'Temporary switching transactions' means the sale of a security and the simultaneous purchase of a closely related security, together with the subsequent resale of the security acquired and simultaneous repurchase of the original holding, the transactions being undertaken for the purpose of exploiting a perceived temporary anomaly in the relative prices of the two securities.

Part 4 – Recommended accounting practice

Scope and application

57 This statement sets out the recommended accounting practice for interests in securities and applies both to the entity accounts of banks and to the consolidated accounts of banking groups. **The provisions of the statement need not be applied to immaterial items.**

58 All securities should be accounted for in accordance with this statement unless:

(a) they derive from transactions which are in substance agreements to lend money, or they are held only for the purpose of recovering advances; or
(b) they are investments in subsidiary or associated undertakings, or other participating interests.

Methods of valuation

59 Subject to paragraphs 60 (large holdings), 61 (hedging) and 62 (investment securities) below, interests in quoted securities should be valued at market price and interests in unquoted securities carried at directors' estimate of market value.

60 Where a holding of a quoted security (other than one to which paragraph 61 or 62 applies) is so large that it could be disposed of only at an unfavourable price or over an extended period, it should be valued at an appropriate discount to the market price. The discount should be sufficient to reflect the reduction in price resulting from the size of the holding or all future costs likely to be incurred in disposing of the interest over time in the ordinary course of business.

61 Interests in securities maintained for the purpose of hedging should be carried at a value which properly reflects the hedge, having regard to

the accounting treatment of the item or items so hedged.

62 Investment securities should be carried at cost, measured in the relevant currency, but the carrying value should be adjusted:

(a) in the case of securities redeemable on or before a given date and not subject to abnormal risk of default, to allow for the amortisation of the premium or discount representing the difference between cost and the redemption proceeds; and
(b) in other cases, to reflect any diminution in their value which is expected to be other than temporary.

Where the profits trend would otherwise be materially distorted, amortisation of premiums and discounts on dated securities should be reckoned so as to give expression to a level gross redemption yield over the period from the date of acquisition to the relevant redemption date. In the case of index-linked securities, the book value and the amount of the amortisation should be updated at each balance sheet date to reflect the movement in the relevant index.

63 Where investment securities have been the subject of temporary switching transactions, their cost may be taken to be the original cost of acquiring the securities before the switching transactions were undertaken. This treatment should not be adopted unless:

(a) appropriate documentation exists of the circumstances in which temporary switching transactions are to be undertaken and of the procedures for executing them; and
(b) the transactions in question are clearly identifiable as complying with those circumstances and procedures.

If this treatment is adopted, then, while the switching transaction is outstanding, the security purchased should be valued at market price. The security which has been sold should be treated as a notional long position valued as though the security were still held, combined with a notional short position valued at market price. If they are material, the amounts concerned should be disclosed.

64 Where quoted securities, or unquoted securities ranking equally with a class of quoted securities and not subject to restrictions on resale, are received by way of fee, their cost should be deemed to be the market value at the start of dealings.

65 In the rare instances when securities are reclassified from dealing portfolios to investment portfolios or from investment portfolios to dealing portfolios, the transfer should be effected at market price (or, in the case of unquoted securities, at directors' estimate of market value) and any consequent profit or loss accounted for through the profit and loss account. There should be appropriate documentary evidence of the circumstances giving rise to the reclassification. The amount of any consequent profit or loss should, if material, be disclosed.

Balance sheet recognition

66 Interests in securities should be recognised as assets or, in the case of short positions, liabilities from the date on which the bank is bound by the contract which gives rise to them.

67 Interests in securities should continue to be recognised as such while the securities are lent, or when they are sold subject to a commitment to repurchase them at a predetermined price. However, where securities are sold subject to a repurchase agreement, the terms of which do not leave substantially all the risks and rewards of ownership with the seller, the transaction should be accounted for as an outright sale and the commitment to repurchase accounted for separately.

Profit and loss account recognition

68 Income from securities held should be brought into the profit and loss account:

(a) in the case of debt securities not subject to abnormal risk of default, as it accrues;
(b) in the case of debt securities which are subject to abnormal risk of default, as it is received;
(c) in the case of equity securities, as dividends are announced or (in the case of quoted securities) when the quotation changes to an 'ex-dividend' basis.

69 Where securities are valued in accordance with paragraphs 59 and 60, profits and losses on disposals and movements in the carrying value of positions held should whenever practicable be measured by reference to the relevant currency for the security. They should be brought into the profit and loss account as they arise. That part of the amount brought into profit which represents the accretion or depletion of discounts or premiums on redeemable debt securities, calculated on the basis set out in paragraph 62, should, if it is material, be segregated and recorded as interest.

70 Profit and losses on disposal of investment securities should be brought into account at the date of disposal and should be separately disclosed. Adjustments to the carrying value of investment securities made in accordance with paragraph 62 should be taken to the profit and loss account; the accretion or depletion of discounts or premiums to redemption should be recorded as interest.

71 Profits and losses arising from movements in the exchange rates of the relevant currencies in which securities are booked should be treated as exchange differences and recorded in the profit and loss account under the appropriate caption.

72 Selling fees should be distinguished from other fees arising from securities issues and should be deducted from the cost of the holding acquired as a result of the issue. Other fees, if not subject to deductions, should be recognised in full when receivable; where a fee is subject to a contingency, it should be recognised only to the extent that it can prudently be expected to exceed the contingent costs.

Disclosure

73 The accounting policies adopted for securities should be disclosed. Where more than one method of valuation is employed, there should be an explanation of the circumstances in which each is applicable.

74 The analyses of securities positions in the notes to the accounts should be given separately at least for investment securities and for other securities. In addition to the required analyses between listed and unlisted securities and between public and private sector debt securities, an analysis should, where practicable, be provided of public sector debt securities between government and other public sector securities. Bank and building society certificates of deposit should be distinguished from other debt securities.

75 Short positions in securities should be recorded in the balance sheet as liabilities and should be analysed in the notes to the accounts in the same way as long positions.

76 The market value of investment securities should be given along with the book value for each category of such securities disclosed in accordance with paragraph 74.

77 Profits less losses from securities trading should be shown separately. In particular, they should not be combined with profits or losses arising from foreign exchange movements.

78 Profits less losses arising on disposal of investment securities should be shown separately. Provisions made in accordance with paragraph 62(b) should be shown separately from other provisions.

Implementation

79 Banks are encouraged to apply the provisions of this SORP as soon as is reasonably practicable, and at the latest in respect of the first accounting year beginning on or after 1 January 1993 (with comparative figures for the year beginning on or after 1 January 1992) to coincide with the implementation of the EC Bank Accounts Directive.

Part 5 – Note on legal requirements

The statutory basis

80 The form and content of the accounts of *non-banking* companies incorporated in Great Britain are governed by section 226 of the Companies Act 1985 (as amended by the Companies Act 1989); the detailed requirements are in Schedule 4 to the Act. (There are parallel provisions for Northern Ireland.) These provisions implement the Fourth EC Company Law Directive (78/660/EEC) and they apply in particular to subsidiaries of banks which are not themselves banks, for example securities companies. The accounts of banks, on the other hand, may be prepared in accordance with section 255 and Schedule 9, which are essentially the rules that applied to all companies before the implementation of the Fourth Directive. It is expected that by the end of 1990 Parliament will have approved a new version of Schedule 9, to take effect for accounting periods beginning on or after 1 January 1993, implementing the Bank Accounts Directive (86/635/EEC). Some banks, mainly merchant banks and discount houses, are permitted to prepare their accounts according to the special rules in Part III of Schedule 9, which allow the maintenance of undisclosed reserves and impose more limited disclosure requirements. These special rules are expected to disappear, however, when the directive is implemented, putting all banks on the same footing.

81 Section 255A of the Act permits the consolidated accounts of a banking group to be prepared in accordance with Schedule 9. A banking group for this purpose is either a group headed by a bank or a group where at least one of the members is an authorised institution under the Banking Act 1987 and where the predominant activities of the group are such as to make it inappropriate to prepare group accounts in accordance with the formats in Schedule 4.

82 Once the new Schedule 9 rules come into force, they will be compulsory for banks and for groups falling within the new definition of a banking group.

Valuation and recognition

83 The existing Schedule 9 rules lay down no particular valuation methods for securities. Any method is therefore permissible so long as it provides a 'true and fair view'. In particular, market value accounting and the use of cost plus accrual of discount are both permissible. Both methods are expressly permitted under the Bank Accounts Directive and so will continue to be permissible when the Directive is implemented, assuming that the United Kingdom exercises the relevant member state options. However, as noted in paragraph 26 above, where a debt security is held as a 'financial fixed asset', only a cost-based method will be permissible. The Directive

does permit revaluation of 'financial fixed assets' but the surplus or deficit must be taken to a revaluation reserve, not to the profit and loss account.

84 This SORP applies to the entity accounts of banks and to the group accounts of banking groups, so it is the Schedule 9 and the Bank Accounts Directive rules that are relevant. In practice, however, banks are likely to adopt the same policies for preparing the entity accounts of their non-banking subsidiaries and it is therefore necessary to have regard to the Schedule 4 rules also. The normal rules (Section B of Part II of the Schedule) do not permit market value accounting for any category of security: paragraphs 22 and 23 require all current assets to be valued at the lower of cost and net realisable value. The alternative rules (Section C of Part II of the Schedule), which are intended to provide a legal basis for current cost accounting, do permit securities to be carried at market value, but they provide that movements in the market value of securities held be taken to a revaluation reserve, not to profit and loss account.

85 Accordingly, a non-banking company can adopt market value accounting only by invoking the 'true and fair override' of section 226(5). This allows departures from the rules laid down in Schedule 4 to the extent that they are *necessary* to provide a true and fair view. The reasons for the departure and the effect of it must be given in the notes to the accounts. It is considered, for the reasons given in paragraphs 14 and 15 above, that it is indeed necessary for securities dealing subsidiaries of banks to value securities at market value in order to give a true and fair view.

86 Paragraph 12 of Schedule 4 requires that only profits realised at the balance sheet date may be included in the profit and loss account. This too may be overridden by virtue either of section 226(5) or of paragraph 15 of the Schedule. In the case of banks a similar requirement will apply once the Directive is implemented, but there will be no doubt about the ability to take profits from movements in the market value of securities to profit and loss account since the Directive makes express provision for market value accounting. However, by virtue of section 263 of the Act a company, whether a bank or a non-bank, may not pay a dividend except out of realised profits. It is important therefore to establish that profits arising from movements in market value are realised.

87 Realised profits are defined in paragraph 91 of Schedule 4 as such profits as fall to be treated as realised profits in accordance with generally accepted accounting principles. It is considered that the use of market value accounting, and the treatment of the resultant profits as realised, is sufficiently widespread to have become 'generally accepted', and that such profits are therefore realised for the purposes of the Act. To qualify as being in accordance with 'generally accepted

accounting principles' a method must, however, be in accordance with fundamental principles, including the principle of prudence. This underlines the importance, stressed in paragraphs 19 and 21 above, of using techniques for assessing market value which do not entail any premature recognition of profit. The subject of realised profits in relation to banking is discussed in the paper 'Distributable profits of banks and deposit taking institutions' (TR556) published by the Consultative Committee of Accounting Bodies.

Disclosure

88 The existing Schedule 9 rules do not prescribe in detail how securities are to be recorded on the face of the balance sheet, although paragraph 4(2) requires that fixed assets, current assets and those that are neither fixed nor current be separately identified. Paragraph 10(1)(a) requires that the aggregate amounts of listed and unlisted securities be shown separately either in the balance sheet or in the notes. Income from listed and unlisted securities must also be separately shown (paragraph 14(1)(g)). The total of listed securities must be further analysed to show those listed on a recognised stock exchange (paragraph 10(3)). The market value of listed securities must be given where it differs from the book value (paragraph 13(13)).

89 The Schedule 4 requirements are similar, except that there is a prescribed balance sheet format. This requires a two-fold distinction to be made between securities held as current assets and securities held as fixed assets. For fixed asset investments, the gross movements must be disclosed.

90 The requirements of the Bank Accounts Directive are more extensive. The balance sheet must distinguish three categories of securities in addition to subsidiaries, associated companies and participating interests: 'treasury bills and other bills eligible for refinancing with central banks'; 'debt securities including fixed-income securities'; and 'shares and other variable-yield securities'.

91 The first of these new categories must be analysed, either in the balance sheet itself or in the notes, between treasury bills and other bills. The second and third categories must be analysed between listed and unlisted securities and between those held as 'financial fixed assets' and those not so held. As explained in paragraph 26 above, it is recommended that the required distinction between 'financial fixed asset' securities and other securities be aligned with the distinction which should be drawn between investment securities (subject to cost-based valuation) and other securities (carried at market value). Debt securities must also be analysed between those issued by public sector entities and those which are not.

92 Interest from fixed-income securities must be shown in the profit and

loss account separately from other income from securities. In the case of 'financial fixed assets', the gross movements must be disclosed, as must the total of premiums and discounts in the course of amortisation and of provisions for impairment in value.

93 Where holdings of securities have been revalued, the Directive requires that their cost be disclosed. The other required disclosures are in relation to holdings of: securities issued by group companies; securities issued by companies in which the group has a participating interest; securities subordinated to the rights of other creditors; securities due for repayment within one year; and the cost of securities valued at market value. The amount of securities pledged, analysed by the liability or contingent liability for which they are pledged, is also required to be shown.

Requirements in the Republic of Ireland

94 In the Republic of Ireland, the Fourth EC Company Law Directive is implemented by the Companies (Amendment) Act 1986. However, licensed banks are exempted from most of the provisions of that Act and they continue to prepare their accounts under the previous provisions, which are to be found in section 148 of the Companies Act 1963 and the Sixth Schedule to that Act. Similarly, the consolidated accounts of a banking group are prepared in accordance with the Sixth Schedule.

95 The provisions relating to banks will shortly be amended in order to implement the EC Bank Accounts Directive. The references in the foregoing paragraphs to the requirements of the Directive are, of course, equally applicable to banks incorporated in the Republic. The Seventh Company Law Directive has also yet to be implemented in the Republic of Ireland.

96 The provisions of the Sixth Schedule mirror closely those of Schedule 9 to the UK Companies Act 1985. (Part III of the Sixth Schedule gives banks an exemption from many of the requirements, but banks do not normally make use of these exemptions.) The references to the Schedule 9 requirements above may therefore generally be taken as applicable also to banks incorporated in the Republic. In particular paragraph 4(4) of the Sixth Schedule requires fixed assets to be distinguished from current assets; paragraph 8(a) requires that the aggregate amounts of quoted and unquoted securities be separately shown; and paragraph 11(7) requires disclosure of the market value of quoted investments. ('Quoted' has the same meaning as 'listed' in the UK legislation.) However, there is no requirement to distinguish between securities listed on a recognised stock exchange and those listed elsewhere. Income from investments must be disclosed (paragraph 12(g)), but there is no requirement to analyse this between listed and unlisted securities.

Appendix A – Illustration of the analyses in the notes to the accounts

	Investment securities		Other securities	
	Book Value £m	Market Value £m	Long positions £m	Short positions £m
1 **Treasury bills and other bills eligible for refinancing with central banks**				
Treasury bills	x	x	x	x
Other bills eligible for refinancing with central banks	x	x	x	x
	X	X	X	X
2 **Debt securities including fixed-income securities**				
Gorvernment securities	x	x	x	x
Other public sector securities	x	x	x	x
Bank and building society certificates of deposit	x	x	x	x
Other debt securities including fixed-income securities	x	x	x	x
	X	X	X	X
Listed	x	x	x	x
Unlisted	x	x	x	x
	X	X	X	X
3 **Shares and other variable-yield securities**				
Listed	x	x	x	x
Unlisted	x	x	x	x
	X	X	X	X

4. The total historical cost of long positions in securities other than investment securities was £Ym.

EC DIRECTIVE ON THE ANNUAL ACCOUNTS AND CONSOLIDATED ACCOUNTS OF BANKS AND OTHER FINANCIAL INSTITUTIONS

THE COUNCIL OF THE EUROPEAN COMMUNITIES,

Having regard to the Treaty establishing the European Community, and in particular Article 54(3)(g) thereof,

Having regard to the proposal from the Commission[1],

Having regard to the opinion of the European Parliament[2],

Having regard to the opinion of the Economic and Social Committee[3],

Whereas Council Directive 78/660/EEC of 25 July 1978, based on Article 54(3)(g) of the Treaty, on the annual accounts of certain types of companies[4], as last amended by Directive 84/569/EEC[5], need not be applied to banks and other financial institutions, hereafter referred to as 'credit institutions', pending subsequent coordination; whereas in view of the central importance of these undertakings in the Community, such coordination is necessary;

Whereas Council Directive 83/349/EEC of 13 June 1983, based on Article 54(3)(g) of the Treaty, on consolidated accounts[6], provides for derogations for credit institutions only until expiry of the deadline imposed for the application of this Directive; whereas this Directive must therefore also include provisions specific to credit institutions in respect of consolidated accounts;

---

(1) OJ No C 130, 1.6.1981, p.1, OJ No C 83, 24.3.1984, p.6 and OJ No C 351, 31.12.1985, p.24.

(2) OJ No C 242, 12.9.1983, p.33 and OJ No C 163, 10.7.1978, p.60.

(3) OJ No C 112, 3.5.1982, p.60.

(4) OJ No L 222, 14.8.1978, p.11.

(5) OJ No L 314, 4.12.1984, p.28.

(6) OJ No L 193, 18.7.1983, p.1.

Whereas such coordination has also become urgent because more and more credit institutions are operating across national borders; whereas for creditors, debtors and members and for the general public improved comparability of the annual accounts and consolidated accounts of these institutions is of crucial importance;

Whereas in virtually all the Members States of the Community credit institutions within the meaning of Council Directive 77/780/EEC of 12 December 1977 on the coordination of laws, regulations and administrative provisions relating to the taking up and pursuit of the business of credit institutions[7], having many different legal forms, are in competition with one another in the banking sector; whereas it therefore seems advisable not to confine coordination in respect of these credit institutions to the legal forms covered by Directive 78/660/EEC but rather to opt for a scope which includes all companies and firms as defined in the second paragraph of Article 58 of the Treaty;

Whereas as far as financial institutions are concerned the scope of this Directive should however be confined to those financial institutions taking one of the legal forms referred to in Directive 78/660/EEC; whereas financial institutions which are not subject to that Directive must automatically come under this Directive;

Whereas a link with coordination in respect of credit institutions is necessary because aspects of the provisions governing annual accounts and consolidated accounts will have an impact on other areas of that coordination, such as authorization requirements and the indicators used for supervisory purposes;

Whereas although, in view of the specific characteristics of credit institutions, it would appear appropriate to adopt a separate Directive on the annual accounts and consolidated accounts of such institutions, this does not imply a new set of rules separate from those under Directives 78/660/EEC and 83/349/EEC; whereas such separate rules would be neither appropriate nor consistent with the principles underlying the coordination of company law since, given the important role which they play in the Community economy, credit institutions cannot be excluded from a framework of rules devised for undertakings generally; whereas, for this reason, only the particular characteristics of credit institutions have been taken into account and this Directive deals only with exceptions to the rules contained in Directives 78/660/EEC and 83/349/EEC;

---

[7] OJ No L 322, 17.12.1977, p.30.

Whereas the structure and content of the balance sheets of credit institutions differ in each Member State; whereas this Directive must therefore prescribe the same layout, nomenclature and terminology for the balance sheets of all credit institutions in the Community; whereas derogations should be allowed if necessitated by the legal form of an institution or by the special nature of its business;

Whereas, if the annual accounts and consolidated accounts are to be comparable, a number of basic questions regarding the disclosure of various transactions in the balance sheet and off the balance sheet must be settled;

Whereas, in the interests of greater comparability, it is also necessary that the content of the various balance sheet and off-balance sheet items be determined precisely;

Whereas the same applies to the layout and definition of the items in the profit and loss account;

Whereas the comparability of figures in the balance sheet and profit and loss account also depends crucially on the values at which assets and liabilities are entered in the balance sheet;

Whereas, in view of the particular risks associated with banking and of the need to maintain confidence, provision should be made for the possibility of introducing a liabilities item in the balance sheet entitled 'Fund for general banking risks'; whereas it would appear advisable for the same reasons that the Member States be permitted, pending subsequent coordination, to allow credit institutions some discretion, especially in the valuation of loans and advances and of certain securities; whereas, however, in this last case the Member States should allow these same credit institutions to create the 'Fund for general banking risks' mentioned above; whereas it would also appear appropriate to permit the Member States to allow credit institutions to set off certain charges and income in the profit and loss account;

Whereas, in view of the special nature of credit institutions, certain changes are also necessary with regard to the notes on the accounts;

Whereas, in the desire to place on the same footing as many credit institutions as possible, as was the case with Directive 77/780/EEC, the relief under Directive 78/660/EEC is not provided for in the case of small and medium-sized credit institutions; whereas, nevertheless, if in the light of experience such relief were to prove necessary it would be possible to provide for it in subsequent coordination; whereas for the same reasons the scope allowed the Member States under Directive 83/349/EEC to exempt parent undertakings from the consolidation requirement if the undertakings to be consolidated do not together exceed a certain size has not been extended to credit institutions;

Whereas the application of the provisions on consolidated accounts to credit institutions requires certain adjustments to some of the rules applicable to all industrial and commercial companies; whereas explicit rules have been provided for in the case of mixed groups and exemption from subconsolidation may be made subject to additional conditions;

Whereas, given the scale on which banking networks extend beyond national borders and their constant development, the annual accounts and consolidated accounts of a credit institution having its head office in one Member State should be published in all the Member States in which it is established;

Whereas the examination of problems which arise in connection with the subject matter of this Directive, notably concerning its application, requires the cooperation of representatives of the Member States and the Commission in a contact committee; whereas, in order to avoid the proliferation of such committees, it is desirable that such cooperation take place in the Committee provided for in Article 52 of Directive 78/660/EEC; whereas, nevertheless, when examining problems concerning credit institutions, the Committee will have to be appropriately constituted;

Whereas, in view of the complexity of the matter, the credit institutions covered by this Directive must be allowed a longer period than usual to implement its provisions;

Whereas provision should be made for the review of certain provisions of this Directive after five years' experience of its application, in the light of the aims of greater transparency and harmonization,

HAS ADOPTED THIS DIRECTIVE:

SECTION 1
PRELIMINARY PROVISIONS AND SCOPE

Article 1

1 Articles 2, 3, 4(1), (3) to (5), 6, 7, 13, 14, 15(3) and (4), 16 to 21, 29 to 35, 37 to 41, 42 first sentence, 45(1), 46, 48 to 50, 51(1), 54, 56 to 59 and 61 of Directive 78/660/EEC shall apply to the institutions mentioned in Article 2 of this Directive, except where this Directive provides otherwise.

2 Where reference is made in Directives 78/660/EEC and 83/349/EEC to Articles 9 and 10 (balance sheet) or to Articles 23 to 26 (profit and loss account) of Directive 78/660/EEC, such references shall be deemed to be references to Articles 4 (balance sheet) or to Articles 27 and 28 (profit and loss account) of this Directive.

3 References in Directives 78/660/EEC and 83/349/EEC to Articles 31 to 42 of Directive 78/660/EEC shall be deemed to be references to those Articles, taking account of Articles 35 to 39 of this Directive.

4 Where reference is made in the aforementioned provisions of Directive 78/660/EEC to balance sheet items for which this Directive makes no equivalent provision, such references shall be deemed to be references to the items in Article 4 of this Directive which include the assets and liabilities in question.

Article 2

1 The coordination measures prescribed by this Directive shall apply to

(a) credit institutions within the meaning of the first indent of Article 1 of Directive 77/780/EEC which are companies or firms as defined in the second paragraph of Article 58 of the Treaty;
(b) financial institutions having one of the legal forms referred to in Article 1(1) of Directive 78/660/EEC which, on the basis of paragraph 2 of that Article, are not subject to that Directive.

For the purposes of this Directive 'credit institutions' shall also include financial institutions unless the context requires otherwise.

2 The Member States need not apply this Directive to:

(a) the credit institutions listed in Article 2(2) of Directive 77/780/EEC;
(b) institutions of the same Member State which, as defined in Article 2(4)(a) of Directive 77/780/EEC, are affiliated to a central body in that Member State. In that case, without prejudice to the application of this Directive to the central body, the whole constituted by the central body and its affiliated institutions must be the subject of consolidated accounts including an annual report which shall be drawn up, audited and published in accordance with this Directive;
(c) the following credit institutions:

- in Greece: ETEBA (National Investment Bank for Industrial Development) and Τράπεζα Επενδύσεων (Investment Bank),
- in Ireland: Industrial and Provident Societies,
- in the United Kingdom: Friendly Societies and Industrial and Provident Societies.

4 Without prejudice to Article 2(3) of Directive 78/660/EEC and pending subsequent coordination, the Member States may:

(a) in the case of the credit institutions referred to in Article 2(1)(a) of this Directive which are not companies of any of the types listed in Article 1(1) of Directive 78/660/EEC, lay down rules derogating from this Directive where derogating rules are necessary because of such institutions' legal form;
(b) in the case of specialized credit institutions, lay down rules derogating from this Directive where derogating rules are necessary because of the special nature of such institutions' business.

Such derogating rules may provide only for adaptations to the layout, nomenclature, terminology and content of items in the balance sheet and the profit and loss account; they may not have the effect of permitting the institutions to which they apply to provide less information in their annual accounts than other institutions subject to this Directive.

The Member States shall inform the Commission of those credit institutions, possibly by category, within six months of the end of the period stipulated in Article 47(2). They shall inform the Commission of the derogations laid down to the end.

These derogations shall be reviewed within 10 years of the notification of this Directive. The Commission shall, if appropriate, submit suitable proposals. It shall also submit an interim report within five years of the notification of this Directive.

SECTION 2

GENERAL PROVISIONS CONCERNING THE BALANCE SHEET AND THE PROFIT AND LOSS ACCOUNT

Article 3
In the case of credit institutions the possibility of combining items pursuant to Article 4(3)(a) or (b) or Directive 78/660/EEC shall be restricted to balance sheet and profit and loss account sub-items preceded by lower-case letters and shall be authorized only under the rules laid down by the Member States to that end.

SECTION 3

LAYOUT OF THE BALANCE SHEET

Article 4
The Member States shall prescribe the following layout for the balance sheet.

Assets

1 Cash in hand, balances with central banks and post office banks

2 Treasury bills and other bills eligible for refinancing with central banks:

(a) Treasury bills and similar securities
(b) Other bills eligible for refinancing with central banks (unless national law prescribes that such bills be shown under Assets items 3 and 4)

3 Loans and advances to credit institutions:

(a) repayable on demand
(b) other loans and advances

4 Loans and advances to customers

5 Debt securities including fixed-income securities:

(a) issued by public bodies
(b) issued by other borrowers, showing separately:
 – own-debt securities (unless national law requires their deduction from liabilities).

6 Shares and other variable-yield securities

7 Participating interests, showing separately:
– participating interests in credit institutions (unless national law requires their disclosure in the notes on the accounts)

8 Shares in affiliated undertakings, showing separately:
– shares in credit institutions (unless national law requires their disclosure in the notes on the accounts)

9 Intangible assets as described under Assets headings B and C.I of Article 9 of Directive 78/660/EEC, showing separately:
– formation expenses, as defined by national law and in so far as national law permits their being shown as an asset (unless national law requires their disclosure in the notes on the accounts)
– goodwill, to the extent that it was acquired for valuable consideration (unless national law requires its disclosure in the notes on the accounts)

10 Tangible assets as described under Assets heading C.II of Article 9 of Directive 78/660/EEC, showing separately:
– land and buildings occupied by a credit institution for its own activities (unless national law requires their disclosure in the notes on the accounts)

11 Subscribed capital unpaid, showing separately:

– called-up capital (unless national law provides for called-up capital to be included under liabilities, in which case capital called but not yet paid must be included either in this Assets item or in Assets item 14)

12 Own shares (with an indication of their nominal value or, in the absence of a nominal value, their accounting par value to the extent that national law permits their being shown in the balance sheet)

13 Other assets

14 Subscribed capital called but not paid (unless national law requires that called-up capital be shown under Assets item 11)

15 Prepayments and accrued income

16 Loss for the financial year (unless national law provides for its inclusion under Liabilities item 14)

Total assets

Liabilities

1 Amounts owed to credit institutions:

(a) repayable on demand
(b) with agreed maturity dates or periods of notice

2 Amounts owed to customers:

(a) savings deposits, showing separately:
– those repayable on demand and those with agreed maturity dates or periods of notice where national law provides for such a breakdown (unless national law provides for such information to be given in the notes on the accounts)
(b) other debts
(ba) repayable on demand
(bb) with agreed maturity dates or periods of notice

3 Debts evidenced by certificates:
(a) debt securities in issue
(b) others

4 Other liabilities

5 Accruals and deferred income

6 Provisions for liabilities and charges:
(a) provisions for pensions and similar obligations
(b) provisions for taxation
(c) other provisions

7 Profit for the financial year (unless national law provides for its inclusion under Liabilities item 14)

8 Subordinated liabilities

9 Subscribed capital (unless national law provides for called-up capital to be shown under this item. In that case, the amounts of subscribed capital and paid-up capital must be shown separately)

10 Share premium account

11 Reserves

12 Revaluation reserve

13 Profit or loss brought forward

14 Profit or loss for the financial year (unless national law requires that this item be shown under Assets item 16 or Liabilities item 7)

Total liabilities

Off-balance sheet items

1 Contingent liabilities, showing separately:
- acceptances and endorsements
- guarantees and assets pledged as collateral security

2 Commitments, showing separately:
- commitments arising out of sale and repurchase transactions

Article 5

The following must be shown separately as sub-items of the items in question:
- claims, whether or not evidenced by certificates, on affiliated undertakings and included in Assets items 2 to 5,
- claims, whether or not evidenced by certificates, on undertakings with which a credit institution is linked by virtue of a participating interest and included in Assets items 2 to 5,
- liabilities, whether or not evidenced by certificates, to affiliated undertakings and included in Liabilities items 1, 2, 3 and 8,
- liabilities, whether or not evidenced by certificates, to undertakings with which a credit institution is linked by virtue of a participating interest and included in Liabilities items 1, 2, 3 and 8.

Article 6

1 Subordinated assets shall be shown separately as sub-items of the items of the layout and the sub-items created in accordance with Article 5.

2 Assets, whether or not evidenced by certificates, are subordinated if, in the event of winding up or bankruptcy, they are to be repaid only after the claims of other creditors have been met.

Article 7

The Member States may permit the disclosure of the information referred to in Articles 5 and 6, duly broken down into the various relevant items, in the notes on the accounts.

Article 8

1 Assets shall be shown under the relevant balance sheet headings even where the credit institution drawing up the balance sheet has pledged them as security for its own liabilities or for those of third parties or has otherwise assigned them as security to third parties.

2 A credit institution shall not include in its balance sheet assets pledged or otherwise assigned to it as security unless such assets are in the form of cash in the hands of that credit institution.

Article 9

1 Where a loan has been granted by a syndicate consisting of a number of credit institutions, each credit institution participating in the syndicate shall disclose only that part of the total loan which it has itself funded.

2 If in the case of a syndicated loan such as described in paragraph 1 the amount of funds guaranteed by a credit institution exceeds the amount which it has made available, any additional guarantee portion shall be shown as a contingent liability (in Off-balance sheet item 1, second indent).

Article 10

1 Funds which a credit institution administers in its own name but on behalf of third parties must be shown in the balance sheet if the credit institution acquires legal title to the assets concerned. The total amount of such assets and liabilities shall be shown separately or in the notes on the accounts, broken down according to the various Assets and Liabilities items. However, the Member States may permit the disclosure of such funds off the balance sheet provided there are special rules whereby such funds can be excluded from the assets available for distribution in the event of the winding-up of a credit institution (or similar proceedings).

2 Assets acquired in the name of and on behalf of third parties must not be shown in the balance sheet.

Article 11

Only those amounts which can at any time be withdrawn without notice or for which a maturity or period of notice of 24 hours or one working day has been agreed shall be regarded as repayable on demand.

Article 12

1 Sale and repurchase transactions shall mean transactions which involve the transfer by a credit institution or customer (the 'transferor') to another credit institution or customer (the 'transferee') of assets, for example, bills, debts or transferable securities, subject to an agreement that the same assets will subsequently be transferred back to the transferor at a specified price.

2 If the transferee undertakes to return the assets on a date specified or to be specified by the transferor, the transaction in question shall be deemed to be a genuine sale and repurchase transaction.

3 If, however, the transferee is merely entitled to return the assets at the purchase price or for a different amount agreed in advance on a date specified or to be specified, the transaction in question shall be deemed to be a sale with an option to repurchase.

4 In the case of the sale and repurchase transactions referred to in paragraph 2, the assets transferred shall continue to appear in the transferor's balance sheet; the purchase price received by the transferor shall be shown as an amount owed to the transferee. In addition, the value of the assets transferred shall be disclosed in a note in the transferor's accounts. The transferee shall not be entitled to show the assets transferred in his balance sheet; the purchase price paid by the transferee shall be shown as an amount owed by the transferor.

5. In the case of the sale and repurchase transactions referred to in paragraph 3, however, the transferor shall not be entitled to show in his balance sheet the assets transferred; those items shall be shown as assets in the transferee's balance sheet. The transferor shall enter under Off-balance sheet item 2 an amount equal to the price agreed in the event of repurchase.

6 No forward exchange transactions, options, transactions involving the issue of debt securities with a commitment to repurchase all or part of the issue before maturity of any similar transactions shall be regarded as sale and repurchase transactions within the meaning of this Article.

SECTION 4

SPECIAL PROVISIONS RELATING TO CERTAIN BALANCE SHEET ITEMS

Article 13

Assets: Item 1 – Cash in hand, balances with central banks and post office banks

1 Cash in hand shall comprise legal tender including foreign notes and coins.

2 This item may include only balances with the central banks and post office banks of the country or countries in which a credit institution is established. Such balances must be readily available at all times. Other claims on such bodies must be shown as loans and advances to credit institutions (Assets item 3) or as loans and advances to customers (Assets item 4).

Article 14

Assets: Item 2 – Treasury bills and other bills eligible for refinancing with central banks

1 This item shall comprise, under (a), treasury bills and similar securities, i.e. treasury bills, treasury certificates and similar debt instruments issued by public bodies which are eligible for refinancing with the central banks of the country or countries in which a credit institution is established. Those debt instruments issued by public bodies which fail to meet the above condition shall be shown under Assets sub-item 5(a).

2 This item shall comprise, under (b), bills eligible for refinancing with central banks, i.e. all bills held in portfolio that were purchased from credit institutions or from customers to the extent that they are eligible, under national law, for refinancing with the central banks of the country or countries in which a credit institution is established.

Article 15

Assets: Item 3 – Loans and advances to credit institutions

1. Loans and advances to credit institutions shall comprise all loans and advances arising out of banking transactions to domestic or foreign credit institutions by the credit institution drawing up the balance sheet, regardless of their actual designations.

The only exception shall be loans and advances represented by debt securities or any other security, which must be shown under Assets item 5.

2 For the purposes of this Article credit institutions shall comprise all undertakings on the list published in the *Official Journal of the European Communities* pursuant to Article 3(7) of Directive 77/780/EEC, as well as central banks and official domestic and international banking organizations and all private and public undertakings which are not established in the Community but which satisfy the definition in Article 1 of Directive 77/780/EEC.

Loans and advances to undertakings which do not satisfy the above conditions shall be shown under Assets item 4.

Article 16

Assets: Item 4 – Loans and advances to customers

Loans and advances to customers shall comprise all types of assets in the form of claims on domestic and foreign customers other than credit institutions, regardless of their actual designations.

The only exception shall be loans and advances represented by debt securities or any other security, which must be shown under Assets item 5.

Article 17

Assets: Item 5 – Debt securities including fixed-income securities

1 This item shall comprise negotiable debt securities including fixed-income securities issued by credit institutions, by other undertakings or by public bodies; such securities issued by the latter, however, shall be included only if they are not to be shown under Assets item 2.

2 Securities bearing interest rates that vary in accordance with specific factors, for example the interest rate on the inter-bank market or on the Euromarket, shall also be regarded as debt securities including fixed-income securities.

3 Only repurchased and negotiable own-debt securities may be included in sub-item 5(b).

Article 18

Liabilities: Item 1 – Amounts owed to credit institutions

1. Amounts owed to credit institutions shall include all amounts arising out of banking transactions owed to other domestic or foreign credit institutions by the credit institution drawing up the balance sheet, regardless of their actual designations.

The only exception shall be liabilities represented by debt securities or by any other security, which must be shown under Liabilities item 3.

2 For the purposes of this Article credit institutions shall comprise all undertakings on the list published in the *Official Journal of the European Communities* pursuant to Article 3(7) of Directive 77/780/EEC, as well as central banks and official domestic and international banking organizations and all private and public undertakings which are not established in the Community but which satisfy the definition in Article 1 of Directive 77/780/EEC.

Article 19

Liabilities: Item 2 – Amounts owed to customers

1 Amounts owed to customers shall include all amounts owed to creditors that are not credit institutions within the meaning of Article 18, regardless of their actual designations.

The only exception shall be liabilities represented by debt securities or by any other security, which must be shown under Liabilities item 3.

2 Only deposits which satisfy the conditions laid down in national law shall be treated as savings deposits.

3 Savings bonds shall be shown under the corresponding sub-item only if they are not represented by negotiable certificates.

Article 20

Liabilities: Item 3 – Debts evidenced by certificates

1. This item shall include both debt securities and debts for which negotiable certificates have been issued, in particular deposit receipts, '*bons de caisse*' and liabilities arising out of own acceptances and promissory notes.

2 Only acceptances which a credit institution has issued for its own refinancing and in respect of which it is the first party liable ('drawee') shall be treated as own acceptances.

Article 21

Liabilities: Item 8 – Subordinated liabilities

Where it has been contractually agreed that, in the event of winding up or of bankruptcy, liabilities, whether or not evidenced by certificates, are to be repaid only after the claims of all other creditors have been met, the liabilities in question shall be shown under this item.

Article 22

Liabilities: Item 9 – Subscribed capital

This item shall comprise all amounts, regardless of their actual designations, which, in accordance with the legal structure of the institution concerned, are regarded under national law as equity capital subscribed by the shareholders or other proprietors.

Article 23

Liabilities: Item 11 – Reserves

This item shall comprise all the types of reserves listed in Article 9 of Directive 78/660/EEC under Liabilities item A.IV, as defined therein. The Member States may also prescribe other types of reserves if necessary for credit institutions the legal structures of which are not covered by Directive 78/660/EEC.

The types of reserve referred to in the first paragraph shall be shown separately, as sub-items of Liabilities item 11, in the balance sheets of the credit institutions concerned, with the exception of the revaluation reserve which shall be shown under item 12.

Article 24

Off-balance sheet: Item 1 – Contingent liabilities

This item shall comprise all transactions whereby an institution has underwritten the obligations of a third party.

Notes on accounts shall state the nature and amount of any type of contingent liability which is material in relation to an institution's activities.

Liabilities arising out of the endorsement of rediscounted bills shall be included in this item only if national law does not require otherwise. The same shall apply to acceptances other than own acceptances.

Sureties and assets pledged as collateral security shall include all guarantee obligations incurred and assets pledged as collateral security on behalf of third parties, particularly in respect of sureties and irrevocable letters of credit.

Article 25

Off-balance sheet: Item 2 – Commitments

This item shall include every irrevocable commitment which could give rise to a risk.

Notes on accounts shall state the nature and amount of any type of commitment which is material in relation to an institution's activities.

Commitments arising out of sale and repurchase transactions shall include commitments entered into by a credit institution in the context of sale and repurchase transactions (on the basis of firm agreements to sell with options to repurchase) within the meaning of Article 12(3).

SECTION 5

LAYOUT OF THE PROFIT AND LOSS ACCOUNT

Article 26

For the presentation of the profit and loss account, the Member States shall prescribe one or both of the layouts provided for in Articles 27 and 28. If a Member State prescribes both layouts it may allow undertakings to choose between them.

Article 27

Vertical layout

1 Interest receivable and similar income, showing separately that arising from fixed-income securities

2 Interest payable and similar charges

3 Income from securities:

(a) Income from shares and other variable-yield securities
(b) Income from participating interests
(c) Income from shares in affiliated undertakings

4 Commissions receivable

5 Commissions payable

6 Net profit or net loss on financial operations

7 Other operating income

8 General administrative expenses:

(a) Staff costs, showing separately:
– wages and salaries
– social security costs, with a separate indication of those relating to pensions
(b) Other administrative expenses

9 Value adjustments in respect of Assets items 9 and 10

10 Other operating charges

11 Value adjustments in respect of loans and advances and provisions for contingent liabilities and for commitments

12 Value re-adjustments in respect of loans and advances and provisions for contingent liabilities and for commitments

13 Value adjustments in respect of transferable securities held as financial fixed assets, participating interests and shares in affiliated undertakings

14 Value re-adjustments in respect of transferable securities held as financial fixed assets, participating interests and shares in affiliated undertakings.

15 Tax on profit or loss on ordinary activities

16 Profit or loss on ordinary activities after tax

17 Extraordinary income

18 Extraordinary charges

19 Extraordinary profit or loss

20 Tax on extraordinary profit or loss

21 Extraordinary profit or loss after tax

22 Other taxes not shown under the preceeding items

23 Profit or loss for the finanacial year

Article 28

Horizontal layout

A *Charges*

1 Interest payable and similar charges

2 Commissions payable

3 Net loss on financial operations

4 General administrative expenses:
(a) Staff costs, showing separately:
– wages and salaries
– social security costs, with a separate indication of those relating to pensions
(b) Other administrative expenses

5 Value adjustments in respect of Assets items 9 and 10

6 Other operating charges

7 Value adjustments in respect of loans and advances and provisions for contingent liabilities and for commitments

8 Value adjustments in respect of transferable securities held as financial fixed assets, participating interests and shares in affiliated undertakings

9 Tax on profit or loss on ordinary activities

10 Profit or loss on ordinary activities after tax

11 Extraordinary charges

12 Tax on extraordinary profit or loss

13 Extraordinary loss after tax

14 Other taxes not shown under the preceding items

15 Profit for the financial year

B *Income*

1 Interest receivable and similar income, showing separately that arising from fixed-income securities

2 Income from securities:
(a) Income from shares and other variable-yield securities
(b) Income from participating interests
(c) Income from shares in affiliated undertakings

3 Commissions receivable

4 Net profit on financial operations

5 Value re-adjustments in respect of loans and advances and provisions for contingent liabilities and for commitments

6 Value re-adjustments in respect of transferable securities held as financial fixed assets, participating interests and shares in affiliated undertakings

7 Other operating income

8 Profit or loss on ordinary activities after tax

9 Extraordinary income

10 Extraordinary profit after tax

11 Loss for the financial year

SECTION 6

SPECIAL PROVISIONS RELATING TO CERTAIN ITEMS IN THE PROFIT AND LOSS ACCOUNT

Article 29

Article 27, items 1 and 2 (vertical layout)

Article 28, items A 1 and B 1 (horizontal layout)

Interest receivable and similar income and interest payable and similiar charges.

These items shall include all profits and losses arising out of banking activities, including:

(1) all income from assets entered under Assets items 1 to 5 in the balance sheet, however calculated. Such income shall also include income arising from the spreading on a time basis of the discount on assets acquired at an amount below, and liabilities contracted at an amount above, the sum payable at maturity;

(2) all charges arising out of liabilities entered under Liabilities items 1, 2, 3 and 8, however calculated. Such charges shall also include charges arising from the spreading on a time basis of the premium on assets acquired at an amount above, and liabilities contracted at an amount below, the sum payable at maturity;

(3) income and charges resulting from covered forward contracts, spread over the actual duration of the contract and similar in nature to interest;

(4) fees and commission similar in nature to interest and calculated on a time basis or by reference to the amount of the claim or liability.

Article 30

Article 27, item 3 (vertical layout)

Article 28, item B 2 (horizontal layout)

Income from shares and other variable-yield securities, from participating interests, and from shares in affiliated undertakings.

This item shall comprise all dividends and other income from variable-yield securities, from participating interests and from shares in affiliated undertakings. Income from shares in investment companies shall also be included under this item.

Article 31

Article 27, items 4 and 5 (vertical layout)

Article 28, items A 2 and B 3 (horizontal layout)

Commissions receivable and commissions payable

Without prejudice to Article 29, commissions receivable shall include income in respect of all services supplied to third parties, and commissions payable shall include charges for services rendered by third parties, in particular
- commissions for guarantees, loans administration on behalf of other lenders and securities transactions on behalf of third parties,
- commissions and other charges and income in respect of payment transactions, account administration charges and commissions for the safe custody and administration of securities,
- commissions for foreign currency transactions and for the sale and purchase of coin and precious metals on behalf of third parties,
- commissions charged for brokerage services in connection with savings and insurance contracts and loans.

Article 32

Article 27, item 6 (vertical layout)

Article 28, item A 3 or item B 4 (horizontal layout)

Net profit or net loss on financial operations.

This item covers:

1 the net profit or loss on transactions in securities which are not held as financial fixed assets together with value adjustments and value re-adjustments on such securities, taking into account, where Article 36(2) has been applied, the difference resulting from application of that article; however, in those Member States which exercise the option provided for in Article 37, these net profits or losses and value adjustments and value re-adjustments shall be included only in so far as they relate to securities included in a trading portfolio;

2 the net profit or loss on exchange activities, without prejudice to Article 29, point 3;

3 the net profits and losses on other buying and selling operations involving financial instruments, including precious metals.

Article 33

Article 27, items 11 and 12 (vertical layout)

Article 28, items A 7 and B 5 (horizontal layout)

Value adjustments in respect of loans and advances and provisions for contingent liabilities and for commitments.

Value re-adjustments in respect of loans and advances and provisions for contingent liabilities and for commitments.

1 These items shall include, on the one hand, charges for value adjustments in respect of loans and advances to be shown under Assets items 3 and 4 and provisions for contingent liabilities and for commitments to be shown under Off-balance sheet items 1 and 2 and, on the other hand, credits from the recovery of written-off loans and advances and amounts written back following earlier value adjustments and provisions.

2 In those Member States which exercise the option provided for in Article 37, this item shall also include the net profit or loss on transactions in securities included in Assets items 5 and 6 which are neither held as financial fixed assets as defined in Article 35(2) nor included in a trading portfolio, together with value adjustments and value re-adjustments on such securities taking into account, where Article 36(2) has been applied, the difference resulting from application of that article. The nomenclature of this item shall be adapted accordingly.

3 The Member States may permit the charges and income covered by these items to be set off against each other, so that only a net item (income or charge) is shown.

4 Value adjustments in respect of loans and advances to credit institutions, to customers, to undertakings with which a credit institution is linked by virtue of participating interests and to affiliated undertakings shall be shown separately in the notes on the accounts where they are material. This provision need not be applied if a Member State permits setting-off pursuant to paragraph 3.

Article 34

Article 27, items 13 and 14 (vertical layout)

Article 28, items A 8 and B 5 (horizontal layout)

Value adjustments in respect of transferable securities held as financial fixed assets, participating interests and shares in affiliated undertakings

Value re-adjustments in respect of transferable securities held as financial fixed assets, participating interests and shares in affiliated undertakings.

1 These items shall include, on the one hand, charges for value adjustments in respect of assets shown in Assets items 5 to 8 and, on the other hand, all the amounts written back following earlier value adjustments, in so far as the charges and income relate to transferable securities held as financial fixed assets as defined in Article 35(2), participating interests and shares in affiliated undertakings.

2 The Member States may permit the charges and income covered by these items to be set off against each other, so that only a net item (income or charge) is shown.

3 Value adjustments in respect of these transferable securities, participating interests and shares in affiliated undertakings shall be shown separately in the notes on the accounts where they are material. This provision need not be applied if a Member State permits setting off pursuant to paragraph 2.

SECTION 7

VALUATION RULES

Article 35

1 Assets items 9 and 10 must always be valued as fixed assets. The assets included in other balance sheet items shall be valued as fixed assets where they are intended for use on a continuing basis in the normal course of an undertakings's activities.

2 Where reference is made to financial fixed assets in Section 7 of Directive 78/660/EEC, this term shall in the case of credit institutions be taken to mean participating interests, shares in affiliated undertakings and securities intended for use on a continuing basis in the normal course of an undertaking's activities.

3 (a) Debt securities including fixed-income securities held as financial fixed assets shall be shown in the balance sheet at purchase price. The Member States may, however, require or permit such debt securities to be shown in the balance sheet at the amount repayable at maturity.

(b) Where the purchase price of such debt securities exceeds the amount repayable at maturity the amount of the difference must be charged to the profit and loss account. The Member States may, however, require or permit the amount of the difference to be written off in instalments so that it is completely written off by the time when the debt securities are repaid. The difference must be shown separately in the balance sheet or in the notes on the accounts.

(c) Where the purchase price of such debt securities is less than the amount repayable at maturity, the Member States may require or permit the amount of the difference to be released to income in instalments over the period remaining until repayment. The difference must be shown separately in the balance sheet or in the notes on the accounts.

Article 36

1 Where transferable securities which are not held as financial fixed assets are shown in the balance sheet at purchase price, credit institutions shall disclose in the notes on their accounts the difference between the purchase price and the higher market value of the balance sheet date.

2 The Member States may, however, require or permit those transferable securities to be shown in the balance sheet at the higher market value at the balance sheet date. The difference between the purchase price and the higher market value shall be disclosed in the notes on the accounts.

Article 37

1 Article 39 of Directive 78/660/EEC shall apply to the valuation of credit institutions' loans and advances, debt securities, shares and other variable-yield securities which are not held as financial fixed assets.

2 Pending subsequent coordination, however, the Member States may permit:

(a) loans and advances to credit institutions and customers (Assets items 3 and 4) and debt securities, shares and other variable-yield securities included in Assets items 5 and 6 which are neither held as financial fixed assets as defined in Article 35(2) nor included in a trading portfolio to be shown at a value lower than that which would result from the application of Article 39(1) of Directive 78/660/EEC, where that is required by the prudence dictated by the particular risks associated with banking. Nevertheless, the difference between the two values must not be more than 4% of the total amount of the assets mentioned above after application of the aforementioned Article 39;

(b) that the lower value resulting from the application of subparagraph (a) be maintained until the credit institution decides to adjust it;

(c) where a Member State exercises the option provided for in subparagraph (a), neither Article 36(1) of this Directive nor Article 40(2) of Directive 78/660/EEC shall apply.

Article 38

1 Pending subsequent coordination, those Member States which exercise the option provided for in Article 37 must permit and those Member States which do not exercise that option may permit the introduction of a Liabilities item 6A entitled 'Fund for general banking risks'. That item shall include those amounts which a credit institution decides to put aside to cover such risks where that is required by the particular risks associated with banking.

2 The net balance of the increases and decreases of the 'Fund for general banking risks' must be shown separately in the profit and loss account.

Article 39

1 Assets and liabilities denominated in foreign currency shall be translated at the spot rate of exchange ruling on the balance sheet date. The Member States may, however, require or permit assets held as financial fixed assets and tangible and intangible assets, not covered or not specifically covered in either the spot or forward markets, to be translated at the rates ruling on the dates of their acquisition.

2 Uncompleted forward and spot exchange transactions shall be translated at the spot rates of exchange ruling on the balance sheet date.

The Member States may, however, require forward transactions to be translated at the foward rate ruling on the balance sheet date.

3 Without prejudice to Article 29(3), the differences between the book values of the assets, liabilities and forward transactions and the amounts produced by translation in accordance with paragraphs 1 and 2 shall be shown in the profit and loss account. The Member States may, however, require or permit differences produced by translation in accordance with paragraphs 1 and 2 to be included, in whole or in part, in reserves not available for distribution, where they arise on assets held as financial fixed assets, on tangible and intangible assets and on any transactions undertaken to cover those assets.

4 The Member States may provide that positive translation differences arising out of forward transactions, assets or liabilities not covered or not specifically covered by other forward transactions, or by assets or liabilities shall not be shown in the profit and loss account.

5 If a method specified in Article 59 of Directive 78/660/EEC is used, the Member States may provide that any translation differences shall be transferred, in whole or in part, directly to reserves. Positive and negative translation differences transferred to reserves shall be shown separately in the balance sheet or in the notes on the accounts.

6 The Member States may require or permit translation differences arising on consolidation out of the re-translation of an affiliated undertaking's capital and reserves or the share of a participating interest's capital and reserves at the beginning of the accounting period to be included, in whole or in part, in consolidated reserves, together with the translation differences arising on the translation of any transactions undertaken to cover that capital and those reserves.

7 The Members States may require or permit the income and expenditure of affiliated undertakings and participating interests to be translated on consolidation at the average rates of exchange ruling during the accounting period.

SECTION 8

CONTENTS OF THE NOTES ON THE ACCOUNTS

Article 40

1 Article 43(1) of Directive 78/660/EEC shall apply, subject to Article 37 of this Directive and to the following provisions.

2 In addition to the information required under Article 43(1)(5) of Directive 78/660/EEC, credit institutions shall disclose the following information relating to Liabilities item 8 (Subordinated liabilities):

(a) in respect of each borrowing which exceeds 10% of the total amount of the subordinated liabilities:

(i) the amount of the borrowing, the currency in which it is denominated, the rate of interest and the maturity date or the fact that it is a perpetual issue;

(ii) whether there are any circumstances in which early repayment is required;

(iii) the terms of the subordination, the existence of any provisions to convert the subordinated liability into capital or some other form of liability and the terms of any such provisions.

(b) an overall indication of the rules governing other borrowings.

3 (a) In place of the information required under Article 43(1)(6) of Directive 78/660/EEC, credit institutions shall in the notes on their accounts state separately for each of the Assets items 3(b) and 4 and the Liabilities items 1(b), 2(a), 2(b)(bb) and 3(b) the amounts of those loans and advances and liabilities on the basis of their remaining maturity as follows:

– not more than three months,
– more than three months but not more than one year,
– more than one year but not more than five years,
– more than five years.

For Assets item 4, loans and advances on call and at short notice must also be shown.

If loans and advances or liabilities involve payment by instalments, the remaining maturity shall be the period between the balance sheet date and the date on which each instalment falls due.

However, for five years after the date referred to in Article 47(2) the Member States may require or permit the listing by maturity of the assets and liabilities referred to in this Article to be based on the originally agreed maturity or period of notice. In that event, where a credit institution has acquired an existing loan not evidenced by a certificate, the Member States shall require classification of that loan to be based on the remaining maturity as at the date on which it was acquired. For the purposes of this subparagraph, the originally agreed maturity for loans shall be the period between the date of first drawing and the date of repayment; the period of notice shall be deemed to be the period between the date on which notice is given and the date on which repayment is to be made; if loans and advances or liabilities are redeemable by instalments, the agreed maturity shall be the period between the date on which such loans and advances or liabilities arose and the date on which the last instalment falls due. Credit institutions shall also indicate for the balance sheet items referred to in this subparagraph what proportion of those assets and liabilities will become due within one year of the balance sheet date.

(b) Credit institutions shall, in respect of Assets item 5 (Debt securities including fixed-income securities) and Liabilities item 3(a) (Debt securities in issue), indicate what proportion of assets and liabilities will become due within one year of the balance sheet date.

(c) The Member States may require the information referred to in subparagraphs (a) and (b) to be given in the balance sheet.

(d) Credit institutions shall give particulars of the assets which they have pledged as security for their own liabilities or for those of third parties (including contingent liabilities); the particulars should be in sufficient detail to indicate for each Liabilities item and for each Off-balance sheet item the total amount of the assets pledged as security.

4 Where credit institutions have to provide the information referred to in Article 43(1)(7) of Directive 78/660/EEC in Off-balance sheet items, such information need not be repeated in the notes on the accounts.

5 In place of the information required under Article 43(1)(8) of Directive 78/660/EEC, a credit institution shall indicate in the notes on its accounts the proportion of its income relating to items 1, 3, 4, 6 and 7 of Article 27 or to items B 1, B 2, B 3, B 4 and B 7 of Aricle 28 by geographical markets, in so far as, taking account of the manner in which the credit institution is organized, those markets differ substantially from one another. Article 45(1)(b) of Directive 78/660/EEC shall apply.

6 The reference in Article 43(1)(9) of Directive 78/660/EEC to Article 23(6) of that Directive shall be deemed to be a reference to Article 27(8) or Article 28(A4) of this Directive.

7 By way of derogation from Article 43(1)(13) of Directive 78/660/EEC, credit institutions need disclose only the amounts of advances and credits granted to the members of their administrative, managerial and supervisory bodies, and the commitments entered into on their behalf by way of guarantees of any kind. That information must be given in the form of a total for each category.

Article 41

1 The information prescribed in Article 15(3) of Directive 78/660/EEC must be given in respect of assets held as fixed assets as defined in Article 35 of this Directive. The obligation to show value adjustments separately shall not, however, apply where a Member State has permitted set-offs between value adjustments pursuant to Article 34(2) of this Directive. In that event value adjustments may be combined with other items.

2 The Member States shall require credit institutions to give the following information as well in the notes on their accounts:

(a) a breakdown of the transferable securities shown under Assets items 5 to 8 into listed and unlisted securities;
(b) a breakdown of the transferable securities shown under Assets items 5 and 6 into securities which, pursuant to Article 35, are or are not held as financial fixed assets and the criterion used to distinguish between the two categories of transferable securities;
(c) the value of leasing transactions, apportioned between the relevant balance sheet items;
(d) a breakdown of Assets item 13, Liabilities item 4, items 10 and 18 in the vertical layout or A 6 and A 11 in the horizontal layout and items 7 and 17 in the vertical layout or B 7 and B 9 in the horizontal layout in the profit and loss account into their main component amounts, where such amounts are important for the purpose of assessing the annual accounts, as well as explanations of their nature and amount;

(e) the charges paid on account of subordinated liabilities by a credit institution in the year under review;
(f) the fact that an institution provides management and agency services to third parties where the scale of business of that kind is material in relation to the institution's activities as a whole;
(g) the aggregate amounts of assets and of liabilities denominated in foreign currencies, translated into the currency in which the annual accounts are drawn up;
(h) a statement of the types of unmatured forward transactions outstanding at the balance sheet date indicating, in particular, for each type of transaction, whether they are made to a material extent for the purpose of hedging the effects of fluctuations in interest rates, exchange rates and market prices, and whether they are made to a material extent for dealing purposes. These types of transaction shall include all those in connection with which the income or expenditure is to be included in Article 27, item 6, Article 28, items A 3 or B 4 or Article 29(3), for example, foreign currencies, precious metals, transferable securities, certificates of deposit and other assets.

SECTION 9

PROVISIONS RELATING TO CONSOLIDATED ACCOUNTS

Article 42

1 Credit institutions shall draw up consolidated accounts and consolidated annual reports in accordance with Directive 83/349/EEC, in so far as this section does not provide otherwise.

2 Insofar as a Member State does not have recourse to Article 5 of Directive 83/349/EEC, paragraph 1 of this Article shall also apply to parent undertakings the sole object of which is to acquire holdings in subsidiary undertakings and to manage such holdings and turn them to profit, where those subsidiary undertakings are either exclusively or mainly credit institutions.

Article 43

1 Directive 83/349/EEC shall apply, subject to Article 1 of this Directive and paragraph 2 of this Article.

2 (a) Articles 4, 6, 15 and 40 of Directive 83/349/EEC shall not apply.
(b) The Member States may make application of Article 7 of Directive 83/349/EEC subject to the following additional conditions:
– the parent undertaking must have declared that it guarantees the commitments entered into by the exempted undertaking; the existence of that declaration shall be disclosed in the accounts of the exempted undertaking;

– the parent undertaking must be a credit institution within the meaning of Article 2(1)(a) of this Directive.

(c) The information referred to in the first two indents of Article 9(2) of Directive 83/349/EEC, namely:
– the amount of the fixed assets and
– the net turnover

shall be replaced by:

– the sum of items 1, 3, 4, 6 and 7 in Article 27 or B 1, B 2, B 3, B4 and B7 in Article 28 of this Directive.

(d) Where, as a result of applying Article 13(3)(c) of Directive 83/349/EEC, a subsidiary undertaking which is a credit institution is not included in consolidated accounts but where the shares of that undertaking are temporarily held as a result of a financial assistance operation with a view to the reorganization of rescue of the undertaking in question, the annual accounts of that undertaking shall be attached to the consolidated accounts and additional information shall be given in the notes on the accounts concerning the nature and terms of the financial assistance operation.

(e) A Member State may also apply Article 12 of Directive 83/349/EEC to two or more credit institutions which are not connected as described in Article 1(1) or (2) of that Directive but are managed on a unified basis other than pursuant to a contract or provisions in the memorandum or articles of association.

(f) Article 14 of Directive 83/349/EEC, with the exception of paragraph 2, shall apply subject to the following provision.

Where a parent undertaking is a credit institution and where one or more subsidiary undertakings to be consolidated do not have that status, those subsidiary undertakings shall be included in the consolidation if their activities are a direct extension of banking or concern services ancillary to banking, such as leasing, factoring, the management of unit trusts, the management of data processing services or any other similar activity.

(g) For the purposes of the layout of consolidated accounts:
– Articles 3, 5 to 26 and 29 to 34 of this Directive shall apply;
– the reference in Article 17 of Directive 83/349/EEC to Article 15(3) of Directive 78/660/EEC shall apply to the assets deemed to be fixed assets pursuant to Article 35 of this Directive.

(h) Article 34 of Directive 83/349/EEC shall apply in respect of the contents of the notes on consolidated accounts, subject to Articles 40 and 41 of this Directive.

SECTION 10
PUBLICATION

Article 44

1 The duly approved annual accounts of credit institutions, together with the annual reports and the reports by the persons responsible for auditing the accounts shall be published as laid down by national law in accordance with Article 3 of Directive 68/151/EEC[1].

National law may, however, permit the annual report not to be published as stipulated above. In that case, it shall be made available to the public at the company's registered office in the Member State concerned. It must be possible to obtain a copy of all or part of any such report on request. The price of such a copy must not exceed its administrative cost.

2 Paragraph 1 shall also apply to the duly approved consolidated accounts, the consolidated annual reports and the reports by the persons responsible for auditing the accounts.

3 However, where a credit institution which has drawn up annual accounts or consolidated accounts is not established as one of the types of company listed in Article 1(1) of Directive 78/660/EEC and is not required by its national law to publish the documents referred to in paragraphs 1 and 2 of this Article as prescribed in Article 3 of Directive 68/151/EEC, it must at least make them available to the public at its registered office or, in the absence of a registered office, at its principal place of business. It must be possible to obtain copies of such documents on request. The prices of such copies must not exceed their administrative cost.

4 The annual accounts and consolidated accounts of a credit institution must be published in every Member State in which that credit institution has branches within the meaning of the third indent of Article 1 of Directive 77/780/EEC. Such Member States may require that those documents be published in their official languages.

5 The Member States shall provide for appropriate sanctions for failure to comply with the publication rules referred to in this Article.

SECTION 11
AUDITING

Article 45

A Member State need not apply Article 2(1)(b)(iii) of Directive 84/253/EEC[2] to public savings banks where the statutory auditing of the documents of those undertakings referred to in Article 1(1) of that Directive is reserved to an existing supervisory body for those savings banks at the time of the entry into force of this Directive and where the person responsible complies at least with the conditions laid down in Article 3 to 9 of Directive 84/253/EEC.

---

(1) OJ No L 65, 14.3.1968, p.8. (2) OJ No L 126, 12.5.1984, p.20.

SECTION 12

FINAL PROVISIONS

Article 46

The Contact Committee established in accordance with Article 52 of Directive 78/660/EEC shall, when meeting as constituted appropriately, also have the following functions:

(a) to facilitate, without prejudice to Articles 169 and 170 of the Treaty, harmonized application of this Directive through regular meetings dealing in particular with practical problems arising in connection with its application;

(b) to advise the Commission, if necessary, on additions or amendments to this Directive.

Article 47

1 The Member States shall bring into force the laws, regulations and administrative provisions necessary for them to comply with this Directive by 31 Decemeber 1990. They shall forthwith inform the Commission thereof.

2 A Member State may provide that the provisions referred to in paragraph 1 shall first apply to annual accounts and consolidated accounts for financial years beginning on 1 January 1993 or during the calendar year 1993.

3 The Member States shall communicate to the Commission the texts of the main provisions of national law which they adopt in the field governed by this Directive.

Article 48

Five years after the date referred to in Article 47(2), the Council, acting on a proposal from the Commission, shall examine and if need be revise all those provisions of this Directive which provide for Member State options, together with Articles 2(1), 27, 28 and 41, in the light of the experience acquired in applying this Directive and in particular of the aims of greater transparency and harmonization of the provisions referred to by this Directive.

Article 49

This Directive is addressed to the Member States.

Done at Brussels, 8 December 1986.

For the Council
The President
N. LAWSON

Chapter 16

INSURANCE COMPANIES

Annexes

INSURANCE COMPANIES

Introduction

16.1 Insurance is primarily a mechanism for spreading risk and minimising financial loss from identified risks that have occurred during a specified period. It involves the acceptance of risk by an insurer for a consideration, which is the premium. Life business (often referred to as long-term business) includes life, annuity, pension, permanent health, capital redemption and pension fund management business. Life products can provide life cover only, but will often have a savings element. General business (often referred to as non- life or property/casualty business) is insurance business other than life business and includes marine and aviation, property damage (commercial and domestic fire and theft policies and motor), liability (such as employers' liability) and accident and health business where this is not long-term business.

16.2 Insurance business in the UK is carried on by:

- Companies limited by shares incorporated under the *Companies Act 1985*, where the members are investors rather than policyholders (proprietary companies).
- Companies limited by guarantee, where the members are the policyholders (mutuals).
- Overseas insurers.
- The Lloyd's market, an international insurance and reinsurance market dealing with almost any type of risk and in which business is accepted on behalf of individual members ('names') who are personally liable for their share of any of their syndicate's losses.
- Trades unions' or employers' associations which provide benefits or strike benefits only for their members (see chapter 10).
- Other organisations such as registered friendly societies and industrial and provident societies (see chapters 11 and 21 respectively).

16.3 Companies writing business in the UK include composite insurers, writing both life and general business, specialist life and non-life companies and UK subsidiaries or branches of overseas insurers. The London insurance market is one of the most important worldwide insurance markets and it contributes significantly to UK invisible earnings and the balance of payments. Specialist non-life companies writing business in this market are known as London Market companies, and typically write similar sorts of business to Lloyd's.

16.4 This chapter is primarily concerned with companies incorporated under the *Companies Act 1985* that carry on insurance business. As can be seen from the comments made in this chapter, the accounting requirements for insurance companies are changing. Practice is therefore still evolving in respect of those requirements recently enacted and further changes are under consideration.

Legislation

16.5 The conduct of insurance business in the UK is regulated principally by the DTI. The primary purpose of regulation is to ensure the protection of policyholders. Because of the long term nature of insurance transactions, legislation has been enacted to ensure that the DTI is capable of much closer supervision of, and control over, insurance companies than over many other non-financial services industries.

16.6 No person may carry on insurance business in the UK unless authorised to do so under section 3 or 4 of the *Insurance Companies Act 1982*, the principal legislation governing the conduct of insurance business in the United Kingdom. [ICA 1982 Sec 2]. Companies authorised to carry on insurance business in the UK are required to restrict their business to insurance business. [ICA 1982 Sec 16]. As a consequence, groups of companies that include an authorised insurance company, but which want to carry on non-insurance activities will generally use separate non-insurance companies for the purpose and frequently have a non- insurance holding company.

16.7 Other legislation has been established for the protection of policyholders such as the *Policyholders Protection Act 1975*. Under this Act, in certain circumstances, payments will be made to policyholders who are individuals that are prejudiced financially by failure of an authorised insurance company. Such failures are funded by means of a levy on the industry.

16.8 The Lloyd's market as a whole is subject to certain requirements of the *Insurance Companies Act 1982*, which deal with financial resources and powers of intervention. [ICA 1982 Sec 84]. This market is largely self-regulated by the Council of Lloyd's under the *Lloyd's Act 1982* and the *Insurance (Lloyd's) Regulations 1983* (SI 1983/224). Other specialist businesses are governed in addition by specific legislation, such as the *Friendly Societies Act 1974* applicable to friendly societies.

16.9 Regulations have been issued by statutory instrument under powers contained in the *Insurance Companies Act 1982* of which the following are particularly important:

- The *Insurance Companies Regulations 1981* (SI 1981/1654) as amended, which contain requirements concerning, *inter-alia*, authorisation, minimum solvency margins and the valuation and matching of assets and liabilities.

- The *Insurance Companies (Accounts and Statements) Regulations 1983* (SI 1983/1811) as amended, which prescribe the form and content of the annual monitoring return to be submitted to the DTI.

16.10 In addition, insurance companies writing life assurance and pensions contracts that have an investment element are also regulated under the *Financial Services Act 1986*, which was enacted for the purposes of controlling the conduct of investment business (see further chapter 26). Insurance companies selling such contracts must register either with the SIB or with LAUTRO to which the SIB has delegated powers.

16.11 The key features of the *Insurance Companies Act 1982*, some of which are discussed in more detail below, are:

- The need for persons carrying on insurance business to have authorisation to do so. [ICA 1982 Secs 3, 4].

- Arrangements for the ongoing supervision of insurance enterprises, such as the requirement to submit an annual monitoring Return. [ICA 1982 Sec 17].

- Powers for the DTI to intervene if necessary in the management of an insurance enterprise for the protection of policyholders. [ICA 1982 Sec 37].

- Requirements for the proper separation of assets attributable to life policyholders (and between certain policyholders), being the life fund or funds, and assets attributable to shareholders, being the general funds, and the need for transactions between the individual life fund or funds and the general funds to be on an arm's length basis. [ICA 1982 Secs 28, 31A].

- A requirement for a company carrying on life business to appoint an actuary. [ICA 1982 Sec 19].

- A regulatory framework for the conduct of insurance business generally, covering such matters as insurance advertisements. [ICA 1982 Sec 72].

Regulation

16.12 The primary purpose of regulation of insurance business is to protect policyholders and potential policyholders against the risk that the company may be unable to meet its liabilities or, in the case of long-term business, to fulfil the reasonable expectations of policyholders or potential policyholders.

16.13 The DTI has responsibility for the regulation of the insurance industry in the UK, including authorisation, ongoing supervision and, if necessary, powers to intervene in the management of an insurance enterprise. Ultimately, the DTI has powers to wind up an insurance operation if it is trading in a manner contrary to the interests of the policyholders.

Authorisation

16.14 The DTI currently authorises companies to carry on either life or general business although no new authorisations are granted for composite insurers. Authorisation is given for particular classes of business specified in Schedule 1 (long-term business) or Schedule 2 (general business) of the *Insurance Companies Act 1982*. Within these two main categories there are a number of classes of business. Companies require authorisation to write each specific class of business. [ICA 1982 Sec 3].

16.15 The procedures for obtaining authorisation are complex. Authorisation under section 3 will not be granted until the insurance company has submitted detailed business proposals, financial forecasts and other information required by the *Insurance Companies Act 1982* and the Secretary of State is satisfied on the basis of that and any other information received by him that the application ought to be granted. [ICA 1982 Sec 5(1)]. The information to be submitted is specified in the *Insurance Companies Regulations 1981*, Schedule 4 (long-term business) and Schedule 5 (general business) and includes, *inter-alia*:

- Details of the company, its directors, controllers, managers and main agents.
- Particulars of the classes of insurance business for which authorisation is being sought.
- The scheme of operations, including the sources of business.
- Projections for each of the first three years following authorisation, including forecast balance sheets, estimates of income and expenditure and estimates of financial resources

intended to cover underwriting liabilities and the margin of solvency.

- Details of the types of investments to be held, of reinsurance treaties and agreements with managers, brokers and agents.

- In the case of life business, a certificate by the appointed actuary of his agreement with certain of the items in the proposals submitted to the DTI.

16.16 Under the provisions of the second non-life directive (now enacted in the UK in the *Insurance Companies Act 1982*), Member States must allow companies to write direct non-life insurance of 'large risks' (as defined in the legislation) in the EC on a 'services' basis, other than through an establishment in the member state in which the risk is situated. The second non-life directive also allows mass risks to be written on a 'services' basis, but this was not mandatory. The UK, however, has not exercised the more restrictive controls over provision of insurance of mass risks that some other member states have. EC companies that are not already authorised in the UK, intending to provide insurance in the UK, not through an establishment in the UK, are required to notify the Secretary of State and furnish certain certificates and other information. [ICA 1982 Sec 81(A)(B)(C)].

16.17 Reinsurers have to be authorised in the same way as other insurance operations, although certain of the supervision requirements are less onerous for pure reinsurers.

16.18 Approval is needed in advance for a change in a controller, director or manager of an insurance company. A controller is a person in accordance with whose instructions the directors are accustomed to act or who exercises 15 per cent or more of the company's voting power. [ICA 1982 Secs 7, 62].

<u>Supervision</u>

16.19 Ongoing supervision of insurance companies is mainly by means of the annual DTI return, which has to be submitted by all authorised insurance companies within six months of their balance sheet date. [ICA 1982 Sec 17]. Unaudited quarterly returns, for which the DTI may modify the standard reporting requirements so less information is given, are usually required from newly authorised companies. The detailed format and content of the DTI return is set out in the *Insurance Companies Regulations 1981* and the *Insurance Companies (Accounts and Statements) Regulations 1983*, as amended. The returns comprise a large numbers of forms, containing very detailed financial information about the insurance company. This information is available to the public since the return is filed with the Registrar of Companies and is available for inspection.

16.20 The DTI return is required primarily to demonstrate the solvency of the insurance company and to allow the DTI to monitor the profitability of the business written, assessing retrospectively the adequacy of claims provisions. There are often differences between amounts (principally asset values) shown in the DTI return and the corresponding amounts as stated in the shareholders' financial statements as the bases of preparation are not the same.

16.21 All insurers carrying on business in the UK are required at all times to maintain assets in excess of liabilities by a specified margin, being such amount as may be prescribed from time to time by the regulations in force. [ICA 1982 Sec 32]. This is referred to as the margin of solvency. The solvency position is determined by comparing the net assets of the company with the solvency margin requirement, both calculated in accordance with the relevant regulations. [ICR 1981, Parts II, V and VI]. An insurance enterprise that fails to meet the required minimum margin of solvency must, at the request of the DTI, submit a plan for the restoration of a sound financial position. If the margin of solvency falls below the absolute minimum required, submission of a short-term financial scheme may be necessary. [ICA 1982 Sec 33].

16.22 The annual DTI return includes certificates in relation to specified matters from the directors, the appointed actuary (in respect of life business) and the auditors. A directors' certificate is required stating *inter alia* that:

- The value of assets and liabilities has been calculated in accordance with the regulations.
- For the purposes of preparing the return proper accounts and records have been maintained and that an appropriate system of internal control has been established and maintained.
- There has been proper separation of life policyholders' funds (and between life funds where relevant) and the general (shareholders') funds and appropriate arrangements are in force to ensure that transactions have not operated unfairly between them.

16.23 Auditors are required to state whether the directors' certificate and those parts of the return subject to audit have been properly prepared in accordance with the regulations and whether it is reasonable for the directors giving the certificates to have made the statements therein.

Intervention

16.24 The *Insurance Companies Act 1982* gives wide powers of intervention to the DTI if there is a risk that the company cannot meet its liabilities or in the case of long-term business, the reasonable expectations of policyholders or if the DTI is not satisfied with regard to certain other matters (for example, with the reinsurance arrangements).

16.25 In these circumstances, the company can be required to take such action as is considered appropriate. These powers include the authority to:

- Regulate the type of investments made and require that assets are held by an authorised custodian. [ICA 1982 Secs 38, 40].
- Place limits on premium income. [ICA 1982 Sec 41].
- Object to the appointment of a new managing director, chief executive or controller. [ICA 1982 Secs 60(3), 61(2)].
- Request a plan for the restoration of a sound financial position if an adequate margin of solvency is not maintained and a short-term financial scheme if the margin of solvency falls below certain minimum requirements. [ICA 1982 Secs 32(4), 33].
- Withdraw authorisation. [ICA 1982 Sec 11].

Financial statements

Form and content

16.26 The law dealing with shareholders' financial statements for insurance companies is contained in the *Companies Act 1985*. The *Companies Act 1985* permits, but does not require, insurance companies to prepare their financial statements in accordance with Part 1 of Schedule 9 to the *Companies Act 1985* rather than Schedule 4 to that Act. [CA 1985 Sec 255 (1)]. The accounting and disclosure requirements of Schedule 9 are less extensive than those of Schedule 4 and, in addition, insurance companies are exempted from certain of the disclosure requirements contained in Schedule 9. The principal exemptions relate to disclosure of the amounts of, and movements in, reserves and provisions. The detailed disclosure requirements and exemptions are discussed in paragraphs 16.117 to 16.136 below.

16.27 Schedule 9 to the *Companies Act 1985* does not set out specified formats for the financial statements of insurance companies. Consequently, in practice the form, and to some extent the content, of insurance companies' financial statements varies more widely than for many other companies. An insurance company's financial statements will normally include:

- One or more revenue accounts, which record the results of the company's underwriting activities.

- A profit and loss account, to which the underwriting result is transferred from the revenue account and which shows the results of other corporate activities including investment activities.
- One or more balance sheets (for example, general business and long-term business).
- A statement of source and application of funds.

16.28 An insurance company that writes both general and long-term business will normally include in its financial statements separate revenue accounts and balance sheets for each type of business. This is not a legal requirement, but arises from the dissimilar nature of the two types of insurance business as well as the requirement of the *Insurance Companies Act 1982* that separate records must be maintained to identify the assets and liabilities attributable to long-term business and restrictions governing the transfer of assets representing long-term business funds. [ICA 1982 Secs 28, 29]. In addition, companies may produce separate revenue accounts for different classes of general business, particularly where classes are managed separately or are reported using different bases of accounting.

16.29 The parent company of an insurance group may prepare consolidated financial statements under Schedule 4A as modified by Part II of Schedule 9 to the *Companies Act 1985*. [CA 1985 Sec 255A(1)]. An insurance group is referred to in the *Companies Act 1985* as a group where the parent company is an insurance company or the predominant activity of the group is insurance business and activities that are a direct extension of or ancillary to insurance business. [CA 1985 Sec 255A(4)]. Most insurance groups preparing their financial statements under Schedule 9 to the *Companies Act 1985* meet these criteria. However, a non-insurance parent company with insurance subsidiaries must prepare its own balance sheet in accordance with Schedule 4 to that Act.

16.30 An Interim Statement on 'Consolidated Accounts' issued by the Accounting Standards Board on 11th December 1990 addresses the issue of exclusion of subsidiaries from the consolidated financial statements where their activities are different from those of the rest of the group. The statement is effective for financial years commencing on or after 23rd December 1989 and has the force of an Accounting Standard. The ASB believes that the circumstances under which a subsidiary undertaking's activities are so different, that its inclusion in the consolidated financial statements would be incompatible with the obligation to give a true and fair view, are so exceptional that it would be misleading to link them to any particular contrast of activities. Therefore, unless there are conclusive grounds for believing that their inclusion is incompatible with the obligation to give a true and fair view, an insurance subsidiary of a non-insurance parent company should be consolidated. In the event of exclusion, the grounds for considering that inclusion is not compatible with the obligation to give a true and fair view must be explained in a note to the financial statements.

16.31 Where insurance companies or groups prepare their financial statements in accordance with Schedule 9 to the *Companies Act 1985*, those financial statements must contain a statement to that effect. [CA 1985 Secs 255(2), 255A(2)].

16.32 An insurance company or group is exempt only from those requirements of chapter 1 of Part VII of and Schedules 4 and 4A to the *Companies Act 1985* that govern the preparation of financial statements. It is not exempt from provisions contained elsewhere in that Act.

16.33 The Secretary of State may also modify any of the disclosure requirements that apply to insurance companies and groups in order to adapt them to a particular company's circumstances. This modification may be made either on the application of the company's directors or with their consent. However, this does not affect the requirement that the financial statements must give a true and fair view within the requirements of Schedule 9 to the *Companies Act 1985* and the disclosure exemptions permitted under that Schedule. [CA 1985 Secs 255(4), 255A(6), 9 Sch 28(2)].

<u>EC directive on insurance accounts</u>

16.34 The EC has almost completed the process of developing a directive on the annual accounts and consolidated accounts of insurance undertakings, which is expected to cover in respect of insurance companies most of the general provisions of the 4th and 7th Company Law Directives. The directive is expected to cover the following matters:

- The format and content of the balance sheet, profit and loss account and revenue accounts.
- Definition of items to be included under each statement heading.
- Additional disclosures to be made in the notes to the financial statements.
- Special valuation rules for certain balance sheet and profit and loss account items.
- Adaptations in respect of the requirement to prepare consolidated financial statements.

- Requirements dealing with publication and the scope of the auditors' opinion.

16.35 Once the directive is adopted by the EC, it will in due course be implemented by legislation in the UK. The new legislation will supersede the rules currently set out in the *Companies Act 1985* that relate specifically to insurance companies and effectively bring them into line, in a manner appropriate for insurers, with those applicable to the generality of companies governed by the *Companies Act 1985*.

Accounting policies and standards

16.36 Insurance companies are required to adopt accounting policies that are applied consistently within the same financial statements and from one financial year to the next. [CA 1985 9 Sch 18A(1)]. In addition, SSAP 2 requires any significant accounting policies a company has adopted in preparing its financial statements to be stated in the notes to the financial statements.

16.37 A company's directors are permitted to change the company's accounting policies where there are special reasons to do so. If they do so, however, the notes to the financial statements must give particulars of the departure from the principle of consistent application, the directors' reasons for it and its effect. [CA 1985 9 Sch 18A(2)].

16.38 The need to give a true and fair view, as noted in paragraph 16.33 above within the requirements of Schedule 9 to the *Companies Act 1985*, means that an insurance company should follow applicable Accounting Standards unless there are good reasons not to do so. The *Companies Act 1989* introduced for the first time the requirement for insurance companies to state, in the notes to the financial statements, whether those financial statements have been prepared in accordance with Accounting Standards that are applicable to the company. In addition, if there are material departures from these standards, the particulars and the reasons for the departure must be given in the notes. [CA 1985 9 Sch 18B].

16.39 There is no accounting standard in the UK that deals specifically with the financial accounting and reporting requirements of insurance companies. However, insurance companies still have to comply with SSAPs to the extent that the *Companies Act 1985* does not provide exemptions. The explanatory foreword to SSAPs says that "*where accounting standards prescribe specific information to be contained in accounts, such disclosure requirements do not override exemptions from disclosure requirements given to and utilised by special classes of companies under Statute*". Consequently, insurance companies may, without contravening any requirements of SSAPs, take advantage of those exemptions in paragraph 28(1) of Schedule 9 to the *Companies*

Act 1985 that relate to disclosure. In practice, SSAP 6, 'Extraordinary items and prior year adjustments', is probably the accounting standard where these exemptions are most invoked since many insurance companies consider that reserve accounting is appropriate in certain circumstances.

16.40 The absence of a specific accounting standard on insurance business has generally led to a wide divergence of accounting practices amongst UK insurance companies. The Association of British Insurers (ABI) issued a SORP on Accounting for Insurance Business in May 1990 which was franked by the ASC, but the SORP does not have the status of an accounting standard. The primary aim of the ABI SORP is to narrow the areas of difference and variety in the accounting treatments of matters unique to insurance business. The ABI SORP, which is intended to supplement accounting standards, sets out recommended accounting practice in respect of both general and long-term insurance business. The recommendations of the franked ABI SORP will now be strongly persuasive, but not mandatory. Companies are encouraged to disclose any departure from the recommendations and the reasons for such departure. A copy of the ABI SORP is included as annex 2 to this chapter.

True and fair view

16.41 Insurance companies are still bound by the overriding requirement that the balance sheet and the profit and loss account must give a true and fair view of the company's state of affairs and profit or loss for the financial period, although this requirement is modified as explained in more detail in paragraph 16.45 below. [CA 1985 226(2)].

16.42 In addition, where compliance with the disclosure provisions of the *Companies Act 1985* (including Part I of Schedule 9) would not be sufficient to give a true and fair view, then an insurance company should disclose the additional information in the notes to the financial statements. This additional information needs to be of sufficient detail to ensure that its disclosure enables the financial statements to give a true and fair view. [CA 1985 Secs 226(4), 255(3)].

16.43 Furthermore, if in 'special circumstances' compliance with any of the Act's provisions (including Part I of Schedule 9) would be inconsistent with the requirements to give a true and fair view, the directors of an insurance company must depart from that provision to the extent necessary to give a true and fair view. Where such a departure is necessary, the particulars of the departure, the reasons for it and its effect should be given in a note to the financial statements. [CA 1985 Secs 226(5), 255(3)].

16.44 Similar provisions to those discussed above apply to insurance groups that prepare consolidated financial statements in accordance with

Schedule 4A as modified by Part II of Schedule 9 to the *Companies Act 1985*. [CA 1985 Secs 227(3)(5)(6), 255A(5)].

16.45 As stated in paragraph 16.26 above, an insurance company is exempt from many of the disclosure requirements of Schedule 9 to the *Companies Act 1985*. Where these exemptions are adopted in the preparation of an insurance company's financial statements, the financial statements will not be deemed not to give a true and fair view by reason only of the fact that disclosure exemptions have been used. [CA 1985 9 Sch 28(2)]. However, the auditors will modify their opinion (see further para 16.159).

General business revenue account

Introduction

16.46 The general business revenue account contains items making up the underwriting profit or loss for the period. These will usually include premiums written or earned, claims paid or incurred and underwriting and claims handling expenses. There are no prescribed rules regarding the allocation of expenses between the revenue account and the profit and loss account and in practice many companies allocate all management expenses to the revenue account other than such items as interest payable and certain corporate expenses.

16.47 General insurance business may be accounted for on an 'annual', 'deferred annual' or 'funded' basis. Each of these bases, together with an indication of the circumstance under which they may be appropriate, is outlined below.

The annual basis of accounting

16.48 The ABI SORP recommends that the annual basis of accounting should be used where the underwriting result can be determined with reasonable certainty at the end of each accounting period for business written in that period. [ABI SORP para 84]. This will be the situation for classes of business where premiums and claims are reported to the insurance company relatively quickly, such as direct property and casualty insurance.

16.49 Under the annual basis of accounting, claims, net of reinsurance recoveries, incurred in the financial year are charged against the premiums, net of reinsurance premiums ceded, earned in the financial year. The principal features of the annual basis are that:

- All premiums should be accounted for in the year in which they incept and the accounts should include an estimate of premiums in respect of risks incepting in the period, which have not yet been recorded in the accounting records. [ABI SORP para 86].

- Premium income should be recognised in the accounts over the period of risk. At the end of an accounting period provision should be made for unearned premiums, representing the unexpired portion of policies in issue with periods of cover extending into the following accounting period. [ABI SORP paras 18, 91].

- Unearned premiums are usually computed on the daily pro rata (365ths) basis or the monthly pro rata (24ths) basis and should be computed gross of commission and other acquisition expenses. [ABI SORP paras 91, 93].

- Deferred acquisition expenses should be calculated as accurately as possible and should be carried forward without limitation. Both the basis of calculation and the amount of the deferred acquisition expenses carried forward should be disclosed. [ABI SORP paras 107 - 109].

- Provision should be made for 'unexpired risks', in addition to unearned premiums, where the latter are likely to be insufficient to meet future losses arising on business in force at the balance sheet date. Investment income on assets representing technical provisions may be taken into account in calculating the unexpired risk provision. Such a provision has to be separately disclosed in the DTI Return and should be disclosed in the shareholders' financial statements, as should the accounting policy adopted to assess the requirement for the provision. [ABI SORP paras 128-131].

- When estimating the cost of incurred claims, provision is made for outstanding claims including claims incurred, but not reported (IBNR). The provision for outstanding claims is based on the best estimate of the ultimate cost of settlement and includes provision for expenses, such as legal fees directly attributable to individual claims. Provision should also be made for the overhead expenses of the insurance company that will be incurred after the balance sheet date in settling outstanding claims. [ABI SORP paras 113 -114].

Table 16.1 illustrates disclosures made under the annual basis of accounting.

The deferred annual basis of accounting

16.50 For some classes of direct and reinsurance business, such as proportional treaties, it is not possible to obtain the information necessary to determine the results at the end of the financial period in which the business incepted. However, where this information becomes available during the following financial period, the 'deferred

Table 16.1: Illustration of disclosures made under the annual (and deferred annual) bases of accounting

Extract from Commercial Union Assurance Company plc Annual Report & Accounts 31st December 1989.

Notes on the accounts (extract)

2. UNDERWRITING RESULT

The analysis of the underwriting result is:	1989 £m	1989 £m	1988 £m	1988 £m
Gross premiums written (B)		3,022.5		2,655.0
Outward reinsurance		(521.3)		(467.6)
Net premiums written		2,501.2		2,187.4
Transfer to unearned premiums (B)		(47.2)		(49.3)
Net premiums earned		2,454.0		2,138.1
Gross claims incurred (C)	(2,420.7)		(1,908.6)	
Outward reinsurance	530.2		313.4	
Net claims incurred	(1,890.5)		(1,595.2)	
Commission	(461.2)		(397.8)	
Expenses	(365.9)		(291.9)	
Transfer to deferred acquisition costs (D)	18.6		17.6	
		(2,699.0)		(2,267.3)
Underwriting result (A)		(245.0)		(129.2)

annual' basis of accounting may be appropriate. The ABI SORP recommends the use of the deferred annual basis in these circumstances. [ABI SORP para 84]. Under this basis:

- All items in the revenue account are reported one accounting period in arrears, but otherwise this basis is the same as the annual basis of accounting. The revenue account for the current financial period includes all items relating to the previous accounting period (known as the 'closed year'). The transactions for the current financial period (known as the 'open year') are deferred and included in the revenue account of the next accounting period.

- Alternatively the transactions for the open year may be recorded in the current financial year and carried forward in the balance sheet as a fund.

If the information available for the open year indicates that a loss is likely to arise then a provision for the deficiency should be made. [ABI SORP paras 94, 115].

The funded basis of accounting

16.51 For classes of business for which long delays are experienced in the notification of premiums and settlement of claims (such as marine, aviation and transport business, certain types of liability business and non-proportional treaty reinsurance) the funded basis of accounting is normally adopted.

16.52 Under the funded basis of accounting, premiums are related back to an 'underwriting' year. This is usually the year in which the policy incepts but other methods of allocation may be used, such as the year in which the policy is written. Claims are allocated to the same underwriting year as the related premium irrespective of the date of occurrence of the event giving rise to the claim.

16.53 Underwriting transactions are included in the revenue account in the financial year in which they are notified and it is unusual for estimates to be made of written but unreported premiums.

16.54 The 'three year' basis is the usual form of the funded basis of accounting, although longer or shorter periods are sometimes used. On this basis, in respect of each underwriting year a 'fund' is created consisting of the balance of premiums received, less the related commissions, expenses and claims paid. A separate fund is usually established for each class of business accounted for on this basis, although more than one class may be grouped together if these classes are managed together. [ABI SORP para 14]. At the end of an underwriting year and at the end of the following financial year the balance on the fund is carried forward in the balance sheet and no underwriting profits are released (that is, the underwriting year is left 'open'). When two years have elapsed since the end of the underwriting year, the year is 'closed' and the underwriting profit is determined by calculating the balance of the 'fund' that needs to be carried forward to settle the remaining liabilities of that underwriting year. Expenses should be accounted for in the accounting period on an incurred basis and allocated to the appropriate underwriting year.

16.55 The fund carried forward in respect of each open underwriting year must be sufficient to cover the estimated ultimate liabilities, including claims not yet reported, which will have to be settled from that fund. Any premiums for the underwriting year not yet recorded can be taken into account in determining the fund required. If the fund appears likely to be insufficient, provision must be made to cover the deficiency. [ABI SORP para 115]. Transfers from one fund to another to cover deficiencies, the cost of which will otherwise be met by means of a charge to the profit and loss account (known as 'cross-funding'), are not permitted although transfers between classes of business within the same fund and underwriting year may be made. [ABI SORP para 115].

16.56 The underwriting result for the accounting period will, therefore, comprise the results of the year that has just been closed, adjustments to estimates used in arriving at the results of previously closed years and provisions for anticipated deficiencies and adjustments to provisions previously established for the open years. At the balance sheet date, the fund will comprise the outstanding liabilities of the closed years, the net income less outgo (that is claims and expenses) for each open year and any provisions for anticipated deficiencies for the open years. Table 16.2 illustrates a revenue account prepared on the funded basis of accounting.

Investment income

16.57 Most insurance companies have tended to show investment income in the profit and loss account rather than the revenue account. However, some companies allocate the income earned on investments representing insurance technical provisions to the revenue account, with income earned on investments representing shareholders' funds remaining in the profit and loss account. This method of allocation recognises the fact that the timing of premium receipts and claims payments and the investment income which will consequently be generated, are factors affecting the profitability of underwriting. Where a company discounts its claims provisions, as explained in paragraph 16.62 below, an allocation of investment income to the revenue account will be necessary in order to match the amortisation of the discount. Accounting for investment income and expenses, and investment gains in the profit and loss account is discussed further in paragraphs 16.83 to 16.87 below.

Reinsurance ceded

16.58 The general rule regarding the accounting treatment of reinsurance premiums ceded and reinsurance recoveries due is that it should follow the treatment of the related inwards premiums written and claims incurred. [ABI SORP paras 96, 118]. In practice, the accounting may be difficult (for example, in relation to whole account reinsurance contracts) and an appropriate basis of apportionment of reinsurance premiums and claims recoveries between different classes of business, or different underwriting years, is required.

16.59 One of the most difficult areas of insurance accounting relates to reinsurance contracts that transfer little or no risk from the cedant to the reinsurer. These are generally known as 'financial reinsurance' contracts. A detailed discussion of financial reinsurance is beyond the scope of this chapter, but in summary:

- The forms of financial reinsurance contracts are many and varied, but typically they provide a level of cover which is determined primarily having regard to the time value of money. In other

Table 16.2: Illustration of disclosures made under the funded basis of accounting

Extract from Terra Nova Insurance Company Limited Report and Accounts 31st December 1989.

Underwriting Revenue Account

for the year ended 31st December 1989

	Notes		$'000		1988 $'000
Gross premiums		285,624			290,529
less: reinsurance ceded		(102,673)			(89,053)
Premiums, less reinsurance			182,951		201,476
Gross claims paid		(297,725)		(208,406)	
less: reinsurance recovered		184,602		118,448	
Claims paid, less reinsurance			(113,123)		(89,958)
Commission			(43,199)		(47,711)
Expenses	1(d) & (e)		(9,709)		(9,600)
			16,920		54,207
Insurance fund brought forward		577,709		519,260	
Foreign exchange revaluation		(4,288)		(2,576)	
			573,421		516,684
Underwriting loss transferred to profit and loss account	1(c)		46,964		6,818
Insurance fund carried forward	1(f) & 13(e)		637,305		577,709

words, the premium paid is based on the net present value of anticipated future claims payments plus an allowance for the reinsurer's expenses and profit.

- The timing and amounts of payments by the reinsurer under the contract may be restricted, for example through specified payment schedules, delayed payment clauses or formulae that delay payments to the cedant.

- There are generally clauses that allow for the return to the cedant of any 'excess' profit earned on the contract, for example by way of return of premium or profit commission.

16.60 The ABI SORP recommends that *"reinsurance arrangements, where the amount of risk transferred is not significant should be accounted for having regard to their economic substance"*. [ABI SORP para 98]. However, no guidance is given on what constitutes significant transfer of risk and the range and complexity of financial reinsurance contracts is evolving rapidly.

16.61 The ABI SORP can be interpreted as requiring financial reinsurance contracts to be accounted for by the cedants as deposits placed with the reinsurer and not passed through the revenue account or used to reduce insurance liabilities. However, many companies consider the wording of the ABI SORP to be sufficiently imprecise to allow for such contracts to be accounted for as normal reinsurance policies, although disclosure of the existence and financial effect of the contracts is sometimes made and is considered good practice where material.

Discounting of claims provisions

16.62 The ABI SORP permits explicit discounting of outstanding claims provisions, provided a satisfactory estimate of the liability can be made and there is adequate past experience on which a reasonable model of the timing of the run-off of the liability can be constructed. The discount rate should not exceed the rate of investment income likely to be earned over the claims settlement period. [ABI SORP paras 124, 125].

16.63 Where claims are discounted, an appropriate accounting policy note should be included in the financial statements and the ABI SORP recommends that disclosure should be made of:

- The classes or groupings of businesses involved.
- The method applied, including the discount rates used and the mean term of the liabilities.
- The treatment of the attributable investment income.
- The effect of discounting on pre-tax profits or losses and on net assets.

[ABI SORP para 126].

16.64 Implicit discounting, involving the failure to provide fully for liabilities on the grounds that any shortfall will be covered by investment income or the application of present value techniques to a claims provision without disclosure that this has been done, is not acceptable. [ABI SORP para 124].

Long-term business revenue account

Introduction

16.65 The ABI SORP defines long-term business as insurance business, the benefits under which are payable primarily on the survival of the policyholder to a stipulated age or death. Long-term business will include life, annuity, pension, permanent health, capital redemption and pension fund management business.

16.66 Long-term insurance business is categorised in the *Insurance Companies Act 1982* as being either ordinary long-term insurance business, which is defined as long-term business that is not industrial assurance business, or industrial assurance business. Industrial assurance business is defined in the *Industrial Assurance Act 1923* as life assurance where the premiums are received by means of collections and certain provisions relating to the frequency and amount of collection are met. These types of business are treated under the *Insurance Companies Act 1982* as separate classes, and hence are accounted for separately. No distinction is required in respect of disclosure of the types of business in *Companies Act 1985* shareholders' financial statements, although separate information by class is often shown in the financial statements of companies writing industrial assurance business.

16.67 An insurance company that carries on long-term business must record separately the assets and liabilities of policyholders and shareholders. [ICA 1982 Sec 29]. This segregation is often reflected in the financial statements in that a long-term revenue account and a long-term balance sheet are shown separately from other revenue accounts and other balance sheets, although there is no requirement for this.

16.68 The long-term revenue account shows the movements in the year on the long-term insurance fund. The ABI SORP requires all long-term insurance business to be accounted for on a funded basis whereby premiums and investment income are credited to the fund and claims and revenue expenses are charged to the fund.

16.69 The results recognised in the profit and loss account in respect of long-term business are determined based on the advice of the company's actuary appointed under section 19 of the *Insurance Companies Act 1982*.

16.70 The appointed actuary is required to provide an annual certificate in the DTI return that includes statements to the effect that proper books and records have been kept for the purpose of actuarial valuation and that the mathematical reserves represent proper provision for the liabilities under long-term business contracts. [IC(AS)R 1983, as amended, para 26(b)]. The auditor is required to reach an opinion as to whether the financial statements of an insurance company, subject to the disclosure exemptions permitted to insurance companies under *Companies Act 1985*, give a true and fair view. In reaching his opinion, the auditor's responsibilities include obtaining reasonable assurance from the actuary that the long-term funds are adequate to meet the related liabilities. The responsibilities of the appointed actuary and auditor of an insurance company conducting long-term business are set out in the ICAEW Technical Release, 'Auditors' relationship with actuaries concerning actuarial valuation of long-term business funds of insurance companies', (TR 568)

Profit recognition

16.71 It is important to distinguish between those profits from long-term business which accrue to shareholders and those which accrue to policyholders. In order to do this it is necessary to distinguish between conventional life and pensions business and unit-linked and pension fund management business.

- Conventional business is either:
  - Non-participating, whereby all profits (or losses) accrue to shareholders. Profits may be retained within the long-term insurance fund until such time, on the advice of the appointed actuary, as a transfer is made to the shareholders' profit and loss account. Any deficiency must be made good when it arises by a transfer from the shareholders' profit and loss account or from the investment reserve.
  - Participating or 'with profit' business, whereby policyholders share in the profits (but not losses) of the business by way of reversionary bonuses (usually declared annually as a guaranteed increase to the sum assured) and terminal bonuses (payable only on policies maturing or terminating). When a bonus is declared, on the advice of the appointed actuary, the value of the liability to policyholders increases and an amount, normally ten per cent of the total cost of bonuses, although this may vary depending on the company's articles of association, is released to shareholders by way of a transfer to the profit and loss account. When declaring bonuses, the actuary is required professionally to maintain equity between different generations of policyholders and between policyholders and shareholders and to maintain the required solvency.
- Unit-linked business and pension fund management business are principally savings business whereby the insurance company collectively manages investments on behalf of policyholders. All

investment income and gains and losses accrue to policyholders. Management charges are made on the funds and the excess of these charges over the expenses incurred accrues to shareholders.

16.72 The traditional method of profit measurement delays the recognition of shareholders' life profits, and understates shareholders' interest in the long-term business fund. Consequently, a few insurance companies have recently used the embedded value basis of profit recognition. An embedded valuation includes, in addition to the reported shareholders' net assets, the present value of estimated future shareholders' profits relating to the business in force. The movement in the embedded value during the year would be included in the profit and loss account on this basis of profit recognition.

16.73 The sources of shareholders' profit are:

- Release of surplus in respect of conventional non-participation business.
- Shareholders' share of the cost of bonus in respect of conventional participation business.
- The excess of management charges over expenses in respect of unit-linked or pensions management business.

16.74 In response to the current varied practice, the ABI released a consultative document and draft proposals in September 1990 entitled 'Accounting for shareholders' profit in long-term insurance business'. The proposed method of accounting, 'the accruals method', is based on the principle that *"the total profit earned over the whole term of each contract or group of contracts is respread over such term in a consistent manner related to risk borne and work performed"*. Revised proposals are expected to be issued in 1991.

Gains and losses on investments

16.75 The treatment of realised and unrealised gains and losses on investments held to match long-term insurance funds differs depending on the types of business written.

- In respect of conventional business, unrealised gains and losses are typically taken to an 'investment reserve', which is deducted from the carrying value of investments in the balance sheet and from (or to) which the appointed actuary may make transfers to (or from) the long-term insurance fund. Alternatively, realised and unrealised gains may be taken direct to the revenue account, and hence the long-term fund, or they may be accounted for separately with realised gains and losses being taken to the revenue account and unrealised gains and losses being taken to the investment reserve.

- In respect of unit-linked and pension management business, realised and unrealised gains and losses accrue to policyholders and are, therefore, taken to the revenue account and hence included in the long-term insurance fund.

Accounting policies

16.76 The ABI SORP recommends the following accounting policies for items in the long-term business revenue accounts:

- Premiums.

  Premiums for investment linked policies should be recorded in the accounting period in which the related liability is established. Conventional business premiums should be recorded when due for payment, including reasonable estimates of contracted renewal premiums where actual information is not available. [ABI SORP paras 133 -135].

- Claims.

  Claims should be charged to the revenue account in respect of investment linked business when the policy ceases to participate in the long-term insurance fund. In respect of conventional business, claims should be recorded when the insured event occurs or becomes due (and this includes amounts payable under long-term disability or annuity contracts) or is notified. [ABI SORP paras 145 - 147].

- Reinsurance.

  Reinsurance premiums and claims recoveries under reinsurance contracts should be accounted for in the same period as the related premium and claim. [ABI SORP paras 136, 148].

- Expenses.

  All revenue expenses should be charged to the fund. [ABI SORP para 144]. Acquisition costs are not normally deferred although the timing of the payment of expenses will be taken into account in the valuation of the fund. Revenue expenses for long-term business are classified as for general business between underwriting, investment and other.

- Investment income.

Investment income is generally credited to the revenue account in respect of all types of long-term business. Investment expenses may be deducted from investment income, but should be disclosed by way of a note to the accounts. [ABI SORP para 112].

Table 16.3 shows an example of a long-term revenue account.

Table 16.3: Example of a long-term business revenue account

Extract from Laurentian Life plc Report & Accounts 30th September 1989.

Consolidated Long-Term Revenue Account for the year ended 30th September 1989

	Note	Year ended 30th September 1989 £'000	9 months ended 30th September 1988 £'000
INCOME			
Premiums	3	217,373	109,353
Investment Income	4	73,846	40,137
Transfer from investment reserve	1, 9	3,143	2,045
Realised and unrealised gains on unit-linked investments	1	89,113	34,551
		383,475	186,086
EXPENDITURE			
Policyholder benefits	5	125,868	71,174
Commissions	1	22,432	16,470
Expenses	6	37,222	26,189
Taxation	7	9,711	1,901
Transfer to profit and loss account	1	5,600	2,600
		200,833	118,334
INCREASE IN FUNDS RESULTING FROM TRADING DURING THE PERIOD		182,642	67,752
FUNDS BROOUGHT FORWARD		854,059	786,307
FUNDS CARRIED FORWARD		1,036,701	854,059

Taxation

16.77 Shareholders' life profits bear tax in the life fund and the transfer from the life fund is net of tax. The profits are usually notionally 'grossed up' to arrive at shareholders' life profit before taxation and the taxation charge that is required to be disclosed in accordance with paragraph 22 of SSAP 8. The rate of tax used for grossing up is either the underlying tax rate of the life fund or the standard corporation tax rate.

Profit and loss account and reserves

General rules

16.78 Schedule 9 to the *Companies Act 1985* does not specify the format that an insurance company's profit and loss account should follow. There are, however, certain requirements concerning what is included in the profit and loss account which are set out in paragraphs 16.79 to 16.90 below. An example of an insurance company's profit and loss account is shown in Table 16.4.

Table 16.4: Example of an insurance company's profit and loss account

Extract from Sphere Drake Insurance plc Report & Financial Statements 31st December 1989.

Profit and Loss Account
for the year ended 31st December, 1989

	Notes	1989 £000s	1988 £000
Investment Income	1	23,095	20,996
Underwriting Losses:			
Three Year Accounts		(8,815)	(307)
One Year Account		(4,363)	(7,796)
		(13,178)	(8,103)
General Expenses	2	(621)	(904)
Exceptional Item – Relocation Costs		–	(1,118)
Profit before Taxation		9,296	10,871
Taxation	3	(2,006)	(13)
Profit for the year		7,290	10,858
Dividends	4	(2,000)	(19,250)
Retained profit brought forward		2,346	10,738
Retained profit carried forward		£7,636	£2,346

16.79 The disclosure exemptions contained in Schedule 9 to the *Companies Act 1985* provide that an insurance company need not show the aggregate amounts of reserves and provisions and the movements on such reserves and provisions during the year. As a result, insurance companies may hold 'hidden' or 'undisclosed' reserves or provisions. Insurance companies taking advantage of these exemptions should, however, identify any balance sheet heading that has been arrived at after taking into account a reserve or provision which has not been separately disclosed and explain how such reserves and provisions have been treated in the profit and loss account. [CA 1985 9 Sch 28 (1)].

16.80 The ABI SORP provides guidance as to the items that should be included in the revenue account, but does not deal with the profit and loss account. Insurance company practice in this area varies, particularly the treatment of realised and unrealised gains on investments. Some of the practices adopted are described in paragraphs 16.84 to 16.87 below. However, many companies follow the general principle that income and expenses relating to insurance funds (and this may include the investment return on insurance funds) should be dealt with in the revenue account and income and expenses relating to other corporate activities or shareholders' funds should be dealt with in the profit and loss account. There are also items that insurance companies may account for through reserves, relying on *Companies Act 1985* disclosure exemptions, which would not be taken to reserves by companies that are required to comply with Schedule 4 to the *Companies Act 1985*.

16.81 The items that may be dealt with in an insurance company's profit and loss account include the following:

- Transfer to/from general business revenue account.
- Transfer from long-term business revenue account.
- Investment income.
- Investment gains.
- Other income.
- Loan interest.
- Taxation.

16.82 Where the accounting treatment adopted by insurance companies in respect of these items differs from that adopted by Schedule 4 companies, this is explained below.

Investment income

16.83 Accounting practice in respect of investment income varies. Broadly, investment income represents a return on shareholders' and insurance funds. To the extent that the income represents a return on general business insurance funds, some insurance companies credit this investment income to the general business revenue account, although many insurance companies choose to credit all investment income to the profit and loss account. Investment expenses for general business are usually deducted from investment income in the profit and loss account, but the ABI SORP requires them to be shown separately. [ABI SORP para 112]. Investment income earned on long-term business funds is credited to the long-term business revenue account.

Realised investment gains and losses

16.84 Insurance companies' treatment of realised investment gains and losses varies. As described in paragraph 16.75 above, realised gains on investments supporting long-term insurance liabilities are generally taken to the revenue account or investment reserve, as appropriate.

16.85 The treatment in respect of realised gains and losses on investments held in the shareholders' balance sheet in support of general business insurance funds and shareholders' funds differs. The practices adopted include crediting (or charging) net realised gains (or losses) to:

- Reserves.
- The profit and loss account but after the profit and loss before taxation.
- Profit and loss before taxation.

Some companies include an averaged amount of realised and unrealised gains and losses in the profit before taxation, transferring the unrealised element back to an undistributable reserve.

Unrealised investment gains and losses

16.86 The accounting policies adopted for recognition of unrealised investment gains and losses also vary. The policy adopted is, of course, influenced by the policy used for the valuation of investments. Some companies account for investments at cost, less provision for any permanent diminution in value, in which case unrealised gains and losses will not be recognised in the financial statements. For companies which include investments at market value, it is common to take such gains and losses direct to a separate non-distributable reserve. As noted in paragraph 16.85 above, those companies that take 'average' investment gains to profit before taxation will transfer the unrealised portion back to reserves as an appropriation of the profit after taxation for the period.

16.87 Where unrealised gains and losses are recognised in the financial statements it is necessary to make appropriate provision for deferred taxation in accordance with the requirements of SSAP 15.

Loan interest

16.88 Loans generally form part of the net assets representing shareholders', rather than insurance, funds and interest thereon is charged to the profit and loss account. However, where loans are, for example, entered into by the life funds of a company, the interest thereon is charged to the long-term revenue account.

Foreign exchange

16.89 Insurance companies should comply with the provisions of SSAP 20 (see 'Manual of Accounting - volume I' chapter 18 for further guidance). However, the ABI SORP states that:

> *"Where SSAP 20 requires companies to include exchange differences within the profit and loss account, for insurance enterprises they may be more appropriately dealt with in the general business or long-term business revenue accounts."* [ABI SORP para 45].

16.90 SSAP 20 has no special exemptions for insurance companies. However, foreign currency insurance operations (where the liabilities are substantially covered by foreign current assets) can be treated as a foreign branch and the liabilities and assets translated into the reporting currency at the closing rate. [ABI SORP para 45]. Such operations include overseas branches and London Market business.

Balance sheet

General rules

16.91 Schedule 9 to the *Companies Act 1985* exempts insurance companies from making many of the balance sheet disclosures required to be made by companies that prepare their financial statements in accordance with Schedule 4 to that Act. However, the ABI SORP requires additional disclosures to be made by insurance companies and these are described further below. This section is applicable to both general and long-term business unless otherwise stated.

16.92 Neither Schedule 9 to the *Companies Act 1985* nor the ABI SORP specify the format that an insurance company's balance sheet must follow. However, the financial statements are required to disclose certain information in respect of balance sheet items. An illustration of a consolidated balance sheet of an insurance group prepared in accordance with Schedule 9 to the *Companies Act 1985* and the ABI SORP is given in Table 16.5.

16.93 The balance sheet should show amounts for share capital, assets and liabilities with such details that explain the general nature of the assets and liabilities. [CA 1985 9 Sch 2].

16.94 Insurance companies are not required, due to Schedule 9 exemptions, to distinguish between fixed, current and other assets. [CA 1985 9 Sch 4(2)].

16.95 Insurance companies are exempt from the requirement to disclose where the balance sheet value of an asset is considered to be greater than the amount it would realise in the ordinary course of the company's business. [CA 1985 9 Sch 13(12)]. However, generally accepted practice and the SSAP 2 requirement for prudence require that an asset should be included at no more than its net realisable value.

16.96 Unlike the provisions that relate to Schedule 4 companies, insurance companies may capitalise and state under separate headings, the following items if they have not been written off:

- Preliminary expenses

- Expenses incurred in connection with any issue of share capital or debenture.

- Any commission paid in respect of any shares or debentures.

- Any amount allowed by way of discount in respect of debentures.

- The amount of the discount allowed on any issue of shares .

General business technical provisions

16.97 The technical provisions contained in an insurance company's balance sheet will depend upon the basis of accounting adopted.

16.98 On the annual and deferred annual bases of accounting the following technical provisions are required:

Table 16.5: Example of general and long-term business balance sheets

Extract from Royal Insurance Holdings plc Annual Report & Accounts 31st December 1989.

CONSOLIDATED BALANCE SHEETS

as at 31st December 1989

		Notes	General 1989 £m	General 1988 £m	Long-term 1989 £m	Long-term 1988 £m
CAPITAL AND RESERVES	Shareholders' Funds					
	Share Capital: Authorised £155m Issued (shares of 25p, fully paid)	2	121	120		
	Share Premium Account		134	131		
	Retained Profits and Reserves	1	838	718		
			1,093	969		
	Investment Fluctuation Account		1,033	721		
	Long-term Insurance Business Reserve		509	425		
			2,635	2,115		
	Minority Interests in Subsidiaries		28	19		
			2,663	2,134		
BORROWINGS	For Group financing	3	568	484	15	23
	For onward lending		241	196	3	—
			809	680	18	23
GENERAL INSURANCE FUNDS	Unearned Premiums	13	1,663	1,458		
	Outstanding Claims	13	4,040	3,171		
			5,703	4,629		
LONG-TERM INSURANCE FUNDS					6,216	4,668
LONG-TERM INSURANCE INVESTMENT RESERVE		4			1,150	743
DEFERRED TAXATION		12	58	56	19	5
SUNDRY LIABILITIES AND PROVISIONS		5	752	603	295	120
			9,985	8,102	7,698	5,559
Represented by INVESTMENTS	British Government Securities		413	399	762	802
	Overseas Government Securities		952	851	134	92
	Local Authority Securities		498	514	33	35
	Debentures		2,284	1,583	1,055	457
	Preference Stocks and Shares		122	111	51	51
	Ordinary Stocks and Shares		1,367	1,095	3,617	2,598
	Mortgages and loans		307	300	422	156
	Freehold and Leasehold Property		397	364	918	817
	Cash on Deposit		376	317	334	317
			6,716	5,534	7,326	5,325
ASSOCIATED COMPANIES		6	405	297		
VALUE OF LONG-TERM INSURANCE BUSINESS			580	470		
OTHER ASSETS		5	2,284	1,801	372	234
			9,985	8,102	7,698	5,559

- Unearned premium provision, which represents the unearned portion of written premiums, accounted for on the annual basis relating to periods of risk after the end of the accounting period, recognition of which is deferred to subsequent accounting periods. The unearned premium provision should be shown gross of any amount of deferred acquisition expenses which should be disclosed separately. In practice, some companies deduct deferred acquisition costs from the unearned premiums provision or from general insurance technical provisions, but disclose the gross amounts in the notes to the financial statements. [ABI SORP para 93].

- Outstanding claims provision, which includes provision for both notified but unsettled claims and IBNR claims (see para 16.49), as well as any additional costs expected to arise on settled claims which may be reopened.

- The unexpired risk provision (see para 16.49) should be disclosed separately.

16.99 On the funded basis of accounting all insurance technical provisions are included within the 'insurance fund'. The insurance fund covers:

- The outstanding claims liabilities of the closed years.

- Accumulated net income less outgo on the open years.

- Provision for anticipated deficiencies on the open years.

- Any profits on closed years not yet released to the profit and loss account.

Long-term business technical provisions

Long-term insurance fund

16.100 The long-term insurance fund represents the balance of accumulated premiums and investment income less claims paid and revenue expenses, adjusted for release of shareholders' profit and transfers to and from investment reserves or gains and losses on investments as appropriate. At the end of each financial year, an insurance company is required to carry out an actuarial valuation of the liabilities of the company attributable to long-term business. [ICA 1982 18(1)(2)]. The balance of the fund at the end of each accounting period should be at least adequate to meet long-term business liabilities. [ABI SORP para 132]. The long-term insurance fund, therefore, comprises the liability to policyholders, as determined by the appointed actuary, together with any unappropriated surplus.

Outstanding claims

16.101 An outstanding claims provision is required for the liability to pay notified claims. All other liabilities to policyholders should be taken into account by the appointed actuary in determining the required fund so the provision for outstanding claims is usually small.

Investment reserves

16.102 The circumstances in which the investment reserve of the long-term business fund may be used to account for realised and unrealised gains and losses are described in paragraph 16.75 above. The investment reserve will usually represent accumulated realised gains (net of losses), unrealised gains (net of losses) as at the year end, less accumulated transfers to and from the investment reserve to the long-term insurance fund.

An example of a long-term balance sheet is given in Table 16.6.

Investments

Securities

16.103 There are no *Companies Act 1985* disclosure or accounting requirements in respect of investments held by insurance companies with certain exceptions which are discussed in paragraph 16.122 below.

16.104 The *Insurance Companies Regulations 1981* (SI 1984/1654) require listed investments, subject to certain limits on the size of holdings, to be valued at middle market value in the DTI return. Whilst it is not a *Companies Act 1985* requirement, most UK insurance companies also carry investments at market value in their shareholders' financial statements. In certain circumstances, it may be appropriate to value redeemable fixed interest securities at amortised cost, for example when it is expected the investments will be held to maturity, but this practice is not common in the UK.

16.105 Unlisted investments are normally included at directors' valuation applying general accepted principles in arriving at an appropriate valuation. There are, however, specific requirements set out in paragraph 44 of the *Insurance Companies Regulations 1981* (SI 1984/1654) in respect of the valuation of unlisted securities in the DTI returns and there may, therefore, be instances where the valuation for shareholders' financial statements and DTI returns differs.

Table 16.6: Example of an insurance company's long-term balance sheet.

Extract from Laurentian Life plc Report & Accounts 30th September 1989.

Consolidated Balance Sheet at 30th September 1989

	Notes	1989 £'000	1988 £'000
INVESTMENTS			
Ordinary stocks and shares		413,143	290,518
Fixed-interest securities		277,054	289,710
Authorised unit trusts		97,115	66,634
Property		82,870	77,638
Mortgages and loans		10,211	10,711
Interest bearing deposits		223,543	169,152
	8(a)	1,103,936	904,363
Less investment reserve	9	(23,110)	(22,151)
		1,080,826	882,212
OTHER ASSETS	10	45,033	53,250
TOTAL ASSETS		1,125,859	935,462
CREDITORS	11	(54,117)	(51,366)
DEFERRED TAXATION	1(h)	(12,144)	(7,191)
NET ASSETS		1,059,598	876,905
CAPITAL AND RESERVES			
Share capital	12	16,600	16,600
Other reserves	13	6,045	6,045
Profit and loss account		252	201
		22,897	22,846
LIFE ASSURANCE FUNDS		1,036,701	854,059
		1,059,598	876,905

16.106 Listed companies and companies that are traded on the USM have to comply also with the requirements that relate to investments that are outlined in The International Stock Exchange's Continuing Obligations and in the USM's General Undertaking respectively. These requirements are discussed in 'Manual of Accounting - volume I' chapter 9.

Land and buildings

16.107 Insurance companies are significant investors in property. Many carry their property investment at market value. As noted in paragraph 16.39 above, insurance companies should comply with SSAPs to the extent appropriate to their circumstances. SSAP 12 'Accounting for depreciation' and SSAP 19 'Accounting for investment properties' are relevant in principle to insurance companies. For example, SSAP 19 states that in respect of long-term insurance business, changes in value should be dealt with in the relevant fund accounts. However where, for example, investment properties represent only a small part of the overall investment portfolio companies may choose not to make all the specific disclosures included in the SSAPs. Insurance companies often occupy their investment properties for their own use, but do not depreciate them on the grounds that such depreciation would not be material to the results and the properties are revalued regularly. Reference should be made to 'Manual of Accounting - volume I' chapter 8 for further guidance.

Goodwill, patents and trademarks

16.108 The accounting and disclosure requirements for insurance companies in respect of goodwill are governed by SSAP 22. The SSAP 22 requirements (from which insurance companies have no exemptions) are considered further in 'Manual of Accounting - volume I' chapter 7.

Other assets and liabilities

16.109 The disclosure requirements in respect of other assets and liabilities are considered in the paragraphs that follow.

Fixed assets

16.110 Schedule 9 to the *Companies Act 1985* exempts insurance companies from making disclosures in respect of fixed assets and many avail themselves of this exemption since fixed assets are not usually material to an insurance operation. However, Schedule 9 does require that where an amount has been provided for depreciation of an asset (including provisions for renewals or for diminution in value), or an amount has been provided for a liability, and the directors consider that the amount provided is excessive, they must treat the excess as a reserve rather than as a provision. [CA 1985 9 Sch 32 (2)].

Broker, agent and reinsurer balances

16.111 Amounts due to and by brokers, agents and reinsurers are frequently 'netted off' in the balance sheet by insurance companies. There is no Schedule 9 *Companies Act 1985* requirement which deals with this practice, although netting off is not allowed by Schedule 4. However, the *Insurance Companies (Accounts and Statements) Regulations 1983* (SI 1983/1811) acknowledge the practice by requiring companies that do so to disclose in the DTI return the fact that amounts due to or by a person or intermediary have been included net, where the effect is significant.

Deferred taxation

16.112 Insurance companies should comply with the provisions of SSAP 15 (see 'Manual of Accounting - volume I' chapter 11).

Contingent liabilities

16.113 Schedule 9 to the *Companies Act 1985* requires that the notes to the financial statements should show the general nature of any other contingent liabilities that have not been provided for, together (where practicable) with the aggregate amount of or an estimate of the liabilities. [CA 1985 9 Sch 13 (7)]. Insurance companies are exempt from such disclosures. [CA 1985 9 Sch 28 (1)(a)]. It should, however, be noted that estimates of outstanding claims, including IBNR should represent the expected claims liabilities of an insurance company as calculated in accordance with the company's accounting policies, even though the quantum of any liability may be contingent on other subsequent events. Despite the exemption, insurance companies generally disclose non-insurance contingent liabilities in accordance with the requirements of SSAP 18 and disclosure of such contingent liabilities is required in the DTI return. For further guidance on the application of SSAP 18 see 'Manual of Accounting - volume I' chapter 11.

Statement of source and application of funds

16.114 SSAP 10 requires the disclosure of the increase or decrease in working capital sub-divided into its component parts, and movements in liquid funds. Working capital is difficult to define for an insurance operation and it is necessary therefore for insurance companies to present their statement of source and application of funds in a manner appropriate to their business. The predecessor to the ABI issued a recommended format for insurance company statements of sources and application of funds which is followed by many companies. The recommended format includes the disclosure of movements in invested funds, rather than working capital, and the cash generated from operations. An example is given in Table 16.7.

Table 16.7: Example of an insurance company's Statement of Source and Application of Funds

Extract from Sun Alliance Group plc Report and Accounts 31st December 1989.

Consolidated Statement of Source and Application of Funds

for the year ended 31st December, 1989 (excluding long-term insurance business)

	1989 £m	1988 £m
Source of funds		
Profit after taxation (per the profit and loss account)	227.7	262.1
Realised investment profits less losses, after taxation	41.6	26.5
Other movements in retained profits	(8.5)	4.5
Adjustments to convert revenue and expenditure onto a cash basis:–		
Increase in insurance funds	370.6	235.0
Increase in agents and other balances	(72.3)	(38.6)
Depreciation of capitalised equipment	29.9	17.7
Funds generated from operations	589.0	507.2
Increase (decrease) in borrowings	(34.8)	88.5
Issue of shares	1.9	0.1
	556.1	595.8
Application of funds		
Dividends paid (including dividends to minority shareholders)	88.9	72.5
Net investment in subsidiary and associated companies	43.0	40.4
Purchase of capitalised equipment	49.4	29.4
Increase (decrease) in invested funds at cost:–		
Fixed interest securities	(50.2)	126.3
Ordinary stocks and shares	345.1	74.7
Property	58.8	52.3
Mortgages and loans	18.8	5.7
Short-term deposits	(34.6)	189.6
	337.9	448.6
Movement in bank balances	36.9	4.9
	556.1	595.8

16.115 An exposure draft on cash flow statements (ED 54) was issued by the ASC which will replace the statement of source and application of funds required by SSAP 10. Broadly, the proposed statement requires the reporting of movements of cash and cash equivalents, classified between the major economic activities (that is, operating, investing and financing). Some insurers already prepare their statement of source and application of funds on these lines. The proposed statement is currently being considered by the ASB and will be issued as an Accounting Standard in 1991.

16.116 The movements in the long-term balance sheets are not normally reflected in the statement of source and application of funds because such movements are disclosed in the long-term revenue account and are considered sufficient to meet the requirements of SSAP 10.

Specific disclosure requirements

16.117 The paragraphs that follow highlight disclosure requirements that are of particular concern to insurance companies and groups. The purpose is not to set out a complete checklist of matters for disclosure in an insurance company's financial statements. Reference should be made to 'Manual of Accounting - volume I' and the text of Schedule 9 to the *Companies Act 1985* which is reproduced, in the extract of accounting provisions in this book, to ensure that more general disclosure requirements have been complied with. The paragraphs that follow consider:

- The disclosure exemptions afforded to insurance companies and groups by paragraph 28(1) of Schedule 9 to the *Companies Act 1985.*

- The recommendations of the ABI SORP.

It should also be borne in mind that many insurance companies make disclosures over and above any requirement of Schedule 9 and the ABI SORP.

General

16.118 The notes to the financial statements should state those accounting policies dealing with items that are judged material or critical in determining the profit or loss for the year and in stating the financial position. In particular, the ABI SORP recommends that:

- The accounting basis or bases adopted should be disclosed. Where the deferred annual or fund accounting basis is used, the classes of business involved and the extent of the time deferral for profit recognition should also be disclosed. [ABI SORP para 85].

- The accounting policy adopted for premium recognition should be stated and where the annual or deferred accounting bases are used, the basis of calculating the unearned premium provision should be disclosed. [ABI SORP para 99].

- The basis for determining deferred acquisition expenses should be disclosed. [ABI SORP para 107].

- The policies adopted with regard to the recognition of the following should be disclosed:

  - Notified claims.

  - IBNR.

  - Claims handling expenses.

  - Salvage and other recoveries.

  [ABI SORP para 121].

- Any discounting of provisions for claims outstanding and direct claims handling expenses should be disclosed (see para 16.63). [ABI SORP para 126].

- The accounting policies in respect of life insurance business premiums and claims should also be disclosed. [ABI SORP para 126].

Balance sheet exemptions

16.119 Insurance companies are exempt from many of the disclosure requirements of Schedule 9 to the *Companies Act 1985*. [CA 1985 9 Sch Part I 28(1)]. The exemptions extend to the consolidated financial statements of the group where the parent company heading the group is entitled to the exemptions. [CA 1985 9 Sch Part II 5(1)].

16.120 The exemptions granted by paragraph 28(1) of Part I of Schedule 9 to the *Companies Act 1985* to insurance companies and groups are discussed in the paragraphs that follow. The references given in round brackets are to the paragraph numbers in Part I of Schedule 9 to the *Companies Act 1985* with which insurance companies and groups need not comply.

Fixed assets

16.121 Assets need not be analysed between fixed assets, current assets and those that are neither fixed nor current. (CA 1985 9 Sch Part I 4(2)). Following from this exemption, an insurance company need not:

- State the method that has been used to arrive at the amount for each category of fixed asset. (CA 1985 9 Sch Part I 4(3)).

- Include fixed assets in the balance sheet at cost (or valuation) less any provisions for depreciation or diminution in value, or disclose the cost and accumulated depreciation of fixed assets. (CA 1985 9 Sch Part I 5).

- Give details of any valuation of assets. (CA 1985 9 Sch Part I 13(9)).

- Give details of additions and disposals of fixed assets. (CA 1985 9 Sch Part I 13(10)).

- Analyse land between freehold, long leasehold and short leasehold. (CA 1985 9 Sch Part I 13(11)).

- State if the directors consider that the realisable value of certain current assets is less than the value at which they are included in the balance sheet. (CA 1985 9 Sch Part I 13(12)).

Investments

16.122 In respect of investments, an insurance company need not:

- Analyse investments between listed investments and unlisted investments. (CA 1985 9 Sch Part I 10(1)(a), 3).

- Show the aggregate market value and the stock exchange value (if applicable) of listed investments. (CA 1985 9 Sch Part I 13(13)).

- Give the following information regarding unlisted investments:

  - ☐ The aggregate amount of income the company received from them during the year.

  - ☐ The total of the company's share of their profits less losses before and after taxation.

  - ☐ The company's share of their accumulated post-acquisition undistributed profits less losses.

  - ☐ The manner in which any losses the unlisted companies have incurred have been dealt with in the company's financial statements.

  (CA 1985 9 Sch Part I 6).

16.123 However, where an insurance company at the end of its financial year has a 'significant holding' of shares in another undertaking, other than a subsidiary undertaking, the *Companies Act 1985* requirement to disclose certain information in accordance with Schedule 5 applies equally to insurance companies. Similarly, where an insurance company has a 'significant holding' in an undertaking (which is not a subsidiary) amounting to 20 per cent or more of the nominal value of the shares in the undertaking, additional information should be given as set out in Schedule 5. [CA 1985 5 Sch 9(1)(a)(b)]. The matters to be disclosed are given in 'Manual of Accounting - volume I' chapter 9.

Reserves, provisions and liabilities

16.124 In general, insurance companies need not classify reserves, provisions and liabilities under headings appropriate to the company's business. (CA 1985 9 Sch Part I 4(1)).

16.125 The financial statements need not disclose the aggregate amount of reserves and provisions separately. (CA 1985 9 Sch Part I 7).

16.126 Where an amount has been provided for depreciation of an asset (including provisions for renewals or the diminution in value), or an amount has been provided for a liability, and the directors consider that the amount provided is excessive, the excess must be treated as a reserve, rather than as a provision. (CA 1985 9 Sch Part I 32(2)).

16.127 Schedule 9 requires that any share premium account must be shown separately. (CA 1985 9 Sch Part I 2(c)). Any capital redemption reserve must also be disclosed. [CA 1985 Sec 170].

16.128 Notwithstanding the statutory exemptions with respect to the separate disclosure of provisions and reserves, the ABI SORP makes the following recommendations with which insurance companies should comply:

- Claims provisions should be disclosed gross with outstanding reinsurance recoveries being shown separately either on the face of the balance sheet or in the notes to the financial statements. [ABI SORP para 123].

- The amount of the provision for unexpired risks in respect of general insurance business together with a note of changes in the amount of the provision from one accounting period to the next should be disclosed. [ABI SORP para 131].

- The unearned premium reserve in respect of annually accounted business should be disclosed without any deduction for deferred acquisition expenses. [ABI SORP para 93]. In addition, the gross amount of the provision and any reinsurance thereon should be shown separately. [ABI SORP para 101].

- The provision for long-term business claims should be shown gross in the balance sheet with outstanding reinsurance claims recoveries shown separately. [ABI SORP para 151].

- In relation to general insurance business accounted for on a deferred annual or fund accounting basis the amount and source of any transfers from the fund and the return of excessive transfers to the fund should be disclosed. [ABI SORP paras 115, 116].

The revenue account and profit and loss account

16.129 In general the financial statements of an insurance company prepared under Schedule 9 to the *Companies Act 1985* must show the following:

Turnover

16.130 The turnover for the year, and the method used to arrive at the figure for turnover. No definition is given of turnover in the *Companies Act 1985.* In the past insurance companies have disclosed various combinations of gross and net, written and earned premiums. The ABI SORP has sought to close the divergence in insurance companies' practice by recommending that companies disclose as much detail as possible. The specific recommendations of the ABI SORP in this regard are considered in paragraphs 16.131 and 16.132 below.

16.131 In respect of general insurance business turnover, the ABI SORP recommends the following disclosure in the financial statements, the directors' report or a business review:

- The total amount of written premiums should be shown inclusive of direct business and inwards reinsurance business on a gross basis with reinsurance cessions shown as a deduction, therefore, displaying the amount of business written and retained. [ABI SORP para 100].

- An analysis of gross premiums into principal classes of business should be disclosed. The company should determine its own principal classes. [ABI SORP para 102].

- An analysis of aggregate gross premiums into geographical areas should be disclosed. [ABI SORP para 103]. With marine, aviation, transport and reinsurance inwards business, it may not be possible to categorise the business into geographical areas, in which case the classes of business involved should be disclosed separately. [ABI SORP para 103].

16.132 In respect of long-term insurance business turnover, the ABI SORP recommends that the following matters should be disclosed in the financial statements, the directors' report or a business review:

- Premium income should be shown on a gross basis with reinsurance cessions shown as a reduction, therefore, displaying the amount of business transacted and retained. [ABI SORP para 138].

- An analysis of premiums into life, annuity, pension and permanent health insurance business with a separate indication in each situation of the amounts of group and unit linked business should be disclosed. [ABI SORP para 139].

- An analysis of premium into geographical areas should be disclosed. [ABI SORP para 140].

- An analysis of the annualised value for new annual premiums and the amount of new single premiums into the classes specified in the second point above should be disclosed. [ABI SORP para 141].

Expenses and claims

16.133 The ABI SORP has also sought to standardise the treatment of expenses and claims in the revenue account. The ABI SORP makes the following recommendations in respect of general insurance business expenses and claims:

- The amount of deferred acquisition costs should be separately disclosed and not deducted from the unearned premium provision. [ABI SORP para 109].

- The movement in deferred acquisition expenses should be disclosed as an adjustment to expenses in the revenue account. [ABI SORP para 108].

- Investment expenses should be separately disclosed. Expenses such as stamp duty and brokerage, which are regarded as part of the capital cost of the investment, are not treated as investment expenses. [ABI SORP para 112].

- Expenses should be classified under the headings of underwriting, claims handling, investments and other. [ABI SORP para 105].

- The effect of discounting on the profit or loss before taxation and on the net assets at the end of the accounting period should be disclosed. [ABI SORP para 126].

- If an enterprise alters its accounting policy for providing for outstanding claims from a discounted basis to a non-discounted basis, this should be dealt with as prior year adjustment in accordance with SSAP 6 and the facts disclosed. [ABI SORP para 127].

- All claims should be shown gross of reinsurance in the revenue account and the reinsurance recoveries shown as a deduction giving a net cost of claims. [ABI SORP para 122].

16.134 The recommendations in respect of long-term business expenses and claims are less extensive:

- Revenue expenses should be classified under the headings of underwriting, investments and other. All revenue expenses should be charged to the fund. [ABI SORP paras 143, 144].

- All life insurance business claims should be shown in the revenue account with the reinsurance recoveries being shown as a deduction to give the net cost for claims. [ABI SORP para 150].

Exceptional and extraordinary items

16.135 The financial statements should give details of any exceptional or extraordinary items and of the effect of any changes in bases of accounting. [CA 1985 9 Sch Part I 18(6)]. Compliance with SSAP 6 will ensure that the financial statements comply with this requirement of the *Companies Act 1985*.

Statutory exemptions

16.136 Insurance companies are granted specific exemptions from certain profit and loss account disclosures by virtue of paragraph 28(1) of Schedule 9 to the *Companies Act 1985*. An insurance company need not disclose the following information (the references in round brackets refer to the paragraph numbers in Schedule 9 to the *Companies Act 1985* with which the company need not comply):

- The amount of any depreciation charge and any amount provided for either renewals or diminution in the value of fixed assets. (CA 1985 9 Sch Part I 14(1)(a), (3)).

- Details of the amount set aside to, or proposed to be set aside to, or withdrawn from, reserves or provisions. (CA 1985 9 Sch Part I 14(1)(e)(f), (2)).

- The amount of income from both listed investments and unlisted investments. (CA 1985 9 Sch Part I 14(1)(g)).

- The amount of rent received. (CA 1985 9 Sch Part I 14(1)(h)).

- Any amount charged for the hire of plant and machinery. (CA 1985 9 Sch Part I 14(1)(j)).

- Whether an amount charged for either depreciation or the diminution in value of any asset has been based on a value other than the value at which that asset is included in the balance sheet. (CA 1985 9 Sch Part I 14(4)).

Consolidated financial statements

16.137 The disclosure requirements applicable to the consolidated financial statements of insurance groups are, under section 255A of and Schedule 4A (as modified by Part II of Schedule 9) to the *Companies Act 1985*, similar to those of individual companies.

16.138 With certain exceptions, the requirement to prepare consolidated financial statements, the methods that should be used to produce them, and their form and content are exactly the same for an insurance group as for a non-insurance group. Consequently, the requirements set out in 'Manual of Accounting - volume II' should be followed. However, the application of the provisions of Part II of Schedule 9 to the *Companies Act 1985* in respect of the following items in particular should be considered:

- The general application of provisions applicable to individual accounts by reference to Schedule 9, not Schedule 4.

- The value and amortisation of goodwill. [CA 1985 9 Sch Part II 3(1)(2)].

- The disclosure of information concerning minority interest and associated undertakings. [CA 1985 9 Sch Part II 4].

16.139 Insurance groups may continue to prepare group accounts in a form other than consolidated financial statements for any financial year ending prior to 1st January 1994. For financial years beginning on or after 1st January 1994, group accounts must be in consolidated form. Where group accounts are prepared in a form other than consolidated financial statements, they may be prepared in either of the following forms:

- More than one set of consolidated accounts.

- A collection of individual accounts of subsidiaries in the parent company's individual accounts.

- Any combination of the above forms.

16.140 Insurance groups can only take advantage of the above provision in the following situations:

- An undertaking within the group is authorised to carry out both long-term and general business.

- The group comprises one or more undertakings authorised to carry out long-term business and one or more undertakings authorised to carry out general business.

[SI 1990/355 2 Sch Part I (3)].

The directors' report

16.141 The information to be included in the directors' report of an insurance company is essentially similar to that of a Schedule 4 company (see further 'Manual of Accounting - volume I' chapter 20). All the requirements of Schedule 7 to the *Companies Act 1985* apply equally to insurance companies and groups. However, there are some specific matters that apply to directors' reports of insurance companies and groups and these are discussed below.

16.142 The directors' report is allowed to contain the following information that would otherwise be given elsewhere in the financial statements:

- Information required under paragraph 6 of Part I of Schedule 9 to the *Companies Act 1985* (directors' valuation of unlisted investments).

- Information required under paragraph 8 of Part I of Schedule 9 to the *Companies Act 1985* (movements on reserves and provisions).

- Information required under paragraph 13 of Part I of Schedule 9 to the *Companies Act 1985* (share options, forfeited and surrendered shares, dividend arrears and contracted capital expenditure).

[CA 1985 Sec 255C(2)].

16.143 In addition, if an item is included in the directors' report that would normally have been included elsewhere in the financial statements, the directors' report must be treated as forming part of the financial statements. Consequently, it must be audited to the extent that it gives information that would otherwise be shown elsewhere in the financial statements. [CA 1985 Sec 255C(2)].

16.144 As with any other companies, the directors must state, in their report, the amount that they propose to be carried to reserves. In this context, the amount proposed to be carried to reserves should be construed within the meaning of Part I of Schedule 9 to the *Companies Act 1985*, and does not therefore prevent an insurance company from having hidden reserves. [CA 1985 Sec 255C(3)].

16.145 An insurance company or group that has taken advantage of the exemptions conferred by paragraph 28 of Part I of Schedule 9 to the *Companies Act 1985* need not give details of the following in the directors' report:

- Significant changes in fixed assets of the company or any of its subsidiary undertakings. [CA 1985 Sec 255C (4), 7 Sch 1(1)].

- Significant differences between the book value and the market value of interests in land. [CA 1985 Sec 255C(4), 7 Sch 1(2)].

16.146 In addition, Schedule 10 to the *Companies Act 1985* sets out certain information that the directors' report of all insurance companies must contain. This information is considered below.

Issue of shares or debentures

16.147 If the company has issued any shares or debentures during the year, the directors' report must state:

- The reason for making the issue.

- The classes of shares or debentures issued and in respect of each class of shares or debentures issued:

  - The number of shares or the amount of debentures issued.

  - The consideration the company received for the issue.

[CA 1985 10 Sch 1(1)(2)].

Disaggregated information

16.148 An insurance group that prepares consolidated financial statements must disclose, in the directors' report, the information set out below. However, this requirement applies only if the company carries on business of two or more classes (for example, general insurance business and long-term insurance business) that, in the directors' opinion, are substantially different. If, however, two classes of business do not differ substantially from each other, they should be treated as one class. [CA 1985 10 Sch 2(4)]. The information required is:

- A description of each class of business (see para 16.131 and 16.132).

- The proportion of turnover for the year that is attributable to each class of business (see para 16.131 and 16.132).

- The amount of the profit or loss before taxation that is, in the directors' opinion, attributable to each class of business.

[CA 1985 10 Sch 2(1)(2)].

16.149 If the insurance company is either listed on The International Stock Exchange or traded on the USM, it will have to comply also with The International Stock Exchange's Continuing Obligations or the USM's General Undertaking as appropriate as to the disclosure of disaggregated information for turnover and profit. This requirement is discussed in 'Manual of Accounting - volume I' chapter 13.

Employees and their remuneration

16.150 The directors' report of an insurance company or group must disclose:

- The average number of people the company or group employed in the UK during each week of the year. This figure should be calculated by first adding up the total number of people employed under contracts of service for each week of the year. These weekly totals should then be added, and the total should be divided by the number of weeks in the year.

- The total remuneration paid or payable in respect of the year to these people. For this purpose, remuneration is the gross remuneration, including bonuses, that was paid or payable.

[CA 1985 10 Sch 3(1)-(4), (6)].

16.151 However, none of the above information has to be given if either the company is a wholly-owned subsidiary of another company incorporated in Great Britain or the company (together with subsidiaries, if applicable) employs on average fewer than 100 people each week in the UK. [CA 1985 10 Sch 3(5), (7)].

Non-insurance holding company

16.152 A situation may arise where a non-insurance holding company prepares its financial statements in accordance with Schedule 4 to the *Companies Act 1985*, but the consolidated financial statements are prepared in accordance with Schedule 9 to that Act (because the predominant activity of the group is insurance business and activities which are a direct extension of or ancillary to insurance business). As the directors' report is attached to the holding company's balance sheet, it should comply with the requirements of Schedule 7 to the *Companies Act 1985*. However, because the consolidated financial statements are prepared in accordance with Schedule 9 to the *Companies Act 1985*, the directors' report should contain also the information required by paragraphs 2 and 3 of Schedule 10 to that Act. These paragraphs require the disaggregation of turnover and profit or loss before tax by class of business, and also the disclosure of the average number of employees and their aggregate remuneration. [CA 1985 Sec 255C(5)].

Auditors' consideration of the directors' report

16.153 As with Schedule 4 companies, auditors are required to consider if, in their opinion, the directors' report is consistent with the financial statements. If there is an inconsistency, auditors are required to draw attention to that fact in their report. [CA 1985 Sec 235(3)]. The directors' report does not form part of the financial statements on which the auditors report. However, as stated in paragraph 16.143 above, where information that would normally be shown in the company's financial statements is included in the directors' report, the auditors' report should cover that information.

Loans to directors and officers

16.154 In general, all the provisions of the *Companies Act 1985* that prevent relevant and non-relevant companies from making loans and quasi-loans to directors or their connected persons are applicable to relevant and non-relevant insurance companies. However, insurance companies (both relevant and non-relevant) may take advantage of a number of further exemptions that are available to money-lending companies under section 338 of the *Companies Act 1985*. In particular, insurance companies may make loans on beneficial terms to directors of either the company or its parent company for the purpose of house purchase or improvement up to a maximum amount of £100,000, provided the company makes similar loans of that type available to its employees on no less favourable terms. The special rules that cover the legality of these transactions for insurance companies are set out in 'Manual of Accounting - volume I', chapter 21.

Distributable profits

16.155 The principles for determining distributable profits are no different for an insurance company than for any other company. Distributions can only be made out of profits available for the purpose, being accumulated realised profits less accumulated realised losses. [CA 1985 Sec 263].

16.156 Other considerations such as the restrictions on distribution of assets available to public companies apply equally to insurance companies. The requirements of section 270 of the *Companies Act 1985* for determining a distribution by reference to the company's relevant accounts apply, but Schedule 11 to the *Companies Act 1985* modified the rules for determining distributable profits when the relevant accounts are those of an insurance company. [CA 1985 Sec 279]. The principal provisions of Schedule 11 are outlined below:

- Provisions stated in accordance with the definition in Part 1 of Schedule 9 to the *Companies Act 1985* should be used to calculate the distributable profits of an insurance company, as opposed to provisions stated in accordance with the tighter definition in Schedule 4 to that Act. [CA 1985 11 Sch 1, 2(a), 4(a), 7(a)].

- If an asset is included in an insurance company's relevant accounts as neither a fixed asset nor a current asset then it shall be treated as a fixed asset for the purpose of determining whether a provision for the diminution in the value of an asset is realised or unrealised. [CA 1985 11 Sch 7(b)].

- The Schedule 4 rule that capitalised development costs should be treated as a realised revenue loss does not apply. [CA 1985 11 Sch 3].

16.157 It should be noted that the requirement that the relevant accounts should be properly prepared does not prevent an insurance company from taking advantage of the exemptions in paragraph 28(1) of Schedule 9 to the *Companies Act 1985* in preparing those financial statements. [CA 1985 11 Sch 5(a), 6(b)].

16.158 The amount transferred to the profit and loss account from a surplus in the life fund or funds, or any deficit in the fund, is considered to be a realised profit or loss. The surplus in the life fund has to be proved by an actuarial investigation under the requirements of the *Insurance Companies Act 1982*. [CA 1985 Sec 268]. There is currently a debate over whether life profits if determined under the proposed accruals method, and not as a transfer of surplus in the fund shown by an actuarial investigation, will qualify as distributable profits.

Audit report

16.159 The auditor's responsibilities in relation to the financial statements of insurance companies under the *Companies Act 1985* are the same as those for the generality of companies. However, where an insurance company is entitled to, and has availed itself of, the disclosure exemptions permitted by Schedule 9 to the *Companies Act 1985*, the auditors are only required to report whether, in their opinion, the balance sheet and the profit and loss account have been properly prepared in accordance with the *Companies Act 1985*. [CA 1985 9 Sch Part I 28A]. Similar requirements apply to consolidated financial statements of an insurance group where the group has taken advantage of the exemptions from the disclosure requirements of Part I of Schedule 9 to that Act. [CA 1985 9 Sch Part II 5(2)]. An example of an unqualified audit report of an insurance company that has availed itself of the disclosure exemptions allowed by paragraph 28(1) of Schedule 9 to the *Companies Act 1985* is given below.

REPORT OF THE AUDITORS TO [NAME OF INSURANCE COMPANY]

We have audited the financial statements on pages [] to [] in accordance with Auditing Standards.

In our opinion the financial statements have been properly prepared in accordance with the provisions of the Companies Act 1985 applicable to insurance companies.

[Name of firm]

Chartered Accountants,

[Address].

[Date of report].

16.160 In March 1991, the APC issued an Auditing Guideline 'General business insurers in the United Kingdom' (AG 3.301). The guideline gives guidance on the special factors to be considered in the application of auditing standards to authorised insurance companies writing general insurance and reinsurance business in the UK.

SECTIONS OF THE COMPANIES ACT 1985 THAT APPLY SPECIFICALLY TO INSURANCE COMPANIES

Section	**Description**
209	Interests to be disregarded
246	Exemptions for small and medium-sized companies
248	Exemptions for small and medium-sized groups
255	Special provisions for banking and insurance companies
255A	Special provisions for banking and insurance groups
255C	Directors' report where accounts prepared in accordance with special provisions
262A	Index of defined expressions
268	Realised profits of insurance company with long-term business
279	Distributions by banking or insurance companies
449	Provisions for security of information obtained
450	Punishment for destroying mutilating etc. company documents
451A	Disclosure of information by Secretary of State or inspector
452	Privileged information
460	Order on application of Secretary of State
720	Certain companies to publish periodical statement
735	'Company' etc.
744	Expressions used generally in this Act

Section	Description
Sch 9	Special provisions for banking and insurance companies and groups
Sch 10	Directors' report where accounts prepared in accordance with special provisions for banking or insurance companies or groups
Sch 11	Modification of Part VIII where company's accounts prepared in accordance with special provisions for banking or insurance companies

ABI SORP – ACCOUNTING FOR INSURANCE BUSINESS

Contents

Paragraphs

STATEMENT OF RECOMMENDED PRACTICE ACCOUNTING FOR INSURANCE BUSINESS

(Issued by the Association of British Insurers in May 1990)

This Statement of Recommended Practice ('SORP'), which has the approval of the Accounting Standards Committee, sets out recommendations, intended to represent current best practice, on the form and content of financial statements of enterprises (other than Lloyd's syndicates) authorised to conduct insurance business in the United Kingdom.

The provisions of this Statement should be read in conjunction with the Explanatory Foreword to SORPs. Although SORPs are not mandatory, entities falling within their scope are encouraged to follow them and to state in their accounts that they have done so. They are also encouraged to disclose any departure from the recommendations and the reasons for such departure. The provisions of this Statement need not be applied to immaterial items.

Part 1 – Explanatory note

Introduction

1 The objective of this Statement is to set out recommended accounting practice, but not presentation, for insurance enterprises in order to narrow the areas of difference and variation in accounting treatment and to enhance the usefulness of published accounting information. The Statement deals basically with issues affecting the underwriting result.

2 The Statement is intended to apply only to the financial statement prepared in accordance with the requirements of the Companies Acts (or the related legislation for entities not subject to the Companies Acts) and not to the regulatory returns drawn up under the Insurance Companies Act 1982 (or similar legislation applicable to certain insurers). However, Regulation 52 of the Insurance Companies Regulations 1981 states that, subject to the more detailed rules in Part VI of the Regulations, the amount of liabilities of an insurance enterprise in respect of its general and long-term business shall be determined 'in accordance with generally accepted accounting concepts, bases and policies or other generally accepted methods appropriate for insurance enterprises'.

Reporting framework

3 The framework for financial reporting for insurance enterprises is derived basically from the following sources:

(i) Statutory requirements
– Companies Acts 1985 and 1989
– Insurance Companies Act 1982
– Friendly Societies Act 1974
– Industrial and Provident Societies Act 1965
– Industrial Assurance Acts 1923 to 1968.

(ii) Statements of Standard Accounting Practice (SSAPs).

(iii) Insurance industry practice.

4 Section 226(2) of the Companies Act 1985 requires that the balance sheet of a company shall give a true and fair view of the state of affairs of the company as at the end of the financial year and the profit and loss account shall give a true and fair view of the profit or loss of the company for the financial year. Section 227(3) of the Companies Act 1985 imposes the same requirement in relation to the undertakings included in group accounts so far as members of the company are concerned. Although insurers are exempted from certain disclosure requirements by virtue of Section 255 and Paragraph 28 of Schedule 9 of the Companies Act 1985 the principal effect of which is to permit them to establish and maintain undisclosed reserves, the recommendations in the Statement have been made without regard to the available exemptions except insofar as these relate to long-term insurance funds. Life insurers generally include in their balance sheet as a liability the long-term fund which may exceed the amount reasonable necessary to meet the liabilities of the long-term business: the long-term fund in the balance sheet may therefore include undisclosed reserves.

5 The Insurance Companies Act and the related regulations provide the legal framework for regulatory returns to the supervisory authorities which are prepared on a different basis from that adopted for financial statements. However, this legislation has an impact on finanacial statements of enterprises writing long-term business in two particular areas – the amount of the surplus which may be allocated to shareholders from the long-term fund and the declaration of dividends. In the case of long-term business, the actuary appointed in accordance with the Section 19 of the Insurance Companies Act 1982 has a statutory responsibility under Section 18 of the Act to carry out an investigation into the financial condition of the long-term business.

6 SSAPs are applicable to all financial statements the purpose of which is to give a true and fair view of an enterprise's financial position as at the accounting date and profit or loss for the accounting period to that date. Accordingly, all enterprises are expected to follow SSAPs unless to do so would conflict with the presentation of a true and fair view. The concept of 'prudence', which is presumed to have been applied in financial statements unless there is an indication to the contrary, is defined in SSAP 2 as: 'revenue and profits are not anticipated, but are recognised by inclusion in the profit and loss account only when

realised in the form either of cash or of other assets the ultimate cash realisation of which can be assessed with reasonable certainty; provision is made for all known liabilities (expenses and losses) whether the amount of these is known with certainty or is a best estimate in the light of the information available.' The prudence concept does not justify the taking of precautionary margins in the estimation of liabilities to create undisclosed reserves.

7 The financial effects of any significant departures from SSAPs should be estimated and disclosed unless this would be impracticable or misleading in the context of giving a true and fair view. If the financial effects of such departures are not disclosed, the reasons for such non-disclosure should be stated. Where SSAPs prescribe that specific information should be contained in financial statements, such requirements do not override disclosure exemptions available to, and utilised by, insurers.

8 The European Community has recognised the need for special accounting rules for insurance enterprises by publishing a proposal for an insurance accounts directive. Accordingly, insurance companies are exempt from the requirements of the EC Fourth Council Directive on the Annual Accounts of Certain Types of Companies (78/660/EEC). However, the principles of this directive will be applied to insurance companies when the proposed EC Directive on the Annual Accounts and Consolidated Accounts of Insurance Undertakings is implemented into Member State legislation.

General insurance business

Base of accounting

9 General insurance business may be accounted for on an annual accounting basis, a deferred annual accounting basis or on a fund accounting basis.

10 The annual accounting basis is adopted where an underwriting result can be determined with reasonable certainty at the end of each accounting period for business written in that period. The underwriting result disclosed in the financial statements will comprise the result for the current accounting period and any adjustments during the current accounting period to estimates used in arriving at the results of prior accounting periods.

11 For some classes of business it is not possible to obtain the data necessary to determine a result with the required degree of certainty using the annual accounting basis. Where, however, sufficient information is available in the succeeding accounting period to permit a result to be determined with the required degree of certainty, the deferred annual basis of accounting is appropriate.

12 There are two different versions of the deferred annual accounting basis, either of which may be applied. The first version involves accounting for all items in the revenue account one accounting period in arrears but is otherwise the same as the annual accounting basis. The revenue account for the current accounting period will comprise items relating to the previous accounting period (closed year) and any adjustments during the current accounting period to estimates used in arriving at the results of previously closed years. Any revenue notified in respect of the current accounting period (open year) is deferred to the following accounting period. Under the second version of the deferred annual accounting basis, the same principles are followed but items are recorded in the revenue account of the accounting period in which they are notified. The aggregate net revenue notified to date in respect of the open year, after adjustments for any anticipated losses, is carried forward as a fund.

13 Under both versions of the deferred annual basis, if on the basis of the limited amount of information available it appears likely that a loss will arise in respect of the open year, provision should be made to cover the anticipated deficiency. The underwriting result disclosed in the financial statements for an accounting period will comprise the result of the closed year, adjustments to estimates used in arriving at the results of previously closed years and provisions for anticipated deficiencies in respect of the open year. The fund at the end of an accounting period will comprise the outstanding liabilities of the closed years, the net income for the open year and any provision for an estimated deficiency of the open year.

14 The fund – or underwriting year – accounting basis is used where, even by the end of the following accounting period, a result cannot be determined with reasonable certainty. This accounting basis may be appropriate for marine, aviation and transport business and some non-proportional reinsurance business in respect of which long reporting delays can be expected. All items recorded in respect of open years will be shown in the revenue account in the accounting period in which they are notified. A fund is created for each underwriting year to which premiums written on all policies or contracts incepting during that year are allocated together with the related claims and other expenditure. A fund can consist of either one class or more than one class of business provided those classes are managed together.

15 The fund for each underwriting year is not closed until sufficient information is available for a result to be determined with reasonable certainty which may not be until a number of accounting periods have elapsed. The recognition of profit is therefore deferred until the underwriting year is closed. Whilst no profits may be recognised for open years, any anticipated deficiencies for those years should be recognised in the financial statements as soon as it appears likely that they will arise. The underwriting result disclosed in the financial

statements relating to business accounted for on a fund basis will comprise the result for the underwriting year closed at the end of the accounting period, adjustments to the estimates used in arriving at the results of previously closed years, provisions for anticipated deficiencies in respect of the open years and adjustments to provisions previously established for open years. The fund at the end of an accounting period will comprise the outstanding liabilities of the closed years, the net income for each open year and any provisions for anticipated deficiencies for the open years.

Premiums

16 Under the annual basis of accounting, written premiums should be accounted for in the revenue account of the accounting period in which the related policies incept. Where the deferred annual basis of accounting is adopted, premiums should be recorded in the accounting period in which they are notified. Open year premiums may be deferred in the balance sheet and included in the revenue account of the accounting period following that in which they are notified or, alternatively, they may be included in the revenue account of the accounting period in which they are notified. Under the fund accounting basis, all written premiums notified in an accounting period are to be accounted for in the revenue account for that accounting period and attributed to the appropriate underwriting year.

17 The accounting treatment of outwards reinsurance should follow the accounting treatment of the direct or inwards reinsurance business being reinsured.

18 Few written premiums will be for a period of risk which coincides with the accounting period of the enterprise. Under the annual basis of accounting, and in accordance with the accruals concept in SSAP 2, a premium should be regarded as earned over the period of risk and, to the extent that this period bridges the end of an accounting period, it will be necessary to carry forward as at that date a proportion of the premium as unearned. The provision for unearned premiums is a deferral of premiums and represents the premiums to be earned in a subsequent accounting period. By adopting this accounting practice the premium is treated as earned over the duration of the risk.

19 For the majority of policies or contracts the level of risk does not fluctuate to a substantial extent during the risk period and in these circumstances premiums may be regarded as having been earned evenly over the risk period. Accordingly, the provision for unearned premiums should be determined on the basis of time apportionment of the written premiums. When the level of risk is expected to fluctuate during the risk period – for example in the case of seasonal risks such as hail and frost – a basis other than time apportionment of the written premiums may be appropriate. The basis to be used should reflect the profile of the risk during the period of insurance.

20 If the risk exposure period is for more than one year, the total written premium should be accounted for and the portion not relating to the current accounting period should be included within the unearned premium provision.

21 Under the deferred annual basis of accounting, provisions for unearned premiums are determined only at the end of the closed year; at the end of open years written premiums for those years will form part of the open year funds. Under the fund basis of accounting written premiums for both open and closed years will form part of the fund for the relevant year.

Expenses

22 A clear and consistent policy should be adopted for distinguishing between capital and revenue expenditure. Expenses (including depreciation of capital expenditure) should be classified according to both their nature and the activity to which they relate. For the purpose of determining the appropriate accounting treatment, the nature of the activity to which the expenses are attributable should be identified for classification under the following headings:

- Underwriting
- Claims handling
- Investment
- Other.

The Appendix to this Statement provides some guidance on the classification of expenses.

Underwriting expenses

23 Underwriting expenses should be sub-divided into acquisition expenses (being those expenses incurred in the acquisition and renewal of insurance policies/contracts) and maintenance expenses (being those expenses incurred in servicing such policies/contracts already in force). In particular, maintenance expenses should include irrecoverable amounts due from reinsurers (which should not be netted off against premiums).

24 Acquisition expenses incurred are attributable to the insurance business written in the accounting period. To the extent that a proportion of the premiums written in the accounting period is deferred to a subsequent accounting period, it is appropriate under the annual and deferred annual bases of accounting and in accordance with the accruals concept to defer an equivalent proportion of the related acquisition expenses. For this purpose it will be necessary to allocate acquisition expenses to classes of business in order that a provision for deferred acquisition expenses for each class of business may be determined. Such an allocation may not always be possible for reinsurance inwards business since the ceding enterprise, when

advising the reinsurer of the unearned premium provision, may include in that provision an amount for deferred acquisition expenses. In these circumstances, and in the absence of specific advices, it will be necessary to estimate the amount of the deferred acquisition expenses.

Claims

25 Where the annual basis of acounting is adopted, the revenue of an accounting period is, in accordance with the accruals concept, charged with the cost of settling all claims, including the related claims handling expenses, arising from events which have occurred up to the end of that period whether or not reported by the end of the period. The charge for claims incurred for an accounting period will comprise amounts paid during the acounting period in respect of claims occurring during that period, provisions for such claims which are outstanding at the end of the period, the claims handling expenses relating to the claims occurring during the accounting period and current period adjustments to the provisions brought forward for claims occurring in previous accounting periods.

26 The provision for claims outstanding which have been notified before the end of the acounting period is necessarily the result of a series of estimates and judgements utilising the information available and should be based on individual case estimates, statistical calculations and management judgement, as appropriate, and should include a provision for claims handling expenses. A provision is also to be made for the estimated ultimate cost of claims arising out of events that have occurred before the end of the accounting period but have not been notified to the insurance enterprise by that date i.e. claims incurred but not reported (IBNR claims). The provision for IBNR claims, which will include a provision for claims handling expenses, is to be estimated on the basis of the latest information available at the time of the preparation of the financial statements and will take into consideration matters such as the previous experience of claims notification patterns, trends in claims frequencies, changes in the nature and volume of business written and variations in average incurred costs per claim.

27 Under the deferred annual and fund bases of accounting, the fund at the end of each open year should be tested for adequacy against the anticipated liabilities, including attributable claims handling expenses and after allowance for the estimated future income. If the fund to be carried forward at the end of an accounting period for any open year is deemed to be insufficient to meet the expected emerging liabilities, an amount should be added to the fund to cover the anticipated deficiency by a transfer from the profit and loss account.

28 Under the deferred annual and fund bases of accounting, specific provisions for outstanding claims, including attributable claims handling expenses, will only be determined at the end of the closed years.

29 Under the annual, deferred annual and fund bases of accounting, if reinsurance recoveries are offset in the revenue account without disclosure against the claims to which they relate, the full cost of the claims for which the enterprise has a primary liability will not be displayed.

Claims equalisation and catastrophe reserves

30 Due to the uneven incidence of claims, and particularly isolated claims of a catastrophic nature, substantial variations can occur from year to year in the general insurance business results reported by an insurance enterprise. Insurance enterprises are required to maintain a minimum level of surplus assets, after providing for all known liabilities, as a solvency margin to cover principally any shortfall in the insurance technical provisions, adverse fluctuations in asset values and unprofitable future trading. In practice most insurance enterprises maintain a solvency margin substantially in excess of the legal minimum, which is estimated to be sufficient to cover, *inter alia*, major fluctuations in claims experience and catastrophes when they arise. Claims equalisation and catastrophe reserves equivalent to that part of the solvency margin set aside to meet such fluctuations may be separately designated and disclosed in the balance sheet.

Discounting

31 Under current accounting practice, the provision for general business claims usually represents the total ultimate cost of settling outstanding claims including claims handling expenses. Accordingly the provision allows for increases in claims costs between the date at which the financial statements are prepared and the date of actual settlement but does not anticipate the future income from any funds held pending the settlement of claims.

32 There is a distinction to be drawn between long-term business claims and general business claims. Long-term business insurance policies are reasonably certain in their terms both as regards the risks that are insured against and the amount of cover provided and it is appropriate to discount the ultimate liability to present value. In the case of general business, the policies will normally specify the type of risks insured against the cover provided. The amount of a claim under such a policy will not be certain but will depend upon the circumstances giving rise to the claim. There can be considerable uncertainty therefore as to the actual liability in respect of a claim until all the relevant information has been collated. In the interm period it will be necessary to estimate the amount of the liability based upon available information including the anticipated settlement date.

33 Paragraph 32(2) of Schedule 9 of the Companies Act 1985 states that where 'any amount retained by way of providing for any known liability is in excess of that which in the opinion of the directors is reasonably necessary for the purpose, the excess shall be treated for

the purposes of this Schedule as a reserve and not as a provision. Given the uncertainty inherent in the estimation of claims provisions, the amount 'reasonably necessary' will almost always be at least equal to the prudent estimate of the total ultimate cost of settling claims and that any reduction in this amount will, accordingly, result in the provision being insufficiently prudent. There is also a view, however, that the amount 'reasonably necessary for the purpose' will not necessarily be the full amount of the liability since income may be earned on the amount retained before the liability is settled. Therefore, in the case of general business claims outstanding where there is expected to be a delay before the claims are settled, there is an argument that the provision should be discounted to take account of the investment income on the funds held to meet the liabilities.

34 In practice, the time taken to determine and settle a claim can vary from weeks in, for example, the case of material damage to twenty years or more in, for example, the case of industrial disease. Furthermore, some claims, such as those for certain classes of liability business, give rise to liabilities payable at regular intervals over many years. Where claims are notified, agreed and settled in a comparatively short time period, as with motor claims not involving personal injury, discounting may not have a significant financial effect. However, where the notification of claims, their agreement and settlement is spread over a considerable period of time, the effect is more likely to be material. Where there is a sound basis for the evaluation of the likely amounts and timing of claims, there is a case for discounting these liabilities to reflect anticipated future investment income by recording claims outstanding provisions and attributable direct claims handling expenses at the present value of anticipated cash payments. Where the inherent uncertainty in estimating future liabilities and the timing of the payment of them is significant, discounting would be imprudent.

Unexpired risks

35 Under the annual basis of accounting, written premiums attributable to the succeeding accounting period are treated as unearned and deferred in accordance with the accruals concept. Where anticipated claims and related expenses under contracts incepting in the current or a prior accounting period exceed the amount of premiums carried forward as unearned, the prudence concept overrides the accruals concept by requiring a provision to be established for unexpired risks.

36 The question of whether or not to set up an unexpired risks provision will usually be considered by an insurance enterprise on the basis of the underwriting experience of the aggregage of all classes of business being written and not from the underwriting experience of each separate class. If, however, within a single enterprise certain classes are managed separately, then the provision may be calculated having regard to these separate classes. It would be in accordance with the

accruals concept to recognise that premiums are not the only source of revenue generated by underwriting and therefore it is permissible to take account of the investment income on assets representing technical funds in the calculation of the unexpired risks provision. Where an insurance enterprise discounts certain provisions for outstanding claims, the investment income of the assets hypothecated to the discounted claims provisions should be excluded from the calculation of the unexpired risks provision.

37 There are two bases of presenting an unexpired risks provision:-

the shortfall in the unearned premium provision is first recognised by writing off deferred acquisition expenses to the revenue account and, if the shortfall is greater than the amortised acquisition expenses, a provision is made for the excess; or

deferred acquisition expenses are disregarded and a provision is made for the entire shortfall in the unearned premium provision with deferred acquisition expenses being carried forward separately.

The first alternative is based on the theory that, where the recovery of deferred acquisition expenses is in doubt, such expenses should be written off before any additional liabilities are recorded. The second alternative is based on the theory that although the unearned premium provision, defered acquisition expenses and the possibility of a loss arising in a subsequent accounting period in respect of existing business are related issues, the requirement for a provision for unexpired risks arises from independent circumstances related primarily to claims experience and accordingly the unearned premium provision and deferred acquisition expenses should be considered separately.

The second alternative is preferable in that income and expenditure are properly segregated and, unlike the first alternative, it does not result in the distortion of operating ratios.

Long-term insurance business

Basis of accounting

38 Long-term business should be accounted for on a fund accounting basis. The balance of the fund at the end of the accounting period is tested for adequacy by comparison with the actuarial valuation of long-term business liabilities. Any distributable surplus emerging from the valuation is available for distribution to policyholders by way of bonus and/or to shareholders by way of profit.

Premiums

39 Annual premiums, single premiums and considerations for the granting of immediate and deferred annuities should be accounted for when due for payment.

40 For investment linked policies, since the entitlement of policyholders is related to the value of the assets underlying the policies, premiums should be recorded in the acounting period in which the liability is established.

41 The accounting treatment of outward reinsurance premiums should follow the accounting treatment of the direct or inwards business being reinsured.

42 The size of an insurance enterprise's operation is presented more clearly if the total premiums are shown with reinsurance cessions shown as a deduction thus displaying the amount of business written and retained.

Expenses

43 Similar considerations will apply to long-term insurance business expenses as for general insurance business expenses as set out in paragraph 22. In particular, underwriting expenses will include irrecoverable amounts due from reinsurers which should not be netted off against written premiums.

Claims

44 The treatment of a claim liability will depend upon whether or not the claim is due or has been notified by the accounting date. All claims due or notified during an accounting period should be charged to the fund for that period with a specific provision being made in the financial statements for claims due or notified but not settled by the end of the accounting period. The actuarial valuation of long-term business liabilities will take into account liabilities under all claims not yet due or to be notified after the end of the accounting period and therefore no specific provision is required for such claims in the financial statements.

General and long-term insurance business

Foreign currency translation

45 Where SSAP 20 requires companies to include exchange differences within the profit and loss account, for insurance enterprises they may be more appropriately dealt with in the general business or long-term business revenue accounts. Where the assets and liabilities of an insurance enterprise are denominated mainly in a foreign currency, SSAP 20 requires that the closing rate/net investment method of translating the local currency financial statement should normally be

used. Under the closing rate/net investment method of foreign exchange translation, exchange differences arising from the retranslation of the opening net investment in a foreign enterprise at the closing rate of exchange should be recorded as a movement on reserves. In the context of an insurance undertaking, a foreign enterprise may comprise, in addition to a subsidiary company or branch the assets and liabilities of which are denominated in a foreign currency, a business operation with foreign currency liabilities which are covered substantially by the holding of foreign currency assets.

Terminology

46 Unless the text requires otherwise, all references in this Statement to premiums, claims and expenses are to the gross amounts, that is before any deductions for reinsurance and, in the case of premiums, before deductions for commission.

Part 2 – Definition of terms

47 *Accounting period* means a period in respect of which a revenue account and/or a profit and loss account is prepared.

48 *Acquisition expenses* are:-

General business – all expenses which vary with, and are primarily related to, the acquisition or renewal of insurance contracts. They include both expenses which vary directly, such as commissions, and those which vary indirectly, such as the salaries of underwriting staff.

Long-term business – all expenses which vary with, and are primarily related to, the acquisition of new insurance contracts.

49 *Actuarial valuation* is the valuation of the long-term insurance business liabilities determined from an actuarial investigation that a company transacting long-term insurance business is required to carry out once in every twelve month period under Section 18(1) of the Insurance Companies Act 1982.

50 *Actuary* means the actuary appointed under Section 19 of the Insurance Companies Act 1982 to carry out the duties prescribed in Sections 18 and 42 of that Act relating to long-term insurance business.

51 *Cedant* – see reinsurance business inwards and outwards – paragraph 75.

52 *Claim* means the amount payable under a contract of insurance arising from the occurrence of an insured event, for example, the destruction of or damage to property; death or disability of the insured; the maturity of an endowment policy; the attainment of pensionable age; the amount payable on the surrender of a policy.

53 *Claims handling expenses* are expenses incurred by an insurance enterprise which are attributable to the handling of claims whether the expenses are incurred through the employment of the enterprise's own staff or by using the services of third parties. Direct claims handling expenses are those which are readily attributable to a particular claim. Indirect claims handling expenses comprise the expenses of running a claims operation which are not readily attributable to specific claims.

54 *Claims incurred* are the aggregate of all claims and claims handling expenses paid during the accounting period adjusted by the movement in the claims outstanding provisions between the beginning and end of the accounting period.

55 *Claims incurred but not reported (IBNR)* are claims arising out of events which have occurred by the end of the accounting period but have not been reported to the enterprise by that date.

56 *Claims outstanding* are:-

General business – the amounts provided to cover the estimated ultimate cost of settling claims arising out of events which have occurred by the end of the accounting period, including claims incurred but not reported and claims handling expenses, less amounts already paid in respect of those claims.

Long-term business – the amount provided to cover the estimated ultimate cost of settling claims arising out of events which have been notified by the end of the accounting period, less amounts already paid in respect of those claims.

57 *Co-insurance* is an arrangement whereby two or more insurance enterprises enter into a single contract with the insured to cover a risk in agreed proportions at an overall premium.

58 *Deferred acquisition expenses* are acquisition expenses relating to the unexpired period of risk which are carried forward from one accounting period to the next.

59 *Direct business* is all business where the insurer has a direct contractual relationship with the insured including co-insurance business.

60 *Discounting* is the reduction to present value at a given date of a future cash transaction at an assumed date by the application of an appropriate discount factor.

61 *Earned premiums* are the premiums earned in an accounting period to meet the risk exposure of the enterprise during that period and are determined as written premiums adjusted by the unearned premium provisions at the beginning and end of the accounting period.

62 *General business* is insurance business other than long-term business.

63 *General business premiums* are the amounts receivable by an enterprise for underwriting general business risks.

64 *Inception of risk* is the time at which the risk commences under a policy or contract of insurance. For this purpose, a policy or contract providing continuing open cover is deemed to commence on each anniversary date of the contract.

65 *Indirect business* is business accepted as a result of a reinsurance agreement.

66 *Investment income* comprises interest, dividends and rents receivable.

67 *Investment expenses* comprise the expenses relating to the buying, holding and selling of investments. Expenses such as stamp duty and brokerage, which are directly attributed to acquiring or disposing of an investment, are not investment expenses but an integral part of the cost of the purchase of investments or a reduction in the sale proceeds.

68 *Long-term business* is insurance business the benefits under which are payable primarily on the survival of the policyholder to a stipulated age or on death. Long-term business will include life, annuity, pension, permanent health, capital redemption and pension fund management business.

69 *Long-term business premiums* are the amounts receivable by an enterprise for underwriting long-term business risks.

70 *Maintenance expenses* are:-

General business – expenses which vary with the level of acquisition and renewal of business but which are distinguished from acquisition expenses by the fact that they are incurred to service such business after it has been acquired or renewed.

Long-term business – the cost of maintaining existing business subsequent to the acquisition of such business which will include the costs of amendment and renewal of in-force contracts.

71 *Non-proportional reinsurance* is reinsurance whereby, in return for a premium, the reinsurer accepts liability for losses or claims incurred by the cedant in excess of an agreed amount which is normally subject to an upper limit.

72 *Portfolio claims* are amounts payable in respect of the transfer between a cedant and a reinsurer of the liability under a reinsurance contract for claims incurred prior to a fixed date, normally the date at which the contract commences or ends.

73 *Portfolio premiums* are amounts payable in respect of the transfer between a cedant and a reinsurer of the liability under a reinsurance contract for premiums expiring after a fixed date, normally the date on which the contract commences or ends.

74 *Proportional reinsurance* is reinsurance whereby, in return for a proportion of the original premium, the reinsurer accepts liability for the same proportion of each related claim incurred by the reinsured.

75 *Reinsurance business inwards and outwards* may be on the basis of individual inwards and outwards risks (facultative) or groups of risks (treaty). The acceptance of risks is known as reinsurance inwards and the placing of risks is known as reinsurance outwards; the enterprise accepting the risks is the reinsurer and the enterprise ceding the risks is the cedant. Where the reinsurance consists of the placing of inwards reinsurance which the cedant has already received, it is known as retrocession and the recipient as the retrocessionaire. In this Statement references to reinsurance include retrocession.

76 *Reinsurer* – see reinsurance business inwards and outwards – paragraph 75.

77 *Retrocession* – see reinsurance business inwards and outwards – paragraph 75.

78 *Revenue account* is an account which shows a financial summary of the insurance related revenue transctions for the accounting period.

79 *Unearned premiums* are the portion of written premiums relating to a period of risk after the accounting date and which are deferred to subsequent accounting periods.

80 *Underwriting expenses* are:-

the costs of acquiring and, in the case of general insurance business, renewing insurance contracts (acquisition expenses), and

the costs associated with the maintenance of, and in the case of life insurance business, the renewal of contracts already in force (maintenance expenses).

81 *Underwriting year* means the accounting period in which the contract of insurance incepted.

82 *Unexpired risks provisions* are the estimated amounts required over and above provisions for unearned premiums to meet future claims and related expenses on business in force at the end of the accounting period.

83 *Written premiums* are premiums in respect of contracts which incept during the accounting period.

Part 3 – Recommended Practice

General insurance business

Basis of accounting

84 The annual basis of accounting should be used whenever an underwriting result can be determined with reasonable certainty at the end of the accounting period. The deferred annual basis of accounting should be adopted when the underwriting result for an accounting period cannot be determined with reasonable certainty using the annual basis of accounting but can be so determined twelve months thereafter. The fund accounting basis should only be adopted when the underwriting result cannot be determined with reasonable certainty using the annual or the deferred annual bases of accounting.

85 The accounting basis or bases adopted should be disclosed. Where the deferred annual or fund accounting basis is used, the classes of business involved and the extent of the time deferral for profit recognition should also be disclosed.

Premiums

Annual basis of accounting

86 Written premiums should be accounted for in the accounting period in which the policy incepts. Estimates, where appropriate, should be made in order to comply with this basic principle.

87 Where an enterprise debits the renewal premium before acceptance by the insured, a lapse rate should be determined based on previous experience and other relevant information in order to calculate a provision for premiums which have been debited but are expected to be cancelled in a subsequent accounting period.

88 If direct business premiums are to be received by instalments during the period of risk of the policies or contracts, the total written premiums should be accounted for at inception, with outstanding instalments being treated as debtors.

89 For some classes of business, where premiums are notified and accounted for net of brokerage and commission, the premiums should be grossed up, on an estimated basis if necessary, to reflect the gross premium and brokerage/commission deduction.

90 If written premiums are subject to a reduction, an adjustment for such a reduction should be made as soon as it can be foreseen. Where written premiums are subject to an increase retrospectively, for example based on the declaration of sums insured or on claims experience, recognition of potential increases should be deferred until the additional premiums can be ascertained with reasonable certainty.

91 Written premiums should be regarded as earned evenly over the life of the policy, unless the exposure to risk is uneven in which case the written premiums should be regarded as earned in accordance with the risk profile. Provisions for unearned premiums at the end of an accounting period should be calculated accordingly.

92 Where additional or return written premiums arise these should be related to the life of the policy concerned in determining the period over which such premiums are to be regarded as earned and unearned premium provisions are to be calculated in accordance with paragraph 91.

93 The unearned premium provision should be disclosed without any deduction for deferred acquisition expenses.

Deferred annual basis of accounting

94 Premiums should be recorded in the accounting period in which they are notified. Open year premiums may be deferred in the balance sheet and recorded in the revenue account of the accounting period following that in which they are notified or, alternatively, should be included in the revenue account of the accounting period in which they are notified.

Fund accounting basis

95 All premiums notified in an accounting period are to be accounted for in the revenue account for that period and attributed to the appropriate underwriting year. The recommendations in paragraphs 89 and 90 apply when this accounting basis is adopted.

Reinsurance

96 The accounting treatment of reinsurance premiums payable or receivable follows the basic principles for direct written premiums referred to in paragraphs 86 and 91 for business accounted for on an annual accounting basis, paragraph 94 for business accounted for on the deferred annual basis and paragraph 95 for business accounted for on a fund accounting basis. All outwards reinsurance premiums should be accounted for in the same accounting period as the premiums for the related direct or inwards reinsurance business.

97 Portfolio premiums receivable or payable by the enterprise should be included with written premiums or the unearned premium provision according to the nature of the transaction.

98 Reinsurance arrangements, where the amount of risk transferred is not significant, should be accounted for having regard to their economic substance. In addition, sufficient disclosure should be made in the financial statements to enable the nature and the financial effect of the agreement to be understood.

Additional disclosures

99 The accounting policy adopted for premium recognition should be stated and, when adopting the annual or deferred annual accounting bases, the basis of calculating the unearned premium provision should be disclosed.

100 The total amount of written premiums should be shown inclusive of direct business and inwards reinsurance business on a gross basis with reinsurance cessions shown as a deduction thus displaying the amount of business written and retained.

101 The unearned premium provision relating to direct and reinsurance inwards business should be shown with the unearned premium provision relating to reinsurance outwards being shown as a deduction therefrom.

102 An analysis of gross written premiums into the principal classes of business transacted by the insurance enterprise should be disclosed.

103 An analysis of the aggregate gross written premiums into geographical areas should be disclosed. With marine, aviation, transport and reinsurance inwards business it may not be possible to categorise the business into geographical areas in which case the classes of business involved should be disclosed separately.

104 The disclosures described in paragraphs 102 and 103 may be included in the financial statements, the directors' report or in a business review issued in conjunction with the financial statements.

Expenses

Classification

105 Expenses should be classified under the following headings:

- Underwriting
- Claims handling
- Investment
- Other.

Underwriting expenses

106 Under the annual and the deferred annual bases of accounting, a proportion of that element of underwriting expenses regarded as acquisition expenses should be deferred to a subsequent accounting period to match the deferral to a subsequent accounting period of a proportion of the written premiums to which the acquisition expenses relate. The deferral of acquisition expenses should be calculated separately for each class of business applying the ratio of unearned premiums to written premiums applicable to that class of business. When the fund basis of accounting is adopted there will not be a deferral of acquisition expenses but all expenses should be charged as incurred with an allocation to the appropriate underwriting year being made.

107 The basis adopted for determining deferred acquisition expenses should be disclosed.

108 The movement in deferred acquisition expenses between the beginning and the end of the accounting period should be disclosed as an addition to/deduction from expenses in the revenue account.

109 The amount of deferred acquisition expenses should be disclosed separately and not deducted from the unearned premium provision.

Claims handling expenses

110 Provisions should be made at the end of an accounting period for claims handling expenses to cover the anticipated costs of negotiating and settling claims which have occurred – whether notified or not – by that date. The provisions should include the anticipated costs of the general claims administration relating to such claims.

111 Claims handling expenses should be charged against the revenue of the accounting period in which the claims occurred. The claims handling expense provision should be included with the claims outstanding provision.

Investment expenses

112 Investment expenses should be separately disclosed.

Claims

Annual basis of accounting

113 Provision should be made at the end of the accounting period for the estimated ultimate cost of all claims not settled at that date after the deduction of amounts already paid, whether arising from events occurring during that period or earlier periods and whether or not notified before the close of the accounting period.

114 The provision for claims outstanding should represent the best estimate in the light of information available having regard to prudent assumptions about the level at which claims are expected to be settled and should take into account anticipated levels of inflation and other factors which may be specific to certain categories of claim such as increases in court awards. The provision for claims outstanding will include a provision for claims incurred but not reported and an amount for the additional costs expected to arise on claims settled prior to the end of the accounting period but which it is anticipated will be reopened. Any amounts receivable as a direct result of salvage by, for example obtaining the legal ownership of insured property, or by subrogation by acquiring the rights of the policyholder against third parties following the settlement of a claim, should be taken into account in determining provisions for outstanding claims.

Deferred annual and fund bases of accounting

115 The balance carried forward at the end of an open year should be sufficient to cover anticipated liabilities and, if necessary, a provision should be made to cover any anticipated loss by means of a disclosed transfer from the profit and loss account. Transfers between different funds (i.e. cross-funding) are not acceptable, but transfers between different classes of business within the same fund are acceptable if within the same underwriting year.

116 Where an amount has been added to a fund in an accounting period for an underwriting year and at the end of a subsequent accounting period (other than when the fund is closed) it is evident that the amount added to the fund for that underwriting year was excessive, a transfer out of the fund may be made up to but not exceeding the amount transferred into the fund at the end of the previous accounting period. Such a transfer should be made to the profit and loss account and disclosed.

117 Specific provisions for unearned premiums and outstanding claims (including claims handling expenses) should be made only at the end of a closed year.

Reinsurance

118 Amounts recoverable under reinsurance arrangements in respect of claims incurred by the enterprise should be taken into account using estimates where necessary.

119 Any portfolio claims assumed or transferred by the enterprise should be included with claims paid, claims outstanding or written premiums according to the nature of the transaction.

120 Reinsurance arrangements, where the amount of risk transferred is not significant, should be accounted for having regard to their economic substance. Sufficient disclosure should be made in the

financial statements to enable the nature and the financial effect of the arrangements to be understood.

Additional disclosure

121 The accounting policies adopted for claims recognition should be disclosed and should include a statement of the policies adopted and bases used with regard to:-

- Notified claims
- IBNR claims
- Claims handling expenses
- Salvage and other recoveries.

122 All claims should be stated gross of reinsurance in the revenue account with reinsurance recoveries being shown as a deduction to display a net cost of claims.

123 Claims provisions should be stated gross in the balance sheet with outstanding reinsurance claims recoveries being shown separately and not deducted from the gross claims provisions.

Discounting

124 Implicit discounting (i.e. an accounting practice which places a present day value on an outstanding claims provision without disclosure of that fact) is not acceptable. Explicit discounting of provisions for outstanding claims is acceptable if a satisfactory estimate of the amount of the liability can be made and there is adequate past experience on which a reasonable model of the timing of the run-off of the liability can be constructed. It is for the insurance enterprise to decide whether or not it is appropriate to discount. Where claims provisions are discounted, the related reinsurance recoveries should also be discounted.

125 The rate used for discounting claims liabilities should not exceed a conservative estimate of the rate of investment income which the enterprise considers is most likely to be earned on its investment portfolio over the term during which the claims are to be settled.

126 The accounting policy adopted for any discounting of provisions for claims outstanding and direct claims handling expenses should be disclosed in the financial statements. In particular, disclosure should be made of:

- the classes or groupings of business involved,
- the methods applied, including:
  - the range of discount rates used,
  - the mean term of the liabilities,
- the treatment of the attributable investment income,
- the effect of discounting on the profit or loss before taxation for

the accounting period and on the net assets at the end of the accounting period.

127 If an enterprise alters its accounting policy for providing for outstanding claims from a non-discounted basis to a discounted basis or from a discounted basis to a non-discounted basis, the change should be dealt with as a prior year adjustment in accordance with the requirements of SSAP 6.

Unexpired risks

128 Under the annual and deferred annual bases of accounting, where anticipated claims and related expenses under existing contracts exceed the amount of unearned premium provision carried forward, a provision for unexpired risks should be established to cover the losses expected to emerge in the subsequent accounting period. An insurance enterprise will usually consider the need for a provision for unexpired risks on the basis of the underwriting experience of the aggregate of all classes of business being written and not from the underwriting experience of each separate class.

129 The question of whether or not to set up an unexpired risks provision should be considered by an insurance enterprise on the basis of the underwriting experience of the aggregate of all classes of business being written and not from the underwriting experience of each separate class.

130 When an unexpired risks provison is established, the provision should be calculated on the basis that deferred acquisition expenses should not be amortised.

131 The accounting policy adopted in assessing the requirement for an unexpired risks provison, and whether investment income has been taken into account, should be disclosed together with the amount of the unexpired risks provision and changes in the amount of the provision from one accounting period to the next.

Long-term insurance business

Basis of accounting

132 The fund accounting basis should be used. The balance of the fund at the end of the accounting period should be at least adequate to meet the long-term business liabilities.

Premiums

Non-profit and with-profit business

133 Annual premiums, single premiums and considerations for the

granting of immediate and deferred annuities should be accounted for when due for payment.

134 When it is impracticable to determine the actual contracted renewal premium, which can arise with pension business due to time delays, a reasonable estimate should be made for premiums based on the latest available information.

Investment-linked business

135 Premiums should be accounted for in the same accounting period as the relevant policy liability is established.

Reinsurance

136 The accounting treatment for reinsurance premiums payable or receivable, should follow the basic principles in paragraphs 133 to 135 with all outwards reinsurance premiums accounted for in the same accounting period as the premiums for the related direct or inwards reinsurance business.

Additional disclosures

137 The accounting policy adopted for premium recognition should be disclosed in the financial statements.

138 Premium income should be shown on a gross basis with reinsurance cessions shown as a deduction thus displaying the amount of business transacted and retained.

139 An analysis of premiums into life, annuity, pension and permanent health insurance business with a separate indication in each case of the amounts of group and unit-linked business should be disclosed.

140 An analysis of premiums into geographical areas should be disclosed.

141 An analysis of the annualised value of new annual premiums and the amount of new single premiums into the classes specified in paragraph 139 should be disclosed.

142 The disclosures described in paragraphs 139 to 141 may be included in the financial statements, the directors' report or in a business review issued in conjunction with the financial statements.

Expenses

143 Revenue expenses should be classified under the following headings:-

– Underwriting
– Investment
– Other.

144 All revenue expenses should be charged to the fund.

Claims

Non-profit and with-profit business

145 The accounting liability for claims outstanding relating to non-profit and with-profit insurance policies or contracts should be accrued when the insured event becomes due or is notified. It will not be necessary to establish a separate IBNR claims provision since, until recorded as a claim, the liability will be included in the actuarial valuation of long-term business liabilities.

146 Where a claim is payable and the policy or contract remains in force, as arises under a continuous disability policy or in the settlement of an annuity contract, the amounts payable should be treated as claims due. The remaining liabilities should be included in the actuarial valuation of long-term business liabilities.

Investment-linked business

147 The accounting liability for claims outstanding relating to investment linked business should be accounted for at the time when the policy or contract ceases to participate in the long-term business fund.

Reinsurance

148 Where a claim has been incurred on a policy which has been reinsured, claims recoveries, estimated where appropriate, should be accounted for in the same accounting period as the cost of the related claim.

Additional disclosure

149 The accounting policy adopted for claims recognition should be disclosed.

150 All claims should be stated gross in the revenue account with reinsurance recoveries being shown as a deduction to display the net cost of claims.

151 Claims provisions should be shown gross in the balance sheet with outstanding reinsurance claims recoveries being shown separately and not deducted from the gross claims provisions.

Part 4 – Note on legal requirements in Great Britain and Northern Ireland

152 Paragraphs 153 to 155 apply to insurance companies preparing accounts in compliance with the Companies Acts 1985 and 1989. The

equivalent Northern Ireland legislation is the Companies (Northern Ireland) Order 1986.

153 Section 255 of the Companies Act 1985 permits but does not require an insurance company to prepare accounts in compliance with Part I of Schedule 9 of the Companies Act 1985, as amended by Schedule 7 of the Companies Act 1989, instead of in accordance with Schedule 4 of the Companies Act 1985, as amended by Schedule 1 of the Companies Act 1989.

154 Paragraph 28(1) of Schedule 9 of the Companies Act 1985 grants certain disclosure exemptions to insurance companies from the requirements in Schedule 9.

Paragraph 28(2) of Schedule 9 of the Companies Act 1985, provides that the accounts of a company shall not be deemed, by reason only of the fact that they do not comply with any requirement of paragraphs 2 to 18 of that Schedule from which the company is exempt by virtue of Paragraph 28(1), not to give the true and fair view required by the Companies Act 1985. Paragraph 28A of Schedule 9 of the Companies Act 1985, provides that, where an insurance company is entitled to, and has availed itself of, any of the provisions of Paragraph 28 of Schedule 9 of the Companies Act 1985, Section 235(2) of the Companies Act 1985 only requires the auditors to state whether in their opinion the accounts have been properly prepared in accordance with the Companies Act 1985.

155 Section 268 of the Companies Act 1985 states that amounts properly transferred to the profit and loss account from a surplus in the fund or funds maintained by the company in respect of long-term business shall be treated as realised profits.

Appendix

This appendix is for guidance only and does not form part of the Statement.

Possible Classification of Expenses

1 **Underwriting**

(a) Acquisition

The cost of acquiring and, in the case of general insurance business, renewing insurance contracts which may include:-

Commission.
Direct advertising for new business.
Salary, accommodation and other costs of sales, sales administration, new business and renewal department staff.
Processing costs related to new policies and renewals.
Premium taxes borne by the enterprise.
Marketing.
Underwriting.
Medical fees.

Acquisition expenses exclude expenses such as those of general management and image marketing which are not related primarily to the acquisition of insurance contracts.

(b) Maintenance

The costs associated with the maintenance of, and in the case of life insurance business, the renewal of contracts already in force which may include:-

Policy endorsements.
Risk reviews and surveys undertaken in accordance with the policy terms.
Cost of maintenance and preparation of statistics and reports.
Commission.
Processing costs.

2 **Claims handling**

Expenses relating to the negotiation and settlement of claims may include:-

Legal and survey fees connected with claims.
Salary, accommodation and other costs of claims handling department staff.

3 Investment

All expenses relating to the buying, holding and selling of all types of investments, including the salary costs and related expenses of the staff involved, their office space, computer usage etc., but excluding stamp duty, brokerage etc., which are part of the cost of investments.

4 Self occupied properties

Where insurance enterprises occupy premises which they own, the imputed notional commercial rent on such premises may be reflected as investment income and expenses.

Chapter 17

INVESTMENT COMPANIES AND APPROVED INVESTMENT TRUSTS

Chapter 17

INVESTMENT COMPANIES AND APPROVED INVESTMENT TRUSTS

Introduction

17.1 The primary function of investment companies is to invest money raised from the issue of shares and loan capital in a wide range of shares of other companies. Investment companies, therefore, derive their income mainly from dividends received from their investment holdings. From an investor's point of view, particularly one with limited resources both in terms of time and expertise, investment companies provide a means of investing in a range of investment thus spreading the risks of investment. Investment companies are designed to offer shareholders both income and capital growth over the medium and long-term.

17.2 Investment companies are 'closed-end' companies whose shares can be bought only from existing shareholders, normally through The International Stock Exchange or upon new issue. Unit trusts on the other hand are 'open-ended', the units being sold to and repurchased from investors by the trust, through the managers (see chapter 7).

17.3 Investment companies are limited liability companies and are, therefore, subject to the regulations of the *Companies Act 1985*. Although the word 'trust' appears in the title of many of these companies, they are not trusts in the sense that their actions are governed by a trust deed, as in the case of unit trusts. The word 'trust' has been used for purely historical reasons and the Registrar of Companies will no longer allow a limited liability company to use the word trust in its title, unless consent is obtained from the Secretary of State (see the *Companies and Business Names Regulations 1981* (SI 1981/1685) para 3).

17.4 Although all investment companies operate primarily under the *Companies Act 1985*, the great majority seek to establish 'approved' status. An investment company that has satisfied certain requirements of the *Income and Corporation Taxes Act 1988* will be able to obtain Inland Revenue approval as an 'approved investment trust' for tax purposes. The conditions that have to be met in order to achieve this status are stated in paragraph 17.10 below. Approved investment trusts have an advantage over unapproved investment companies in that they are entitled to various tax concessions (see para 17.11). This chapter considers the special provisions of the *Companies Act 1985* that relate to investment companies generally. Investment companies that have obtained Inland Revenue approval are referred to in this chapter as 'approved investment trusts'.

Formation and constitution

17.5 To form an investment company or an approved investment trust it is necessary to set up a *public* company in the usual manner. The company must then give notice in the prescribed form (Form 266(1)) to the Registrar of Companies of its intention to carry on business as an investment company. In addition, the company must, since the date of that notice, comply with the requirements of section 266 of the *Companies Act 1985* as specified below:

- The company's business consists of investing its funds principally in securities, with the aim of spreading the investment risk and of giving its members the benefit of the results of its management of its funds.
- None of the company's holdings in companies (other than in 'approved investment trusts' - see para 17.10) represents more than 15 per cent of the value of its total holdings. This requirement does not apply where an investment's value exceeds the 15 per cent limit only because it has been revalued.
- The distribution of the company's capital profits is prohibited by either its memorandum or articles of association.
- The company has not retained (during any accounting reference period) more than 15 per cent of the income it derives from securities, unless it was prohibited from making a distribution under the provisions of that Act.

[CA 1985 Sec 266(2)].

17.6 Memorandum and articles of association appropriate to a public company should be used to form the constitution of an investment company. The constitution must satisfy the requirements of paragraph 17.5 above. As mentioned, the company's memorandum or articles of association must prohibit the distribution, by way of dividend, of capital profits realised on the sale of investments (see para 17.10). To be eligible for listing by The International Stock Exchange there must be a similar prohibition although this is expressed in relation to 'surpluses' and not 'capital profits' (see paras 17.14 and 17.15).

17.7 The *Companies Act 1985* requires that investment companies must indicate their public status both on their letterheads and on their order forms. [CA 1985 Sec 351(1)(c)].

17.8 A company will cease to be an investment company if it revokes the notice that it has previously given to the Registrar of Companies. It may do this by giving notice to him, in the prescribed form (Form 266(3)), that it no longer wishes to be an investment company. [CA 1985 Sec 266(3)].

Portfolio management

17.9 Investment trusts originally operated as a separate entity with the board of directors assuming responsibility for both the formulation of overall investment policy and its day to day implementation. However, with the increasing sophistication of portfolio management techniques, the day to day running of an investment trust is often delegated to a professional management organisation that manages investment portfolios on behalf of one or more investment trusts. The directors of the trust still remain responsible for overall policy and are accountable to the shareholders in the same manner as before. Although a professional management organisation is, by far, the most popular organisational structure today, there are some trusts that still maintain their independent status.

Approved investment trusts

17.10 As stated in paragraph 17.4 above, an investment company may obtain 'approved' status by satisfying the Inland Revenue that it complies with the following conditions that are set out in the *Income and Corporation Taxes Act 1988*.

- It is resident in the UK.
- Its income is derived either wholly or mainly from shares or securities.
- No investment represents more than 15 per cent of the value of the investing company's assets (unless that investment is in another investment trust). However, this requirement does not apply in the following situations where:
  - An investment exceeds the 15 per cent limit only because it has been subsequently revalued.
  - An investment was acquired before 6th April 1965 and which on that date represented not more than 25 per cent by value of the investing company's investments and no further addition has been made to the holding since then.
  - An investment was acquired and which on the date of purchase represented not more than 15 per cent by value of

the investing company's investments and no further addition has been made since that date.

- It is a public company and its shares are listed on The International Stock Exchange. If the company has more than one class of shares (for example, income and capital shares), then each class of shares must be listed.

- Its memorandum or its articles of association prohibit the distribution, by way of dividend, of capital profits realised on the sale of investments.

- It retains no more than 15 per cent of its income derived from shares and securities.

- It is not a 'close' company.

[ICTA 1988 Sec 842].

17.11 The above conditions are very similar to those that a company must satisfy in order to qualify as an investment company under the *Companies Act 1985*. (However, an investment trust must satisfy the Inland Revenue that it complies with these conditions.) The main advantage of qualifying as an 'approved investment trust' is that chargeable capital gains realised on disposal of investments are not taxable.

17.12 Furthermore, since approved status requires an investment company to seek listing on The International Stock Exchange, it must satisfy additional listing requirements that are more onerous than those imposed on other listed investment companies that are not approved investment trusts (see para 17.15).

Listed investment companies

17.13 An investment company must be a public company, but it may be either listed or unlisted. In order to obtain a listing on The International Stock Exchange, an investment company must first comply with the conditions outlined in 'Admission of Securities to Listing' (the Yellow Book) chapter 3, section 10 paragraphs 4 and 7. It should be noted, however, that the Yellow Book refers to both investment companies and approved investment trusts and sets out different listing and accounting requirements for each category.

17.14 The main listing requirements that an investment company, which is not an approved investment trust, must comply with are as follows:

- The company must undertake not to take legal control or management control of any of its investments (except insofar as the investments take the form of partnerships, or joint ventures or other forms of non-corporate investment).

- Not more than 20 per cent of the group's assets (before deducting borrowed money) may be invested in the securities of any one company.
- The company must adhere to its policy statement set out in the listing particulars or equivalent offering document for at least three years following listing.
- Dividends must be paid only out of income received from investments, shares of profits of associated companies being unavailable for this purpose unless, and until, distributed to the company.
- Shareholders' approval must be sought to realise any investment that has a directors' valuation amounting to 50 per cent or more of the investment portfolio.
- Where the company has a policy to subscribe for shares in another company or fund in which its assets are, or are proposed, to be principally invested, which itself invests in a portfolio of securities, it must ensure that its directors comprise a majority of the directors of that company or fund. This is to ensure that the investment company's directors control that company's or fund's underlying policies.
- The memorandum or articles of association must prohibit the distribution as dividends of surpluses arising from the sale of investments.

17.15 Investment companies seeking an initial listing on The International Stock Exchange as an investment trust must comply with the following conditions specified in section 10, chapter 3 of the Yellow Book.

- Where the company is incorporated and resident in the UK, it must be approved by the Inland Revenue as an investment trust for its most recent accounting period or have announced that it will direct its affairs so as to continue to be eligible.
- The company must have expressed an intention that its income will be derived wholly or mainly from shares or other securities.
- The memorandum or articles of association must prohibit the distribution as dividend of surpluses arising from the sale of investments.

- The investment policy must prescribe that:
  - Not more than 10 per cent of the group's assets (before deducting borrowed money) may be either lent to or invested in the securities of any one company (other than another approved investment trust).
  - Not more than 25 per cent of the group's assets (before deducting borrowed money) may be invested in the aggregate of securities not listed on any recognised stock exchange or quoted on the NASDAQ system in the US or Canada and holdings in which the group's interest amounts to 20 per cent or more of the total equity capital (including any capital that has an element of equity) of any one listed company. However, this restriction does not apply if such investments are in other approved investment trusts.

17.16 It can be seen from the above paragraphs that there is no restriction on the proportion of unlisted investments that a listed investment company may hold although, any new investment is limited to not more than 20 per cent of the company's shares at the time it is made.

17.17 Once listed, the investment company becomes subject to The International Stock Exchange's Continuing Obligations and has to disclose additional information in its annual financial statements. There are different disclosure requirements for approved investment trusts and investment companies. Basically, the requirements for investment companies demand more detailed information on individual investments. This is because investment companies can invest to a greater extent in unlisted companies about which there may be little public information available. These disclosure requirements are considered in paragraphs 17.39 and 17.40 below.

Split capital trusts

17.18 An interesting feature of listed investment companies is that the market price of the company's shares is often less than the corresponding net asset value per share. In this situation, the shares are said to be standing at a discount. One way that managers have been able to reduce the discount to net asset value at which many investment trusts shares tend to trade is to establish a split capital structure. However, from an investor's point of view a discount to net assets will represent a higher yield.

17.19 At their simplest form split capital investment trusts have two classes of shares, *viz* income shares and capital shares. They usually have a limited or determinable life. Income shares receive all of the income plus a fixed repayment of capital when the trust is wound up. Capital shares receive little or no income during the life of the trust, but benefit from the capital growth achieved by the trust's investments. These shares take their gain on liquidation of the trust as they are entitled to the assets remaining once the income shares have been repaid. The capital structures of trusts are becoming increasingly complex with a combination of income shares, capital shares, zero dividend preference shares, stepped preference shares and warrants.

Financial statements

Form and content

17.20 Investment companies are subject to the requirements of the *Companies Act 1985* in the same way as are all other companies incorporated under that Act. In addition, the financial statements of investment companies must also comply with SSAPs. Therefore, the form and content of the financial statements of an investment company or group are essentially similar to most other companies. However, there are a number of differences and these are discussed in the paragraphs that follow.

17.21 Many investment companies use the term 'revenue account' instead of the term 'profit and loss account' in their financial statements. Although 'revenue account' is not a term recognised in the *Companies Act 1985* Schedule 4 formats, its usage is based on the concept that, since capital profits and losses of investment companies are not dealt with through this account, it ceases to be a statement of all profits and losses. Therefore, in order to emphasise the distinction between revenue and capital profits, the term 'revenue account' is more commonly used. An example of a revenue account is illustrated in Table 17.1

17.22 It has also been questioned whether an investment company can show investment income under the heading 'Turnover' in the profit and loss account formats. On the grounds that such income is the company's principal source of revenue, this disclosure appears to be acceptable. In practice, investment companies disclose their income from operations under the headings 'Revenue' or 'Investment income'. The legality of changing the wordings of headings and sub-headings used in the Schedule 4 Formats is discussed in 'Manual of Accounting - volume I' chapter 6.

Special accounting provisions

17.23 Investment companies are exempted from some of the alternative accounting rules as outlined in Part V of Schedule 4 to the *Companies Act 1985*. These exemptions are discussed in paragraphs 17.24 and 17.25 below.

Table 17.1: Illustration of a revenue account for an investment trust company.

Extract from the Alliance Trust PLC Report and Accounts at 31st January 1990.

REVENUE ACCOUNT

for the year ended 31st January 1990

	Notes	1990		1989	
INCOME FROM ASSETS					
Income from Investments		£000 Listed	£000 Unlisted	£000 Listed	£000 Unlisted
UK dividends		14,879	39	11,300	27
UK interest		106	20	56	20
Overseas dividends		7,814	20	6,871	42
Overseas interest		69	22	247	14
Dividends from subsidiary		—	350	—	350
Interest on loan to subsidiary		—	382	—	289
		22,868	833	18,474	742
Total Income from Investments			23,701		19,216
Other Income					
Interest received	2	2,566		4,152	
Mineral royalties		304		228	
Underwriting commission		88		62	
			2,958		4,442
Total Revenue			26,659		23,658
EXPENSES, INTEREST & TAXATION					
Management expenses		1,078		927	
Audit fee		10		9	
Administration expenses	1	1,088		936	
Interest payable	2	102		80	
			1,190		1,016
Revenue before Taxation			25,469		22,642
Taxation	3		7,389		6,815
Revenue after Taxation			18,080		15,827
DIVIDENDS					
Preference Stock			68		68
			18,012		15,759
Ordinary Stock:					
Interim paid — 10.0p (8.75p)		5,040		4,410	
Final proposed — 25.0p (22.25p)		12,600		11,214	
			17,640		15,624
REVENUE RESERVE					
Surplus revenue for the year			372		135
Balance at 1st February 1989			8,288		8,153
Balance at 31st January 1990			8,660		8,288
Earnings per ordinary stock unit	4		35.74p		31.27p

The notes on pages 18 to 20 form part of these accounts.

17.24 An investment company is not required to credit or debit to a revaluation reserve any profit or loss that arises from including investments in the balance sheet, either at their market value or at some appropriate valuation other than historical cost. Instead, they may be credited or debited to any other reserve. [CA 1985 4 Sch 71(1)]. In practice, such unrealised gains and losses on investments held at the balance sheet date are either credited or debited to an unrealised appreciation/depreciation reserve. The effect of this provision is to exempt any such profits or losses from the restrictions that the *Companies Act 1985* places on the uses of the revaluation reserve (see 'Manual of Accounting - volume I' chapter 5). However, the use of these profits or losses is restricted by the company's articles of association.

17.25 Where an investment company writes down the value of its fixed asset investments to account for either a temporary or a permanent fall in value, the amount of this write-down need not be charged to the profit and loss account. This applies, however, only if either the write-down is charged to a reserve account to which revaluation surpluses that arose on the revaluation of investments have been credited, or the write-down is disclosed separately in the balance sheet under the sub-heading 'Other reserves'. [CA 1985 4 Sch 71(2)]. It appears, therefore, that in this situation it is acceptable for an investment company to have a debit balance on either of these reserves.

17.26 Where the holding company of a group of companies is an investment company, the consolidated financial statements can be prepared taking advantage of the exemptions available to investment companies that are outlined in the paragraphs above. [CA 1985 4A Sch 1(3)].

Valuation of investments

Securities

17.27 The vast majority of investment companies value their investment securities that are listed on The International Stock Exchange or a stock exchange of repute outside Great Britain, at market value. Unlisted investment securities are normally valued at directors' valuation. An example of an accounting policy on investments is shown in Table 17.2.

17.28 Because investment companies are prohibited from distributing profits realised on the sale of investments, gains and losses on disposal of investments are credited or debited to a realised capital reserve. Unrealised capital gains and losses on investments held at the balance sheet are credited or debited to a separate unrealised appreciation or depreciation account. In some situations, unrealised gains and losses are taken to the same capital reserve to which realised gains and

Table 17.2: Illustration of an accounting policy on investments.

Extract from Globe Investment Trust P.L.C. Report and Accounts 31st March 1990.

Accounting policies (extract)

Investments

Listed investments are stated at market value which is based upon middle market prices at the accounting date. Investments in overseas companies listed both abroad and on The International Stock Exchange, London are classified as investments listed overseas.

Unlisted investments are stated at values determined by the Directors. Investment properties are valued annually by the Directors. The aggregate surplus or deficit is transferred to a revaluation reserve. No depreciation is provided in respect of freehold investment properties or leasehold investment properties with over 20 years to run. The Directors consider that this accounting policy results in the accounts giving a true and fair view.

Unrealised appreciation or depreciation on forward currency contracts is included in unlisted investments at the relevant middle market forward foreign exchange rate.

Investments held for dealing and shown as current assets are individually stated at the lower of cost and value at middle market price or Directors' valuation.

losses are taken with the unrealised element disclosed in a note to the financial statements. Table 17.3 illustrates the disclosure of reserves by an investment trust company.

17.29 The above treatment is also consistent with SSAP 6 which states:

> *"In the special circumstances of investment trust companies, the major part of whose assets consists of readily marketable securities, it may not be appropriate to deal with losses or gains whether realised or unrealised in the profit and loss account; in such cases realised and unrealised gains or losses should be shown prominently in the balance sheet or in a note to the accounts."* [SSAP 6 para 24].

Properties

17.30 Investment companies may also carry investment properties in their balance sheet. These investment properties are valued on an 'open market value' basis and any changes in the value are taken to an unrealised appreciation/depreciation reserve in accordance with SSAP 19. However, where the amount of the unrealised appreciation reserve in respect of investment properties is insufficient to cover a deficit, investment companies need not take the excess deficit to the profit and loss account. In such situations, however, the deficit should be shown prominently in the financial statements. [SSAP 19 para 13].

Table 17.3: Illustration of disclosure of reserves by an investment trust company.

Extract from Electra Investment Trust P.L.C. Report & Accounts 30th September 1990.

NOTES TO THE ACCOUNTS

19. Reserves	30th Sept 1990 Group £'000	Company £'000
a. Realised Profits - Non Distributable*		
At 1 October 1989	365,061	369,931
Share premium arising during the year	119	119
Exchange differences arising on consolidation	(1,117)	—
Profit less losses on realisation of investments during the year	47,554	47,885
Profit on part sale of subsidiary	4,260	2,478
Unrealised net appreciation at 1 October 1989 on investments sold during the year	3,027	990
Unrealised net depreciation at 1 October 1989 on currency loans repaid during the year	(146)	(146)
Net defecit on revaluation of overseas bank balances	(57)	(57)
At 30 September 1990	418,701	421,200
b. Unrealised Profits - Non Distributable		
At 1 October 1989	153,288	147,360
Unrealised net appreciation at 1 October 1989 on investments sold during the year transferred to realised profits	(3,027)	(990)
Unrealised net depreciation at 1 October 1989 on currency loans repaid during the year transferred to realised profits	146	146
Decrease in value of fixed asset investments	(161,764)	(149,560)
Profit on revaluation of currency loans	2,736	2,677
Profit on revaluation of 9% promissory notes	3,271	3,271
At 30 September 1990	(5,350)	2,904
c. Profit & Loss Account - Distributable		
At 1 October 1989	11,708	8,847
Exchange differences arising on consolidation	(193)	—
Transfer from profit and loss account	5,066	2,437
At 30 September 1990	16,581	11,284
Total reserves at 30 September 1990	429,932	435,388
Total reserves at 30 September 1989	530,057	526,138

The amount of the reserves of Electra Investment Trust P.L.C. which may legally be distributed under Section 265(1) of the Companies Act 1985 is £11,284,000 (1989 £8,847,000).

*Includes share premium at 30 September 1990 £1,981,000 (1989 £1,862,000)

Recognition of income

Dividend income

17.31 Dividend income is by far the major source of revenue for all investment companies. However, the dividend income recognition policies vary from company to company. Some investment companies account for their dividend income in their financial statements on a 'cash received' basis, whereas other investment companies have accrued dividends. Dividends could be accrued from the time when any one of the following occurs:

- The dividends are declared.
- The paying company's shares are quoted ex-dividend.
- The dividends are due and payable.

17.32 Generally, investment companies account for dividends receivable on the date when they become due for payment. The 'cash received' basis seems to conflict with paragraph 13 of Schedule 4 to the *Companies Act 1985* which requires all income to be brought into account without regard to the date of receipt or payment. The difference between accounting for investment income under the three accruals bases outlined above can be significant. An example of an accounting policy on investment income is shown in Table 17.4.

Table 17.4: Illustration of an accounting policy on income from investments.

Extract from The First Scottish American Trust PLC Annual Report 31st January 1990.

Note extract

1 Accounting basis and policies

The accounts have been prepared under the historical cost convention, modified to include the revaluation of fixed assets.

(a) Revenue, Expenses and Interest payable—Income from investments including taxes deducted at source and imputed tax credits, is included in revenue by reference to the date on which it is receivable except in the case of securities covered by the Finance Act 1985. Where a security of this type is purchased or sold, an adjustment is made to income to reflect the accrued interest in the transaction. Foreign income is converted at the exchange rate applicable at the time of receipt. Interest receivable on short term deposits, expenses and interest payable are treated on an accruals basis.

Income arising on fixed interest securities

17.33 Whereas the treatment of dividend income discussed above is one of timing and not of measurement because the amount of dividend income is fixed when it is declared, recognition of income arising from fixed interest securities involves both timing and measurement considerations.

17.34 In the past, a number of investment companies had indulged in what was termed 'bond-washing'. This process essentially involved the disposal of fixed interest securities on which interest was accrued but not yet paid. The benefit of the accrued interest was reflected in higher disposal proceeds rather than income, thus giving rise to a higher capital gain. Since capital gains are tax-free in an approved investment trust, the treatment of accrued income as capital rather than income was highly popular. The accounting treatment also followed the tax treatment.

17.35 However, during 1986, the Inland Revenue introduced anti-avoidance measures under which interest accrued on variable or fixed interest securities at the date of disposal is to be taxable as income and not as capital gains. The accrued income scheme provisions of the *Income and Corporation Taxes Act 1988* made many investment trust companies change their accounting policy for interest income. An example of an accounting policy for income covered by accrued income scheme is shown in Table 17.4.

Management fees

17.36 As stated in paragraph 17.9 above, the directors of most investment companies sub-contract the day to day management of their investment portfolio to professional investment managers. The management fee, which is generally based on a percentage of the market value of the managed portfolio, is charged as an expense to the revenue account. However, some approved investment trusts charge a proportion of the management fee to capital reserve on the basis that part of their management is directed towards managing the capital growth of the fund. In certain circumstances, it might also be acceptable to charge other expenses including finance costs to the capital reserve.

Foreign currency transactions

17.37 Many investment companies and approved investment trusts have overseas investments and, consequently, enter into hedging transactions to reduce the effects of exchange rate fluctuations on the value of those investments. The intention is to protect the capital value of the investments and, therefore, exchange gains or losses arising on hedging transactions are often taken to capital reserve or unrealised appreciation reserve. There are a number of methods that investment companies use to minimise the risk of exchange rate fluctuations. They range from back-to-back loans, forward contracts and currency options and futures. In all these situations, the profit or loss on hedging instruments are accounted for through capital reserves. Since the currency effects on the value of the investments are also taken to capital reserve, this treatment is in accordance with the 'cover method' described in SSAP 20.

International Stock Exchange requirements

17.38 In addition to complying with the accounting and disclosure requirements of the *Companies Act 1985*, listed investment companies must also comply with The International Stock Exchange's Continuing Obligations. There are different disclosure requirements for investment companies and approved investment trusts and these requirements are considered below.

17.39 A listed investment company that is not an approved investment trust must give the following information in its financial statements:

- A summary of (at least) the investment company's ten largest investments, with corresponding amounts. In addition, the investing company should summarise any other investments that it owns that have a value greater than five per cent of its assets. The type of information that is required to be summarised is as follows:

  - A brief description of the business.
  - The proportion of the company's share capital that is owned.
  - The cost of the investment.
  - The directors' valuation of the investment.
  - The dividends received during the year (with an indication of any abnormally large dividends).
  - The dividend cover or the underlying earnings.
  - Any extraordinary items.
  - The net assets attributable to the investment (that is, the company's share of the net assets of the company that it has invested in).

- ■ An analysis of any provision for the diminution in value of its investments. The notes should state which investments have been provided against, and also:
  - □ The original cost of the investment concerned.
  - □ The amount of the provision made against the investment.
  - □ The book value of the investment after the provision has been made.
- ■ An analysis of realised and unrealised surpluses, with a separate statement of profits and losses (whether realised or not) split between listed and unlisted investments.

[CO 21(s)].

17.40 For an approved investment trust which is listed, The International Stock Exchange's Continuing Obligations require the trust's financial statements to give the following information:

- ■ A statement that the Inland Revenue has approved the company as an approved investment trust, specifying the last accounting period in respect of which such approval has been given, and confirming that the company has conducted its affairs in such a way that it will continue to be approved. (A new investment trust must state that it will direct its affairs so as to enable it to seek approval.)
- ■ An analysis of the investment portfolio:
  - □ By broad geographical area (based on the countries of incorporation of the companies that the investment trust has invested in).
  - □ By broad industrial or commercial sector.
  - □ Between equity capital, securities that have an equity element (for example, convertible loan stock) and fixed income securities.
- ■ A list of the investment trust's largest investments by market value, stating the market value for each such investment.
- ■ An analysis of income between:
  - □ Dividends.
  - □ Interest.

- □ Other income (distinguishing, where material, between underwriting income and the results of dealing by subsidiaries.)

- ■ An analysis, where material to an application of the investment trust's financial position, of realised and unrealised profits and losses, with a separate statement of profits and losses (whether realised or not), split between listed and unlisted investments.
- ■ The name of the group or company that manages the investment portfolio, together with an indication of the terms and duration of its appointment and the basis for its remuneration.

[CO 21(r)].

Consolidated financial statements

Subsidiary undertakings

17.41 Investment companies that have subsidiary undertakings are required to prepare consolidated financial statements in accordance with section 227 of the *Companies Act 1985*. Consolidated financial statements should cover the parent and all its subsidiary undertakings unless one, or more of the subsidiary undertakings fall to be excluded from consolidation for any of the reasons specified in section 229 of the *Companies Act 1985*.

17.42 Previously some investment companies have excluded a subsidiary from consolidation on the grounds that its activities were so different from the rest of the group that it would be misleading to include it in the consolidation. However, section 5 of the *Companies Act 1989* substituted a new section 229(4) of the *Companies Act 1985* that tightens the previous condition by requiring that a subsidiary must be excluded from consolidation on this ground only if its inclusion in the consolidated financial statements would be incompatible with the obligation to give a true and fair view.

17.43 Investments held by investment companies need not be limited to shares and securities, but may take the form of partnership arrangements, participations, joint-ventures and other forms of non-corporate investment. Where these investments are material and satisfy the definition of a subsidiary undertaking, they should be consolidated unless their activities are so different from the rest of the group that their inclusion in the consolidated financial statements would be incompatible with the obligation to give a true and fair view. This possibility, however, is likely to be rare. In the event of exclusion, the grounds for considering that inclusion is not compatible with the obligation to give a true and fair view must be explained in a note to the financial statements (see further 'Manual of accounting - volume II chapter 3).

Associated undertakings

17.44 In the past where an investment company owned between 20 per cent and 50 per cent of another company's equity share capital, there was an apparent reluctance for the investment company to account for that other company under the equity method of accounting in accordance with SSAP 1 in its consolidated financial statements. The reason frequently cited was that it would be misleading or inappropriate to do so, because investment companies are by their very nature merely passive investors and do not seek to exert significant influence over, or actively participate in, the activities or policy decisions of the investee company.

17.45 However, since the introduction of the *Companies Act 1989* it is now provided in law that a company's associated undertakings should be accounted for under the equity method of accounting in the consolidated financial statements (see 'Manual of Accounting – volume II' chapter 11). Consequently, where an investment trust has a participating interest of more than 20 per cent in another undertaking, it is presumed that the investment trust has significant influence unless otherwise shown. Where this is so, the undertaking should be accounted for on an equity basis thereby consolidating its share of that undertaking's profits or losses and net assets.

17.46 Where the investment company does not prepare consolidated financial statements, SSAP 1 would not, in any event, permit the inclusion of the associated undertaking's share of profits or losses in the investment company's own financial statements. However, SSAP 1 requires certain supplementary information to be disclosed in the notes to the financial statements (such as the investor's share of the associated company's profit before taxation, taxation, extraordinary items and retained profits) in these circumstances. For a more detailed explanation of equity accounting see 'Manual of Accounting - volume II' chapter 11.

17.47 Where the investment company (like any other company) includes in its revenue account its share of profits of the associated undertaking, those profits cannot be distributed until received in the form of dividends. Furthermore, if the associated undertaking is subsequently sold, an investment trust is prohibited from distributing any surplus arising on the disposal by its memorandum and articles of association as this will represent a capital profit and must be credited to the realised capital reserve.

Distributions

17.48 Investment companies may make a distribution either on the basis of the *capital maintenance* test applicable to all public companies (see 'Manual of Accounting - volume I' chapter 19) or on the basis of an *asset ratio* test (see para 17.51). However, where a distribution reduces an investment company's net assets below the aggregate of its called-up capital and undistributable reserves, this fact must be disclosed in the notes to the financial statements. [CA 1985 4 Sch 72(1); 9 Sch 13(4)].

17.49 Subject to the conditions listed in paragraph 17.50 below, an investment company may make a distribution at any time out of those of its accumulated realised *revenue* profits that have not previously been either distributed or capitalised, *less* its accumulated *revenue* losses (realised and unrealised, and only insofar as they have not been previously written off in a reduction or reorganisation of capital). The advantage of this is that capital losses may be ignored, although the other side of the coin is that realised capital profits cannot be included and the asset ratio test in paragraph 17.51 below must be satisfied. An investment company is, therefore, able to satisfy the Inland Revenue condition of non-retention of income because it may make distributions even where the value of its investments has fallen.

17.50 The conditions which must be satisfied before an investment company may make a distribution on this basis are:

- ■ The company's shares must be listed on a recognised investment exchange other than an overseas investment exchange within the meaning of the *Financial Services Act 1986*. [CA 1985 Sec 265(4)(a)].

- ■ During the period beginning with the first day of the accounting reference period immediately preceding that in which the proposed distribution is to be made (or, where the distribution is proposed to be made during the company's first accounting reference period, the first day of that period) and ending with the date of that distribution, the company must not have:

  - □ Distributed any of its capital profits.

  - □ Applied any unrealised profits or any capital profits (whether realised or unrealised) in paying up debentures or any amounts unpaid on any of its issued shares. This means that companies may not distribute indirectly any amounts that are not available for distribution directly. [CA 1985 Sec 265(4)(5)].

- The company must have given the Registrar of Companies the notice required in section 266(1) of the *Companies Act 1985* at one of the following times:
  - ☐ Before the beginning of the period referred to in the point immediately above.
  - ☐ As soon as reasonably practicable after the date on which the company was incorporated.

  [CA 1985 Sec 265(6)].

  This condition is necessary to prevent companies adopting investment company status merely for a particular distribution and who might then revoke that status only to adopt it again for the purpose of the next distribution.

- The amount of the company's assets must be at least 50 per cent greater than the aggregate of its liabilities. [CA 1985 Sec 265(1)(a)]. In this context, 'liabilities' includes any provision other than for depreciation or diminution in the value of assets. [CA 1985 Sec 265(2), 4 Sch 89]. However, the company must not include any uncalled share capital as an asset in those financial statements that are used to determine the legality of any distribution. [CA 1985 Sec 265(3)].

17.51 Where all the above conditions are satisfied an investment company may make a distribution, but only to the extent that the distribution does not reduce the company's assets below 150 per cent of the aggregate of its liabilities. [CA 1985 Sec 265(1)(b)].

17.52 The following example sets out extracts from the balance sheets of four companies. The example shows how investment companies calculate their distributable profits and contrasts this with how other companies calculate their distributable profits:

		Company 1		Company 2		Company 3		Company 4	
		£	£	£	£	£	£	£	£
A	Share capital		1,000		1,000		1,000		1,000
B	Share premium		100		100		100		100
C	Unrealised capital profits	600		600		600		600	
D	Unrealised revenue profits	–		–		100		100	
E	Unrealised capital losses	–		(700)		(700)		(700)	
F	Unrealised revenue losses	–		(250)		(250)		(250)	
G	Net unrealised reserves		600		(350)		(250)		(250)
H	Realised revenue profits	1,200		1,200		1,200		1,200	
I	Realised capital profits	–		–		100		100	
J	Realised capital losses	–		–		–		(600)	
K	Realised revenue losses	–		–		(150)		(150)	
L	Net realised reserves		1,200		1,200		1,150		550

		Company 1	Company 2	Company 3	Company 4
		£	£	£	£
M	Share capital and reserves	2,900	1,950	2,000	1,400
N	Total liabilities	1,300	1,300	1,300	1,300
O	Total assets	4,200	3,250	3,300	2,700
	Maximum distributable profits - Special rules for an investment company				
(i)	per section 265 The lower of:				
	(a) Realised revenue profits(H) less accumulated revenue losses (K + F)	1,200	950	800	800
	(b) 150 per cent asset test, O – (1½ x N)	2,250	1,300	1,350	750
	Amount distributable	1,200	950	800	750
	Normal rules for a public company				
(ii)	per section 264 (The lower of L and (L + G))	1,200	850	900	300

Audit requirements

17.53 The audit requirements for investment companies are no different to any other public companies incorporated under the *Companies Act 1985.* Consequently, auditors should have regard to Auditing Standards and Guidelines when conducting the audit of investment companies and approved investments trusts.

Audit report

17.54 The auditors' report on an investment company's financial statements is no different from the report given for normal companies limited by shares.

SECTIONS OF THE COMPANIES ACT 1985 THAT APPLY SPECIFICALLY TO INVESTMENT COMPANIES

Section	Description
265	Other distributions by investment companies
266	Meaning of 'investment company'
351(1)(c)	Particulars in correspondence etc.
4 Sch Part V	Form and content of company accounts (Special provisions where the company is an investment company)
4A Sch 1(3)	Form and content of group accounts (General rules)

Chapter 18

OVERSEA COMPANIES

Annexes

Chapter 18

OVERSEA COMPANIES

Introduction

18.1 Companies incorporated outside Great Britain frequently establish branches to trade in Great Britain. It is, therefore, necessary for the protection of the public that such companies are brought, to some extent, within the regulatory framework applicable to companies incorporated in Great Britain. This is done by requiring the registration of oversea companies with the Registrar of Companies and extending wide exemptions to them so as not to discourage them establishing a place of business in Great Britain.

18.2 Oversea companies are regulated in accordance with Part XXIII of the *Companies Act 1985*. This provides for:

- Registration of oversea companies, including the regulation of names used by oversea companies.
- Preparation and filing of financial statements.
- Registration of charges.

Definition

18.3 An 'oversea company' is defined as any 'company' incorporated outside Great Britain which has established a 'place of business' in Great Britain. [CA 1985 Sec 744]. This definition includes a company that is incorporated in Northern Ireland, or in the Isle of Man, or in the Channel Islands, and has a place of business in Great Britain.

18.4 The definition of 'company' in section 735(1)(a) of the *Companies Act 1985* is *"a company formed and registered under this Act, or an existing company [which is a company formed and registered under the former Companies Acts]"*. Accordingly, that definition does not apply to the word 'company' as used in the definition of an oversea 'company'. No alternative definition is, however, given.

18.5 There is no comprehensive statutory or common law definition of what constitutes a 'place of business'. The term is defined only as to include a share transfer or share registration office. [CA 1985 Sec 744]. The extent of this is not clear. Accordingly, unless it is desired to register a place of business in Great Britain, share register and transfer books should not be kept at an office in Great Britain. It is quite common for a company incorporated overseas to be acquired off-the-shelf. All documents concerning the company may be sent to the purchaser of the company and could include the share register and transfer books. If these are then kept at an office in Great Britain that office could constitute a share register or transfer office which would be a place of business.

18.6 Subject to the above, whether a place of business has been established must be a question of fact in each particular circumstance. Guidance regarding the term 'place of business' can be found by reference to decided cases.

18.7 The general principle is that an oversea company must occupy premises from which its officers and/or employees carry on activities in furtherance of the company's business. Case law illustrates the following principles:

- Level of corporate activity required.

  It is sufficient that the company carries on some business activity at its place of business. It does not matter if that business does not form a substantial part of its activities (*South India Shipping Corporation Limited v Export-Import Bank of Korea (1985) 1 WLR 585*). However, a company will not be regarded as having established a place of business if it carries on its activities through an agent (*Lord Advocate v Huron & Erie Loan and Savings Co. 1911 SC 612*). Furthermore, a foreign company that operates in Great Britain through a subsidiary company will not, simply by virtue of that fact, have a place of business in Great Britain (*Deverall v Grant Advertising Inc. (1955) Ch. 111*).

- Corporate presence of company officers.

  A hotel that a director frequently stays in and from which he transacts the company's business may be a place of business (*Re. Tovarishestvo Manufactur Liudvig-Rabenek (1944) Ch 404*). However, the mere presence of the directors in their private residence will not make the residence a place of business (*Re. Oriel Limited (1985) Financial Times 2nd July 1985*).

Registration of oversea companies

18.8 There is no obligation upon a company incorporated outside Great Britain to register unless it has established a place of business here. When it does so, it must deliver certain documents to the Registrar of Companies for registration within one month. [CA 1985 Sec 691(1)]. These are:

- A certified copy of the instrument constituting or defining the constitution of the company and a certified translation of it, if it is not in English, with a list of the documents delivered (on Form 691). [CA 1985 Sec 691(1)(a), (b)(iii)].

- A list (on Form 691) of the company's directors and secretary. [CA 1985 Sec 691(1)(b)(i)]. As in the rest of the *Companies Act 1985* this requirement applies to shadow directors as well. [CA 1985 Sec 741]. The following particulars must be given of the company's directors and secretary:

  - In the case of an individual, his present and any former Christian name (or other forename) and surname and his usual residential address. A director must also given his nationality, date of birth and any business occupation, or if none, any other directorships held.

  - In the case of a corporation or Scottish firm, its corporate or firm name and registered or principal address.

  [CA 1985 Sec 691].

- A list (on Form 691) of the names and addresses of a person or persons resident in Great Britain authorised to accept service on behalf of the company. [CA 1985 Sec 691(1)(b)(ii)].

- A statutory declaration (on Form 691), by one of the persons listed in the second point above, of the date on which the company's place of business in Great Britain was established. [CA 1985 Sec 691(1)(b)(iv)].

18.9 Any changes in the instrument constituting or defining the constitution of the company or particulars relating to its directors and company secretary must be registered (on Forms 692(1)(a) and 692(1)(b) respectively 21 days after the date on which the Form could have been received in Great Britain or in the due course of post (if despatched with due diligence)). [CA 1985 Sec 692(3)(b)].

18.10 Any change in names or addresses of persons authorised to accept service on behalf of an oversea company must be registered (on Form 692(1)(c)) 21 days after it is made. [CA 1985 Sec 692(3)(a)].

Duty to keep accounting records

18.11 There are no provisions requiring an oversea company registered in Great Britain to keep adequate, or even any, accounting records. This is despite the detailed requirements (see paras 18.12 below) to prepare and file financial statements.

Duty to prepare financial statements

18.12 Every oversea company must prepare financial statements in respect of each accounting reference period. These must be made up by reference to such dates and contain the same information as if the company had been formed and registered under the *Companies Act 1985.* [CA 1985 Sec 700(1)]. The Secretary of State, however, has taken advantage of the power contained in section 700(2) and (3) of the *Companies Act 1985* to modify these requirements or exempt oversea companies from them. The statutory instrument giving effect to this exemption is *The Oversea Companies (Accounts) (Modifications and Exemptions) Order 1990* (SI 1990/440).

18.13 Oversea companies must prepare their financial statements in accordance with the requirements of sections 258 and 259 of and Schedule 9 to the *Companies Act 1985* as applied before it was amended by the *Companies Act 1989* as if they were old special category companies in so far as those requirements applied. [SI 1990/440 para 2(1)(b)]. Oversea companies are not required to refer to the fact that their financial statements are drawn up in compliance with section 258 or section 259 of and Schedule 9 to the unamended *Companies Act 1985*. [SI 1990/440 Sch 5]. Oversea companies are, of course, permitted to give additional information, including that required by Schedule 4 to the *Companies Act 1985*.

18.14 Any information that an oversea company was to include in its financial statements may alternatively be disclosed in a statement annexed to the financial statements.

18.15 Oversea companies may not take advantage of the exemptions available to small, medium-sized or dormant companies. [SI 1990/440 para 2(2)].

18.16 An unlimited oversea company that, if it were a company registered in Great Britain, would be exempt from the requirement to *deliver* financial statements to the Registrar of Companies in respect of a particular accounting period under section 241(4) of the *Companies Act 1985*, is also exempt from the requirement to *prepare* (and hence deliver) such annual financial statements. [CA 1985 Sec 700(3)].

Exemptions from reporting requirements

18.17 Oversea companies are not required to provide the following information:

- An audit report (see para 18.25)

- A directors' report. This exemption covers all the information that a company that prepares its financial statements in accordance with Schedule 9 is required to disclose in its directors' report (such as, disaggregated information in respect of turnover and profit before tax, particulars of the average number of employees and their remuneration).

- Taxation information:
  - The basis of computation and amount of any provision, or charge to revenue for UK corporation tax (ignoring double tax relief) and UK income tax.
  - The amount of any charge to revenue for taxation imposed outside the UK on profits, income and capital gains (to the extent that these are credited to revenue).
- The amount of turnover (where it exceeds £1,000,000) and the method by which it is arrived at.
- Details in the parent company's financial statements of the identities of, the place of incorporation of, and particulars of the company's shareholdings in subsidiaries.
- Details of investments that exceed one-tenth of the nominal value of any class of the issued equity share capital of another body corporate, and details of any investment that exceeds one-tenth of the company's own assets.
- Details of the name and place of incorporation of the company's ultimate holding company.
- Particulars of the chairman's and the highest-paid director's emoluments and the banding of all director's emoluments.
- Details of any emoluments that directors have waived.
- Details of the bandings of higher-paid employees' emoluments.
- Particulars of transactions with directors and officers.

[SI 1990/440 Sch 2 - 6].

18.18 Where an oversea company avails itself of the above exemptions, the contents of its financial statements will be substantially different from those of a company incorporated in Great Britain. Consequently, it is recommended that any oversea company that takes advantage of the provisions of the regulation should disclose this fact in the notes to its financial statements. This recommendation applies whether or not those financial statements are audited.

Stock Exchange listed or USM traded oversea companies

18.19 Regardless of any of the exemptions or modifications referred to in paragraph 18.17 above, any oversea company that has obtained a listing on The International Stock Exchange is bound by the requirements of the Exchange's Continuing Obligations to circulate annual audited financial statements to its members. These provide that:

> *"In the case of a company incorporated in a non-member state [of the EC] which is not required to draw up its accounts so as to give a true and fair view, but is required to draw them up to an equivalent standard, the latter may be sufficient. References must, however, be made to the [Quotations] Department [of the International Stock Exchange]."* [CO 20.1].

18.20 Consequently, depending on the requirements that the Quotations Department imposes, a listed oversea company may be unable to take advantage of many of the exemptions listed in paragraph 18.17.

18.21 These considerations will also apply to any oversea companies traded on the USM.

Accounting reference period

18.22 An oversea company's accounting reference period is determined in the same way as for a company incorporated under the *Companies Act 1985*. Except that the date of incorporation of a company registered under that Act is equivalent to the date on which an oversea company establishes a place of business in Great Britain. [CA 1985 Sec 701]. Accounting reference periods are considered further in 'Manual of Accounting - volume I' chapter 2.

Duty to submit accounts and reports

18.23 All oversea companies must deliver a copy of their financial statements for each accounting reference period to the Registrar of Companies within 13 months from the end of the relevant accounting reference period. [CA 1985 Sec 702(2)]. This is longer than the time limits for companies incorporated in Great Britain which are allowed ten months for a private company, and seven months for a public company.

18.24 If the oversea company's first accounting reference period exceeds 12 months, the period allowed is 13 months from the first anniversary of the company establishing a place of business in Great Britain. [CA 1985 Sec 702(3)].

Audit requirements

18.25 No requirement for an audit is imposed by the *Companies Act 1985*, although the law of the oversea company's country of incorporation may still do so. This is subject to the obligations on oversea companies which are listed on The International Stock Exchange or traded on the USM as discussed in paragraphs 18.19 - 18.21 above.

SECTIONS OF THE COMPANIES ACT 1985 THAT APPLY TO OVERSEA COMPANIES

Section	Description
72	Prospectus of oversea company
691	Documents to be delivered to registrar
692	Registration of altered particulars
693	Obligation to state name and other particulars
694	Regulation of oversea companies in respect of their names
695	Service of documents on oversea company
696	Registrar to whom documents to be delivered
697	Penalties for non-compliance
698	Definitions for this Chapter
699	Channel Islands and Isle of Man companies
700	Preparation of accounts and reports by oversea companies
701	Oversea company's financial year and accounting reference periods
702	Delivery to registrar of accounts and reports of oversea company
703	Penalty for non-compliance
703A	Introductory provisions
703B	Charges requiring registration
703C	The register
703D	Company's duty to deliver particulars of charges for registration

Section	Description
703E	Registrar to whom particulars etc. to be delivered
703F	Effect of failure to deliver particulars, late delivery and effect of errors and omissions
703G	Delivery of further particulars or memorandum
703H	Further provisions with respect of voidness of charges
703I	Additional information to be registered
703J	Copies of instruments and register to be kept by company
703K	Power to make further provision by regulations
703L	Provisions as to situation of property
703M	Other supplementary provisions
703N	Index of defined expressions
705	Companies' registered number
744	Expressions used generally in this text
744A	Index of defined expressions

THE OVERSEA COMPANIES (ACCOUNTS) (MODIFICATIONS AND EXEMPTIONS) ORDER 1990 (SI 1990/440)

Made	*5th March 1990*
Laid before Parliament	*7th March 1990*
Coming into force	*1st April 1990*

The Secretary of State, in exercise of the powers conferred by section 700(2) and (3) of the Companies Act 1985(**a**) and of all other powers enabling him in that behalf, hereby makes the following Order:

1 (1) This Order may be cited as the Oversea Companies (Accounts) (Modifications and Exemptions) Order 1990 and shall come into force on 1st April 1990.

(2) In this Order:

"the 1989 Act" means the Companies Act 1989(**b**);

"the 1985 Act" means the Companies Act 1985 as amended by the 1989 Act; and

"the unamended 1985 Act" means the provisions of the 1985 Act prior to their amendment by the 1989 Act.

(3) The Oversea Companies (Accounts) (Modifications and Exemptions) Order 1982(**c**) is hereby revoked.

2 (1) The requirements referred to in section 700(1) of the 1985 Act shall, for the purposes of their application to oversea companies, be modified as follows:

(a) subject to the following provisions of this article, Part VII of the 1985 Act shall apply as if it had not been amended by the 1989 Act and as if any provision of the 1985 Act necessary for the interpretation of that Part had not been amended or repealed by the 1989 Act;

(b) sections 228 and 230 of the unamended 1985 Act shall not apply in relation to such companies but sections 258 and 259 of the unamended 1985 Act shall apply as if such companies were special category companies within the meaning of section 257(1) of that

---

(**a**) 1985 c.6; section 700 was substituted by section 23 of, and paragraph 13 of Schedule 10, to the Companies Act 1989 (c.40). (**b**) 1989 c.40. (**c**) S.I. 1982/676.

Act and in particular shall (subject to the provisions of those sections) require the balance sheet, profit and loss account and group accounts of such companies to comply with the requirements of Schedule 9 to the unamended 1985 Act so far as applicable; and

(c) sections 245 and 247 to 253 of, and Schedule 8 and paragraph 29 of Schedule 9 to, the unamended 1985 Act shall not apply to such companies.

(2) Oversea companies shall be exempt from such requirements of the unamended 1985 Act referred to in section 700(1) of the 1985 Act as are specified in the Schedule to this Order.

(3) Oversea companies which would be exempt under section 700(3) of the unamended 1985 Act from compliance with that section (independent company with unlimited liability) shall be exempt from the requirements referred to in section 700(1) of the 1985 Act.

John Redwood
Parliamentary Under-Secretary of State,
5th March 1990 Department of Trade and Industry

SCHEDULE Article 2(2)

REQUIREMENTS OF THE UNAMENDED 1985 ACT FROM WHICH OVERSEA COMPANIES ARE EXEMPT

1 Sections 231 and 260 and Schedule 5, except for the disclosure in the accounts of overseas companies, or in a document annexed thereto, of the information required to be given in paragraphs 22 and 28 to 34 of the said Schedule 5 and section 260(2) so far as it relates to those paragraphs.

2 Sections 232 to 234 and Schedule 6.

3 Sections 235 and 261 and Schedules 7 and 10.

4 Sections 236, 238(3), so far as that subsection requires the auditors' report to be attached to the balance sheet, and 262.

5 Section 257(3).

6 Paragraphs 13(17), 14(1)(c), 17 and 18(3) of Schedule 9.

EXPLANATORY NOTE

(This note is not part of the Order)

This Order modifies the requirements of the Companies Act 1985 relating to the preparation of accounts and related documents for the purpose of their application to oversea companies. It also exempts oversea companies from the requirements listed in the Schedule to the Order. Certain oversea companies with unlimited liability are exempted altogether from such requirements of the 1985 Act.

The Order revokes and remakes the Oversea Companies (Accounts) (Modifications and Exemptions) Order 1982 to reflect, with minor exceptions, the consolidation in the 1985 Act of the provisions referred to in the 1982 Order. The Order also disapplies the amendments made by the Companies Act 1989 to such provisions in relation to oversea companies. The provisions of this Order are subject to the transitional and saving provisions relating to such companies which are provided in the Companies Act 1989 (Commencement No. 4 and Transitional and Saving Provisions) Order 1990 (S.I. 1990/355).

Chapter 19

COMPANIES INCORPORATED BY ROYAL CHARTER

Chapter 19

COMPANIES INCORPORATED BY ROYAL CHARTER

Introduction

19.1 The Crown has power at common law to incorporate by charter any association of persons who consent to be incorporated. More recently, such companies have been incorporated under the *Chartered Companies Act 1837*. That Act empowers the Crown to grant, by letters patent under the Great Seal, to any association of persons any privilege that the Crown can grant at common law to them by any charter of incorporation. [CCA 1837 Sec 2]. Furthermore, the *Chartered Companies Act 1837* empowers the Crown to apply the provisions of that Act to companies incorporated by Royal Charter. [CCA 1837 Sec 29].

19.2 Chartered companies are not uncommon. The British Broadcasting Corporation was incorporated by Royal Charter for a period of ten years from 1st January 1927. Its incorporation has been continued by subsequent charters. Livery companies are also examples of companies incorporated by Royal Charter.

Application of company law

19.3 A company will have the *Chartered Companies Act 1837* as its prime source of regulation in the following circumstances:

- It has been incorporated under that Act.
- The Crown in granting the charter of incorporation applies (under section 29 of the *Chartered Companies Act 1837*) the provision of that Act to the company.

19.4 Where the provision of the *Chartered Companies Act 1837* do not apply to a company, then its charter will be its prime source of regulation.

19.5 However, certain provisions of the *Companies Act 1985* will apply to the company, unless it is one of the following:

- A company whose purpose is not to carry on business with the object of acquiring gain for itself or for its members.

- A company exempted by the Secretary of State (or before him by the Board of Trade).

[CA 1985 Secs 718(2)(4)].

19.6 Where the *Companies Act 1985* applies to a chartered company, this does not mean the charter or letters patent will no longer apply. It does mean, however, that any part of the Royal Charter or the letters patent that is inconsistent with the relevant provisions of the *Companies Act 1985* will no longer apply to the company. [CA 1985 Sec 718(5)].

19.7 The provisions of the *Companies Act 1985* that apply to chartered companies are listed in Schedule 22 to that Act. These provisions may be varied by regulations that can be made by the Secretary of State. [CA 1985 Sec 718(3)]. The *Companies (Unregistered Companies) Regulations 1985* (SI 1985/680) as amended by SI 1990/438, 1990/1394 and 1990/2571 were made under section 718(3) of the *Companies Act 1985* and implement certain requirements in the list given in Schedule 22 to the *Companies Act 1985*. The provisions that apply to chartered companies are given in annex 1.

Formation

19.8 The procedure for forming a chartered company under the *Chartered Companies Act 1837* is very slow compared with companies registered under the *Companies Act 1985*. In order to form a chartered company, the following procedures have to be followed:

- The persons seeking incorporation must enter into a deed of partnership, a deed of association or an agreement in writing that is similar in nature.
- The deed or agreement must specify the number of shares the undertaking will be divided into.
- The deed or agreement must also specify:
  - The company's name.
  - The names of the company's members.
  - The date of the company's commencement.
  - The business or purpose for which the company is being formed.
  - The principal or only place of business.

- ☐ The appointment of two or more officers to sue, or to be sued, on behalf of the company.

  [CCA 1837 Sec 5].

- ■ An application for letters patent must be made to the Crown, who will refer it to the DTI. Notice of the application must be inserted by the persons concerned in three issues of the London Gazette at intervals of not less than one week. In addition, the notice must also be inserted in one or more newspapers that circulate in the country where the company's principal place of business is to be established. [CCA 1837 Sec 32].

- ■ The company must make a return in the form of Schedule A to the *Chartered Companies Act 1837* within three calendar months of being granted letters patent. This return must contain the following information:

  - ☐ The date the company was granted letters patent.
  - ☐ The company's name or style.
  - ☐ The business or purpose for which it is formed.
  - ☐ The principal or only place for carrying on that business.
  - ☐ The total number of the company's shares.
  - ☐ The amount to which each share will render the holder liable.
  - ☐ The names and (except where the member is a corporation) the addresses of all the members, including the numbers of the shares they hold.
  - ☐ The names and descriptions of the officers appointed by the company to sue, or to be sued, on its behalf.

  [CCA 1837 Sec 6].

Duty to keep accounting records

19.9 Chartered companies that are regulated by the *Chartered Companies Act 1837* are subject to the same requirements to keep accounting records and to their form and preservation as apply to limited companies generally (see 'Manual of Accounting - volume I'). For chartered companies not governed by the *Chartered Companies Act 1837*, the only requirements concerning accounting records will be contained in the constitution of the company. In addition, with regard to the preservation of records, regulations for such companies will be contained in other legislation, or will be required by commercial practice (see 'Manual of Accounting - volume I' chapter 2).

Duty to prepare financial statements

19.10 The requirements that apply to normal limited companies concerning the preparation of individual company financial statements, or to consolidated financial statements, also apply generally to chartered companies. However, there are certain modifications as follows:

- Balance sheet formats.

  The heading 'share premium account' is not required and should be omitted (items K II and A II). [SI 1985/680 para 6(h)(i)].

- The requirement to disclose outstanding loans, made under the authority of sections 153(4)(b) or (c) of the *Companies Act 1985*, and the requirement to disclose financial assistance for the purchase of a company's own shares under section 155 of that Act do not apply. [SI 1985/680 para 6(h)(ii)].

- Investment companies.

  The disclosure requirements in Part V of Schedule 4 to the *Companies Act 1985* for investment companies do not apply. [SI 1985/680 para 6(h)(iii)].

- Merger relief provisions.

  The disclosure requirements in Part VI of Schedule 4 to the *Companies Act 1985*, where a company has entered into arrangements that are subject to merger relief, do not apply. [SI 1985/680 para 6(h)(iv)].

- Preliminary expenses.

  Preliminary expenses and the expenses of, or commission on, any issue of shares and debentures are normally not permitted to be treated as an asset in a company's balance sheet. However, for a chartered company this provision does not apply in relation to such expenses incurred before 1st January 1985. [SI 1985/680 para 5(d)].

- Distributions.

  The requirement to disclose any distribution made by an investment company that reduces the amount of its net assets to less than the aggregate of its called up share capital and undistributable reserves, does not apply. [SI 1985/680 para 6(i)].

Duty to submit an annual return

19.11 Where the *Chartered Companies Act 1837* applies to chartered companies, they are placed under the same duty to submit an annual return as limited companies generally. For chartered companies not governed by that Act, it is unlikely that they would need to submit returns of this nature.

Appointment and removal of auditors

19.12 Chartered companies governed by the *Chartered Companies Act 1837* are subject to the same provisions with respect to auditors as for normal limited companies. However, where a chartered company is not governed by that Act any audit requirements will depend on the wording of the company's constitution.

Audit report

19.13 The audit report of chartered companies governed by the *Chartered Companies Act 1837* will be the same as those used for normal companies limited by shares. The audit report of a chartered company which is not governed by that Act, but whose constitution requires an audit would depend on the terms of the appointment. Generally, the report should be along the same lines as that for a company limited by shares except that reference to the *Companies Act 1985* is not relevant and should be replaced where applicable by the *Chartered Companies Act 1837* or in other cases, the letter of appointment or Charter provision or both.

SECTIONS OF THE COMPANIES ACT 1985 THAT APPLY TO COMPANIES INCORPORATED BY ROYAL CHARTER

Section	Description
18	Amendments of memorandum or articles to be registered
35	A company's capacity not limited by its memorandum
35A	Power of directors to bind the company
35B	No duty to enquire as to capacity of the company or authority of directors
36	Company contracts: England and Wales
36A	Execution of documents: England and Wales
36B	Execution of documents: Scotland
36C	Pre-incorporation contracts, deeds and obligations
40	Official seal for share certificates etc.
42	Events affecting a company's status
56	Matters to be stated, and reports to be set out, in prospectus
57	Attempted evasion of section 56 to be void
58	Document offering shares etc. for sale deemed a prospectus
59	Rule governing what is an 'offer to the public'
60	Exceptions from rule in section 59
61	Prospectus containing statement by expert
62	Meaning of 'expert'
63	Prospectus to be dated
64	Registration requirement applicable in all cases

Section	Description
65	Additional requirements in case of prospectus issued generally
66	Directors, etc. exempt from liability in certain cases
67	Compensation for subscribers misled by statement in prospectus
68	Exemption from section 67 for those acting with propriety
69	Indemnity for innocent director or expert
70	Criminal liability for untrue statements
71	Interpretation for sections 56 to 70
82	Application for, and allotment of, shares and debentures
86	Allotment of shares, etc. to be dealt in on stock exchange
87	Operation of section 86 where prospectus offers shares for sale
185(4)	Duty of company as to issue of certificates (exemption from duty to prepare certificates where shares etc. are issued to a stock exchange nominee)
186	Certificate as evidence of title
221	Duty to keep accounting records
222	Where and for how long records to be kept
223	A company's financial year
224	Accounting reference periods and accounting reference date
225	Alteration of accounting reference date
226	Duty to prepare individual company accounts
227	Duty to prepare group accounts
228	Exemption for parent companies included in accounts of larger group
229	Subsidiary undertakings included in the consolidation

Section	Description
230	Treatment of individual profit and loss account where group accounts prepared
231	Disclosure required in notes to accounts: related undertakings
232	Disclosure required in notes to accounts: emoluments and other benefits of directors and others
233	Approval and signing of accounts
234	Duty to prepare directors' report
234A	Approval and signing of directors' report
235	Auditors' report
236	Signature of auditors' report
237	Duties of auditors
238	Persons entitled to receive copies of accounts and reports
239	Right to demand copies of accounts and reports
240	Requirements in connection with publication of accounts
241	Accounts and reports to be laid before company in general meeting
242	Accounts and reports to be delivered to the registrar
242A	Civil penalty for failure to deliver accounts
243	Accounts of subsidiary undertakings to be appended in certain cases
244	Period allowed for laying and delivering accounts and reports
245	Voluntary revision of annual accounts or directors' report
245A	Secretary of State's notice in respect of annual accounts
245B	Application to court in respect of defective accounts
245C	Other persons authorised to apply to court

Section	Description
246	Exemptions for small and medium-sized companies
247	Qualification of company as small or medium-sized
248	Exemption for small and medium-sized groups
249	Qualification of group as small or medium-sized
250	Resolution not to appoint auditors
251	Provision of summary financial statement to shareholders
254	Exemption from requirement to deliver accounts and reports
255	Special provisions for banking and insurance companies
255A	Special provisions for banking and insurance groups
255B	Modification of disclosure requirements in relation to banking company or group
255C	Directors' report where accounts prepared in accordance with special provisions
255D	Power to apply provisions to banking partnerships
256	Accounting standards
257	Power of Secretary of State to alter accounting requirements
258	Parent and subsidiary undertakings
259	Meaning of 'undertaking' and related expressions
260	Participating interests
261	Notes to the accounts
262	Minor definitions
262A	Index of defined expressions
287	Registered office
322A	Invalidity of certain transactions involving directors etc.
343	Record of transactions not disclosed in company acocunts

Section	Description
344	Exceptions from section 343
345	Power to increase financial limits
346	'Connected persons' etc.
347	Transactions under foreign law
351(1), (2), (5)(a)	Particulars in correspondence etc
363	Duty to deliver annual returns
364	Contents of annual return: general
364A	Contents of annual return: particulars of share capital and shareholders
365	Supplementary provisions: regulations and interpretation
384	Duty to appoint auditors
385	Appointment at general meeting at which accounts laid
387	Appointment by Secretary of State in default of appointment by company
388	Filling of casual vacancy
388A	Dormant company exempt from obligation to appoint auditors
389A	Rights to information
390	Right to attend company meetings etc.
390A	Remuneration of auditors
390B	Remuneration of auditors or their associates for non-audit work
391	Removal of auditors
391A	Rights of auditors who are removed or not re-appointed
392	Resignation of auditors

Section	Description
392A	Rights of resigning auditors
394	Statement by person ceasing to hold office as auditor
394A	Offences of failing to company with section 394
711	Public notice by registrar of receipt and issue of certain documents
720	Certain companies to publish periodical statement
Sch 3	Mandatory contents of prospectus
Sch 4	Form and content of company accounts
Sch 4A	Form and content of group accounts
Sch 5	Disclosure of information: related undertakings
Sch 6	Disclosure of information: emoluments and other benefits of directors and others
Sch 7	Matters to be dealt with in directors' report (except paras 2 to 2B, 7, and 8)
Sch 8	Exemptions for small and medium-sized companies
Sch 9	Special provisions for banking and insurance companies and groups (except paras 2(a) to (d), 3(c) to (e) and 10(1)(c))
Sch 10	Directors' report where accounts prepared in accordance with special provisions for banking or insurance companies or groups
Sch 10A	Parent and subsidiary undertakings: supplementary provisions

Chapter 20

COMPANIES INCORPORATED BY SPECIAL STATUTORY PROVISIONS

COMPANIES INCORPORATED BY SPECIAL STATUTORY PROVISIONS

Introduction

20.1 The Victorian age was the great era for establishing and expanding public utilities, including railways, water, gas and electricity. It was also the era that saw the development of harbour undertakings. These undertakings were set up as companies by private Act of Parliament in order to take advantage of corporate status. Many of the well known limited companies today were incorporated by their own Act of Parliament, for example LLoyd's of London and the Bank of England.

20.2 In order, to avoid the necessity of repeating in each private Act certain provisions relating to the constitution and management of these entities, which by their nature were usually similar, various statutes were passed to provide a standard set of provisions that could be applied where appropriate to these companies. These provisions are now contained in five statutes:

The Companies Clauses Consolidation Act 1845

20.3 The provisions of this Act apply to all companies incorporated by special Act of Parliament after 8th May 1845, except where the special Act expressly varies or exempts the company from complying with the *Companies Clauses Consolidation Act 1845*. The Act deals with:

- Share capital.
- Share transfers.
- Payment and non-payment of calls on share capital.
- Remedies against shareholders.
- Powers to borrow and lend money.
- General meetings.
- Directors' appointment and rotation.
- Directors' powers.
- Proceedings of directors.

- Auditors.
- Accountability of officers.
- Accounts.
- Dividends.
- Miscellaneous matters, such as notices.

The Companies Clauses Act 1863

20.4 Most of the *Companies Clauses Act 1863* applies to special statutory companies only where it is expressly included by the special Act incorporating the company. The *Companies Clauses Act 1863* deals with:

- Cancellation and surrender of shares.
- Raising additional capital.
- Name changes.

20.5 There are also provisions in the *Companies Clauses Act 1863* that concern the creation and issue of debenture stock, which apply to all companies incorporated by special Act of Parliament that have the power to raise money on mortgage or a bond.

The Companies Clauses Act 1869

20.6 This Act amends the *Companies Clauses Act 1863* in relation to the provisions that cover debentures.

The Companies Clauses Consolidation Act 1888

20.7 This Act amends the *Companies Clauses Consolidation Act 1845* concerning the provisions that cover proxies for voting at meetings.

The Statutory Companies (Redeemable Stock) Act 1915

20.8 The *Statutory Companies (Redeemable Stock) Act 1915* was passed to enable companies established by a special Act of Parliament that were permitted to carry on certain public works (such as a railway) to issue redeemable preference shares or debenture stock.

The Companies Act 1985

20.9 Although the statutes mentioned above determine the constitution of statutory companies, in addition certain provisions of the *Companies*

Act 1985 also apply to them, unless the company is in either of the following situations:

- The company was formed for a purpose other than carrying on a business to acquire gain for itself or its members.
- The company is exempted by a direction from the Secretary of State (or before him, the Board of Trade).

[CA 1985 Sec 718(2)(4)].

20.10 The effect of the two exemptions above is not to repeal the earlier Acts or the special Act incorporating the company. However, any part of those Acts that is inconsistent with the relevant provisions of the *Companies Act 1985* is suspended and, therefore, no longer applies. [CA 1985 Sec 718(5)].

20.11 The provisions of the *Companies Act 1985* that apply to statutory companies are identical to the provisions that apply to chartered companies and these are considered further in chapter 19.

Duty to keep accounting records

20.12 The directors of statutory companies are under an obligation under sections 115 and 119 of the *Companies Clauses Consolidation Act 1845* to appoint a bookkeeper to keep *"full and true accounts"* of all receipts and payments and of the matters to which these relate in books to be provided for the purpose. This obligation would still seem to arise because it is not inconsistent with the duty to keep proper accounting records included in the *Companies Act 1985* (see 'Manual of Accounting - volume I').

Duty to prepare financial statements

20.13 The duty in section 116 of the *Companies Clauses Consolidation Act 1845* to prepare financial statements is expressed in the following manner:

> *"The books of the company shall be balanced at the prescribed periods, and if no periods be prescribed, fourteen days at least before each ordinary meeting; and forthwith on the books being so balanced an exact balance sheet shall be made up, which shall exhibit a true statement of the capital stock, credits, and property of every description belonging to the company, and the debts due by the company, at the date of making such balance sheet, and a distinct view of the profit or loss which shall have arisen on the transactions of the company in the course of the preceding half year; and previously to each ordinary meeting*

such balance sheet shall be examined by the directors, or any three of their number, and shall be signed by the chairman or deputy chairman of the directors."

20.14 These requirements are, however, superseded by those of the *Companies Act 1985* in particular, the requirement of the *Companies Act 1985* that the financial statements should give a *"true and fair"* view. [CA 1985 Sch 22].

Duty to submit an annual return

20.15 A statutory company is placed under the same duty to submit an annual return as any normal limited company incorporated under the 'Manual of Accounting - volume I').

Appointment and renewal of auditors

20.16 The provisions of the *Companies Clauses Consolidation Act 1845* that concern the appointment and renewal of auditors would be difficult to comply with now. For example, there are provisions that:

- Require the election of a prescribed number of auditors and if no number is prescribed two auditors would be elected. [CCCA 1845 Sec 101].
- Require the auditor to have a shareholding in the company as qualification to be an auditor. [CCCA 1845 Sec 102].
- Require the rotation of one auditor each year. The outgoing auditor being eligible for re-election. [CCCA 1845 Sec 103].
- Empower the auditors to employ accountants to report on the financial statements. [CCCA 1845 Sec 108].

20.17 However, the provisions of the *Companies Clauses Consolidation Act 1845* are again superseded by the provisions of the *Companies Act 1985* and, consequently, the normal rules for companies apply (see 'Manual of Accounting - volume I'). [CA 1985 Sch 22].

Audit report

20.18 The audit report of special statutory companies will be the same as those used for normal companies limited by shares.

Chapter 21

INDUSTRIAL AND PROVIDENT SOCIETIES

Chapter 21

INDUSTRIAL AND PROVIDENT SOCIETIES

Background

21.1 In 1834 legislation was introduced to enable friendly societies to be established for any lawful purpose (see chapter 11). Various friendly societies were known as 'industrial and provident societies', because those who worked for, or subscribed to, such societies were entitled to a distribution of a proportion of the society's profits. The remaining profits had to be retained in the society or applied for 'provident' purposes, such as the relief of sick members. This distinctive type of operation led to societies becoming more widely known as 'co-operatives'. These friendly societies were unincorporated associations and were similar to partnerships, in that the liability of their members was unlimited.

21.2 The *Industrial and Provident Societies Act 1852* first specifically recognised and regulated such societies. A further Act of 1862 conferred incorporation on societies registered under it and limited the liability of their members. These two Acts were consolidated in the *Industrial and Provident Societies Act 1893* (now repealed), which was subject to further amending Acts until the present statutory framework was established. A co-operative society carrying on any industry, trade or business intended to be conducted for the benefit of the community may apply to be registered as an industrial and provident society under the *Industrial and Provident Societies Act 1965*.

21.3 Co-operative societies vary in size and function. Examples are:

- Workers' co-operatives.
- Consumer co-operatives.
- Housing co-operatives.
- Agricultural co-operatives.

Current legislation

21.4 The current legislative framework is set out in a series of Acts commencing with the *Industrial and Provident Societies Act 1965*, which is the principal regulating statute. In particular, this covers the following matters:

- Criteria for, and effect of, registration.

- Rules.
- Membership.
- Contracts.
- Accounts and annual return.
- Officers.
- Registers and books.
- Amalgamation, transfers of engagement and dissolution.

21.5 The *Industrial and Provident Societies Act 1967* deals with the borrowing powers of societies, whilst the *Friendly and Industrial and Provident Societies Act 1968* (so called because it originally covered friendly societies as well) makes further provision for their financial statements and audits. The latter is particularly important and covers:

- Record keeping requirements.
- Auditors' appointment and removal.
- Auditors' rights.
- Group accounts.

21.6 When these statutes were enacted they brought societies into line with the provisions applying to companies generally (see 'Manual of Accounting - volume I'). The changes effected by the *Companies Act 1985*, have not been reflected by any changes in the requirements imposed on individual societies. Where a society has a subsidiary or subsidiaries, which can be either an industrial and provident society or some other body corporate, the *Friendly and Industrial and Provident Societies Act 1968* lays down further requirements, and detailed rules have been made under it in respect of group accounts. These are contained in the *Industrial and Provident Societies (Group Accounts) Regulations 1969*, (SI 1969/1037), and are referred to as the 'Regulations' in this chapter.

21.7 The *Industrial and Provident Societies Acts of 1975 and 1978* provide for the following:

- An increase in the limit on the shareholding of individual members under the *Industrial and Provident Societies Act 1965*.

- An increase in the maximum deposits that a society can take from a depositor without being treated as carrying on a banking business.

Specialised co-operative activities

21.8 There are a number of specialised activities that a society may be involved in which may bring it within the scope of additional legislation. These additional legal requirements are usually encountered in connection with banking, insurance, housing, agricultural, horticultural and forestry societies which are considered below.

Banking business

21.9 There is no prohibition on a society carrying on a banking business provided that its share capital is not withdrawable. [IPSA 1965 Sec 7(1)]. However, a society will not be regarded as carrying on a banking business unless it accepts deposits in excess of £400 in total from any one depositor. [IPSA 1978, Sec 2(1); SI 1981/394].

21.10 If a society does accept such deposits, it would fall under the regulatory framework of the *Banking Act 1987* (see chapter 15). On the first Monday in February and August each year, all deposit accepting societies must make out a statement of their capital, and of their liabilities and assets as at the first day of the preceding month. [IPSA 1965 Sec 7(2), Sch 2]. This statement must be displayed in a conspicuous position in the society's registered office, and in every other office or place of business belonging to the society where banking business is carried on, until the next such Monday. [IPSA 1965 Sec 7(2)].

Insurance business

21.11 Societies may carry out insurance business and, if they do so, they are subject to the *Insurance Companies Act 1982*. The group accounting rules (paras 21.41 to 21.47) are modified in respect of such societies.

21.12 Societies that carry on industrial assurance business are 'industrial assurance companies' within the meaning of the *Industrial Assurance Acts 1923 to 1968* and, consequently, are subject to those Acts. Societies that carry on long-term insurance business would be subject to the provisions of the *Financial Services Act 1986* and would probably be regulated by LAUTRO (see chapters 16 and 26).

Housing associations

21.13 A society may be a housing association. These societies are considered in chapter 24.

Credit unions

21.14 These are special co-operative societies concerned with savings and loans and are dealt with in chapter 22.

Agricultural, horticultural and forestry societies

21.15 Where a society consists mainly of members who are involved in agriculture or horticulture or persons engaged in forestry (or organisations of such producers or persons), certain special provisions apply to them concerning the following matters:

- The ability to grant advances without security.

- Qualification for agricultural grants.

[IPSA 1965 Sec 12].

Charitable status

21.16 The purpose of a society may be charitable and this status entitles the society to certain privileges (see chapter 25). However, societies are not required to register under the *Charities Act 1960*. [ChA 1960 Sec 4(4)(a), Sch 2(g)].

Formation of societies

21.17 An industrial and provident society is a society (often a co-operative society) that has been registered and as a result incorporated under the *Industrial and Provident Societies Acts 1965 to 1978*. Whilst co-operative societies can be formed without being registered as industrial and provident societies, there are consequential disadvantages depending on what other legal form the co-operative takes. For example:

- A partnership.

  A partnership has the disadvantages of not possessing corporate status and must carry on business with a view to profit (see chapter 4). A co-operative may not satisfy this requirement, depending upon its aims and consequently it would have to be constituted in some other form. Furthermore, if a co-operative is formed as a partnership, it will be restricted to 20 members (see chapter 4).

- An unincorporated association.

  An unincorporated association has the disadvantages of not possessing corporate status. An unincorporated association that has as its objects the acquisition of gain is prohibited from becoming an industrial and provident society if the number of its members exceeds 20 (see chapter 9). However, if an unincorporated association is formed to carry out its purpose otherwise than for profit, there is no restriction on the number of members (see chapter 9). Even if a co-operative can be formed as an unincorporated association, it will be restricted to 20 members, where its business is carried on for gain.

- A company.

  An unlimited company registered under the *Companies Act 1985* is a fairly flexible business vehicle and could well be an appropriate form for a co-operative (see chapter 12). Other types of company will usually be inappropriate, because of restrictions on the transfer of share capital.

21.18 Consequently, co-operative societies are usually formed by registering an industrial and provident society in accordance with the *Industrial and Provident Societies Acts 1965 to 1978*.

Registration of societies

21.19 There are two categories of society eligible for registration:

- *Bona fide* co-operative societies. This does not include a society that carries on, or intend to carry on, business with the object of making profits to pay interest, dividends or bonuses on money invested with the society (or any other person). [IPSA 1965 Secs 1(1)(a), 1(2)(a), (1)(3)].
- Societies whose business is, or is intended to be, conducted for the community's benefit. There must be special reasons for the society to be registered under the *Industrial and Provident Societies Act 1965* rather than being registered as a company. [IPSA 1965 Secs 1(1)(a), 1(2)(b)].

21.20 An application to register a society must be made to the Registrar of Friendly Societies (see chapter 11) on Form A. This must be signed by seven members and the secretary of the society and must be sent to the Registrar with two printed copies of the society's rules. [IPSA 1965 Sec 2(1)(b)]. Societies frequently use specimen rules supplied by interested organisations and a lower fee is payable for registration where these are used. All societies registered prior to 1st January 1966 under previous legislation are deemed registered under the *Industrial and Provident Societies Act 1965*. [IPSA 1965 Sec 4].

21.21 A society will be registered if it complies with the following:

- The Registrar is satisfied that it is eligible for registration (see above). [IPSA 1965 Sec 1(1)(a)].

- Its rules contain provision for specified matters (see para 21.26). [IPSA 1965 Sec 1(1)(b)]. The rules must provide for the society's registered office to be situated in Great Britain or the Channel Islands. [IPSA 1965 Sec 1(1)(c)].

- It has seven or more members. [IPSA 1965 Sec 2(1)(a)].

- The Registrar does not consider that its name is undesirable. [IPSA 1965 Sec 5(1)]. The last word in the name of a society must be 'limited' unless the Registrar is satisfied that its objects are wholly charitable or benevolent. [IPSA 1965 Secs 5(2)(5)].

21.22 There are special provisions in respect of those societies that carry on the business of banking, insurance, or of providing housing (see paras 21.8 to 21.15).

21.23 Where the Registrar is satisfied that a society has complied with all the statutory requirements outlined above, he must issue the society with an acknowledgement of registration. This is conclusive evidence that the society is properly registered. [IPSA 1965 Sec 2(3)].

21.24 The principal effects of registration are:

- The society becomes a corporate body and this confers the following benefits:

  □ The right to sue and be sued in its own name.

  □ Perpetual succession (that is the society continues to exist regardless of changes in its members).

  □ Limited liability.

  □ Power to hold land.

- All property held on trust for the society prior to registration vests in the society.

[IPSA 1965 Sec 3].

21.25 The Registrar of Companies also maintains an index of societies registered under the *Industrial and Provident Societies Act 1965* or the *Industrial and Provident Societies Act (Northern Ireland) 1969*. [CA 1985 Sec 714(1)(g)].

Constitution

21.26 An industrial and provident society's constitution is contained in its rules. Schedule 1 of the *Industrial and Provident Societies Act 1965* lays down in detail the matters that a society's rules must deal with. These include the matters listed below:

- The society's name.
- The society's objects.
- The society's registered office.
- The society's rules in respect of:
  - Members' admission
  - Holding meetings, voting rights and the alteration of rules.
  - Appointing and removing a committee (whatever called).
  - Appointing and removing managers or other officers and their powers and remuneration.
  - The maximum shareholdings of any individual member.
  - Whether it can make loans or receive deposits from members or others and, if so, on what terms.
  - Whether its shares are transferable or withdrawable and, if so, on what terms.
  - The audit of its financial statements by one or more auditors appointed by it under the *Friendly and Industrial and Provident Societies Act 1968*.
  - Whether members can leave the society and, if so, how.
  - Provisions governing deceased or bankrupt members.
  - The mode of application of its profits.
  - Custody and use of its seal.
  - Whether and, if so, how its funds can be invested.

21.27 In addition societies may make any other lawful rules. [IPSA 1965 Sec 13(4)].

21.28 A society's members are bound by the rules in the same way as shareholders in a company are bound by the company's Memorandum and Articles of Association under section 14(1) of the *Companies Act 1985*..

Share capital

21.29 The legislation does not regulate the share capital of societies very extensively. Co-operatives usually regard the holding of their shares as a form of membership. The rules frequently, therefore, limit members to holding a single share each. In accordance with the principle that dividends are paid by reason of purchases from, or work put into, a society, the dividend payable on shares will frequently only be a nominal amount. Furthermore, the share capital of a society will fluctuate, depending upon the number of members and, consequently, the number of shares issued. Societies do not have to authorise the maximum share capital that may be issued, although they may do so if they wish. Members of a society are not permitted to acquire a shareholding in the society in excess of £10,000. [IPSA 1965 Sec 6(1) (as amended by IPSA 1975 Sec 1(1)); SI 1981/394]. The principal exception to this is where the shareholding is owned by another registered society. The rules of a society must specify the maximum share capital that it has adopted.

21.30 The legislation only refers to two types of share capital:

- Withdrawable shares.

  These are shares that the rules of a society permit members to withdraw. Members are entitled to be paid the value of the shares withdrawn. These may not be issued by a banking co-operative (see para 21.9).

- Transferable shares.

  The rules of a society must specify whether shares are to be transferable from one person to another. [IPSA 1965 1 Sch 9]. It is unusual for rules to permit this. If they do, however, the rules must provide for a form of transfer, registration of the transfer and the consent of the committee.

21.31 There is no reason in principle why other classes of shares should not be issued by a society, such as preference shares or deferred shares if the rules permit. In addition, there is no reason why, in addition to share capital, a society should not raise finance by loan capital if the rules permit.

Duty to keep accounting records

21.32 Every registered society must keep proper books of account relating to its transactions, assets and liabilities as are necessary in order to give a true and fair view of the state of the society's affairs and to explain its transactions. [FIPSA 1968 Sec 1(1)(a), 2]. Books of account may be kept in either bound books or in some other form. [FIPSA

1968 Sec 2(1)]. If they are kept in another format, adequate precautions must be taken to guard against falsification and to facilitate their discovery. [FIPSA 1968 Sec 2(2)].

Duty to establish and maintain a system of control

21.33 Every registered society must establish and maintain a satisfactory system of control of its books of account, cash holdings and all receipts and remittances. [FIPSA 1968 Sec 1(1)(b)].

Duty to prepare financial statements

Revenue account

21.34 Every society must prepare a revenue account for each year of account. Two alternative forms of presentation are permitted:

- A revenue account dealing with the affairs of the society as a whole. [FIPSA 1968 Sec 3(2)(a)]. This must give a true and fair view of the income and expenditure for the period to which it relates. [FIPSA 1968 Sec 3(1)(a)].
- Two or more revenue accounts dealing separately with particular businesses conducted by the society. [FIPSA 1968 Sec 3(2)(b)]. However, each revenue account must give a true and fair view of the income and expenditure in respect of the business to which it relates. [FIPSA 1968 Sec 3(1)(a)]. Also, when they are viewed together, they must give a true and fair view of the income and expenditure of the society as a whole. [FIPSA 1968 Sec 3(3)].

Balance sheet

21.35 The legislation does not expressly require the preparation of a balance sheet, but this is implied by the regulations that require the society's balance sheet to be audited. Furthermore, every balance sheet of a society must give a true and fair view of the state of the society's affairs at the balance sheet date. [FIPSA 1968 Sec 3(4)].

Duty to prepare consolidated financial statements

21.36 Where at the end of a year of account a registered society has subsidiaries, it must prepare consolidated financial statements for that year. These financial statements must deal with the state of affairs and income and expenditure of the society and its subsidiaries. [FIPSA 1968 Sec 13(1)].

21.37 There are two sets of rules to determine whether a body is a 'subsidiary' in this context, depending upon whether the potential subsidiary is a company (which for this purpose includes any body corporate other than an industrial and provident society) or another society [FIPSA 1968 Sec 15].

Companies

21.38 The rules are closely based on those that determine whether a company was deemed a subsidiary of another under the *Companies Act 1985* before it was amended by the *Companies Act 1989*. Consequently, if a parent owns more than half of the equity share capital of the company or controls the composition of its board, that company is a subsidiary [FIPSA 1968 15(1)(2)]. This section of the *Friendly and Industrial and Provident Societies Act 1968* appears not to have been amended subsequently after the implementation of the changes in definitions brought about by the *Companies Act 1989*. Therefore, the principal difference of the *Friendly and Industrial and Provident Societies Act 1968* compared to the provision of the *Companies Act 1985* (as amended by the *Companies Act 1989*) is that the definition of a subsidiary in the *Friendly and Industrial and Provident Societies Act 1968* depends on legal ownership rather than control. In addition, the *Companies Act 1989* regulations include three additional reasons for treating an undertaking as a subsidiary which do not appear in the *Friendly and Industrial and Provident Societies Act 1968* as follows:

- Right to exercise a dominant influence via a control contract.

  There is no equivalent provision to that of section 258(2)(c) of the *Companies Act 1985*.

- Control pursuant to an agreement with the shareholders.

  There is no equivalent provision to section 258(2)(d) of the *Companies Act 1985* which says a subsidiary arises where a member of the undertaking can control alone, pursuant to an agreement with other shareholders, a majority of the voting rights of an undertaking.

- Dominant influence or management on a unified basis.

  There is no equivalent provision to section 258(4) of the *Companies Act 1985* whereby a subsidiary relationship can arise when the investing undertaking has a participating interest in another undertaking and actually exercises a dominant influence over it or manages it on a unified basis.

Societies

21.39 The legislation deems subsidiaries in the same way as for companies under the unamended *Companies Act 1985* as explained above, subject to the following differences.

- Terminology.

  Instead of referring to a director in respect of a board of directors the provisions refer to members of the committee. [FIPSA 1968 Sec 15(5)].

- Control.

  Control is determined not by references to holding equity share capital, but by the ability to exercise a majority of the votes to which members of the 'subsidiary' society are entitled. [FIPSA 1968 Sec 15(5)]. This is similar to the change to the *Companies Act 1985* brought about by the *Companies Act 1989*.

- Control of the committee.

  For a company there is deemed to be power to appoint a director where the company actually holds that directorship, whereas for a society it is necessary not only to be a member of the committee, but also to be able to appoint and remove the remaining members of that committee or appoint and remove sufficient members as, together with itself, would constitute a majority. [FIPSA 1968 Sec 15(6)]. This is similar to the new requirement in section 258(2)(b) of the amended *Companies Act 1985*.

21.40 Consolidated financial statements are not required for a society, however, in the following two situations:

- Where the society is, at the end of its accounting year, the wholly owned subsidiary of another body corporate incorporated in Great Britain. [FIPSA 1968 Sec 14(1)]. It will be deemed wholly-owned if it has no members except that other body corporate and the wholly-owned subsidiaries of that body and its or their nominees. [FIPSA 1968 Sec 14(4)].

- Where the Chief Registrar of Friendly Societies approves the opinion of the society's committee that consolidated financial statements need not deal with a subsidiary because one or more of the following reasons exists:

  - ☐ It would be impracticable.

- ☐ It would be of no real value to members of the society, in view of the insignificant amounts involved.
- ☐ It would involve expense or delay out of proportion to the value to members.
- ☐ The result would be misleading.
- ☐ The result would be harmful to the business of the society or any of its subsidiaries.
- ☐ The business of the society and that of the subsidiary are so different that they cannot reasonably be treated as a single undertaking.

[FIPSA 1968 Sec 14(2)].

Where the committee's opinion is approved by the Chief Registrar in respect of all of a society's subsidiaries, consolidated financial statements are not required. [FIPSA 1968 Sec 14(3)].

Form and content of consolidated financial statements

21.41 Consolidated financial statements must give a true and fair view of the state of affairs and income and expenditure of the society and its subsidiaries dealt with as a whole, so far as concerns the society's members. [FIPSA 1968 Sec 13(2)]. The consolidated financial statements should normally comprise:

- ■ A consolidated balance sheet.

  This should deal with the state of the society's affairs and subsidiaries' affairs dealt with in those accounts.

- ■ A consolidated revenue account.

  This should deal with the society's income and expenditure and the income and expenditure of those subsidiaries.

[FIPSA 1968 Sec 13(3); SI 1969/1037].

21.42 However, if the society's committee considers that some other form (other than consolidated financial statements) is better for the purpose of presenting the same or equivalent information, so that it may be readily appreciated by the society's members, group accounts may be prepared in that other form. [FIPSA 1968 Sec 13(3); SI 1969/1037]. In particular, group accounts may consist of the following:

- More than one set of consolidated accounts dealing respectively with the society and one group of subsidiaries and with other groups of subsidiaries.

- Separate accounts dealing with each of the subsidiaries to be dealt with in the group accounts.

- Statements expanding the information about those subsidiaries in the society's own accounts.

- Any combination of the three bases above.

[FIPSA 1968 Sec 13(3); SI 1969/1037].

Disclosure requirements

21.43 Consolidated financial statements must comply with Schedule 1 to the Regulations. [SI 1969/1037]. The requirements are very detailed and differ from those now contained in the *Companies Act 1985*.

Balance sheet

21.44 The balance sheet must disclose:

- Share capital.

  The amount paid up on shares and (except for withdrawable shares) the amount of issued shares.

- Reserves, provisions, liabilities and assets.

  These must be classified under appropriate headings for the society and its subsidiaries' businesses. If any heading is not material it can be included under another heading. Furthermore, where any asset within one heading cannot be separated from those of another, they can be included together.

- The general nature of liabilities and assets.

- Fixed, current and other assets must be separately identified.

- The method of arriving at fixed asset headings.

- The following must be disclosed under separate headings:

  - ☐ Preliminary expenses.

  - ☐ Material reserves and provisions (other than for depreciation, renewals or diminution in value).

- ☐ Quoted and unquoted investments respectively.
- ☐ Bank loans and overdrafts.
- ☐ Other loans.
- ☐ Any amount set aside to prevent undue fluctuations in tax charges.
- ☐ Any security given.

Notes to the balance sheet

21.45 Certain matters must be disclosed in either a note to the balance sheet or in an annexed statement or report. These matters are detailed below:

- ■ Fixed assets.
  - ☐ Provision for their replacement.
  - ☐ Any valuation particulars.
  - ☐ Acquisitions and disposals.
  - ☐ Whether any land held is freehold or leasehold.
- ■ Stock and work-in-progress.

  Where these are material the basis for their computation.
- ■ Current assets and unquoted investments.

  Whether the committee considers the stated value exceeds the realisable value.
- ■ Quoted investments.

  Market value where different from that stated and Stock Exchange value where lower than the market value.
- ■ Reserves and provisions.

  Where these are separately disclosed (see para 24.1) in the balance sheet and material increases or decreases have occurred since the previous year end, the source of the increases and the application of the decreases.

- Contingent liabilities.

  The general nature of any contingent liability not provided for and its estimated value if material.

- Capital expenditure.

  Contracts for capital expenditure (not provided for) and authorised capital expenditure (not contracted) of both the society and any subsidiaries.

- UK corporation tax.

  The basis of computation.

- Subsidiaries.

  Their names, specifying those that are not dealt with in the consolidated financial statements and the reasons for excluding them.

- Comparative figures.

Revenue account

21.46 The revenue account must disclose the following detail:

- Fixed assets.

  Any provision for depreciation, renewals or diminution in value (stating the latter separately).

- Plant and machinery.

  Material amounts charged to revenue for hire.

- UK corporation tax charge.

- Interest on bank loans, overdrafts or other loans to the society or its subsidiaries.

- Income from quoted and unquoted investments respectively.

- Rents (if they form a substantial part of revenue).

- Fees and expenses paid to the committee's members or the society's management.

- The auditor's remuneration (including expenses) for the society and its subsidiaries.

Notes to the revenue account

21.47 Certain matters must be disclosed in either a note to the balance sheet or in an annexed statement or report. These include the following matters:

- Turnover.

  This must be stated with the method of ascertaining it. Banking and discounting business must be excluded.

- Depreciation.

  The method of providing for depreciation or replacement of fixed assets must be stated if made other than by a charge or provision. If no provision is made that fact must be stated.

- Basis of the UK corporation tax charge and certain other tax details.

- Any items materially affected by:

  - Transactions of a sort not usually undertaken by the society and its subsidiaries.

  - Circumstances of an exceptional or non-recurrent nature.

  - Any change in the basis of accounting.

Duty to submit an annual return

21.48 A society must send to the Chief Registrar of Friendly Societies a return relating to its affairs, usually no later than 31st March. [IPSA 1965 Sec 39]. There are detailed requirements that relate to the period the return should cover. In general, the return must be made up to include the financial statements prepared in respect of the year of account to which the return relates. [IPSA 1965 Sec 39]. The annual return must include the following information:

- The revenue accounts for the year.

- A balance sheet at the end of the year.

- Consolidated financial statements, where required.

- A copy of the auditors report on the financial statements.

21.49 The annual return should not, however, contain any accounts other than the revenue accounts, unless they have been audited. [FIPSA 1968 Sec 11(2)(b)].

Appointment and removal of auditors

21.50 A society must appoint one or more qualified auditors in each year of account to audit its financial statements for that year [FIPSA 1968 Sec 4(1)]. Where a society is exempt from this requirement it may instead appoint two or more unqualified persons, subject to any direction given by the Chief Registrar of Friendly Societies. [FIPSA 1968 Sec 4(5)].

21.51 A society may be exempt from the above requirement in any year of account if the following criteria apply:

- Its receipts and payments in respect of the preceding year of account did not exceed £5,000 in aggregate.
- The number of members at the end of that year did not exceed 500.
- The value of its assets at the end of that year did not exceed £5,000 in aggregate.

[FIPSA 1968 Sec 4(2)]

21.52 These limits may be changed by regulation and so care should be taken to ensure that they have not recently been changed.

21.53 There are detailed provisions that specify the procedures to be adopted when appointing or removing an auditor. These are, in general terms, similar to those for auditors appointed under the *Companies Act 1985*. [FIPSA 1968 Secs 5 to 8].

Auditors' rights

21.54 The auditors have the following rights:

- Access at all times to the society's books, deeds and accounts and to all other documents relating to its affairs. [FIPSA 1968 Sec 9(5)(a)].
- To require from the officers such information and explanations as they think necessary to perform their duties. [FIPSA 1968 Sec 9(5)(b)].

- To attend any general meeting and to receive all notices of, and other communications relating to, general meetings that any member is entitled to receive. [FIPSA 1968 Sec 9(7)(a)].

- To be heard at any meeting that they attend on any part of the business of the meeting that concerns them as auditors. [FIPSA 1968 Sec 9(7)(b)].

Audit report

21.55 The auditors of a society must make a report to the society on the accounts examined by them and on the revenue accounts and the balance sheet for the year of account. [FIPSA 1968 Sec 9(1)].

21.56 The audit report must state the following:

- Whether the revenue accounts and the balance sheet for that year comply with the *Industrial and Provident Societies Acts 1965 to 1978.* [FIPSA 1968 Sec 9(2)].

- Whether the revenue accounts give a true and fair view (in accordance with the statutory requirements) of the income and expenditure of the society as a whole for the year. In addition, if revenue accounts have been prepared separately in respect of any particular business they must be reported on and give a true and fair view. [FIPSA 1968 Sec 9(2)(a)].

- Whether the balance sheet gives a true and fair view (in accordance with the statutory requirements) either of the state of affairs of the society or, as the case may require, of its assets and current liabilities and the resulting balances of its funds. [FIPSA 1968 Sec 9(2)(b)].

- Where consolidated financial statements have been prepared, whether they have been properly prepared in accordance with the *Industrial and Provident Societies Acts 1965 to 1978* and whether in their opinion those financial statements give a true and fair view of the state of affairs and income and expenditure of the society and its subsidiaries. [FIPSA 1968 Sec 13(2)].

- If the auditors have not received satisfactory explanations on any of the matters they are required to investigate and form an opinion on. These matters are whether:

  - ☐ The society has kept proper books of account.

  - ☐ The society has maintained a satisfactory system of control over its transactions.

- ☐ The revenue accounts and any other accounts being reported on and the balance sheet are in agreement with the books of account

- ■ The auditors must, however, find that there has been a failure to comply with these requirements. [FIPSA 1968 Sec 9(4)].

21.57 Guidance on reporting to industrial and provident societies is given in the ICAEW's Members' Handbook statement, 'Auditors' reports - registered friendly and industrial and provident societies' (MH 3.910). Examples for the suggested wording for an unqualified industrial and provident society audit report are:

An individual society's financial statements

REPORT OF THE AUDITORS TO THE MEMBERS OF THE [NAME OF INDUSTRIAL AND PROVIDENT SOCIETY]

We have audited the financial statements on pages [] to [] in accordance with Auditing Standards.

In our opinion the financial statements give a true and fair view of the state of the affairs of the society at [date] and of its excess of [income over expenditure/expenditure over income] and source and application of funds for the [period] then ended and comply with the Friendly and Industrial and Provident Societies Act 1968, the Industrial and Provident Societies Acts 1965 to 1978.

[Name of the firm]

Chartered Accountants,

[Address].

[Date of report].

A group's financial statements

REPORT OF THE AUDITORS TO THE MEMBERS OF THE [NAME OF INDUSTRIAL AND PROVIDENT SOCIETY]

We have audited the financial statements on pages [] to [] in accordance with Auditing Standards.

In our opinion the financial statements give a true and fair view of the state of the affairs of the society and of the group at [date] and of the excess of [income over expenditure/ expenditure over income] and source and application of funds of the group for the [period] then ended and comply with the Friendly and Industrial and Provident Societies Act 1968, Industrial and Provident Societies Acts 1965 to 1978 and the Industrial and Provident Societies (Group Accounts) Regulations 1969.

[Name of the firm]

Chartered Accountants,

[Address].

[Date of report].

Remuneration of auditors

21.58 Maximum rates of remuneration to be paid by societies for the audit of their financial statements may be prescribed by regulations. [FIPSA 1968 Sec 10(1)]. However, none has yet been made.

Chapter 22

CREDIT UNIONS

Chapter 22

CREDIT UNIONS

Background

22.1 The concept of the credit union is still relatively unfamiliar in the UK, although credit unions are commonly encountered elsewhere in Europe and in the US. Essentially, a credit union is a special form of co-operative society, which takes deposits from members in order to lend the money back to some of its members. In many ways they are like the original building societies, with members expecting to be net depositors for part of the time and net borrowers at other times. The main difference between credit unions and building societies is that the purpose of loans made by credit unions is usually for some form of consumer purchase.

22.2 Credit unions are, therefore, an alternative to a bank or other savings institution. They are usually established to help poorer people and, in particular, they aim to protect people from moneylenders who might charge excessive rates of interest. Frequently, credit unions now assist people in getting out of debt repayment crises with credit card companies. Accordingly, credit unions try to provide loans to members at low rates of interest. These low rates of interest can be achieved by using voluntary administration to run the credit union and by paying only a low rate of interest on the deposits that members invest. Because there is usually little or no security given for loans made to members there can be a high risk of default. Consequently, the statutory framework for credit unions outlined below ensures that there is a 'common bond' between members. For example, members of a particular credit union might live in the same community or work for the same company.

22.3 Although credit unions take deposits from members, they are regarded as exempt persons as specified in Schedule 2 to the *Banking Act 1987* for the purposes of carrying on a deposit taking business. Consequently, they are not subject to regulations contained in the *Banking Act 1987*. This is a general prohibition on credit unions taking deposits unless the deposit is from a person by way of subscription for its shares. [CUA 1979 Sec 8(1)].

22.4 Before 1979, it was possible to establish a credit union as a limited company, industrial and provident society, or unincorporated association. However, since the enactment of the *Credit Unions Act 1979* any society that wishes to, or continues to, use the name 'credit union' must register as a credit union under the *Industrial and Provident Societies Act 1965*, provided that it fulfils the conditions laid down in the *Credit Unions Act 1979*. The legislation governing industrial and provident societies (see chapter 21), therefore, applies to such credit unions, except for the modifications contained in the *Credit Unions Act 1979*. This legislation was enacted to protect credit union members, because they frequently have little knowledge of financial matters and are particularly susceptible to the risk of fraud or error in the handling of their money by a credit union's management.

22.5 The supervisory system contained in the *Credit Unions Act 1979* covers the following matters with regard to the regulation of credit unions:

- Registration as a credit union under the *Industrial And Provident Societies Act 1965*.
- Name to include 'credit union'.
- Constitution.
- Members' numbers and rights.
- Money raising.
- Power to hold land for united purposes.
- Investments.
- Profit computation and application.
- Insurance against fraud and other dishonesty.
- Power to protect depositors through arrangements with insurance companies, or other credit unions.
- The Registrar of Friendly Societies' powers.
- Amalgamation, transfers of engagements and conversions.
- Audit of financial statements.
- Prohibition on owning subsidiaries.
- Management.

22.6 There is no specific guidance, however, in the legislation on how to account for, or audit, a credit union.

The Registrar of Friendly Societies

22.7 The functions of the Registrar of Friendly Societies are considered in chapter 21. The Registrar has been given additional powers with regard to credit unions to complement those given in respect of his responsibilities for industrial and provident societies (see chapter 21). These additional powers are to ensure that the credit union's members and potential members are adequately protected and include the following matters:

- The Registrar may require a credit union to give him a financial statement or periodic financial statement in such form and containing such information as he may require. [CUA 1979 Sec 17(2)].
- The Registrar may appoint an inspector to investigate a credit union's affairs. [CUA 1979 Sec 18(1)].
- The Registrar may call a meeting of the credit union's members to consider its affairs. [CUA 1979 Sec 18(1)].
- The Registrar may issue a direction prohibiting or restricting a credit union from:
  - ☐ Borrowing money.
  - ☐ Accepting new subscriptions.
  - ☐ Lending money.
  - ☐ Repaying share capital.

  This power may be exercised where the Registrar considers it necessary, having regard to the interests of all the credit union's members or potential members and provided the Treasury agrees. [CUA 1979 Sec 19(1)].
- The Registrar has powers to cancel or suspend a credit union's registration and to petition for its winding up. [CUA 1979 Sec 20].

Registration of credit unions

22.8 The *Credit Union Act 1979* provides that a society may register as a credit union under the *Industrial and Provident Societies Act 1965* if it satisfies the Chief Registrar of Friendly Societies that its objects, membership and rules comply with that Act's requirements.

Objects

22.9 The society's objects can only include the following:

- Promoting thrift among the society's members by accumulating their savings.
- Creating sources of credit to benefit the society's members at a fair and reasonable rate of interest.
- Using and controlling members' savings for their mutual benefit.
- Members' training and education in the wise use of money and in the management of their financial affairs.

[CUA 1979 Secs 1(1)(a), 1(2)(a), 1(3)].

Membership

22.10 A leading principle in establishing credit unions is that they should lend to members on the basis of the knowledge that members have of each other, rather than on other bases that might, for example, depend upon a member's status. The *Credit Unions Act 1979* accordingly provides that a specific qualification for admission to a society must be included in its rules. This qualification must apply regardless of any other qualifications that may also be included in the rules. The purpose for requiring such a qualification is to ensure that a 'common bond' exists between the society's members. [CUA 1979 Sec 2(b)].

22.11 Appropriate qualifications for admission that are listed in the *Credit Union Act 1979* are noted below:

- Following a particular occupation.
- Residing in a particular locality.
- Being employed in a particular locality.
- Being employed by a particular employer.
- Being a member of a *bona fide* organisation or otherwise being associated with the society's members for a purpose other than forming a society registered as a credit union.
- Any other qualifications approved by the Chief Registrar of Friendly Societies.

[CUA 1979 Sec 1(4)].

22.12 There are two situations when a credit union's rules may allow people to become members who do not satisfy the test of a 'common bond':

- Where the person is a member of the same household and is a relative of a person who qualified directly as a credit union's member. [CUA 1979 Sec 1(6)].

- Where the person ceases to qualify for credit union membership (for example, by leaving the locality, or by leaving a certain employer). [CUA 1979 Sec 5(5)].

22.13 Different interpretations of this membership requirement led the Registrar of Friendly Societies to issue a Guidance Note in April 1986. This guidance sets out what the Registry looks for in deciding whether, as a consequence of the membership qualification, a 'common bond' exists between the society's members and states that the critical test is whether:

"... the particular features of the proposed union [are] such that there is a reasonable expectation that it will be able and willing to safeguard properly the money of members placed with it ..."

Constitution

22.14 A credit union's constitution is found in its rules. Schedule 1 to the *Credit Unions Act 1979* sets out certain matters that must be provided for in a society's rules. These matters include:

- Its name.

- Its objects.

- Its registered office.

- The qualifications for, and the terms of, admission to membership including any special provision for members to be insured in relation to their shares.

- The mode of holding meetings, including the quorum necessary for business to be transacted.

- The mode of making, altering or rescinding rules.

- The appointment and removal of a committee (whatever called) managers and other officers, with their respective powers and remuneration.

- The maximum amount of the interest that a member may hold in the credit union's shares.

- How shares may be withdrawn and the balance due on them paid.
- How and in what circumstances loans are to be made to, and repaid by, members.
- Custody and use of the society's seal.
- Audit of financial statements by one or more appointed auditors.
- Withdrawal of members from the society and any claims arising.
- Termination of membership.
- The society's dissolution.

Distributions

22.15 There are a number of controls imposed on computing and applying a credit union's profit or loss. In general terms, these controls reduce members' freedom to make distributions by requiring the creation of a general reserve and by restricting the proportion of any surplus that can be used for 'social, cultural and charitable purposes'.

Profit or loss

22.16 All operating expenses in an accounting year must be deducted from the credit union's profit (or added to its loss). These deductions include payments of interest, depreciation, tax and provisions for bad debts. However, no provision for dividends to members is permitted to be made out to these profits before the provisions in paragraphs 22.17 and 22.18 are complied with. [CUA 1979 Sec 14(1)]. The result for the year is then added to, or deducted from, the revenue account.

General reserve

22.17 Once profits have been calculated, a transfer to or from the general reserve may have to be made. The reserve must be at least 10 per cent of the credit union's total assets, but cannot be more than 20 per cent of those assets. If the reserve stands at less than 10 per cent of assets, then at least 20 per cent of the current year's profits must be transferred to it. If, however, the reserve stands at more than 20 per cent of assets, the surplus must be transferred from the general reserve to the revenue account. Provided that the general reserve is between 10 per cent and 20 per cent of total assets, the credit union in general meeting may freely transfer any amount from a particular year's profits to the general reserve and from the general reserve to the revenue account. [CUA 1979 Sec 14(2)].

Compulsory distribution

22.18 The balance on the revenue account after the adjustments referred to above is available for distribution. At least 90 per cent of the revenue account's balance *must* be distributed as the general meeting decides between:

- The members as a dividend of not more than eight per cent on their paid up shares.
- The members as a rebate proportionate to interest paid or due on loans to the society during that accounting year.
- 'Social, cultural or charitable purposes' provided that a dividend of at least three per cent has been paid on shares. However, not more than 10 per cent of the revenue account balance may be distributed in this way and only after a dividend of not less than 3 per cent has been paid on all paid-up shares.

[CUA 1979 Secs 14(3) to (5)].

22.19 The requirement to establish a general reserve, however, is not as onerous as it may first appear. Up to 10 per cent of the balance available for distribution may be left unallocated in the revenue account after adjustment with the general reserve. In addition, the amounts to be distributed may be placed in funds earmarked for that purposes (as mentioned in the last two points above) to be expended from time to time in the future. [CUA 1979 Sec 14(6)].

Accounting and audit requirements

22.20 Credit unions are subject to the general rules that apply to industrial and provident societies (see chapter 21) in respect of:

- Requirements for accounting records (see chapter 21 para 21.32).
- Requirements for financial statements (see chapter 21 paras 21.34 and 21.35). There is no requirement for consolidated financial statements to be prepared, because a credit union is not permitted to have any subsidiaries under section 15 of the *Friendly and Industrial and Provident Societies Act 1968*. [CUA 1979 Sec 26].
- Requirement for annual returns (see chapter 21 para 21.48).
- Appointments and removal of auditors (see chapter 21 paras 21.50 to 21.53).
- Auditors' rights (see chapter 21 para 21.54).

- The audit report (see chapter 21 paras 21.55 to 21.57). However, a credit union may in certain circumstances display interim accounts at its registered office without having them audited. [CUA 1979 Sec 24].

- Auditors' remuneration (see chapter 21 para 21.58).

Audit Report

22.21 The wording for an unqualified credit union audit report would be similar to the one given for Industrial and Provident Societies in chapter 21 para 21.55.

Chapter 23

BUILDING SOCIETIES

Annex

Chapter 23

BUILDING SOCIETIES

Background

23.1 Building societies are mutual institutions incorporated under a succession of statutes, though their roots were among the incorporated associations of the nineteenth century. The associations were made up of people who pooled their savings together to buy land and build houses for themselves (not unlike modern 'self-build' schemes). Regulation of these societies became essential because of the size of the funds they held and the risks this entailed. Accordingly, the *Building Societies Act 1874* was passed. It provided that any society established to raise, by members' subscriptions, a stock or fund in order to make secured advances to members by way of mortgage had to become incorporated under that Act. Such societies were subject to a detailed regulatory code, which was extensively amended, and the system of regulation was completed by the *Building Societies Act 1894*.

23.2 Further restrictions were placed on societies by the *Building Societies Act 1939*, which included regulations governing the type of security that was acceptable when advances were made. The *Building Societies Act 1960* placed restrictions on the power of building societies to make advances and the *Building Societies Act 1962* consolidated the above legislation.

23.3 For more than 20 years the 1962 Act appeared to serve the movement well. With the exception of one or two spectacular collapses (the Wakefield and Grays societies were the most significant) building societies maintained their high reputation in the financial market, attracting savings from a largely unsophisticated public, advancing money on first mortgages and investing surplus funds in government securities.

23.4 In the early 1980s, however, the financial markets opened up, so that building societies' traditional sources of business were open to competition. For example, banks started actively marketing mortgages, the UK government's privatisation policy sought to turn ordinary savers into active investors and many foreign financial institutions (mainly from Europe, the US and Japan) saw the attraction of the UK as an additional base of operations. Building societies, therefore, saw the need to be more commercial in their approach in order to survive. They needed to broaden the range of their operations to introduce savings and mortgage products that differentiated them from their competitors. In addition, they needed to move into other financial service areas that were currently closed to them.

The Building Societies Act 1986

23.5 The *Building Societies Act 1986* extended the powers available to building societies while at the same time strengthening the regulatory regime. The *Building Societies Act 1986* provides *inter alia* for the following matters:

- The establishment of a Building Societies Commission ('Commission') to regulate societies and the determination of its powers.
- The establishment of a Building Societies Investor Protection Board and Investor Protection Fund.
- The regulation of societies' establishment, constitution and management.
- The regulation of societies' powers to raise funds, invest in advances, loans and other assets and provide services.
- The introduction of a stricter duty to keep accounting records and to maintain systems of internal control, inspection and report together with more stringent requirements for accounts and their audit.
- Provision for a society's dissolution, winding up, merger or transfer of business to a limited company.

The Building Societies Commission

23.6 The Commission is a body corporate established by statute under the Treasury's control. It is composed of between four and ten members, under a Chairman, who is known as the First Commissioner.

23.7 The general functions of the Commission are as follows:

- To promote the protection by each building society of the investments of its shareholders and depositors.
- To promote building societies' financial stability generally.
- To secure that building societies' principal purpose remains that of raising funds, primarily from their members, for making advances to members secured upon land for their residential use.
- To administer the system of statutory regulation of building societies.

- To advise and make recommendations to the Treasury or other government departments on any matter relating to building societies.

[BSA 1986 Sec 1(4)].

23.8 Specific functions are provided in the appropriate sections of the *Building Societies Act 1986*. Section 1(5) gives the Commission the power to do anything calculated to facilitate, or incidental or conducive to the discharge of its functions, which makes it one of the most powerful regulators in the UK financial scene.

The Investor Protection Scheme

23.9 The Building Societies Investor Protection Board has been established to hold, manage and apply the Building Societies Investor Protection Fund. The purpose of this fund is to compensate investors when a building society becomes insolvent and it is financed in part from levies on the building societies themselves. The detailed provisions relating to investor protection are contained in Part IV of the *Building Societies Act 1986*.

Establishment

23.10 As mentioned above, a society may only be established in order to raise funds from its members to lend to other members, those loans being secured on land for the members' residential use. [BSA 1986 Sec 5(1)]. A society is 'established' under the *Building Societies Act 1986* when it has complied with the requirements summarised below. It is 'incorporated' when it is registered by the Central Office of the Registry of Friendly Societies. Building societies incorporated under the repealed legislation are deemed to be registered and, therefore, incorporated under the *Building Societies Act 1986*. [BSA 1986 Sec 5(4)]. Ten or more people may establish a society by sending to the Central Office four copies (signed by at least ten of those people) of its memorandum and rules. The memorandum reflects the society's purpose or principal purpose and the extent of its powers, which must comply with the *Building Societies Act 1986* requirements. The rules, which must also comply with the Act's requirements, govern the regulation of the society. Changes to the memorandum or the rules require the passing of a special resolution of members.

Constitution

23.11 A society's constitution is found in its rules. Paragraph 3(4) of Schedule 2 to the *Building Societies Act 1986* includes a table specifying certain matters that must be provided in a society's rules. These matters include:

- Its name.
- The address of its principal office.
- How the society's stock or funds is, or are, to be raised.
- How the terms on which shares are to be issued are to be determined and shareholders informed of any changes.
- Whether any preferential or deferred shares are to be issued and, if so, within what limits.
- How advances are to be made and repaid and the conditions for early redemption.
- How losses are to be ascertained and provided for.
- How membership is to cease.
- How the society's auditors are to be remunerated.
- The manner of electing directors, whether they may be co-opted and any requirement with regard to share qualification.
- How directors are to be remunerated and rules regarding pensions.
- The powers and duties of the board of directors.
- The custody of mortgage deeds and other securities belonging to the society.
- The form, custody and use of the society's common seal.
- Calling and holding meetings.
- The members' entitlement on the society's winding up or dissolution.

23.12 A society's rules bind its members and officers and anybody claiming on a member's account. These people are also deemed to have notice of the rules. [BSA 1986 2 Sch 3(2)].

Management

23.13 Part VII of the *Building Societies Act 1986* deals with the management of building societies and contains detailed requirements with regard to the appointment, election and retirement of directors and their dealings with their society. It also contains requirements for the appointment of a chairman, a chief executive and a secretary.

23.14 The provisions relating to dealings between a society and its directors cover:

- Prohibitions of tax-free and income tax related remuneration. [BSA 1986 Sec 62].
- The disclosure of directors' interests in contracts and other transactions or arrangements. [BSA 1986 Sec 63].
- The prohibition of certain transactions involving the acquisition or disposal of substantial non-cash assets of societies from or to directors or their connected persons. [BSA 1986 Sec 64].
- Restrictions with regard to loans and advances, the leasing or hiring of property and payments in respect of any service specified in Part I of Schedule 8 to the *Building Societies Act 1986*, to a director or his connected persons and the provision of any guarantee or security in respect of such a transaction. [BSA 1986 Sec 65].
- The prohibition of directors' and others' receiving commission in connection with any loan made by a society. [BSA 1986 Sec 67].
- The maintenance of a register of transactions with directors and their connected persons. [BSA 1986 Sec 68].
- The recording of certain particulars of transactions with directors or officers who are also directors of, or partners in, business associates of the society. [BSA 1986 Sec 69].

23.15 One of the requirements of the legislation is that societies and their directors meet seven criteria of prudent management, which are set out in section 45(3) of the *Building Societies Act 1986*, and the Commission is entitled to assume that the failure to satisfy one or more of them will prejudice the security of the investments of shareholders or depositors. The criteria are:

1. Maintenance of adequate reserves and other designated capital resources.
2. Maintenance of a structure of commercial assets which satisfies the requirements of Part III of the *Building Societies Act 1986*.
3. Maintenance of adequate assets in liquid form.

4. Maintenance of the requisite arrangements for assessing the adequacy of securities for advances secured on land.

5. Maintenance of the requisite accounting records and systems of control of business and of inspection and report.

6. Direction and management:

   - □ Conducted by a sufficient number of persons who are fit and proper to be directors or, as the case may be, officers in their respective positions.

   - □ Conducted by them with prudence and integrity.

7. Conduct of the business with adequate professional skills.

23.16 In interpreting the criteria of prudent management, the definitions contained in section 45(10) are particularly important, namely:

- ■ 'Adequate', except with reference to liquidity, means adequate having regard to the range and scale of the society's business. The adequacy of capital resources was one of the first matters the Commission considered after the passing of the *Building Societies Act 1986*, and its Prudential Note 1987/1 contains a framework for societies to work to. A supplementary note (Prudential Note 1990/1) adjusted the capital adequacy calculation to reflect the increased risks associated with some of the more innovative mortgage products introduced by many societies.

- ■ 'Adequate', with reference to liquidity, means of such proportion and composition as is required by section 21(1) and 'liquid form', in relation to assets, means assets which are of an authorised character for the purposes of that subsection. Liquid assets have to be at least sufficient to enable the society to meet its liabilities as they arise, but cannot exceed one third of total assets. Authorised liquid assets are those described in the *Building Societies (Liquid Asset) Regulations 1987* (SI 1987/1499) as amended.

- ■ 'Business' includes business the society proposes to carry on and references to the business of the society include, where other bodies are associated with it, references to the business of those associated bodies. Associated bodies are one or more of those:

   - □ In which the society holds shares or corresponding membership rights.

- ☐ To which the society is linked by resolution, that is, by a resolution of the board of the society's directors that is still in force.

- ☐ In which a body described above holds shares or corresponding membership rights by virtue of Commission consent given under section 18(8)(b).

The definition of 'business' means that the fifth criterion requires systems of control to be in place before any new business areas are embarked upon.

- ■ 'Requisite', with reference to the arrangements for assessing the adequacy of securities, means such as are required by section 13, which requires an appropriate internal independent assessment supported by a written valuation report.

- ■ 'Requisite', with reference to accounting records and systems of control, means such as are required by section 71. Section 71 is one of the most significant sections of the *Building Societies Act 1986* and its provisions are covered in detail in paragraphs 23.29 to 23.42 below.

- ■ 'Sufficient' with reference to the number of directors and officers, means sufficient having regard to the range and scale of the society's business.

Powers

23.17 Although the *Building Societies Act 1986* and subsequent regulations have increased greatly the scope of the activities available to building societies, their powers are still significantly restricted to those matters described in paragraphs 23.18 to 23.28 below.

23.18 They may raise retail funds from their members and borrow money and receive deposits from anyone, as long as sections 7, 8 and 9 of the *Building Societies Act 1986* are complied with. These sections provide, *inter alia*, that:

- ■ Non-retail funds should not exceed a prescribed amount. This is currently 40 per cent of total share and deposit liabilities, although in general societies work to internally set limits that are significantly smaller. [BSA 1986 Sec 7(3)].

- ■ Including accrued interest, deposits should not exceed 50 per cent of the total of shares and deposits, excepting certain specified types of share or deposit. [BSA 1986 Sec 8(1)].

23.19 They may make advances to members secured on land, being either of the following:

- Class 1 advances, which are to individuals, secured on land occupied as residents by them or their dependants, of an amount which is not more than the value of the security, and where there is no equal or prior mortgage to another lender. [BSA 1986 Sec 11(2)].

- Class 2 advances, which do not meet one or more class 1 criteria but are secured on land, of an amount which is no more than the aggregate of the values of the security and any additional security as prescribed, and where there is no more than one equal or prior mortgage to another lender. [BSA 1986 Sec 11(4)].

23.20 They may make to members or non-members mobile home loans and certain other secured and unsecured loans (in prescribed circumstances). [BSA 1986 Secs 15, 16].

23.21 They may acquire, hold and dispose of land in the UK as a commercial asset to be used primarily for residential purposes or for purposes incidental to adjoining residential property. [BSA 1986 Sec 17].

23.22 They may invest in, and support, subsidiaries and other associated bodies. [BSA 1986 Sec 18]. Support, in this context, refers to any of the following services:

- Loans of money, whether or not secured and whether or not at interest.

- Grants of money, whether or not repayable.

- Guarantees of the discharge of the subsidiaries' or associates' liabilities.

- The use of the society's services or property, whether or not for payment.

Where the support is to be provided to a body corporate in which the society does not hold shares or corresponding membership rights, that body must be *"linked by resolution"* of the society's board of directors. The resolution must specify the power exercisable by the society in relation to the body corporate.

23.23 The assets described in paragraphs 23.20 to 23.22 and certain other assets so designated by the Treasury constitute class 3 assets. Class 3 assets were restricted by section 20(3) of the *Building Societies Act 1986* to 5 per cent and class 2 and 3 assets combined to 10 per cent, of total commercial assets as shown in the society's latest balance sheet. *The Building Societies (Limits on Commercial Assets) Order 1988* (SI 1988/1142) increased those percentages in three stages between 1st January 1990 and 1st January 1993 as follows:

	Limit of class 3 assets as % of total commercial assets	Limit of class 2 and class 3 assets as % of total commercial assets
	%	%
30th June 1988 to 31st December 1990	7½	17½
1st January 1991 to 31st December 1992	10	20
After 31st December 1992	15	25

23.24 They may hold sufficient liquid assets to enable them to meet their liabilities as they arise and hold all their liquid assets (which may not exceed one-third of total assets) in a form authorised in liquid asset regulations made by the Commission with Treasury consent. [BSA 1986 Sec 21(1)].

23.25 They may enter into hedging contracts of a prescribed description for the purpose of reducing the risk of loss arising from changes in interest rates, currency rates or other prescribed factors. [BSA 1986 Sec 23(1)].

23.26 Except where the legislation specifically provides otherwise, most categories of class 3 assets and hedging instruments are available only to societies whose latest balance sheet showed commercial assets in excess of £100m.

23.27 They may provide services described in Schedule 8 to the *Building Societies Act 1986*. [BSA 1986 Sec 34(1)]. When first enacted, Schedule 8 was prescriptive, setting out in detail all the services societies and their associated bodies could provide. *The Building Societies (Commercial Assets and Services) Order 1988* (SI 1988/1141) amended Schedule 8, making it permissive, so that societies may now provide services under six broad headings, with exceptions specifically precluded or restricted elsewhere in the schedule. The six categories are:

- Investment services.
- Insurance services.
- Banking services.
- Trusteeship.
- Executorship.
- Land services.

23.28 Certain powers, such as insurance underwriting and estate agency, are available only through subsidiaries or other associated bodies. Other powers, such as the power to establish and manage unit trust schemes for the provision of pensions, are available only to societies with total assets of more than £100m. All powers covered by schedule 8 have to be adopted by a society in its memorandum before they can be used.

Accounting records

23.29 Every society must keep accounting records. [BSA 1986 Sec 71(1)(a)]. The accounting records must be kept in an orderly manner and must:

- Explain the society's transactions.
- Disclose, with reasonable accuracy and promptness, the state of the society's business at any time.
- Enable the directors properly to discharge their duties under the *Building Societies Act 1986* and their functions relating to the direction of the society's affairs.
- Enable the society to properly discharge its duties under the *Building Societies Act 1986*.

[BSA 1986 Sec 71(2)].

23.30 The accounting records must contain, in particular:

- Entries from day to day of all sums received and paid by the society and the matters in respect of which they are received or paid.
- Entries from day to day of every transaction entered into by the society which will, or may reasonably be expected to, give rise to liabilities or assets. This requirement does not include insignificant liabilities or assets in respect of the management of the society, but it does extend the areas covered by the records to mortgage commitments, capital commitments and contingent liabilities.
- A record of the society's assets and liabilities. The record must contain, in particular, assets and liabilities of any class specifically regulated by Parts II and III of the *Building Societies Act 1986*.

[BSA 1986 Sec 71(3)].

23.31 Where a society has subsidiaries or other associated bodies linked by resolution, it must also ensure that such accounting records are kept by the society and the subsidiaries or other associated bodies to enable the society to comply with the requirements to keep accounting records in relation to the business of the society and those subsidiaries and other associated bodies. [BSA 1986 Sec 71(10)].

23.32 Accounting records must be kept at the society's principal office or at such other place or places as the directors decide. They must be open to inspection by the directors at all times and be preserved for six years from the date on which they were made. [BSA 1986 Sec 71(8)(9)]. (It should be borne in mind that other regulations may require such records to be kept for longer periods.)

Systems of control, inspection and report

23.33 Every society must establish and maintain a system of control of its business and records and a system of inspection and report. [BSA 1986 Sec 71(1)(b)].

23.34 A system of control means a system for the control of the following:

- The conduct of the society's business in accordance with the *Building Societies Act 1986* and the decisions of the society's board of directors.
- The accounting and other records of the society's business.

[BSA 1986 Sec 71(4)].

23.35 A detailed written statement of the system of control actually in operation must be available to the board. Otherwise no system of control will be treated as having been established or maintained under the *Building Societies Act 1986*. [BSA 1986 Sec 71(6)].

23.36 A system of inspection and report means a system of inspection on behalf of, and report to, the board of directors on the operation of the system of control. [BSA 1986 Sec 71(5)].

23.37 The systems of control and of inspection and report must enable:

- The directors and the society respectively to discharge their duties under the *Building Societies Act 1986* properly.
- The directors to direct the affairs of the society properly.

[BSA 1986 Sec 71(6)].

23.38 The systems must be such as to ensure that the society's business is conducted and its records kept so that:

- Information that the directors and the society need in order to discharge their duties and functions is sufficiently accurate for this to be done and is regularly available. This means that a system should cover matters such as management information, planning, human resource management and the organisation itself.

- Information regularly obtained by, or given to, the Commission in accordance with the *Building Societies Act 1986* is sufficiently accurate for that purpose.

23.39 In this context, 'regularly' includes that regularity requested by or agreed with the Commission. [BSA 1986 Sec 71(7)].

23.40 Where the society has subsidiaries or it has other associated bodies linked by resolution (see para 23.22), it must also secure that systems of control and of inspection and report are established and maintained by the society and those subsidiaries or associated bodies to enable the society to comply with the *Building Societies Act 1986* in relation to the business of the society and those subsidiaries and other associated bodies. [BSA 1986 Sec 71(10)].

23.41 The requirements of section 71 are extremely onerous, and this is one area where the extensive powers of the Commission are often seen most clearly by societies. The Commission has a role to guide societies and their officers in their efforts to meet their responsibilities under the *Building Societies Act 1986* and, in particular, the criteria for prudent management. Accordingly, it has published a number of Prudential Notes that give authoritative guidance on how the statutory requirements should be met in practice. One of the most significant is the Prudential Note on systems (1987/4), which covers in some detail the ways that societies and directors might meet their section 71 responsibilities.

23.42 The directors and chief executive of every society must make an annual statement of their opinion as to whether the requirements in respect of accounting records and systems of control and of inspection and report have been complied with. This statement should be signed by the chairman on behalf of the board of directors and by the chief executive and sent to the Commission within three months of the end of every financial year. [BSA 1986 Sec 71(11)].

Accounts and related provisions

23.43 The directors of every building society are required to prepare in respect of each financial year:

- Annual accounts.
- An annual business statement.
- A directors' report.
- A summary financial statement.

23.44 The business statement and the directors' report accompany the accounts, which are laid before the society at the annual general meeting and filed with the Commission and the Central Office of the Registry of Friendly Societies. The summary financial statement, which is an extract of the other three documents, is sent to members and given to individuals becoming members or depositors for the first time. It is also filed as above. The annual accounts are also available on demand to members and depositors.

23.45 The above paragraph is a general statement that is intended to give a brief overview of the various annual statements and how they interrelate. The detailed requirements for their preparation and audit, set out in sections 72 to 81 of the *Building Societies Act 1986* and related regulations, are more complex. They are considered in the following paragraphs. The comprehensive nature of the requirements means that although building societies are not governed by the Companies Acts there are substantial similarities between the two sets of accounting regulations. Other elements of GAAP in the UK that are contained in relevant accounting standards and exposure drafts also apply. The areas of commonality are dealt with fully in 'Manual of accounting - volumes I and II' and readers should refer to those volumes for appropriate guidance. This chapter concentrates on accounting and auditing matters that relate specifically to building societies.

Accounts

23.46 Section 72(1) of the *Building Societies Act 1986* requires the directors of every building society to prepare with respect to each financial year an income and expenditure account, a balance sheet and a statement of the source and application of funds, collectively referred to as the 'annual accounts'. If at the end of a financial year a society has subsidiaries it must (except as referred to in paragraph 23.47) also produce group accounts and, where it does so, the annual accounts need not include a statement of the source and application of funds of the society itself. However, unlike a company, a building society producing group accounts still has to produce its own income and expenditure account in addition to a consolidated one for the group. The *Building Societies Act 1986* contains no equivalent provision to section 230 of the *Companies Act 1985*.

23.47 Group accounts need not deal with a subsidiary if the society's directors consider that any one of the following situations applies:

- It is impracticable, or would be of no real value to the society's members, in view of the insignificant amounts involved.

- It would involve expense or delay out of proportion to the value to members.

- The result would be misleading or harmful to the business of the society or any of its subsidiaries (in which case prior approval is usually required from the Commission).

[BSA 1986 Sec 72(5)(6)].

23.48 While considering the requirement for group accounts it should be noted that the *Building Societies Act 1986* ties the definition of 'subsidiary' to the definition given in section 258 of the *Companies Act 1985*. Accordingly, the definition changed on 1st November 1990 when section 144 of the *Companies Act 1989* came into effect (see 'Manual of accounting - volume II' chapter 3). However, the requirement to consolidate subsidiary 'undertakings', rather than just subsidiary companies, introduced by that Act in relation to consolidated financial statements, does not apply to building societies which are only required to consolidate subsidiary companies.

23.49 The annual accounts are required to give a true and fair view of:

- The income and expenditure of the society for the financial year.

- The state of affairs of the society as at the end of the financial year.

- The manner in which the business of the society has been financed and in which its financial resources have been used during the financial year.

[BSA 1986 Sec 71(1)-(4)].

23.50 Group accounts have to meet similar criteria by reference to the society and (so far as it concerns the members of the society) the subsidiaries dealt with therein. [BSA 1986 Sec 73(5)].

Business statement

23.51 In addition to the annual accounts, the directors of every building society are required to prepare an 'annual business statement', which is a statement relating to prescribed aspects of the society's (and, where applicable, the group's) business during the year. The annual business statement must be prepared by reference to the accounts and other records and information at the directors' disposal and it must give a true representation of the matters in respect of which it is given. [BSA 1986 Sec 74(1)(5)].

23.52 As is the case with group accounts, the annual business statement is annexed to the society's balance sheet. [BSA 1986 Sec 80(2)].

Directors' report

23.53 Building society directors are required, as are company directors, to prepare for submission to the annual general meeting a report on the business of the society containing:

- A fair review of the development of its business (and, where applicable, of the business of the society and its subsidiaries and associated bodies) during the year and the position at the end of it.
- Prescribed information.
- A statement whether any and, if so, what activities carried on during the year are believed to have been carried on outside the powers of the society.

[BSA 1986 Sec 75(1)(2)].

23.54 The directors' report is attached to the balance sheet, as is the auditors' report. [BSA 1986 Sec 80(2)(4)].

Summary financial statement

23.55 With respect to each financial year the directors are required to prepare a 'summary financial statement', which is a statement derived from the annual accounts, business statement and directors' report (and, where applicable, the group accounts). It gives a summary account of the financial development and position of the society and its subsidiaries and other associated bodies. [BSA 1986 Sec 76(1)(2)].

23.56 The summary financial statement must also include statements to the effect that:

- It is only a summary of information in the accounts, business statement and directors' report.
- The accounts have been audited.

- From a specified date the accounts, business statement and directors' report will be available to members and depositors free of charge on demand at every office of the society.

[BSA 1986 Sec 76(4)].

23.57 In addition, the summary financial statement has to include a statement of the auditors' opinion as to it's consistency with the accounts, business statement and directors' report and its conformity with relevant legislation. [BSA 1986 Sec 76(5)].

Form and contents

23.58 The form and contents of the annual accounts, group accounts, business statement, directors' report and summary financial statement were delegated in the *Building Societies Act 1986* to the Commission, with the consent of the Treasury. [BSA 1986 Secs 73(7), 74(3), 75(1)(b), 76(3)]. They are contained in *The Building Societies (Accounts and Related Provisions) Regulations 1987* (SI 1987/2072) (the 'Accounts Regulations'), which came into force on 31st December 1987 and applied (with some transitional relief) to financial years ending on and after that date. (The first major revision of the Accounts Regulations is currently in progress and is likely to affect accounting periods commencing on or after 1st January 1993.)

23.59 The Accounts Regulations were based largely on the *Companies Act 1985* (though before that Act was amended by the *Companies Act 1989*) but were also intended to incorporate the requirements of the EC Directive of 8th December 1986 on the accounts of banks and other financial institutions. [86/635/EEC]. The Accounts Regulations are reproduced in full in annex 1 to this chapter.

Annual accounts formats

23.60 Schedules 1, 2 and 3 to the Accounts Regulations contain prescribed formats for annual accounts. Unlike companies, building societies are not given two balance sheet and four income and expenditure account formats from which to choose their accounts' presentation they are restricted to one format for each. Another difference from companies legislation is the presence of a prescribed format for the statement of the source and application of funds. [SI 1987/2072 para 3].

23.61 As with companies, assets may not be set off against liabilities, and *vice versa*, and similarly income may not be set off against expenditure. However, for building societies there are exceptions in respect of set-offs specifically required or permitted by the Accounts Regulations. [SI 1987/2072 5 Sch 20].

23.62 Group accounts (see paragraph 23.46 above) combine the information contained in the society's own accounts with that contained in the accounts of its relevant subsidiaries (that is, the subsidiaries required by section 72 of the *Building Societies Act 1986* to be dealt with in the group accounts), adjusted so far as is necessary to consolidate those accounts. [SI 1987/2072 para 4(2)]. Investments in bodies corporate that are not relevant subsidiaries may be dealt with by equity accounting where the closeness of the relationship justifies the use of that method. [SI 1987/2072 para 3(6)].

23.63 The directors of every building society that has subsidiaries are required to ensure that subsidiaries' financial years coincide with the society's, unless in their opinion there are good reasons against it. [BSA 1986 Sec 72(3)]. Where they differ, the group accounts will incorporate the relevant subsidiary's accounts for the financial year ending next before the society's financial year end unless the directors of the society consider there are good reasons against it and they disclose those reasons in the notes to the accounts. [SI 1987/2072 para 4(1)]. The notes must also disclose, in respect of each such subsidiary, the reasons why the society's directors consider that its financial year should differ from the society's and the financial year ends (or the earliest and latest financial year ends) of such subsidiaries. [SI 1987/2072 para 4(3)].

Income and expenditure accounts

23.64 The prescribed format of a building society's income and expenditure account is shown in annex 1. [SI 1987/2072 1 Sch Part I].

23.65 The format of the consolidated income and expenditure account (SI 1987/2072 1 Sch Part II) is similar to the above except that it allows for 'other' interest receivable (item 1(c)), extends the tax charge on the society's profit on ordinary activities to include relevant subsidiaries (item 11(a)) and provides for the elimination of minority interests in the profit on ordinary activities after tax.

23.66 Part III of Schedule 1 to the Accounts Regulations sets out a number of provisions applicable to the income and expenditure account formats, all of which are special to building societies:

- Items 1(a) and (b) include all income from advances and loans, and interest, other income and profits net of losses arising from liquid assets. [SI 1987/2072 1 Sch 1].

- In item 1(a)(i) secured advances includes loans secured other than on land as well as advances secured on land. [SI 1987/2072 1 Sch 2].

- Items 4(a) and 11(b) apply only where the equity method of accounting is used. [SI 1987/2072 1 Sch 3].

- Item 5(a) includes income in respect of all services supplied for the account of third parties and item 5(b) includes charges for the use of services of third parties including specified categories of such third party transactions (other than relevant agency payments to appointed agents) which would otherwise be capable of inclusion elsewhere. [SI 1987/2072 1 Sch 4(1)(2)].

- Net profits or losses on financial instruments are included in item 5(c) or item 5(d) as appropriate. Profits net of losses on development properties are included in item 5(e). Financial instruments are hedging instruments prescribed under section 23 of the *Building Societies Act 1986*, options to buy or sell any liquid asset and (for the purposes of the consolidated income and expenditure account) instruments on which interest or a dividend is capable of being received but which is not an advance, a loan or a liquid asset. [SI 1987/2072 1 Sch 5(1)(2)].

23.67 An example of a consolidated income and expenditure account is given in Table 23.1. Table 23.2 illustrates certain income and expenditure items expanded in the notes.

Table 23.1: Illustration of a building society consolidated income and expenditure account

Extract from Yorkshire Building Society Report & Accounts 31st December 1989.

GROUP INCOME AND EXPENDITURE ACCOUNT
FOR THE YEAR ENDED 31ST DECEMBER 1989

	Notes	1989 £000	1988 £000
Interest receivable	2	379,978	276,432
Interest payable	3	317,151	219,229
Net interest receivable		62,827	57,203
Other income and charges	4	13,628	10,916
		76,455	68,119
Management expenses	5	34,696	30,608
		41,759	37,511
Provisions for loans, advances and guarantees	11	728	154
Profit on ordinary activities before tax		41,031	37,357
Tax on profit on ordinary activities	9	14,234	13,032
Profit for the Financial Year	20	26,797	24,325

Table 23.2: Illustration of disclosure of income and expenditure in the notes to the accounts of a building society.

Extract from Yorkshire Building Society Report & Accounts 31st December 1989.

Note extract

2. INTEREST RECEIVABLE	Group		Society	
	1989	1988	1989	1988
	£000	£000	£000	£000
On secured advances	319,672	227,673	319,672	227,673
On fixed-interest liquid assets				
Interest	56,756	43,584	56,756	43,584
Profit net of losses	524	3,343	524	3,343
On other liquid assets				
Interest	3,026	1,832	3,026	1,832
	379,978	276,432	379,978	276,432
3. INTEREST PAYABLE				
a) On retail funds and deposits	281,833	201,599	281,833	201,599
On non-retail funds and deposits	33,189	17,630	33,122	17,630
On subordinated liabilities	2,129	–	2,129	–
	317,151	219,229	317,084	219,229
b) Interest payable on retail funds, non-retail funds, deposits and subordinated liabilities				
Interest	256,179	172,619	256,112	172,619
Income tax on interest	60,972	46,610	60,972	46,610
	317,151	219,229	317,084	219,229
4. OTHER INCOME AND CHARGES				
Commissions receivable	9,766	8,947	9,766	8,947
Commissions payable	(352)	(87)	(352)	(87)
Other operating income				
Rent receivable	965	779	965	779
Other	3,249	1,277	1,906	1,274
	13,628	10,916	12,285	10,913

Balance sheets

23.68 The prescribed format of a building society's balance sheet is shown in annex 1. [SI 1987/2072 2 Sch Part I]:

23.69 The format of the consolidated balance sheet (SI 1987/2072 2 Sch Part II) is similar to the above except for the addition of other operating assets and minority interests, which are respectively items 5 and 19.

23.70 Part III of Schedule 2 to the Accounts Regulations sets out a number of provisions applicable to the balance sheet formats:

- The balance sheet heading 'shares and deposits' may be expressed as 'shares, deposits and loans', provided that the same expression is used in the consolidated balance sheet and 'other deposits' is replaced by 'other deposits and loans'. [SI 1987/2072 2 Sch 1].

- Any asset in or liability to, an associated body (or, in the case of a consolidated balance sheet, an associated body that is not a relevant subsidiary) is shown separately. [SI 1987/2072 2 Sch 2].

- Cash in hand and with banks (item (a)) includes cash* and deposits* (other than marketable securities*) with the Bank of England or any Banking Act authorised institution*. UK Government securities (item 1(b)) includes marketable securities issued in the UK by HM Government or by other issuers where payment is guaranteed by HM Government. Other securities (item 1(c)) includes all liquid assets not included in items 1(a) or 1(b). Within item 1(c) any asset corresponding to a liability of or a security issued by HM Government, a Government Department, a relevant authority* or any other body exercising statutory functions falls within item 1(c)(i) and any other asset, including securities issued by a nationalised industry, falls within item 1(c)(ii). [SI 1987/2072 2 Sch 3]. The terms asterisked are defined in *The Building Societies (Liquid Asset) Regulations 1987* (SI 1987/1499).

- Advances secured on residential property correspond to class 1 advances and other advances secured on land to class 2 advances as defined in Part III of the *Building Societies Act 1986*. [SI 1987/2072 2 Sch 4].

- Other commercial assets represent class 3 assets as defined in Part III of the *Building Societies Act 1986*. Mobile home loans are included under item 4(a). [BSA 1986 Sec 15]. Secured loans (item 4(c)) include loans made under section 16 on any security (whether partial or full and whether comprising property or a guarantee). Unsecured loans (item 4(b)) includes any other section 16 loans. Residential properties (item 4(d)) includes all properties held under section 17 for rental or development other than properties acquired for business purposes but only partially used as such, which are included in fixed assets despite being classified as class 3 assets by section 17(6). The subdivisions of other commercial assets described above apply in respect of the consolidated balance sheet to any asset of a relevant subsidiary which would fall within a subdivision were that subsidiary the society. [SI 1987/2072 2 Sch 5, 6].

- Intangible assets included in item 5(a)(i) (item 6(a)(i) in the consolidated balance sheet format) must have been either acquired for valuable consideration (and should not be shown under goodwill) or created by the society itself (or, for the purposes of the consolidated accounts, by the society or a relevant subsidiary). [SI 1987/2072 2 Sch 7]. Goodwill, on the other hand, must have been acquired for valuable consideration to be included in the balance sheet. [SI 1987/2072 2 Sch 8].

- Deferred shares (including shares issued as deferred shares under previous legislation) are included as such and not as shares. [SI 1987/2072 2 Sch 9].

- In the consolidated balance sheet liabilities in respect of deposits of a relevant subsidiary that, were they liabilities of the society, would be included as non-retail funds and deposits are so included and any other such liabilities of the relevant subsidiary are included in retail funds and deposits. Any shares of a relevant subsidiary that are included in the consolidated balance sheet are included in minority interests. [SI 1987/2072 2 Sch 10].

- Amounts owed to banks include sums deposited by (or by a trustee for) a Banking Act authorised institution or an overseas institution falling within Part IV of the *Banking Act 1987*, except for qualifying time deposits, which are included in time deposits, and transferable bearer and non-bearer instruments, which are included in certificates of deposit, negotiable bonds or fixed and floating rate notes depending upon their nature. [SI 1987/2072 2 Sch 11]. Qualifying time deposits and non-bearer instruments are defined in section 7(19) of the *Building Societies Act 1986*.

- Subordinated loan capital of the society must be included in subordinate liabilities as, in the consolidated balance sheet, are subordinated liabilities of relevant subsidiaries. [SI 1987/2072 2 Sch 12].

23.71 Every balance sheet of a building society must be signed by two directors on behalf of the board and by the chief executive, after the income and expenditure account, the statement of the source and application of funds and the annual business statement, together with any group accounts, have been approved by the board and annexed to the balance sheet. The directors' report and auditors' report are attached to the balance sheet. Failure to comply with the above before the balance sheet is issued, circulated or published, is a criminal offence punishable by a fine. [BSA 1986 Sec 80].

23.72 An example of a balance sheet is given in Table 23.3. Table 23.4 gives extracts from the notes analysing other commercial assets and non-retail funds and deposits.

Table 23.3: Illustration of a building society balance sheet.

Extract from Leeds Permanent Building Society Annual Accounts and Directors' Report 30th September 1990.

SOCIETY BALANCE SHEET

At 30th September 1990

ASSETS	Notes	1990 £m	1989 £m
Liquid assets	11	2,370.8	2,074.5
Commercial assets			
• Advances secured on residential property		11,878.4	10,541.4
• Other advances secured on land		46.7	42.6
• Other commercial assets	12	154.1	68.4
Fixed assets			
• Tangible assets	14	151.7	144.9
Other assets		48.5	45.6
Total assets		14,650.2	12,917.4
LIABILITIES AND RESERVES			
Shares and deposits			
• Retail funds and deposits	15	10,799.4	9,693.0
• Non-retail funds and deposits	16	2,839.2	2,350.3
Other liabilities	17	216.1	184.2
Provisions for liabilities and charges	18	10.4	16.5
Subordinated liabilities	19	156.3	155.7
Total liabilities		14,021.4	12,399.7
General reserve	20	628.8	517.7
Total liabilities and reserves		14,650.2	12,917.4

The notes on pages 28 to 36 form part of these Accounts.
Approved by the Board of Directors on 6th November 1990.
J. Malcom Barr, President
R. B. Strachan, Vice President
J. M. Blackburn, Director and Chief Executive

Statement of the source and application of funds

23.73 The directors of every building society, unlike company directors, have a statutory obligation to produce for each financial year a statement of the source and application of the society's funds, unless at the end of that year it has relevant subsidiaries, in which case a consolidated statement will suffice. The statement must give a true and fair view of the manner in which the business of the society (or group) has been financed and in which its financial resources have been used during the financial year and it must be prepared in a prescribed format. [BSA 1986 Sec 73(4)]. Such a statement for a building society is shown in annex 1. [SI 1987/2072 3 Sch Part I].

23.74 The format for a consolidated statement of the source and application of funds is similar although, in addition, it provides for the change in

Table 23.4: Illustration of disclosure of assets and liabilities in the notes to the accounts of a building society.

Extract from Leeds Permanent Building Society Annual Accounts and Directors' Report 30th September 1990.

Note extract

12 OTHER COMMERCIAL ASSETS		Group 1990 £m	Group 1989 £m	Society 1990 £m	Society 1989 £m
	Unsecured loans	118.8	34.4	118.8	34.4
	Others (incl. development properties)	13.3	12.6	13.3	12.6
	Investments in associated bodies (see note 13):				
	• Shares in associated bodies	0.6	0.6	15.8	11.7
	• General reserve	0.2	0.4	–	–
	• Loans to associated bodies	6.2	9.7	6.2	9.7
		139.1	57.7	154.1	68.4

The Group's share of the net assets of its associated company, Leeds Permanent Financial Services Ltd included in the above figures, is £0.6m (1989 –£0.9m).

16 NON-RETAIL FUNDS AND DEPOSITS	a) Non-retail funds and deposits comprise:				
	Amounts owed to banks*	193.9	316.1	193.4	312.3
	Certificates of Deposit	654.8	608.1	654.8	608.1
	Time deposits	176.8	348.0	176.8	348.0
	Fixed and Floating Rate Notes	1,289.5	921.3	1,289.5	921.3
	Other deposits	291.1	160.6	524.7	160.6
		2,606.1	2,354.1	2,839.2	2,350.3

* Including subsidiaries' bank loans of £0.5m (1989 – £3.8m).

b) Repayable from the date of the balance sheet in the ordinary course of business as follows:

SOCIETY	Amounts owed to banks £m	Certificates of Deposit £m	Time Deposits £m	Fixed & Floating Rate Notes £m	Other deposits £m	Total £m
At 30th September 1990						
Repayable on demand	–	–	–	–	248.9	248.9
In not more than 3 months	105.2	441.6	123.8	–	272.9	943.5
In more than 3 months but not more than 1 year	28.0	173.2	42.1	125.0	–	368.3
In more than 1 year but not more than 5 years	59.0	20.0	6.0	538.0	–	623.0
In more than 5 years	–	–	–	596.1	–	596.1
	192.2	634.8	171.9	1,259.1	521.8	2,779.8
Accrued interest	1.2	20.0	4.9	30.4	2.9	59.4
	193.4	654.8	176.8	1,289.5	524.7	2,839.2

Of £524.7m included in Other deposits, £233.6m relates to monies deposited by a subsidiary. The subsidiaries' bank loans of £0.5m (1989 – £3.8m) are repayable on demand.

As explained in the accounting policy note on deposits, deposits taken by the Group's offshore subsidiary are lent to the Society and are repayable on demand. The resulting inter-company account balance of £229.1m (1989 £nil) is treated as a non-retail deposit in the Society's balance sheet and is treated as a retail deposit in the consolidated balance sheet.

At 30th September 1989						
Repayable on demand	–	–	–	–	21.6	21.6
In not more than 3 months	168.7	253.0	308.9	–	137.0	867.6
In more than 3 months but not more than 1 year	36.5	314.4	30.1	–	–	381.0
In more than 1 year but not more than 5 years	105.0	18.7	5.0	355.0	–	483.7
In more than 5 years	–	–	–	546.1	–	546.1
	310.2	586.1	344.0	901.1	158.6	2,300.0
Accrued interest	2.1	22.0	4.0	20.2	2.0	50.3
	312.3	608.1	348.0	921.3	160.6	2,350.3

other operating assets and the impact of minority interests in subsidiaries. [SI 1987/2072 3 Sch Part II].

23.75 Part III of Schedule 3 to the Accounts Regulations sets out a number of provisions applicable to the formats of statements of the source and application of funds:

- Properties acquired for business purposes but only partially used as such are included in fixed assets despite being classified as commercial assets by section 17(6) of the Act. [SI 1987/2072 3 Sch 1]. Any other assets which arise from the activity of a relevant subsidiary and would, if they were assets of the society, be classed as commercial assets are included in commercial assets in the consolidated statement. [SI 1987/2072 3 Sch 2].

- Subordinated loan capital cannot be treated as retail or non-retail funds and deposits. Any other liabilities of any relevant subsidiary that, were they liabilities of the society, would be included as non-retail funds and deposits are so included in the consolidated statement and any other such liabilities of the relevant subsidiary are included in retail funds and deposits [SI 1987/2072 3 Sch 3].

- Where relevant subsidiaries have been acquired or disposed of during the year, the effects of the acquisitions or disposals are shown in aggregate as a footnote to the statement, quite separate from the notes to the accounts.

- The notes to the accounts should include analyses of such changes in other commercial and other operating assets as are material to the way in which the business has been financed and in which the financial resources have been used. [SI 1987/2072 3 Sch 5].

- Where amounts included within the statement (but not within the section headed 'increase in free capital') have a positive description (that is, increase receipt or profit) but the amount is negative, the corresponding negative term (that is, decrease outflow or loss) is used and the item transferred to the opposite grouping in the format. For example, a decrease in liquid assets would be described as such and included under the heading 'source of funds'. [SI 1987/2072 3 Sch 6].

23.76 There are two anomalies within the format for consolidated statements of the source and application of funds:

- Dividends paid to minority shareholders (item 19) are not required, since minority interests are already deducted in arriving at the profits included as item 13.

- The definition of free capital is the aggregate of total reserves as shown in the balance sheet (plus subordinated liabilities) and general loss provisions, less fixed assets. Item 15(f) (minority interests in retained profits) does not fall within that definition and so should be included under source of funds.

Notes to annual accounts

23.77 Schedule 4 to the Accounts Regulations sets out requirements for disclosure in the notes to annual accounts, additional to matters required to be disclosed by other provisions of the Accounts Regulations. [SI 1987/2072 para 5(1)]. The information disclosed is also required in respect of the group, except for information required by Schedule 4 paragraph 4 (directors' emoluments) and paragraph 21 (directors' loans and transactions). [SI 1987/2072 paras 5(2)-(4)].

23.78 The notes should include a statement of the accounting policies adopted by the society in determining the amounts to be included in respect of items shown in the balance sheet and in determining the income and expenditure and the source and application of funds. Unlike the *Companies Act 1985*, the Act specifies five items as a minimum, for which the policies adopted should be stated:

- Depreciation and diminution in value of assets.
- Translation of amounts denominated in foreign currencies.
- Accounting for and valuation of UK Government and other securities.
- Valuation of investment properties.
- Provision for losses on advances and loans.

23.79 Where any accounting policy departs from generally accepted accounting principles or practice, the reasons for the departure must be stated. [SI 1987/2072 4 Sch 1]. This is a similar provision to the new paragraph 36A of Schedule 4 to the *Companies Act 1985*, though the latter provision is narrower, confining itself to departures from applicable accounting standards. Furthermore, companies legislation does not specify a minimum list of policies to be disclosed, although SSAP 2 includes a list of some which may be appropriate.

23.80 Information required in respect of employees is similar to that required for companies, except that for building societies the average number of employees is calculated on a monthly, rather than weekly basis. In addition, numbers of employees earning £30,000 and above in bands of £5,000 are required to be disclosed. This is the same as the disclosure required by Part VI of Schedule 5 to the *Companies Act 1985* before it was repealed by the *Companies Act 1989*. The emoluments concerned include amounts paid to or receivable by the employee from the society, an associated body or any other person in respect of services as an employee of the society or an associated body or as a director of an associated body (directors of the society are excluded from these requirements). [SI 1987/2072 4 Sch 2, 3].

23.81 Directors' emoluments disclosures are similar to those required by the *Companies Act 1985*, with the following principal differences:

- Emoluments include those paid in respect of services to the society and any associated body, rather than just subsidiary undertakings.

- Emoluments do not include those in respect of a person's accepting office as director (that is, 'golden hellos').

- Full disclosure is required from all societies, not just those whose directors' emoluments aggregate to £60,000 or more.

- Payments to third parties in respect of directors' services are not included.

- References to a person are to the person alone, and do not include persons connected with him or companies controlled by him.

[SI 1987/2072 4 Sch 4].

23.82 In respect of interest receivable, interest derived from associated bodies is shown separately. [SI 1987/2072 4 Sch 5(1)]. There is no requirement to identify income from listed investments.

23.83 In respect of interest payable, separate disclosure is required of amounts payable to associated bodies and of any income tax on interest on shares and deposits accounted for by the society. [SI 1987/2072 4 Sch 5].

23.84 Disclosure is also required of the amount of any income from rent payable to the society in respect of premises or other land. [SI 1987/2072 4 Sch 5(3)]. By way of contrast with companies legislation, this disclosure is required whether or not a substantial part of the income for the financial year consists of rents and no deduction is allowed for ground rents, rates or other outgoings.

23.85 There are also disclosure requirements in respect of the hire of equipment, fixtures, fittings, vehicles, auditors' remuneration, including expenses and any material component of income from associated bodies or other income and charges. [SI 1987/2072 4 Sch 5(4)-(6)].

23.86 Where interest in respect of development projects has been capitalised during the year, the Accounts Regulations require disclosure of the amount capitalised, together with an indication of the amount and treatment of any related tax relief. [SI 1987/2072 4 Sch 5(6)].

23.87 Taxation disclosures are similar to those required for companies (see 'Manual of accounting - volume I' chapter 14) except that the basis of the tax charge is specifically stated to include the charge for deferred tax. [SI 1987/2072 4 Sch 6(1)]. In practice, however, most companies include deferred tax within the tax charge for that purpose. The other principal difference is that the *Building Societies Act 1986* does not require disclosures to be made separately in respect of the tax charged on ordinary activities and on any extraordinary profit or loss.

23.88 The last note requirement in respect of the income and expenditure account is similar to the *Companies Act 1985* disclosure of prior year, extraordinary and exceptional items. [SI 1987/2072 4 Sch 7].

23.89 Specific maturity analysis is required of the various components of the heading 'liquid assets', with separate disclosure of the book and market values of listed investments. [SI 1987/2072 4 Sch 8].

23.90 The notes to annual accounts include details of provisions for losses on each sub-heading of loans and advances classified as commercial assets, with the exception of loans to associated bodies. The details required relate to the movements on provisions during the year, with separate disclosure for specific and general provisions. [SI 1987/2072 4 Sch 9].

23.91 Where at the end of its financial year a building society (or, if the society prepares group accounts, a group) has any associated body that is at that time carrying on business, considerable information about that body is required, including:

- Whether it is a subsidiary, an associated body linked by resolution or another associated body of the society (see para 23.22).

- Its name.

- How it is constituted.

- Its place of registration.
- Where relevant, particulars of the shares held and the proportion held by the society (or group), distinguishing between holdings of, or of a nominee for, the society and those of subsidiaries and their nominees.
- The nature of its business.
- The principal country in which it operates.
- Whether it is a direct or indirect associate body of the society.
- Where it is not included in the annual accounts either by way of the equity method of accounting or by inclusion in group accounts, the aggregate of its capital and reserves as at the end of its financial year ending with or within the financial year of the society and its profit or loss for that year.
- Where the investment constitutes listed shares, the aggregate amount in respect of all such investments of book value, market value and, if lower than market value, stock exchange value.

[SI 1987/2072 4 Sch 10].

A 'direct associated body' is one in which the society itself holds shares or corresponding membership rights or with which the society itself is linked by resolution. An 'indirect associated body' is one where the association exists only through another associated body, as in the case of a sub-subsidiary.

23.92 Fixed asset disclosures are the same as those applying to companies. [SI 1987/2072 4 Sch 11]. Other assets falling due after more than one year are separately identified. [SI 1987/2072 4 Sch 12].

23.93 Specific maturity analysis is required of the totals of retail and non-retail funds and deposits, as well as the amount and the nature of any security given in respect of each component thereof. [SI 1987/2072 4 Sch 13, 14].

23.94 Disclosure in the notes to the annual accounts is also made in respect of:

- Deferred shares.
- Creditors for taxation and social security.
- 'Other liabilities' falling due after one year.

- Movements on provisions and reserves.
- Subordinated liabilities.
- Guarantees and other financial commitments.

[SI 1987/2072 4 Sch 15-19].

23.95 The following information is given in respect of certain loans to, and transactions and other arrangements with, directors of building societies and their connected persons:

- The aggregate amounts outstanding.
- The numbers of persons for whom they were made.
- Where relevant, the existence of the register of transactions with directors and others maintained under section 68 of the *Building Societies Act 1986* and the availability of the requisite particulars for inspection.

Accounting principles and rules

23.96 The accounting principles governing annual accounts of building societies are similar to those that apply to companies and other entities that are required to prepare true and fair accounts, namely:

- The presumption of a going concern.
- The consistent application of accounting policies from one financial year to the next.
- The adoption of a prudent accounting basis and, in particular, the inclusion in the income and expenditure account of all losses and liabilities incurred or likely to have been incurred by the balance sheet date, including those that become apparent only between the balance sheet date and the date the balance sheet is signed on behalf of the board.
- The adoption of the accruals basis.
- The separate determination of each individual asset or liability when arriving at an aggregate amount.

[SI 1987/2072 5 Sch Part I].

23.97 Departure from those principles is allowed only where there appear to the directors to be special reasons, in that case the notes to the annual accounts must give particulars of the departure, the reasons for it and its effect. [SI 1987/2072 5 Sch Part II].

23.98 There is no statutory requirement for consistency within the same accounts or for the inclusion in income of only realised profits, although both requirements apply by virtue of accounting standards. [SSAP 2 para 14].

23.99 Subject to any provision for depreciation, amortisation or permanent diminution in value, fixed assets are included in the balance sheet at their purchase price, although tangible fixed assets may be included at market value at the date of their last valuation or at their current cost. [SI 1987/2072 5 Sch 8]. Commercial assets falling within the balance sheet headings 4(d) (residential properties) and 4(f) (other) are accounted for in the same way as fixed assets where they are intended for use on a continuing basis in the normal course of a society's (or group's) activities. [SI 1987/2072 5 Sch 11]. Investments in associated bodies may be included either at their latest market value or by another appropriate valuation method. In the latter situation, the notes to the accounts must include particulars of, and the reasons for adopting, the method used. [SI 1987/2072 5 Sch 15(2)].

23.100 The rules regarding depreciation and other provisions against fixed assets and the operation of the revaluation reserve, are similar to those applying to companies.

23.101 Commercial assets, other than those included in the balance sheet headings 4(d) to (f), are included, after deducting loss provisions, at the amount of the outstanding advance or loan or the capital repayment amount if lower, in any case where the capital repayable is variable. [SI 1987/2072 5 Sch 17].

23.102 UK government and other securities are included in the balance sheet at cost (whether or not adjusted) or at market value. [SI 1987/2072 5 Sch 18]. To the extent that cost is used, the method used to determine that cost must be disclosed. [SI 1987/2072 5 Sch 19]. However, the publication in September 1990 of the SORP on accounting for securities, although aimed primarily at banks (see chapter 15) may be persuasive in encouraging building societies to use market value for any on-balance sheet transferable security.

Directors' report

23.103 Schedule 6 to the Accounts Regulations sets out the disclosure requirements in respect of directors' reports (the prescribed information referred to in para 23.53 above). The requirements are as follows:

- The names of those persons who were directors at any time during the year. [SI 1987/2072 6 Sch 1].

- A statement of the business objectives and activities of the society and its associated bodies, particulars of important post balance sheet events and the directors' opinion as to likely future developments. [SI 1987/2072 6 Sch 2].

- Particulars of any significant changes in fixed assets during the year and, where the directors believe that members should be made aware of it, any significant difference between the market value and the balance sheet value of land. [SI 1987/2072 6 Sch 3].

- Certain particulars of political and/or charitable donations. [SI 1987/2072 6 Sch 4].

- Particulars of directors' interests in associated bodies. [SI 1987/2072 6 Sch 5].

- Where the society has on average employed more than 250 persons during the year, particulars of:

  - Employment policies in respect of disabled persons.

  - Arrangements for specified forms of employee involvement.

  [SI 1987/2072 6 Sch 6].

- The percentages of share and deposit liabilities of the society or, where applicable, the group represented respectively by free capital and gross capital. [SI 1987/2072 6 Sch 7].

- The number of mortgage accounts twelve or more months in arrears and the total amount of those arrears.

23.104 An example of specialised aspects of a building society's directors' report is given in Table 23.5.

Annual business statement

23.105 The requirement to prepare an annual business statement is referred to in paragraph 23.51 above. The aspects of the business that are dealt with in the statement are prescribed in Schedule 7 to the Accounts Regulations. They fall within the following categories:

- Summary ratios and percentages.

- Other percentages.
- Information relating to directors and other officers.
- Average rates.
- Associated bodies not carrying on business.
- Information about new activities.

Table 23.5: Illustration of the specialised disclosures in a building society directors' report.

Extract from Bradford & Bingley Building Society Annual Report & Accounts 31st December 1989.

Directors' Report extract

Capital

At 31st December 1989, the group's free capital amounted to 3.64 per cent of share, deposit and loan liabilities. Gross capital amounted to 4.92 per cent of share, deposit and loan liabilities.

Liquid assets

The liquid assets of the group increased during the year by £254m to £1,278m representing 17.86 per cent of total assets.

Commercial assets

At 31st December 1989, there were 759 mortgages where repayments were twelve months or more in arrear. The total amount of arrears in these cases was £3,966m.

23.106 The following paragraphs set out the detailed disclosure requirements within those categories.

Summary ratios and percentages

23.107 The following percentages are shown as at the balance sheet date [SI 1987/2072 Sch para 1]:

- Non-retail funds and deposits as a percentage of shares and deposits.
- Deposits as a percentage of shares and deposits.
- Advances secured on residential property as a percentage of total commercial assets.

- Advances secured on land, other than residential property, as a percentage of total commercial assets.

- Commercial assets not included in the above two classes of advance as a percentage of total commercial assets.

- The aggregate of commercial assets, other than advances secured on residential property, as a percentage of total commercial assets.

[SI 1987/2072 7 Sch 1].

23.108 Where a percentage described above is subject to a statutory limit, it is expressed as one element of a ratio and the statutory limit is expressed as the other.

23.109 The annual business statement also includes an explanation of what is represented by each component of the statutory ratios and percentages disclosed, including the statutory limits. [SI 1987/2072 7 Sch 1(2)].

23.110 Schedule 7 also prescribes how the disclosure requirements in respect of statutory ratios and percentages are interpreted where a society has an associated body's assets or liabilities attributed to it. The relevant rules are either the *Building Societies (Aggregation) Rules 1990* (SI 1990/2362) made under section 7(10), 8(3) or 20(9) of the *Building Societies Act 1986* or alternative rules requested by a particular society and approved by the Commission under section 7(13), 8(5) or 20(12). [SI 1987/2072 7 Sch 1(4)]. For an understanding of the detailed requirements reference should be made to the relevant rules and the associated guidance note issued by the Commission in November 1990.

23.111 An example of the disclosure of statutory ratios and percentages is given in Table 23.6.

Other percentages

23.112 The following percentages are shown in relation to the current and previous financial year.

- Gross capital as a percentage of share and deposit liabilities.

- Free capital as a percentage of share and deposit liabilities.

- Liquid assets as a percentage of total assets.

- Profit or loss after tax as a percentage of mean reserves.

- Profit or loss after tax as a percentage of mean total assets.

- Where in either year there are extraordinary items, the ordinary profit or loss after tax as a percentage of mean reserves and mean total assets.

[SI 1987/2072 7 Sch 2(1)].

Mean reserves and mean total assets are arrived at by halving the aggregate of those amounts shown in the current and the previous balance sheets.

Table 23.6: Illustration of disclosure of statutory ratios and percentages in a building society annual business statement.

Extract from Leeds Permanent Building Society Annual Accounts and Directors' Report 30th September 1990.

Annual business statement extract

1 STATUTORY RATIOS AND PERCENTAGES

Calculated in accordance with the Building Societies Act 1986

	Ratio at 30 Sept 1990 %	Statutory Limit %
As percentage of Shares, Deposits and Subordinated Liabilities		
Non-retail funds and deposits	20.2	40.0
Deposits	23.1	50.0
As percentage of total commercial assets		
Advances secured on residential property (class 1 assets)	98.3	N/A
Advances secured on land other than residential property (class 2 assets)	0.4	N/A
Other commercial assets (class 3 assets)	1.3	7.5
Class 2 and class 3 assets	1.7	17.5

The ratios and percentages have been calculated on the following balances:

	Retail (Note 15) £m	Non-Retail £m	Total £m
Total shares, deposits & subordinated liabilities	11,028.5	2,762.4	13,790.9
Less accrued interest	382.8	65.7	448.5
	10,645.7	2,696.7	13,342.4
Represented by:			
Shares	10,255.0	–	10,255.0
Deposits	390.7	2,546.7	2,937.4
Subordinated liabilities	–	150.0	150.0
	10,645.7	2,696.7	13,342.4

Non-retail funds above comprise those detailed in note 16 to the Accounts together with subordinated liabilities of £156.3m including accrued interest of £6.3m.

Commercial assets per Group Balance Sheet	
Advances secured on residential property (class 1)	11,878.4
Other advances secured on land (class 2)	46.7
Other commercial assets (class 3)	157.5
	12,082.6
Other commercial assets represent:	
Other commercial assets (Note 12 to the accounts)	154.1
Business premises included in tangible fixed assets	3.4
	157.5

23.113 The descriptions used in the previous paragraph are all defined in paragraph 2(5) of Schedule 7 to the Accounts Regulations and have to be explained within the statement, as does the basis upon which the information is included by societies presenting group accounts. [SI 1987/2072 7 Sch 2(4)].

Information relating to directors and other officers

23.114 The annual business statement should include the following information relating to every person who was a director of the society at the year end:

- His name.
- His home address (or an address, other than the society's, where documents may be served on him).
- His business occupation.
- His other directorships.
- His date of birth.
- His date of appointment as a director.

[SI 1987/2072 7 Sch 3(1)(a)].

23.115 In relation to any other person who was an officer of the society at the year end the statement should show:

- His name.
- His business occupation.
- Any other directorships.

[SI 1987/2072 Sch 3(1)(b)].

23.116 An officer of a building society means a director, chief executive, secretary or manager of the society. 'Manager' means an employee (other than the chief executive) who, under the immediate authority of a director or the chief executive, exercises managerial functions or is responsible for maintaining accounts or other records of the society. [BSA 1986 Sec 119(1)].

23.117 The annual business statement also includes particulars of any service contract between a society and a director or chief executive and of any arrangement for the acquisition or disposal of any non-cash asset of the society or a relevant subsidiary, where the other party is a director of the society or a person connected with him. [SI 1987/2072 7 Sch 3(2)(3)].

23.118 An example of the disclosure of information relating to directors and other officers is given in Table 23.7.

Table 23.7: Illustration of disclosure of information relating to directors and officers in a building society annual business statement.

Extract from Leeds Permanent Building Society Annual Accounts and Directors' Report 30th September 1990.

Annual business statement (extract)

6 INFORMATION RELATING TO DIRECTORS AND OTHER OFFICERS

a) Directors (extract)

Name and Address	Date of Birth	Date of Appointment	Occupation
J. Malcolm Barr CBE MA LLM, President, Kirkby House, Kirkby Overblow Harrogate HG3 1HJ	23.12.26	21.8.72	Company Director

Other Directorships
Chairman. Barr & Wallace Arnold Trust PLC and subsidiary companies.

Director. British Equestrian Promotions Limited. The British Show Jumping Association. Hickson International PLC.

Name and Address	Date of Birth	Date of Appointment	Occupation
J. M. Blackburn, FCIB CBIM Director & Chief Executive c/o Booth & Co, Dept WLT, Sovereign House, South Parade, Leeds LS1 1HQ	16.12.41	1.10.87	Building Society Chief Executive

Other Directorships
Chairman. Leeds Permanent Estates Limited. Leeds Permanent Group Limited.

Director. Headrow Enterprises Limited. Headrow Home Services Limited. Leeds Permanent Development Services Limited. Leeds Permanent Financial Planning Limited. Leeds Permanent Financial Services Limited. Leeds Permanent Overseas Limited. Leeds Permanent Pension Scheme Trustees Limited. Lovell Park Housing Management Limited. Lovell Park Mortgage Services Limited. Moneybox Limited. Property Leeds (UK) Limited. Royal Philharmonic Orchestra Limited.

Table 23.7 continued

b) Other Officers

Name	Occupation	Other Directorships
R.F. Bennett FCA ACMA IPFA	General Manager Finance & Estates	Director Leeds Permanent Financial Planning Limited Leeds Permanent Financial Services Limited
H.J. Briggs BCom FCA	Secretary	Director Headrow Enterprises Limited Headrow Home Services Limited Leeds Permanent Estates Limited Leeds Permanent Group Limited Lovell Park Housing Management Limited Lovell Park Mortgage Services Limited

Average rates

23.119 In respect of each of the four major categories of interest bearing assets and liabilities (that is, liquid assets, secured advances and retail and non-retail funds and deposits) the annual business statement should include the following particulars in respect of the year under review:

- The average amount outstanding.
- Interest earned or paid.
- Average yield on assets.
- Average rate paid on liabilities.

[SI 1987/2072 7 Sch 4(1)].

23.120 The descriptions used in the previous paragraph are all defined in paragraph 4(4) of Schedule 7 to the Accounts Regulations and have to be explained within the statement. In addition, the basis upon which the information is included by societies presenting group accounts must be explained. [SI 1987/2072 7 Sch 4(4)]

23.121 An example of the disclosure of average rates is given in Table 23.8.

Associated bodies not carrying on business

23.122 For every associated body not carrying on business at the end of the financial year, the statement contains the following particulars:

- Whether it is a subsidiary, an associated body linked by resolution (see para 23.22) or another associated body of the society.

- Its name.
- How it is constituted.
- Where relevant, particulars of the shares held and the proportion held by the society (or group).
- Whether it is a direct or indirect associated body of the society.

[SI 1987/2072 7 Sch 5].

Table 23.8: Illustration of disclosure of average rates in a building society annual business statement.

Extract from Leeds & Holbeck Building Society Annual Report 31st December 1989.

Annual business statement extract

4. Average Rates	Average amount outstanding during year £000	Interest earned £000	Interest paid £000	Average yield	Average rate paid
Assets					
Liquid assets	207,539	26,577		12.81%	
Secured advances	1,044,662	144,322		13.81%	
Liabilities					
Retail funds and deposits	1,047,709		127,940		12.21%
Non-retail funds and deposits	107,477		14,637		13.62%

The above items represent the major categories of interest-bearing assets and liabilities.

In order to give a true representation of the average rates, the figures shown for average amount outstanding during the year are based on the relevant amounts at the end of each month during the year, excluding accrued interest. These average rates are not calculated in accordance with the Building Societies (Accounts and Related Provisions) Regulations. However, the Regulations allow additional information to be used if this will assist in giving a true representation of the relevant average rates.

The figures for interest earned or paid are taken from the accounts shown on pages 6 to 22.

The information required by the Building Societies (Accounts and Related Provisions) Regulations in respect of average amount outstanding during the year, average yield and average rate paid is as follows:

	Average amount outstanding during year £000	Average yield	Average rate paid
Liquid assets	246,277	10.79%	
Secured advances	1,066,029	13.54%	
Retail funds and deposits	1,066,315		12.00%
Non-retail funds and deposits	169,695		8.62%

The average amounts outstanding shown in accordance with the Regulations are taken from the accounts shown on pages 6 to 22.

Information about new activities

23.123 Where a society (including bodies corporate associated with it) has for the first time during the year exercised any adopted power (that is, a power included in a society's Memorandum of Powers) of the society, the annual business statement must state that fact in respect of each such power. [SI 1987/2072 7 Sch 6].

Summary financial statement

23.124 The requirement to prepare a summary financial statement is referred to in paragraph 23.55 above. The format of the statement, prescribed under section 76(3) and (4) of the Act, is contained in Part I of Schedule 8 to the Accounts Regulations, and Part II of that schedule contains the detailed rules for its compilation and its derivation from the annual accounts, the directors' report and the annual business statement.

23.125 An example of a summary financial statement of a building society is given in Table 23.9.

Audit requirements

23.126 Every building society is required at each annual general meeting to appoint an auditor or auditors to hold office from the conclusion of that meeting until the conclusion of the next annual general meeting. Schedule 11 to the *Building Societies Act 1986* contains the detailed provisions relating to the appointment, qualification, disqualification, removal and resignation of auditors. [BSA 1986 Sec 77].

23.127 The extent of the reports required annually from building societies' auditors is much greater than for auditors of companies. They report on the following matters:

- The annual accounts. [BSA 1986 Sec 78(11)].
- The annual business statement. [BSA 1986 Sec 78(3)].
- The directors' report. [BSA 1986 Sec 78(3)].
- The summary financial statement. [BSA 1986 Sec 76(5)].
- The conduct of business. [BSA 1986 Sec 82(11)].
- The statement of particulars of certain transactions with directors and their connected persons. [BSA 1986 Sec 78(9)].

Table 23.9: Illustration of a building society summary financial statement.

Extract from Britannia Building Society Summary Financial Statement 31st December 1989.

Summary Financial Statement
For year ended 31st December, 1989

This summary financial statement is only a summary of information in the annual accounts, directors' report and annual business statement. Insofar as this summary financial statement summarises the information in the annual accounts, those accounts have been audited. The annual accounts, directors' report and annual business statement will be available to members and depositors on demand at every office of Britannia Building Society from 11th April, 1990.

SUMMARY DIRECTORS' REPORT

The primary business objectives of the Society are to continue to pursue a sound and prudent financial policy, to provide a high standard of customer service and to maintain a competitive position in the savings and lending markets.

Summary review of the business

1989 was a very successful year with Group profits of £50,504,000. This was an increase of 23 per cent on the previous year. Assets grew by 18 per cent to £6,298,238,000. The total of reserves (capital) stood at £309,276,000. There was a heavy demand for mortgages. A total of £1,437,452,000 was advanced and the number off mortgages completed was 35,970.

The Society continued to use wholesale markets as a cost effective way of providing additional funds for home loans.

Summary review of events

A major event in the year was the successful conclusion of negotiations for the acquisition of FS Assurance, a life assurance company based in Glasgow, which commenced trading as Britannia Life Limited on 1st January, 1990.

A number of innovative mortgage products were launched during the year. A personal loan pilot scheme with Lloyds Bowmaker was introduced. From April all branch offices offered foreign currency as well as a varied travellers' cheques facility. A European research project group was established during the year to identify opportunities and threats of 1992.

A further 43 branch offices were converted to a semi-open plan lay-out.

Summary indication of likely events

Your Directors will seek to maintain a satisfactory level of lending to home owner-occupiers, with particular emphasis being given to helping first-time buyers. The provision of residential accommodation is planned by joint ventures in selected areas. A further 62 branches have been selected for semi-open plan conversion. The Society will strengthen its offshore operations by establishing a wholly owned subsidiary company to administer operations through the existing office at Douglas, Isle of Man. The implementation of new equipment in branch offices is planned to take advantage of advances in information technology.

Your Directors record their appreciation to all Staff and Agents for their loyal service and enthusiastic support in a very busy and successful year.

The continuing support and confidence of our Members is very much appreciated and ensures the successful progress of the Society.

On behalf of the Board of Directors.

J. L. HILL
Chairman
31st January, 1990

Table 23.9 continued

	1989 £M	1988 £M
RESULTS FOR THE YEAR		
Profit for the year after taxation	50.5	41.0
FINANCIAL POSITION AT END OF YEAR		
Assets		
Liquid assets	960.8	850.3
Mortgages	5,218.4	4,408.8
Other commercial assets	6.6	0.5
Fixed and other assets	112.4	83.2
	6,298.2	5,342.8
Liabilities and capital		
Shares	4,702.4	4,151.7
Deposits and Loans	1,162.9	825.7
Other liabilities	123.6	111.1
Capital	309.3	254.3
	6,298.2	5,342.8

	1989 %	1988 %
SUMMARY OF KEY FINANCIAL RATIOS		
As a percentage of share, deposit and loan liabilities:–		
(a) Gross Capital	5.3	5.1
(b) Free Capital	3.5	3.5
Liquid assets as a percentage of total assets	15.3	15.9
Profit for the year as a percentage of average gross capital	17.9	17.6

Approved by the Board of Directors 31st January, 1990.

J. L. Hill	Chairman
S. J. Sebire	Joint Deputy Chairman
F. M. Shaw	Managing Director
T. J. Bayley	Finance Director

Auditors' Report to the Members of Britannia Building Society

We have examined the summary financial statement on pages 1 and 2.

In our opinion the summary financial statement is consistent with the accounts, business statement and directors' report for the year ended 31st December, 1989 and conforms with the requirements of section 76 of the Building Societies Act 1986 and regulations thereunder.

1st February, 1990 PRICE WATERHOUSE
MANCHESTER Chartered Accountants

23.128 The above are the legal requirements for annual reports by auditors contained in building society legislation. There could be additional reporting requirements under other legislation, for example the *Financial Services Act 1986*, but such requirements will vary according to the circumstances and are not dealt with in this chapter. The professional requirements of auditors are contained in Auditing Standards, issued by the APC. The APC has also developed guidelines to amplify the requirements laid down in Auditing Standards, most of which are applicable to the audit of building societies. The Auditing Guideline 'Building Societies in the United Kingdom' (AG 3.302) issued in its revised form in March 1989, is essential reading for anyone involved in a building society audit.

Annual accounts

23.129 The auditors' report to members on the annual accounts is required to state whether they have been prepared so as to conform with the requirements of Part VIII of the *Building Societies Act 1986* and the regulations made under it and whether, in the auditors' opinion, they give a true and fair view of the following matters:

- In the case of the income and expenditure account, of the income and expenditure for the year.
- In the case of the balance sheet, of the state of the society's affairs at the year end.
- In the case of the statement of the source and application of funds, of the manner in which the business of the society has been financed and in which its financial resources have been used during the year.

[BSA 1986 Sec 78(4)].

23.130 In relation to group accounts section 78(4) of the *Building Societies Act 1986* applies to the society and (so far as it concerns members of the society) the subsidiaries dealt with therein. [BSA 1986 Sec 78(5)].

23.131 As with companies, there are situations where additional matters are dealt with in the auditors' report to members as follows:

- Where, in the auditors' opinion, the annual accounts are not in agreement with the accounting records. [BSA 1986 Sec 79(2)].
- Where the auditors fail to obtain all the information and explanations and the access to documents which, to the best of their knowledge and belief, are necessary for the purposes of their audit. [BSA 1986 Sec 79(6)].

23.132 There is, however, no requirement to include in the auditors' report to members qualifications regarding the accounting records or the systems, unless the shortcomings impact on a true and fair view. Such qualifications will be reported to the Commission under section 82(2) of the *Building Societies Act 1986* (see paras 23.142 - 23.149 below).

Annual business statement

23.133 The auditors' report on the annual business statement does not deal with any matters which are prescribed not to be reported on by them. [BSA 1986 Sec 78(8)]. It therefore does not deal with information relating to directors and other officers required to be included in the annual business statement by paragraph 3 of Schedule 7 to the

Accounts Regulations. [SI 1987/2072 para 8(4)]. In respect of the rest of the statement it states whether it has been prepared so as to conform to the requirements of section 74 of the *Building Societies Act 1986* and whether, in the auditors' opinion, it gives a true representation of the matters in respect of which it is given. [BSA 1986 Sec 78(7)].

Directors' report

23.134 Unlike company auditors' reports, the auditors' report to the members of building societies covers the directors' report. They report whether it has been prepared to conform with the requirements of section 75 of the *Building Societies Act 1986* and whether, in their opinion, the information it gives is consistent with the accounting records and the annual accounts for the year. [BSA 1986 Sec 78(7)].

23.135 The auditors deal with the annual business statement and the directors' report within their report to members on the annual accounts. [BSA 1986 Sec 78(3)].

23.136 The following is a form of unqualified auditors' report to members of societies that do not have subsidiaries:

REPORT OF THE AUDITORS TO THE MEMBERS OF [NAME OF BUILDING SOCIETY]

We have audited the accounts on pages [] to [] in accordance with Auditing Standards.

In our opinion the accounts give a true and fair view of the state of affairs of the Society at [date], of the income and expenditure of the Society for the year then ended, and of the manner in which the business of the Society was financed and in which its financial resources were used during the year.

We have examined the annual business statement on pages [] to [] other than the details of directors and officers upon which we are not required to report. In our opinion the information which we have examined gives a true representation of those matters referred to therein.

We have examined the directors' report on pages [] to []. In our opinion the information given therein is consistent with the accounting records and the annual accounts.

In our opinion the accounts, the business statement and the directors' report have each been prepared so as to conform to the requirements of Part VIII of the Building Societies Act 1986 and regulations thereunder.

[Name of firm]

Chartered Accountants,

[Address].

[Date of report].

23.137 Where a society has subsidiaries, the unqualified report on the truth and fairness of the accounts takes the following form, the other paragraphs remaining unchanged:

We have audited the accounts on pages [] to [] in accordance with auditing standards.

In our opinion the accounts give a true and fair view of the state of affairs of the Society and of the Group at [date], of the income and expenditure of the Society and of the Group for the year then ended, and of the manner in which the business of the Group was financed and in which the Group's financial resources were used during the year.

23.138 The requirement to report on income and expenditure, rather than profit or loss, will normally involve additional audit work on the revenue account, and auditors of building societies that have limited companies as subsidiaries need to be satisfied that the scope of the subsidiaries' audits is sufficient to enable them to form an opinion on the income and expenditure of the group.

Summary financial statement

23.139 As noted in paragraph 23.55 above, the summary financial statement includes a statement of the auditors' opinion as to its consistency with the accounts, business statement and directors' report and its conformity with relevant legislation. [BSA 1986 Sec 76(5)]. It is interesting that the auditors' opinion on the summary financial statement is addressed not only to the members of the society, but also to its depositors. This is because section 76(1) of the *Building Societies Act 1986* requires the statement to be prepared for members and depositors. However, the *Building Societies Act 1986* does not provide for summary financial statements to be given to depositors except when they first deposit money with the society.

23.140 The following is a form of unqualified auditors' report on a summary financial statement:

REPORT OF THE AUDITORS TO THE MEMBERS AND DEPOSITORS OF [NAME OF BUILDING SOCIETY] ON THE SUMMARY FINANCIAL STATEMENT FOR THE YEAR ENDED [DATE]

We have examined the summary financial statement above.

In our opinion the summary financial statement is consistent with the accounts, business statement and directors' report for the year ended [date] and conforms to the requirements of section 76 of the Building Societies Act 1986 and regulations thereunder.

[Name of firm]

Chartered Accountants,

[Address].

[Date of report].

23.141 Where the auditors' report on the annual accounts is qualified in respect of their truth and fairness, it has to accompany every copy of the summary financial statement that is sent to a member entitled to receive notice of the annual general meeting, to the Commission and to the Central Office of the Registry of Friendly Societies, no later than 21 days before the annual general meeting. Furthermore, it has to be given to a new member or depositor and given to any other member on request. [BSA 1986 Sec 78(6)].

Conduct of business

23.142 In addition to their duties to report to members and depositors, outlined in the previous paragraphs, auditors of building societies are required to report annually to the Commission on the conduct of the society's business during the year in respect of:

- Its accounting records kept under section 71.
- The systems of control of its business and records and of inspection and report maintained under section 71.
- The system of safe custody of all documents relating to property mortgaged to the society maintained under section 12(12).

[BSA 1986 Sec 82(1)].

23.143 The report to the Commission must contain the auditors' opinion on whether each of the matters specified above complies with the relevant legislation and, if not, each specific requirement not complied with and the respects in which it was not complied with. [BSA 1986 Sec 82(3)].

23.144 Where, at any time during the year, a society had a subsidiary or other associated body linked by resolution, the auditors' report to the Commission must also cover the society's responsibilities, in respect of section 71(10). These responsibilities are to ensure that the accounting records and systems of control and inspection and report maintained by the society and those other bodies will enable the society to comply with section 71 in relation to the business of the society and those other bodies. [BSA 1986 Sec 82(4)].

23.145 The section 82 report has to be submitted by the society to the Commission within 90 days of its financial year end, a similar time limit to that imposed by section 71(11) in respect of the directors' own opinion on compliance. Unless the society agrees to a later date the auditors' report to the Commission has to be submitted to the society within 72 days of the year end (but not so as to prevent it meeting the 90 day limit). [BSA 1986 Sec 82(5)].

23.146 Qualifications of auditors' opinions in their reports to members and depositors are the exception rather than the rule, but in the case of reports to the Commission the opposite is the case, as can be seen by the example given in the Auditing Guideline, 'Building Societies in the United Kingdom' (AG3.302), outlined below:

AUDITORS' REPORT TO THE BUILDING SOCIETIES COMMISSION ON [NAME OF BUILDING SOCIETY] FOR THE YEAR ENDED [DATE]

We have examined the accounting records, the systems of control and of inspection and report and the system of safe custody of documents maintained by the society during the year ended [date].

Our examination was carried out in accordance with the Auditing Guideline 'Building Societies in the United Kingdom'. The scope of our work was limited to consideration of whether the foregoing records and systems complied with the requirements of sections 12 and 71 of the Building Societies Act 1986 (the Act).

In our opinion during the year ended [date].

either [some or all of (a) to (d)]

(a) [except for the matters set out at paragraph x of the appendix to this report/subject to the matters set out at paragraph x of the appendix to this report], the accounting records complied with the requirements of section 71 of the Act;

(b) [except for the matters set out at paragraph x of the appendix to this report/subject to the matters set out at paragraph x of the appendix to this report], the system of control of the business and records of the society complied with the requirements of section 71 of the Act;

(c) [except for the matters set out at paragraph x of the appendix to this report/subject to the matters set out at paragraph x of the appendix to this report], the system of inspection and report complied with the requirements of section 71 of the Act; and

(d) [except for the matters set out at paragraph x of the appendix to this report/subject to the matters set out at paragraph x of the appendix to this report], the system of safe custody of documents complied with the requirement of section 12(12) of the Act.

and/or [some or all of the following or other qualification] the accounting records/systems of control/systems of inspection and report/system of safe custody of documents were not established and maintained in accordance with the requirements of [specify section and sub-section of the Act] in the respects set out in the appendix attached to this report.

[Name of firm]

Chartered Accountants,

[Address].

[Date of report].

23.147 The content of auditors' reports on the conduct of business is confidential to the auditors, the client societies and the Commission. This confidentiality allows auditors to make positive comments on relevant matters without the risk of adverse comment in the public arena, which might result in unjustified loss of confidence among investors. The Commission too reacts positively to the reports as can be seen from the following extract from a letter to all Chief Executives, dated 2nd October 1990:

> *"The Commission is pleased to note the general high quality of the review and reporting process. It appreciates the commitment of the societies and their auditors to its success. Discussion of systems issues with societies on the basis of full and accurate reports now forms a useful part of the supervisory system."*

23.148 Reference is made above (para 23.130) to the Auditing Guideline 'Building Societies in the United Kingdom' (AG 3.302), is essential reading for anyone involved in a building society audit and that is particularly so in respect of compliance with section 71 of the *Building Societies Act 1986*. The Commission's principal Prudential Note on systems (1987/4) is reproduced as an appendix to the guideline and contains specific guidance for societies and for auditors.

23.149 The confidential nature of the dialogue between auditors, societies and the Commission is a pre-requisite for the *ad hoc* reporting provisions contained in the *Building Societies Act 1986*. Where at any time auditors are satisfied that it is expedient to do so, in order to protect the investments of shareholders or depositors, or the Commission (on its being so satisfied) asks them to do so, they are entitled to give the Commission information on business conduct. This right is notwithstanding any obligation of client confidentiality or even the interests of the society. [BSA 1986 Sec 82(8)]. Clearly to report to the Commission without the knowledge of the society is a step to be taken in only the most extreme situations. On the other hand the Commission will usually call for a specific systems report from auditors (via the society) before consenting to the commencement of a new business venture.

Transactions with directors

23.150 Building societies are required to keep registers of certain transactions and arrangements made with a director or connected person in the current financial year and the previous ten financial years. [BSA 1986 Sec 68(1)]. Each year a statement must be prepared giving particulars of those transactions and must be made available for inspection by members at the annual general meeting and for fifteen days before that meeting. [BSA 1986 Sec 68(3)]. Copies of the particulars must also be sent to the Commission and put on the society's public file at the Central Office of the Registry of Friendly Societies. [BSA 1986 Sec 68(5)].

23.151 Before the section 68(3) statement is made available for inspection it must be examined by the auditors, who report to the members on it. Their report is annexed to the statement before it is made available for inspection. [BSA 1986 Sec 68(9)].

23.152 The particulars to be included in the statement are the requisite particulars (which are those specified in Schedule 9 to the *Building Societies Act 1986*) of those transactions and arrangements that were included in the register at any time during the last completed year. Auditors are not required to identify transactions that are not included in the register, merely to conclude whether the statements contain the requisite particulars of those transactions that are included in the register and, if not, include the missing details in their report. [BSA 1986 Sec 68(10)].

23.153 The following is a form of unqualified section 68(9) report:

REPORT OF THE AUDITORS TO THE MEMBERS OF [NAME OF BUILDING SOCIETY] ON THE STATEMENT OF PARTICULARS OF TRANSACTIONS AND ARRANGEMENTS INCLUDED IN THE SECTION 68(1) REGISTER AT ANY TIME DURING THE YEAR ENDED [DATE]

We have examined the foregoing statement of particulars of transactions and arrangements with directors and persons connected with them falling within section 65(1) of the Building Societies Act 1986.

In our opinion the statement contains the requisite particulars, as required by section 68 of the Building Societies Act 1986, in relation to those transactions recorded by the society in the register of transactions and arrangements maintained under section 68(1) of that Act.

[Name of firm]

Chartered Accountants,
[Address].

[Date of report].

Dissolution, winding up, mergers and transfer of business

23.154 Part X of the *Building Societies Act 1986* contains provisions for the termination of societies, which can be by dissolution or winding up.

23.155 Dissolution of a society will take place:

- By an instrument of dissolution, consented to and signed by three quarters of a society's members holding not less than two thirds of its shares. [BSA 1986 Sec 87].

- Upon its merging with another society to form a new one. [BSA 1986 Sec 93].

- Upon its engagements being transferred to another society which undertakes to fulfil them. [BSA 1986 Sec 94].

- Upon the transfer of the whole of its business to an existing company or one specially formed for the purpose. [BSA 1986 Sec 97].

23.156 Winding up may be voluntary, by passing a special resolution, or compulsorily by the court, under modified winding up legislation. [BSA 1986 Secs 88, 89].

23.157 The rules governing the various methods of terminating a building society are specialised and often complex. They are beyond the scope of this book and readers meeting those situations for the first time should seek specialist help.

THE BUILDING SOCIETIES (ACCOUNTS AND) RELATED PROVISIONS) REGULATIONS 1987 (SI 1987/2072)

Made - - - -	*24th November 1987*
Laid before Parliament	*7th December 1987*
Coming into force -	*31st December 1987*

ARRANGEMENT OF REGULATIONS

The Building Societies Commission, with the consent of the Treasury, in exercise of the powers conferred on it by sections 73, 74(3) and (6), 75(1) and 76(3) of the Building Societies Act 1986**(a)**, and of all other powers enabling it in that behalf, hereby makes the following Regulations:

Citation and commencement

1. These Regulations may be cited as the Building Societies (Accounts and Related Provisions) Regulations 1987 and shall come into force on 31st December 1987.

Interpretation

2.—(1) In these Regulations–

"the Act" means the Building Societies Act 1986;

"group accounts society" means a society the directors of which are obliged by section 72 of the Act (duty of directors to prepare annual accounts) to prepare group accounts;

"particular account" means an income and expenditure account, a balance sheet, or a statement of the source and application of funds;

"relevant subsidiary" means a subsidiary of a group accounts society with which the group accounts of the society are required by section 72 of the Act to deal;

"single accounts society" means a society which is not a group accounts society; and

"society" means a building society.

(a) 1986 c.53.

(2) Nothing in these Regulations shall be taken to imply that the carrying on by a society of any activity provision for the recording of which is contained in these Regulations is, by virtue of that provision, within the powers of that society.

Annual accounts

3.—(1) In respect of the annual accounts of any single accounts society–

(a) every income and expenditure account shall be prepared in the format set out in Part I of Schedule 1 below,

(b) every balance sheet shall be prepared in the format set out in Part I of Schedule 2 below, and

(c) every statement of the source and application of funds shall be prepared in the format set out in Part I of Schedule 3 below,

and in accordance with the relevant provisions, and every such document shall, subject to the following paragraphs of this Regulation, be prepared in the order and under the headings and sub-headings in the format applicable to it.

(2) In respect of the annual accounts of any group accounts society–

(a) the provisions of this Regulation shall apply subject to the provisions of Regulation 4 below, the supplementary provisions of which shall also have effect in relation to those accounts, and

(b) within those accounts–

(i) every income and expenditure account relating to the society shall be prepared in the format set out in Part I of Schedule 1 below,

(ii) every income and expenditure account relating to the society and its relevant subsidiaries shall be prepared in the format set out in Part II of Schedule 1 below,

(iii) every balance sheet relating to the society shall be prepared in the format set out in Part I of Schedule 2 below,

(iv) every balance sheet relating to the society and its relevant subsidiaries shall be prepared in the format set out in Part II of Schedule 2 below, and

(v) every statement of the source and application of funds of the society and its relevant subsidiaries shall be prepared in the format set out in Part II of Schedule 3 below, and if such a statement is also prepared in relation to the society alone, that further statement shall be prepared in the format set out in Part I thereof,

and in accordance with the relevant provisions, and every such document shall, subject to the following paragraphs of this Regulation, be prepared in the order and under the headings and sub-headings in the format applicable to it.

(3) Paragraphs (1) and (2) above are not to be read as–

(a) requiring the heading or sub-heading for any item to be distinguished by any letter or number assigned to that item in the format in which it appears, or

(b) prohibiting the showing of any item in a particular account in greater detail than is required by the format for that particular account.

(4) Items preceded by lower case letter or Roman numeral in any format set out in Schedule 1, 2 or 3 may be combined in a society's annual accounts for any financial year if either:–

(a) their individual amounts are not material to assessing–

(i) in respect of an income and expenditure account, the income and expenditure of the society (or, as the case may be, the society and its relevant subsidiaries) for that year, and

(ii) in respect of a balance sheet, the state of affairs of the society (or, as the case may be, the society and its relevant subsidaries) as at the end of that year, and

(iii) in respect of a statement of the source and application of funds, the manner in which the business of the society (or, as the case may be, the society and its relevant subsidiaries) has been financed and in which its (or their) financial resources have been used during that year, or

(b) their combination facilitates that assessment,

but where subparagraph (b) above applies, the individual amounts of any items so combined shall be disclosed in a note to the annual accounts.

(5) Subject to paragraph (7) below, a heading or sub-heading for an item contained in any format set out in Schedule 1, 2 or 3 shall not be included if there is no amount to be shown for that item in respect of the financial year to which the annual accounts relate (and a total need not be included if, as a result of this paragraph, it would be composed of a single item).

(6) The annual accounts may deal with an investment of the society or any relevant subsidiary in the shares of any body corporate which is not a relevant subsidiary by way of the equity method of accounting in any case where that body corporate is so closely associated with the society or that relevant subsidiary as to justify the use of that method in dealing with that investment in the shares of that body corporate.

(7) For the purpose of comparing particular accounts with those for the preceding financial year–

(a) in respect of every item shown in a balance sheet, income and expenditure account and statement of the source and application of funds, the corresponding amount for the preceding financial year shall be shown,

(b) where that corresponding amount is not comparable with the amount to be shown for the item in question in respect of the financial year to which the annual accounts relate the former amount shall be adjusted and particulars of the adjustment and the reasons for it shall be disclosed in a note to the annual accounts, and

(c) paragraph (5) above does not apply in any case where an amount can be shown for the item to which the heading or sub-heading relates in respect of the preceding financial year, and in such a case that amount shall be shown under the heading or sub-heading required for that item.

(8) In this Regulation, "the relevant provisions" means, in relation to any particular account, Part III of the Schedule below Parts I and II of which contain formats of that particular account.

Group accounts–supplementary provisions

4.—(1) If the financial year of any relevant subsidiary does not coincide with that of the society, the components of the annual accounts relating to the society and its relevant subsidiaries shall, so far as they relate to that subsidiary, relate to its financial year ending last before the end of the financial year of the society dealt with in the annual accounts unless–

(a) the directors of the society are of the opinion that there are good reasons against it, and

(b) they disclose those reasons in the notes to the annual accounts.

(2) Each particular account which is a group account shall combine the information contained in the particular account of the society and the accounts of its relevant subsidiaries from which it is derived, adjusted so far as is necessary to consolidate those accounts.

(3) Where a society has subsidiaries whose financial years do not end with that of the society, the following information shall be given in relation to each such subsidiary by way of a note to the annual accounts, that is to say–

(a) the reasons why the society's directors consider that the subsidiaries' financial years should not end with that of the society, and

(b) the dates on which the subsidiaries' financial years ending last before that of the society respectively ended or the earliest and latest of those dates.

Notes to annual accounts

5.—(1) The annual accounts of any single accounts society shall, subject to paragraph (5) below, include notes to them containing the material specified, set out in the manner specified, in Schedule 4 below, as well as the notes required to be included by other provisions of these Regulations.

(2) The annual accounts of any group accounts society shall, subject to paragraph (5) below and any provision in Schedule 4 below which indicates otherwise, include notes to them containing–

(a) in respect of the society, and

(b) in respect of the society and its relevant subsidiaries in combination,

the material specified, set out in the manner specified, in Schedule 4 below, as well as the notes required to be included by other provisions of these Regulations.

(3) For the purposes of paragraph (2)(b) above–

(a) any reference in a relevant provision of Schedule 4 below to a society shall be taken as a reference to the society and its relevant subsidiaries in combination, and

(b) each associated body of the society which is not a relevant subsidiary shall be treated as an associated body of theirs.

(4) In paragraph (3) above "relevant provision" means, in relation to Schedule 4 below, a provision thereof other than paragraphs 4 and 21.

(5) Paragraphs (1) and (2) above are not to be read as prohibiting the disclosing of any material in the notes to the annual accounts in greater detail than is required by these Regulations.

Accounting principles and rules

6. Each society shall prepare its annual accounts in accordance with the accounting principles and rules set out in Schedule 5 below.

Directors' report

7. Each directors' report of a society prepared under section 75 of the Act (directors' report) shall contain, in addition to the other matters required to be contained in it by the Act, the material specified, set out in the manner specified, in Schedule 6 below.

Annual business statement

8.—(1) Each annual business statement of a society prepared under section 74 of the Act (duty of directors to prepare annual business statement) shall, subject to paragraphs (2) and (3) below, contain the material specified in Schedule 7 below.

(2) Nothing in this Regulation–

(a) requires the setting out of the material specified in Schedule 7 below in any particular manner, or

(b) prohibits the inclusion, for the purpose of the giving in the annual business statement of a true representation of the matters to which that material relates, of material additional to that required to be included by this Regulation.

(3) Any material required or permitted by this Regulation to be contained in the annual business statement may be included instead in the notes to the annual accounts or the directors' report and, where any such material is so included, the annual business statement shall specify where in those notes or (as the case may be) that report that material is to be found.

(4) The material required to be contained in the annual business statement by virtue of paragraph 3 of Schedule 7 below shall not be the subject of report by auditors under section 78 of the Act (auditors' report).

Summary financial statement

9.—(1) Subject to paragraph (2) of this Regulation, each summary financial statement of a society prepared under section 76 of the Act (summary financial statement for members and depositors) shall be prepared in the order and under the headings and sub-headings shown in the formats (and as directed by the notes) set out in Part I, and in accordance with the provisions of Part II, of Schedule 8 below, so as to contain–

(a) a statement in the prescribed form for the purposes of section 76(4) of the Act,
(b) a summary directors' report,
(c) a summary statement, and
(d) a summary of key financial ratios,

followed by the statement of the auditors' opinion required to be included by section 76(5) of the Act, and so as to give a summary account of the relevant matters.

(2) Paragraph (1) above is not to be read as–

(a) requiring the heading or sub-heading for any item to be distinguished by any letter or number assigned to that item in the format in which it appears,
(b) requiring the headings in Section B of Part I of Schedule 8 below to contain any particular wording,
(c) prohibiting the inclusion, in place of the words "THIS YEAR" and "LAST YEAR" in Sections C and D of Part I of Schedule 8 below, of other column headings consistent with paragraph 2 of Part II of that Schedule, or
(d) prohibiting the inclusion, for the purpose of assisting the giving in the summary financial statement of a summary account of the relevant matters, of material additional to that required to be included by this Regulation.

(3) In this Regulation "the relevant matters" are, in relation to a financial year of a society with which a summary financial statement deals, the financial development (during the year) and the financial position (at the end of the year) of–

(a) where section 76(2) of the Act does not apply, the society, and
(b) where section 76(2) of the Act applies, the society and its relevant subsidiaries.

Interpretation of Schedules

10. Schedule 9 below shall have effect for the interpretation of the Schedules to these Regulations.

Transitional provisions

11. Where any provision of these Regulations requires–

(a) the recording of a particular item for the entirety of a financial year, and–
   (i) that financial year began before the coming into force of these Regulations, and
   (ii) the legislation in force during the period beginning with the start of the financial year and ending immediately before the coming into force of these Regulations did not require the recording of, or the making of a return of, that particular item, or
(b) the recording of a particular item as at the end of a previous financial year, and–
   (i) that previous financial year ended before the coming into force of these Regulations, and
   (ii) the legislation in force as at the end of that previous financial year did not require the recording of, or the making of a return of, that particular item,

then if the records of the society are so kept as to enable that particular item to be identified, it shall be identified and so recorded, but if the records of the society are not so kept, it shall instead be included on the basis of an estimate.

In witness whereof the common seal of the Building Societies Commission is hereto fixed, and is authenticated by me, a person authorised under paragraph 14 of Schedule 1 to the Building Societies Act 1986, on 19th November 1987.

D. B. Severn
Secretary to the Commission

We consent to this Order.

Peter Lloyd
Tony Durant
Two of the Lords Commissioners of
Her Majesty's Treasury

24th November 1987

SCHEDULE 1

Regulation 3

PART I

FORMAT OF SOCIETY INCOME AND EXPENDITURE ACCOUNT

1. Interest receivable:
   (a) (i) On secured advances
   (ii) On other lending
   (b) (i) On fixed-interest liquid assets
   (ii) On other liquid assets.

2. Interest payable:
   (a) On retail funds and deposits
   (b) On non-retail funds and deposits

3. Net interest receivable

4. Income from associated bodies:
   (a) Share of profits of associated companies
   (b) Other

5. Other income and charges:
   (a) Commissions receivable
   (b) Commissions payable
   (c) Other financial income
   (d) Other financial charges
   (e) Other operating income

6. Amortisation of intangible fixed assets

7. Management expenses:
   (a) Staff costs, showing separately–
   (i) Wages and salaries
   (ii) Social security costs
   (iii) Other pension costs
   (b) Depreciation and other amounts written off tangible fixed assets
   (c) Other expenses

8. Provisions for loans, advances and guarantees

9. Provisions for interests and shares in associated bodies

10. Profit or loss on ordinary activities before tax

11. Tax on profit or loss on ordinary activities:
    (a) Society
    (b) Associated companies

12. Profit or loss on ordinary activities after tax

13. Extraordinary income

14. Extraordinary charges

15. Extraordinary profit or loss

16. Tax on extraordinary profit or loss

17. Extraordinary profit or loss after tax

18. Profit or loss for the financial year

PART II

FORMAT OF CONSOLIDATED INCOME AND EXPENDITURE ACCOUNT

1. Interest receivable:
   (a) (i) On secured advances
   (ii) On other lending
   (b) (i) On fixed-interest liquid assets
   (ii) On other liquid assets
   (c) Other

2. Interest payable:
   (a) On retail funds and deposits
   (b) On non-retail funds and deposits

3. Net interest receivable

4. Income from associated bodies:
   (a) Share of profits of associated companies
   (b) Other

5. Other income and charges:
   (a) Commissions receivable
   (b) Commissions payable
   (c) Other financial income
   (d) Other financial charges
   (e) Other operating income

6. Amortisation of intangible fixed assets

7. Management expenses:
   (a) Staff costs, showing separately–
   (i) Wages and salaries
   (ii) Social security costs
   (iii) Other pension costs
   (b) Depreciation and other amounts written off tangible fixed assets
   (c) Other expenses

8. Provisions for loans, advances and guarantees

9. Provisions for interests and shares in associated bodies

10. Profit or loss on ordinary activities before tax

11. Tax on profit or loss on ordinary activities:
    (a) Society and relevant subsidiaries
    (b) Associated companies

12. Profit or loss on ordinary activities after tax

13. Minority interests

14. Profit or loss before extraordinary items

15. Extraordinary income

16. Extraordinary charges

17. Extraordinary profit or loss

18. Tax on extraordinary profit or loss

19. Extraordinary profit or loss after tax

20. Profit or loss for the financial year

PART III

PROVISIONS APPLICABLE TO PARTS I AND II

1. Item 1(a) and (b) in each of Parts I and II above shall include–

(a) all income from assets entered under Asset items 2, 3, and 4(a), (b) and (c) in the balance sheet in the corresponding Part of Schedule 2 below, however calculated,

(b) interest receivable on–

(i) in the case of Part I above, advances and loans to associated bodies, and

(ii) in the case of Part II above, advances and loans to associated bodies other than relevant subsidiaries, and

(c) (in item 1(b) in each case) interest, other income and profits net of losses arising from liquid assets,

and the notes to the annual accounts shall disclose the amount of profits net of losses arising from liquid assets and the amount of interest and other income arising from them as separate amounts unless those two amounts are separately stated under each of item 1(b)(i) and 1(b)(ii) in each case.

2. Item 1(a)(i) in Parts I and II above shall include all income to which paragraph 1 above refers arising from secured loans which are not advances secured on land as well as from advances secured on land.

3. Items 4(a) and 11(b) in Parts I and II above shall only be included where the equity method of accounting is used.

4.—(1) Item 5(a) in Parts I and II above shall include income in respect of all services supplied for the account of third parties, and item 5(b) in those Parts shall include charges for the use of services of third parties.

(2) Any amount, apart from an appointed agency payment, which represents–

(a) commissions for guarantees and loan administration,

(b) commissions and other charges and income in respect of payment transactions, account administration charges and commissions for the safe custody and administration of deeds, securities or other related documents,

(c) commissions for foreign currency transactions,

(d) commissions and other charges and income in connection with insurance and pension contracts, or

(e) commissions and other charges and income in connection with arranging brokerage services,

and which falls within subparagraph (1) above but would also be capable of being included within an item other than those referred to in that subparagraph shall be included within the items so referred to.

(3) For the purposes of subparagraph (2) above, an appointed agency payment is a payment for a relevant agency function to a person who, by virtue of an appointment by a society, acts as its agent in that function, and a relevant agency function comprises action as an agent of the society for the purpose of receipt of sums in respect of shares or deposits or the making of advances secured on land.

5.—(1) Item 5(c) in Parts I and II above shall include the net profits, and item 5(d) the net losses, on financial instruments, and item 5(e) of those Parts shall, where it relates to development properties, include the profits net of losses on them.

(2) In subparagraph (1) above "financial instrument" means–

(a) in relation to Parts I and II above, an instrument the powers of the society in relation to which are derived from section 23 of the Act (power to hedge) and any option to purchase or sell any liquid asset, and

(b) additionally in relation to Part II above, an instrument on which interest or a dividend is capable of being received and which is not an advance, a loan or a liquid asset.

SCHEDULE 2

Regulation 3

PART I

FORMAT OF SOCIETY BALANCE SHEET

ASSETS

1. LIQUID ASSETS
   (a) Cash in hand and with banks
   (b) UK Government securities
   (c) Other securities–
      (i) Issued by public bodies
      (ii) Issued by other borrowers

Commercial Assets

2. ADVANCES SECURED ON RESIDENTIAL PROPERTY

3. OTHER ADVANCES SECURED ON LAND

4. OTHER COMMERCIAL ASSETS
   (a) Loans for mobile homes
   (b) Unsecured loans
   (c) Secured loans
   (d) Residential properties
      (i) Held for rental
      (ii) Development properties
         (aa) Completed
         (ab) Work in progress
   (e) Investments in associated bodies
      (i) Shares held in associated bodies
      (ii) Loans to associated bodies
   (f) Other

- - - - - - - -

5. FIXED ASSETS
   (a) Intangible assets
      (i) Concessions, patents, licences, trade marks and similar rights and assets
      (ii) Goodwill
   (b) Tangible assets
   (i) Land and buildings
   (ii) Equipment, fixtures, fittings and vehicles
   (iii) Payments on account and assets in course of construction

6. OTHER ASSETS

7. TOTAL ASSETS

LIABILITIES AND RESERVES

Shares and Deposits

8. RETAIL FUNDS AND DEPOSITS
   (a) Shares
   (b) Deposits
   (c) Deferred shares

9. NON-RETAIL FUNDS AND DEPOSITS
   (a) Amounts owed to banks
   (b) Time deposits
   (c) Certificates of deposit
   (d) Negotiable bonds
   (e) Fixed and floating rate notes
   (f) Other deposits
   (g) Shares
   (h) Deferred shares

– – – – – – – –

10. OTHER LIABILITIES
   (a) Income tax
   (b) Corporation tax
   (c) Other creditors

11. PROVISIONS FOR LIABILITIES AND CHARGES
   (a) Provisions for pensions and similar obligations
   (b) Provisions for taxation
   (c) Other provisions

12. SUBORDINATED LIABILITIES

13. TOTAL LIABILITIES

Reserves

14. General Reserve

15. Revaluation Reserve

– – – –

16. Other Reserves

17. TOTAL RESERVES

18. TOTAL LIABILITIES AND RESERVES

PART II

FORMAT OF CONSOLIDATED BALANCE SHEET

ASSETS

1. LIQUID ASSETS
   (a) Cash in hand and with banks
   (b) UK Government securities
   (c) Other securities–
      (i) Issued by public bodies
      (ii) Issued by other borrowers

Commercial Assets

2. ADVANCES SECURED ON RESIDENTIAL PROPERTY

3. OTHER ADVANCES SECURED ON LAND

4. OTHER COMMERCIAL ASSETS
   (a) Loans for mobile homes
   (b) Unsecured loans
   (c) Secured loans
   (d) Residential properties
      (i) Held for rental
      (ii) Development properties
         (aa) Completed
         (ab) Work in progress
   (e) Investments in associated bodies
      (i) Shares held in associated bodies
      (ii) Loans to associated bodies
   (f) Other

\- - - - - - - -

5. OTHER OPERATING ASSETS
   (a) Loans
   (b) Other

6. FIXED ASSETS
   (a) Intangible assets
      (i) Concessions, patents, licences, trade marks and similar rights and assets
      (ii) Goodwill
   (b) Tangible assets
      (i) Land and buildings
      (ii) Equipment, fixtures, fittings and vehicles
      (iii) Payments on account and assets in course of construction

7. OTHER ASSETS

8. TOTAL ASSETS

LIABILITIES AND RESERVES

Shares and Deposits

9. RETAIL FUNDS AND DEPOSITS
   - (a) Shares
   - (b) Deposits
   - (c) Deferred shares

10. NON-RETAIL FUNDS AND DEPOSITS
    - (a) Amounts owed to banks
    - (b) Time deposits
    - (c) Certificates of deposit
    - (d) Negotiable bonds
    - (e) Fixed and floating rate notes
    - (f) Other deposits
    - (g) Shares
    - (h) Deferred shares

– – – – – – – – –

11. OTHER LIABILITIES
    - (a) Income tax
    - (b) Corporation tax
    - (c) Other creditors

12. PROVISIONS FOR LIABILITIES AND CHARGES
    - (a) Provisions for pensions and similar obligations
    - (b) Provisions for taxation
    - (c) Other provisions

13. SUBORDINATED LIABILITIES

14. TOTAL LIABILITIES

Reserves

15. General Reserve

16. Revaluation Reserve

17. Other Reserves

– – – –

18. TOTAL RESERVES

19. MINORITY INTERESTS

20. TOTAL LIABILITIES AND RESERVES

PART III

PROVISIONS APPLICABLE TO PARTS I AND II

1. The heading "Shares and Deposits" in the balance sheet in Part I above may instead be expressed as "Shares, Deposits and Loans" and if it is so expressed–

(a) the corresponding heading in the balance sheet in Part II above shall be similarly expressed, and

(b) in the balance sheets in Parts I and II above the expression "Other deposits" shall be replaced by the expression "Other deposits and loans".

2. Any asset in or liability to–

(a) in the case of Part I above, an associated body, and

(b) in the case of Part II above, an associated body which is not a relevant subsidiary,

shall be shown separately as a component of the item within which is it included.

3. In Asset item 1 of Parts I and II above–

(a) there shall be included in item 1(a)–

(i) cash, and

(ii) deposits (not being marketable securities) with the Bank of England or any Banking Act authorised institution,

(b) there shall be included in item 1(b)–

(i) marketable securities issued in the United Kingdom by Her Majesty's Government, and

(ii) marketable securities issued in the United Kingdom in respect of which the obligations of the issuer as to payment are guaranteed by Her Majesty's Government, and

(c) there shall be included in item 1(c) all liquid assets other than those included in item 1(a) or (b), and within item 1(c)–

(i) any asset which represents a liability of, or comprises a security issued by, Her Majesty's Government, a Government Department, a relevant authority or any other body exercising statutory functions shall be included in item 1(c)(i), and

(ii) any asset which comprises a security issued by a nationalised industry or otherwise does not fall to be included in item 1(c)(i) shall be included in item 1(c)(ii),

and for the purposes of this paragraph the expressions "cash", "deposit", "marketable security", "Banking Act authorised institution" and "relevant authority" have the meanings which they have for the purposes of the Building Societies (Liquid Asset) Regulations 1987**(a)**.

4. In Asset items 2 and 3 in Parts I and II above the expression "ADVANCES SECURED ON RESIDENTIAL PROPERTY" shall correspond to advances which are class 1 advances, and the expression "OTHER ADVANCES SECURED ON LAND" to advances which are class 2 advances, for the purpose of the requirements of Part III (advances, loans and other assets) of the Act for the structure of commercial assets.

5. Within Asset item 4 of Parts I and II above–

(a) in item 4(a) there shall be included mobile home loans,

(b) in item 4(b) there shall be included loans to which section 16 (power to lend to individuals) of the Act applies and which do not fall to be included in item 4(c),

(c) in item 4(c) there shall be included loans on any security (whether partial or full and whether comprising property or a guarantee) to which section 16 of the Act applies, and

(d) in item 4(d) there shall be included all property to which section 17 of the Act (power to hold and develop land), other than section 17(6), applies,

and each subdivision of that Asset item shall in Part II above also apply to any asset which arises from the activity of a relevant subsidiary and would, were that relevant subsidiary the society, be an asset to which that subdivision would apply.

(a) S.I. 1987/1499.

6. Premises to which section 17(6) of the Act applies (and premises of a relevant subsidiary which would, were they premises of a society, be premises to which that provision would apply) shall be included in Asset item 5(b)(i) (and not in Asset item 4(f)) in Part I above, and in Asset item 6(b)(i) (and not in Asset item 4(f)) in Part II above.

7. Amounts in respect of assets shall be included in Asset item 5(a)(i) in Part I above (or, as the case may be, 6(a)(i) in Part II above) only if either–

(a) the assets were acquired for valuable consideration and are not required to be shown under goodwill, or

(b) the assets in question were created by the society (or, as the case may be, the society or a relevant subsidiary).

8. Amounts shall be included in Asset item 5(a)(ii) in Part I above or 6(a)(ii) in Part II above to represent goodwill only to the extent that the goodwill was acquired for valuable consideration.

9. In Liability items 8 and 9 of Part I above and 9 and 10 of Part II above all deferred shares shall be included as such (and not as shares) and for the purposes of this paragraph shares (of whatever nominal value) to which Article 3 of the Building Societies (Designated Capital Resources) Order 1986**(a)** (shares issued as deferred shares under previous legislation) applies shall be treated as deferred shares.

10.—(1) All liabilities of a relevant subsidiary of a society in respect of deposits shall be included in Liability item 10 of Part II above where they would, were they liabilities of the society, be classifiable as non-retail funds and deposits, and any other such liabilities of the relevant subsidiary shall be included in liability item 9 thereof.

(2) Any liabilities of a relevant subsidiary of a society in respect of shares, where included in the balance sheet in Part II above, shall be included in Liability item 19 thereof.

11.—(1) In Liability item 9 of Part I above and 10 of Part II above–

(a) in "Amounts owed to banks" there shall be included liabilities to which subsection (4)(bb) of section 7 of the Act applies (or, where in Part II above the liability is that of a relevant subsidiary, would apply were that relevant subsidiary the society);

(b) in "Time deposits" there shall be included liabilities to which subsection (4)(b) of that section applies (or, where in Part II above the liability is that of a relevant subsidiary, would apply were that relevant subsidiary the society);

(c) in item 9(c), (d) and (e) of Part I above and 10(c), (d) and (e) of Part II above there shall be included liabilities to which subsection (4)(a) and (aa) of that section applies (or, where in Part II above the liability is that of a relevant subsidiary, would apply were that relevant subsidiary the society).

(2) For the purpose of those Liability items–

(a) "certificate of deposit" and "floating rate note" have the respective meanings which they have in the Building Societies (Liquid Asset) Regulations 1987, and

(b) "fixed rate note" means a note which embodies a right, transferable to any person by delivery or by a method specified in the note, to receive a principal sum and interest at a rate which is fixed as specified in the note.

12. Any subordinated loan capital of the society shall be included in Liability item 12 in Part I above and 13 in Part II above and in no other such Liability item, but this requirement shall not be taken to exclude the obligation to include in Liability item 13 in Part II above subordinated liabilities of relevant subsidiaries.

(a) S.I. 1986/1878.

SCHEDULE 3

Regulation 3

PART I

FORMAT OF SOCIETY STATEMENT OF THE SOURCE AND APPLICATION OF FUNDS

Source of Funds

1. Increase in free capital

2. Advances and loans repaid by borrowers

3. Net receipts from retail funds and deposits

4. Net receipts from non-retail funds and deposits

5. Other items

6. Total source of funds

Application of Funds

7. Increase in liquid assets

8. Advances and loans made to borrowers

9. Increase in other commercial assets

10. Other items

11. Total application of funds

Increase in Free Capital

Source of Funds

12. Profit on ordinary activities after tax

13. Extraordinary profit after tax

14. Adjustment for items not involving the movement of funds:
   (a) Depreciation and other amounts written off tangible fixed assets
   (b) Amortisation of intangible fixed assets
   (c) Profit on disposal of fixed assets
   (d) Increase in general provision for loans, advances and guarantees
   (e) Profits retained in associated companies

15. Funds generated from operations

16. Funds from other sources:
   (a) Disposal of tangible fixed assets
   (b) Disposal of intangible fixed assets
   (c) Issue of subordinated loan capital

Application of Funds

17. Purchase of fixed assets:
   (a) Purchase of tangible fixed assets
   (b) Purchase of intangible fixed assets

18. Increase in free capital

PART II

FORMAT OF CONSOLIDATED STATEMENT OF THE SOURCE AND APPLICATION OF FUNDS

Source of Funds

1. Increase in free capital
2. Advances and loans repaid by borrowers
3. Net receipts from retail funds and deposits
4. Net receipts from non-retail funds and deposits
5. Other items
6. Total source of funds

Application of Funds

7. Increase in liquid assets
8. Advances and loans made to borrowers
9. Increase in other commercial assets
10. Increase in other operating assets
11. Other items
12. Total application of funds

Increase in Free Capital

Source of Funds

13. Profit on ordinary activities after tax less minority interests
14. Extraordinary profit after tax
15. Adjustment for items not involving the movement of funds:
    (a) Depreciation and other amounts written off tangible fixed assets
    (b) Amortisation of intangible fixed assets
    (c) Profit on disposal of fixed assets
    (d) Increase in general provision for loans, advances and guarantees
    (e) Profits retained in associated companies
    (f) Minority interests in retained profits
16. Funds generated from operations
17. Funds from other sources:
    (a) Disposal of tangible fixed assets
    (b) Disposal of intangible fixed assets
    (c) Issue of subordinated loan capital

Application of Funds

18. Purchase of fixed assets:
    (a) Purchase of tangible fixed assets
    (b) Purchase of intangible fixed assets
19. Dividends paid to minority shareholders
20. Increase in free capital

PART III

PROVISIONS APPLICABLE TO PARTS I AND II

1. In Parts I and II above assets to which section 17(6) of the Act applies shall be treated as fixed assets and not as commercial assets.

2. In Part II above–

(a) any asset which arises from the activity of a relevant subsidiary and would, were the relevant subsidiary the society, be a commercial asset, shall (subject to subparagraph (b) below) be treated as a commercial asset, but

(b) assets to which section 17(6) of the Act would apply by the operation of subparagraph (a) above shall be treated as fixed assets and not as commercial assets.

3.—(1) No subordinated loan capital shall, in Part I or II above, be treated as retail or non-retail funds and deposits.

(2) Subject to subparagraph (1) above, in Part II above the liabilities of any relevant subsidiary of a society in respect of deposits which would, were they liabilities of the society, be classifiable as non-retail funds and deposits shall be treated as non-retail funds and deposits and any other such liabilities of the relevant subsidiary shall be treated as retail funds and deposits.

4. Where relevant subsidiaries have been acquired or disposed of during a financial year to which a statement of the source and application of funds relates, the effect of such acquisitions or disposals shall be summarised in aggregate by way of a footnote to the statement which shall be separate from the notes to the annual accounts.

5.—(1) There shall be inserted in the notes to the annual accounts such analyses of the relevant items as are material to the assessment of the key factors.

(2) For the purposes of subparagraph (1) above–

(a) the relevant items are item 9 in Part I above and items 9 and 10 in Part II above, and

(b) the key factors, in relation to any statement of the source and application of funds, are–

(i) in Part I above, the manner in which the business of the society has been financed and in which its financial resources have been used, and

(ii) in Part II above, the manner in which the business of the society and its relevant subsidiaries has been financed and in which their financial resources have been used,

during the financial year to which the statement relates.

6.—(1) Where in any item in a statement in Part I or II above a positive term is used, and the amount referable thereto represents its corresponding negative term, the corresponding negative term shall be used instead and, where that change falls to be made within the relevant section of the statement, the format of the relevant section of the statement shall be changed so far as necessary to include that item in the grouping opposite to that specified for it in the format.

(2) For the purposes of paragraph (1) above the positive terms are increase, receipt and profit, their respective corresponding negative terms are decrease, outflow and loss, the groupings are source of funds and application of funds, and the relevant section of the statement comprises–

(a) in Part I above, the section ending with item 11, and

(b) in Part II above, the section ending with item 12.

SCHEDULE 4

Regulation 5

NOTES TO ANNUAL ACCOUNTS

Accounting policies

1. The accounting policies adopted by the society in determining the amounts to be included in respect of items shown in the balance sheet and in determining the income and expenditure and the source and application of funds of the society shall be stated, and that statement will include at least a statement of the policies in respect of–

(a) the depreciation and diminution in value of assets,

(b) the translation of amounts denominated in foreign currencies (if applicable),

(c) the accounting for and valuation of UK Government and other securities,

(d) the valuation of investment properties (if applicable), and

(e) the provision for losses on advances and loans,

and where any policy stated under this paragraph or any practice used in preparing the annual accounts departs from generally accepted accounting principles or practice, there shall be a statement of the reasons for the departure.

Employees

2.—(1) The following information shall be given with respect to the employees of the society–

(a) the average number of persons employed by the society in the financial year; and

(b) the average number of persons so employed within each category of persons employed by the society.

(2) The average number required by subparagraph (1)(a) or (b) above shall be determined by dividing the relevant annual number by the number of complete calendar months in the financial year, and that relevant annual number shall be determined by ascertaining for each complete calendar month in the financial year–

(a) for the purposes of subparagraph (1)(a), the number of persons employed under contracts of service by the society in that month (whether throughout the month or not), and

(b) for the purposes of subparagraph (1)(b), the number of persons in each such category of persons so employed,

and, in either case, adding together all the monthly numbers.

(3) In respect of all persons employed by the society during the financial year who are taken into account in determining the relevant annual number for the purposes of subparagraph (1)(a) above there shall also be stated the aggregate amounts respectively of–

(a) wages and salaries paid or payable in respect of that year to those persons,

(b) social security costs incurred by the society on their behalf, and

(c) other pension costs so incurred,

save in so far as those amounts or any of them are stated in the income and expenditure account.

(4) The categories of persons employed by the society by reference to which the number required to be disclosed by subparagraph (1)(b) is to be determined shall be such as to assist the assessment of the manner in which the society's activities are organised.

Higher paid employees' emoluments

3.—(1) There shall be shown by reference to each pair of adjacent points on a scale whereon the lowest point is £30,000 and the succeeding ones are successive integral multiples of £5,000 beginning with that in the case of which the multiplier is 7, the number (if any) of persons in the society's employment whose several emoluments exceeded the lower point but did not exceed the higher.

(2) The persons whose emoluments are to be taken into account for the purposes of this paragraph do not include–

(a) directors of the society, or

(b) persons (other than directors of the society) who–

(i) if employed by the society throughout the financial year, worked wholly or mainly during that year outside the United Kingdon, or

(ii) if employed by the society for part only of that year, worked wholly or mainly during that part outside the United Kingdom.

(3) For the purposes of this paragraph, a person's emoluments include any amount paid to or receivable by him from the society, an associated body and any other person in respect of his services as a person in the employment of the society or an associated body of it or as a director of an associated body of the society (except sums to be accounted for to the society or any of its associated bodies), and the term "emoluments" shall be taken to include fees and percentages, any sums paid by way of expenses allowance (in so far as those sums are charged to United Kingdom income tax), and the estimated money value of any other benefits received by a person otherwise than in cash.

(4) The amounts to be brought into account for the purpose of complying with subparagraph (1) above are the sums receivable in respect of the financial year (whenever paid) or, in the case of sums not receivable in respect of a period, the sums paid during that year, but where–

(a) any sums are not brought into account for the financial year on the ground that the person receiving them is liable to account for them as mentioned in subparagraph (3) above, but the liability is wholly or partly released or is not enforced within the period of two years, or

(b) any sums paid to a person by way of expenses allowance are charged to United Kingdom income tax after the end of the financial year,

those sums shall, to the extent to which the liability is released or not enforced or they are charged as above mentioned (as the case may be), be brought into account for the purposes of complying with subparagraph (1) on the first occasion on which it is practicable to do so.

(5) References in subparagraph (3) to a society's associated body shall be taken as referring to a body which was an associated body at the time the services referred to in that subparagraph were rendered.

Directors' emoluments

4.—(1) There shall be shown the aggregate amount of the directors' emoluments, and this amount–

(a) shall include any emoluments paid or receivable by a person in respect of his services as director of the society or in respect of his services, while director of the society, as a director of any associated body of it or otherwise in connection with the management of the affairs of the society or any associated body of it, and

(b) shall distinguish between emoluments in respect of services as director, whether of the society or its associated bodies, and other emoluments.

(2) For purposes of this paragraph "emoluments", in relation to a director, includes fees and percentages, any sums paid by way of expenses allowance (in so far as those sums are charged to United Kingdom income tax), any contributions paid in respect of him under any pension scheme and the estimated money value of any other benefits received by him otherwise than in cash.

(3) If one person has been chairman of the board of directors throughout the financial year, there shall be shown his emoluments, and otherwise there shall be shown with respect to each person who has been chairman during the year his emoluments so far as attributable to the period during which he was chairman.

(4) With respect to all the directors (other than any who discharged their duties as such wholly or mainly outside the United Kingdom), there shall be shown–

(a) the number (if any) who had no emoluments or whose several emoluments amounted to not more than £5,000); and

(b) by reference to each pair of adjacent points on a scale whereon the lowest point is £5,000 and the succeeding ones are successive integral multiples of £5,000, the number (if any) whose several emoluments exceeded the lower point but did not exceed the higher.

(5) If, of the directors (other than any who discharged their duties as such wholly or mainly outside the United Kingdom), the emoluments of one only exceed the relevant amount, his emoluments (so far as so ascertainable) shall also be shown.

(6) If, of the directors (other than any who discharged their duties as such wholly or mainly outside the United Kingdom), the emoluments of two or more exceed the relevant amount, the emoluments of him (or them, in the case of equality) who had the greater or, as the case may be, the greatest shall also be shown.

(7) For the purposes of subparagraphs (5) and (6) above "the relevant amount"–

(a) if one person has been chairman throughout the financial year, means the amount of his emoluments; and

(b) otherwise, means an amount equal to the aggregate of the emoluments, so far as attributable to the period during which he was chairman, of each person who has been chairman during the financial year.

(8) There shall under subparagraphs (3) to (6) above be brought into account as emoluments of a person all such amounts (other than contributions paid in respect of him under a pension scheme) as in his case are to be included in the amount shown under subparagraph (1) above.

(9) There shall be shown–

(a) the number of directors who have waived rights to receive emoluments in the present financial year or in the future which, but for the waiver, would have fallen to be included in the amount shown under subparagraph (1) above in the present annual accounts or in future annual accounts; and

(b) the aggregate amount of those emoluments.

(10) For the purposes of subparagraph (9) above, it shall be assumed–

(a) that a sum not receivable in respect of a period would have been paid at the time at which it was due to be paid, and

(b) that if such a sum (being a sum the right to receive which has been waived) was payable only on demand, it was due to be paid at the time of the waiver.

(11) There shall be shown the aggregate amount of directors' or past directors' pensions.

(12) The amount referred to in subparagraph (11) above shall not include any pensions paid or receivable under a pension scheme if the scheme is such that the contributions under it are substantially adequate for the maintenance of the scheme but, subject to that, shall include any pension paid or receivable in respect of any such services of a director or past directors as are mentioned in subparagraph (1) above, whether to him or by him or, on his nomination or by virtue of dependence on or other connection with him, to or by any other person.

(13) The amount shown under subparagraph (11) above shall distinguish between pensions in respect of services as director, whether of the society or its associated bodies, and other pensions.

(14) There shall be shown the aggregate amount of any compensation to directors or past directors in respect of loss of office, and that amount–

(a) shall include any sums paid to or receivable by and any benefit received otherwise than in cash by a director, or past director, by way of compensation for loss of office as director of the society or for the loss, while director of the society or on or in connection with his ceasing to be a director of it, of any other office in connection with the management of the society's affairs or of any office as director or otherwise in connection with the management of the affairs of any associated body of the society, and

(b) shall distinguish between compensation in respect of the office of director, whether of the society or its associated body, and compensation in respect of other offices,

and for this purpose compensation for loss of office shall be taken to include sums paid as consideration for or in connection with a person's retirement from office.

(15) The amount to be shown under this paragraph includes in each case all sums relevant to that case paid by or receivable from–

(a) the society,

(b) the society's associated bodies, and

(c) any other person,

and the amount to be shown under subparagraph (14) shall distinguish between the sums respectively paid by or receivable from the society, the society's associated bodies and persons other than the society and its associated bodies.

(16) The amount to be shown for any financial year under this paragraph comprises the sums receivable in respect of that year (whenever paid) or, in the case of sums not receivable in respect of a period, the sums paid during that year, but where any sums paid by way of expenses allowance in that financial year are charged to United Kingdom income tax after the end of that financial year, those sums shall, to the extent to which the liability is charged, instead be shown in a note to the first accounts in which it is practicable to show them and shall be distinguished from the amounts to be shown apart from this provision.

(17) Regulation 5(2)(b) above shall not apply to this paragraph.

(18) In this paragraph–

(a) "pension" includes any superannuation allowance, superannuation gratuity or similar payment,

(b) "pension scheme" means a scheme for the provision of pensions in respect of services as director or otherwise which is maintained in whole or in part by means of contributions,

(c) "contribution" in relation to a pension scheme, means any payment (including an insurance premium) paid for the purposes of the scheme by or in respect of persons rendering services in respect of which pensions will or may become payable under the scheme, except that it does not include any payment in respect of two or more persons if the amount paid in respect of each of them is not ascertainable, and

(d) references to a society's associated body, in respect of any services to it, shall be taken as referring to a body which was an associated body at the time at which those services were rendered.

Other income and expenditure items

5.—(1) In respect of interest receivable, the amount of interest derived from associated bodies shall be shown separately from interest derived from other sources.

(2) In respect of interest payable–

(a) the amount payable to associated bodies shall be shown separately, and

(b) the amount of any income tax on interest on shares and deposits accounted for by the society shall be separately disclosed.

(3) There shall be shown the amount of any income from rent payable to the society in respect of premises or other land.

(4) There shall be shown the amount charged in respect of sums payable in respect of the hire of equipment, fixtures, fittings and vehicles.

(5) There shall be shown the amount of the remuneration of the auditors, including any sums paid by the society in respect of the auditors' expenses.

(6) There shall be shown the amount of any interest capitalised by the society in respect of development projects during the year, together with an indication of the amount and treatment of any related tax relief.

(7) Where separate disclosure of any component of item 4(a), 4(b), 5(a), 5(b), 5(c), 5(d) or 5(e) in Part I or II of Schedule 1 above would be material to the assessment of income and expenditure for a financial year, that component shall be separately disclosed.

Taxation

6.—(1) The basis on which the charge for United Kingdom corporation tax, deferred tax and United Kingdom income tax is computed shall be stated.

(2) Particulars shall be given of any special circumstances which affect liability in respect of taxation of profits, income or capital gains for the financial year or liability in respect of taxation of profits, income or capital gains for succeeding financial years.

(3) The following amounts shall be stated–

(a) the amount of the charge for United Kingdom corporation tax;

(b) if that amount would have been greater but for relief from double taxation, the amount which it would have been but for such relief; and

(c) the amount of the charge for taxation imposed outside the United Kingdom on profits, income and (so far as charged to the income and expenditure account) capital gains.

Miscellaneous matters

7.—(1) Where any amount relating to any preceding financial year is included in any item in the income and expenditure account, the effect of that inclusion shall be stated.

(2) Particulars shall be given of any extraordinary profits or losses arising in the financial year.

(3) The effect shall be stated of any transactions that are exceptional by virtue of size or incidence though they fall within the ordinary activities of the society.

Liquid assets

8.—(1) The amounts of loans and advances classifiable in the balance sheet as "cash with banks" shall be shown on the basis of their remaining maturity as follows:

(a) repayable on demand; and
(b) others with remaining maturity of–
(i) not more than three months,
(ii) more than three months but not more than one year,
(iii) more than one year but not more than five years, and
(iv) more than five years.

(2) The amounts classifiable in the balance sheet as UK Government securities shall be shown on the basis of their remaining maturity as follows–
(a) not more than one year,
(b) more than on year but not more than five years, and
(c) more than five years.

(3) The amounts classifiable in the balance sheet as "other securities" shall be shown on the basis of their remaining maturity as follows–
(a) not more than one year, and
(b) more than one year.

(4) In respect of the aggregate amount shown under subparagraph (2) above there shall be stated how much of that amount is ascribable to listed investments and, where it differs from the amount so stated, the aggregate market value, and the same shall apply in respect of the aggregate amount shown under subparagraph (3) above.

Provision for losses

9.—(1) In respect of any provision for losses deducted from Asset items 2, 3, 4(a), 4(b) and 4(c) in the balance sheet there shall be shown the following information, in respect of each item–
(a) the amount of the provision as at the date of the beginning of the financial year and as at the balance sheet date respectively, showing separately–
(i) specific provisions for losses, and
(ii) general provisions for losses,
(b) any amounts transferred to or from each of the provisions referred to in paragraph (a) above during the year, and
(c) the source and application respectively of any amounts so transferred.

(2) For the purposes of subparagraph (1) above a "specific provision" shall be any provision determined by reference to a particular advance or loan and all other provisions shall be "general provisions".

Investment in associated bodies

10.—(1) Where a society, at the end of its financial year, has any associated body which is carrying on business as at the end of that financial year there shall be stated as at the end of that financial year the following particulars of the associated body:
(a) whether it is a subsidiary, an associated body linked by resolution, or another associated body of the society;
(b) its name;
(c) how it is constituted;
(d) its place of registration;
(e) where it is a company limited by shares, the particulars of each class of its shares held, and the proportion of the nominal value of the allotted shares of that class represented by the shares held, by the society;
(f) the nature of the business carried on by it;
(g) the principal country of operation of the associated body; and
(h) whether it is a direct or indirect associated body of the society.

(2) For the purposes of this paragraph an associated body of a society is a direct associated body of the society if it is one–
(a) in which the society holds shares or corresponding membership rights, or
(b) to which the society is linked by resolution,
and is otherwise an indirect associated body of the society.

(3) The particulars required by subparagraph (1) above include, with reference to the proportion of the nominal value of the allotted shares of a class represented by shares held by the society, a statement of the extent (if any) to which it consists in shares held by, or by a nominee for, a subsidiary of the society and the extent (if any) to which it consists in shares held by, or by a nominee for, the society itself.

(4) Details required by subparagraphs (1) to (3) above need not be given in the case of an associated body which has not yet traded or had ceased to trade before the start of the financial year and had not, before its end, recommenced trading.

(5) In respect of each associated body particulars of which are disclosed under subparagraph (1) the additional information specified in subparagraph (6) below shall be given unless–

(a) the society prepares group accounts which include the accounts of the associated body, or

(b) the investment of the society in the shares of the associated body is included in, or in a note to, the annual accounts by way of the equity method of valuation.

(6) The information required by this subparagraph is the aggregate amount of the capital and reserves of the body as at the end of its relevant financial year, and its profit or loss for that year, and for this purpose the relevant financial year is–

(a) if the financial year of the body ends with that of the society giving the information in a note to its accounts, that financial year, and

(b) if not, the body corporate's financial year ending last before the end of the financial year of the society giving that information.

(7) Where an item stated in a balance sheet includes listed investments in an associated body–

(a) the aggregate amount referable to those investments within that item shall be stated and so shall their aggregate market value, and

(b) where the aggregate market value of those listed investments is higher than their aggregate stock exchange value, both of those aggregate values shall be stated.

Fixed assets

11.—(1) In respect of each item which is shown under "fixed assets" in the balance sheet the following information shall be given–

(a) the appropriate amounts in respect of that item as at the date of the beginning of the financial year and as at the balance sheet date respectively; and

(b) the effect on any amount shown in the balance sheet in respect of that item of–

(i) any revision of the amount in respect of any assets included under that item made during that year on any basis mentioned in paragraph 14 of Schedule 5 below,

(ii) acquisition during that year of any assets,

(iii) disposals during that year of any assets, and

(iv) any transfers of assets to and from that item during that year.

(2) The reference in subparagraph (1)(a) above to the appropriate amounts in respect of any item as at any date there mentioned is a reference to amounts representing the aggregate amounts determined, as at that date, in respect of assets falling to be included under that item on either of the following bases, that is to say–

(a) on the basis of purchase price,

(b) on any basis mentioned in paragraph 14 of Schedule 5 below,

(leaving out of account in either case any provisions for depreciation or diminution in value).

(3) In respect of each item within subparagraph (1) above–

(a) the cumulative amount of provisions for depreciation or diminution in value of assets included under that item as at each date mentioned in subparagraph (1)(a),

(b) the amount of any such provisions made in respect of the financial year,

(c) the amount of any adjustments made in respect of any such provisions during that year in consequence of the disposal of any assets, and

(d) the amount of any other adjustments made in respect of any such provisions during that year,

shall also be stated.

(4) Where any fixed assets of the society are included in the society's balance sheet at an amount determined on any basis mentioned in paragraph 14 of Schedule 5, the following information shall be given–

(a) the years (so far as they are known to the directors) in which the assets were severally valued and the several values; and

(b) in the case of assets that have been valued during the financial year, the names of the persons who valued them or particulars of their qualifications and (whichever is stated) the bases of valuation used by them.

(5) In relation to any amount which is or would but for Regulation 3(4) above be shown in respect of the item "land and buildings" in the balance sheet there shall be stated–

(a) how much of that amount is ascribable to land of freehold tenure and how much to land of leasehold tenure; and

(b) how much of the amount ascribable to land of leasehold tenure is ascribable to land held on long lease and how much to land held on short lease.

(6) In any case where any goodwill which has been acquired is shown or included as an asset in the balance sheet the period chosen for writing off the consideration for that goodwill and the reasons for choosing that period shall be disclosed.

Other assets

12. Any amount classifiable among "other assets" in the balance sheet and falling due after more than one year from the balance sheet date shall be separately disclosed.

Retail funds and deposits

13. The total of the amounts shown in the balance sheet as "retail funds and deposits" shall be analysed by division into–

(a) amounts repayable on demand, and

(b) amounts repayable from the balance sheet date in the ordinary course of business and whether by virtue of the giving of a period of notice or otherwise–

(i) in not more than three months,

(ii) in more than three months but not more than one year,

(iii) in more than one year but not more than five years, and

(iv) in more than five years.

Non-retail funds and deposits

14.—(1) The total of the amounts shown in the balance sheet as "non-retail funds and deposits" shall be analysed by division into–

(a) amounts repayable on demand, and

(b) amounts repayable from the balance sheet date in the ordinary course of business and whether by virtue of the giving of a period of notice or otherwise–

(i) in not more than three months,

(ii) in more than three months but not more than one year,

(iii) in more than one year but not more than five years, and

(iv) in more than five years.

(2) In respect of each item shown under "non-retail funds and deposits" in the balance sheet there shall be stated–

(a) the aggregate amount of any debts included under that item in respect of which any security has been given; and

(b) an indication of the nature of any security so given.

Deferred shares

15. Details of the terms of any deferred shares recorded in the balance sheet shall be given.

Other liabilities

16.—(1) Any amount classifiable among "other liabilities" in the balance sheet and falling due after more than one year from the balance sheet date shall be separately disclosed.

(2) The amount for creditors in respect of taxation and social security shall be separately disclosed.

Provisions and reserves

17.—(1) Where any amount is transferred–

(a) to or from any reserves,

(b) to any provisions for liabilities and charges, or

(c) from any provisions for liabilities and charges otherwise than for the purpose for which the provision was established,

and the reserves or provisions are shown or would but for Regulation 3(4) above be shown as separate items in the society's balance sheet, the information required by the following subparagraph shall be given in respect of the aggregate of reserves or provisions included in items in the balance sheet to which any such transfer relates.

(2) The information required by this subparagraph is–

(a) the amount of the reserves or provisions as at the date of the beginning of the financial year and as at the balance sheet date respectively,

(b) any amounts transferred to or from the reserves or provisions during that year, and

(c) the source and application respectively of any amounts so transferred.

(3) Particulars shall be given of each provision included in the item "Provisions for liabilities and charges" in the balance sheet.

Subordinated liabilities

18. Details of the terms of subordinated liabilities included in the balance sheet shall be given, and the reason for the issue of any instrument by which those liabilities were incurred shall be given in the financial year of the issue.

Guarantees and other financial commitments

19.—(1) Particulars shall be given of any charge on the assets of the society to secure the liabilities of any other person, including, where practicable, the amount secured.

(2) The following information shall be given with respect to any other contingent liability not provided for in the balance sheet (including contingent liabilities of any associated body which is not a relevant subsidiary where those liabilities are guaranteed by the society or otherwise are relevant to the assessment of the state of its affairs at the end of the financial year):

(a) where practicable, the amount or estimated amount of that liability;

(b) its legal nature; and

(c) whether any valuable security has been provided by the society in connection with that liability and if so, what.

(3) There shall be stated, where practicable–

(a) the aggregate amount or estimated amount of contracts for capital expenditure, so far as not provided for in the balance sheet, and

(b) the aggregate amount or estimated amount of capital expenditure authorised by the directors which has not been contracted for.

(4) Particulars shall be given of–

(a) any pension commitments included under any provision shown in the balance sheet, and

(b) any such commitment for which no such provision has been made,

and, where any such commitment relates wholly or partly to pensions payable to past directors of the society separate particulars shall be given of that commitment so far as it relates to such pensions.

(5) Particulars shall also be given of any other financial commitments which have not been provided for in the balance sheet and are relevant to assessing the society's state of affairs at the end of the financial year.

(6) Commitments within any of the preceding subparagraphs undertaken on behalf of or for the benefit of any associated body of the society shall be stated separately from the other commitments within that subparagraph.

Other miscellaneous matters

20.—(1) Subject to the following subparagraph, in respect of every item stated in a note to the annual accounts the corresponding amount for the financial year immediately preceding that to which the accounts relate shall also be stated and where it is not reasonable to compare the corresponding amount, it shall be adjusted and particulars of the adjustment and the reasons for it shall be given.

(2) Subparagraph (1) above does not apply in relation to any amounts stated by virtue of any of the following provisions of this Schedule:

- (a) paragraph 9;
- (b) paragraph 11(1) to (4);
- (c) paragraph 17(1) and (2); and
- (d) paragraph 21.

(3) Where the notes to the annual accounts set out the remaining maturity of a liability or an asset comprising an advance or loan and that advance or loan involves payment by instalments, the period between the balance sheet date and the date on which each instalment falls due shall be treated as the remaining maturity in respect of each instalment.

Directors' loans and transactions

21.—(1) This paragraph applies, subject to subparagraph (5) below, in relation to–

- (a) loans from and other transactions and arrangements with the society described in section 65 of the Act (which restricts loans to and other transactions and arrangements with directors and persons connected with them), other than those to which section 65(5) and (6) of the Act applies, and
- (b) in the case of a group accounts society, loans from and other transactions and arrangements with a relevant subsidiary of the society to which paragraph (a) above would apply were the society rather than the relevant subsidiary a party to them.

(2) The notes to the annual accounts shall contain a statement, in relation to such loans, transactions, and arrangements showing as follows–

- (a) the aggregate amounts outstanding under them at the end of the financial year, and
- (b) the numbers of persons for whom such loans, transactions and arrangements were made.

(3) The notes to the annual accounts shall, in relation to any loan or other transaction or arrangement subsisting during or at the end of the financial year, make the following disclosures:–

- (a) where a copy of it or a memorandum of its terms is included in the register maintained under section 68 of the Act (which requires the maintenance of such a register), the existence of the register and the availability of requisite particulars from it for inspection shall be disclosed;
- (b) where it comes within subparagraph (1)(b) above, its particulars shall be disclosed unless it was one which would, had the relevant subsidiaries of the society formed part of the society, have been excepted from the obligations imposed by section 68 of the Act.

(4) Regulation 5(2)(b) above shall not apply to this paragraph.

(5) So far as this paragraph applies to loans to and other transactions and arrangements with persons who are not directors of the society, it applies to those to which the society (or, in the case of any relevant subsidiary incorporated in the United Kingdom, the relevant subsidiary) has notice of the application of this paragraph, and for this purpose notice of the connection of any such person with a director of the society shall be treated as notice of the application of this paragraph.

SCHEDULE 5

Regulation 6

ACCOUNTING PRINCIPLES AND RULES

PART I

ACCOUNTING PRINCIPLES

1. Subject to paragraph 7 below, the amounts to be included in respect of all items shown in a society's annual accounts shall be determined in accordance with the principles set out in this Part of this Schedule.

2. The society shall be presumed to be carrying on business as a going concern, and so, where group accounts are prepared, shall the society and its relevant subsidiaries.

3. Accounting policies shall be applied consistently from one financial year to the next.

4.—(1) The amount of any item shall be determined on a prudent basis, and in particular all liabilities and losses which have arisen or are likely to arise in respect of the financial year to which the accounts relate or a previous financial year shall be taken into account, including those which only become apparent between the balance sheet date and the relevant date.

(2) For the purposes of subparagraph (1) above, the relevant date is the date of signature of the balance sheet of the society on behalf of the board of directors under section 80 of the Act (signing of balance sheet and annexing of documents).

5. Except so far as these Regulations otherwise specify, income and charges relating to the financial year to which the accounts relate shall be taken into account without regard to the date of receipt or payment.

6. In determining the aggregate amount of any item the amount of each individual asset or liability that falls to be taken into account shall be determined separately.

PART II

DEPARTURE FROM ACCOUNTING PRINCIPLES

7. If it appears to the directors of a society that there are special reasons for departing from any of the principles stated in Part I above in preparing annual accounts in respect of any financial year they may do so, but particulars of the departure, the reasons for it, and its effect shall be given in a note to the annual accounts.

PART III

FIXED ASSETS

8.—(1) Subject to any provision for depreciation or diminution in value made in accordance with paragraph 9 or 10 below, the amount to be included in respect of any fixed asset shall be its purchase price unless it is valued in accordance with paragraph 14 below.

(2) In this Schedule "fixed asset" means an asset which falls to be classified as a fixed asset in a balance sheet.

9. In the case of any fixed asset which has a limited useful economic life, the amount of–

(a) the purchase price, or

(b) where it is estimated that any such asset will have a residual value at the end of the period of its useful economic life, its purchase price less that estimated residual value,

shall be reduced by provisions for depreciation calculated to write off that amount systematically over the period of the asset's useful economic life.

10.—(1) Provisions for diminution in value shall be made in respect of any fixed asset which has diminished in value if the reduction in its value is expected to be permanent (whether its useful economic life is limited or not), and the amount to be included in respect of it shall be reduced accordingly, and any such provisions which are not shown in the income and expenditure account shall be disclosed (either separately or in aggregate) in a note to the accounts.

(2) Where the reasons for which any provision in respect of fixed assets (whether or not it is one to which subparagraph (1) above applies) was made have ceased to apply to any extent, that provision shall be written back to the extent that it is no longer necessary, and any amounts written back in accordance with this subparagaph which are not shown in the income and expenditure account shall be disclosed (either separately or in aggregate) in a note to the accounts.

11. Assets included in Asset items 4(d) and (f) in a balance sheet shall be valued according to methods set out for valuation of fixed assets in this Part of this Schedule where they are intended for use on a continuing basis in the normal course of a society's activities.

12.—(1) The application of paragraphs 8 to 10 above in relation to goodwill (in any case where goodwill is treated as an asset) is subject to subparagraph (2) below.

(2) The amount of the consideration for any goodwill acquired by a society shall be reduced by provisions for amortisation calculated to write off that amount systematically over a period which shall not exceed the useful economic life of the goodwill in question.

PART IV

ACCOUNTING RULES

13. Subject to paragraphs 15 and 16 the amounts to be included in respect of assets of any description mentioned in paragraph 14 may be determined on any basis so mentioned.

14.—(1) Tangible fixed assets may be included at a market value determined as at the date of their last valuation or at their current cost.

(2) Investments of any description falling to be included in the balance sheet as investments in associated bodies may be included either–

(a) at a market value determined as at the date of their last valuation; or

(b) at a value determined by use of a different method of valuation appropriate to the valuation of the investment in the particular body in respect of which that method is used;

and where paragraph (b) above applies particulars of the method of valuation adopted and of the reasons for adopting it shall be disclosed in a note to the accounts.

15. Where the value of any asset of a society is determined on any basis mentioned in paragraph 14 above that value shall be, or (as the case may require) be the starting point for determining, the amount to be included in respect of that asset in the society's accounts, instead of its purchase price or any value previously so determined for that asset, and methods for depreciation to be used pursuant to these Regulations shall apply accordingly in relation to any such asset with the substitution for any reference to its purchase price of a reference to the value most recently determined for that asset on any basis mentioned in paragraph 14 above.

16.—(1) With respect to any determination of the value of an asset of a society on any basis mentioned in paragraph 14, the amount of any profit or loss arising from that determination (after allowing, where appropriate, for any provisions for depreciation or diminution in value made otherwise than by reference to the value so determined and any adjustments of any such provisions made in the light of that determination) shall be credited or (as the case may be) debited to a separate reserve (referred to in these Regulations as "the revaluation reserve").

(2) The revaluation reserve shall be reduced to the extent that the amounts standing to the credit of that reserve are no longer necessary for the purpose of the accounting policies adopted by the society, but an amount may only be transferred from that reserve to the income and expenditure account if either–

(a) the amount in question was previously charged to that account, or

(b) it represents a realised profit.

(3) The treatment for taxation purposes of amounts credited or debited to the revaluation reserve shall be disclosed in a note to the accounts.

17. Advances and loans disclosed under items 2, 3 and 4(a) to (c) in the balance sheet Part I or, as the case may be, Part II of Schedule 2 above shall be included (after deduction of provisions for losses) at the amount of the outstanding loan or advance or the capital repayment amount, if lower, in the case where the capital repayable is variable.

18.—(1) This paragraph applies to liquid assets within a relevant category in a balance sheet (that is to say item 1(b), 1(c)(i) or 1(c)(ii)).

(2) The balance sheet shall show liquid assets within a relevant category at cost (whether or not adjusted), at market value or at a combination of the two.

19. To the extent that a relevant category of liquid assets under paragraph 18 above includes liquid assets at cost, the method of arriving at their cost shall be disclosed in the notes to the annual accounts.

20. In any particular account, unless these Regulations otherwise require or permit, amounts in respect of items representing assets or income may not be set off against amounts in respect of items representing liabilities or expenditure (as the case may be), or vice versa.

SCHEDULE 6

Regulation 7

DIRECTORS' REPORT

1. There shall be stated the names of the persons who, at any time during the financial year, were directors of the society.

2. The directors' report shall contain–

(a) a statement of the business objectives and activities of the society and its associated bodies,

(b) particulars of any events which have occurred since the end of the financial year and which are considered by the directors of the society to have an important effect on the society or any of its associated bodies, and

(c) an indication of the opinion of the directors of the society as to the developments which they consider likely to happen in the business of the society and its associated bodies.

3.—(1) If significant changes in the fixed assets of the society or of any relevant subsidiary have occurred in the financial year, the report shall contain particulars of the changes.

(2) If, in the case of such of those fixed assets as consist in interests in land and buildings, their market value (as at the end of the financial year) differs substantially from the amount at which they are included in the balance sheet, and the difference is, in the directors' opinion, of such significance as to require that the attention of members of the society should be drawn to it, the report shall indicate the difference with such degree of precision as is practicable.

4.—(1) The following applies if the society or any relevant subsidiary of the society has in the financial year given money for political purposes or charitable purposes or both.

(2) If the money given exceeded £200 in amount, there shall be contained in the directors' report for the year–

(a) in the case of each of the purposes for which the money has been given, a statement of the amount of money given for that purpose, and

(b) in the case of political purposes for which money has been given, the following particulars (so far as is applicable):

(i) the name of each person to whom money has been given for those purposes exceeding £200 in amount and the amount of money given; and

(ii) if money exceeding £200 in amount has been given by way of donation or subscription to a political party, the identity of the party and the amount of money given.

(3) For the purposes of this paragraph a society or a relevant subsidiary is to be treated as giving money for political purposes if, directly or indirectly–

(a) it gives a donation or subscription to a political party of the United Kingdom or any part of it, or

(b) it gives a donation or subscription to a person who, to the society's knowledge (or, as the case may be, that of the relevant subsidiary), is carrying on, or proposing to carry on, any activities which can, at the time at which the donation or subscription was given, reasonably be regarded as likely to affect public support for such a political party as is mentioned above.

(4) For the purposes of this paragraph money given for charitable purposes to a person who, when it was given, was ordinarily resident outside the United Kingdom shall be left out of account.

(5) In this paragraph, "charitable purposes" means purposes which are exclusively charitable; and, as respects Scotland, "charitable" is to be construed as if it were contained in the Income Tax Acts.

5.—(1) Subject to subparagraphs (2) and (3) below, the directors' report shall state the following, with respect to each person who, at the end of the financial year, was a director of the society–

(a) whether or not he was at the end of that year interested in shares in, or debentures of, any associated body of the society;

(b) if he was so interested–

(i) the number and amount of shares in, and debentures of, each such body (specifying it) in which he was then interested,

(ii) whether or not he was, at the beginning of that year (or, if he was not then a director, when he became one), interested in shares in, or debentures of, that or any other such body, and

(iii) if he was, the number and amount of shares in, and debentures of, each body (specifying it) in which he was interested at the beginning of the financial year or (as the case may be) when he became a director.

(2) The particulars required by paragraph (1) above may be given by way of notes to the society's annual accounts in respect of the financial year, instead of being stated in the directors' report.

(3) Particulars required by paragraph (1) above are not required to be given in respect of directors' nominee shareholdings, held on behalf of the society.

(4) Any changes, in the details disclosed under paragraph (1) above, between the end of the year and the relevant date must be disclosed in the directors' report and any such change after that date may be so disclosed.

(5) For the purposes of subparagraph (4) above "the relevant date" is–

(a) the date one month prior to the date of the notice of the society's annual general meeting, or

(b) if earlier, the date on which approval, under section 80 of the Act, of components of the annual accounts is completed.

6.—(1) This paragraph applies to the directors' report where the average number of persons employed by the society in each month during the financial year exceeded 250.

(2) For the purposes of subparagraph (1) above the average number is the quotient derived by dividing, by the number of complete calendar months in the financial year, the number derived by ascertaining, in relation to each of those months, the number of persons who, under contracts of service, were employed in the month (whether throughout it or not) by the society, and adding up the numbers ascertained.

(3) The directors' report shall where this paragraph applies contain a statement describing such policy as the society has applied during the financial year–

(a) for giving full and fair consideration to applications for employment by the society made by disabled persons, having regard to their particular aptitudes and abilities,

(b) for continuing the employment of, and for arranging appropriate training for, employees of the society who have become disabled persons during the period when they were employed by the society, and

(c) otherwise for the training, career development and promotion of disabled persons employed by the society.

(4) The directors' report shall where this paragraph applies also contain a statement describing the action that has been taken during the financial year to introduce, maintain or develop arrangements aimed at–

(a) providing employees systematically with information on matters of concern to them as employees,

(b) consulting employees or their representatives on a regular basis so that the views of employees can be taken into account in making decisions which are likely to affect their interests,

(c) encouraging the involvement of employees in the society's performance, and

(d) achieving a common awareness on the part of all employees of the financial and economic factors affecting the performance of the society.

(5) In this paragraph–

(a) "employment" means employment other than employment to work wholly or mainly outside the United Kingdom, and "employed" and "employee" shall be construed accordingly; and

(b) "disabled person" means the same as in the Disabled Persons (Employment) Act 1944(**a**) and the Disabled Persons (Employment) Act (Northern Ireland) 1945(**b**).

7.—(1) The directors' report shall disclose, in accordance with subparagraph (2) below–

(a) free capital as a percentage of the total of the share and deposit liabilities in the balance sheet,

(b) gross capital as a percentage of the total of the share and deposit liabilities in the balance sheet,

and, where consistency with the use of expression in the balance sheet so requires, the expression "share, deposit and loan liabilities" shall be used in the directors' report in place of the expression "share and deposit" liabilities.

(2) The matters required to be disclosed by subparagraph (1) above shall be disclosed–

(a) where the society is a single accounts society, in relation to the society, and

(b) where the society is a group accounts society, in relation to the society and its relevant subsidiaries.

8. The directors' report shall also disclose the number of mortgage accounts twelve or more months in arrears and the total amount of such arrears.

(**a**) 1944 c.10.
(**b**) 1945 c.6 (N.I.).

SCHEDULE 7

Regulation 8

ANNUAL BUSINESS STATEMENT

Statutory ratios and percentages

1.—(1) Subject to the following provisions of this paragraph, the annual business statement of a society shall state, as at the end of the financial year with which it deals, the following ratios and particulars:

(a) a ratio showing–
   (i) as its first quantity, non-retail funds and deposits as a percentage of shares and deposits, and
   (ii) as its second quantity, the relevant statutory limit for that percentage;

(b) a ratio showing–
   (i) as its first quantity, deposits as a percentage of shares and deposits, and
   (ii) as its second quantity, the relevant statutory limit for that percentage;

(c) advances secured on residential property as a percentage of total commercial assets;

(d) advances secured on land other than residential property as a percentage of total commercial assets;

(e) a ratio showing–
   (i) as its first quantity, commercial assets other than advances secured on land as a percentage of total commercial assets, and
   (ii) as its second quantity, the relevant statutory limit for that percentage; and

(f) a ratio showing–
   (i) as its first quantity, the aggregate of the assets to which paragraphs (d) and (e)(i) refer as a percentage of total commercial assets, and
   (ii) as its second quantity, the relevant statutory limit for that percentage.

(2) The annual business statement shall include an explanation of what is represented by–

(a) each of the quantities specified in subparagraph (1) above;

(b) the description of advances referred to in–
   (i) subparagraph (1)(c) above, and
   (ii) subparagraph (1)(d) above; and

(c) each of the relevant statutory limits specified in subparagraph (1) above.

(3) In subparagraph (1) above–

(a) in paragraph (a), the first quantity shall be shown in accordance with subsection (3) of section 7 of the Act (power to raise funds and borrow money) and accordingly–
   (i) "non-retail funds and deposits" means liabilities of the society in respect of its non-retail funds and deposits less those of them which are among the particular liabilities to which subsection (14) of that section refers, and
   (ii) "shares and deposits" means the total liabilities of the society in respect of shares and deposits less the particular liabilities to which subsection (14) of that section refers;

(b) in paragraph (b), the first quantity shall be shown in accordance with subsection (1) of section 8 of the Act (proportion of liabilities to be in form of shares) and accordingly–
   (i) "deposits" means the amount of the principal of, and interest payable on, sums deposited with the society less that part of it which comes within the particular liabilities to which subsection (2) of that section refers, and
   (ii) "shares and deposits" means the aggregate of the principal of, and interest payable on, sums deposited with the society and the principal value of, and interest payable on, shares in the society less the particular liabilities to which subsection (2) of that section refers;

(c) in paragraph (c), "advances secured on residential property" means those commercial assets which are class 1 assets for the purpose of the requirements of Part III of the Act for the structure of commercial assets;

(d) in pragraph (d), "advances secured on land other than residential property" means those commercial assets which are class 2 assets for the purpose of the requirements of Part III of the Act for the structure of commercial assets; and

(e) "relevant statutory limit" shall be construed–

(i) subject to subparagraph (ii) below, in accordance with section 36 of the Act (powers in event of breach of limits), and

(ii) where the relevant statutory limit imposed by subsection (2) (or (3)) of section 20 (commercial asset structure requirement) in respect of a particular financial year of a society is the amount imposed by paragraph (b) of that subsection, as if that amount were expressed as a percentage of the total commercial assets of the society as at the end of that financial year.

(4) Where relevant rules are in force so as to attribute to a society assets or liabilities of a body corporate associated with it, the ratios and particulars required to be shown by this paragraph shall be shown so as to take that attribution into account, and–

(a) where such relevant rules make provision for the disregarding of assets or liabilities of the society, those ratios and particulars shall be shown so as to take that provision into account, and

(b) in this paragraph "relevant rules" means–

(i) aggregation rules under section 7(10), 8(3) or 20(9) of the Act, or

(ii) rules approved under section 7(13), 8(5) or 20(12) of the Act.

Other percentages

2.—(1) Subject to the following provisions of this paragraph, the annual business statement of a society shall state the following particulars in respect of the society both in relation to the financial year with which it deals and in relation to the previous financial year:

(a) as a percentage of the share and deposit liabilities as at the balance sheet date–

(i) the gross capital as at that date, and

(ii) the free capital as at that date;

(b) the liquid assets as at the balance sheet date as a percentage of the total assets as at that date;

(c) the profit or loss after taxation as a percentage of–

(i) the mean reserves, and

(ii) the mean total assets; and

(d) (except where there is no extraordinary profit or loss shown in the income and expenditure account in relation to either of those financial years) the ordinary profit or loss after taxation as a percentage of–

(i) the mean reserves, and

(ii) the mean total assets.

(2) Where the society is a group accounts society, the particulars required to be stated by paragraph (1) above in respect of the society shall be stated in respect of the society and its relevant subsidiaries, but this subparagraph shall not be taken to prohibit the stating in addition by a society of those particulars in respect of the society alone.

(3) Any matter required by subparagraph (1) above to be stated as a particular in, or to be used as a factor in calculating a particular required by this Regulation to be stated in, the annual business statement and which relates to a previous financial year is required to be so stated or used for purposes of assisting the assessment of the corresponding particular for the financial year with which the annual business statement deals and accordingly shall, where it can be derived from an amount in annual accounts adjusted in accordance with Regulation 3(7)(b) above, be derived from that amount as so adjusted.

(4) The annual business statment shall include an explanation of what is represented by each of the particulars referred to in subparagraph (1) above and, where subparagraph (2) above applies, a statement of the basis on which particulars are stated by virtue of that subparagraph.

(5) Subject to subparagraph (3) above, in this paragraph–

(a) "share and deposit liabilities" means the aggregate of liabilities in the balance sheet representing retail and non-retail funds and deposits;

(b) "liquid assets" and "total assets" shall be taken from the items so named in the balance sheet;

(c) "the profit or loss after taxation" shall be taken from item 18 in Part I (or, as the case may be, item 20 in Part II) of Schedule 1 above;

(d) "the ordinary profit or loss after taxation" shall be taken from item 12 in Part I (or, as the case may be, item 14 in Part II) of Schedule 1 above;

(e) "mean reserves" means, in respect of a financial year, the amount produced by halving the aggregate of total reserves as stated in the balance sheet in respect of that and the previous financial year; and

(f) "mean total assets" means, in respect of a financial year, the amount produced by halving the aggregate of total assets as stated in the balance sheet in respect of that and the previous financial year.

Information relating to directors and other officers

3.—(1) The annual business statement of a society shall state–

(a) in relation to each person who was, at the end of the financial year with which it deals, a director of the society:

(i) his name;

(ii) his home address or an address, other than that of the society, at which documents may be served on him;

(iii) his business occupation;

(iv) the bodies (other than the society) of which he is a director, if any;

(v) his date of birth; and

(vi) his date of appointment as director; and

(b) in relation to each person who was, at the end of the financial year with which it deals, an officer (but not a director) of the society:

(i) his name;

(ii) his business occupation; and

(iii) the bodies of which he is a director, if any.

(2) The annual business statement of a society shall state, in relation to each person who was, at the end of the financial year with which it deals, a director or the chief executive of the society, particulars of his service contract (if any) with the society.

(3) The annual business statement of a society shall state particulars of any arrangement entered into during the financial year with which it deals whereby–

(a) a director of the society or a person connected with him acquired, or arranged to acquire, any non-cash asset from a relevant body, or

(b) a relevant body acquired, or arranged to acquire, any non-cash asset from a director of the society or a person connected with him,

and for the purposes of this subparagraph "non-cash asset" and "connected with" shall be construed in accordance with Part VII (Management of Societies) of the Act, and "relevant body" means the society or any relevant subsidiary of the society.

Average rates

4.—(1) Subject to the following provisions of this paragraph, the annual business statement of a society shall state the following particulars in respect of the society, in relation to the financial year with which it deals, with regard to each of the major categories of interest bearing assets and liabilities:

(a) the average amount outstanding during the financial year;

(b) the interest earned on such assets;

(c) the interest paid on such liabilities;

(d) the average yield on such assets; and

(e) the average rate paid on such liabilities.

(2) Where the society is a group accounts society, the particulars required to be stated by paragraph (1) above in respect of the society shall be stated in respect of the society and its relevant subsidiaries, but this subparagraph shall not be taken to prohibit the stating in addition by a society of those particulars in relation to the society alone.

(3) The annual business statement shall include an explanation of what is represented by each of the particulars referred to in subparagraph (1) above and, where subparagraph (2) above applies, a statement of the basis on which particulars are stated by virtue of that subparagraph.

(4) In this paragraph–

(a) the major categories of interest bearing assets are–

(i) liquid assets; and

(ii) secured advances;

(b) the major categories of interest bearing liabilities are–

(i) retail funds and deposits; and

(ii) non-retail funds and deposits;

(c) "the average amount outstanding during the financial year", in respect of each major category of interest bearing assets and liabilities, means the amount produced by halving the aggregate of the assets (or, as the case may be, liabilities) attributable to that category in the balance sheet in respect of that and the preceding financial year, and for this purpose the amount attributable to secured advances shall be the aggregate of the amounts in Asset items 2, 3, 4(a) and 4(c) of the balance sheet in Part I (or, in the case when group accounts are used, Part II) of Schedule 2 above;

(d) "the interest earned", in respect of each major category of interest bearing assets, means the amount (or aggregate amount) shown as interest receivable in the income and expenditure account which is attributable to that category;

(e) "the interest paid", in respect of each major category of interest bearing liabilities, means the amount shown as interest payable in the income and expenditure account which is attributable to that category;

(f) "the average yield", in respect of each major category of interest bearing assets, means the amount (or aggregate amount) in paragraph (d) above attributable to that category as a percentage of the amount in paragraph (c) above attributable to that category; and

(g) "the average rate paid", in respect of each major category of interest bearing liabilities, means the amount in paragraph (e) above attributable to that category as a percentage of the amount in paragraph (c) above attributable to that category.

Associated bodies not carrying on business

5. The annual business statement of a society shall state, in respect of each associated body of the society which is not carrying on business at the end of the financial year with which the annual business statement deals, the particulars required by paragraph 10(1)(a), (b), (c), (e) and (h) of Schedule 4 above to be stated in the notes to the annual accounts in respect of associated bodies carrying on business at that time.

Information about new activities

6.—(1) The annual business statement of a society shall state, in respect of each adopted power of the society which has been exercised by the society for the first time during the financial year with which the annual business statement deals, the fact that it has been so exercised.

(2) In determining for the purposes of subparagraph (1) above whether a power has been exercised by a society, the society shall be treated as including bodies corporate associated with it.

SCHEDULE 8

Regulation 9

SUMMARY FINANCIAL STATEMENT

PART I

FORMAT OF SUMMARY FINANCIAL STATEMENT

SECTION A

PRESCRIBED FORM OF STATEMENT FOR THE PURPOSES OF SECTION 76(4) OF THE ACT

1. This summary financial statement is only a summary of information in the annual accounts, directors' report and annual business statement.

2. Insofar as this summary financial statement summarises the information in the annual accounts, those accounts have been audited.

3. The annual accounts, directors' report and annual business statement will be available to members and depositors on demand at every office of .... [NOTE 1] from/after [NOTE 2] .... [NOTE 3].

NOTE 1 : Insert name of society.
NOTE 2 : Delete as appropriate.
NOTE 3 : Insert appropriate date.

SECTION B

FORMAT OF SUMMARY DIRECTORS' REPORT

1. Summary review of the business.

2. Summary review of events.

3. Summary indication of likely developments.

SECTION C

FORMAT OF SUMMARY STATEMENT

RESULTS FOR THE YEAR	THIS YEAR £	LAST YEAR £
1. Profit/Loss [NOTE 1] for the year after taxation	....	....
FINANCIAL POSITION AT END OF YEAR		
Assets		
2. Liquid assets	....	....
3. Mortgages	....	....
4. Other commercial assets	....	....
5. Fixed and other assets	....	....
Liabilities and Capital		
6. Shares	....	....
7. Deposits [NOTE 2]	....	....
8. Other liabilities	....	....
9. Capital	....	....

NOTE 1 : Delete as appropriate
NOTE 2 : Add "and loans" where required for consistency with balance sheet.

SECTION D

FORMAT OF SUMMARY OF KEY FINANCIAL RATIOS

	THIS YEAR %	LAST YEAR %
1. As percentage of share and deposit [NOTE 1] liabilities–		
(a) Gross capital	....	....
(b) Free capital	....	....
2. As percentage of total assets–		
Liquid assets	....	....
3. As percentage of average gross capital–		
(a) Profit/Loss [NOTE 2] for the year before extraordinary items	....	....
(b) Profit/Loss [NOTE 2] for the year	....	....

NOTE 1 : For "share and deposit" substitute "share, deposit and loan" where required for consistency with balance sheet.
NOTE 2 : Delete as appropriate.

PART II

PROVISIONS APPLICABLE TO PART I

1. In section B of Part I above–
   (a) the summary review of the business shall comprise–
      (i) in the case of a single accounts society, a summary review of the business of the society during, and a commentary on its financial position at the end of, the relevant year, and
      (ii) in the case of a group accounts society, a summary review of the business of the society and its relevant subsidiaries during, and a commentary on their financial position at the end of, the relevant year;
   (b) the summary review of events shall comprise a summary review of the events during the relevant year considered by the directors of the society to have an important effect–
      (i) in the case of a single accounts society, on the society, and
      (ii) in the case of a group accounts society, on the society and its relevant subsidiaries; and
   (c) the summary indication of likely developments shall comprise a summary indication of the opinion of the directors of the society as to the developments considered by them to be likely to happen–
      (i) in the case of a single accounts society, in the business of the society, and
      (ii) in the case of a group accounts society, in the business of the society and its relevant subsidiaries.

2. In sections C and D of Part I above "year" means "financial year", "this year" means the relevant year, and "last year" means the financial year preceding the relevant year.

3.. Any amount or percentage required to be included in section C or D of Part I above in the column headed "LAST YEAR" is required to be included for the purposes of assisting the assessment of the corresponding amount or percentage in the column headed "THIS YEAR" and accordingly shall, where it is derived from an amount in annual accounts adjusted in accordance with Regulation 3(7)(b) above, be derived from that amount as so adjusted.

4. Sections C and D of Part I above shall be completed–
   (a) in relation to a single accounts society, in relation to the society, and
   (b) in relation to a group accounts society, in relation to the society and its relevant subsidiaries.

5. Subject to paragraph 3 above, in section C of Part I above–

(a) item 1 shall be derived from item 18 in Part I (or, as the case may be, item 20 in Part II) of Schedule 1 above,

(b) item 2 shall be derived from item 1 in Part I (or, as the case may be, Part II) of Schedule 2 above,

(c) item 3 shall be derived from items 2 and 3 in Part I (or, as the case may be, Part II) of Schedule 2 above,

(d) item 4 shall be derived from item 4 in Part I (or, as the case may be, Part II) of Schedule 2 above,

(e) item 5 shall be derived from items 5 and 6 in Part I (or, as the case may be, items 5, 6 and 7 in Part II) of Schedule 2 above,

(f) item 6 shall be derived from items 8(a), 8(c), 9(g) and 9(h) in Part I (or, as the case may be, items 9(a), 9(c), 10(g) and 10(h) in Part II) of Schedule 2 above,

(g) item 7 shall be derived from items 8(b) and 9(a) to (f) in Part I (or, as the case may be, items 9(b) and 10(a) to (f) in Part II) of Schedule 2 above,

(h) item 8 shall be derived from items 10 and 11 in Part I (or, as the case may be, items 11, 12 and 19 in Part II) of Schedule 2 above, and

(i) item 9 shall be derived from items 12 and 17 in Part I (or, as the case may be, items 13 and 18 in Part II) of Schedule 2 above.

6. Unless there are no extraordinary items in the income and expenditure accounts for the relevant year and the previous financial year, there shall be disclosed in a note to the summary statement the format of which is set out in section C of Part I above–

(a) whether there are any extraordinary items in the income and expenditure account for the relevant year and, if there are, a summary statement of them, and

(b) such information in relation to the matters to which subparagraph (a) above relates as respects the previous financial year as can be used to assist the assessment of the summary statement required by subparagraph (a) above.

7. Subject to paragraph 3 above, in section D of Part I above–

(a) item 1 shall be derived from the particulars required to be stated in the annual business statement by paragraph 2(1)(a) of Schedule 7 above,

(b) item 2 shall be derived from the particulars required to be stated in the annual business statement by paragraph 2(1)(b) of Schedule 7 above, and

(c) in item 3–

(i) where there is no extraordinary profit or loss shown in the income and expenditure account for the relevant year and the previous financial year, item 3(a) is not required to be included,

(ii) where item 3(a) is included, the profit or loss for the year before extraordinary items to be used as a factor in that item shall be derived from item 12 in Part I (or, as the case may be, item 14 in Part II) of Schedule 1 above, and

(iii) the profit or loss for the year to be used as a factor in item 3(b) shall be derived from item 18 in Part I (or, as the case may be, item 20 in Part II) of Schedule 1 above.

8. In this Schedule–

(a) "relevant year", in relation to a summary financial statement of a society, means the financial year of the society with which the summary financial statement deals, and

(b) "average capital" means, in respect of a financial year, the amount produced by halving the aggregate of the amounts in items 12 and 17 in Part I (or, as the case may be, items 13 and 18 in Part II) of Schedule 2 above for that and the previous financial year.

SCHEDULE 9

Regulation 10

INTERPRETATION OF SCHEDULES

1. The following paragraphs apply for the purposes of the interpretation of the Schedules to these Regulations.

Associated companies and bodies

2. Where reference is made to an associated body of a society, a body corporate associated with a society or an associated company of a society–

(a) a reference to either of the first two shall be construed in accordance with section 18 of the Act (power to invest), but

(b) in the case of a reference to the last, in determining whether or not a company is an associated company, generally accepted accounting principles shall be used.

Balance sheet date

3. "Balance sheet date", in relation to a balance sheet, means the date as at which the balance sheet was prepared.

Leases

4. In respect of leases–

"long lease" means a lease in the case of which the portion of the term for which it was granted remaining unexpired at the end of the financial year is not less than 50 years,

"short lease" means a lease which is not a long lease, and

"lease" includes an agreement for a lease.

Listed investments

5. "Listed investment"–

(a) except in relation to Northern Ireland, has the meaning given to it in paragraph 84 in Part VII of Schedule 4 to the Companies Act 1985**(a)** (Form and Content of Company Accounts) and, from the coming into force of paragraph 23(b) of Schedule 16 to the Financial Services Act 1986**(b)**, shall have the meaning so given to it in that former paragraph as amended by that latter paragraph, and

(b) in relation to Northern Ireland, has the meaning given to it in paragraph 83 in Part VII of Schedule 4 to the Companies (Northern Ireland) Order 1986**(c)** (Form and Content of Company Accounts) and, from the coming into force of paragraph 38(b) of Schedule 16 to the Financial Services Act 1986, shall have the meaning so given to it in that former paragraph as amended by that latter paragraph.

Materiality

6. No provision of these Regulations requiring the inclusion of amounts in a particular account, or in notes to the annual accounts (other than paragraphs 3, 4 and 21 of Schedule 4 above), shall be taken to prohibit the disregarding of an amount which, in the particular context of that provision, is immaterial.

Provisions

7.—(1) References to provisions for depreciation or diminution in value of assets are to be taken as references to any amount written off by way of providing for depreciation or diminution in value of assets.

(2) Any reference in an income and expenditure account to the depreciation of, or amounts written off, assets of any description is to be taken as a reference to any provision for depreciation or diminution in value of assets of that description.

(3) References to provisions for liabilities and charges are to be taken as a reference to any amount retained as reasonably necessary for the purpose of providing for any liability or loss which is either likely to be incurred, or certain to be incurred but uncertain as to amount or as to the date on which it will arise.

(a) 1985 c.6.
(b) 1986 c.60.
(c) S.I. 1986/1032 (N.I.6).

Purchase price

8. References (however expressed) to the purchase price of any asset of a society include any consideration (whether in cash or otherwise) given by the society in respect of that asset.

Scots land tenure

9. In the application of these Regulations in Scotland, "land of freehold tenure" means land in respect of which the society is the proprietor of the dominium utile or, in the case of land not held on feudal tenure, is the owner, and "land of leasehold tenure" means land of which the society (or, as the case may be, a relevant subsidiary) is the tenant under a lease.

Staff costs

10.—(1) "Social security costs" means any contribution by the society to any state social security or pension scheme, fund or arrangement.

(2) "Pension costs" includes any other contributions by the society for the purposes of any pension scheme established for the purpose of providing pensions for persons employed by the society, any sums set aside for that purpose, and any amounts paid by the society in respect of pensions without first being set aside.

(3) Any amount stated in respect of either of the above items or in respect of the item "wages and salaries" in the society's income and expenditure account shall be determined by reference to payments made or costs incurred in respect of all persons employed by the society during the financial year.

Capital

11.—(1) "Gross capital" means total reserves as shown in the balance sheet plus any subordinated liabilities as shown in the balance sheet.

(2) "Free capital" means the aggregate of gross capital and general loss provisions less fixed assets.

Amounts repayable

12. Only those amounts which can at any time be withdrawn without notice or for which a maturity or period of notice of twenty-four hours or one working day has been agreed shall be regarded as repayable on demand.

Other definitions

13. In the Schedules to these Regulation–

"liquid asset" means an asset which a society is, by virtue of regulations in force for the time being under section 21 (liquid assets) of the Act, empowered to hold or to continue to hold;

"retail funds and deposits" means those funds and deposits of a society which–

(a) come within section 7 (power to raise funds and borrow money) of the Act, and

(b) are not, by virtue of that section, classified as non-retail funds and deposits,

and includes, in the case of a society which has made an effective election for the purposes of subsection (5) of that section, those funds and deposits which would, but for that election, be classified as non-retail;

"subordinated loan capital" means, in respect of a society, any liability (not being a liability in respect of a share) specified in an order for the time being in force under section 45(5) of the Act (capital resources which may be aggregated with reserves for certain purposes); and

"third party" means a person who is neither the society nor a body corporate associated with it.

EXPLANATORY NOTE

(This note is not part of the Regulations)

These Regulations prescribe the format and content of building society annual accounts (the income and expenditure account, balance sheet and statement of the source and application of funds) and make provision for notes to the annual accounts and accounting principles and rules. They also provide for the inclusion of specific material in building society directors' reports and annual business statements, and prescribe the format and content of building society summary financial statements.

The annual accounts, directors' report and annual business statement are required by sections 80 and 81 of the Building Societies Act 1986 to be laid before a building society at its annual general meeting. The summary financial statement, which is derived from those documents, is required by section 76 of that Act to be sent to every society member entitled to receive notice of the annual general meeting.

Chapter 24

HOUSING ASSOCIATIONS

Annexes

Chapter 24

HOUSING ASSOCIATIONS

Background

24.1 Housing associations provide an alternative to local authority and private enterprise housing. They account for nearly 25 per cent of all public capital expenditure on housing, benefitting from over £1,000 million annually of public money, and provide homes for over one million people. Housing associations improve properties and build new homes, primarily for rent, in inner cities, towns and remote rural areas. They also provide homes for sale through special schemes to help people on lower incomes wishing to become home owners.

24.2 Housing association schemes may be either wholly public funded or mixed funded with private finance. A significant recent development has been the transfer of local authority housing stock to housing associations arising from the introduction of 'Tenant's Choice' in the *Housing Act 1988*.

24.3 A housing association is not a separate category of legal entity as there are a number of ways in which a housing association can be established in law. The legislative framework that applies to housing associations is, therefore, determined by the type of legal entity used. For example, if a housing association has been formed as an industrial and provident society, the *Industrial and Provident Societies Acts 1965 to 1978* will apply (see chapter 21). Only housing associations that have been registered under the *Charities Act 1960* or the *Industrial and Provident Societies Acts 1965 to 1978* may register with the Housing Corporation as a 'registered housing association' under the *Housing Associations Act 1985*. Registration of housing associations is considered in detail below (see para 24.14). The significance of registration is that only a registered association is eligible to receive certain loans, grants and subsidies that are payable under the *Housing Associations Act 1985* as amended by the *Housing Act 1988* (see para 24.30).

24.4 The *Housing Associations Act 1985,* as amended by the *Housing Act 1988,* provides a comprehensive legislative framework for registered housing associations. It consolidated provisions that were previously contained in the *Housing Acts 1957 to 1980* and, in particular, it covers:

- Registration of housing associations.
- Their constitution.

- Accounting and audit requirements.

- Their supervision by the Housing Corporation.

- Their finances, in particular grants made to them.

- The Housing Corporation's constitution, powers and finances.

24.5 The sections of the *Housing Associations Act 1985*, dealing with grants, were subsequently repealed and revised sections introduced by the *Housing Act 1988*.

24.6 This framework does not, however, supersede the regulation of registered housing associations that are governed by the *Charities Act 1960* or that are governed by the *Industrial and Provident Societies Acts 1965 to 1978*.

24.7 In addition, all registered housing associations are required to comply with the *Registered Housing Associations (Accounting Requirements) Order 1988* (SI 1988/395) and the *Registered Housing Associations (Accounting Requirements) (Amendment) Order 1989* (SI 1989/327) (see annex 1).

Accounting and auditing background

24.8 Housing associations are subject to various legal restrictions and so special factors need to be considered in relation to their audit. A specific Auditing Guideline, 'Housing Associations' (AG 3.304) was issued by the APC in November 1984 to give guidance on the audit of such associations. However, it must be borne in mind that this guideline was written before the enactment of the *Housing Associations Act 1985* and the *Housing Act 1988*.

The Housing Corporation

24.9 The Housing Corporation funds and supervises registered housing associations. Since 1st April 1989 this has been restricted to England as the *Housing Act 1988* transferred the Housing Corporation's responsibilities in Scotland and in Wales to Scottish Homes and Housing for Wales (Tai Cymru) respectively. (References to the Housing Corporation in this chapter should generally be taken to include also these two other bodies.) The general functions of these bodies are to:

- Promote and assist the development of registered housing associations and unregistered self-build societies.

- Facilitate the proper performance of the functions of registered housing associations and unregistered self-build societies.

- Publicise the aims and principles of registered housing associations and unregistered self-build societies.

- Maintain a register of housing associations (see para 24.14).

- Exercise supervision and control over registered housing associations (see para 24.33).

- Determine housing association grant payments to registered housing associations.

- Undertake, to the extent considered necessary, the provision and management of dwellings (for letting or sale) and hostels. This may be by construction, acquisition, conversion, improvement or otherwise.

[HAA 1985 Sec 75].

24.10 Under the *Housing Act 1988* the Housing Corporation took over responsibility from the Department of the Environment for paying capital and revenue grants to associations and recouping surplus rental income from associations.

24.11 The Housing Corporation also provides mortgage loan finance, although such loans are diminishing as housing associations increasingly fund new schemes with a combination of housing association grant and loans from the private sector.

24.12 The Housing Corporation guarantees bank overdrafts and issues guidance and policy circulars.

Other institutions

24.13 The other principal bodies that are concerned with housing associations' financial statements or audit are:

- The Department of the Environment, Scottish Office and the Welsh Office.

  These government departments work jointly to determine and control housing policy.

- The National Federation of Housing Associations (NFHA).

  This is the central representative body for housing associations. It provides common services to members and represents them in discussions with the Government, local authorities and others.

- The Housing Finance Corporation Limited.

  This company arose out of a joint initiative by The Housing Corporation and the NFHA. The purpose of the company is to raise private sector funding for housing.

Registration of housing associations

24.14 The *Housing Associations Act 1985* recognises any society, body of trustees or company as a housing association, that is established *inter alia* to provide, construct, improve, manage, or to facilitate or encourage the construction or improvement of, housing accommodation. [HAA 1985 Sec 1(1)]. However, such associations must not trade for profit and their constitution or rules must prohibit the issue of capital with interest or dividend exceeding such rate as may be prescribed by the Treasury.

24.15 Housing associations may be registered with the Housing Corporation. A registered charity that satisfies the requirements for a 'housing association' in paragraph 24.14 will automatically be eligible for registration as a housing association. [HAA 1985 Sec 4(1)(a)]. However, the charity must not be an 'exempt' charity within the meaning of the *Charities Act 1960*. A full list of exempt charities is given in chapter 25 paragraph 25.21. The most important for this purpose are registered friendly societies and their branches.

24.16 A registered industrial and provident society (see chapter 21) may also be eligible for registration as a housing association if it satisfies the requirements for registration as a 'housing association' in paragraph 24.14 and, furthermore, fulfils the following conditions:

- It must be established for the purpose of, or include amongst its objects or powers, the provision, construction, improvement or management of the following properties:

  - ☐ Houses to be kept available for letting.

  - ☐ Houses for occupation by the association's members, where the association's rules restrict membership to persons who may be entitled to occupy a house provided or managed by the association.

  - ☐ Hostels.

  [HAA 1985 Sec 4(2)].

- Any additional purposes or objects must be restricted to:
  - ☐ Providing land, amenities or services, or providing, constructing, repairing or improving buildings, for the benefit of the association's residents, either exclusively or together with other persons.
  - ☐ Acquiring, or repairing and improving, or creating by the conversion of houses or other property, houses to be disposed of on sale, on lease or on shared ownership terms.
  - ☐ Constructing houses to be disposed of on shared ownership terms.
  - ☐ Managing houses which are held on leases or other lettings not being houses referred to in section 4(2) (see above) or blocks of flats.
  - ☐ Providing services of any description for owners or occupiers of houses in arranging or carrying out works of maintenance, repair or improvement, or encouraging or facilitating the carrying out of such works.
  - ☐ Encouraging and giving advice on the formation of other housing associations or providing services for and giving advice on the running of such associations and other voluntary organisation's concerned with housing or matters connected with housing.

  [HAA 1985 Sec 4(3)].

24.17 The Housing Corporation may refuse to register a housing association, that is otherwise eligible for registration, if the housing association does not satisfy the additional criteria set out in paragraphs 24.18 to 24.25 below. [HAA 1985 Sec 5(1)].

Control of the association

24.18 The association must be under the control of responsible persons of appropriate experience and must be organised in such a way that it is an acceptable body for handling public finance and the continuing proper use of publicly funded assets.

24.19 The association's constitution (or rules of law relating to its continuation) must provide that the control of the association's affairs is vested in a management committee, or body of trustees or other governing body. The skills and experience of the persons exercising this control should be such that the affairs of the association are likely to be conducted in a responsible and effective manner.

24.20 The governing body must be able to demonstrate that it is not under the control of, or subject to influence from, another person or organisation such that its independence is prejudiced, unless that organisation is a registered housing association or, exceptionally, a registered charity and the influence or control operates in the best interests of the association.

24.21 Persons with whom the association has a contract of employment and their close relatives should not be members of the governing body of the association.

24.22 The association must demonstrate that there is no conflict of interest between the association and the members of its governing body and their close relatives. Associations registered under the *Industrial and Provident Societies Act 1965* are prohibited from granting any benefit or payment, with some exemptions, to its committee members, officers, or employees. This extends to any close relatives of these individuals and any business owned or managed by them and applies for 12 months after they cease to hold office or employment with the association. [HAA 1985 Sec 15]. Under the Housing Corporation's registration criteria, associations that are registered charities and subsidiaries of all registered associations are expected to comply with these requirements.

Financial requirements

24.23 The association must be able to demonstrate that it is operating (or will operate) on a sound and proper financial basis, and in particular:

- It must, to the satisfaction of the Housing Corporation, keep proper accounting records, have adequate systems of control and produce annual financial statements that must be audited by a properly qualified auditor.

- It must demonstrate that its capital commitments can be fully financed (whether by loan or otherwise) and that its income will be sufficient to meet its outgoings and to ensure its future financial stability.

- Its constitution (or the legal rules relating to it) must prohibit it from distributing any surplus funds or assets to either its members or management committee. The restriction on distributions applies to other related parties as well, subject otherwise to the Housing Corporation's consent.

- The association's overheads (including salaries and expenses) must be reasonable having regard to the association's size and level of its activity.

Managerial efficiency

24.24 The Housing Corporation takes into account both the property development and housing management skills of associations. The association must be able to show that with regard to its size and level of its activity it has access to professional skills relevant to the provision and management of housing, either within the association itself, or externally. Where the association is already established, it must be able to show an efficient performance in the provision and management of housing schemes. Furthermore, the housing scheme must have been provided skilfully and expeditiously and managed competently, at reasonable cost and with proper regard to its tenants' welfare.

Applications to register

24.25 The application must be made on a questionnaire issued by the Housing Corporation and its completion is taken as conveying the association's agreement to the following matters:

- That the requirements of these criteria are observed at all times.
- To allow the Housing Corporation access to its books of account and records, and to its offices and housing schemes at all reasonable times.
- To validate or substantiate any information provided on the application form and to furnish any additional information the Housing Corporation may require.
- To authorise its auditors, banks, solicitors and any other consultants or advisors to disclose to the Housing Corporation such information as it might require.
- To submit an annual return (see para 24.66).
- To observe any other procedures or conditions that the Housing Corporation may specify.
- To notify the Housing Corporation of any proposed constitutional changes.
- To maintain a complete register of all properties in which the association has an interest.

24.26 Once the Housing Corporation has registered a housing association it must notify the Charity Commissioners or Chief Registrar of Friendly Societies (as appropriate) of the fact. [HAA 1985 Sec 5(3)].

Co-ownership societies

24.27 A co-ownership society is an industrial and provident society (see chapter 21) that has registered as a housing association and that satisfies both of the following conditions:

- Its rules must restrict membership to persons who are tenants or prospective tenants of the association and must preclude it from granting or assigning tenancies to non-members.
- The tenancy or membership agreement must entitle each tenant or member to a sum calculated by reference to the value of his housing accommodation upon his ceasing to be a member.

[SI 1988/395 para 2].

24.28 Co-ownership societies are subject to specific accounting requirements, for example in relation to the form of their income and expenditure account. [SI 1988/395].

Almshouses

24.29 An almshouse is defined as:

> *"A corporation or body of persons which is a charity and which is prevented by its rules or constituent instrument from granting tenancies of dwellings occupied for the purposes of the charity."* [SI 1988/395 para 2].

Almshouses are exempt from certain accounting requirements. [SI 1988/395 para 4(b)].

Benefits of registration

24.30 The main benefits of registration lie in the complex array of grants available from the Housing Corporation. Prior to the implementation of the *Housing Act 1988*, these grants were made at the discretion of the Department of the Environment. The grants now fall into two main categories.

Capital grants

24.31 The Housing Corporation may make grants to registered housing associations in respect of expenditure incurred, or to be incurred, by them in connection with housing activities. The Housing Corporation is responsible for specifying:

- The procedure to be followed in relation to applying for a grant.

- The circumstances in which a grant is or is not to be payable.

- The method for calculating, and any limitations on, the amount of a grant.

- The manner in which, and time or times at which, a grant is to be paid.

[HA 1988 Sec 45].

Revenue grants

24.32 The Housing Corporation may make a grant (revenue deficit grant) to a registered association if the association's expenditure exceeds its income for any period in relation to:

- All housing activities of the association.

- Housing activities of the association of a particular description.

- Particular housing activities of the association.

[HA 1988 Sec 46].

Responsibilities of registration

24.33 The responsibilities of registration as a housing association include the following:

- Increased accounting and audit requirements.

- Supervision by the Housing Corporation, which covers *inter alia*:

  - Approval of some land disposals. [HAA 1985 Sec 9].

  - Control over payments to members and former members. [HAA 1985 Secs 13 - 15].

  - Powers of appointment and removal of committee members where certain types of grant have been made. [HAA 1985 Secs 16 - 18].

  - Control over constitutional matters. [HAA 1985 Secs 19 - 21].

  - Power to petition for winding up. [HAA 1985 Sec 22].

  - Power to initiate an inquiry or special audit into a housing association's affairs, where certain types of grant have been made. [HAA 1985 Secs 28 - 32].

Performance expectations

24.34 The Housing Corporation has issued a set of performance expectations ('Performance Expectations: Housing Association Guide to Self-Monitoring') that set down the standards expected of an efficient and well managed registered housing association. These expectations form a series of clear criteria against which an association can be monitored by the Corporation. The performance expectations cover the following areas:

- Committee and association accountability.
- Management control.
- Finance.
- Race equality and equal opportunity.
- Access to housing.
- Housing management service.
- Maintenance.
- Development.

24.35 Larger associations (those with over 250 units and developing associations with 100 - 250 units, but excluding almshouses, co-ownerships and self-build associations) can use the performance expectations to develop a plan for self-monitoring and are required to report the results of the self-monitoring to the Corporation. Separate performance expectations are available for co-operatives.

24.36 The areas of particular relevance include:

- Expectation 3.8 - Produce and file audited financial statements in accordance with the law and the relevant statutory instruments. The commentary accompanying this expectation adds that committee members of housing associations are expected to understand what the financial statements show in order to exercise proper control.
- Expectation 3.12 - Make full use of external auditors by following the Corporation's code of audit practice (see para 24.72).

Duty to keep accounting records

24.37 Housing associations governed by the *Industrial and Provident Societies Acts 1965 to 1978* or the *Companies Act 1985* must comply with the obligations imposed under those Acts. Housing associations that are registered as charitable trusts are subject to a lesser standard of accountability (see chapter 25). Accordingly, such charitable associations are subject to provisions that correspond to those contained in the *Friendly and Industrial and Provident Societies Act 1968* (see chapter 11). [HAA 1985 Sec 26(1), 3 Sch].

24.38 All registered housing associations are required by the Housing Corporation (see para 24.23) to keep proper accounting records and, in particular, to keep a complete register of all properties in which the association has an interest. In addition, the Housing Corporation must be allowed access to an association's books and records when it considers that this is necessary.

Duty to establish and maintain a system of control

24.39 Housing associations governed by the *Industrial and Provident Societies Acts 1965 to 1978* are subject to a duty to establish and maintain a system of control. Housing associations that are registered charitable trusts are not subject to any specific legal duty in this respect (see chapter 25 para 25.34), but are made subject to provisions that correspond with those contained in the *Friendly and Industrial and Provident Societies Act 1968* (see chapter 11 para 11.31).

24.40 The Auditing Guideline identifies controls of particular significance to housing associations, in respect of:

- Rents.
- Service charges and, where appropriate, rates.
- Property development.
- Housing land disposals.
- Grants and loans.
- Housing accommodation.
- Repairs.

Duty to prepare financial statements

24.41 Housing associations governed by the *Industrial and Provident Societies Acts 1965 to 1978* or the *Companies Act 1985* must comply with the obligations imposed under those Acts.

24.42 Housing associations that are registered charitable trusts may not be under any specific duty to prepare financial statements. Requirements corresponding to those under the *Friendly and Industrial and Provident Societies Act 1968* were intended, but slightly different requirements were finally imposed. Consequently, charitable housing associations are required to prepare:

- A revenue account for each accounting period. This must give a true and fair view of its income and expenditure in that period, so far as these arise in connection with its housing activities. [HAA 1985 Sec 26, 3 Sch 2(1)(a)].
- A balance sheet as at the end of each accounting period. This must give a true and fair view of its affairs at that date. [HAA 1985 Sec 26, 3 Sch 2(1)(b)].

Accounting period

24.43 The accounting period of a housing association will be determined by reference to its legal form. Housing associations are required by the *Housing Associations Act 1985* to adopt an accounting period of 12 months. However, a housing association may set a period of between 6 and 18 months with the consent of the Housing Corporation. [HAA 1985 Sec 26, 3 Sch 7].

Accounting requirements common to all housing associations

24.44 In addition to the requirements already imposed upon housing associations by virtue of their legal form, the Secretary of State was given power to lay down accounting requirements that apply to all registered housing associations. This is to ensure that the financial statements of every registered housing association are prepared in the requisite form. They should also give a true and fair view of the state of the association's affairs, so far as its housing activities are concerned and of the disposition of funds and assets which are, or at any time have been, in its hands in connection with those activities.

24.45 These accounting requirements are set out in the *Registered Housing Associations (Accounting Requirements) Order 1988* (SI 1988/395) which consolidated, with amendments, three earlier Orders, and was further amended by the *Registered Housing Associations (Accounting Requirements) (Amendment) Order 1989* (SI 1989/327).

24.46 The Order does not prejudice or affect any statutory duties that require the financial statements of a housing association to give a true and fair view, for example, by the requirements of the *Companies Act 1985* if they apply. Accordingly, where it is necessary to depart from the disclosure requirements in Schedule 1 to the Order in order to give a true and fair view, nothing in the Order prevents this. However, the fact of any such departure, the reasons for it and its effect, must be recorded in the notes to the financial statements. [SI 1988/395 para 4(3)].

24.47 Furthermore, the Order does not prevent an association from giving more information than it is required to. [SI 1988/395 para 4(4)].

24.48 The *Registered Housing Associations (Accounting Requirements) Order 1988* (SI 1988/395) is included as annex 1 to this chapter and has been charged for the 1989 amendment Order (SI 1989/327). The effect of the 1989 Order was to substitute references to the rent surplus fund for the grant redemption fund. This is because section 53 of the *Housing Associations Act 1985*, which provided for a grant redemption fund was replaced by section 55 of the *Housing Act 1988* which provided for a rent surplus fund to be kept by registered housing associations.

Disclosure requirements

24.49 The information a housing association needs to disclose in its financial statements is set out in Schedule 1 to the Order (see annex 1).

Balance sheet

24.50 Part I of Schedule 1 to the Order details the information that must be shown in the balance sheet, which comprises:

- Corresponding amounts for the previous balance sheet date.
- The nature of each item, disclosing separately between the association's different activities where applicable.
- Housing land which must be distinguished from other assets.
- Housing land must be included at its net book value. This is the difference between its cost (including both the acquisition cost and the cost of any work carried out on it) and the sum of the amount provided for depreciation, housing association grant received and amounts transferred to the property equity account in respect of the land. Where the association is a co-ownership society the net book value of housing land must be calculated in accordance with that society's housing cost and finance statement (see para 24.59).
- Other fixed assets must be included at net book value, which is calculated at cost less depreciation.
- The aggregate amounts of the following items must be disclosed:
  - ☐ Reserves.

- ☐ Provision for future cyclical repairs and maintenance to housing accommodation.

- ☐ Other provisions (except in respect of depreciation or bad debts).

- ☐ The rent surplus fund.

- ☐ Investments.

- ■ Loans to the association must be distinguished between those:

  - ☐ Incurred to acquire, or carry out, work on housing land.

  - ☐ Incurred for other purposes.

- ■ The amount included with current assets in respect of revenue deficit grant and hostel deficit grant receivable must be disclosed (see para 24.32).

24.51 Part II of Schedule 1 to the Order specifies the information that may be shown either in the balance sheet, or in the notes to the financial statements, which comprises:

- ■ Movements in the fixed assets and related accounts disclosed in sufficient detail to show their nature and cause.

- ■ Movements in reserves disclosed in detail.

- ■ Housing land distinguishing between long leases, other leases and all other land.

- ■ The method used to arrive at the provision for future cyclical repairs and maintenance to housing accommodation.

- ■ Considerable detail must be given in respect of loans to an association. The following must be itemised:

  - ☐ Amounts lent by category of lender, for example, by the Housing Corporation or local authorities.

  - ☐ Details of security, itemising amounts of loans secured by a charge on the association's assets and amounts secured by a charge on the assets of other persons (with their names).

  - ☐ The names of any guarantors for each loan.

- Loans by an association to a member of an association's managing body, or officer, must be disclosed and particulars given. For officers, this means:

  - ☐ The date the loan was made.
  - ☐ The borrower's name.
  - ☐ Whether it was made under the officer's contract of employment.
  - ☐ The total amount outstanding.
  - ☐ The terms of repayment, including the interest rate.

- Loans by an association to employees must be disclosed and particulars given. This means:

  - ☐ The aggregate number of loans.
  - ☐ The aggregate amount of loans outstanding.
  - ☐ The purposes of the loans.
  - ☐ The terms of repayment, including the interest rate.

- In addition, certain other matters must be disclosed:

  - ☐ Arrears of rent carried as current assets (together with amounts deducted for bad or doubtful debts).
  - ☐ Grants relating to rent phasing (which are not otherwise shown in the property revenue account).
  - ☐ Charges on the association's assets to secure another person's liabilities.
  - ☐ Basis on which the amount set aside for tax is calculated.
  - ☐ Capital commitments, including the means by which and the persons by whom they will be financed.
  - ☐ Contingent liabilities.

<u>Income and expenditure account</u>

24.52 Schedules 2 and 3 to the Order specify the form required for the income and expenditure accounts of housing associations, which are:

- Societies other than co-ownership societies (Schedule 2).
- Co-ownership societies (Schedule 3).

24.53 Schedule 2 comprises the following major components in arriving at the surplus/deficit before taxation and deficit grant.

- Property revenue account summary. This consists of total income less expenditure and the transfer to the rent surplus fund.
- Development administration. Being grants receivable less management expenses and any abortive development costs.
- Fees for architects' and surveyors' services.
- Managed associations. This represents fees less management expenses in relation to any association whose affairs are managed by the association.
- Sales of housing accommodation. This is made up of proceeds of sales less net book value and management expenses.
- Housing accommodation held for disposal, representing proceeds of sales and grants receivable less management expenses and cost of sales.
- Other income and expenditure, analysed under separate headings for housing activities and non-housing activities.

24.54 The equivalent requirements under Schedule 3 are as follows:

- Income made up of rents less losses arising from vacant accommodation and bad debts.
- Investment income, that is, interest and dividends receivable.
- Other income.
- Expenditure.
- Amounts transferred to the rent surplus fund.

24.55 Both Schedules 2 and 3 require corresponding amounts for the previous accounting period.

Notes to the financial statements

24.56 Part III of Schedule I to the Order specifies the information that must be detailed in the notes to the financial statements. This information comprises:

- The average number of the association's employees.
- The total remuneration of the association's employees.
- Social security costs.
- Other pension costs.
- The total remuneration (including expenses) of the association's auditors.
- Any fees, remuneration or expenses paid to an association's member who is not a member of the association's managing body, or an officer or employee of it.
- Any fees, remuneration or expenses paid to a member of the managing body who is neither an officer or employee of the association.
- Any fees, remuneration or expenses paid to an officer of the association who is not an employee.
- Any payment made or benefit granted to specified persons.
- Any material amount withdrawn from a provision other than for the purpose for which it was set up.

Statement of source and application of funds

24.57 All registered housing associations must prepare a statement of source and application of funds for the accounting period, with comparative figures. This is defined as a statement that shows:

> *"... the disposition during the period of account and the previous period of account of all funds received or receivable by the association in each period, and the sources thereof."* [SI 1988/395 para 7].

Other financial statements required

24.58 Societies other than co-ownership societies must prepare in addition to the above statements:

- A property revenue account in the form set out in Schedule 4 to the Order.
- A statement of housing administration costs in the form set out in Schedule 5 to the Order.

[SI 1988/395 para 8(a)(b)].

24.59 Co-ownership societies must prepare a housing cost and finance statement in the form set out in Schedule 6 to the Order. [SI 1988/395 para 8(c)].

24.60 These additional financial statements provide the Housing Corporation and the Department of the Environment with a more detailed analysis of an association's activities.

24.61 Almshouses are exempted from the Order's provisions that relate to the obligation to prepare an income and expenditure account, additional financial statements and a source and application of funds statement. [SI 1988/395 para 4(1)(b)].

Recommended form of published accounts

24.62 The Housing Corporation in association with the NFHA and the ICAEW has compiled the 'Recommended form of published accounts for housing associations'. This does not carry any statutory authority, but nevertheless it does provide sufficient detailed guidance on housing association accounting to enable an association to comply with the legal requirements and also to adopt the most suitable accounting policies and form of presentation for its annual financial statements. It reflects the financial framework within which housing associations operate.

24.63 If an association adopts the form set out in the document it will, when it applies for certain grants, probably find it easier to deal with the Housing Corporation.

24.64 The recommended form is published in loose-leaf form and is updated from time to time. The recommendations include two sets of specimen housing association accounts. Association B is reproduced as annex 2 to this chapter. This set of housing association accounts reflects changes in arrangements for housing association grant and rent surplus fund

24.65 The NFHA produces guidance on the more limited accounting arrangements for small associations with fewer than 250 dwellings ('Accounts: A Guide for small housing associations').

Duty to submit an annual return

24.66 With regard to submitting annual returns, housing associations governed by the *Industrial and Provident Societies Acts 1965 to 1978* or the *Companies Act 1985* must comply with the obligations imposed under those Acts. There are no reasons why associations' financial statements that are filed should not contain additional information in order to comply with the requirements of any other Act. Housing associations that are registered charitable trusts do not need to file their financial statements with the Charity Commissioners unless specifically requested to do so.

Returns to the Housing Corporation

<u>Annual returns</u>

24.67 The Housing Corporation is under a statutory duty to maintain a register of housing associations. To fulfil this duty, the Housing Corporation requires associations to complete an annual return to provide information that will update the information provided on its initial registration or on previous annual returns. There are two types of return:

- Form HAR 10 which is the usual return.
- Form HAR 10/CO which is the return for all registered Housing Corporation funded co-ownership societies.

24.68 Various constitutional and staff changes must be recorded on the annual return. Associations should send the annual return to the Housing Corporation within two months of 31st March each year, together with a further return (HAR 10/1) which contains statistical information.

<u>Financial statements and auditors' management letters</u>

24.69 Associations should also send the Housing Corporation copies of their audited annual financial statements within six months of the end of the accounting period. [HAA 1985 Sec 24(4)]. Copies of the auditors' annual management letters should be submitted with these statements, or as soon as possible thereafter.

<u>Rent surplus fund return</u>

24.70 Every association that is providing accommodation on which a rent surplus fund liability may arise from increased rental income is required to complete a rent surplus fund return. The completed return (forms RSF 1, 2 and 3) should be sent to the Corporation with the audited financial statements. Form RSF 1 includes an auditors' report requiring an opinion whether the amounts stated in the return have been properly calculated in accordance with the rent surplus fund determination 1989 and 1990. The auditors should be the same firm of auditors who audited the annual financial statements.

Applications for grants

24.71 Applications for grants such as hostel deficit grant and supplementary management grant also need to be audited to confirm that the statements and information provided are correct and in accordance with the Corporation's regulations and instructions.

Housing association audit practice

24.72 Housing Corporation Circular 45/89 'Code of Housing Association Audit Practice' issued in June 1989 describes best audit practice and advises housing associations of their own responsibilities with respect to their auditors. The Corporation expects all larger associations (250 or more dwellings) to adhere to the code and small associations are advised to do so for their own well being.

24.73 The code places responsibilities on the association in the following areas:

- The appointment of the auditor.
- Agreeing the scope of the audit.
- Liaising with the auditor on staff assigned to the audit.
- Agreeing the audit plan and budget.
- Receiving reports.
- Reviewing the fees to be charged.
- Liaising with the auditor on the work to be carried out arising from the management letter.
- Reviewing the service provided by the auditor in deciding whether or not to re-appoint for the next year.

Appointment and removal of auditors

24.74 With regard to the appointment and removal of auditors, housing associations governed by the *Companies Act 1985* must comply with the obligations in that Act. All housing associations governed by the

Industrial and Provident Societies Acts 1965 to 1978 must comply with its requirements concerning auditors, regardless of whether or not they would otherwise be exempt from complying with other provisions of that Act on the grounds of size. [HAA 1985 Sec 25; FIPSA 1968 Sec 4(2)].

24.75 Housing associations that are registered charitable trusts have corresponding audit requirements in relation to their housing activities. The general requirement is that such housing associations must appoint a qualified auditor in each accounting period to audit their financial statements. [HAA 1985 Sec 26, 3 Sch 3(1)].

24.76 The *Housing Associations Act 1985* has no provisions that cover the auditors' resignation, or his removal.

Auditors' rights

24.77 The rights of the housing association's auditors are governed by the *Companies Act 1985* or the *Industrial and Provident Societies Acts 1965 to 1978*. The rights of auditors of registered charitable trust housing associations are as follows:

- Access at all times to the books, deeds and accounts and to all other documents of the housing association, so far as they relate to its housing activities. [HAA 1985 Sec 26, 3 Sch 6(a)].

- To require from the housing association's trustees or officers such information and explanations as they think necessary for the performance of their duties. [HAA 1985 Sec 26, 3 Sch 6(b)].

24.78 There are no rights to protect the auditor from removal from office.

Audit report

24.79 The audit report of a housing association governed by the *Companies Act 1985* or the *Industrial and Provident Societies Acts 1965 to 1978* will have to comply with the provisions of those Acts.

24.80 The audit report of a housing association that is a registered charitable trust should be made to the housing association and must state:

- Whether, in the auditors' opinion, the revenue account gives a true and fair view of the state of income and expenditure of the association in respect of its housing activities and of any other matters to which it relates. [HAA 1985 Sec 26, 3 Sch 4(2a)].

- Whether, in the auditors' opinion, the balance sheet gives a true and fair view of the state of affairs of the association as at the end of the accounting period. [HAA 1985 Sec 26, 3 Sch 4(2b)].
- If, in the auditors' opinion, the association has failed to keep, in respect of its housing activities, proper books of account or the association has failed to maintain a satisfactory system of control over its transactions or if the accounts are not in accordance with the association's books. [HAA 1985 Sec 26, 3 Sch 5].
- If the auditor has failed to obtain all the information and explanations that, to the best of his knowledge and belief, are necessary for the purposes of his audit. [HAA 1985 Sec 26, 3 Sch 6].

24.81 An example of the suggested wording for an unqualified housing association's audit report, where the housing association is an industrial and provident society, is as follows:

REPORT OF THE AUDITORS TO [NAME OF SOCIETY]

[Name of society] is a housing association registered under section 5 of the Housing Associations Act 1985.

We have audited the financial statements on pages [] to [] in accordance with Auditing Standards.

In our opinion, the financial statements give a true and fair view of the state of the society's affairs at [date] and of its income and expenditure and source and application of funds for the [period] then ended and comply with the requirements of the Industrial and Provident Societies Acts 1965 to 1978 and section 24(1) of the Housing Associations Act 1985 and the Registered Housing Associations (Accounting Requirements) Order 1988 as amended.

[Name of firm]

Chartered Accountants,

[Address].

[Date of report].

24.82 An example of the suggested wording for an unqualified audit report, where the housing association is a registered charity is as follows:

REPORT OF THE AUDITORS TO [NAME OF CHARITY] AND ITS [TRUSTEES/ MEMBERS]

[Name of charity] is a housing association registered under section 5 of the Housing Associations Act 1985.

We have audited the financial statements on pages [] to [] in accordance with Auditing Standards.

In our opinion, the financial statements give a true and fair view of the state of the charity's affairs at [date] and of its income and expenditure and source and application of funds for the [period] then ended and comply with [the Trust Deed dated [date] / the Companies Act 1985] [Schedule 3 of the Housing Associations Act 1985] and the Registered Housing Associations (Accounting Requirements) Order 1988 as amended.

[Name of firm],

Chartered Accountants,

[Address].

[Date of report].

THE REGISTERED HOUSING ASSOCIATIONS (ACCOUNTING REQUIREMENTS) ORDER 1988 (SI 1988/395) (AS AMENDED BY SI 1989/327)

Made - - -	*4th March 1988*
Laid before Parliament	*11th March 1988*
Coming into force	*1st April 1988*

The Secretary of State for the Environment as respects England, the Secretary of State for Wales as respects Wales, and the Secretary of State for Scotland as respects Scotland, in exercise of the powers conferred upon them by section 24(1), (2) and (5) of the Housing Associations Act 1985(**a**), and of all other powers enabling them in that behalf, hereby make the following Order:

Citation, commencement and revocation

1.—(1) This Order may be cited as the Registered Housing Associations (Accounting Requirements) Order 1988, and shall come into force on 1st April 1988.

(2) Subject to article 3 of this Order, the Registered Housing Associations (Accounting Requirements) Order 1982(**b**), the Registered Housing Associations (Accounting Requirements for Almshouses) Order 1983(**c**) and the Registered Housing Associations (Limited Accounting Requirements) Order 1984(**d**) are hereby revoked.

Interpretation

2. In this Order, unless the context otherwise requires–

"the 1965 Act" means the Industrial and Provident Societies Act 1965(**e**);

"the 1968 Act" means the Friendly and Industrial and Provident Societies Act 1968(**f**);

"the 1985 Act" means the Housing Associations Act 1985;

"accounts" means the balance sheet, the income and expenditure account, the statement of source and application of funds and additional financial statements required by this Order, and notes to the accounts;

"almshouse" means a corporation or body of persons which is a charity and which is prevented by its rules or constituent instrument from granting tenancies of dwellings occupied for the purposes of the charity;

"association" means a registered housing association within the meaning of the 1985 Act;

"1965 Act society" means an association which is registered under the 1965 Act;

(**a**) 1985 c.69. (**b**) S.I. 1982/828. (**c**) S.I. 1983/207.
(**d**) S.I. 1984/1833. (**e**) 1965 c.12. (**f**) 1968 c.55.

"balance sheet" means the balance sheet required for the purposes of section 39(1) of the 1965 Act(**a**) or, as the case may be, paragraph 2(1) of Schedule 3 to the 1985 Act;

"balance sheet date" means the date on which the period of account ends;

"co-ownership society" means a 1965 Act society in the case of which–

(i) the rules of the society restrict membership to persons who are tenants or prospective tenants of the association and preclude the granting or assignment (or, in Scotland, assignation) of tenancies to persons other than members, and

(ii) each tenant (or his personal representatives) will, under the terms of the tenancy agreement or of the agreement under which he became a member of the society, be entitled, on his ceasing to be a member and subject to any conditions stated in either agreement, to a sum calculated by reference directly or indirectly to the value of his housing accommodation;

"grant for rent phasing" means as much of the housing association grant for a project as does not exceed the amount, taken into account in the calculation of that grant, which relates to the inability of the association to recover the full amount of the fair rent registered under Part VI of the Rent Act 1977(**b**) or, in Scotland, Part VI of the Rent (Scotland) Act 1984(**c**) by reason of the provisions thereof;

"housing cost and finance statement" means the statement required by article 8(c) of this Order;

"housing land" means land and buildings held by an association for the purpose of providing housing accommodation (including accommodation to be provided by disposal on sale or on lease);

"income and expenditure account" means the revenue account required for the purposes of section 3(2) of the 1968 Act or, as the case may be, paragraph 2(1) of Schedule 3 to the 1985 Act;

"large association" means, in relation to a period of account, an association which on the day when that period begins, is providing more than 250 units of accommodation;

"long lease" means a lease the unexpired term of which at the balance sheet date is not less than 50 years and, in Scotland, includes a lease which is the subject of a decree under Section 9(4) of the Land Tenure Reform (Scotland) Act 1974(**d**);

"managing body" means–

(a) in relation to a 1965 Act society, the committee of management or other directing body of the society;

(b) in relation to a charity which is a company within the meaning of the Companies Act 1985(**e**), the board of directors of the company;

(c) in relation to any other charity, the trustees of the charity;

"notes to the accounts" means notes to the balance sheet, the income and expenditure account, the statement of source and application of funds and the additional financial statements required by this Order;

"period of account" means the period to which the income and expenditure account relates;

"property equity account" means an account showing the extent to which the association's capital expenditure on its property has been financed from its own resources;

"property revenue account" means the account required by article 8(a) of this Order;

"public authority" means any body of persons authorised by or under any Act to carry on a railway, dock, water or other public undertaking;

"rent", in relation to housing accommodation, includes any sum payable for or in consideration of the use or occupation of that accommodation;

"small association" means, in relation to a period of account, an association which, on the day when that period begins, is providing 250 or less units of accommodation;

"unit of accommodation" means, in the case of a hostel, the accommodation

(**a**) Section 39(1) was amended by section 11(1) of the 1968 Act. (**b**) 1977 c.42. (**c**) 1984 c.58.
(**d**) 1974 c.38. (**e**) 1985 c.6.

provided for one individual, and in any other case, a dwelling; and "vacant accommodation" means housing accommodation available for occupation which has been vacant at any time during the period of account.

Application

3. This Order applies in relation to the accounts of every association in respect of any period of account commencing on or after the date when this Order comes into force; and in respect of any earlier period of account, the Orders revoked by this Order shall apply as if those Orders had not been revoked.

General accounting requirements

4.—(1) The accounts of every large association and every co-ownership society shall comply–

(a) if the association is not an almshouse, with the requirements contained in this Order except Schedule 7 hereto;

(b) if the association is an almshouse, with the requirements contained in this Order except articles 6, 7 and 8 and Schedules 2 to 7 hereto.

(2) The accounts of every small association which is not a co-ownership society shall comply either with the requirements specified in paragraph (1)(a) or (b) of this article (as appropriate) or with those requirements amended by Schedule 7 to this Order.

(3) Nothing in this Order shall prejudice or affect the duties imposed by section 3(1) of the 1968 Act or, as the case may be, paragraph 2 of Schedule 3 to the 1985 Act insofar as they require a true and fair view to be given of the state of affairs of an association and of its income and expenditure; and accordingly where it is necessary to depart from the requirements of this Order so as to give such a true and fair view–

(a) nothing in this Order shall prevent such a departure from those requirements, but

(b) the fact of any such departure, the reasons for it and its effect shall be recorded in the notes to the accounts of the association.

(4) Nothing in this Order shall prevent the accounts of an association from giving more information than is required by this Order.

(5) Save for the information required to be shown in accordance with Part I of Schedule 1 to this Order, paragraph 12 of Part II of Schedule 1 to this Order and paragraph 14(f) to (i) of Part III of Schedule 1 to this Order, amounts which in the particular context of any provision of this Order are not material may be disregarded for the purposes of that provision.

(6) Any requirement in this Order to prepare information in a specified form shall be satisfied if it is prepared in a form substantially to the like effect.

Balance sheet and notes to the accounts

5.—(1) The information referred to in Part I of Schedule 1 to this Order shall be shown, in the manner thereby required, in the balance sheet.

(2) The information referred to in Part II of Schedule 1 to this Order shall be shown, in the manner thereby required, in the balance sheet or in notes to the accounts.

(3) The information referred to in Part III of Schedule 1 to this Order shall be shown, in the manner thereby required, in notes to the accounts.

Income and expenditure account

6. The income and expenditure account of an association–

(a) which is not a co-ownership society, shall be in the form set out in Schedule 2 to this Order;

(b) which is a co-ownership society, shall be in the form set out in Schedule 3 to this Order.

Preparation of statement of source and application of funds

7. An association shall prepare a statement of source and application of funds which shall show the disposition during the period of account and the previous period of account of all funds received or receivable by the association in each period, and the sources thereof.

Preparation of additional financial statements

8. In addition to the balance sheet, income and expenditure account, statement of source and application of funds, notes to the accounts and any other accounts which it is required to prepare apart from this Order, an association shall prepare the following additional financial statements–

(a) unless it is a co-ownership society, a property revenue account in the form set out in Schedule 4 to this Order;

(b) unless it is a co-ownership society, a statement of housing administration costs in the form set out in Schedule 5 to this Order; and

(c) if it is a co-ownership society, a statement showing the cost of the housing accommodation of the society and the finance thereof ("the housing cost and finance statement") in the form set out in Schedule 6 to this Order.

Method of distinguishing housing activities in the accounts

9.—(1) Where an association undertakes any activities which are not housing activities the method by which that association shall distinguish in its accounts between its housing activities and other activities shall be as set out in paragraph (2) of this article.

(2) The method shall be–

(a) to identify those items which relate solely to housing activities; and

(b) to apportion those items which relate to housing and other activities.

[Constitution of the Rent Surplus Fund

10.—(1) The Rent Surplus Fund of an association required to maintain such a Fund shall be constituted and shown in the accounts according to the method set out in this article, and in this article "Fund" means Rent Surplus Fund.

(2) The surpluses calculated in the manner determined under section 55(3) of the Housing Act 1988 shall be shown as such in the property revenue account.

(3) The Fund shall be shown in the balance sheet, and the sums shown under paragraph (2) of this article shall be transferred to that Fund.

(4) Where sums stand in the Fund in respect of previous periods, they shall be accumulated with any sums transferred to the Fund in respect of the period of account.]

Nicholas Ridley
1st March 1988 — Secretary of State for the Environment

Peter Walker
2nd March 1988 — Secretary of State for Wales

Malcolm Rifkind
4th March 1988 — Secretary of State for/ Scotland

[ ] Inserted by SI 1989/327

SCHEDULE 1

Article 5

BALANCE SHEET AND NOTES TO THE ACCOUNTS

PART I

INFORMATION TO BE SHOWN IN THE BALANCE SHEET

1. All amounts shown in the balance sheet for the balance sheet date shall be accompanied by the corresponding amounts for the preceding balance sheet date (if any).

2. The various items shown in the balance sheet shall be sufficiently particularised to disclose their nature and the distinction where applicable between different activities of the association.

3. Housing land shall be distinguished from other assets.

4.—(1) Fixed assets shall be entered in the balance sheet at their net book value, calculated in accordance with this paragraph.

(2) The net book value of the fixed assets which comprise housing land of an association which is not a co-ownership society shall be accompanied in the balance sheet by the elements in that calculation.

(3) The net book value of any fixed asset other than housing land is the difference between the cost of that asset and the amount provided for depreciation thereof.

(4) The net book value of any housing land belonging to a co-ownership society shall be calculated in accordance with the housing cost and finance statement of that society.

(5) The net book value of any other housing land shall be calculated according to the difference between its cost and the sum of–

(a) the total amount provided for depreciation;

(b) all housing association grant received in respect thereof; and

(c) the total amount transferred to the property equity account (if any) in respect of that land.

(6) The cost to be entered under this paragraph for any asset is the cost of its acquisition and the cost of any works carried out thereupon.

5. There shall be itemised the aggregate amount (where applicable) for each of the following–

(a) reserves;

(b) provision for future cyclical repairs and maintenance to housing accommodation;

(c) any other provision (not being in respect of depreciation of assets or bad debts);

(d) the [Rent Surplus] Fund; and

(e) investments.

6. The balance sheet shall distinguish between loans to the association which–

(a) were incurred for the purposes of the acquisition of, or works upon, housing land; or

(b) were incurred for other purposes.

7. The balance sheet shall show the amount included with current assets in respect of revenue deficit grant and hostel deficit grant receivable.

PART II

INFORMATION TO BE SHOWN IN THE BALANCE SHEET OR IN NOTES TO THE ACCOUNTS

8.—(1) Where during the period of account any of the following events have occurred–

(a) fixed assets have been acquired or disposed of;

(b) amounts provided for depreciation have been increased or adjusted;

(c) housing association grant has been received in relation to fixed assets; or

(d) amounts have been transferred to or from the property equity account (if any) of the association,

the resulting variations in the cost, the total amount provided for depreciation, the total housing association grant received, the balance on the property equity account, and the net book value of or in relation to the fixed assets of the association shall be stated in accordance with this paragraph.

(2) The variations referred to above shall be set out in sufficient detail to show their nature and cause, together with the relevant opening and closing amounts.

[ ] Inserted by SI 1989/327

(3) Where the amount of the reserves or the provisions for the balance sheet date differs from the corresponding amount for the previous balance sheet date, or where amounts have been transferred to or from the reserves or the provisions during the period of account the following shall be stated–

(a) the amounts transferred to or from the reserves or the provisions as the case may require;

(b) the source of all amounts transferred to the reserves or, as the case may be, provisions; and

(c) in the case of a transfer occasioned otherwise than by applying a provision to the purpose for which it was established, how the amounts transferred have been applied.

9. Housing land belonging to the association shall be itemised according to the amounts attributable to–

(a) land held by it under a long lease;

(b) land held by it under other leases;

(c) all other land held by it.

10. The method used to arrive at the provision for future cyclical repairs and maintenance to housing accommodation shall be stated.

11.—(1) There shall be itemised the total amounts of all loans advanced to the association by each of the following–

(a) the Public Works Loan Commissioners;

(b) local authorities;

(c) the Housing Corporation;

(d) building societies (within the meaning of the Building Societies Act 1986 (**a**)) and banks;

(e) present or former members of the association; and

(f) any other persons.

(2) In relation to each loan referred to in this paragraph the names of the guarantors (if any) shall be stated.

(3) In relation to secured loans, there shall be itemised the total amounts of–

(a) all loans secured by a charge on the assets of the association;

(b) all loans secured by a charge on the assets of other persons, together with the names of such persons.

12.—(1) Where a 1965 Act society has made a loan to a member of its managing body or to an officer of the society, there shall be stated–

(a) the date on which the loan was made;

(b) the name of the borrower;

(c) whether the loan, if made to an officer, was made under his contract of employment with the association (if any);

(d) the total amount outstanding in respect of the loan; and

(e) the terms; including the rate of interest, on which the loan is, or purports to be, repayable.

(2) Where a 1965 Act society has made a loan to an employee other than an officer of the society, there shall be stated–

(a) the aggregate number of loans to such employees;

(b) the aggregate amount of such loans outstanding;

(c) the purposes of the loans; and

(d) the terms, including the rates of interest, on which the loans are, or purport to be, repayable.

13. The following items shall be stated where applicable, namely–

(a) the amount included with current assets in respect of arrears of rent, together with the amount deducted therefrom for bad or doubtful debts;

(b) so much of any grant for rent phasing received as is not shown in the property revenue account (if any);

(c) particulars of any charge on the assets of the association to secure the liabilities of another person;

(d) the basis on which the amount set aside for tax is calculated;

(**a**) 1986 c.53.

(e) the total amount or estimated amount of any material capital expenditure not provided for, distinguishing the amount contracted for and the amount not contracted for but decided upon by the association;
(f) the means by which and the persons by whom the expenditure referred to in the foregoing sub-paragraph is intended to be financed;
(g) the general nature and the total estimated amount of any other material contingent liabilities not provided for.

PART III

INFORMATION TO BE SHOWN IN NOTES TO THE ACCOUNTS

14. There shall be stated–
(a) the average number of employees of the association, as ascertained from the average number of persons employed in each week of the period of account;
(b) the total remuneration of the employees of the association in the period of account;
(c) the total of the social security costs incurred by the association on behalf of such employees;
(d) the total of other pension costs so incurred;
(e) the total remuneration, including expenses, of the auditors of the association;
(f) any payments by way of fees or other remuneration or by way of expenses to a member of the association, being neither a member of the managing body nor an officer nor an employee thereof;
(g) any payments by way of fees or other remuneration or by way of expenses to a member of the managing body, being neither an officer nor an employee of the association;
(h) any payments by way of fees or other remuneration or by way of expenses to an officer of the association, not being an employee;
(i) any other payments or benefits granted, to the persons referred to in section 15(1)(a) to (d) of the 1985 Act.

15. Any material amount withdrawn from a provision otherwise than for the purpose for which that provision was established shall be stated.

SCHEDULE 2

Article 6(a)

INCOME AND EXPENDITURE ACCOUNT OF AN ASSOCIATION WHICH IS NOT A CO-OWNERSHIP SOCIETY

INCOME AND EXPENDITURE ACCOUNT OF (NAME OF ASSOCIATION) FOR THE PERIOD ENDED

			Preceding period	
	£	£	£	£
Property revenue account summary				
Total income				
less				
Expenditure before transfer to [Rent Surplus] Fund				
Transfer to [Rent Surplus] Fund				
Surplus/(deficit) for the period				
Development administration				
Grant receivable for acquisition and development (Note 1)				
Grant receivable for projects where completion has become impossible				
less				
Management expenses				
Abortive development costs (Note 2)				
Surplus/(deficit) for the period				

[ ] Inserted by SI 1989/327

	£	£	£	£
Fees for architects' and surveyors' services (Note 3)				
Fees receivable				
less				
Management expenses				
Surplus/(deficit) for the period				
Managed associations (Note 4)				
Fees and recoveries				
less				
Management expenses				
Surplus/(deficit) for the period				
Sales of housing accommodation (Note 5)				
Proceeds of sale				
less				
Net book value of accommodation sold representing–				
Loan debt repayable				
Housing association grant repayable to the Secretary of State				
Other				
Management expenses				
Surplus/(deficit) for the period				
Housing accommodation held for disposal (Note 6)				
Proceeds of sales				
Housing association grant receivable (other than grant for acquisition and development) (Note 1)				
Grant receivable for acquisition and development				
less				
Management expenses				
Cost of sales				
Surplus/(deficit) for the period				
Other income and expenditure (housing activities)				
Income				
Gross investment income				
Donations				
Other				
less Expenditure				
Interest not attributable to housing accommodation				
Interest on [Rent Surplus] Fund				
Other – specify				
Surplus/(deficit) for the period				
Other income and expenditure (non-housing activities)				
Income				
less				
Expenditure				
Surplus/(deficit) for the period				
Total surplus/(deficit) for the period before taxation and deficit grant				

[ ] Inserted by SI 1989/327

	£	£	£	£
Taxation				
less				
Grant receivable from the Secretary of State under section 62 of the 1985 Act(**a**)				
add				
Revenue deficit grant receivable				
Hostel deficit grant receivable				
Total surplus/(deficit) for the period after taxation and deficit grants				
Surplus/(deficit) at beginning of period				
Prior period adjustments				
Transfers to/from reserves				
Surplus/(deficit) at end of period				

Notes

1. *Grant receivable for acquisition and development* means so much of the housing association grant payable as relates to the administrative cost of acquiring and developing housing accommodation.

2. *Abortive development costs* means costs incurred on projects abandoned prior to completion.

3. *Fees for architects' and surveyors' services* means fees payable to the association in respect of the services of architects and surveyors employed by the association.

4. *Managed associations* means associations whose affairs are managed by the association to which the account relates in consideration of a fee.

5. *Sales of housing accommodation* includes leases granted in consideration of a premium.

6. *Houses held for disposal* means houses disposed of by the association after it has exercised the powers referred to in section 4(3)(c), (d) and, in Scotland, (h) of the 1985 Act(**b**).

SCHEDULE 3

Article 6(b)

INCOME AND EXPENDITURE ACCOUNT OF A CO-OWNERSHIP SOCIETY

INCOME AND EXPENDITURE ACCOUNT OF (NAME OF ASSOCIATION) FOR THE PERIOD ENDED

	£	£	*Preceding period* £	£
Income				
Rents				
less Losses arising from vacant accommodation and bad debts				

(**a**) Section 62 was amended by the Housing and Planning Act 1986 (c.63), Schedule 5, Part I, paragraph 8(1).
(**b**) Paragraph (h) was added to section 4(3) by section 13(1) of the Housing (Scotland) Act 1986 (c.65).

	£	£	£	£
Interest and dividends receivable				
Other				
Total income				
less Expenditure				
Expenses of management				
Repairs and maintenance–				
Current repairs and maintenance (Note 1)				
Cyclical repairs and maintenance (including provision for future repairs and maintenance) (Note 2)				
Service costs				
Interest payable on loans by Housing Corporation				
Interest payable on loans by a building society				
Other interest payable				
Depreciation				
(a) equal to repayment of loan principal				
(b) other				
Gross surplus/(deficit) for the period before taxation				
less Taxation				
Surplus/(deficit) for the period after taxation				
Surplus/(deficit) at beginning of period				
Prior period adjustments				
Transfers to/from reserves				
Surplus/(deficit) at end of period				

Notes

1. *Current repairs and maintenance* means works of repair or maintenance undertaken from time to time as the occasion requires.

2. *Cyclical repairs and maintenance* means works of repair or maintenance undertaken at intervals in accordance with a programme of works.

SCHEDULE 4

Article 8(a)

PROPERTY REVENUE ACCOUNT OF AN ASSOCIATION WHICH IS NOT A CO-OWNERSHIP SOCIETY

PROPERTY REVENUE ACCOUNT OF (NAME OF ASSOCIATION) FOR THE PERIOD ENDED

	Housing accommodation (excluding hostels and shared ownership schemes) (Note 3)	*Hostels*	*Shared ownership schemes (Note 3)*	*Total*	*Preceding period*
	£	£	£	£	£
INCOME					
Rents (excluding service charges) receivable					
Service charges receivable					
less Rates (including domestic water rates) recoverable from tenants					
Losses arising from vacant accommodation and bad debts					
Payments from central and local government					
Grant for rent phasing					
Other					
Total income					
EXPENDITURE					
Management expenses					
Repairs and maintenance–					
Current repairs and maintenance (Note 1)					
Cyclical repairs and maintenance (including provision for future repairs and maintenance) (Note 2)					
Service costs					
Interest (attributable to housing accommodation) payable on loans from–					
(a) the Public Works Loan Commissioners, local authorities and the Housing Corporation;					
(b) present or past members of the association;					
(c) a bank;					
(d) other persons					
Depreciation–					
(a) equal to repayment of loan principal					
(b) other					
Other					
Total expenditure					

Surplus/(deficit) for the period before transfer to [Rent Surplus] Fund
Transfer to [Rent Surplus] Fund

Surplus/(deficit) for the period transferred to general income and expenditure account

Notes

1. *Current repairs and maintenance* means works of repair or maintenance undertaken from time to time as the occasion requires.

2. *Cyclical repairs and maintenance* means works of repair or maintenance undertaken at intervals in accordance with a programme of works.

3. *Shared ownership schemes* means housing accommodation the subject of a shared ownership lease or, in Scotland, a shared ownership agreement.

[ ] Inserted by SI 1989/327

SCHEDULE 5

Article 8(b)

STATEMENT OF HOUSING ADMINISTRATION COSTS OF AN ASSOCIATION WHICH IS NOT A CO-OWNERSHIP SOCIETY

Notes

1. *Management costs* means management expenses taken from the property revenue account and *maintenance costs* means the repairs and maintenance costs from the same account.

2. *Maintenance allowances* and *management allowances* are the allowances determined by the Secretary of State for the purposes of calculating expenditure under sections 54(3) and 55(3) of the 1985 Act.

3. *Averages* in Part A are calculated by dividing the total by–
   (i) for Table 1, the number of units of accommodation occupied or available for occupation excluding any unit occupied by a warden or caretaker;
   (ii) for Table 2, the number of such units so occupied or available but including any unit occupied by a warden or caretaker,

where the number of units is the arithmetical average of those at the beginning and end of the period of account.

PART A – Housing accommodation (excluding hostels)

	Total £	*Average per unit* £
Table 1 Management		
Management costs		
Maximum management allowances		
Cost over/(under) maximum allowances		
Table 2 Current maintenance		
Current maintenance costs		
Maximum current maintenance allowances		
Cost over/(under) maximum allowances		

	Total £
Table 3 Total maintenance	
Current maintenance costs	
Cyclical maintenance costs	
Total maintenance costs	
Maximum current maintenance allowances	
Maximum cyclical maintenance allowances	
Total maximum maintenance allowances	
Total costs over/(under) total maximum allowances	

PART B – Hostels

Table 1 Management	*Total* £
Management costs	
Maximum management allowances	
Cost over/(under) maximum allowances	

Table 2 Current maintenance	*Total* £
Current maintenance costs	
Maximum current maintenance allowances	
Cost over/(under) maximum allowances	

Table 3 Total maintenance	*Total* £
Current maintenance costs	
Cyclical maintenance costs	
Total maintenance costs	
Maximum current maintenance allowances	
Maximum cyclical maintenance allowances	
Total maximum maintenance allowances	
Total costs over/(under) total maximum allowances	

SCHEDULE 6

Article 8(c)

HOUSING COST AND FINANCE STATEMENT OF A CO-OWNERSHIP SOCIETY

PART A – COST OF HOUSING LAND AND ACCOMMODATION FOR THE PERIOD ENDED

		Preceding period
	£	£
COST		
At beginning of period		
Additions during period		
Sales during period (Note 1)	( )	( )
At end of period		
HOUSING ASSOCIATION GRANT		
At beginning of period		
Additions during period		
Repayments made to the Secretary of State	( )	( )
At end of period		
REVALUATION ON RE-LETTINGS (Note 2)		
At beginning of period		
Movement during period attributable to re-lettings		
Movement during period attributable to sales (Note 1)	( )	( )
At end of period		
DEPRECIATION		
At beginning of period		
Charge during period		
Attributable to sales (Note 1)	( )	( )
At end of period		
NET BOOK VALUE OF LAND AND HOUSING ACCOMMODATION AT END OF PERIOD		
CAPITALISED UNPAID INTEREST ON LOANS TO THE ASSOCIATION		
At beginning of period		
Capitalised during period		
At end of period		

PART B – FINANCE OF HOUSING ACCOMMODATION FOR THE PERIOD ENDED

		Preceding period
	£	£
LOANS AND ACCRUED INTEREST ON LOANS BY THE HOUSING CORPORATION		
At beginning of period		
Advanced during period		
Interest accrued during period		

	£	£
Interest accrued and capitalised during period		
Repaid during period	( )	( )
At end of period		

LOANS AND ACCRUED INTEREST ON LOANS BY A BUILDING SOCIETY

At beginning of period		
Advanced during period		
Interest accrued during period		
Interest accrued and capitalised during period		
Repaid during period	( )	( )
At end of period		

REVALUATION RESERVE

At beginning of period		
Addition to reserve on relettings during period		
Amount distributed to past members during period	( )	( )
Transfer from general reserve during period		
Reduction attributable to sales (Note 1)	( )	( )
At end of period		

Notes

1. *Sales*, in relation to housing accommodation, includes leases granted in consideration of a premium.

2. *Revaluation on re-lettings* means the valuation made when vacant housing accommodation is re-let.

SCHEDULE 7

Article 4(2)

MODIFIED ACCOUNTING REQUIREMENTS FOR APPLICATION TO SMALL ASSOCIATIONS IN ACCORDANCE WITH ARTICLE 4(2)

1. In article 2 (interpretation), there shall be substituted for the definition of "accounts" and "notes to the accounts" the following–

" "accounts" means the balance sheet, income and expenditure account, and notes to the accounts;

"notes to the accounts" means notes to the balance sheet, income and expenditure account and the additional financial statement required by this Order;".

2. For article 6 (income and expenditure account), there shall be substituted–

"**Income and expenditure account**

6.—(1) The income and expenditure account shall show the following information–

(a) as income–

(i) rents (excluding service charges) receivable after deducting rates (including domestic water rates) recoverable from tenants and losses arising from vacant accommodation and bad debts;

(ii) service charges receivable;

(iii) grants and subsidies receivable from the Secretary of State or a public authority (distinguishing between payments for acquisition and development of housing accommodation and those for projects where completion has become impossible but excluding grant receivable under section 62 of the 1985 Act);
(iv) interest and dividends from investments;
(v) net surpluses from sales of property (including leases granted at a premium);
(vi) all other income;

(b) as expenditure–
(i) management expenses;
(ii) the costs of repairs and maintenance, including provision for future works;
(iii) service costs, showing separately those relating to hostels and those relating to other housing accommodation;
(iv) interest on loans attributable to housing land;
(v) depreciation equal to repayment of loan principal;
(vi) other depreciation;
(vii) amounts transferred to the Grant Redemption Fund;
(viii) administrative costs of acquiring and developing housing accommodation;
(ix) cost of housing projects where completion has become impossible;
(x) all other expenditure.

(2) The income and expenditure account shall also show–
(a) the gross surplus or deficit for the period of account, ascertained by deducting expenditure from income, but before deducting the tax or crediting the grant referred to below;
(b) the amount charged to revenue for corporation tax and income tax, together with grant receivable under section 62 of the 1985 Act;
(c) the overall surplus or deficit for the period of account, after deducting the tax and crediting the grant referred to in (b) above;
(d) amounts transferred to or withdrawn from reserves.

(3) All amounts shown in the income and expenditure account for the period of account shall be accompanied by the corresponding amounts for the preceding period (if any)."

3. Article 7 (statement of source and application of funds) shall be omitted.

4. For article 8 (preparation of additional financial statements) there shall be substituted–

"**Preparation of additional financial statement**

8. In addition to any other accounts which it is required to prepare apart from those required by virtue of this Order, the association shall prepare a statement of housing administration costs which shall be in the form set out in Schedule 5 to this Order."

5. For article 10(2) there shall be substituted–

"(2) The surpluses calculated in the manner determined by the Secretary of State under [section 55(3) of the Housing Act 1988] shall be shown as such in the income and expenditure account.".

6. In paragraph 4 of Part I of Schedule 1 (value of fixed assets in the balance sheet), the words "which is not a co-ownership society" in sub-paragraph (2), and sub-paragraph (4), shall be omitted.

7. Schedules 2, 3, 4 and 6 shall be omitted.

[ ] *Inserted by SI 1989/327*

EXPLANATORY NOTE

(This note is not part of the Order)

This Order consolidates with amendments the Registered Housing Associations (Accounting Requirements) Order 1982 (S.I. 1982/828), the Registered Housing Associations (Accounting Requirements for Almshouses) Order 1983 (S.I. 1983/207) and the Registered Housing Associations (Limited Accounting Requirements) Order 1984 (S.I. 1984/1833). The amendments made are as follows–

(1) limited accounting requirements are applied to associations providing 250 or less units of accommodation (formerly 100 under the 1984 Order) (article 4(2));

(2) the requirement, where it applied, for a summary income and expenditure account is removed;

(3) provision is made for disregarding amounts which are immaterial (article 4(5));

(4) some items required by Schedule 1 to the 1982 Order to be shown in the balance sheet or notes to the accounts are omitted;

(5) further items are required to be shown in the income and expenditure account of an association which is not a co-ownership society (Schedule 2);

(6) the requirement to show in relation to hostels the housing administration costs for each bedspace is omitted (Schedule 5).

In addition there are drafting amendments.

PRO-FORMA HOUSING ASSOCIATION ACCOUNTS

Reproduced on the pages that follow is a pro-forma set of housing association accounts for Association B. Association B is extracted from the Housing Corporation's 'Recommended form of published accounts for housing associations'.

ASSOCIATION B

THE BRAVO HOUSING ASSOCIATION LIMITED
ACCOUNTS FOR THE YEAR ENDED
31 MARCH 1990

INDEX

ASSOCIATION B

Auditors Report to the members of The Bravo Housing Association Limited

We have audited the finanacial statements on pages 4 to 20 in accordance with Auditing Standards.

In our opinion the financial statements, give a true and fair view of the state of the association's affairs at 31 March 1990 and of its income and expenditure and source and application of funds for the year then ended and have been properly prepared in accordance with the Industrial and Provident Societies Acts 1965 to 1978, the Housing Associations Act 1985 and the Registered Housing Associations (Accounting Requirements) Order 1988 as amended.

Brighton
22 June 1990

The Auditors

ASSOCIATION B

ACCOUNTS FOR THE YEAR ENDED 31 MARCH 1990
BALANCE SHEET AT 31 MARCH 1990

Schedule 1, S1, 1988 No. 395 Ref — Text Reference

	Notes	1990 £	1990 £	1989 £	1989 £
FIXED ASSETS	2				
Housing properties					
At cost			17,819,363		15,774,404
Less:					
Housing Association Grant		15,465,465		11,551,935	
Property equity account		35,345		34,682	
Depreciation		83,454		75,730	
			15,584,264		11,662,347
			2,235,099		4,112,057
Deferred Indexation account	3		15,783		–
			2,250,882		4,112,057
Other	4		169,319		144,336
Investments	5		55,000		30,000
TOTAL FIXED ASSETS			2,475,201		4,286,393
CURRENT ASSETS					
Stock & work-in-progress	6	55,826		34,742	
Hostel deficit grant receivable	7	6,141		5,495	
Investments	5	3,214,000		–	
Debtors	8	263,377		183,650	
Cash		114,318		110,250	
		3,653,662		334,137	
Less:					
CURRENT LIABILITIES					
Rent Surplus Fund	9	3,288		–	
Grant Redemption Fund	9	–		21,642	
Creditors	10	224,616		196,747	
Bank Overdraft		67,845		69,591	
		295,749		287,980	
NET CURRENT ASSETS			3,357,913		46,157
Less:					
Provisions for:					
Future cyclical repairs and maintenance	11	(24,396)		–	
Furniture replacement	12	(10,854)		(7,499)	
Major repairs	13	(22,525)		–	
			(57,775)		(7,499)
			£5,775,339		£4,325,051
FINANCED BY:					
Housing Property Finance:					
Loans:					
Allocated to properties			4,859,898		3,997,966
Unallocated			514,000		–
Share capital	15		42		40
Accumulated surplus			57,899		44,218
Reserves:	16				
General charitable reserve		228,373		161,800	
Capital reserve		28,455		28,455	
			256,828		190,255
Non-housing loans	14		86,672		92,572
			£5,775,339		£4,325,051

A Smith — Chairman
B Jones — Member
C Brown — Secretary

22 June 1990

ASSOCIATION B

INCOME AND EXPENDITURE ACCOUNT FOR THE YEAR ENDED 31 MARCH 1990

Text Ref

	Notes	1990 £	1990 £	1989 £	1989 £
PROPERTY REVENUE ACCOUNT SUMMARY					
Total Income		1,220,721		1,017,278	
Less:					
Expenditure before transfer to Rent Surplus Fund		1,224,492		1,006,547	
Transfer to Rent Surplus Fund	5	3,288		21,642	
		1,227,780		1,028,189	
(Deficit) for the year			(7,059)		(10,911)
DEVELOPMENT ADMINISTRATION					
Percentage on-costs receivable		14,927		–	
Grant receivable for acquisition and development		25,058		41,260	
		39,985		41,260	
Less:					
Management expenses	17	28,229		30,950	
Interest		940		80	
Direct costs	18	9,107		5,645	
		38,276		36,675	
Surplus for year			1,709		4,585
FEES FOR ARCHITECTS' SURVEYORS' SERVICES					
Fees receivable		69,908		59,088	
Less:					
Management expenses	17	66,882		49,798	
Surplus for year			3,026		9,290
MANAGED ASSOCIATIONS					
Development and and management fees		91,052		89,426	
Less:					
Management expenses	17	85,640		79,012	
Surplus for year	7		5,412		10,414
OTHER INCOME AND EXPENDITURE (housing activities)					
Covenants and donations		60,736		75,949	
Interest		7,139		97	
Fees		5,548		–	
		73,423		76,046	
Less:					
Penalty interest		1,735		–	
Surplus for year			71,688		76,046
Total surplus for year before deficit grant			74,776		89,424
Add:					
Hostel deficit grant receivable	7		6,141		–
			80,917		89,424
Surplus at beginning of year			44,218		35,243
Transfers to reserves:	16				
General charitable reserve		(66,573)		(80,449)	
Property equity account – non-qualifying costs	2	(663)		–	
			(67,236)		(80,449)
Surplus at year end			£57,899		£44,218

ASSOCIATION B

PROPERTY REVENUE ACCOUNT FOR THE YEAR ENDED 31 MARCH 1990

Schedule 1 SI 1988 No 395 Ref | Text Ref

	Notes	1990 Housing Association	1990 Hostels	1990 Total	1989 Total
		£	£	£	£
INCOME					
Rents (excluding service charges) receivable		968,636	369,674	1,338,310	1,144,895
Service charges receivable		78,467	–	78,467	45,337
Less:					
Rates, including water rates recoverable from tenants		(221,829)	–	(221,829)	(172,131)
Losses from:					
Vacant accommodation		(12,733)	(9,002)	(21,735)	(26,232)
Bad debts		(14,248)	(6,032)	(20,280)	(28,721)
Net rental income		798,293	354,640	1,152,933	963,148
Payments from central and local government		1,501	57,607	59,108	44,891
Other:					
charitable contributions		–	8,680	8,680	9,239
Net rental income		799,794	420,927	1,220,721	1,017,278
EXPENDITURE					
Management expenses	17	101,363	125,943	227,306	215,884
Repairs and maintenance					
Current repairs and maintenance	17	123,970	15,185	139,155	115,455
Cyclical repairs and maintenance including provision	11	109,320	8,569	117,889	100,620
Major repairs provision	13	22,525	–	22,525	–
Service costs	17	107,271	292,648	399,919	311,336
Interest, attributable to housing accommodation, payable on loans from:					
a) local authorities and the Housing Corporation		285,775	1,817	287,592	257,634
b) building societies		20,650	–	20,650	–
Depreciation equal to repayment of loan principal		7,697	27	7,724	5,618
Other:					
Transfer to deferred indexation account	3	1,732	–	1,732	–
Total expenditure		780,303	444,189	1,224,492	1,006,547
Surplus/(Deficit) for the year before transfer to the Rent Surplus Fund		19,491	(23,262)	(3,771)	10,731
Less:					
Transfer to Rent Surplus Fund	9	(3,288)	–	(3,288)	(21,642)
Surplus/(Deficit) for the year transferred to Income and Expenditure account		£16,203	£(23,262)	£(7,059)	£(10,911)

ASSOCIATION B

STATEMENT OF SOURCE AND APPLICATION OF FUNDS FOR THE YEAR ENDED 31 MARCH 1990

	1990		1989		Schedule 1 SI 1988 No 395 Ref	Text Ref
	£	£	£	£		
Overall net surplus for the year		80,917		89,424		5 of Ch 2
Adjustment for items not involving movement of funds:						
Provision for:						
Cyclical maintenance	24,396		–			
Furniture replacement	3,355		1,867			
Major repairs	22,525		–			
Depreciation	24,648		16,596			
(Profit) on disposal of fixed assets	(359)		–			
Deferred indexation account	(15,783)		–			
		58,782		18,463		
		139,699		107,887		
SOURCE OF CAPTIAL FUNDS						
Share capital – net – increase	2		–			
Mortgages and other loans received	2,688,082		1,870,056			
Housing association grant received	3,913,530		2,526,796			
Net sale proceeds on disposal of fixed assets	2,772					
		6,604,336		4,396.852		
APPLICATION OF CAPITAL FUNDS						
Purchase and development of housing properties	2,044,959		2,008,515			
Purchase of other fixed assets	44,270		7,087			
Purchase of fixed asset investments	25,000		–			
Loans redeemed by housing	1,304,426		2,526,796			
Loan repayments:	13,624		11,038			
		(3,432,279)		(4,553,436)		
INCREASE/(DECREASE) IN WORKING CAPITAL		£3,311,756		£ (48,697)		
REPRESENTED BY MOVEMENTS IN:						
Investments		3,214,000		–		
Stock and Work-in-progress		21,084		(8,419)		
Hostel deficit grant receivable		646		36,639		
Debtors		79,727		(32,967)		
Grant Redemption Fund		21,642		(21,642)		
Rent Surplus Fund		(3,288)		–		
Creditors		(27,869)		(74,352)		
		3,305,942		(100,741)		
Net liquid funds		5,814		52,044		
		£3,311,756		£ (48,697)		

NOTES TO THE ACCOUNTS FOR THE YEAR ENDED 31 MARCH 1990

1. ACCOUNTING POLICIES — Comments

(a) *Introduction and Accounting Basis*

The principle accounting policies of the Association are set out in paragraphs (b) to (n) below. These financial statements are prepared under the historical cost convention, are based on the Housing Corporation's Recommended Form of Published Accounts for Housing Associations, and comply with the Registered Housing Associations (Accounting Requirements) Orders 1988 and 1989. In the case of Rent Surplus Fund, as set out in the Recommended Form, paragraph 4(3) of the Order has taken precedence over other detailed requirements of the Order.

(b) *Finance*

The financial statements have been prepared on the basis that the capital expenditure referred to in Note 2 will be grant aided, funded by loan or met out of reserves.

(c) *Mortgages*

Mortgage loans are advanced by local authorities, the Housing Corporation or building societies under the terms of individual mortgage deeds in respect of each property or housing scheme. Advances are available only in respect of those developments which have been given approval for housing association grant by the Department of the Environment or the Housing Corporation. Mortgage loans in the balance sheet include amounts due but not received (Note 1 (g)).

(d) *Housing Association Grants*

Housing Association Grants (HAG) are made by the Housing Corporation and are utilised to reduce the amount of mortgage loan in respect of an approved scheme to the amount which it is estimated can be serviced by the net annual income of the scheme. The amount of HAG is calculated on the qualifying costs (Note 1 (g)) of the scheme in accordance with instructions issued from time to time by the Housing Corporation. The grants are paid direct to the lending authority and are reflected in the financial statements of the Association only when the payment has been made and the relevant mortgage loan reduced. For schemes developed with new fixed HAG, see Note 1(g) below. HAG is repayable under certain circumstances, primarily following sale of a property but will normally be restricted to net proceeds of sale.

(e) *Revenue and Hostel Deficit Grants (Note 7)*

Revenue and hostel deficit grants are payable to the Association at the discretion of the Department of the environment or the Housing Corporation. They are credited to the income and expenditure account in the year in which the deficits occur. The amount credited to the income and expenditure account has been evaluated in accordance with the principles used by the Housing Corporation for assessing claims for Hostel Deficit Grant published by the Department of the Environment in 1983, and amended in March 1989, and the Revenue Deficit Grant General Determination, 1989 issued by the Housing Corporation.

Notes to the Accounts (continued)

Comments

(f) *Housing Association Grant*
Acquisition and Development Allowances Receivable

Acquisition and development allowances are determined by the Housing Corporation and are advanced as mortgage loans. They are intended to finance certain internal administrative costs relating to the acquisition and development of housing properties for approved schemes. Development allowances become available in instalments according to the progress of work on the scheme. Amounts equal to these allowances are added to housing properties and are released to the income and expenditure account when they are receivable.

This is illustrative of one particular policy. An alternative is where the association credits the allowances when work covered by them is carried out.

For schemes developed with new fixed HAG, on-costs replace development allowances, and cover all costs associated with the development except for land or property purchase and works.

(g) *Fixed Assets – Housing Properties (Note 2)*

Housing properties are stated at cost. The development cost of housing properties funded with traditional HAG or under earlier funding arrangements includes the following:

(i) cost of acquiring land and buildings
(ii) development expenditure
(iii) interest charged on the mortgage loans raised to finance the scheme
(iv) amounts equal to acquisition and development allowances receivable.

These costs are either termed "qualifying costs" by the Housing Corporation for approved housing association grant schemes and are considered for mortgage loans by the relevant lending authorities, or are met out of the Association's reserve.

All invoices and architects' certificates relating to capital expenditure incurred in the year at net value after retentions are included in the financial statements for the year, provided that the dates of issue or valuation are prior to the year end. Related mortgage advances receivable from lending authorities are also included (see Note 8).

Alternative policies are permissable so long as the related mortgage advances receivable are brought in to match expenditure for which loan had been received at the balance sheet date and which have been dealt with as fixed assets.

If expenditure does not qualify for housing association grant it is nevertheless capitalised and an equivalent amount is transferred from the surplus to property equity account.

Expenditure on schemes which are subsequently aborted is written off in the year in which it is recognised that the scheme will not be developed to completion.

Interest on the mortgage loan financing the development is capitalised up to the relevant date of interim HAG application. Interest on the residual mortgage loan after this date is charged to the property revenue account. Interm relevant date for each scheme is determined in accordance with guidelines laid down in circulars from time to time. At present the guidelines provide for interim relevant date to occur three months after the last day of the month in which practical completion occurs. Interest on advances made after the interim HAG application is capitalised up to the final relevant date for the scheme, guidelines for which are determined by the Housing Corporation and laid down in circulars from time to time.

Notes to the Accounts (continued) | Comments

For schemes developed with new fixed HAG, the above also applies but with the following modifications.

Items (iii) and (iv) and the fees and expenses element of (ii) are replaced by on-costs and the one relevant date for capitalization of interest is two months after the last day of the month in which practical completion occurs.

Schemes are classified in the relevant note as being "completed" or "under construction". Schemes are transferred to completed schemes on the relevant date for capitalisation of interest.

(h) *Depreciation*

(i) **Housing properties:**

Depreciation of housing properties is effectively recognised:-

(a) by housing association grant which reduces the net investment in housing properties, and in particular land, net investment being cost less housing association grant, to an amount which can be recovered from the expected net rental income;

and

(b) in respect of that proportion of cost not financed by housing association grant, by making periodic charges for depreciation in the property revenue account equivalent to related loan principal repayments in the year over the period of the loan, (but see Note 1(m) below);

and

(c) in respect of that proportion of cost not financed by either housing association grant or by long term loan by making a transfer from reserves to property equity account.

(ii) **Other fixed assets:**

Office equipment (15% except photocopier 25%) and motor vehicles (25%) have been depreciated on a reducing balance basis. Property fixtures and fittings have been depreciated at 25% per annum on cost.

Comment: Other methods of providing depreciation to other fixed assets are equally legitimate

(iii) **Freehold office building** – as for housing properties.

(i) *Provision for future cyclical repairs and maintenance (Note 11)*

The provision is based on the association's liability to maintain the properties in accordance with a planned programme of works, but limited to the amount of a full provision which is likely to be fully utilised over the course of the cycle. External decoration is planned to take place every four years, internal decoration of hostel bedspaces every three years and internal decoration of common areas every five years. It is considered that all other forms of periodic maintenance will be funded by housing association grant or from major repairs provision, as may be appropriate, when the work becomes necessary; accordingly no provision has been made for such work.

Notes to the Accounts (continued) | Comments

(j) *Provision for Major Repairs*

A provision has been established this year to fund major repairs for those schemes for which housing association grant can not be paid for such work. Annual contributions are made to the reserve at 1% of current value of those schemes.

This is a new requirement. See paragraph 5 of the introduction to the Specimen Accounts and paragraph 8 of Chapter 4.

A provision has also been established for earlier schemes to the extent that the provision can be fully funded by 70% of the net rental income in the Rent Surplus fund calculation. No provision for major repairs has been made for the remaining schemes which can not be so funded, but HAG can be paid to fund major repairs on those schemes.

(k) *Apportionment of Employee Administration Costs (Note 17)*

Direct employee, adminstration and operating costs have been apportioned to the proerty revenue account and the relevant sections of the income and expenditure account on the basis of the actual expenditure. Management, finance and administration costs are further apportioned on the basis of staff salaries.

(l) *VAT*

The association is VAT registered but a large proportion of its income, rents, is exempt for VAT purposes and therefore give rise to a partial exemption calculation. For 1990 only 10% of VAT paid was reclaimable. Expenditure is therefore shown inclusive of VAT and the Input VAT recovered is shown in the schedule of overheads. (Note 17.)

(m) *Deferred Indexation Account (Note 3)*

This represents the cumulative effect of annual revaluation of index-linked loans, less the sum of principal repayments in excess of those treated as depreciation.

(n) *Pensions*

The Association operates a defined contribution pension scheme, the cost of which is written off to the income and expenditure accouint on an accruals basis. The assets of the scheme are held separately from those of the Association in an independently administered fund.

Notes to the Accounts (continued)

2. FIXED ASSETS

	1990 Completed Schemes £	1990 Under Construction £	1990 Total £	1989 Total £	Schedule 1 SI 1988 No 395 Ref	Text Ref
Cost:						
At beginning of year	13,830,804	1,943,600	15,774,404	13,765,889		
Additions during year	189,509	1,855,450	2,044,959	2,008,515		
Transferred on completion	2,614,400	(2,614,400)	–	–		
At end of year	16,634,713	1,184,650	17,819,363	15,774,404		
Less:						
Housing Association Grant						
At beginning of year	9,703,795	1,848,140	11,551,935	9,025,139		
Received during year	184,140	3,729,390	3,913,530	2,526,796		
Transferred on completion	1,926,400	(1,926,400)	–	–		
At end of year	11,814,335	3,651,130	15,465,465	11,551,935		
Property equity account:						
At beginning of year	34,682	–	34,682	34,682		
Transferred from income and expenditure account	663	–	663	–		
At end of year	35,345	–	35,345	34,682		
Depreciation						
At beginning of year	75,730	–	75,730	70,112		
Charged during year	7,724	–	7,724	5,618		
At end of year	83,454	–	83,454	75,730		
Net book value:						
At beginning of year	£4,016,597	£95,460	£4,112,057	£4,635,956		
At end of year	£4,701,579	£(2,466,480)	£2,235,099	£4,112,057		

3. DEFERRED INDEXATION ACCOUNT

	1990 £	£	
At beginning of year		–	Annex 3 to Appendix IV
Indexation of loan in year		17,515	
		17,515	
Transfer from Property Revenue Account:			
Principal repaid	2,363		
less: Depreciation	631		
At end of year		1,732	
		£15,783	

This relates to a 40 year loan, taken out in 1989, of £352,653 at that time, on the following terms. Interest rate of 5.856% per annum, indexation at Retail Price Index. (1990 – 5%).

Notes to the Accounts (continued)

4. FIXED ASSETS – OTHER

	1990						1989
	Motor V'cles	Maint Equip	Office Equip	Property Furniture & Fittings	F'hold Offices	Total	
	£	£	£	£	£	£	£
Cost:							
At beginning of year	14,705	1,073	31,864	4,620	146,455	198,717	191,630
Additions during year	11,172	–	13,382	19,716	–	44,270	7,087
Disposals	(5,872)	–	(154)	–	–	(6,026)	–
At end of year	20,005	1,073	45,092	24,336	146,455	236,961	198,717
Less:							
Depreciation							
At beginning of year	8,799	738	16,225	3,191	25,428	54,381	43,403
Charge for year	3,693	50	2,612	4,669	5,900	16,924	10,978
Disposals	(3,566)	–	(97)	–	–	(3,663)	–
At end of year	8,926	788	18,740	7,860	31,328	67,642	54,381
Net Book value							
At beginning of year	£5,906	£335	£15,639	£1,429	£121,027	£144,336	£148,227
At end of year	£11,079	£285	£26,352	£16,476	£115,127	£169,319	£144,336

5. INVESTMENTS

(a) **Fixed Assets**	1990	1989	Schedule 1 SI 1988 No 395 Ref	Text Ref
	£	£		2.4.1 of Ch 2
Cost:				
At beginning of year	30,000	30,000		
Additions during year	25,000	–		
At end of year	£55,000	£30,000		
Market value at end of year	£55,294	£29,310		

(b) **Current Assets**	1990	
	Cost	Market Value
	£	£
Public and local authorities investments	500,000	497,355
Other investments:		
Money on deposit	2,714,000	2,714,000
	£3,214,000	£3,211,355

Public and local authority investments are redeemable within one year.

6. STOCK AND WORK-IN-PROGRESS

	1990	1989	Text Ref
	£	£	2.2.5 and 2.5.1. of Ch 2
Maintenance stock	2,000	2,000	
Work-in-progress			
Development Department	36,326	15,742	
Architects and Surveyors	17,500	17,000	
	£55,826	£34,742	

Notes to the Accounts (continued)

		Schedule 1 SI 1988 No 395 Ref	Text Ref
7. DEFICIT GRANTS		7	2.6.1 of Ch 2

There is no requirement for Revenue Deficit Grant for 1990 (1989 – Nil). Hostel Deficit Grant of £6,141 is receivable for the year (1989 – Nil) after offsetting development administration surplus.

Amount receivable, as stated in the Balance Sheet, is computed as follow:

	£
Receivable 1 April 1987	4,575
Receivable for year to 31 March 1988	5,495
Received from Secretary of State in year	(4,575)
	5,495
Receivable for year to 31 March 1989	–
Received from Secretary of State in year	–
Balance Sheet, March 1989	5,495
Claim for year to 31 March 1990	6,141
Transferred from Grant Redemption Fund by Direction of Secretary of State	(5,495)
	£6,141

8 DEBTORS 13(a) 2.8.2 of Ch 2

	1990 £	1989 £
Arrears of rent and service charges	19,478	29,767
Mortgage advances receivable	99,270	51,427
Other debtros	13,611	22,220
Staff car loans	2,445	4,563
Management fees	13,265	13,408
Development allowances	6,013	15,875
Architects' and Surveyors' fees	7,600	9,348
Bravo Family Trust	49,430	15,769
Other managed associations	26,765	4,773
Corporation tax refund on deeds of covenant	25,500	16,500
	£263,377	£183,650

Staff car loans of £2,445 consist of loans to two employees. Both loans are repayable over five years and bear interest at 3% per annum. 12(2)

9. GRANT REDEMPTION FUND AND RENT SURPLUS FUND

(a) **Grant Redemption Fund**

	1990 £	1989 £
At beginning of year	21,642	–
Transferred from income and expenditure and property revenue accounts	–	21,642
Applied to Hostel Deficit Grant by Direction of Secretary of State	(5,495)	–
Paid to Secretary of State	(16,147)	–
At end of year	–	£21,642

(b) **Rent Surplus Fund**

	1990 £
At beginning of year	–
Net relevant income	21,918
Less:	
Transfer to major repairs provisions	15,343
Rent Surplus Fund	6,575
Retention	3,287
Payable	£ 3,288

Notes to the Accounts (continued)

As the Housing Corporation has indicated that only 50% of the Fund will be collected, the amount included in Current Liabilities has been restricted accordingly; see Note 1(a).

Rent Surplus fund replaced Grant Redemption Fund for accounting years ending after 31 March 1989. Although both funds are shown in the Balance Sheet, for clarity reference to Grant Redemption Fund, which relates to the prior year, has been omitted from the Income and Expenditure and Property Revenue Accounts.

10. CREDITORS	1990 £	1989 £	Schedule 1 SI 1988 No 395 Ref	Text Ref
Rents in development period	–	7,311		
Loan principal and interest	130,216	104,093		
Maintenance expenditure	8,978	8,250		
Capital expenditure on housing properties	36,360	29,724		
Other	31,311	32,276		
PAYE and National Insurance	–	15,093		
Managing agent – deficit	17,751	–		
	£224,616	£196,747	8(3) Ch 2	2.11.1(c) of

11. PROVISION FOR FUTURE CYCLICAL REPAIRS AND MAINTENANCE	1990 £	1989 £		
			6.12-6.2.1 of Ch 4	
Provision at beginning of year	NIL	NIL		
Expenditures: Note 17	(93,493)	(100,620)		
Charge to property revenue account	117,889	100,620		
At end of year	£ 24,396	NIL		
The provision required if calculated on a full rather than a partial provision basis; see note 1(i)	£156,107	£124,295	10	2.11.1(d) of Ch 2

12. PROVISION FOR FURNITURE REPLACEMENT	1990 £	1989 £	8(3)	2.11.1(c) of Ch 2
At beginning of year	7,499	5,632		
Charged to services costs: Note 17	5,737	5,068		
Expenditure	(2,382)	(3,201)		
At end of year	£10,854	£7,499		

13. PROVISION FOR MAJOR REPAIRS

(a) **"New" HAG Schemes**

	1990 £	£		2.11.1.(c) of Ch 2 Appendix III
At beginning of year	–			
Charged to Property Revenue	7,182			
At end of year		7,182		

(b) **Rent Surplus Fund Retention**

At beginning of year	–	
Charged to Property Revenue	15,343	
At end of year		15,343
At end of year		£22,525

The provision funded from Rent Surplus Fund retention provides a full provision for al properties completed after 31st March 1989 and a 21% cover for those completed during 1988/89.

No provision has been made for older properties; the association is still eligible to apply for HAG for major Repairs for those properties, subject to a free reserves test.

Notes to the Accounts (continued)

	Guarantor	1990 £	1989 £	Schedule 1 SI 1988 No 395 Ref	Text Ref
14. LOANS					
Housing Proprerty Finance				11 Ch 2	2.9.1 of of 2.12 of Ch 3
(a) **Allocated housing loans**:					
(i) For completed schemes, advanced to the housing association by:					
Local Authorities	–	438,203	441,356		
The Housing Corporation	–	3,303,024	3,554,654		
Building Societies & Bank	–	966,135	1,956		
Present or former member of the association		–	–		
Other; Housing Association Charitable Trust		10,000	–		
		4,717,362	3,997,966		
(ii) For schemes, under construction, advanced by:					
The Housing Corporation	–	142,536	–		
Total allocated housing loans		£4,859,898	£3,997,966		2.9.2 of Ch 2
(b) **Unallocated loans** advanced to the association for future development work by a Building Society		£ 514,000	–		
Non-Housing Loan					
Insurance Company loan Secured on freehold offices		£ 86,672	£ 92,572		

Allocated housing loans for completed schemes are equal to the sum of the net book value of completed schemes and the deferred indexation account. As HAG has been received for schemes under construction prior to the related costs being incurred in full, loans for these schemes is not equal to net book value, which is negative, as shown in Note 2.

15. SHARE CAPITAL

	1990 £	1989 £
Shares of £1 each fully paid and issued at beginning of year	40	40
Shares issued during year	2	–
	£42	£40

16. RESERVES

8(3) Ch 2 — 2.11.1(c) of

(a) *General Charitable Reserves*

	1990 £	1989 £
At beginning of year	161,800	81,351
Transfer from Income and Expenditure Account	66,573	80,449
At end of year	£ 228,373	£ 161,800

Included with the transfer from Income and Expenditure Account is an amount of £6,500 for interest (1988 – £4,500) of which £500 (1988 – £500) is charged to the Property Revenue account, being one of eleven such annual charges from 1986 as repayment of mortgages redeemed early from charitable funds.

(b) *Capital Reserve*

This reserve was created and has been maintained to reflect the proportion of the cost of the freehold offices funded from the resources of the association.

Notes to the Accounts (continued)

17. Management Expenses

	1990								
	HOUSING ACCOMMODATION				HOSTELS				
	M'ment £	Services £	Current Maint £	Cyclical Maint £	M'ment £	Services £	Current Maint £	Cyclical Maint £	Balance to page 18 £
Employee Costs									
Salaries	46,525	32,930	14,676	11,345	85,241	35,217	1,799	888	228,621
Pensions and National Insurance	5,200	3,872	1,640	1,268	9,381	3,782	201	99	25,443
	51,725	36,802	16,316	12,613	94,622	38,999	2,000	987	254,064
Estate Costs									
Cleaning	–	19,327	–	–	–	96,113	–	–	115,440
Insurance	7,287	–	–	–	122	–	–	–	7,409
Garden Maintenance	–	7,711	–	–	–	22,001	–	–	29,712
Heating & Lighting	–	19,079	–	–	–	102,942	–	–	122,021
Repair & Maintenance	–	–	96,259	65,422	–	–	11,789	4,972	178,442
Common Area Rates	–	1,622	–	–	–	4,730	–	–	6,352
Furniture Replacement	–	952	–	–	–	4,785	–	–	5,737
	7,287	48,691	96,259	65,422	122	230,571	11,789	4,972	465,113
Office Overheads									
Rent & Rates	2,453	–	–	–	1,546	–	–	–	3,999
Publicity, printing & stationery	4,110	–	–	–	2,480	–	–	–	6,590
Postage & Telephone	692	–	–	–	1,815	–	–	–	2,507
Motor & Travel	4,598	–	1,740	1,345	356	–	213	106	8,358
Heating & Lighting	45	–	–	–	–	–	–	–	45
Repairs & Renewals	9	–	–	–	–	–	–	–	9
Staff recruitment	169	–	–	–	–	–	–	–	169
Legal & Professional	2,973	–	–	–	360	–	–	–	3,333
Training & Conferences	2,175	–	–	–	228	–	–	–	2,403
Depreciation of:									
Office Equipment	–	–	–	–	–	–	–	–	–
Motor Vehicles	–	–	–	–	–	–	–	–	–
Leasing of Office Equipment	66	–	–	–	–	–	–	–	66
Sundries	–	–	–	–	–	–	–	–	–
	17,290	–	1,740	1,345	6,785	–	213	106	27,479
Other Operating Expenses									
General Insurance	–	–	–	–	–	–	–	–	–
Audit Fees	–	–	–	–	–	–	–	–	–
	–	–	–	–	–	–	–	–	–
Total Costs	76,302	85,493	114,315	79,380	101,529	269,570	14,002	6,065	746,656
Less: VAT recoverable Right to Buy & HOTCHA sales	(5,548)								(5,548)
Net Costs	70,754	85,493	114,315	79,380	101,529	269,570	14,002	6,065	741,108
Development service Finance & Admin re-charged	30,609	21,778	9,655	7,464	24,414	23,078	1,183	584	118,765
Total Charged	101,363	107,271	123,970	86,844	125,943	292,648	15,185	6,649	859,873
1989	96,270	84,289	102,856	93,464	119,614	227,047	12,599	7,156	743,295

Notes to the Accounts (continued)

Text Ref
4.4 of Ch 2
5 of Ch 4

17. Management Expenses (continued)

Balance from page 17 (1990)	New Devt. (1990)	Surveyors' & Architects' Dept. (1990)	Managed Assocs (1990)	Finance & Admin. (1990)	Total (1990)	Total (1989)	
£	£	£	£	£	£	£	£
							Employee Costs
228,621	29,621	27,240	29,463	82,484	397,429	341,208	Salaries
25,443	3,311	3,044	3,293	9,219	44,310	38,184	Pensions and National Insurance
254,064	32,932	30,284	32,756	91,703	441,739	379,392	
							Estate Costs
115,440	–	–	–	–	115,440	95,734	Cleaning
7,409	–	–	–	–	7,409	6,129	Insurance
29,712	–	–	–	–	29,712	27,109	Garden Maintenance
122,021	–	–	–	–	122,021	94,875	Heating & Lighting
178,442	–	–	–	–	178,442	198,430	Repair & Maintenance
6,352	–	–	–	–	6,352	5,778	Common Area Rates
5,737	–	–	–	–	5,737	5,068	Furniture Replacement
465,113	–	–	–	–	465,113	433,123	
							Office Overheads
3,999	–	6,186	2,810	50,830	63,825	23,425	Rent & Rates
6,590	–	1,310	473	12,767	21,140	16,825	Publicity, printing & stationery
2,507	–	947	–	12,486	15,940	12,018	Postage & Telephone
8,358	673	329	2,910	2,370	14,640	13,130	Motor & Travel
45	–	286	193	2,142	2,666	2,402	Heating & Lighting
9	–	1,900	15	6,201	8,125	7,125	Repairs & Renewals
169	–	590	1,838	2,115	4,712	1,775	Staff Recruitment
3,333	–	589	–	3,375	7,297	8,817	Legal & Professional
2,403	136	620	261	563	3,983	2,994	Training & Conferences
							Depreciation of:
–	–	–	–	2,612	2,612	3,071	office Equipment
–	–	–	–	3,693	3,693	1,969	Motor Vehicles
66	–	420	–	11,222	11,708	10,439	Leasing of Office Equipment
–	–	–	–	2,596	2,596	2,021	Sundries
27,479	809	13,177	8,500	112,972	162,937	106,011	
							Other Operating Expenses
–	–	5,500	–	1,649	7,149	7,039	General Insurance
–	–	–	–	3,000	3,000	2,500	Audit Fees
–	–	5,500	–	4,649	10,149	9,539	
746,656	33,741	48,961	41,256	209,324	1,079,938	928,065	Total Costs
				(33,766)	(33,766)	(25,010)	Less: VAT recoverable
(5,548)	–	–	–	–	(5,548)		Right to Buy & HOTCHA sales
741,108	33,741	48,961	41,256	175,558	1,040,624	903,055	Net Cost
–	(25,000)		25,000				Development service
118,765	19,488	17,921	19,384	(175,558)			Finance & Admin re-charged
859,873	28,229	66,882	85,640	–	1,040,624	903,055	Total charged
743,295	30,950	49,798	79,012	–	903,055		1989

Notes to the Accounts (continued)

	1990	1989	Schedule 1 SI 1988 No 395 Ref	Text Ref
18. DIRECT COSTS	£	£		
Architects fee	3,635	1,304		
Legal fees, stamp duty	1,205	2,703		
Home loss and disturbance payments	3,518	1,115		
Other	749	523		
	£9,107	£5,645		

19. CAPITAL COMMITMENTS

	1990 £	1989 £		2.11.1(i) of Ch 2
Contracted less certified	2,316,000	2,462,000		
Authorised by Committee of Management but not contracted	2,558,000	1,600,000		
	£4,874,000	£4,062,000	13(e)	

The total amount contracted for at 31 March 1990 and 1989 is related to approved schemes for which loan approval has been received or for which private finance has been arranged. 13(f)

20. CONTINGENT LIABILITIES

At 31 March 1990 and 1989 there were no known contingent liabilities. 13(g) 2.11.1(j) of Ch 2

21. AUDITORS' REMUNERATION

	1990 £	1989 £		
			14(e)	3.1 of Ch 2
			14(e)	3.1 of Ch 2
The remuneration of the auditors (including expenses) for the year	£3,000	£2,500		

22. PAYMENTS TO MEMBERS, COMMITTEE MEMBERS, OFFICERS, EMPLOYEES ETC.

	1990 £	1989 £		3 of Ch 2
Fees, remuneration or expenses payable to members of the Association who were neither members of the Committee of Management nor employees of the Association	None	None	14(f)	
Fees, remuneration or expenses payable to members of the Committee of Management of the Association who were neither officers nor employees of the Association	None	None	14(g)	
Fees, remuneration or expenses paid to officers of the Association who were not employees	126	68	14(h)	
Payments or gifts made, or benefits granted to the persons referred to in sections 13 and 15 of the Housing Associations Act 1985	None	None	14(i)	

23. AMOUNTS WITHDRAWN FROM PROVISIONS

There were no (1989 nil) material amounts withdrawn from provisions otherwise than for the purpose for which the provisions were established 15 3.1 of Ch 2

Notes to the Accounts (continued)

	Schedule 1 SI 1988 No 395 Ref	Text Ref
24. HOUSING STOCK		6.2 of Ch 2

(a) The number of units of housing and hostel accommodation under development and in management at 31 March 1989 was:

	Units under development		Units in management	
	1990	1989	1990	1989
Housing accommodation for letting:				
New build	93	92	365	307
Rehabilitation	10	6	240	234
	103	98	605	541
Hostel accommodation: bedspaces	47	10	90	80

(b) The number of units of housing accommodation under management for other associations at 31 March 1990 was:

	1990	1989
New build	121	97
Rehabilitation	90	90
	211	187

25. EMPLOYEES AND EMPLOYEE COSTS

	1990	1989	Schedule 1 SI 1988 No 395 Ref	Text Ref
			14(a)-(d)	3.1 of Ch 2
Average number of employees	31	30		
Employee costs during year	£	£		
Wages and salaries	397,429	341,208		
National Insurance contributions	27,390	24,671		
Other pension costs	16,920	13,513		
	£441,739	£379,392		

The pension cost charge represents contributions payable by the Association to the pension fund. Contributions totalling £1,560 (1989: £1,170) were payable to the fund at the year end and are included in creditors.

STATEMEMT OF HOUSING ADMINISTRATION COSTS

Part A – Housing Accommodation

	Total £	Average per unit £
Table 1 – *Management*		
Management Costs	101,363	177
Maximum allowances	134,517	235
Cost (under) maximum allowances	(£33,154)	(£ 58)
Table 2 – *Current Maintenance*		
Current maintenance costs	123,970	216
Maximum current maintenance allowances	119,319	208
Cost over maximum allowances	£ 4,651	£ 8
Table 3 – *Total Maintenance*		
Current maintenance costs	123,970	
Cyclical maintenance costs	109,320	
Total maintenance costs	233,290	
Maximum current maintenance allowances	119,319	
Maximum cyclical maintenance allowances	81,957	
Total maximum maintenance allowances	201,276	
Total costs over total maximum allowances	£ 32,014	

Part B – Hostels

	Total £
Total 1 – Management	
Management Costs	125,943
Maximum management allowances	55,788
Cost over maximum allowances	£ 70,155
Table 2 – *Current Maintenance*	
Current maintenance costs	15,185
Maximum current maintenance allowances	8,270
Cost over maximum allowances	£ 6,915
Table 3 – *Total Maintenance*	
Current maintenance costs	15,185
Cyclical maintenance costs	8,569
Total maintenance costs	23,754
Maximum current maintenance allowances	8,270
Maximum cyclical maintenance allowances	13,889
Total maximum maintenance allowances	22,159
Total costs over total maximum allowances	£1,595

The excess of hostel management cost over maximum allowances at £70,155 is largely offset by other income of £66,287, as shown in the property revenue account, there being no excess rent losses.

Chapter 25

CHARITIES

Annexes

Chapter 25

CHARITIES

Introduction

25.1 Charities come in a variety of forms, such as trusts, associations, societies and companies. Charities also come in a wide variety of sizes. They range from small groups of individuals, giving their own time and having little in the way of assets or income, to multi-national institutions with multi-million pound incomes. An example of the degree of sophistication of some large charities is that in order to meet part of their financing requirements some charities have in recent years launched split capital investment trusts on The International Stock Exchange (see chapter 17 para 17.18).

25.2 It is estimated that UK charities now share income in excess of £15,000 million a year. Much of this growth in income, and importance, has developed since the second world war. However, the regulatory framework for charities has evolved piecemeal and, consequently, substantial anomalies exist. For example, charities constituted as companies are subject to detailed disclosure and audit requirements under the *Companies Act 1985*. Charitable trusts, however, although subject to the *Trustee Act 1925* and *Charities Acts of 1960 and 1985*, may only be required to prepare rudimentary financial statements and these may not require to be audited. This wide range of differences has led to considerable pressure for reform. The ASC issued SORP 2, 'Accounting by Charities' in May 1988 (reproduced as annex 1 to this chapter) and this SORP has lead to greater consistency in charities' financial statements. It should be noted that the Government introduced a White Paper in May 1989 which proposed the audit of charities and effectively the statutory enforcement of certain aspects of the SORP, subject to income criteria. No legislation is expected before Autumn 1991 at the earliest.

Legal background

25.3 Because of the legal privileges charities enjoy, their status has been a matter of concern for many centuries. The Statute of Charitable Uses 1601, usually called the Statute of Elizabeth is still referred to even today in order to set the general parameters for the definition of what is charitable. These parameters are considered below in paragraph 25.17.

25.4 The regulation of charities commenced in the early 19th century, with the *Charitable Trusts Act 1853*. This Act set up a Board of Commissioners to promote the effective use of charitable resources (see paras 25.11 to 25.15).

25.5 This system remained unchanged until the enactment of the *Charities Act 1960*. That Act includes provisions for the following matters:

- The Charity Commissioners' constitution .
- Charities' registration.
- Charities' supervision.
- Imposition of certain duties on charities.

25.6 The *Charities (Statements of Accounts) Regulations 1960* (SI 1960/2425) also deals with certain aspects of charities' financial statements

25.7 Other legislation that affects charities includes the following statutes:

- The *House to House Collections Act 1939*.

  This Act introduced regulations to protect the public when house to house collections are made.

- The *War Charities Act 1940*.

  War charities and charities for disabled persons are subject to more rigorous accounting and audit requirements than other charities.

- The *Charities Act 1985*.

  This Act provides for regulations to be made to increase the accounting requirements that apply to many charities established to relieve poverty.

- The *Companies Act 1989*.

  Section 111 of the *Companies Act 1989* amends certain provisions of the *Charities Act 1960*. These provisions relate to petitions to wind up charity companies, the power to alter a charity company's constitution, the power of its directors to bind the company and the requirement to state in all business letters, notices and official publications etc. the fact that the company is a charity if this in not obvious from its name.

Accounting and auditing background

25.8 The APC issued the Auditing Guideline 'Charities' (AG 3.301) in October 1981. This guideline considers the practical application of Auditing Standards and other Auditing Guidelines in the light of the special factors that apply to charities.

25.9 In 1985 the ASC published an exposure draft on charity accounting. As was mentioned above, this exposure draft became SORP 2, 'Accounting by Charities', in May 1988. The SORP applies to all charities (other than universities) regardless of their constitution, size or complexity, although it is left to the trustees whether they ultimately apply the SORP's recommendations. SORP 2 recommends that every charity should produce a full annual report each year giving legal and administrative details, a trustees' report, and financial statements. The content, form and basis of the financial statements are laid down in detail. These provisions are considered further in paragraphs 25.35 to 25.78. However, the non-mandatory nature of a SORP must be borne in mind when considering these provisions.

25.10 To assist the trustees of small charities, the ASC issued, at the same time as they published SORP 2, some guidance notes entitled 'Accounting by charities: A guide for the smaller charity'. The guidance notes give detailed examples and illustrations of how recommendations in SORP 2 should be implemented by smaller charities. Subject to legislation being introduced in furtherance of the White Paper referred to above SORP 2 and the guidance notes are not mandatory, but they do represent current recommended accounting practice.

The Charity Commissioners

25.11 A Board of Commissioners was first set up by the *Charitable Trusts Act 1853*, although that Act has now been repealed. The Board was supported by a staff of inspectors with powers to enquire into the state of a charity, to give reliable legal advice to its trustees, to sanction transactions in charity property and to control legal action brought by charities.

25.12 This system has remained largely unchanged by the enactment of the *Charities Act 1960*. However, there are now three Commissioners, all of whom are appointed by the Home Secretary. One is elected to be the Chief Charity Commissioner and at least two of the three must be barristers or solicitors. All of these Commissioners are civil servants and operate with a substantial support staff.

25.13 The duties of the Charity Commissioners are to promote the effective use of charitable resources by:

- Encouraging the development of better administration methods.
- Giving charity trustees information or advice on any matter affecting the charity.

- Investigating and checking abuses.

  [ChA 1960 Sec 1(3)].

25.14 Furthermore, the Commissioners act for specific charities in order to help them meet the needs for which they have been set up. However, they are prohibited from helping with the charity's administration. [ChA 1960 Sec 1(4)].

25.15 The responsibilities of the Charity Commissioners include:

- Establishing and maintaining a register of charities.
- Supervision of registered charities (see para 25.27).
- Provision of advice to charity trustees.

The National Council of Voluntary Organisations

25.16 The National Council of Voluntary Organisations (NCVO) is an unofficial charity advice organisation. It is a useful source of information and advice on charities.

Definition of a charity

25.17 Whether or not an institution is a charity will depend on what it has been established to do, rather than on its legal form. A charity is not a category of legal entity, although they are commonly constituted as trusts. Legally a charity is defined as:

> "*...any institution, corporate or not [that is] established for charitable purposes [and that is] subject to the jurisdiction of the High Court in charitable matters.*" [ChA 1960 Sec 45(1)].

25.18 The meaning of this definition is considered in more detail below:

- *"Any institution, corporate or not."*

  Most types of legal entity can be used to establish a charity and, in particular, it is common to see the following types:

  - ☐ Trusts (see chapter 6).
  - ☐ Companies - usually limited by guarantee (see chapter 14).
  - ☐ Unincorporated associations (see chapter 9) - although not partnerships, because trading with a view to making a profit would conflict with the charitable purpose.

- ☐ Friendly societies (see chapter 11).
- ☐ Industrial and provident societies (see chapter 21).
- ☐ Companies established by Royal Charter (see chapter 19).

The Charity Commissioners, however, recommend that charities are set up as limited companies.

- ■ *"Established for charitable purposes."*

The basic classification of charitable trusts was made by Lord Macnaghten in *Income Tax Special Purposes Commissioners v Pemsel (1891) AC 531 at 583*. He did not provide a definition of what is charitable, but did give some indication of what types of activity would be considered charitable. These activities include the following:

- ☐ Trusts for relieving poverty.
- ☐ Trusts for advancing education.
- ☐ Trusts for advancing religion.
- ☐ Trusts for other purposes beneficial to the community that do not fall within the other three categories.

Although this list was given for charitable trusts, there is no reason why it should not be used to determine whether other bodies are charitable.

25.19 A considerable amount of case law has developed concerning what objects are charitable. Where, however, an entity is registered by the Charity Commissioners it is legally presumed to be a charity. [ChA 1960 Sec 5(1)].

Registration of charities

25.20 The concept of a central register of charities is relatively recent and was introduced by the *Charities Act 1960*. Under that Act, a duty is placed on all charity trustees to apply for registration of their charity, unless the charity is exempt or excepted, or falls within the other categories considered below. [ChA 1960 Sec 6(a)].

Exempt charities

25.21 Certain large institutions are specifically exempted from registration under the *Charities Act 1960* and these include:

- The Universities of Oxford, Cambridge, Durham and London, including the colleges and halls of the first three.
- The Church Commissioners and any institution they administer.
- Registered industrial and provident societies (see chapter 21).
- Registered friendly societies and branches (see chapter 11).

[ChA 1960 Sec 4(4)(a), Sch 2].

25.22 The reason for exempting these particular institutions is that they are generally subject to some other form of regulation.

Excepted charities

25.23 In addition, a number of charities have been excepted from registration by specific statutory instruments. [ChA 1960 Sec 4(4)(b)]. These charities include:

- Voluntary schools with no permanent endowment other than their premises. Excepted by the *Charities (Exception of Voluntary Schools from Registration) Regulations 1960* (SI 1960/2366).
- Funds accumulated for local units of the Boy Scouts Association and the Girl Guides Association that are not permanent endowments. Excepted under the *Charities (Exception of Certain Charities for Boy Scouts and Girl Guides from Registration) Regulations 1961* (SI 1961/1044).

Small charities

25.24 Charities need not register under the *Charities Act 1960* if they have none of the following:

- Permanent endowments.
- Income from investments and other property exceeding £15 per annum.
- The use or occupation of any land.

[ChA 1960 Sec 4(4)(c)].

Places of worship

25.25 Furthermore, charities need not register under the *Charities Act 1960* if they are already registered under the *Places of Worship Registration*

Act 1855. [ChA 1960 Sec 4(4)(9)]. This exemption extends to a vestry or caretaker's house situated on the same site as the place of worship and held on the same trusts. However, it does not extend to any other buildings adjacent to the place of worship.

Benefits of registration

25.26 The main benefit of registration is the statutory exemption from taxation where certain conditions are complied with.

Responsibilities of registration

25.27 The responsibilities of registration include various accounting and audit requirements as well as supervision by the Charity Commissioners. This supervision is based, *inter alia,* on the Charity Commissioners' powers to:

- Institute enquiries into specific, or classes of, charities (other than those that are exempt). [ChA 1960 Sec 6(1)].

- Call for charity documents and search charity records. [ChA 1960 Sec 7(1)].

- Request charity financial statements and require their audit (see para 26.86). [ChA 1960 Sec 8(1)(3)].

- Have jurisdiction concurrent with that of the High Court to:

  - ☐ Establish a scheme for the charity's administration. [ChA 1960 Sec 18(1)(a)].

  - ☐ Appoint, discharge or remove a charity's trustee. [ChA 1960 Sec 18(1)(b)].

  - ☐ Remove a charity's officer or servant. [ChA 1960 Sec 18(1)(b)].

  - ☐ Vest or transfer property, or require or entitle any person to call for a transfer or transfer any property or make any payment in respect of a charity. [ChA 1960 Sec 18(1)(c)].

- Act for the protection of charities where there has been misconduct or mismanagement or where it is necessary or desirable to do so to protect or secure the proper application of charitable property. [ChA 1960 Sec 20(1)].

- Establish a common investment fund. [ChA 1960 Sec 22(1)].

Charities for the relief of poverty

25.28 The *Charities Act 1985* came into force on 1st January 1986. It provided a new regulatory structure for charities set up to relieve poverty and, in particular, gives the Secretary of State specific powers to issue regulations governing the Statements of Account that a local charity must send to its local authority.

25.29 The *Charities Act 1985* applies to all registered charities (other than exempt or ecclesiastical charities), whose sole or primary object is to relieve poverty. [ChA 1985 Sec 1]. Their sphere of activity must not generally exceed the area of five adjoining parishes, or of one county or of Greater London. [ChA 1985 Sec 6(1)].

25.30 The Act empowers the Secretary of State to make the following regulations:

- To prescribe the forms in which such statements are to be transmitted.
- To require any such statements to include an itemised schedule (in the prescribed form) of all property currently held for the charity's purposes, with an estimated value assigned to each item.

[ChA 1985 Sec 1(1)(a)(b)].

War charities and charities for disabled persons

25.31 The *War Charities Act 1940* provides a system to regulate war charities. Such charities must register with special 'registration authorities' and are subject to special requirements that apply to their financial statements and audit. Charities for disabled people are also subject to these same requirements. [NAA 1948 Sec 41].

Duty to keep accounting records

25.32 Charity trustees must keep 'proper books of account' regardless of their legal form. [ChA 1960 Sec 32(1)]. This term is not defined, however, in the legislation. Charities established as a legal entity other than a trust may be subject to additional duties to keep accounting records that will be governed by their legal form (for example, for companies, those requirements included in the *Companies Act 1985*).

25.33 War charities and charities for disabled persons are also subject to a specific duty to keep proper books of account. [WCA 1940 Sec 3(b); NAA 1948 Sec 41]. In addition these books of account must be open to inspection. [WCA 1940 Sec 3(d)].

Duty to establish and maintain systems of control

25.34 Charities have no specific legal duty to establish and maintain systems of control, unless the particular legal form of the charity requires this. However, the Auditing Guideline 'Charities' suggests that large charities should have internal controls appropriate to a large enterprise. Consequently, auditors of such charities are required to look for and encourage the implementation of normal internal control and reporting systems in keeping with the charity's scale of operations. [AG 3.301 para 47]. There is no definition of 'large charities' in the Auditing Guideline, but some indication of the internal controls expected in most charities is given. These controls cover the following areas of operation:

- Donations - collecting boxes and tins.
- Donations - postal and cash.
- Deeds of covenant.
- Legacies.
- Fund-raising activities.
- Central and local government grants and loans.
- Branches.
- Fixed assets and depreciation.
- Specific funds.
- Grants to beneficiaries.
- Bank records.

[AG 3.301 paras 52 - 62].

Duty to prepare financial statements

25.35 In general, charities must prepare financial statements appropriate to their legal form. Where a charity is set up as a trust, the trustees are placed under a duty to prepare consecutive Statements of Account. These comprise an income and expenditure account and a balance sheet. [ChA 1960 Sec 32(1)].

25.36 Information to be included in the Statement of Account has been supplemented by *The Charities (Statements of Account) Regulations*

1960 (SI 1960/2425). These provisions and regulations prescribe for the following additional information to be given:

- Particulars of assets, and the persons in whom they are vested, at the charity's year end date, distinguishing between assets forming part of the permanent endowment and other assets.
- The approximate amount of the liabilities on that day.
- The amount of receipts received during the accounting year, classified according to the nature of the receipt and distinguishing between receipts forming part of the permanent endowment and other receipts.
- The amount of payments made during the accounting year, classified according to the nature of the payment and distinguishing between payments made out of the permanent endowment and other payments.

[SI 1960/2425 Sch 1].

25.37 The regulations require a receipts and payments account, whereas the *Charities Act 1960* requires an income and expenditure account. In practice, however, accounts prepared by charitable trusts either on a cash or on an accruals basis are acceptable to the Charity Commissioners, although a cash basis would now conflict with the recommendations of SORP 2 (see below).

Accounting period

25.38 The legal rules regulating the accounting period of a charity will depend upon the legal form of the charity. However, where the charity is a trust, the Statement of Account required must relate to a period of no more than 15 months. The balance sheet must be prepared as at the end of that period. [ChA 1960 Sec 32].

The annual report

25.39 SORP 2 states that the purpose of a charity's annual report is to provide timely and regular information on the charity, enabling the user of the report to gain an understanding of the charity's operations and achievements and of its position at the period end. [SORP 2 para 1]. The responsibility for the annual report lies with the trustees. The annual report should contain:

- Legal and administrative details giving information on the constitution of the charity and its organisation (see para 25.40).

- A trustee's report that further describes the charity's operations, its objectives and strategy and provides a review of activities and information to help interpret the financial statements (see para 25.41).

- Financial statements of the charity including appropriately detailed notes to reflect the charity's transactions and financial position at the period end (see para 25.44).

A checklist to the requirements of SORP 2 is reproduced as annex 2 to this chapter.

Legal and administrative details

25.40 The legal and administrative details recommended to be given by the SORP are to provide background information on the charity's governing instrument or legal status. The SORP suggests that at least the following information should be given:

- An indication of the nature of the governing instrument or legal status of the charity.

- The charity's registration number, and, where applicable, the company's registration number.

- The trustees' names and the name of their nominating body (or other method of appointment or election), the names of any management committee and the names of the charity's principal officers.

- The charity's registered address.

- The names and addresses of any other relevant organisations or persons. These may include the names and addresses of those persons acting as bankers, solicitors, auditors and investment or other advisors.

- Details of any restrictions on the charity's operations. This should include details of any limitations in the trustees' powers of investment including, for example, any restrictions imposed by the *Trustee Investments Act 1961* (see chapter 6).

[SORP 2 para 21].

The trustees' report

25.41 The object of the trustee's report is to explain the charity's organisation, policies, activities, commitments and plans and to comment on and review the financial statements. This will enable the reader to interpret the financial statements more easily. It is recommended, therefore, that the report should include at least the following information:

- A description of the charity's objectives and the strategy adopted during the year in pursuance of its objectives and aims.
- A review of the charity's development, activities and achievements during the year, including an explanation of the significance of any surpluses or deficits or other figures disclosed in the financial statements. Details of how the charity has responded to events that have happened during the year and sufficient information to enable the reader to judge the charity's effectiveness.
- A review of the charity's transactions, and financial position, including an explanation of salient features of the financial statements and an indication of its future plans and commitments, particularly with regard to on-going items of expenditure, projects not yet completed and obligations not yet met.

[SORP 2 para 22].

25.42 Apart from the above purposes of the trustees' report, the SORP clearly intends that the report should, through disclosures, either descriptively or numerically reflect information of importance that is not incorporated into the financial statements. For example, it may not be practicable to evaluate items (such as, voluntary help, donations in kind and other intangible income) and incorporate them into the financial statements. The SORP recommends that where this is so, information relating to these factors should be disclosed in the trustees' report as an alternative to the notes to the financial statements. Other information that the SORP suggests could be disclosed in the trustees' report includes dependency on key donors and progress reports on significant projects. [SORP 2 para 23].

25.43 The trustees' report should be signed by at least two trustees to indicate their approval to it. [SORP 2 para 20].

Content of financial statements

25.44 The aim of a charity's financial statements is to provide a report on its activities and resources. Consequently, the financial statements should include:

- An income and expenditure account for the period.
- A balance sheet at the end of the period.
- A statement of source and application of funds, although this may, in certain circumstances, not be necessary and in that case should therefore not be prepared (see para 25.72).

- An explanation of the accounting policies used to prepare the financial statements.

- Notes, which expand the information given above, or which provide other useful information.

- Corresponding figures and the length of the current and previous accounting periods.

[SORP 2 para 24].

25.45 In addition, the financial statements should provide the following information:

- The resources made available to the charity during the period.

- The charity's expenses incurred during the period.

- How the charity's funds may or, because of restrictions placed on their use, must be utilised.

- Details of the movement on and position of the charity's various funds.

- The relationships between, and analyses of, the above information.

[SORP 2 para 24].

Accounting for separate funds

25.46 The funds of most charities are unrestricted, but some charities have restricted funds and the SORP summarises the legal position concerning such funds as follows:

- The assets and liabilities that represent the charity's various funds need to be distinguished in the accounting records in order to know which assets and liabilities are held in which funds.

- Realised and unrealised profits and losses on assets held in a particular fund form part of that fund. Provisions for depreciation of a particular fund's asset form part of the fund's expenditure.

- Income generated from assets held in a particular fund may be subject to donor-imposed restrictions as to its use, or as to the fund to which it should belong.

[SORP 2 para 25].

25.47 Permanent endowment funds represent a charity's capital and should not be dealt with in the income and expenditure account, but should be dealt with in the permanent endowment fund in the balance sheet.

[SORP 2 para 26]. Income from permanently endowed assets may be subject to donor-imposed restrictions concerning their use and as to the fund that they should belong to. However, where no such restrictions are placed on the income from an asset, it will be unrestricted and, therefore, should be taken to the income and expenditure account. [SORP 2 para 26, 27].

25.48 The SORP states that the financial statements should provide information on the charity's fund structure and on the significance of each major fund balance. The charity may either produce a single set of financial statements covering all the charity's funds with columnar or note analysis of the separate funds or alternatively produce separate sets of statements for each of its funds. [SORP 2 para 29].

25.49 The financial statements should also include a reconciliation of the charity's total opening funds to its total closing funds. This reconciliation should show the income and expenditure balance and movements on all of the charity's funds, analysed between the major funds (for example, see Table 25.1). When disclosing details of movements on major funds, transfers should be shown separately from allocations to designated funds. [SORP 2 para 31].

Table 25.1: Illustration of disclosure of separate funds in the notes to the financial statements of a charity.

Extract from British Agencies for Adoption & Fostering Annual Review and Accounts 1989/90.

Notes to the accounts extract

Balance 1.4.89	Income for year	Expenditure for year	Transfer from/to Income & Expenditure Account	Balance 31.3.90	5 Specific purpose funds
£	£	£	£	£	
					Restricted funds
1,352	96	–	96	1,448	Hilda Lewis Memorial Fund
(5)	5	–	5	–	London Regional Group
16,135	24,351	40,486*	(16,135)	–	Black Issues Project fund
7,814	101,884	109,698*	(7,814)	–	Regional levy
11,500	–	5,750	(5,750)	5,750	Fostering video
10,000	–	–	–	10,000	Publications
	* including staff salaries				
46,796	126,336	155,934	(29,598)	17,198	
	Allocation from I&E Account				*Unrestricted funds*
–	24,000	–	24,000	24,000	Accommodation fund
4,000	6,000	–	6,000	10,000	Capital equipment fund
4,000	6,000	–	6,000	10,000	Rent equalisation
–	10,000	–	10,000	10,000	Computerisation of accounts
–	10,000	–	10,000	10,000	Superannuation reserve
8,000	56,000	–	56,000	64,000	
54,796	182,336	155,934	26,402	81,198	

25.50 In addition, the charity's funds should be analysed between the amount that is realised and the amount that is unrealised. [SORP 2 para 30].

Accounting policies

25.51 The SORP recommends that the notes to the financial statements should explain the accounting policies followed for dealing with items that are judged material in accounting for, or reporting on, the charity's activities and resources. The explanations should be as clear, fair and brief as possible. [SORP 2 para 32]. Examples of areas for which the accounting policies should be explained are as follows:

- Capitalisation and depreciation of fixed assets.
- Commitments not yet met and the use of designated funds.
- The amounts at which assets are included in the balance sheet.
- Donations, legacies and other forms of voluntary income.
- Grants payable and receivable.
- Identification of items to be included in administration expenses, fund-raising expenses and publicity expenses.
- Investment income.
- Netting-off of expenses and related income.
- Realised and unrealised gains and losses on investment and fixed assets.
- Stock.
- Subscriptions for life membership.

[SORP 2 para 33].

Table 25.2 illustrates the disclosures of accounting policies adopted by a charity.

25.52 The SORP recommends that a charity's accounting policies should be applied consistently throughout each accounting period and from one period to the next. The statement recommends that a charity should change an accounting policy only where it considers that the new policy will give a fairer presentation of the charity's activities or financial position. If changes are made, they should be disclosed and if

Table 25.2: Illustration of accounting policies adopted by a charity

Extract from The Spastics Society for people with cerebral palsy Report and Accounts 5th April 1990.

Notes to the Accounts for the year ended 5 April 1990

1. Accounting policies

(a) Accounting bases
These accounts have been prepared under the historical cost convention and in accordance with the Companies Act, 1985, and in compliance with the Statement of Recommended Practice No. 2 (Accounting for Charities).

(b) Tangible assets
The cost of schools and centres properties and central and regional offices have been depreciated over a period of 50 years in the case of freeholds and long leaseholds or over the term of the lease if less. Leasehold shop properties have been depreciated over a period of 5 years or over the term of the lease if less. The proportion of the cost of land included in these properties is not material.
Other fixed assets have been depreciated on a straight line basis over their estimated useful life: Furniture and equipment – 5 years; motor vehicles – 4 years.

(c) Grants to affiliated groups
The Society makes grants to affiliated groups towards the purchase of properties for local centres and legal title to certain of these properties remains with the Society. The amount of the grants has been charged in the income and expenditure account. No value has been attributed to the properties in the balance sheet since the beneficial owherships remain with the groups.

(d) Investments
Profits or losses on sales of investments have been included in the income and expenditure account and those relating to general fund have been transferred to special reserve. Investments are stated in the balance sheet at cost less any provisions for permanent diminutions in value.

(e) Stocks
Stocks and work in progress have been valued at the lower of purchase invoice cost and net realisable value. Finished goods and work in progress include an appropriate element of production overheads.

(f) Income
Income is accounted for on an accruals basis except for appeals and donations income which is accounted for when received. Legacies have been credited to the income and expenditure account and bequests in the form of properties or investments have been included at their estimated value at the time of receipt. Donations in kind to the Society's shops are accounted for when they are sold.

(g) Specific funds
Income and expenditure in respect of specific funds has been included in the income and expenditure account and transferred to the appropriate fund.

(h) Appeals costs
Appeals costs include salaries and costs of staff engaged directly on fund-raising plus an appropriate element of personnel and administrative support, based on numbers of staff, and of Head Office property costs, based on floor area.

(i) Central administrative and financial services
Central administrative and financial services include salaries and costs of central management

Table 25.2 continued

and finance plus an appropriate element of personnel and administrative support, based on numbers of staff, and of Head Office property costs, based on floor area.

(j) **Pension costs**
The expected cost of providing pensions, as calculated periodically by qualified actuaries is charged to the income and expenditure account so as to spread the cost over the service lives of employees in the schemes in such a way that the pension cost is a substantially level percentage of current and expected future pensionable payroll.

(k) **Leases**
Rental costs under operating leases are charged to the income and expenditure account in equal annual amounts over the periods of the leases.

the effect is material then the SORP recommends that any resulting adjustment should be treated as a prior year adjustment in accordance with the normal rules included in SSAP 6, 'Extraordinary items and prior year adjustments'. [SORP 2 para 34].

25.53 The SORP goes on to consider the accounting policies that should be adopted in respect of certain items. These are described briefly below.

Voluntary income

25.54 Voluntary income should be recognised in the income and expenditure account as soon as it is prudent and practicable to do so. This will usually be when the income is received. [SORP 2 para 37]. Exceptions to this general rule may include:

- Restricted income, where the conditions attached to the donations are so onerous that return of the unused income is a possibility (see para 25.58).

- Donated assets where it is impractical to value them. In this situation, receipt of the donated asset and a description of it should be disclosed in a note.

- Cash collections that may have been made but not submitted to the central body or counted, or ongoing collections (such as, from a publicly located collection container) should either be estimated and included in income or excluded from income, although the treatment adopted should be disclosed.

- Life subscriptions should be allocated over a number of years on a practical basis. The SORP suggests a period based on the relationship of a life subscription to an annual subscription.

Restricted income

25.55 Restricted income should be excluded from the income and expenditure account when the conditions attaching to it are so onerous that the return of the income becomes a possibility. [SORP 2 para 38]. Otherwise a restriction should not, in itself, cause the income to be accounted for any differently. [SORP 2 para 28]. Where onerous conditions apply, the income should be carried forward as 'deferred restricted income' and the restrictions explained.

Legacies

25.56 Legacies (other than those received for permanent endowment) should be accounted for as income as soon as received. [SORP 2 para 37]. Legacies that have been notified to the charity, but have not been received, or are not practically capable of quantification, may be treated in the same way as a donated asset, that is they should be disclosed (quantified where possible) in the notes to the financial statements.

Expenditure

25.57 All expenditure should be included in the income and expenditure account as soon as it is incurred. [SORP 2 para 56]. The exceptions given to this rule are capital expenditure, for example, the acquisition of fixed assets and investments, or other expenditure relating to future periods, such as stock. However, the main exceptions will be charitable expenditure and grants. The conceptual justification for this is that no services or goods are received in exchange for expenditure and grants on charitable activities. Thus such expenditure should be recognised when payment becomes due. [SORP 2 para 57].

Gains and losses on investments and fixed assets

25.58 Realised gains and losses on the disposal of investments should be treated in one of the following ways:

- Included as a separate item in the income and expenditure account.

- Disclosed in a statement of investment gains.

25.59 The statement of investment gains required by the SORP is a new idea. An example is given in Appendix 2 to the SORP and is also illustrated in Table 25.3. This statement should be disclosed on the face of the financial statements, not in the notes. [SORP 2 para 46(b)]. The SORP allows investments to be carried at cost or market value, although market value is not defined. Where market value is adopted this will clearly create unrealised gains and losses. [SORP 2 para 68].

Where such gains or losses arise the SORP states that they should be treated in a manner consistent with realised gains and losses. [SORP 2 para 48].

Table 25.3: Illustration of a statement of investment and property gains.

Extract from the Royal National Institute for the Blind Financial Statements 31st March 1990.

Statement of Investment and Property gains/losses for the year ended 31 March 1990

Realised gains on disposal of investments		£	£
General		1,258,126	*5,321,391*
Endowments		66,395	*86,656*
Realised gains on disposal of property	1(i)(a)	8,659,187	—
Net loss on valuation of property in use by RNIB services	8	(656,082)	*(1,579,306)*
Net gain		9,327,626	*3,828,741*
Appropriation to/(from) reserves:			
General Reserve	4	1,258,126	*5,321,391*
Development Fund for new and improved services	4	8,659,187	—
Endowments	6	66,395	*86,656*
Property in use by RNIB services	4	(656,082)	*(1,579,306)*
		9,327,626	*3,828,741*

25.60 In respect of realised and unrealised gains and losses on fixed assets, only realised gains and losses should be taken to the income and expenditure account. Unrealised gains and losses resulting from revaluations should be added to or deducted from the appropriate fund in the balance sheet. [SORP 2 para 49]. The exception to this general rule would be where a revaluation resulted in unrealised losses greater than any unrealised gains previously recorded. In this situation, the deficit below cost would be taken to the income and expenditure account.

Capitalisation and depreciation of fixed assets

25.61 Fixed assets should either be capitalised at cost or, if received as a gift, capitalised at the value at which the gift was included in income. [SORP 2 para 51]. If a fixed asset that has been previously charged to the income and expenditure account is to be capitalised due to a change in accounting policy, the fixed asset should be brought into the balance sheet using the original cost, original valuation (if gifted and included as income) or current value if the original cost or valuation is not available. This would be treated as a prior year adjustment.

25.62 The SORP recommends that the following types of fixed assets need not be capitalised.

- 'Inalienable' assets such as monuments that the charity maintains.
- Fixed assets where, in exceptional situations, neither the cost nor the market value is available.

25.63 If fixed assets are not included in the balance sheet then the SORP recommends that details of such assets should be given in the notes to the financial statements. [SORP 2 para 52].

25.64 The SORP allows the revaluation of fixed assets provided sufficient details of the revaluation are given in the notes to the financial statements. [SORP 2 para 53].

25.65 Fixed assets that have a finite useful life should be depreciated. If fixed assets have been revalued, then depreciation charged should be based on the revalued amount, the residual value and remaining useful life of the asset at the date of the revaluation.

25.66 Where the cost of minor adaptations of fixed assets undertaken before a charity can use the asset are capitalised, this often increases the cost of the asset above its market value. In such circumstances, the options available to the charity are:

- To depreciate the total cost over an estimated useful life.
- To write off, after revaluation, the 'excess cost' (for example, cost of adaptions) immediately and depreciate the market value. The effect here would always go through the income and expenditure account.

Investments including investment properties

25.67 Investments should be included in the balance sheet at their cost or market value. However, if the investments are to be included at cost, then the market value of the investments should be disclosed in the notes to the financial statements. [SORP 2 para 68].

25.68 The SORP seems to allow revaluation of investment properties if they are classified as either fixed assets or investments. If such properties are deemed to be fixed assets, depreciation would have to be charged on the revalued amount to the income and expenditure account (as SSAP 19 is not applicable). If investment properties were to be classed with other investments (for example, stocks and shares) then no depreciation would be passed through the statement of gains and losses on investments or the income and expenditure account (depending on the policy adopted by the charity). In the guidance notes for small charities (see para 5.5(b) Appendix 2 to the SORP 2) investment properties are given as an example of an investment. If this was also the intention behind the SORP, although it has not been specified, then clearly the issue of depreciation does not arise, as the property will be treated with other investments. This treatment appears to be the most appropriate subject to the following practical point.

25.69 It is easy to obtain the market values for listed stocks and shares but determining the market value of properties can be expensive and time consuming and may not be deemed to be an appropriate use of a charity's funds. Consequently, it is likely that charities will have to develop an accounting policy for investment properties separate from other investments that complies with the rules outlined above.

Income and expenditure account

25.70 The basic rule is that the income and expenditure account should be *"sufficient"* and *"appropriate"* in its analysis but not excessively detailed. The following should be shown separately:

- Realised and unrealised gains and losses on investments (if the option to disclose is a separate statement is not used) and, if material, realised gains and losses on fixed assets.
- Fund-raising expenses.
- Publicity expenses.
- Administration expenses.
- Charitable expenditure.

An example of an income and expenditure account is shown in Table 25.4.

Table 25.4: Illustration of an income and expenditure account of a charity.

Extract from The Spastics Society for people with cerebral palsy Report and Accounts 5th April 1990.

Income and Expenditure Account for the year ended 5 April 1990

	1990		1989	
	£000	£000	£000	£000
Proceeds from appeals, donations, legacies and other income		18,013		15,147
Income from investments and rents (note 11)		1,272		1,275
Income from shops		12,219		9,365
Exceptional items (note 12)		1,420		1,242
Fees and grants				
– schools and centres		21,561		20,639
– regional services		3,587		3,655
Total income		58,072		51,323
Less: Expenditure				
Schools and centres	28,116		26,311	
Social work and employment services	3,166		2,594	
Regional services	6,203		5,500	
Development of services	519		284	
Grants				
Research – medical, education and social	708		715	
Affiliated societies and groups	877		880	
Associated charitable work	396		361	
Publications, films and information	884		987	
Services to persons with disabilities	40,869		37,632	
National and regional appeal costs	5,569		4,567	
Shops costs	8,922		6,660	
Central administrative and financial services	1,304		1,109	
Non-recoverable VAT	617		577	
Total expenditure		57,281		50,545
Surplus		791		778
Appropriations				
Transferred to special reserve (note 10)	876		1,242	
Net income in respect of specific funds transferred (note 9)	763		479	
		1,639		1,721
Net deficit for the year after appropriations (note 8)		848		943

The balance sheet

25.71 The balance sheet disclosure recommended is that presented in the example set of financial statements (see Appendix 2 to SORP 2). The balance sheet should be signed by at least two trustees on behalf of all the trustees to show their approval. An example of a balance sheet is shown in Table 25.5.

Table 25.5: Illustration of a balance sheet of a charity

Extract from British Agencies for Adoption & Fostering Annual Review and Accounts 1989/90.

BALANCE SHEET

AS AT 31 MARCH 1990

31.3.89 £	31.3.90 £		*Note*
		Fixed assets	
46,526	39,929	Tangible fixed assets	9
		Current assets	
84,297	87,684	Publications and stationery stocks	
199,666	231,438	Debtors and prepayments	10
12,670	39,926	Cash at bank and in hand	
15,487	28,280	Cash on deposit	
312,120	387,328		
		Creditors: amounts falling due within one year	
48,290	3,153	Bank loans and overdrafts	12
31,387	30,144	Membership fees received in advance	
252,924	226,396	Other creditors including taxation and Social Security	11
332,601	259,693		
(20,481)	127,635	Net current assets/(liabilities)	
26,045	167,564	Total assets less current liabilities	
		Creditors: amounts falling due after more than one year	12
6,829	3,955	Bank loans and overdrafts	
19,216	163,609		
		Reserves	
54,796	81,198	Specific purpose funds	5
(35,580)	82,411	Income and Expenditure Account	
19,216	163,609		

These accounts were approved by the Management Committee on 4 July 1990

David Peryer *Chairperson* W T Leadbetter *Treasurer*

Statement of source and application of funds

25.72 The SORP recognises, that for certain charities, a statement of source and application of funds may not provide any significant additional information and in such circumstances should not be produced. In this respect, the SORP gives the example of a charity that operates on a cash basis as a situation where the funds statement would not be necessary. However, the SORP goes on to note that in certain circumstances a statement of source and application of funds may be more meaningful than the income and expenditure account itself. Where this is so, the SORP suggests that the statement of source and application of funds may be given greater prominence than the income and expenditure account. This type of disclosure might be applicable where the charity is funded on a cash requirement or where its investment activity is directed primarily towards making the proceeds of sales available for charitable purposes. [SORP 2 para 62].

Notes to the financial statements

25.73 The SORP specifies certain information that a charity should normally disclose in the notes to its financial statements. Charitable companies will usually need to disclose further information as required by the *Companies Act 1985*. However, for other charities the requirements are to disclose the following:

- Charitable commitments, whether legally binding or not. These commitments should include details of the movements on commitments previously reported. [SORP 2 para 74].

- Legally binding non-charitable commitments. [SORP 2 para 75].

- Guarantees given by the charity and the conditions under which liabilities may arise. [SORP 2 para 76].

- Loans and other liabilities secured on the charity's assets and their details, together with information about any charges. [SORP 2 para 77].

- The amount and terms of all inter-fund loans. [SORP 2 para 78].

- Any significant transactions, contracts or other arrangements between the charity and any of its employees, trustees or their connected persons, other than contracts of employment. [SORP 2 para 79].

- Particulars of any relevant connection of a charity's trustees or officers (for example, as trustees or officers of charities with which the reporting charity works). [SORP 2 para 80].

- Details of the remuneration trustees receive from the charity and any expenses reimbursed. If no remuneration was paid or expenses reimbursed, this should be stated. [SORP 2 para 81].

- Total emoluments (remuneration and benefits in kind) paid to employees during the accounting period and the average numbers of employees during the period. [SORP 2 para 82].

Simplified financial statements

25.74 The SORP allows simplified financial statements to be appended to the annual report of a charity. However, full financial statements must always be produced and the simplified financial statements should carry a statement explaining that they are not full financial statements and have, therefore, not been audited. [SORP 2 para 7].

Duty to prepare consolidated financial statements

25.75 Depending on its legal form a charity may be under an obligation to prepare consolidated financial statements legal obligations notwithstanding. The SORP recommends preparing consolidated financial statements when the charity has subsidiaries with activities that do not differ fundamentally from its own activities. Where fundamental differences do exist, the charity's financial statements should include in addition a summary of each subsidiary's transactions, assets and liabilities together with an explanation of the subsidiary's activities and its relevance to the charity. [SORP 2 para 72]. Associated companies should be treated in the same way as those subsidiaries that undertake activities that are fundamentally different from that of the charity. [SORP 2 para 73].

Connected charities

25.76 In addition, the SORP considers the wider issue of how charities should account for 'connected' charities. Connected charities are determined for this purpose by considering whether they have all the following characteristics:

- Common trustees.

- Unity of administration.

- Common, parallel or related objects and activities.

[SORP 2 para 70].

25.77 Such a situation may frequently arise where a charity has a number of district branches that have separate constitutions. Where a charity does have such connected charities, the SORP suggests that its annual report should include information about their activities and the resources entrusted to them. [SORP 2 para 71]. The SORP suggests doing this by aggregating the charity's financial statements with those of its connected charities and disclosing a summary of the aggregated information in the charity's financial statements. However, the charity should still produce its own individual financial statements and consolidated financial statements for itself and its subsidiaries.

25.78 Where a charity has connected charities, the annual report should disclose as a minimum:

- Particulars of the connected charities, including principal contact addresses and the nature of the relationship between them.

- Particulars of any material transactions between the charity and the connected charities.

[SORP 2 para 71].

Retention of accounting records and statements of account

25.79 The books of account and statements of account relating to any charity must be preserved for at least seven years, unless the charity ceases to exist or the Charity Commissioners permit them to be destroyed or otherwise disposed of. [ChA 1960 Sec 32(2)]. It should be remembered, however, that other legislation (for example, the *Limitation Act 1980* and the *Latent Damages Act 1986*) may also have a bearing on the period that books and records of transactions should be retained.

Duty to submit an annual return

25.80 Charities must comply with any requirement to submit an annual return imposed on them by their particular legal form. All charities (apart from exempt charities) that have to prepare a Statement of Account must also send it to the Charity Commissioners on request. [ChA 1960 Sec 8].

25.81 Unless they are exempt or excepted, all charities that have a permanent endowment must send the Charity Commissioners a statement relating to the permanent endowment each year. [ChA 1960 Sec 8(1)]. A charity is deemed to have a permanent endowment unless all property held for the purposes of the charity can be *"expended for the purpose without distinction between capital and income"*. [ChA 1960 Sec 45(3)].

25.82 Charities set up to relieve poverty (see para 25.28 above) must send a Statement of Account annually to the appropriate local authority as defined in the *Charities Act 1985*. [ChA 1985 Sec 6(2)].

25.83 War charities and charities for disabled persons must file their financial statements either with the registration authority or the Charity Commissioners. [WCA 1940 Sec 3(d)]. There are no requirements concerning time limits.

Audit requirements

25.84 A charity may require an audit for various reasons. If it is a company limited by guarantee, it is obliged by law to produce financial statements and have them audited every year. [CA 1985 Secs 227, 236]. Charitable friendly societies (see chapter 11), industrial and provident societies (see chapter 21) and housing associations (see chapter 24) are subject to similar requirements, as are war charities, charities for the disabled and charities set up under a special Act of Parliament. [FSA 1974 Sec 31; FIPSA 1968 Sec 9; HA 1988 Sec 26; WCA 1940 Sec 3(b); SI 1940/1533].

25.85 Consequently, war charities and charities for disabled persons (see para 25.31) must have their financial statements audited either annually, or at more frequent intervals as the registration authority may require with the consent of the Charity Commissioners. The auditor must be an independent person who possesses the prescribed qualifications, or a person who is for some other grounds accepted by the registration authority as competent. [WCA 1940 Sec 3(b)].

25.86 Although there is no requirement for an annual audit under the *Charities Act 1960*, the Charity Commissioners can order *"that the conditions and accounts of a charity for such period as they think fit shall be investigated and audited..."*. [ChA 1960 Sec 8(3)]. Many charities have an audit requirement in their constitution or rules although the scope of the audit is often unclear.

25.87 In 1988 the Charity Commission produced a consultation paper which suggested that whilst all charities should produce financial statements, only medium-sized and large- sized charities should file them with the Commission. Medium-sized charities would be required to be independently audited, but not necessarily by professionals. Large charities would be required to be audited by a properly qualified person.

25.88 In May 1989 a White Paper was published called 'Charities: A Framework for the Future'. The changes proposed by the White Paper included:

- The requirement for all registered charities to submit statements to the Charity Commission.
- The introduction of graduated requirements governing the contents and auditing of financial statements.
- The requirement for trustees to make copies of their charity's statements available to the public on request.
- Large charities (income greater than £25,000) must disclose reasons for departure from SORP 2.
- Large charities must be professionally audited.
- Medium sized charities must be *"independently examined"*.

25.89 Legislation enforcing the above recommendations and effectively giving legal status to some aspects of SORP 2 is not expected to be introduced to Parliament before Autumn 1991.

Auditors' rights

25.90 The rights of auditors of charities will depend upon the charity's legal form. However, auditors acting under appointment by the Charity Commissioners have the following rights:

- Access to all books, accounts and documents relating to the charity that are in the possession or control of the charity's trustees, or to which the charity's trustees have access.
- To require from any charity trustee, past or present, and from any past or present officer or servant of the charity, such information and explanations as he thinks necessary for the performance of his duties.

[ChA 1960 Sec 8(4)(a)(b)].

Audit report

25.91 The audit report in respect of a charity will depend on the charity's legal form and constitution. Most charities have a requirement laid down either by law or in their constitution requiring that the audit report should be addressed to the members or to the trustees. For charitable friendly or industrial and provident societies (see chapters 11 and 21), the report must be addressed to the charity itself as is also the case for charitable housing associations (see chapter 24). [FIPSA 1968 Sec 9; HA 1988 Sec 26, 3 Sch 4-6]. An example of an unqualified audit report is given below:

REPORT OF THE AUDITORS TO [NAME OF CHARITY] AND ITS [TRUSTEES/ MEMBERS]

We have audited the financial statements on pages [] to [] in accordance with Auditing Standards.

In our opinion the financial statements give a true and fair view of the state of the charity's affairs at [date] and of its income and expenditure and source and application of funds for the [period] then ended and [comply with the Trust Deed dated [date]] [have been properly prepared in accordance with the Companies Act 1985].

[Name of firm],

Chartered Accountants,

[Address].

[Date of report].

25.92 As stated above the Charity Commission can request an audit to be done. When such an audit is carried out the auditor must at the conclusion of, or during the progress of, the audit make such reports to the Commissioners about the audit or about the charity's financial statements or affairs as he thinks the circumstances require. A copy of any such report must also be sent to the charity's trustees. [ChA 1960 Sec 8(4)(c)]. The auditor must have regard to the Auditing Guideline on Charities (AG 3.301) in conducting his audit and completing his report.

Auditors' remuneration

25.93 Where an auditor is appointed under the terms of section 8(3) of the *Charities Act 1960* the expenses and remuneration in respect of the audit must be paid by the Charity Commissioners. [ChA 1960 Sec 8(5)]. In all other cases they will be paid by the charity itself.

SORP 2 – ACCOUNTING BY CHARITIES

Contents

Accounting by Charities

(Issued by the Accounting Standards Committee in May 1988)

This Statement of Recommended Practice sets out recommendations on the way in which a charity should report annually on the resources entrusted to it and the activities it undertakes.

Although the recommendations are not mandatory, charities are encouraged to follow them and to state in their accounts that they have done so. They are also encouraged to disclose any departure from the recommendations and the reason for it. The recommendations ***need not be applied to immaterial items.***

The recommendations contained in this statement of recommended practice go beyond the requirements of the Charities Act 1960 and the Charities Act 1985 and have been welcomed by the Charity Commission. Accounts prepared in accordance with these recommendations will therefore be acceptable for filing with the Charity Commission and, if necessary, with the appropriate local authority.

Part 1 – Explanatory note

Introduction

1 The purpose of a charity's annual report is to provide timely and regular information on the charity, enabling the user of the report to gain an understanding of the charity's operations and achievements and a full and proper appreciation of the charity's transactions during the period and of its position at the period end. This statement of recommended practice sets out recommendations on the form and content of the annual report and on the way in which the accounts contained in the report should be prepared.

2 The Accounting Standards Committee's purpose in setting out these recommendations is to help improve the quality of financial reporting by charities. It also wishes to provide assistance to those who are responsible for the preparation of charities' annual reports and accounts. The Accounting Standards Committee hopes that the recommendations will assist in reducing the current diversity in accounting practice and presentation although the intention is not to try to standardise them.

3 Universities are not included within the scope of the recommendations. That apart, the statement is intended to be applicable to all charities in the United Kingdom and the Republic of Ireland, regardless of their constitution, size or complexity. However,

it is recognised that some of the recommendations may not be applicable to all charities because of the nature of the particular charity or because of the limited classes or size of the transactions or assets involved. Nevertheless, the full recommendations have been given in this statement, leaving discretion to the trustees of each charity to apply the recommendations according to the character of their charity and the significance of the figures involved.

4 The Accounting Standards Committee has issued 'Accounting by charities: A guide for the smaller charity' in order to assist the trustees of small charities in exercising this discretion.

Interpretation of financial information on charities

5 Charities are highly disparate in character, so any comparison of the financial information they produce must be undertaken with care, even if the charities involved seem to be homogeneous. Also it is important to note that, when interpreting the income and expenditure account of a charity, the amount by which income exceeds expenditure, or expenditure exceeds income, in any one year is not usually a measure of performance or efficiency and does not usually provide an indication of the charity's future needs. Similarly, the balance sheet is not necessarily a measure of the wealth of the charity.

6 This statement recommends that a review and explanation of the accounts be provided in the annual report. It is important that reference be made to this review and explanation by those seeking to interpret the accounts correctly.

Simplified reporting

7 It has been assumed in preparing this statement that a full annual report is to be prepared and that it will include a full set of accounts. However, some charities include simplified accounts in their annual report or include extracts from their annual report in other publications. As the form of such documents will vary considerably depending on the purpose for which they have been prepared, it is not practicable to include detailed recommendations on their preparation in this statement. However, some general principles which ought to be followed are set out below.

(a) Regardless of the intended circulation of any simplified report, a full annual report should always be produced. Details of how this full report can be obtained should be given in the simplified report.

(b) Simplified accounts should carry a statement explaining that they are not the full accounts and that they are not audited.

(c) Simplified accounts should be a fair summary of the full accounts. This means that they should contain information on both the income and expenditure account and the balance sheet and that they should be based on the principles set out in this statement.

Part 2 – Definition of terms

8 A *charity* is any institution established for charitable purposes only. Where the institution is involved in more than one activity, operates more than one fund, or is not centralised into one unit of operation, the term is used in this statement to incorporate all those activities and funds which fall within the scope of a single governing instrument (or instruments supplemental to the main instrument) and any further endowments held within the terms of the original instrument.

9 A *fund* is a pool of unexpended resources, held and maintained separately from other pools because of the circumstances in which the resources were originally received or the way in which they have subsequently been treated. A fund will be one of two kinds: a restricted fund or an unrestricted fund. (The terms 'fund' and 'funds' are used in the statement in this specialised way except when used in the phrases 'fund-raising' and 'statement of source and application of funds'.)

10 *Restricted funds* are funds subject to specific conditions, imposed by the donor* and binding on the trustees. They represent unspent restricted income and/or assets to which restrictions as to their use apply.

11 A *permanent endowment* is a particular form of restricted fund in that the fund must be held permanently, although its constituent assets may change from time to time.

12 A *designated fund* is a particular form of unrestricted fund, consisting of amounts of unrestricted funds which have been allocated or designated for specific purposes by the charity itself. The use of designated funds for their designated purpose will remain at the discretion of the trustees.

13 *Administration expenses* comprise the costs which are not incurred directly on any of the charitable activities or projects of the charity and which are not incurred on fund-raising activities or publicity. Administration expenses will include a proper allocation of items of expenditure involving more than one cost category (eg administration expenses, fund-raising expenses etc), but should not include any apportionment of costs which belong to other cost categories.

14 *Fund-raising expenses* comprise the costs incurred by a charity in inducing others to make voluntary contributions to it. They will also

---

*The conditions may alternatively be imposed not by the donor but by the trusts relating to the donation. For example, if a donation is made in response to a special appeal, its use will be restricted to the purpose of the appeal, notwithstanding the fact that the donor did not impose any restriction on its use.

include a proper allocation of items of expenditure involving more than one cost category (eg administration expenses, fund-raising expenses etc), but should not include any apportionment of costs which belong to other cost categories.

Part 3 – Recommended practice

The scope of the recommendations

15 These recommendations are intended to be applicable to all charities other than universities. Any departure from the recommendations should be disclosed and explained in the annual report.

The annual report

Activities and funds to be reported on

16 The annual report of a charity should contain information on all the activities and funds of the charity and its non-autonomous branches. If a charity has some branches which are autonomous and which are therefore not dealt with in the report, this fact should be explained.

17 In order for the user to gain a full appreciation of the scope of a charity's activities, the annual report should also provide information on charities which are connected with the reporting charity and on its subsidiary and associated companies. Recommendations on the provision of this information are set out in paragraphs 70 to 73.

18 Funds held by a charity as custodian trustee will not usually fall within the scope of the annual report. Nevertheless, an indication of the extent to which the charity acts as a custodian trustee will need to be provided when explaining the charity's unquantifiable charitable work and the level of its administration expenses incurred.

The content of the annual report

19 The annual report should contain:

(a) legal and administrative details. These details will provide background information on the constitution of the charity. Paragraph 21 sets out the information which should usually be disclosed;

(b) a trustees' report or equivalent statement. This report should, as explained in paragraph 22, include a description of the charity and how it operates and a commentary on the figures shown in the accounts; and

(c) the accounts and notes thereto and, if the accounts have been audited, the auditors' report on them. The accounts are a report, expressed in financial terms, on the activities and resources of the charity. Paragraph 24 describes the accounts in detail, and the remainder of this statement sets out recommendations on their preparation.

Although it has been assumed in this statement that the legal and administrative details, the trustees' report, and the accounts will form three separate parts of the annual report, it is recognised that some or all of the legal and administrative details could just as easily be provided in the trustees' report or in the notes to the accounts.

Responsibility for preparing the annual report

20 The trustees are responsible for the preparation of the annual report and therefore for the form and content of the accounts. They should discharge this responsibility by formally approving and adopting the report. The trustees' report and balance sheet should be signed by at least two trustees on behalf of all of them in order to show this approval. The date of approval should also be disclosed.

Legal and administrative details

21 The legal and administrative details provided in the annual report should include the following information:

(a) an indication of the nature of the governing instrument or legal status of the charity. If applicable, the charity registration number and the company registration number should also be provided;
(b) the names of the trustees and their nominating body (or other method of appointment or election), the names of the members of any management committee and the names of the principal officers of the charity;
(c) the principal or registered address of the charity;
(d) the names and addresses of any other relevant organisations or persons. This may include the names and addresses of those acting as bankers, solicitors, auditors, and investment or other advisers;
(e) details of any restrictions in the way in which the charity can operate. This should include details of any limitations in the trustees' powers of investment including, for example, any restrictions imposed by the Trustee Investments Act 1961.

The trustees' report

22 The trustees' report is the main narrative section of the annual report. It should contain:

(a) an explanation of the objectives of the charity and a description of the way in which the charity is organised. The policies that have been adopted in order to try to achieve these objectives should also be explained. If there have been any significant changes in the objectives, organisation or policies since the last report, this should also be made clear. The purpose of this part of the report is to explain what the charity is trying to achieve and how it is going about it;
(b) a review of the development, activities and achievements of the charity during the year. This review should bring the reader up-to-date on the charity's progress and achievements. It should also

explain the important events which have occurred during the year and how the charity has responded to them. It will be in this part of the report that information enabling the reader to judge the effectiveness of the charity will usually be provided;

(c) a review of the transactions and financial position of the charity, and an explanation of the salient features of the accounts. This review should enable the reader to appreciate the significance of any surpluses or deficits disclosed in the accounts and the purposes for which the charity's assets are being held. It will also put the charity's current financial position in the context of its future plans and commitments, particularly with regard to on-going items of expenditure, projects not yet completed and obligations not yet met. The purpose of this part of the report is to help ensure that the accounts are properly interpreted.

23 Other information which, if not included in the accounts, could usefully be provided in the trustees' report includes details of voluntary help, donations-in-kind and other intangible income received during the accounting period (see paragraph 36), an indication of the extent to which the charity is dependent upon certain donors and, if the charity was set up to undertake a specific project, cumulative figures on progress of the project.

The accounts

24 The accounts are a report in financial terms on the activities and resources of the charity. They should comprise:

(a) an income and expenditure account that shows the resources made available to the charity and the expenditure incurred by the charity during the period;

(b) a balance sheet that shows the assets, liabilities and funds of the charity. The balance sheet (or its notes, see (f) below) should also provide some indication of how the funds may or, because of restrictions imposed by donors, must be utilised;

(c) a statement of source and application of funds that shows the flow of cash through the charity. However, as explained more fully in paragraph 64, there may be circumstances in which such a statement is neither necessary nor helpful. If this is the case, the statement should not be prepared;

(d) an explanation of the accounting policies used to prepare the accounts;

(e) details of the movement on, and position of, the various funds of the charity; and

(f) other notes which explain or expand upon the information contained in the accounting statements referred to above or which provide other useful information. This will include notes which show an analysis of the figures in the accounts and notes which explain the relationships between the figures.

The corresponding amounts for the previous accounting period should be given for figures disclosed in the accounts or in the notes to the accounts. The duration of the current and corresponding accounting periods should also be shown.

Accounting for separate funds

25 Most charities will hold unrestricted funds. Some may also hold one or more restricted funds, some of which may be permanent endowment funds. Appendix I explains in detail the legal position as regards transactions involving these various funds. To summarise, the position is as follows.

(a) The assets and liabilities representing the various funds of the charity need to be distinguished in the accounting records so that it is known which assets and liabilities are held in which funds.

(b) Realised and unrealised profits and losses on assets held in a particular fund form part of that fund. Similarly, provisions for depreciation or for a permanent fall in value of an asset form part of the fund in which the asset is held.

(c) Income generated from assets held in a particular fund may be subject to donor-imposed restrictions as to its use or the fund to which it belongs. However, where this is not the case the income will be unrestricted income.

Accounting for permanent endowment funds

26 Permanent endowment funds represent the capital of a charity. A consequence of this is that increases and decreases in the amount of the permanent endowment funds should not be dealt with in the income and expenditure account, but should instead be taken directly to the relevant permanent endowment fund in the balance sheet. A note to the accounts should disclose all movements on permanent endowment funds.

27 Income derived from assets held within a permanent endowment fund may be subject to donor-imposed restrictions as to its use or the fund to which it belongs. However, where this is not the case the income will be unrestricted income: it will not form part of the permanent endowment fund. It should therefore be included in the income and expenditure account in the normal way.

Accounting for other funds

28 The treatment of movements on all other funds should not be affected by the type of fund involved. This means, for example, that restricted income and unrestricted income received at the same time should be included in the income and expenditure account at the same time. Similarly, expenditure out of restricted funds should be included no sooner or later than expenditure made at the same time out of unrestricted funds.

29 The accounts and notes should provide information on the charity's fund structure and on the significance of each of the major fund balances. There are a number of different ways in which this information could be presented. For example, the accounts could consist of a single set of accounting statements with columnar or note analysis. On the other hand, separate sets of statements could be produced for each major fund. The trustees should decide on the presentation to be adopted. In doing so, they should take into account the complexity of the fund structure and the need to avoid confusion between the movements on the various funds.*

30 Whatever the presentation adopted, the accounts or notes should contain a reconciliation of the total opening funds of the charity to the closing funds, showing the income less expenditure figure from the income and expenditure account and details of all other movements on the funds during the period. This reconciliation should be analysed between the major funds of the charity. The amount of each major fund should be analysed between the amount that is realised and the amount that is unrealised. The nature and purpose of each major fund should also be disclosed.

31 When disclosing details of movements on the major funds, transfers should be shown separately from allocations to designated funds. Furthermore:

(a) material transfers and allocations of income received to designated funds should be separately disclosed, without aggregation or netting off, and should be accompanied by a narrative explaination of the nature and objective of the transfer or allocation;

(b) transfers and allocations should, if they are to be included in the income and expenditure account, be shown separately from, and beneath a subtotal of, the income and expenditure for the period.

Accounting policies

32 In order to understand the accounts it is essential that they are accompanied by an explanation of the basis on which they have been prepared. The accounting policies adopted for dealing with material items should therefore be explained in the notes to the accounts. These explanations should be clear, fair, and as brief as possible.

33 Examples of the accounting policies which should be explained include the policies adopted in the following areas:

(a) the capitalisation and depreciation of fixed assets;

*References in the remainder of the statement to 'the income and expenditure account', 'the balance sheet' and 'the statement of source and application of funds' should be taken to be references to all income and expenditure accounts, balance sheets and statements of source and application of funds prepared by the charity.

(b) commitments not yet met and the use of designated funds;
(c) determining the amounts at which assets are included in the balance sheet;
(d) donations, legacies and other forms of voluntary income;
(e) grants payable and receivable;
(f) identifying the items to be included within administration expenses, fund-raising expenses, and publicity expenses;
(g) investment income;
(h) netting off of expenses and related income;
(i) realised and unrealised gains and losses on investments and fixed assets;
(j) stock;
(k) subscriptions for life membership.

Where a charity is involved in specialised activities, such as research, it is particularly important that the accounting policies adopted to account for these activities are explained.

34 The accounting policies should be consistently applied throughout the period and from one period to the next. A change in accounting policy should not be made unless the new policy will give a fairer presentation of the transactions or financial position of the charity than the one it replaces. Any change in accounting policy should be disclosed. If the effect of such a change is material, it should be accounted for by restating the opening balance of the fund or funds involved. The corresponding amounts for the previous period should also be adjusted. Any such restatements should be disclosed and explained.

Voluntary income

35 Voluntary income consists of all incoming resources (whether in the form of cash or other assets or in kind) other than incoming resources received for permanent endowment, government and similar grants, investment income and gains, and payments received for services or goods.

36 A charity may receive assistance in the form of donated facilities, voluntary help or beneficial loan arrangements. Such assistance is generally referred to as 'intangible income' or 'donations-in-kind'. Although some intangible income could be included in the income and expenditure account, it will usually be more appropriate to deal with it in the notes to the accounts or in the trustees' report – particularly as its value will often be impossible to quantify. The information disclosed in respect of such income should be sufficient to give a reasonable appreciation of the benefit derived from it.

37 The value of all other voluntary income should be included in the income and expenditure account as soon as it is prudent and practicable to do so. This will usually be when the income is received. Paragraphs 38 to 44 expand upon this general principle. This means,

for example, that all legacies (other than those received for permanent endowment) should be included in full in the income and expenditure account as soon as they are received.

Restricted income

38 As explained in paragraph 28, the fact that income is restricted should not affect the manner in which it is accounted for in the income and expenditure account or the timing of its recognition as income. The one exception to this rule is when the restrictions imposed are so onerous that it is impossible to use the income in the way intended. In such circumstances the income should be carried forward in the balance sheet under the heading 'deferred restricted income' and the restrictions involved explained.

Donated assets

39 Incoming resources in the form of donated assets should usually be included in the income and expenditure account as soon as they are received. The amount at which they should be included should be a reasonable estimate of their value to the charity. The basis of valuation should be disclosed. This treatment is appropriate regardless of whether the assets were donated for use, sale or distribution.

40 On occasion it may not be practicable to ascertain the value of assets received, in which case their receipt should instead be disclosed in a note to the accounts. If it later becomes practicable to ascertain a value for them, this value should be included in the income and expenditure account as income at the date of valuation. For example, if an asset cannot be valued at the date of receipt but is later sold, the sale proceeds should be included as income at the date of sale. If the amount of assets included in income in a period other than the period of receipt is significant, this fact should be reported and the amounts involved disclosed.

Cash collections

41 When income has been collected for a charity but has not been received by it by the end of the accounting period, an estimate of the amount not received should in theory be included in the income and expenditure account. Similarly, when some of the charity's income is in collection containers at public premises at the period end, an estimate of the amount in the containers should in theory be included as income. However, because of the practical difficulties which will often be involved, it is not necessary to include such estimates in the income and expenditure account. Whatever treatment is adopted to account for such income should be applied consistently and disclosed.

Life subscriptions

42 Life subscriptions purchase for the subscriber facilities or benefits extending over a number of years. In theory a proportion of each subscription received should be allocated to each of the periods for

which it is anticipated the subscription will apply. However, rather than undertake lengthy calculations to estimate the appropriate period to use, it is acceptable to use an approximation, perhaps based on the relationship between the amount of the annual subscription and the amount of the life subscription. The period used should be disclosed.

Grants receivable

43 Government and similar grants should be dealt with in accordance with the terms of the grant. Grants made towards the cost of acquiring a fixed asset should be taken to income and expenditure account over the useful life of the asset concerned (see paragraphs 51 to 55, which deal with accounting for fixed assets). The amount of the grant still to be taken to income and expenditure account should be shown on the balance sheet as a deferred credit or, where appropriate, included in the relevant fund balance.

44 If a grant is to be received after the expenditure to which it relates, a best estimate of the amount to be received should be included in the income and expenditure account.

Gains and losses on investments and fixed assets

45 A realised or unrealised gain or loss arising on an asset will form part of the fund in which the asset involved is (or, in the case of an asset disposed of, was) held.

Realised gains and loses

46 Reaslised gains and losses on the disposal of investments should either be:

(a) included in the income and expenditure account, in which case they should be disclosed separately from other income; or
(b) disclosed in the statement of investment gains (an example of which is shown in Appendix 2) and then added to or deducted from the appropriate fund in the balance sheet. Statements of investment gains should be disclosed on the face of the accounts, not in the notes.

47 Realised gains and losses on the disposal of fixed assets should be included in the income and expenditure account and, if material, disclosed separately from other income.

Unrealised gains and losses

48 As explained in paragraph 68, investments may be carried in the balance sheet at cost or at market value. Where they are carried at cost, there will be no unrealised gains or losses to account for, except in the case of a permanent diminution in value (see paragraph 69). Where they are carried at market value, unrealised gains and losses will arise. Such gains and losses should be accounted for in a manner

which is consistent with realised gains and losses on investments; in other words, if realised gains and losses on investments are included in the income and expenditure account, unrealised gains and losses on investments should be as well.

49 Similarly, unrealised gains or losses will arise if fixed assets are included in the balance sheet at revalued amounts (see paragraph 68). Such gains and losses should not be included in the income and expenditure account: they should be added to or deducted from the appropriate fund in the balance sheet.

Other income

50 If a charity carries out trading activities, the income should be accounted for in accordance with the normal accounting rules for profit-oriented entities. If a charity charges for services which it provides, the charges should be recognised as income in the income and expenditure account as they are earned. For example, if a service is provided over a period of time, the income involved should be recognised over the period of service and not over the period in which the payment is received.

Accounting for fixed assets

Capitalisation of fixed assets

51 All expenditure on the acquisition, production or installation of fixed assets and all receipts of fixed assets by way of gift should be capitalised and included in the balance sheet. This general principle is not affected by the source of finance used to pay for the fixed asset, or the source of finance likely to be used to pay for any future replacement of the asset.

(a) Expenditure on the acquisition, production or installation of fixed assets should be capitalised at the amount expended.

(b) Fixed assets received by way of gift should be capitalised at the value at which the gift was included in income (see paragraph 39).

(c) Fixed assets being capitalised some time after being acquired, for example as a result of a change in accounting policy, should similarly be capitalised at original cost or at the value at which the gift was included in income. However, if neither of these amounts are ascertainable, a reasonable estimate of the asset's current value to the charity should be used.

For the remainder of this statement all of these valuation bases will be referred to as 'cost'.

52 The only exception to this general principle is that a charity need not capitalise a fixed asset which is either:

(a) inalienable (in other words a fixed asset which the charity is prohibited from disposing of) or historic (such as a monument or statue); or

(b) for which neither a cost nor a market value is available. This should be an extremely rare occurrence: it will usually be possible to determine a reasonable estimate of its cost or value without incurring significant expenditure.

A summary of the fixed assets not included in the balance sheet but still in use should be given in the notes to the accounts. These summary details should be sufficient to enable the reader to appreciate the age and scale of fixed assets not included on the balance sheet.

Revaluation of fixed assets

53 If a charity revalues some or all of its fixed assets, this fact, together with the date and bases of valuation, should be stated in the notes to the accounts. In the year of valuation, the names and qualifications of the persons responsible for making the valuation should also be disclosed.

Depreciation of fixed assets

54 Most fixed assets depreciate, that is wear out, get consumed or otherwise suffer a reduction in their useful life through use, the passing of time or obsolescence. Fixed assets which have a finite useful life should be depreciated. Fixed assets which have an indefinite useful life, such as freehold land, should not be depreciated. This means that:

(a) fixed assets with finite useful lives should be included in the balance sheet at cost (or, if revalued, at a revalued amount) less an appropriate provision for depreciation; and

(b) fixed assets with an indefinite useful life should be included at cost (or, if revalued, at a revalued amount).

55 If a fixed asset is revalued its depreciation should be based on the revalued amount, the residual value and remaining useful life of the asset at the date of the revaluation.

Other expenditure and costs

56 All expenditure should be included in the income and expenditure account as soon as it is incurred. The only exception to this is expenditure incurred to acquire assets, that is, expenditure on the acquisition, production or installation of fixed assets, expenditure on stock items, expenditure on the acquisition of investments, advance expenditure or prepayments. Expenditure incurred to acquire assets should be carried forward in the balance sheet.

57 Expenditure is not incurred until consideration for the expenditure has passed, in other words until something is received in exchange for the expenditure. However, in the case of expenditure and grants relating directly to charitable activities an exchange is usually not involved. Where there is no exchange, the expenditure or grant should be

recognised in the income and expenditure account when its payment becomes due. An implication of this is that commitments which extend beyond the end of the accounting period and grants which fall to be paid in future accounting periods should be charged in future income and expenditure accounts. (See also paragraphs 74 and 75).

The income and expenditure account

Presentation

58 The income and expenditure should be analysed in a manner appropriate to the charity. This analysis should enable the user of the accounts to gain a proper appreciation of the principal elements of the income and expenditure of the charity, but should not be excessively detailed. The following items should be shown separately in the analysis:

(a) realised and unrealised gains and losses on investments (if included in the income and expenditure account) and, if material, realised gains and losses on the disposal of fixed assets;
(b) fund-raising expenses;
(c) publicity expenses;
(d) administration expenses; and
(e) expenditure and grants relating directly to charitable activities.

Administration expenses, fund-raising expenses and publicity expenses

59 It is not practicable to produce precise definitions of 'administration expenses', 'fund-raising expenses' and 'publicity expenses' or to set out detailed guidance, applicable to all charities, on what expenditure should be included within each heading. The following principles should however be applied.

(a) Items of expenditure which involve more than one cost category, for example some administration expenses and some expenditure relating directly to charitable activities, should be allocated on a rational basis to the cost categories involved.
(b) Expenditure incurred on activities falling directly within one cost category should not be apportioned to any other cost category.

60 The absence of precise definitions or detailed guidance means that each charity should develop principles for cost allocation suitable to its own circumstances. These principles should be applied consistently. A full description of the items included within each category and of the principles adopted should be disclosed.

Netting off

61 A minimum of 'netting off' of income and expenditure and of assets and liabilities should take place. However, if a charity has received income from, and incurred expenses on, special fund-raising events or activities, it may occasionally be more informative to include only the net figure in the income and expenditure account. Where netting off

takes place, the reason for it and, whenever practicable, the 'gross' figures should be disclosed in the notes.

Tax credits on income

62 Income received after deduction of tax at source and income received by deed of covenant should be grossed up for the tax recoverable and this gross figure included in the income and expenditure account. The tax recoverable should be shown as a debtor until the charity recovers the amount involved.

The statement of source and application of funds

63 The purpose of the statement of source and application of funds is to show the movement of cash through the charity. Some charities believe information on their cash transactions to be more meaningful than information on their income and expenditure because, for example, they are funded on the basis of their cash needs or because their investment activity is directed primarily towards making the proceeds of sales available for charitable purposes. Where this is the case the statement of source and application of funds may be given greater prominence than the income and expenditure account.

64 On the other hand, there may be circumstances in which the preparation of a statement of source and application of funds is neither necessary to give full disclosure of information nor helpful in enabling the user to understand the charity's activities. For example, charities that operate on a cash basis and consequently have no significant assets or liabilities will find that the statement will be similar to their income and expenditure account. In such circumstances, the statement need not be included in the accounts.

65 Where a statement of source and application of funds is prepared:

(a) the analysis of the cash movements and the use of figures which have been netted-off should follow the same principles as those adopted for the income and expenditure account (see paragraphs 35 to 44, and 61); and

(b) the statement should be reconcilable to the income and expenditure account and the balance sheet.

The balance sheet

Presentation

66 The assets of a charity should be analysed in the balance sheet between fixed assets, investments (including investment properties), and current assets; and the liabilities should be analysed between current and long-term liabilities. In addition, the assets and liabilities should be analysed in a way that enables the reader to gain a proper appreciation of their spread and character. The example set of accounts in Appendix 2 illustrates what this might entail.

67 The total amount of the assets less liabilities of a charity should be analysed between its major funds.

(a) Wherever possible it should be made clear which assets and liabilities form part of restricted funds, particularly permanent endowment funds. Where this is not practicable, the notes should provide an indication as to whether or not sufficient resources are held in an appropriate form to enable the funds concerned to be applied in accordance with the restrictions imposed. For example, if a charity has a fund which is to be spent in the near future, it should be made clear in the notes whether or not the assets held in the fund are short-term assets.

(b) Where funds have been divided into wider and narrower ranges under the powers given to trustees by the Trustee Investments Act 1961, the accounts or notes should indicate the investments allotted to each range.

The amounts at which assets and liabilities are included in the balance sheet

68 Except as explained in paragraph 69, the assets and liabilities of a charity should be included in the balance sheet at the following amounts:

(a) fixed assets at cost (or valuation) less an appropriate provision for depreciation;

(b) investments at cost or market value. If the investments are included in the balance sheet at cost, the market value should be disclosed in the notes to the accounts;

(c) current assets at the lower of cost and net realisable value; and

(d) liabilities at their settlement value.

69 If an asset suffers a permanent loss (or diminution) in value, the amount at which the asset is carried in the balance sheet should be reduced to the asset's current value by a provision. Where this provision should be charged will depend on the circumstances involved.

(a) If the asset involved is an investment, the provision should be charged to the same place as realised and unrealised losses on investments (see paragraphs 45 to 48).

(b) If the asset involved is a fixed asset, the provision should be charged to the income and expenditure account to the extent that it is not covered by a previous gain on revaluation of that asset. To the extent that it is covered by a previous gain, the provision should be used to reduce the gain by deducting it from the appropriate fund in the balance sheet.

In determining whether any asset has suffered a permanent loss, gains in the value of other assets should not be taken into account.

Connected charities

70 A charity may be connected with other charities. It will usually be possible to identify whether charities are connected by considering whether they have common trustees, unity of administration, and common, parallel or related objects and activities.

71 If the reporting charity is connected to other charities, information about the other charities' activities and resources should be included in its annual report. This information should include:

(a) particulars of the connected charities, including principal contact addresses and the nature of the relationship between the charities; and

(b) particulars of any material transactions between the charities.

One way in which the relevant information could be given is by aggregating the accounts of the charity with those of its connected charities. If aggregated accounts are prepared, the basis on which they have been prepared should be disclosed. Separate accounts for the reporting charity should still be prepared.

Subsidiary and associated companies

72 A charity may have one or more subsidiary companies.

(a) The activities of a subsidiary may not be fundamentally different from those of the charity. For example, the subsidiary may be an investment-holding company; it might be concerned solely or largely with fund-raising; or it might be the vehicle used to undertake the charitable activities of the charity. If a charity has such a subsidiary or subsidiaries, it should prepare consolidated accounts for itself and its subsidiary or subsidiaries. Separate accounts for the charity itself should still be prepared.

(b) If a subsidiary undertakes activities which are fundamentally different from those of the charity, for example if it is a trading company, it will not be appropriate to consolidate its accounts with those of the charity. Instead, the investment in the subsidiary should be treated in the same way as other investments are treated. A summary of the transactions, assets and liabilities of the subsidiary, together with an explanation of its activities and their relevance to the charity, should be disclosed in the notes to the accounts. As an alternative to providing a summary of its subsidiary's transactions, assets and liabilities, the charity may if it wishes include the accounts of the subsidiary within its annual report.

73 A charity may have one or more associated companies. Investments in associated companies should be treated in the same way as investments in subsidiaries undertaking activities which are fundamentally different from those of the charity (see paragraph 72).

Other disclosure items

Commitments and designated funds

74 Particulars of all material commitments in respect of specific charitable projects, whether they are legally binding or not, should be disclosed in the accounts. These particulars should include the amounts involved, when the commitments are likely to be met, and the movements on commitments previously reported. Particulars of all other material legally binding commitments should also be disclosed.

75 Commitments can be dealt with either by disclosing them in a note to the accounts or by using designated funds to represent committed unrestricted funds. If designated funds are used, they should be disclosed separately from restricted funds and appropriately described.

76 Guarantees given by the charity, and the conditions under which liabilities might arise as a result of guarantees, should be disclosed in a note to the accounts.

Loans and other liabilities

77 If loans or other liabilities are secured on the assets of a charity then this fact, along with details of the security, should be disclosed in the notes to the accounts. The existence of charges against assets should be disclosed in a similar manner.

78 The amount and interest and repayment terms of all inter-fund loans should be disclosed in the notes to the accounts.

Information relating to transactions with trustees and to employees of the charity

79 Particulars, including the amounts involved, of any transaction, contract or other arrangement between a charity and any of its employees or trustees, or persons connected with them, should be disclosed in the notes to the accounts if the transaction, contract or other arrangement is likely to be significant to the user of the accounts. Employees' contracts of employment are an example of contracts which will not usually be significant to the user.

80 Particulars of any relevant connection of the trustees or officers of a charity (for example, as trustees or officers of charities with which the reporting charity works) should also be disclosed.

81 If some or all of the trustees have received remuneration from the charity or have been reimbursed by the charity for expenses which they have incurred, this fact and the amounts involved should be disclosed in the notes to the accounts. An indication of the type of expenses reimbursed should also be provided. If no remuneration was paid or no expenses reimbursed, this should be reported.

82 The total emoluments (ie remuneration and benefits-in-kind) paid to employees during the accounting period and the average number of employees during the period should be disclosed in the notes to the accounts.

Part 4 – Notes on legal requirements in the United Kingdom and the Republic of Ireland

83 A charity constituted in the United Kingdom or the Republic of Ireland may, by virtue of its constitution or activities, be subject to a range of statutory reporting requirements. Some of the more commonly encountered requirements are referred to below. Although the recommendations contained in this statement are intended to represent best practice there may be circumstances in which they conflict with some of the statutory requirements imposed on a charity. This statement cannot overrule such requirements.

84 The recommendations do not incorporate every statutory reporting requirement that may be imposed on a particular charity. For example, an incorporated charity would be required to provide certain additional disclosures and analyses in the notes to the accounts and would also be required to prepare a directors' report containing specified information. Compliance with the recommendations contained in this statement will therefore not necessarily mean that all the statutory reporting requirements that may be imposed on a charity have been met.

England and Wales

Charities Act 1960

85 All charities in England and Wales must comply with the financial reporting requirements of the Charities Act 1960 and the Charities (Statement of Account) Regulations, 1960 ('the 1960 legislation'). This legislation requires charities to keep proper accounting records to enable them to prepare consecutive statements of account. These statements of account should consist of an income and expenditure account relating to a period of not more than fifteen months and a balance sheet relating to the end of that period. Each statement of account should contain:

(a) particulars of the charity's assets at the balance sheet date, distinguishing between assets forming part of the permanent endowment and other assets. These particulars should include the names of the persons in whom the assets are vested;
(b) the approximate amount of the charity's liabilities at that date;
(c) the amount of the receipts during the period, classified according to the nature of the receipt and distinguishing between receipts forming part of the permanent endowment and other receipts; and
(d) the amount of the payments made during the period, classified according to the nature of the payment and distinguishing between

payments made out of the permanent endowment and other payments.

86 All charities having permanent endowments, other than 'expected charities', must automatically send to the Commissioners each year a statement of account. All charities, other than 'exempt charities', must send statements of account to the Commissioners on request.

87 The format in which the income and expenditure account and balance sheet should be prepared, and the accounting policies which should be adopted in preparing them, are not specified in the legislation. Although the Charity Commission provide charities with standard forms for the preparation of statements of account, alternative formats can be used as long as the information provided meets the requirements of the legislation.

Charities Act 1985

88 All local charities whose sole or primary object is the relief of poverty, other than exempt charities (as defined in the 1960 legislation) and ecclesiastical charities, must send statements of account prepared in accordance with the 1960 legislation to the 'appropriate local authority'.

Companies Act 1985

89 Many charities are incorporated as limited companies and, as a consequence, are required to follow the reporting requirements set out in the Companies Act 1985 ('the 1985 Act'). In essence, this Act requires all incorporated charities to prepare, in respect of each accounting period, and file an income and expenditure account, a balance sheet, various notes, a directors' report and an auditors' report. If, at the end of the accounting period, the charity has one or more subsidiaries, then group accounts should also be prepared and filed. The accounts of the charity and its group are required to show a true and fair view and, except where it is not consistent with the showing of a true and fair view, should comply with the detailed requirements set out in Schedule 4 to the 1985 Act.

90 Schedule 4 sets out the formats in which the income and expenditure account and balance sheet should usually be prepared. These formats, and the income and expenditure account formats in particular, are not wholly appropriate for the income and expenditure accounts of charities. It is therefore normally necessary to take advantage of paragraph 3(3) of Schedule 4, which allows the formats to be adapted in respect of items to which an Arabic number has been assigned to reflect the special nature of a charity's operations.

91 Although Schedule 4 requires the disclosure of certain information not referred to in this statement, the statement's recommendations, with the following exceptions, are consistent with the Schedule's requirements:

(a) In paragraph 61 it is recognised that, although the netting off of income and expenditure will usually be inappropriate, it may occasionally be acceptable. Schedule 4, paragraph 5 states that no material netting off of separate items should take place.

(b) In paragraph 66 it is recommended that the assets of a charity be analysed between fixed assets, investments, and current assets. Schedule 4 requires assets to be analysed between fixed assets and current assets. Fixed assets and current assets are designated by capital letters in the balance sheet formats. They cannot, therefore, be adapted under paragraph 3(3). However, provided that all the investments are fixed assets it should be possible to satisfy both the Companies Act formats and the recommendations of the SORP.

Scotland

92 Although the Companies Act 1985 extends to incorporated charities constituted in Scotland, there is no equivalent legislation to the Charities Act 1960 or the Charities Act 1985 in Scotland. This means that, whilst incorporated charities have to prepare and file an income and expenditure account, balance sheet and various notes in respect of each accounting period, unincorporated charities constituted in Scotland are not required by law to prepare accounts.

Northern Ireland

Charities Act 1964

93 In Northern Ireland charities are governed by the Charities Act [Northern Ireland] 1964. However, this Act requires neither registration nor the preparation or filing of accounts.

Companies (Northern Ireland) Order 1986

94 The Companies (Northern Ireland) Order 1986 is the Northern Ireland legislation equivalent to the Companies Act 1985. The references to the Companies Act 1985 in paragraphs 89 to 91 should therefore also be taken to be references to the 1986 Order.

Republic of Ireland

Charities Acts 1961 and 1973

95 In the Republic of Ireland charities are governed by the Charities Acts 1961 and 1973. Neither of these Acts requires charities to register or to prepare and submit accounts.

Companies (Amendment) Act 1986

96 The Companies (Amendment) Act 1986 ('the 1986 Act') is the Republic of Ireland legislation equivalent to the Companies Act 1985. The 1986 Act references that are equivalent to those given in paragraphs 89 to 91 are as follows:

The 1985 Act	*The 1986 Act*
Schedule 4	The Schedule
Paragraph 3(3) of Sch 4	Section 4 (13)

Appendix 1 – The funds of a charity

The purpose of this appendix is to explain the legal position as regards the various funds of a charity and the implications this has for the way in which the funds are accounted for.

The types of funds a charity might have

1 A charity's funds can be categorised into restricted funds and unrestricted funds. Restricted funds are funds subject to specific conditions, imposed by the donor, or the trusts under which the donation was made, and binding on the trustees. All other funds are unrestricted funds, which means that as long as they are used in pursuance of the charity's objectives and in a way which is consistent with the charity's charitable status, their use is at the complete discretion of the trustees.

The need to distinguish between the assets and liabilities held in different funds

2 If a profit is made on the disposal of an asset, the profit will form part of the fund in which the asset was held. An unrealised profit on an asset will also form part of the fund in which the asset is held. Similarly, realised and unrealised losses and provisions for depreciation and for the permanent diminuition in value of an asset reduce the fund in which the asset is (or, in the case of a realised loss, was) held. In order to ensure that profits, losses and provisions are added to or deducted from the correct fund, it is therefore essential to know which assets and liabilities are held in which fund.

3 The trustees of a charity will be in breach of trust if they use restricted income in a way which is not consistent with the restrictions imposed. To this end it is essential that items of income and expenditure are added to, or deducted from, the appropriate fund. It is also important for the trustees to ensure that the assets and liabilities held in a fund are consistent with the fund type: if a fund which, because of donor restrictions, must be used in the short-term is represented by assets which can only be utilised in the long-term, there is a real possibility that the charity will not be able to meet the restrictions.

Income derived from assets held by the charity

4 Although profits arising on the disposal of an asset will form part of the fund in which the asset was held, this will not necessarily be the case with income derived from the asset. Unless the terms on which the asset was donated make it clear that an alternative treatment should be adopted, income derived from an asset already held by the charity will be unrestricted income, even if the asset is held in a permanent endowment fund.

Permanent endowment funds

5 One particular type of restricted fund is known as a permanent endowment fund. Permanent endowment funds must be held indefinitely. This does not however necessarily mean that the assets held in the permanent endowment fund cannot be disposed of – although the terms of the endowment might prohibit this. What it does mean is that the permanent endowment fund cannot be used to make payments to others, and the assets making up the permanent endowment fund cannot be given away. Furthermore, if an asset that is held as part of a permanent endowment fund is disposed of, its place in the fund must be taken by the assets received in exchange.

6 As explained above, if a profit is made on the disposal of an asset held in permanent endowment fund, the profit will become part of the permanent endowment and the amount of the fund will increase. The other means by which permanent endowment funds will be increased will be by receiving incoming resources received for permanent endowment (whether in the form of new permanent endowment funds or additions to existing ones) and recognising unrealised gains on assets held in permanent endowments. On the other hand, income derived from assets held within a permanent endowment fund does not affect the amount of permanent endowment unless either the terms of the original endowment require it to do so or the Charity Commission so order.

7 Similarly, a loss made on the disposal of an asset held in a permanent endowment fund will result in the amount of the fund being decreased. Such losses are in fact the only transactions which can reduce the amount of the permanent endowment. Provisions for the depreciation of assets held in permanent endowment funds or for the permanent diminution in value of assets held in permanent endowment funds, and unrealised losses recognised in the accounts in respect of assets held in permanent endowment funds are the only other means by which a permanent endowment fund can be reduced.

8 Permanent endowment funds, because of their permanence, are tantamount to being the capital of the charity. The statement of recommended practice recognises this by recommending that increases and decreases in the amount of permanent endowment funds are not dealt with in the income and expenditure account.

Appendix 2 – Example set of accounts

INCOME AND EXPENDITURE ACCOUNT YEAR ENDED 31 DECEMBER 1987

	1987		*15 months ended 31.12.86*	
	£	£	£	£
Income				
Donations and gifts		7,920		8,942
Legacies		3,416		19,761
Covenanted income		15,600		15,500
Voluntary income		26,936		44,203
Grants received		2,793		2,749
Investment income		414		481
		30,143		47,433
Indirect expenditure				
Fund-raising expenses	782		656	
Publicity expenses	534		412	
Administration expenses	1,236		1,471	
		2,552		2,539
Income less indirect expenditure		27,591		44,894
Direct charitable expenditure		30,479		41,684
Income less expenditure		(2,888)		3,210

STATEMENT OF INVESTMENT GAINS YEAR ENDED 31 DECEMBER 1987

	1987	*15 months ended 31.12.86*
	£	£
Realised gains on disposal of investments	1,463	912
Change in unrealised gains/(losses) on investments	(1,212)	361
Net investment gains	251	1,273

The income and expenditure account and statement of investment gains should be read in conjunction with the reconciliation and analysis of movements on the funds shown on page . . .

BALANCE SHEET AS 31 DECEMBER 1987

	1987		1986	
	£	£	£	£
Fixed assets		5,461		5,698
Investments		3,913		4,561
Current assets				
Stock	671		631	
Debtors	483		886	
Cash at bank in hand	816		361	
	1,970		1,878	
Current liabilities	421		216	
Net current assets		1,549		1,662
		10,923		11,921
Long-term liabilities		(248)		(225)
		10,675		11,696
Funds				
Permanent endowment funds		1,850		234
Other restricted funds		8,357		5,911
Unrestricted funds		468		5,551
		10,675		11,696

The balance sheet should be read in conjunction with the reconciliation and analysis of movements on the funds shown on page . . .

RECONCILIATION AND ANALYSIS OF MOVEMENT ON THE FUNDS FOR THE YEAR ENDED 31 DECEMBER 1987

	Unrestricted funds			*Restricted funds* (excluding permanent endowment funds)				*Total*	*Permanent endowment funds*
	General £	*Designated* £	*Total* £	*Core* £	*India* £	*Africa* £	*Total* £	£	£
Income	22,038	—	22,038	—	7,112	993	8,105	30,143	—
Indirect expenditure	(1,636)	—	(1,636)	—	(822)	(94)	(916)	(2,552)	—
	20,402	—	20,402	—	6,290	899	7,189	27,591	—
Opening value of funds	938	4,100	5,038	1,513	3,631	1,280	6,424	11,462	234
Funds available for use	21,340	4,100	25,440	1,513	9,921	2,179	13,613	39,053	—
New permanent endowment fund	—	—	—	—	—	—	—	—	1,020
Net investment gains	—	—	—	201	50	—	251	251	596
Charitable expenditure	(15,674)	(7,911)	(23,585)	—	(4,753)	(2,141)	(6,894)	(30,479)	—
	5,666	(3,811)	1,855	1,714	5,218	38	6,970	8,825	1,850
Transfers	(1,387)	—	(1,387)	1,387	—	—	1,387	—	—
Designations	(4,235)	4,235	—	—	—	—	—	—	—
	44	424	468	3,101	5,218	38	8,357	8,825	1,850

Extracts from notes

[NB Although the accounts would normally be accompanied by a full set of notes, only extracts from the notes are included here. The extracts shown illustrate some of the more important or more complex of the recommended disclosures. The notes should be cross referenced to the accounts.]

Fixed assets

	Motor vehicles	*Fixtures and fittings*	*Total*
Cost			
	£	£	£
Opening balance at 1 January 1987	7,531	1,100	8,631
Additions	2,980	—	2,980
Disposals	(2,329)	—	(2,329)
Closing balance at 31 December 1987	8,182	1,100	9,282
Accumulated depreciation			
Opening balance at 1 January 1987	2,383	550	2,933
Charge for the year	2,359	275	2,634
Depreciation on disposals	(1,746)	—	(1,746)
Closing balance at 31 December 1987	2,996	825	3,821
Net book value			
At 31 December 1987	5,186	275	5,461
At 1 January 1987	5,148	550	5,698

ANALYSIS OF FUND BALANCES BETWEEN THE NET ASSETS

	Unrestricted funds	*Restricted funds (excluding permanent endowment funds)*				*Permanent endowment funds*	*Total funds*
		Core	*India*	*Africa*	*Total*		
	£	£	£	£	£	£	£
Fixed assets	—	—	4,106	—	4,106	1,355	5,461
Investments	—	3,101	279	38	3,418	495	3,913
Net current assets	716	—	833	—	833	—	1,549
Long term liabilities	(136)	—	—	—	—	—	(136)
Provisions	(112)	—	—	—	—	—	(112)
	468	3,101	5,218	38	8,357	1,850	10,675
Represented by:							
Realised amounts	468	2,435	5,188	38	7,661	1,619	9,748
Unrealised amounts	—	666	30	—	696	231	927
	468	3,101	5,218	38	8,357	1,850	10,675

COMMITMENTS

(a) *Charitable commitments*

As explained in accounting policy note . . . commitments for specific charitable projects are dealt with by making allocations to designated funds. Therefore, as the reconciliation and analysis of movements on the funds shows, the commitments of the charity in respect of such projects are as follows:

	1987	*1986*
	£	£
Commitments at the beginning of the period	4,100	796
Additional commitments entered into	4,235	8,213
Commitments met	(7,911)	(4,909)
Commitments at the end of the period	424	4,100

It is expected that the commitments outstanding at the period-end will all be met in 1988.

(b) *Other commitments*

In addition to the commitments referred to above, the charity has entered into the following legally-binding commitments:

	1987	*1986*
	£	£
For the purchase of motor vehicles	5,921	2,980

SUBSIDIARY COMPANIES

The charity has a subsidiary, ShopCo Ltd, which undertakes trading activities. As these activities are fundamentally different from the activities of the charity, consolidated accounts have not been prepared. ShopCo Ltd operates three shops, located in various parts of the country. It purchases ornaments and artefacts from manufacturers and sells them to the public. The profits earned are passed to the charity by means of a deed of covenant; a fact which is referred to in the company's publicity material. Two trustees of the charity sit on the board of ShopCo Ltd but receive no remuneration for doing so. A summary of ShopCo Ltd's transactions and financial position is set out below.

(a) *Profit and Loss Account*	*1987*	*1986*
	£	£
Turnover	72,149	68,163
Cost of sales	43,637	40,611
Gross profit	28,512	27,552
Selling costs	9,361	8,800
Administration costs	3,461	3,013
Profit before deed of covenant	15,690	15,739
Deed of covenant	15,600	15,500
Profit before taxation	90	239
Taxation	—	—
Retained profit for the financial year	90	239

(b) *Balance sheet*		
Current assets		
Stock	9,239	12,576
Cash in hand and at bank	1,610	(311)
	10,849	12,265
Creditors: amounts due within one year		
Trade creditors	840	2,346
	10,009	9,919
Represented by:		
Share Capital	10,000	10,000
Profit and loss account	9	(81)
	10,009	9,919

CONNECTED CHARITIES

The trustees of the charity are also the trustees of the Pollington Charity, a charity with which the charity shares administration facilities. Whilst the charity provides assistance and comfort to those being treated for cancer, the Pollington Charity makes grants to persons researching into cures for cancer. From time to time, loans on commercial terms may be made by one of the charities to the other, although there were no such loans outstanding at the year-end. There are no other transactions between the charities. A summarised set of accounts, in which the accounts of the charity and the Pollington charity have been aggregated, are set out below:

(a) *Income and expenditure account*

	1987	*1986*
	£	£
Voluntary income	34,631	57,351
Grants received	33,961	31,621
Investment income	1,321	1,012
	69,913	89,984
Indirect expenditure	7,264	6,982
	62,649	83,002
Direct charitable expenditure	60,192	73,139
Income less expenditure	2,457	9,863

(b) *Statement of investment gains*

Realised gains	2,651	1,101
Change in unrealised gains	381	1,312
Net investment gains	3,032	2,413

(c) *Balance sheet*

Fixed assets	5,461	5,698
Investments	28,140	24,163
Current assets	4,136	2,011
Current liabilities	(4,596)	(6,035)
Long-term liabilities	(248)	(225)
	32,893	25,612
Permanent endowment funds	6,211	4,419
Other restricted funds	10,487	9,321
Unrestricted funds	16,195	11,872
	32,893	25,612

The Pollington charity can be contacted at the following address: . . . (Not shown)

CHECKLIST TO THE RECOMMENDATIONS OF SORP 2 FOR THE PREPARATION OF ANNUAL REPORTS OF CHARITIES

This checklist is designed to help ensure that the requirements of SORP 2 are complied with by a charity when it prepares its annual report. Whilst every effort has been made to make the checklist comprehensive, reference should be made to the SORP on any point of doubt or difficulty. In addition to the steps set out in the checklist the user should also refer to the charity's trust deed or similar document for special requirements in respect of the financial statements. Also the charities constitution might impose other requirements that need to be considered. This will be so in particular where the charity is set up as a company (see further Appendix I to 'Manual of Accounting - volumes I and II').

1. General requirements

1.1 Has the charity produced an annual report which includes: SORP 2 para 19

(a) Legal and administrative details?

(b) A trustees' report?

(c) Financial statements and notes thereto?

1.2 Has the trustees' report and the balance sheet been signed by at least two trustees and dated? SORP 2 para 20

Do the legal and administrative details of the annual report include the following: SORP 2 para 21

(a) Nature of governing instrument or legal status of the charity?

(b) The names of the trustees and their nominating body, the names of the members of any management committees and the names of the principal officers of the charity?

(c) The principal or registered address of the charity?

(d) The names and addresses of any other relevant organisations or persons (such as brokers, solicitors, auditors, investment or other advisers)?

(e) Details of restriction imposed on the way in which the charity can operate

1.3 Does the trustees' report: SORP 2 para 22

(a) Describe the charity's organisation objectives and policies adopted to achieve these objectives?

(b) Describe significant development, activities and achievements of the charity since the last report?

(c) Provide a commentary on the figures in the financial statements?

1.4 Do the financial statements contain the following statements: SORP 2 para 24

(a) An income and expenditure account?

(b) A balance sheet that shows the assets, liabilities and funds available to the charity (together with restrictions placed upon those funds)?

(c) A statement of source and application of funds? If omitted are the reasons valid?

(d) Adequate notes to the accounts explaining:

(i) The accounting policies used?
(ii) The movement on various funds?

(iii) The relationship between figures as well as the analysis of the figures in the accounts?

1.5 Are corresponding figures shown for figures disclosed in the financial statements? SORP 2 para 24

1.6 **Accounting for separate funds**

1.6.1 Do the financial statements and notes provide adequate information on the charity's funds and their significance? In particular: SORP 2 para 29

(a) Is a reconciliation of the total opening funds of the charity to the closing funds provided analysed between the major funds? SORP 2 para 30

(b) Have movements on permanent endowment funds been separately shown in the notes to the accounts? SORP 2 para 26

1.6.2 Are material transfers and allocations of income to designated funds shown separately? SORP 2 para 3(a)

1.6.3 Are such transfers shown separately below the results for the period? SORP 2 para 31(b)

1.7 **Accounting policies**

1.7.1 Are the accounting policies adopted for all material items disclosed in the financial statements? SORP 2 para 33

1.7.2 Are all changes in accounting policies disclosed and if the effect is material have opening balances and corresponding amounts been restated? SORP 2 para 34

2. Income

2.1 Has the charity received significant intangible income? If so, has the charity reflected this in the financial statements or trustees' report? SORP 2 para 36

2.2 Have significant donated assets been accounted for as income at valuation or disclosed in a note where valuation is impracticable? SORP 2 para 39

2.3 Have income where restrictions imposed are so onerous that it is impossible to use the income in the way intended, been carried forward in the balance sheet under the heading 'deferred restricted income' and the restrictions involved explained? SORP 2 para 38

2.4 Have estimates been made of income collected but not received or counted (collection containers at public premises) and included in the income and expenditure account? SORP 2 para 41

2.5 Have income from life subscriptions been properly accounted for? SORP 2 para 42

3. Investment gains and losses

3.1 Are realised gains and losses dealt with and disclosed in the income and expenditure account or else shown in a separate statement of investment gains? SORP 2 para 46

3.2 Have unrealised gains and losses been dealt with and disclosed in a manner that is consistent with the treatment of realised gains and losses? SORP 2 para 48

4. Fixed assets

4.1 Has all expenditure on fixed assets and have all the receipts of fixed assets by way of gift been capitalised? SORP 2 para 51

4.2 Do fixed assets not capitalised fall within the exceptions allowed for by the SORP? SORP 2 para 52

4.3 Is a summary of fixed assets still in use but not included in the balance sheet, shown in the notes to the financial statements? SORP 2 para 52

4.4 Have details of revaluations including date and bases been stated in the notes to the financial statements? SORP 2 para 53

5. Income and expenditure account

5.1 (a) Have all expenditure, other than expenditure relating directly to charitable activities, been included in the income and expenditure account as soon as it is incurred? SORP 2 para 56

(b) Have expenditure or charitable activities been included when its payment becomes due? SORP 2 para 57

5.2 Have the following items been shown separately in the income and expenditure account: SORP 2 para 58

(a) Realised gains and losses on fixed assets, if material?

(b) Fund-raising expenses?

(c) Publicity expenses?

(d) Administration expenses?

(e) Expenditure and grants relating directly to charitable activities?

5.3 Has a full description of the items included within each category and the principles adopted been disclosed? SORP 2 para 60

5.4 Where permissable netting off of income and expenditure has taken place have the reasons and the gross amounts been disclosed in the notes to the financial statements? SORP 2 para 61

5.5 Have income received after deduction of tax at source and income received by deed of covenant been grossed up? Has tax recoverable been shown as a debtor until the charity recovers the amount involved? SORP 2 para 62

6. Source and application of funds

If the charity has prepared a statement of source and application of funds is the statement reconcilable to the income and expenditure account and the balance sheet? SORP 2 para 65

7. The balance sheet

7.1	Have the assets and liabilities been analysed in a manner that is consistent with the example set of financial statements.	SORP 2 para 66, App 2
7.2	Have the funds of the charity been adequately disclosed between restricted and unrestricted funds?	SORP 2 para 67(a)
7.3	Where funds have been divided into wider and narrower groups under the **Investment Trustees Act 1961** do the accounts or notes thereto adequately indicate the investment allotted to each range?	SORP 2 para 67(b)
7.4	Have the following been included appropriately:	SORP 2 para 68
	(a) Fixed assets at cost (or valuation) less an appropriate provision for depreciation?	
	(b) Investments at cost or market value? If included at cost, is market value disclosed?	
	(c) Current assets at the lower of cost and net realisable value?	
	(d) Liabilities at their settlement value?	

8. Connected charities

8.1	Is the charity connected with other charities as defined by SORP 2? If so, is appropriate disclosures in the annual report made?	SORP 2 paras 70, 71
8.2	If the charity's financial statements are aggregated with those of its connected charities is the basis of aggregation adequately disclosed?	SORP 2 para 71
8.3	If aggregated financial statements have been prepared have separate accounts been prepared for the charity?	SORP 2 para 71

9. Subsidiary and associated companies

9.1	If a subsidiary company has been consolidated have separate financial statements for the charity itself been prepared?	SORP 2 para 72(a)
9.2	Where a subsidiary company has not been consolidated for appropriate reasons, has a summary of the transactions, assets and liabilities, and the activities of the subsidiary been adequately disclosed in the notes to the financial statements?	SORP 2 para 72(b)
9.3	Have all associated companies been treated in the same manner as subsidiary companies not consolidated?	SORP 2 para 73

10. Other disclosure items

10.1	Have all material charitable commitments been disclosed whether legally binding or not?	SORP 2 para 74
10.2	If such commitments are dealt with by using designated funds are they disclosed separately from restricted funds and appropriately described?	SORP 2 para 75

10.3	Are all other legally binding commitments disclosed?	SORP 2 para 74
10.4	Are all guarantees and the conditions of crystallisation of a liability disclosed in the notes to the financial statements?	SORP 2 para 76
10.5	Have all charges against assets and security given been adequately disclosed?	SORP 2 para 77
10.6	Are details of amount, interest rate and terms of repayment disclosed for any inter-fund loans?	SORP 2 para 78
10.7	Have transactions between the charity and its trustees and employees been disclosed where appropriate?	SORP 2 para 79
10.8	Have relevant connections of trustees and officers been disclosed?	SORP 2 para 80
10.9	Have trustees remuneration and reimbursement for expenses been disclosed?	SORP 2 para 81
10.10	Do the notes to the financial statements disclose the total emoluments and average number of employees during the period?	SORP 2 para 82

11. Compliance with other statements and requirements

SORP 2 paras 85 - 91

11.1	If the charity is constituted as a company does it comply with the **Companies Act 1985** requirements?	
11.2	Does the charity comply with the **Charities Act 1960**, and the **Charities (Statement of Account) Regulations, 1960**?	
11.3	Does the charity comply with the **Charities Act 1985** if applicable?	

Chapter 26

INVESTMENT BUSINESSES

Chapter 26

INVESTMENT BUSINESSES

Introduction

26.1 Financial regulation for investment businesses is not a totally new concept. An investment business set up as a limited company has for many years had to comply with the accounting requirements of the Companies Acts on accounting records, audited financial statements and (to an extent) capital maintenance. Stockbrokers were regulated by The International Stock Exchange and some security dealers by the National Association of Securities Dealers and Investment Managers (NASDIM).

26.2 The *Financial Services Act 1986* established a new framework for investor protection in the UK. Investment business may now only be carried on by undertakings that have demonstrated to the appropriate regulatory bodies that thay are 'fit and proper'. Once authorised under the *Financial Services Act 1986*, a firm must comply with the relevant rules and regulations. The financial requirements included in these rules and regulations are summarised in this chapter.

The scope of regulation

26.3 The scope of the *Financial Services Act 1986* is wide and affects many different kinds of organisation, some of which may not previously have considered themselves to be carrying on investment business. The *Financial Services Act 1986* applies throughout the UK (excluding the Channel Islands and the Isle of Man) and extends to non-UK organisations carrying on business through a UK branch or supplying investment services of any kind into the UK.

26.4 The *Financial Services Act 1986's* coverage is delineated by the definition of 'investment business', which in turn depends on the meaning of 'investments'. 'Investments' are widely defined and include the following:

- Shares and stock in a company.
- Debentures.
- Government and public securities.
- Warrants or other instruments entitling the holder to subscribe for the three investments mentioned above.

- Certificates representing securities.
- Units in collective investment schemes (see chapter 7).
- Options.
- Futures.
- Contracts for differences.
- Long-term insurance contracts (see chapter 16).
- Rights and interests in investments.

[FSA 1986 1 Sch Part I].

26.5 A person carries on an 'investment business' if he engages in one or more of the following activities:

- Dealing in investments.
- Arranging deals in investments.
- Managing investments.
- Advising on investments.
- Acting in connection with a collective investment scheme.

[FSA 1986 Sec 1(2), 1 Sch Part II].

26.6 Approximately 13,000 businesses became authorised in 1988, the year the legislation was introduced. This figure excludes firms of accountants, solicitors, actuaries and certain registered insurance brokers who obtained their authorisation through membership of a professional body.

26.7 Clearly, with such wide definitions of 'investment' and 'investment business', many activities would have been caught which it is not necessary to regulate. Accordingly, a long list of exemptions has been granted and these are detailed in Schedule 1 to the *Financial Services Act 1986*.

26.8 The following bodies are exempted and, therefore, do not need to be authorised:

- The Bank of England. [FSA 1986 Sec 27].
- Lloyd's. [FSA 1986 Sec 42].

- Recognised investment exchanges and clearing houses. [FSA 1986 Secs 36 to 41].
- Listed money market institutions. [FSA 1986 Sec 43].
- Appointed representatives. [FSA 1986 Sec 44].

Legal constitution

26.9 An investment business may be undertaken using different entities, for example, investment business may be carried out by a body corporate (see chapter 12), a partnership (see chapter 4), an individual (see chapter 2) or an unincorporated association (see chapter 9).

The structure of regulation

26.10 In order to become authorised, a business must apply to one of the regulatory bodies established under the *Financial Services Act 1986*. Most of the relevant supervisory powers have been delegated by the DTI to the Securities and Investments Board (SIB), which in turn relies on various Self-Regulating Organisations (SROs) to authorise and control firms in particular sectors of the financial services industry. A firm may apply for authorisation directly to SIB or to one or more SROs. Separate routes are open to professional firms, insurance companies, friendly societies, companies based in another EC country and, for certain types of activity, banks.

26.11 The regulatory structure as it affects firms carrying on investment business is set out in the diagram below:

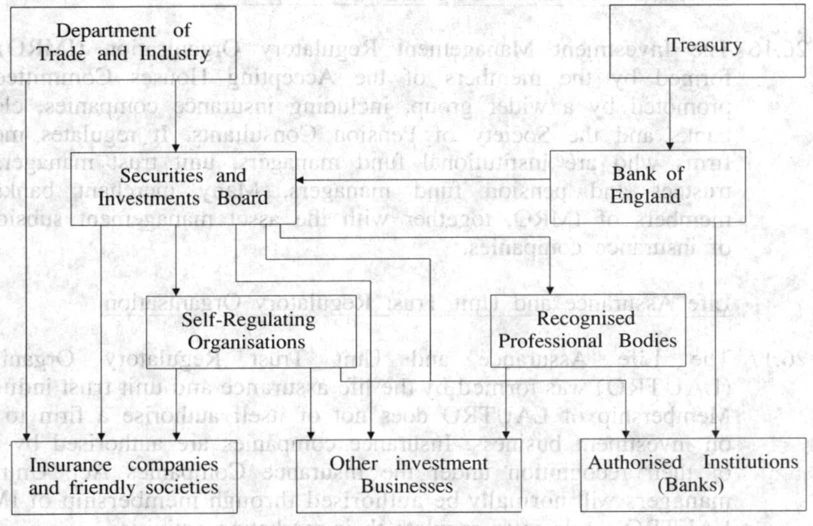

The Securities and Investments Board

26.12 The Securities and Investments Board's (SIB's) most important function is the recognition of the self-regulating organisations. Although SIB can give authorisation of investment businesses directly, this is discouraged. Investment businesses normally seek authorisation from an appropriate SRO.

Self-Regulating Organisations

26.13 There are four SROs, which are considered below.

Financial Intermediaries, Managers and Brokers Regulatory Association

26.14 The Financial Intermediaries, Managers and Brokers Regulatory Association (FIMBRA) grew out of NASDIM. NASDIM was a recognised association of dealers in securities under the *Prevention of Fraud (Investments) Act 1958*.

26.15 FIMBRA regulates member firms whose main business is that of an independent intermediary advising on and arranging transactions in investments (mainly unit trusts and life assurance) or providing investment management services to private investors. FIMBRA is the SRO with the largest number of members, although many of them are quite small businesses.

Investment Management Regulatory Organisation

26.16 The Investment Management Regulatory Organisation (IMRO) was formed by the members of the Accepting Houses Committee and promoted by a wider group, including insurance companies, clearing banks and the Society of Pension Consultants. It regulates member firms who are institutional fund managers, unit trust managers and trustees and pension fund managers. Many merchant banks are members of IMRO, together with the asset management subsidiaries of insurance companies.

Life Assurance and Unit Trust Regulatory Organisation

26.17 The Life Assurance and Unit Trust Regulatory Organisation (LAUTRO) was formed by the life assurance and unit trust industries. Membership of LAUTRO does not of itself authorise a firm to carry on investment business. Insurance companies are authorised by virtue of their recognition under the Insurance Companies Act. Unit trust managers will normally be authorised through membership of IMRO. LAUTRO's role is to regulate their marketing activities.

The Securities and Futures Authority

26.18 The Securities and Futures Authority (SFA) was formed on 1st April 1991 with the merger of the Association of Futures Brokers and Dealers (AFBD) and The Securities Association (TSA).

26.19 TSA was itself the result of a merger between the International Securities Regulatory Organisation and The International Stock Exchange. It regulated member firms dealing and arranging deals in domestic and international securities and advising corporate finance customers. The membership of TSA, therefore, included stockbrokers (formerly regulated by the Stock Exchange) and international securities and bond dealers. AFBD regulated member firms whose activities included broking and dealing in financial and commodity futures and options and providing investment management and advice incidental to that business.

Group registration

26.20 Membership of an SRO is not available to a group, which must arrange for each of its subsidiaries that carry on investment business to apply separately to the appropriate SRO. There are some areas of overlap in the scope of the SROs, so in some situations a firm may have a choice of which regulator to apply to. Conversely, some firms may have to join more than one, in which case the SRO covering the principal activities will generally act as 'lead regulator' for the purposes of financial regulation.

Recognised Professional Bodies

26.21 Whilst most investment businesses will be authorised and regulated by one of the SROs, there are some exceptions, one of which is the Recognised Professional Body (RPB) route. A firm can become authorised to carry on investment business by being a member of, and being 'certified' by, an RPB. [FSA 1986 Sec 15(1)]. RPBs can certify only members that do not undertake investment business as a main activity. There are nine RPBs of which the Insurance Brokers Registration Council (IBRC) has the most extensive financial regulations.

Financial regulations

26.22 Before a firm can be authorised to carry on investment business, it must demonstrate to the relevant regulatory body that it is 'fit and proper'. This term has been interpreted as requiring businesses and their management to be honest, competent and solvent. SIB, the SROs and the RPBs have established admission procedures to satisfy themselves on these matters and have drawn up rulebooks, that are binding on investment businesses, aimed at ensuring that the firms continue to be honest, competent and solvent after they have become authorised.

26.23 A substantial part of each rulebook relates to the financial regulations. These are primarily designed to ensure that investment businesses are adequately capitalised and that they maintain the necessary accounting records and submit financial returns to demonstrate this. An important part of the investor protection is the requirement that a firm maintains sufficient financial resources to carry on the type and level of business for which it is authorised. There are also rules to ensure that a firm properly segregates money and securities that it is holding on behalf of its clients.

26.24 The financial regulations issued under the *Financial Services Act 1986* have had a major effect on most investment businesses. There are many detailed differences in the rules of each regulator, since one set of rules cannot easily be applied to the wide range of investment businesses affected by the *Financial Services Act 1986,* but the coverage is broadly as follows:

- Accounting records and system rules, amplifying the meaning of proper books and records under the *Companies Act 1985*. They usually contain additional requirements related to the nature of a firm's business and the need to demonstrate compliance with the financial resources and client money rules (see para 26.24).

- Financial resources rules under which a firm is required to maintain, at all times, sufficient 'capital' to support the type of business it transacts. The capital requirements are set according to various formulae. 'Capital' is determined by reference to the net tangible assets, usually with adjustments to exclude certain non-liquid assets and sometimes to include other available sources of finance (see para 26.28).

- Financial statements and notification rules, requiring a firm to submit financial reports to the regulator. The frequency varies according to a firm's category of membership, but the minimum requirement for most firms is for an audited annual financial statement. The statement normally comprises a profit and loss account and a balance sheet drawn up to give a true and fair view, together with a financial resources calculation. These statements have to be prepared in addition to other financial statements required by, for example, the *Companies Act 1985* (see para 26.31).

- Client money and asset rules, requiring a business to keep money and securities belonging to clients strictly separate from its own assets (see para 26.37).

Accounting records and controls

26.25 The rules require that the accounting records must be sufficient to show and explain all the firm's transactions, whether effected on its own behalf or on behalf of others, and to enable it to:

- Disclose with reasonable accuracy at any point in time the financial position of the firm.
- Demonstrate whether or not the firm is complying with the requirements of the financial resources rules.
- Prepare all required financial statements within a reasonable time.

26.26 The regulators each provide guidance on the types of records that must be maintained in respect of various activities.

26.27 The records must be kept in sufficient detail and with sufficient cross-referencing to establish an audit trail, including details of money received and expended, income and expenditure, assets and liabilities and movements and location of documents of title. A firm must retain for six years all records required by the rules. The regulators have the right to demand these records at such reasonable time and place as they may specify.

26.28 Certain regulators impose a requirement for adequate systems for the control of the accounting records. This is particularly important in the case of records relating to client money and assets (see para 26.37).

Financial resources

26.29 The rulebooks contain detailed regulations concerning capital adequacy. A 'financial resource requirement', which depends on the nature and scale of a firm's business, is set annually. The firm is required to maintain at least this amount of 'financial resources' (the definition of which varies according to the type of firm) at all times.

26.30 The financial resource requirement may be:

- A specified amount.
- A fraction of annual expenditure.
- A position risk requirement, to reflect the market risk of the firm's own positions in investments (each position is multiplied by prescribed risk percentages, that are suitably weighted, and aggregated).

- A counterparty risk requirement, to reflect the risk that the firm's counterparties will fail to perform on their contracts with it.

- A volume of business requirement based on customers' margin requirements.

- A combination of the above.

26.31 The financial resources may be either net tangible assets, or net current assets or liquid capital. In calculating financial resources, the rules may require certain adjustments to the values included in the balance sheet, for example:

- Investments must be valued at realisable market value.

- Eligible subordinated loans must be ignored.

- Provisions must be made for income tax (partnerships and sole traders) and commissions received on indemnity terms (insurance brokers).

Financial statements and notification

26.32 Each firm must prepare unconsolidated financial statements for the year ending on its annual accounting reference date. The regulator must be informed of the annual accounting reference date. For firms to which the *Companies Act 1985* applies, the date is determined by the provisions in this Act. Other firms should select an equivalent date.

26.33 In addition, certain categories of firm must prepare quarterly statements at each quarter-end date. Only the annual financial statements are subject to audit.

26.34 The annual and quarterly financial statements must consist of:

- A balance sheet.

- A profit and loss account.

- A statement of financial resources.

- If applicable, reconciliation of amounts shown in the annual balance sheet with the amounts shown in the balance sheet of the fourth quarter and of the amounts shown in the annual profit and loss account with the sum of the amounts shown in the four quarterly profit and loss accounts.

26.35 The financial statements must be drawn up in accordance with the appropriate format set out in the rulebook and the balance sheet and profit and loss account must give a true and fair view. However, if in drawing up the financial statements in accordance with the rules there is insufficient information to provide a true and fair view, any necessary additional information should be provided.

26.36 The regulatory bodies set out time limits for the submission of the financial statements.

26.37 A firm must notify the regulator of certain eventualities, for example:

- A breach of the financial resources rules.
- Failure or inability to comply with the client money rules.
- Change of auditors.

Client money and assets

26.38 The rules on client money and other client assets (for example, share certificates and documents of title to investments) are designed to protect money and investments belonging to clients from the claims of the investment business' own creditors.

26.39 Client money must be held on trust in a separate account at an approved bank. The rules contain detailed provisions on the payment of interest and restrictions on the payment of money into and the withdrawal of money from client bank accounts. Adequate accounting records must be maintained. Regular reconciliations must be carried out to ensure that:

- The total of the client bank account balances agrees with the balances recorded as due to clients.
- The cash book agrees with the bank statements.

26.40 Client assets must be separately identified and segregated from the firm's own investments. Adequate records must be maintained and reconciliations carried out.

Audit requirements

26.41 All investment businesses (except for certain categories of 'low risk' firms) must appoint an auditor who must make reports to the regulatory body. This requirement extends to partnerships and sole traders. For companies, the auditor appointed for this purpose would normally be the same as the auditor appointed under the relevant Companies Act.

26.42 Auditors must have specified qualifications and must be independent of the investment business. The rules set out the rights and obligations of the auditor and certain provisions to be included in the engagement letter. When an auditor resigns or is removed from office, he must sign a statement setting out any circumstances connected with his resignation or removal which he thinks should be brought to the attention of the regulator.

26.43 Detailed guidance on auditing investment businesses is given in Coopers and Lybrand Deloitte's book 'Auditing Investment Businesses'.

Audit report

26.44 The auditor must make a report to the regulator on the business's annual financial statements. The exact terms of the report vary according to the regulatory body and the nature of the investment firm's business. A suggested form of an unqualified audit report for a company directly authorised by the SIB is given below.

REPORT OF THE AUDITORS TO THE SECURITIES AND INVESTMENTS BOARD IN RESPECT OF XYZ LIMITED

1. We have audited the annual financial statements on pages [] to [] in accordance with Auditing Standards. We have obtained all the information and explanations which, to the best of our knowledge and belief, were necessary for the purposes of our audit.

2. In our opinion:

(a) the annual financial statements of the company have been prepared in accordance with Schedule 1 to the Financial Supervision Rules 1990 ('the Rules');

(b) the annual financial statements of the company give a true and fair view:

(i) in the case of the annual balance sheet, of the state of affairs of the company at [date]; and

(ii) in the case of the profit and loss account, of the company's profit [loss] for the year ended on that date;

(c) the statement of financial resources has been prepared and calculated in accordance with the Rules and Schedule 1 to those Rules;

[(d) the reconciliations referred to in Rule 7.01.2 have been properly carried out;]

(e) the company has, throughout the financial year, kept accounting records in accordance with Part 9 of the Rules;

(f) the balance sheet and the profit and loss account are in agreement with the company's accounting records and returns;

(g) the company had, as at [date], financial resources of at least the minimum which the company was required at that date to have in order to comply with its financial resources requirements.

3. The directors of the company are responsible for establishing and maintaining adequate accounting and other records and internal control systems. In fulfilling that responsibility, estimates and judgements must be made to assess the expected benefits and related costs of management information and of control procedures. The objective is to provide reasonable, but not absolute, assurance that assets are safeguarded against loss from unauthorised use or disposition, that transactions are executed in accordance with established authorised procedures and are recorded properly, and to enable the directors to conduct the business in a prudent manner.

4. Because of inherent limitations in any accounting and internal control system, errors or irregularities may nevertheless occur and not be detected. Also, projection of any evaluation of the systems to future periods is subject to the risk that management information and control procedures may become inadequate because of changes in conditions or that the degree of compliance with those procedures may deteriorate.

5. In the context of the matters referred to above, in our opinion the company has maintained throughout the year systems to enable it to comply with obligations incumbent upon it by rules and regulations relating to client money and assets.

6. In our opinion the company was in compliance with the Financial Services (Clients' Money) Regulations 1987 as at [date]; and was in compliance with Part 12 of the Financial Services (Conduct of Business) Rules 1987 as at [date].

[Name of firm]

Chartered Accountants,

[Address].

[Date of report].

26.45 Auditors are also required to communicate with SROs or RPBs on an *ad hoc* basis any matters that the auditors believe should be brought to their attention. Guidance on such reports is given in the Auditing Guideline 'Communications between auditors and regulators under sections 109 and 180(1)(q) of the Financial Services Act 1986' (AG 3.309).

Chapter 27

SOLICITORS

Annexes

Chapter 27

SOLICITORS

Background

27.1 Solicitors are the general practitioners of the law who are consulted by individuals, companies or public authorities needing legal advice. There are approximately 8,000 solicitors practising in England and Wales.

27.2 The partnership is the usual vehicle for professions such as solicitors to carry on business (see chapter 4 for further details regarding partnerships). As a profession, solicitors are subject to additional legal requirements as contained in the *Solicitors Act 1974* and the *Solicitors (Amendment) Act 1974*. The Law Society is in turn empowered by sections 32 to 34 of the *Solicitors Act 1974* to monitor and regulate the custody of client's money.

27.3 Chapter 4 considers the accounting and auditing requirements that apply to partnerships generally and this chapter concentrates on the special rules that apply to solicitors concerning the custody of client's money.

Solicitors' Accounts Rules

27.4 Because solicitors handle large amounts of other peoples' money, the Law Society has set up the following series of rules to regulate the solicitors' custody of client's money:

- *Solicitors' Accounts Rules 1986* (SAR) (see annex 1).
- *Solicitors' Trust Account Rules 1986* (STAR) (see annex 2).
- *Solicitors' Accounts (Deposit Interest) Rules 1988* (SA(DI)R) (see annex 3).
- *Accountant's Report Rules 1986* (ARR) (see annex 4).
- *Accountant's Report Amendment Rules 1988* (AR(A)R) (incorporated into ARR reproduced as annex 4).

27.5 The above rules are currently being revised by the Law Society. It is anticipated that new rules will come into effect from January 1992. One of the main changes being proposed is that client ledger balances will have to be reconciled at least every five weeks as opposed to every three months under the current rules (see para. 27.25).

27.6 The fundamental principles that the Rules must meet are:

- Client's money and trust money must be separated and distinguished from the solicitor's money and maintained in separate bank or building society accounts.

- Proper books must be maintained.

- Every solicitor must state in his annual application for a practising certificate if he has held or received client's money.

- An accountant's report stating whether or not the solicitor has complied with the SAR and paragraph 13 of the SIBR, must be submitted by the solicitor if he has held or received client's money.

The above rules are briefly described in paragraphs 27.11 to 27.18.

Solicitors' Investment Business Rules

27.7 As a consequence of the *Financial Services Act 1986* the Law Society drew up the *Solicitors' Investment Business Rules 1990* (SIBR). These Rules give solicitors guidance as to how they should comply with the *Financial Services Act 1986* when giving investment business advice to their clients (see also chapter 26). Solicitor partnerships have to be certified by the Law Society in order to conduct investment business through the partnership.

Guide to professional conduct of solicitors.

27.8 The Law Society republished in 1990 its guide titled 'The guide to professional conduct of solicitors'. The guide is intended to provide a clear and helpful source of reference for solicitors for the day to day conduct of their business. It also includes valuable appendices which reproduce all the solicitors rules, including those given as annexes to this chapter.

Accounting and auditing background

27.9 Before the 1986 and the 1988 rules mentioned in paragraph 27.3 above, the financial statements and the requirement for an accountant's report were governed by the 1975 rules. The 1975 rules were amended principally as a result of the *Financial Services Act 1986.* Changes included:

- Widening the definition of 'client account' to include building society deposit accounts in addition to bank accounts.

- Changing the criteria for when interest on client's money is due and specifying the rate of interest applicable.

27.10 The Rules are strict concerning the scope and nature of the reporting accountant's work. However, the effect of the rules is that in some respects the work involved is less complex than in a normal audit. However, the ensuing responsibility is perhaps more onerous than a normal audit because of the following:

- The complete control that a solicitor exercises over his client's money.
- The risk of error being exposed. The Investigation Accountant's Department of the Law Society undertakes regular reviews and in practice breaches of the rules are exposed. (See para 27.32 for removal or disqualification of reporting accountants.)

Scope of the Solicitors' Accounts Rules

27.11 The object of the SAR is to ensure fair treatment of client's money and to maintain adequate bookkeeping and recording systems. Compliance with the SAR will make it impossible for a solicitor to confuse client's money with his own. Client's money may be held by a solicitor for a variety of reasons. Examples of reasons for holding clients funds include:

- Conveyancing.

  Handling deposits and other sums to purchase real estate for clients.

- Executorship.

  Handling sums of money belonging to estates of deceased persons.

- Investment management.

  Solicitors sometimes act as family advisers on investment.

- Agency.

  Sums are received when a solicitor acts as agent for a client.

- Receipts in advance of billing for professional advice or work.

27.12 Client's money is defined as *"money held or received by a solicitor on account of a person for whom he is acting .... as a solicitor, or in connection with his practice as a solicitor, as agent, trustee, stakeholder or in any other capacity*". [SAR para 2(1)].

27.13 A client account is a bank account (current or deposit account at a bank or building society) in the name of the solicitor and the word 'client' appears in the title of the account. [SAR para 2(1)(b)]. It may be a general account holding money belonging to more than one client or a designated account in favour of one client.

27.14 A solicitor cannot pay his own funds into a client account to finance clients generally. However, a solicitor is allowed to pay in a nominal amount of his own money into a client account in order to keep the account 'alive'. [SAR para 4(b)]. If a solicitor wishes to advance money to a particular client to enable the client to carry out a particular transaction, the sum paid into the client account must be the amount of that specific payment. Once the amount is paid into the client account, the money becomes client's money and no longer belongs to the solicitor. Accountants have to report on compliance with the SAR and paragraph 13 of the SIBR (see para 27.26).

27.15 There is no requirement that the overseas offices of a firm of solicitors should comply with the SAR. However, it would appear to be best practice for them to do so.

Solicitors' Trust Account Rules

27.16 The Solicitors' Trust Account Rules are similar to the SAR except that an accountant's report is not required on money paid into the trust bank account. However, any trust money, whether or not relating to a controlled trust, which is paid into a client account, is subject to the Accountant's Report Rules.

Solicitors' Accounts (Deposit Interest) Rules

27.17 The Solicitors' Accounts (Deposit Interest) Rules prescribes the basis for accounting for interest to the client on client funds held by the solicitor. A person in a fiduciary capacity cannot retain interest earned on another's money. In the case *Brown v CIR (1964) 3 WLR 511*, it was held that interest earned on a client's money did not belong to the solicitor. Where client money is held in a designated account the actual interest earned should be accounted for to the client. [SA(DI)R para 3(a)]. Where client money is held in an undesignated account or a general account interest should be accounted for on a fair and reasonable basis in relation to the amount and time held in accordance the following table:

Number of weeks	Minimum balance
8	£500
4	£1,000
2	£5,000
1	£10,000

Where sums exceeding the relevant figures have been held for lengths of time exceeding the relevant periods, interest becomes payable. [SA(DI)R para 3(b)].

27.18 Where balances held vary significantly over a period, or held intermittently, then interest is payable if it would be fair and reasonable for the client to have earned interest. [SA(DI)R para 3(c)]. The rate of interest to be paid is the deposit rate at the bank or building society where the money is actually held. [SA(DI)R para 4].

Duty to keep accounting records

27.19 In a partnership, the responsibility for maintaining a proper bookkeeping system is shared by all partners (including salaried partners) (see further chapter 4). Under the Solicitors' Accounts Rules a solicitor is required to keep the following books and records:

- Cash book.
- Journal or record of transfers of client's money.
- Client's ledger.
- Record of bills of costs.

[SAR para 11(2)(3)].

27.20 There must be a cash book for each client (bank or building society) account which must also be supported by a ledger account for each client. The books and records must be maintained in such a way that client's money is clearly distinguishable from all other money that the solicitor handles, including trust money (which is dealt through a trust bank account). [SAR para 11(1)].

27.21 Bills of costs (distinguishing between profit costs and disbursements) must be recorded in a bills delivered book or in a file of bills delivered. *"Written intimations of costs"* must also be recorded in the same way as for bills. [SAR para 11(3)].

27.22 Books and records can either be a mechanical or computerised system of accounting, provided there are adequate safeguards in relation to the protection of client's money. [SAR para 11(5)]. (See para 27.37 for a waiver granted by the Law Society in respect of para 4(1)(f) of the ARR.)

27.23 Books of account and supporting records must be kept for at least six years. [SAR para 11(6)]. However, books and records relating to trusts may have to be kept for a considerably longer period. For further information on the length of time books and records must be kept, see 'Manual of Accounting - volume I' chapter 2.

Duty to establish and maintain systems of control

27.24 Paragraph 11(1) of the SAR requires a solicitor, at all times, to keep properly written up such accounts as may be necessary to show all his dealings with client's money and any other money dealt with by him through a client account.

27.25 The SAR also specifically requires the solicitor to carry out reconciliations of client accounts (at banks and building societies) at least once in every three months. [SAR para 11(4)].

Duty to submit an accountant's report

27.26 Every solicitor who handles client money must produce annually a report by a duly qualified accountant (see para 27.31) that the solicitor has complied with the SAR and paragraph 13 of the SIBR. The ARR requires the solicitor to deliver this report to the Council of the Law Society. [ARR para 6].

27.27 An accountant's report is not required where the solicitor has stated in his form of application for a practising certificate that he has not held client's money and that he is not obliged to comply with the SAR. [ARR para 7].

27.28 A separate accountant's report will usually be required from each partner whose name appears on the letter heading of the firm unless the council is satisfied that they have not held or received client's money. However, due to the size of some partnerships the Law Society now allows the submission of a single report for the firm with details of all partners who practised during the period.

27.29 The accountants reports must cover all addresses at which the solicitor practices. If an address is not covered, the reason for not covering it must be stated in the accountant's report.

27.30 The accountant's report must be delivered no later than six months after the end of the accounting period specified in the report.

Appointment and removal of accountant

27.31 The following persons are qualified to give an accountant's report on behalf of a solicitor:

- A member of:
  - The Institute of Chartered Accountants in England and Wales.
  - The Institute of Chartered Accountants in Scotland.
  - The Chartered Association of Certified Accountants.
  - The Institute of Chartered Accountants in Ireland.
- He has not been during the accounting period or subsequently become a partner or employee of the solicitor or any partner of his.

[ARR para 3(1)].

27.32 An accountant may be disqualified from giving an accountant's report if he:

- Has been found guilty by the Disciplinary Tribunal of his professional body.
- Was found negligent in giving a report on a solicitor who has not complied with the provisions of the SAR.

[ARR para 3(2)].

Work to be performed

27.33 The detailed work the accountant must perform in order to give his report is laid down in ARR paragraph 4(1). The accountant must ascertain from the solicitor details of all bank and building society accounts kept for clients. In addition, the rules require the accountant to make the following examination of the solicitors' books, accounts and relevant documents:

- Examine and verify that the bookkeeping system complies with paragraph 11 of SAR and paragraph 13 of SIBR and is designed to ensure that:

- ☐ An appropriate ledger is kept for the client.
- ☐ Such accounts show separately clients' money.
- ☐ Transactions relating to clients' money are dealt with separately in the solicitor's books.

- ■ Check postings to the ledger accounts from records of receipts and payments.
- ■ Check casts of the ledger accounts.
- ■ Compare lodgements and payments as shown in bank and building society statements to the solicitor's records of receipts and payments.
- ■ Enquire into and check the system of recording costs and making transfers for such items from the client account.
- ■ Test examine documents to ascertain and confirm:
  - ☐ The financial transactions (including transfers between ledger accounts) are in accordance with SAR.
  - ☐ Entries in client ledger accounts reflect those transactions.
- ■ Extract client ledger balances at least twice during the period and:
  - ☐ Compare ledger balances with the client cash book balances.
  - ☐ Reconcile client cash book balances to confirmed bank and building society balances.
- ■ Check that client account reconciliations have been kept in accordance with paragraph 11(4) of SAR.
- ■ Test client ledger accounts to ensure payments for particular clients do not exceed the funds held on behalf of that client.
- ■ Check to ascertain whether any client's money has not been paid into a client account.
- ■ Ask for any necessary explanation in respect of the points above.

[ARR para 4].

27.34 The scope of the accountant's examination should not extend beyond the information contained in the relevant documents supplied to him and explanations given to him by the solicitor. In particular, he is not empowered to enquire into the stocks, shares or other securities or documents of title held by the solicitor on his client's behalf. [ARR para 42(a)(b)].

27.35 The work in respect of the accountant's report differs from a normal audit in the following major respects:

- The report relates to compliance with the accounting rules and does not give a true and fair view on a set of financial statements.
- The work is restricted only to the client accounts out of all the accounts in a ledger.
- Because of the sensetive nature of a particular solicitor's work, it may be necessary for the audit partner to perform certain of the work required, especially where this entails reviewing case files.
- The reporting accountant cannot seek external evidence.
- The work to be done is prescribed and has to be completed.

27.36 The introduction of the Solicitors' Investment Business Rule 1990 has not changed the reporting accountant's duties significantly, except that the report now has to confirm that all bills of costs record separately the costs attributable to discrete investment business advice. [SIBR para 13]. The reporting accountant does not have to concern himself with the definition of 'discrete investment business', but only whether the solicitor having identified such income and has a system to record it separately.

Waiver in respect of computerised accounting system

27.37 Where a solicitor uses a computerised or mechanised system of accounting, the Law Society has waived the requirement for the accountant to check all balances of the clients' ledger accounts extracted on the list produced by the computer or machine to the individual records of ledger accounts, insofar as such work merely amounts to a check on the accuracy of the computer or machine. The accountant must, however, assure himself that a satisfactory system of control operates and should test check the extraction against the individual records. Furthermore, he should specify in his report that he has relied on the waiver (see para 27.41).

Accountant's report

27.38 The format of the accountant's report is prescribed by the Law Society (see annex 4 to this chapter).

27.39 For larger firms of solicitors, it may be easier to produce three accountant's reports as follows:

- One covering solicitors who have practised throughout the year.
- One covering solicitors who were appointed to the partnership during the year.
- One covering solicitors who resigned from the partnership during the year.

27.40 The accountant's report may be qualified if the accountant is unable to examine documentation that the solicitor considers to be confidential. The circumstances of such qualification should be set out in the report.

27.41 Under ARR paragraph 4(1)(f) it is necessary to extract and check every balance (see para 27.33 above). If the accountant takes advantage of the waiver (see para 27.37 above) he should add the following wording at the foot of the report:

> This report has been made in reliance on the waiver of rule 4(1)(f) of the Accountant's Report Rules published by the Law Society on 13th June 1979.

Duty to prepare financial statements

27.42 The necessity to prepare financial statements for a solicitor partnership is no different from that of a normal partnership. Such financial statements are considered fully in chapter 4 paragraph 4.28.

Audit

27.43 Similarly, the requirements for an audit of partnerships generally apply equally to solicitor partnerships. These requirements are discussed in chapter 4 paragraph 4.41.

SOLICITORS' ACCOUNTS RULES 1986

Made on the 11th December 1986, by the Council of the Law Society and approved by the Master of the Rolls pursuant to sections 32 of the Solicitors Act 1974 (as amended).

1 These Rules may be cited as the Solicitors' Accounts Rules, 1986, and shall come into operation on the 1st day of January, 1987, whereupon the Solicitors' Account Rules, 1975, shall cease to have effect.

2 (1) In these Rules, unless the context otherwise requires:

'Solicitor' shall mean a solicitor of the Supreme Court and shall include a firm of solicitors;

'Client's Money' shall mean money held or received by a solicitor on account of a person for whom he is acting in relation to the holding or receipt of such money either as a solicitor or, in connection with his practice as a solicitor, as agent, bailee, stakeholder or in any other capacity; provided that the expression 'client's money' shall not include:

(a) money held or received on account of the trustees of a trust of which the solicitor is a solicitor-trustee; or

(b) money to which the only person entitled is the solicitor himself or, in the case of a firm of solicitors, one or more of the partners in the firm;

'Client' shall mean any person on whose account a solicitor holds or receives client's money;

'Trust Money' shall mean money held or received by a solicitor which is not client's money and which is subject to a trust of which the solicitor is a trustee whether or not he is a solicitor-trustee of such trust;

'Client account' shall mean a current or deposit account at a bank or deposit account with a building society in the name of the solicitor and in the title of which account the word 'client' appears;

'Bank' shall mean the branch, situated in England or Wales, of a Bank as defined by section 87(1) of the Solicitors Act 1974, as amended by paragraph 9 of Schedule 6 to the Banking Act 1979;

'Building Society' shall mean the branch, situated in England or Wales, of a building society as defined by paragraph 11(5) of Schedule 18 to the Building Societies Act, 1986;

'Solicitor-Trustee' shall mean a solicitor who is a sole trustee or co-trustee only with one or more of his partners or employees;

'Public Officer' shall mean an officer whose remuneration is defrayed out of moneys provided by Parliament, the revenues of the Duchy of Cornwall or the Duchy of Lancaster, the general fund of the Church Commissioners, the Forestry Fund or the Development Fund;

'Statutory undertakers' shall mean any person authorised by or under an Act of Parliament, to construct, work, or carry on any railway, canal, inland navigation, dock, harbour, tramway, gas, electricity, water or other public undertaking;
'Local Authority' shall have the same meaning as is given to this expression by the Local Government Act, 1972.
(2) Other expressions in these Rules shall except where otherwise stated have the meanings assigned to them by the Solicitors Act 1974.
(3) The Interpretation Act 1989, shall apply to these rules in the same manner as it applies to an Act of Parliament, and for the purposes of section 38 of the said Act the Solicitors' Accounts Rules 1975, shall be deemed to be an enactment repealed by these Rules.

3 Subject to the provisions of Rule 9 hereof, every solicitor who holds or receives client's money, or money which under Rule 4 hereof he is permitted and elects to pay into a client account, shall without delay pay such money into a client account. Any solicitor may keep one client account or as many such accounts as he thinks fit.

4 There may be paid into a client account:

(a) trust money;
(b) such money belonging to the solicitor as may be necessary for the purposes of opening or maintaining the account;
(c) money to replace any sum which for any reason may have been drawn from the account in contravention of paragraph (2) of Rule 8 of these Rules; and
(d) a cheque or draft received by the solicitor which under paragraph (b) of Rule 5 of these Rules he is entitled to split but which he does not split.

5 Where a solicitor holds or received a cheque or draft which includes client's money or trust money of one or more trust:

(a) he may where practicable split such cheque or draft and, if he does so, he shall deal with each part thereof as if he had received a separate cheque or draft in respect of that part; or
(b) if he does not split the cheque or draft, he shall, if any part thereof consists of clients' money, and may, in any other case, pay the cheque or draft into a client account.

6 No money other than money which under the foregoing Rules a solicitor is required or permitted to pay into a client account shall be paid into a client account, and it shall be the duty of a solicitor into whose client account any money has been paid in contravention of this Rule to withdraw the same without delay on discovery.

7 There may be drawn from a client account:

(a) in the case of client's money:

(i) money properly required for a payment to or on behalf of the client;

(ii) money properly required for or towards payment of a debt due to the solicitor from the client or in reimbursement of money expended by the solicitor on behalf of the client;

(iii) money drawn on the client's authority;

(iv) money properly required for or towards payment of the solicitor's costs where there has been delivered to the client a bill of costs or other written intimation of the amount of the costs incurred and it has thereby or otherwise in writing been made clear to the client that money held for him is being or will be applied towards or in satisfaction of such costs; and

(v) money which is transferred into another client account;

(b) in the case of trust money:

(i) money properly required for a payment in the execution of the particular trust, and

(ii) money to be transferred to a separate bank or building society account kept solely for the money of the particular trust;

(c) such money, not being money to which either paragraph (a) or paragraph (b) of this Rule applies, as may have been paid into the account under paragraph (b) of Rule 4 or paragraph (b) of Rule 5 of these Rules; and

(d) money which for any reason may have been paid into the account in contravention of Rule 6 of these Rules;

provided that in any case under paragraph (a) or paragraph (b) of this Rule the money so drawn shall not exceed the total of the money held for the time being in such account on account of such client or trust.

8 (1) No money drawn from a client account under subparagraph (ii) or subparagraph (iv) of paragraph (a) or under paragraph (c) or paragraph (d) of Rule 7 of these Rules shall be drawn except by:

(a) a cheque drawn in favour of the solicitor, or

(b) a transfer to a bank or building society account in the name of the solicitor not being a client account.

(2) No money other than money permitted by Rule 7 to be drawn from a client account shall be so drawn unless the Council upon an application made to them by the solicitor specifically authorise in writing its withdrawal.

9 (1) Notwithstanding the provisions of these Rules, a solicitor shall not be under obligation to pay into a client account client's money held or received by him:

(a) which is received by him in the form of cash and is without delay paid in cash in the ordinary course of business to the client or on his behalf to a third party; or

(b) which is received by him in the form of a cheque or draft which is endorsed over in the ordinary course of business to the client or on his behalf to a third party and is not passed by the solicitor through a bank or building society account; or

(c) which he pays into a separate bank or building society account opened or to be opened in the name of the client or of some person designated by the client in writing or acknowledged by the solicitor to the client in writing.

(2) Notwithstanding the provisions of these Rules, a solicitor shall not pay into a client account money held or received by him:

(a) which the client for his own convenience requests the solicitor to withhold from such account, such request being either in writing from the client or acknowledged by the solicitor to the client in writing; or

(b) which is received by him for or towards payment of a debt to the solicitor from the client or in reimbursement of money expended by the solicitor on behalf of the client; or

(c) which is expressly paid to him either:

(i) on account of costs incurred in respect of which a bill of costs or other written intimation of the amount of the costs incurred has been delivered for payment; or

(ii) as an agreed fee (or on account of an agreed fee) for business undertaken or to be undertaken.

(3) Where a cheque or draft includes client's money as well as money of the nature described in paragraph (2) of this Rule such cheque or draft shall be dealt with in accordance with Rule 5 of these Rules.

(4) Notwithstanding the provisions of these Rules the Council may upon application made to them by a solicitor specifically authorise him in writing to withhold any client's money from a client account.

10 No sum shall be transferred from the ledger account of one client to that of another except in circumstances in which it would have been permissible under these Rules to have withdrawn from client account the sum transferred from the first client and to have paid into client account the sum so transferred to the second client.

11 (1) Every solicitor shall at all times keep properly written up such accounts as may be necessary:

(a) to show all his dealings with:

(i) client's money received, held or paid by him; and

(ii) any other money dealt with by him through a client account; and

(b) (i) to show separately in respect of each client all money of the categories specified in sub-paragraph (a) of this paragraph with is received, held or paid by him on account of that client; and

(ii) to distinguish all money of the said categories received, held or paid by him from any other money received, held or paid by him.

(2)(a) All dealings referred to in sub-paragraph (a) of paragraph (1) of this Rule shall be recorded as may be appropriate:

(i) either in a clients' cash book, or a clients' column of a cash book, or

(ii) in a record of sums transferred from the ledger account of one client to that of another, and in addition:

(iii) in a clients' ledger or a clients' column of a ledger,

and no other dealings shall be recorded in such clients' cash book and ledger or, as the case may be, in such clients' columns, and

(b) All dealings of the solicitor relating to his practice as a solicitor other than those referred to in sub-paragraph (a) of paragraph (1) of this Rule shall (subject to compliance with the Solicitors' Trust Accounts Rules, 1986) be recorded in such other cash book and ledger or such other columns of a cash book and ledger as the solicitor may maintain.

(3) In addition to the books, ledgers and records referred to in paragraph (2) of this Rule, every solicitor shall keep a record of all bills of costs (distinguishing between profit costs and disbursements) and of all written intimations under Rule 7(a)(iv) and under Rule 9(2)(c) of these Rules delivered or made by the solicitor to his clients, which record shall be contained in a bills delivered book or a file of copies of such bills and intimations.

(4) Every solicitor shall within three months of the coming into force of this sub-rule or of his commencing practice on his own account (either alone or in partnership) whichever shall be later and thereafter not less than once in every succeeding period of three months cause the balance of his clients' cash book (or clients' column of his cash book) to be agreed with his client bank and building society pass books or statements and shall keep in the cash book or other appropriate place a reconciliation statement showing this agreement.

(5) In this Rule the expressions 'accounts', 'books', 'ledgers' and 'records' shall be deemed to include loose-leaf books and such cards or other permanent documents or records as are necessary for the operation of any system of book-keeping, mechanical or otherwise.

(6) Every solicitor shall preserve for at least six years from the date of the last entry therein all accounts, books, ledgers and records kept by him under this Rule.

(7) No money may be withdrawn from a bank or building society account, being or forming part of a client account, otherwise than under the signature of one at least of the following (either alone or in conjunction with other persons) namely;

(a) a solicitor who holds a current practising certificate, or

(b) an employee of such a solicitor being either a solicitor or a Fellow of the Institute of Legal Executives who is confirmed by the Institute as being of good standing and who shall have been admitted a Fellow for not less than five years.

12 (1) In order to ascertain whether these Rules have been complied with the Council, acting either:

(a) on their own motion; or
(b) on a written statement and request transmitted to them by or on behalf of the Governing Body of a Local Law Society or a Committee thereof; or
(c) on a written complaint lodged with them by a third party,

may require any solicitor to produce at a time and place to be fixed by the Council, his books of account, bank and building society pass books, loose-leaf bank and building society statements, statements of account, vouchers and any other necessary documents for the inspection of any person appointed by the Council and to supply to such person any necessary information and explanations and such person shall be directed to prepare for the information of the Council a report on the result of such inspection. Such report may be used as a basis for proceedings under the Solicitors Act 1974.

(2) Upon being required so to do a solicitor shall produce such books of account, bank and building society pass books, loose-leaf bank and building society statements, statements of accounts, vouchers and documents at the time and place fixed.

(3) In any case in which the Governing Body of a Local Law Society or a Committee thereof are of opinion that an inspection should be made under this Rule of the books of account, bank and building society pass books, loose-leaf bank and building society statements, statements of account, vouchers and any other necessary documents of a solicitor, it shall be the duty of such Governing Body or Committee to transmit to the Council a statement containing all relevant information in their possession and a request that such an inspection be made.

(4) Before instituting an inspection on a written complaint lodged with them by a third party, the Council shall require prima facie evidence that a ground of complaint exists, and may require the payment by such party to the Council of a reasonable sum to be fixed by them to cover the costs of the inspection and the costs of the solicitor against whom the complaint is made. The Council may deal with any sum so paid in such manner as they think fit.

13 Every requirement to be made by the Council of a solicitor under these Rules shall be made in writing and sent by registered post or the recorded delivery service to the last address of the solicitor appearing in the Roll or in the Register kept by the Society under section 9 of the Solicitors Act, 1974, and, when so made and sent, shall be deemed to have been received by the solicitor within forty-eight hours (excluding Saturdays, Sundays and Bank Holidays) of the time of posting.

14 Nothing in these Rules shall deprive a solicitor of any recourse or right, whether by way of lien, set off, counterclaim, charge or otherwise, against moneys standing to the credit of a client account.

15 These Rules shall not apply to a solicitor acting in the course of his employment as (a) a public officer, or (b) an officer of statutory undertakers, or (c) an officer of a local authority.

Reproduced with the kind permission of the Law Society.

SOLICITORS' TRUST ACCOUNTS RULES 1986

Made on the 11th December 1986, by the Council of the Law Society and approved by the Master of the Rolls pursuant to section 32 of the Solicitors Act 1974 (as amended).

1 These Rules may be cited as the Solicitors' Trust Accounts Rules, 1986, and shall come into operation on the 1st day of January, 1987, whereupon the Solicitors' Trust Accounts Rules, 1975, shall cease to have effect.

2 (1) In these Rules unless the context otherwise requires:

'Client account' shall mean a current or deposit account at a bank or deposit account with a building society, in the title of which the word 'client' appears, kept and operated in accordance with the provisions of the Solicitors' Accounts Rules, 1986;

'Solicitor-trustee' shall mean a solicitor who is a sole trustee or co-trustee only with one or more of his partners or employees;

'Trust account' shall mean a current or deposit account kept at a bank or deposit account kept with a building society in the title of which the word 'trustee' or 'executor' appears, or which is otherwise clearly designated as a trust account, and kept solely for money subject to a particular trust of which the solicitor is a solicitor-trustee;

'Bank' and **'Building Society'** shall have the meaning assigned to them by the Solicitors' Accounts Rules, 1986;

'Public officer' shall mean an officer whose remuneration is defrayed out of moneys provided by Parliament, the revenues of the Duchy of Cornwall or the Duchy of Lancaster, the general fund of the Church Commissioners, the Forestry Fund or the Development Fund;

'Statutory undertakers' shall mean any person authorised by or under an Act of Parliament, or an order having the force of an Act of Parliament, to construct, work, or carry on any railway, canal, inland navigation, dock, harbour, tramway, gas, electricity, water or other public undertaking;

'Local authority' shall have the same meaning as is given to this expression by the Local Government Act, 1972.

(2) Other expressions in these Rules shall except where otherwise stated have the meanings assigned to them by the Solicitors Act 1974.

(3) The Interpretation Act 1889, shall apply to these Rules in the same manner as it applies to an Act of Parliament and for the purposes of section 38 of the said Act, the Solicitors' Trust Accounts Rules, 1975, shall be deemed to be an enactment repealed by these Rules.

3 Subject to the provisions of Rule 9 of these Rules every solicitor-trustee who holds or receives money subject to a trust of which he is a solicitor-trustee, other than money which is paid into a client account as permitted by the Solicitors' Accounts Rules, 1986, shall without delay pay such money into the trust account of the particular trust.

4 There may be paid into a trust account:

(a) money subject to the particular trust;
(b) such money belonging to the solicitor-trustee or to a co-trustee as may be necessary for the purpose of opening or maintaining the account; or
(c) money to replace any sum which for any reason may have been drawn from the account in contravention of Rule 8 of these Rules.

5 Where a solicitor holds or receives a cheque or draft which includes money subject to a trust or trusts of which the solicitor is solicitor-trustee:

(a) he shall where practicable split such cheque or draft and, if he does so, shall deal with each part thereof as if he had received a separate cheque or draft in respect of that part; or
(b) if he does not split the cheque or draft, he may pay it into a client account as permitted by the Solicitors' Accounts Rules 1986.

6 No money, other than money which under the foregoing Rules a solicitor is required or permitted to pay into a trust account, shall be paid into a trust account, and it shall be the duty of a solicitor into whose trust account any money has been paid in contravention of this Rule to withdraw the same without delay on discovery.

7 There may be drawn from a trust account:

(a) money properly required for a payment in the execution of the particular trust;
(b) money to be transferred to a client account;
(c) such money, not being money subject to the particular trust, as may have been paid into the account under paragraph (b) of Rule 4 of these Rules; or
(d) money which may for any reason have been paid into the account in contravention of Rule 6 of these Rules.

8 No money other than money permitted by Rule 7 of these Rules to be drawn from a trust account shall be so drawn unless the Council upon an application made to them by the solicitor expressly authorise in writing its withdrawal.

9 Notwithstanding the provisions of these Rules a solicitor shall not be under obligation to pay into a trust account money held or received by him which is subject to a trust of which he is solicitor-trustee:

(a) if the money is received by him in the form of cash and is without delay paid in cash in the execution of the trust to a third party; or
(b) if the money is received by him in the form of a cheque or draft which is without delay endorsed over in the execution of the trust to a third party and is not passed by the solicitor through a bank or building society account.

10 (1) Every solicitor-trustee shall at all times keep properly written up such accounts as may be necessary:

(a) to show separately in respect of each trust of which he is solicitor-trustee all his dealings with money received, held or paid by him on account of that trust; and

(b) to distinguish the same from money received, held or paid by him on any other account.

(2) Every solicitor-trustee shall preserve for at least six years from the date of the last entry therein all accounts kept by him under this Rule.

11 (1) In order to ascertain whether these Rules have been complied with the Council acting either:

(a) on their own motion; or

(b) on a written statement and request transmitted to them by or on behalf of the Governing Body of a Local Law Society or a Committee thereof; or

(c) on a written complaint lodged with them by a third party,

may require any solicitor-trustee to produce at a time and place to be fixed by the Council, all books of account, bank and building society pass books, loose-leaf bank and building society statements, statements of account, vouchers and documents relating to all or any of the trusts of which he is solicitor-trustee for the inspection of any person appointed by the Council, and to supply to such person any necessary information and explanations and such person shall be directed to prepare for the information of the Council a report on the result of such inspection. Such report may be used as a basis for proceedings under the Solicitors Act 1974.

(2) Upon being required so to do a solicitor-trustee shall produce such books of account, bank and building society pass books, loose-leaf bank and building society statements, statements of account, vouchers and documents at the time and place fixed.

(3) In any case in which the Governing Body of a Local Law Society or a committee thereof are of opinion that an inspection should be made under this Rule of books of account, bank and building society pass books, loose-leaf bank and building society statements, statements of account, vouchers and documents relating to all or any of the trusts of which a solicitor is solicitor-trustee it shall be the duty of such Governing Body or Committee to transmit to the Council a statement containing all relevant information in their possession and a request that such an inspection be made.

(4) Before instituting an insepction on a written complaint lodged with them by a third party, the Council shall require prima facie evidence that a ground of complaint exists, and may require the payment by such party to the Council of a reasonable sum to be fixed by them to cover the costs of the inspection, and the costs of the solicitor-trustee against whom the complaint is made. The Council may deal with any sum so paid in such manner as they think fit.

12 Every requirement to be made by the Council of a solicitor-trustee under these Rules shall be made in writing and sent by recorded or registered delivery service to the last address of the solicitor-trustee appearing in the Roll or in the Register kept by the Society under section 9 of the Solicitors Act 1974, and, when so made and sent, shall be deemed to have been received by the solicitor-trustee within forty-eight hours (excluding Saturdays, Sundays and Bank Holidays) of the time of posting.

13 Nothing in these Rules shall deprive a solicitor of any recourse or right whether by way of lien, set off, counterclaim, charge or otherwise, against money standing to the credit of a trust account.

14 These Rules shall not apply to a solicitor acting in the course of his employment as (a) a public officer, or (b) an officer of statutory undertakers, or (c) an officer of a local authority.

Reproduced with the kind permission of the Law Society.

SOLICITORS' ACCOUNTS (DEPOSIT INTEREST) RULES 1988

Made on the 21st July 1988 by the Council of The Law Society and approved by the Master of the Rolls pursuant to sections 32 and 33 of the Solicitors Act 1974 and section 9 of the Administration of Justice Act 1985.

Citation and commencement

1 These Rules may be cited as the Solicitors' Accounts (Deposit Interest) Rules 1988 and shall come into operation on the 1st day of September 1988 whereupon the Solicitors' Accounts (Deposit Interest) Rules 1987 shall cease to have effect.

Interpretation

2 In these Rules the expression 'a separate designated account' shall mean a deposit account at a bank or building society in the name of the solicitor or his firm in the title of which the word 'client' appears and which is designated by reference to the identity of the client or matter concerned; the expressions 'bank' and 'building society' shall have the meanings assigned to them by the Solicitors' Accounts Rules 1986.

Obligation to account for interest

3 Subject to Rule 6, when a solicitor holds money for a client, the solicitor shall account to the client for interest in the following circumstances:

Separate designated account

(a) Where the money is held in a separate designated account, the solicitor shall account for the interest earned on it.

Undesignated accounts

(b) Where the money is not held in a separate designated account, the following provisions shall apply:

Sums held for specified periods

(i) The solicitor shall account to the client for interest at a rate calculated in accordance with Rule 4, if the money is held for as long as or longer than the number of weeks set out in the left hand column of the table below and the minimum balance held during that period equals or exceeds the corresponding figure in the right hand column of the table.

TABLE

No. of Weeks	Minimum Balance
8	£500
4	£1,000
2	£5,000
1	£10,000

Sums held for less than one week

(ii) The solicitor shall account to the client for interest at a rate calculated in accordance with Rule 4 if he holds a sum of money exceeding £10,000 for less than 1 week and it is fair and reasonable to do so having regard to all the circumstances.

Variable balances

(iii) Where money continuously held for a client varies significantly in amount over the period during which it is held, then having regard to any sum payable under subparagraph (i) the solicitor shall account to the client for such interest (or additional interest) at a rate calculated in accordance with Rule 4 as is fair and reasonable having regard to the varying amounts of money and the length of time for which these are held.

Money held intermittently

(iv) Where a solicitor during the course of acting for a client holds sums of money for the client intermittently, the solicitor shall account to the client for interest at a rate calculated in accordance with Rule 4, if it is fair and reasonable to do so having regard to all the circumstances including the aggregate of the sums held and the periods for which they are held, notwithstanding that no individual sum would have attracted interest under subparagraph (i).

Transfers between designated and undesignated accounts

(c) Where the money is held successively in designated and undesignated accounts, but as a result of the previous paragraphs interest or sum equivalent thereto is not payable on the money for the whole time it is held, then the solicitor shall account to the client for such interest (or additional interest) at a rate calculated in accordance with Rule 4 as is fair and reasonable; for this purpose regard shall be had to the provisions of paragraph (b) as if for the whole time the money was held, it was not held in a separate designated account.

Rate of interest

4 (1) The rate of interest to be applied for the purposes of Rules 3(b) and (c) shall be the rate of interest which would have been earned by the money, or its gross equivalent if the rate would have been net of tax, if the money had been kept in a separate designated account earning interest at a rate not less than that from time to time posted publicly by the relevant bank or building society for small deposits subject to the minimum period of notice of withdrawals.

(2) For the purpose of paragraph (1), the relevant bank or building society shall mean:

(a) the bank or building society where the money is held, or

(b) where the money, or part of it, is held in successive and concurrent client accounts maintained at different banks or building societies, whichever of those banks or building societies was offering the highest rate for small deposits subject to the minimum period of notice of withdrawals on the day when interest payable under Rules 3(b) and (c) commenced to accrue, or

(c) where, contrary to the provisions of the Solicitors' Accounts Rules 1986, the money is not held in a client account, any bank or building society nominated by the client.

Certification by Law Society

5 Without prejudice to any other remedy which may be available to him, any client who feels aggrieved that interest, or a sum equivalent thereto has not been paid to him under these Rules shall be entitled to apply to the Law Society for a certificate as to whether or not interest ought to have been earned for him and, if so, the amount of such interest, and upon the issue of such a certificate the sum certified to be due shall be payable by the solicitor to the client.

Exception

6 Nothing in these Rules shall:

(a) affect any arrangement in writing, whenever made, between a solicitor and his client as to the application of the client's money or interest thereon; or

(b) apply to money received by a solicitor being money subject to a trust of which the solicitor is a trustee.

Reproduced with the kind permission of the Law Society.

ACCOUNTANT'S REPORT RULES 1986 (INCORPORATING AMENDMENTS TO 29TH APRIL 1988)

Made on the 11th December 1986, by the Council of the Law Society pursuant to section 34 of the Solicitors Act 1974 (as amended) with respect to the delivery by solicitors of Accountant's Reports.

1 These Rules may be cited as the Accountant's Report Rules, 1986, and shall come into operation on the 1st day of January, 1987, whereupon the Accountant's Report Rules, 1975, shall cease to have effect.

2 (1) In these Rules the expressions 'client's money', 'client', 'trust money' and 'client account' shall have the meanings respectively assigned to them by the Solicitors' Accounts Rules, 1986, and the expression 'trust account' shall have the meaning assigned to it by the Solicitors' Trust Accounts Rules, 1986, but in the case of a solicitor holding one of the offices to which Rule 15 of the Solicitors' Accounts Rules, 1986, or subsection (2) of section 88 of the Solicitors Act, 1974 applies, 'client's money' shall not extend to money held or received by him in the course of his employment in such office.

(2) Other expressions in these Rules shall except where otherwise stated have the meanings assigned to them by the Solicitors Act, 1974.

(3) The Interpretation Act, 1889, shall apply to these Rules in the same manner as it applies to an Act of Parliament, and for the purposes of section 38 of the said Act the Accountant's Report Rules, 1975, shall be deemed to be an enactment repealed by these Rules.

3 (1) An accountant shall be qualified to give an Accountant's Report on behalf of a solicitor if

(a) he is a member of

   (i) The Institute of Chartered Accountants in England and Wales; or
   (ii) The Institute of Chartered Accountants in Scotland; or
   (iii) The Association of Certified Accountants; or
   (iv) The Institute of Chartered Accountants in Ireland; and

(b) he has neither been at any time during the accounting period to which the Report relates, nor subsequently, before giving the Report, become a partner or employee of such solicitor or any partner of his; and

(c) he is not subject to notice of disqualification under paragraph (2) of this Rule.

(2) In either of the following cases, that is to say, where:

(a) the accountant has been found guilty by the Disciplinary Tribunal of his professional body of professional misconduct or discreditable conduct; or

(b) the Council are satisfied that a solicitor has not complied with the provisions of the Solicitors' Accounts Rules, 1986, in respect of matters not specified in an Accountant's Report and that the accountant was negligent in giving such Report, whether or not an application be made for a grant out of the Compensation Fund, the Council may at their discretion, at any time notify the accountant concerned that he is not qualified to give an Accountant's Report, and they may give notice of such fact to any solicitor on whose behalf he may have given an Accountant's Report, or who may appear to the Council to be likely to employ such accountant for the purpose of giving an Accountant's Report; and after such accountant shall have been so notified, unless and until such notice of disqualification shall have been withdrawn by the Council, he shall not be qualified to give an Accountant's Report. Before coming to their decision the Council shall take into consideration any observations or explanation made or given by such accountant or on his behalf by the professional body of which he is a member.

4 (1) For the purpose of giving an Accountant's Report, an accountant shall ascertain from the solicitor particulars of all bank and building society accounts (excluding trust accounts) kept, maintained or operated by the solicitor in connection with his practice at any time during the accounting period to which his Report relates and subject to paragraph (2) of this Rule make the following examination of the books, accounts and other relevant documents of the solicitor:

(a) so examine the book-keeping system in every office of the solicitor as to enable the accountant to verify that such system complies with Rule 11 of the Solicitors' Accounts Rules, 1986 and Rule 13 of the Solicitors' Investment Business Rules 1988 and is so designed that:

(i) an appropriate ledger account is kept for each client;

(ii) such ledger accounts show separately from other information particulars of all clients' money received, held or paid on account of each client;

(iii) transactions relating to clients' money and any other money dealt with through a client account are recorded in the solicitor's books so as to distinguish such transactions from transactions relating to any other money received, held or paid by the solicitor;

(b) make test checks of postings to clients' ledger accounts from records of receipts and payments of clients' money and make test checks of the casts of such accounts and records;

(c) compare a sample of lodgments into and payments from the client account as shown in bank and building society statements with the solicitor's records of receipts and payments of clients' money;

(d) enquire into and test check the system of recording costs and of making transfers in respect of costs from the client account;

(e) make a test examination of such documents as he shall request the solicitor to produce to him with the object of ascertaining and confirming:

  (i) that the financial transactions, (including those giving rise to transfers from one ledger account to another) evidenced by such documents, are in accordance with the Solicitors' Accounts Rules, 1986; and

  (ii) that the entries in clients' ledger accounts reflect those transactions in a manner complying with the Solicitors' Accounts Rules, 1986;

(f) extract (or check extractions of) balances on the clients' ledger accounts during the accounting period under review at not fewer than two dates selected by the accountant (one of which may be the last day of the accounting period), and at each such date:

  (i) compare the total as shown by such ledger accounts of the liabilities to the clients, including those for whom trust money is held in the client account, with the cash book balance on client account; and

  (ii) reconcile that cash book balance with the client account balance as confirmed direct to the accountant by the bank and building society;

(g) satisfy himself that reconciliation statements have been kept in accordance with Rule 11(4) of the Solicitors' Accounts Rules 1986;

(h) make a test examination of the clients' ledger accounts in order to ascertain whether payments from the client account have been made on any individual account in excess of money held on behalf of that client;

(i) peruse such office ledger and cash accounts and bank and building society statements as the solicitor maintains with a view to ascertaining whether any client's money has not been paid into a client account;

(j) ask for such information and explanations as he may require arising out of subparagraphs (a) to (i) of this paragraph.

(2) Nothing in paragraph (1) of this Rule shall require the accountant

(a) to extend his enquiries beyond the information contained in the relevant documents relating to any client's matter produced to him supplemented by such information and explanations as he may obtain from the solicitor;

(b) to enquire into the stocks, shares, other securities or documents of title held by the solicitor on behalf of his clients;

(c) to consider whether the books of account of the solicitor have been properly written up in accordance with Rule 11 of the Solicitors' Accounts Rules, 1986 and Rule 13 of the Solicitors' Investment Business Rules 1988, at any time other than the time as at which his examination of those books and accounts takes place.

(3) If after making an examination in accordance with paragraphs (1) and (2) of this Rule it appears to the accountant that there is evidence that the Solicitors' Accounts Rules, 1986 have not been complied with he shall make such further examination as he considers necessary in order to complete his Report with or without qualification.
(4) Except where a client's money has been deposited in a separate designated account, nothing in these Rules shall apply to any matter arising under section 33 of the Solicitors Act, 1974, or the Solicitors' Accounts (Deposit Interest) Rules, 1986, notwithstanding any payment into client account of a sum in lieu of interest.
(5) In this Rule the expression 'separate designated account' shall have the same meaning as in Rule 2 of the Solicitors' Accounts (Deposit Interest) Rules, 1986.

5 Nothing in these Rules shall deprive a solicitor of the right on the grounds of privilege as between solicitor and client to decline to produce to the accountant any document which the accountant may consider it necessary for him to inspect for the purposes of his examination in accordance with Rule 4 of these Rules and where the solicitor so declines, the accountant shall qualify his Report to that effect setting out the circumstances.

6 An Accountant's Report delivered by a solicitor under these Rules shall be in the form set out in the Schedule to these Rules or in a form to the like effect approved by the Council.

7 The Council will in each practice year be satisfied that the delivery of an Accountant's Report is unnecessary, and shall not require evidence of that fact, in the case of any solicitor who:
(1) does not hold a practising certificate and:
(a) has never held one; or
(b) having held one has delivered an Accountant's Report covering the accounting period ended on the date upon which he ceased to practice and to hold or receive client's money; or
(2) holds a current practising certificate:
(a) for the first time; or
(b) for the first time, after having for 12 months or more ceased so to do; or
(c) has satisfied the Council that either:
   (i) he is exempt from complying with the Solicitors' Accounts Rules, 1986, by virtue of holding one of the offices to which Rule 15 of those Rules or subsection (2) of section 88 of the Solicitors Act, 1974, applies and has not, during the period to which such application relates, practised alone or in partnership or held or received client's money; or
   (ii) the Solicitors' Accounts Rules, 1986, are not applicable to him because he is employed only as an assistant solicitor by another solicitor or firm of solicitors and has not, during the period to which the said application relates, practised alone

or in partnership or been held out to the public as a partner or held or received client's money; or

(iii) the Solicitors' Accounts Rules, 1986, are not applicable to him because during the period to which the said application relates he has either (a) not practised as a solicitor alone or as a partner or been held out to the public as a partner or (b) not held or received client's money.

8 (1) In the case of a solicitor who:

(a) becomes under an obligation to deliver his first Accountant's Report; or

(b) having been exempt under Rule 7 of these Rules from delivering an Accountant's Report in the preceding practice year, becomes under an obligation to deliver an Accountant's Report,

the accounting period shall begin on the date upon which he first held or received client's money or, after such exemption, began again to hold or receive client's money, and may cover less than twelve months, and shall in all other respects comply with the requirements of subsection (3) of section 34 of the Solicitors Act, 1974.

(2) In the case of a solicitor retiring from practice who, having ceased to hold or receive client's money, is under an obligation to deliver his final Accountant's Report, the accounting period shall end on the date upon which he ceased to hold or receive client's money, and may cover less than twelve months, and shall in all other respects comply with the requirements of subsection (3) of section 34 of the Solicitors Act, 1974.

9 (1) In the case of a solicitor who:

(a) was not exempt under Rule 7 of these Rules from delivering an Accountant's Report in the preceding practice year; and

(b) since the expiry of the accounting period covered by such Accountant's Report has become, or ceased to be, a member of a firm of solicitors, the accounting period may cover less than twelve months and shall in all other respects comply with the requirements of subsection (3) of section 34 of the Solicitors Act, 1974.

(2) In the case of a solicitor who has two or more places of business:

(a) separate accounting periods covered by separate Accountant's Reports may be adopted in respect of each such place of business, provided that the accounting periods comply with the requirements of subsection (3) of section 34 of the Solicitors Act, 1974; and

(b) the Accountant's Report or the Accountant's Reports delivered by him to the Society in each practice year shall cover all clients' money held or received by him.

10 Every notice to be given by the Council under these Rules to a solicitor shall be in writing and sent by registered post or the recorded delivery service to the last address of the solicitor appearing in the Roll or in the Register kept by the Society under section 9 of the Solicitors Act, 1974, and, when so given and sent, shall be deemed to have been received by

the solicitor within forty-eight hours (excluding Saturdays, Sundays and Bank Holidays) of the time of posting.

11 Every notice to be given by the Council under these Rules to an accountant shall be in writing and sent by registered post or the recorded delivery service to the address of the accountant as shown on an Accountant's Report or appearing in the records of the professional body of which the accountant is a member, and, when so given and sent, shall be deemed to have been received by the accountant within forty-eight hours (excluding Saturdays, Sundays and Bank Holidays) of the time of posting.

12 The Council shall have power to waive in writing in any particular case any of the provisions of these Rules, other than those of paragraph (2) of Rule 3.

Reproduced with the kind permission of the Law Society.

Schedule
Section 34, Solicitors Act 1974

FORM OF ACCOUNTANT'S REPORT

Note: In the case of a firm with a number of partners, one copy of the Report may be delivered provided section 1 below is completed with the names of all the individual partners in the firm.

PLEASE INDICATE WHETHER THIS REPORT COVERS ALL THE PARTNERS WITHIN THE FIRM WHO HAVE HELD CLIENTS MONIES DURING THE PERIOD UNDER REVIEW OR WHETHER INDIVIDUAL REPORTS ARE BEING SUBMITTED

TICK AS APPROPRIATE:

COVERS ALL PARTNERS ☐ INDIVIDUAL REPORTS SUBMITTED ☐

(a) BLOCK CAPITALS. 1. Solicitor(s) Full Names (a)

SURNAME FORENAMES

(Continue on separate sheet as necessary)

(b) NOTE– *All addresses at which the Solicitor(s) practise(s) must be covered by an Accountant's Report or Reports. If an address is not so covered the reason must be stated.*

1. Firm(s) Name(s) and Address(es) (b)

(c) NOTE– *The period(s) must comply with Section 34(3) of the Solicitors Act 1974, and the Accountant's Report Rules 1986.*

3. Accounting Period(s) (c)

Beginning . . . . Ending . . . .

Beginning . . . . Ending . . . .

ACCOUNTANT'S REPORT

In compliance with section 34 of the Solicitors Act 1974, and the Accountant's Report rules 1986 made thereunder, I have examined to the extent required by Rule 4 of the said Rules the books, accounts and documents produced to me in respect of the above practice(s) of the above-named solicitor.

1 In so far as an opinion can be based on this limited examination I am satisfied that during the above mentioned period(s) he has complied with the provisions of the Solicitors' Accounts Rules 1986 and Rule 13 of the Solicitors Investment Business Rules 1988 except so far as concerns:

Delete sub-paragraph(s) not applicable.

(a) certain trivial breaches due to clerical errors or mistakes in book-keeping, all of which were rectified on discovery and none of which, I am satisfied, resulted in any loss to any client:

(b) the matters set out in the First Section on the back hereof, in respect of which I have not been able to satisfy myself for the reasons therein stated:

(c) the matters set out in the Second Section on the back hereof, in respect of which it appears to me that the solicitor has not complied with the provisions of the Solicitors' Accounts Rules 1986.

2 The results of the comparisons required under Rule 4(1)(f) of the Accountant's Report Rules 1986, at the dates selected by me were as follows:

Delete (a) or (b) as appropriate.

(i) at ....

(a) the figures were in agreement:

(b) there was a difference computed as follows:

	£
Liabilities to clients as shown by clients' ledger accounts	
Cash held in client account after allowance for outstanding cheques and lodgments cleared after date	
	£

Delete (a) or (b) as appropriate.

(ii) at ....

(a) the figures were in agreement:

(b) there was a difference computed as follows:

	£
Liabilities to clients as shown by clients' ledger accounts	
Cash held in client account after allowance for outstanding cheques and lodgments cleared after date	
	£

3 The following solicitor(s) having retired from active practice as a solicitor ceased to hold client's money on the date indicated and the report covers the period up to the date of cessation:

FULL NAME	DATE CEASED TO HOLD CLIENT'S MONEY

4 The following solicitor(s) having left the firm and ceased to practise under this style, ceased to hold client's money under this style on the date indicated and the report covers the period up to the date of cessation:

FULL NAME	DATE CEASED TO HOLD CLIENT'S MONEY UNDER THIS STYLE

5 The following solicitor(s) have joined the firm during the period under review on the date on which client's money was held under this style: A

FULL NAME	DATE FROM WHICH CLIENT'S MONEY HELD UNDER THIS STYLE

Particulars of the accountant:

Full Name ....

Qualifications ....

Firm Name ....

Address ....

....

Date .... Signature ....

To: The Director
Professional Standards and Development Directorate
Ipsley Court, Redditch
Worcs B98 0TD
(DX 19114 REDDITCH)

First Section

Matters in respect of which the accountant has been unable to satisfy himself and the reasons for that inability:

Second Section

Matters (other than trivial breaches) in respect of which it appears to the accountant that the solicitor(s) has not complied with the provisions of the Solicitors' Accounts Rules 1986:

WAIVER

Accountant's Report Rules 1986 Rule 4(1)(f)
The Council have considered the question of whether or not full compliance with the above Rule is essential where a solicitor uses a computerised or mechanised system of accounting and have decided that some relaxation can be permitted. Accordingly, in so far as Rule 4(1)(f) of the Accountant's Report Rules, 1986 requires an accountant to extract, or check extractions of, balances on the clients' ledger accounts then, where a solicitor uses a computerised or mechanised system of accounting which automatically produces an extraction of all client ledger balances, in so far as such work merely amounts to a check on the accuracy of the computer or machine, the Council waive the requirement of the Rule that all client ledger balances extracted on the list produced by the computer or machine must be checked against the individual records of ledger accounts, provided the accountant is satisfied that a satisfactory system of control is in operation, carries out a test check of the extraction against the individual records and specifies in his report that he has relied on this waiver. It should be noted that the remainder of the Rule is not waived and the appropriate comparisons must continue to be made at not fewer than two dates.

STATEMENTS OF ACCOUNTING PRACTICE AND EXPOSURE DRAFTS

SSAP 1	Accounting for associated companies	Revised April 1982
SSAP 2	Disclosure of accounting policies	Issued Nov. 1971
SSAP 3	Earnings per share	Revised Aug. 1984
SSAP 4	The accounting treatment of government grants	Revised July 1990
SSAP 5	Accounting for value added tax	Issued April 1974
SSAP 6	Extraordinary items and prior year adjustments	Revised Aug. 1986
SSAP 8	The treatment of taxation under the imputation system in the accounts of companies	Revised Dec. 1977
SSAP 9	Stocks and long-term contracts	Revised Sept. 1988
SSAP 10	Statements of source and application of funds	Revised June 1978
SSAP 12	Accounting for depreciation	Revised Jan. 1987
SSAP 13	Accounting for research and development	Revised Jan. 1989
SSAP 14	Group accounts	Issued Sept. 1978
SSAP 15	Accounting for deferred taxation	Revised May 1985
SSAP 17	Accounting for post balance sheet events	Issued Aug. 1980
SSAP 18	Accounting for contingencies	Issued Aug. 1980
SSAP 19	Accounting for investment properties	Issued Nov. 1981

SSAP 20	Foreign currency translation	Issued April 1983
SSAP 21	Accounting for leases and hire purchase contracts	Issued Aug. 1984
SSAP 22	Accounting for goodwill	Revised July 1989
SSAP 23	Accounting for acquisitions and mergers	Issued April 1985
SSAP 24	Accounting for pension costs	Issued May 1988
SSAP 25	Segmental reporting	Issued July 1990
ED 46	Disclosure of related party transactions	Issued April 1989
ED 47	Accounting for goodwill	Issued Feb. 1990
ED 48	Accounting for acquisitions and mergers	Issued Feb. 1990
ED 49	Reflecting the substance of transactions in assets and liabilities	Issued May 1990
ED 50	Consolidated accounts	Issued June 1990
ED 51	Accounting for fixed assets and revaluations	Issued May 1990
ED 52	Accounting for intangible fixed assets	Issued May 1990
ED 53	Fair value in the context of acquisition accounting	Issued July 1990
ED 54	Cash flow statements	Issued Sept. 1990
ED 55	Accounting for investments	Issued Sept. 1990

FRANKED STATEMENTS OF RECOMMENDED PRACTICE AND EXPOSURE DRAFTS

BODIES RECOGNISED TO ISSUE FRANKED SORPS

Body	Industry/sector
Accounting Standards for Local Authorities Group (ASLA)	Local Authorities (E&W)
Association of British Insurers (ABI)	Insurance
British Bankers Association (BBA)	Banking
Building Societies Association (BSA)	Building Societies
Chartered Institute of Public Finance and Accountancy	Public Finance
Committee of Vice Chancellors and Principals (CVCP)	Universities
Investment Management Regulatory Organisation (IMRO)	Unit Trusts
Irish Bankers Federation (IBF)	Banking
Local Authority (Scotland) Accounts Advisory Committee (LA(S)AAC)	Local Authorities (S)
Oil Industry Accounting Committee (OIAC)	Oil/Gas
Unit Trust Association (UTA)	Unit Trusts

FRANKED SORPS AND EXPOSURE DRAFTS

Accounting Standards for Local Authorities (ASLA)

The application of accounting standards (SSAPs) to local authorities in England & Wales — Issued April 1987

(superceded by a franked SORP issued by CIPFA in December 1990 see below)

Association of British Insurers (ABI)

Accounting for insurance business — Issued May 1990

Lloyds syndicates — Issued Feb. 1988

British Bankers Association (BBA) and Irish Bankers Federation (IBF)

Securities — Issued Sept. 1990

Commitments and contingencies — Exposure draft

Chartered Institute Of Public Finance and Accountancy (CIPFA)

Local authority accounting (code of practice) — Issued Nov. 1987

Capital accounting in local authorities — Exposure draft Issued Sept. 1990

Accounting code of practice for local authorities in Great Britain — Issued April 1991 but not yet franked

The application of Accounting Standards to local authorities in Great Britain — Issued Dec. 1990

Committee of Vice Chancellors & Principals (CVCP)

Accounting in UK universities — Issued May 1989

Investment Management Regulatory Organisation (IMRO) and Unit Trust Association (UTA)

Authorised unit trust schemes — Issued April 1991

Local Authority (Scotland) Accounts Advisory Committee (LA(S)AAC)

SORP 1	Disclosure of accounting policies	Issued Jan. 1987
SORP 2	Accounting treatment of Government grants	Issued Jan. 1987
SORP 3	Accounting for Value Added Tax	Issued Jan. 1987
SORP 4	Accounting for post balance sheet events	Issued March 1988
SORP 5	Accounting for contingencies	Issued March 1988
SORP 6	Foreign currency translation	Issued March 1988

(The above six SORPs were superceded by a franked SORP issued by CIPFA in December 1990 see above)

Oil Industry Accounting Committee (OIAC)

Disclosures about oil and gas exploration and production activities	Issued April 1986
Accounting for oil and gas exploration and development of activities	Issued Dec. 1987
Accounting for abandonment costs	Issued June 1988
Accounting for various financing, revenue and other transaction of oil and gas exploration and production companies	Issued Jan. 1991

AUDITING STANDARDS, AUDITING GUIDELINES AND EXPOSURE DRAFTS

Explanatory foreword		Revised Jan. 1989

Auditing Standards

101	The auditor's operational standard	Issued April 1980
102	The audit report	Revised March 1989

Auditing Guidelines - Operational

201	Planning, controlling and recording	Issued April 1980
202	Accounting systems	Issued April 1980
203	Audit evidence	Issued April 1980
204	Internal controls	Issued April 1980
205	Review of financial statements	Issued April 1980

Auditing Guidelines - Industries

301	Charities	Issued Oct. 1981
302	Building societies in the United Kingdom	Revised March 1989
303	Trade unions and employers' associations	Issued Aug. 1984
304	Housing associations	Issued Nov. 1984
305	The impact of regulations on public sector audits	Issued March 1988
306	Pension schemes in the United Kingdom	Issued Nov. 1988
307	Banks in the United Kingdom	Issued March 1989
308	Guidance for internal auditors	Issued June 1990

309	Communications between auditors and Regulators under sections 109 and 180(1)(q) of the Financial Services Act 1986	Issued July 1990
310	General business insurers in the United Kingdom	Issued March 1991

Auditing Guidelines - Detailed operational

401	Bank reports for audit purposes	Issued June 1982
402	Events after the balance sheet date	Issued Nov. 1982
403	Amounts derived from the preceding financial statements	Issued Nov. 1982
404	Representations by management	Issued July 1983
405	Attendance at stocktaking	Issued Oct. 1983
406	Engagement letters	Issued May 1984
407	Auditing in a computer environment	Issued June 1984
408	Reliance on internal audit	Issued Nov. 1984
409	Quality control	Issued Jan. 1985
410	The auditor's considerations in respect of going concern	Issued Aug. 1985
411	Financial information issued with audited financial statements	Issued Sept. 1985
412	Prospectuses and the reporting accountant	Issued Feb. 1986
413	Reliance on other specialists	Issued May 1986
414	Reports to management	Issued Dec. 1986
415	Group financial statements - reliance on the work of other auditors	Issued Dec. 1986
416	Applicability to the public sector of Auditing Standards and Guidelines	Issued July 1987
417	Analytical review	Issued April 1988

418	The auditor's responsibility in relation to fraud, other irregularities and errors	Issued Feb. 1990

Auditing Guidelines - Audit reports

503	Reports by auditors under company legislation in the United Kingdom	Revised Feb. 1991
504	Reports by auditors under company legislation in the Republic of Ireland	Issued June 1989
505	Audit reports and information on the effects of changing prices	Issued Oct. 1989

Exposure drafts

Audit sampling	Issued April 1987
The auditors' statement on the summary financial statement	Issued March 1990
Life insurers in the United Kingdom	Issued Aug. 1990
The auditors responsibility in relation to illegal acts	Issued Oct. 1990
Prospective financial information	Issued Nov. 1990
The Lloyd's market	Issued Feb. 1991
The audit of small businesses	Issued March 1991

Tolley's Companies Legislation

Extracts of accounting provisions

Those sections of, and Schedules to, the Act that are reproduced in full are indicated on the Arrangement of Sections by an asterisk.

The first edition of Tolley's Companies Legislation incorporates all relevant companies legislation (excluding insolvency) up to and including the Companies Act 1989, together with statutory instruments. It not only includes current provisions but also superseded provisions to the extent that these have applied at some time since the Companies Act 1985 came into force. Amending or repealing legislation is both given effect to in the original legislation and referred to in the text of the Act or statutory instrument where it occurs. This includes the Commencement Orders up to and including No 5 (SI 1990 No 713) issued on 23 March 1990.

Free of charge supplements will be issued to subscribers with details of commencement dates of the Companies Act 1989 provisions if these are not known at the time of publication.

TOLLEY PUBLISHING CO. LTD.

Abbreviations

BNA	=	Business Names Act 1985
CA 1989	=	Companies Act 1989
CC(CP)A	=	Companies Consolidation (Consequential Provisions) Act 1985
CDDA	=	Company Directors Disqualification Act 1986
CS(ID)A	=	Company Securities (Insider Dealing) Act 1985
FSA	=	Financial Services Act 1986
FTA	=	Fair Trading Act 1973
Pt	=	Part
Reg	=	Regulation
s	=	Section
Sch	=	Schedule
4 Sch 10	=	4th Schedule, paragraph 10
Sec	=	Section
SI	=	Statutory Instrument

Companies Act 1985

1985 Chapter 6 — Royal Assent 11 March 1985 incorporating Companies Act 1989, Chapter 40 — Royal Assent 16 November 1989

ARRANGEMENT OF SECTIONS

Part III Capital Issues

CHAPTER I ISSUES BY COMPANIES REGISTERED, OR TO BE REGISTERED, IN GREAT BRITAIN

The prospectus

56 Matters to be stated, and reports to be set out, in prospectus.
57 Attempted evasion of s 56 to be void.
58 Document offering shares etc. for sale deemed a prospectus.
59 Rule governing what is an "offer to the public".
60 Exceptions from rule in s 59.
61 Prospectus containing statement by expert.
62 Meaning of "expert".
63 Prospectus to be dated.

Registration of prospectus

64 Registration requirement applicable in all cases.
65 Additional requirements in case of prospectus issued generally.

Liabilities and offences in connection with prospectus

66 Directors, etc. exempt from liability in certain cases.
67 Compensation for subscribers misled by statement in prospectus.
68 Exemption from s 67 for those acting with propriety.
69 Indemnity for innocent director or expert.
70 Criminal liability for untrue statements.

Supplementary

71 Interpretation for ss 56 to 70.

CHAPTER II ISSUES BY COMPANIES INCORPORATED, OR TO BE INCORPORATED, OUTSIDE GREAT BRITAIN

72* Prospectus of oversea company.
73 Attempted evasion of s 72 to be void.
74 Prospectus containing statement by expert.
75 Restrictions on allotment to be secured in prospectus.
76 Stock exchange certificate exempting from compliance with Sch. 3.
77* Registration of oversea prospectus before issue.
78 Consequences (criminal and civil) of non-compliance with ss 72 to 77.
79 Supplementary.

Part IV Allotment of Shares and Debentures

General provisions as to allotment

80 Authority of company required for certain allotments.
80A Election by private company as to duration of authority.
81* Restriction on public offers by private company.
82 Application for, and allotment of, shares and debentures.
83 No allotment unless minimum subscription received.

84 Allotment where issue not fully subscribed.
85 Effect of irregular allotment.
86 Allotment of shares, etc. to be dealt in on stock exchange.
87 Operation of s 86 where prospectus offers shares for sale.
88* Return as to allotments, etc.

Pre-emption rights

89 Offers to shareholders to be on pre-emptive basis.
90 Communication of pre-emption offers to shareholders.
91 Exclusion of ss 89, 90 by private company.
92 Consequences of contravening ss 89, 90.
93 Saving for other restrictions as to offers.
94 Definitions for ss 89-96.
95 Disapplication of pre-emption rights.
96 Saving for company's pre-emption procedure operative before 1982.

Commissions and discounts

97 Power of company to pay commissions.
98 Apart from s 97, commissions and discounts barred.

Amount to be paid for shares; the means of payment

99 General rules as to payment for shares on allotment.
100 Prohibition on allotment of shares at a discount.
101 Shares to be allotted as at least one-quarter paid-up.
102 Restriction on payment by long-term undertaking.
103 Non-cash consideration to be valued before allotment.
104 Transfer to public company of non-cash asset in initial period.
105 Agreements contravening s 104.
106 Shares issued to subscribers of memorandum.
107 Meaning of "the appropriate rate".

Valuation provisions

108 Valuation and report (s 103).
109 Valuation and report (s 104).
110 Entitlement of valuer to full disclosure.
111 Matters to be communicated to registrar.
111A Rights to damages, etc. not affected.

Other matters arising out of allotment, etc.

112 Liability of subsequent holders of shares allotted.
113 Relief in respect of certain liabilities under ss 99 ff.
114 Penalty for contravention.
115 Undertakings to do work, etc.
116 Application of ss 99 ff to special cases.

Part V Share Capital, its Increase, Maintenance and Reduction

CHAPTER I GENERAL PROVISIONS ABOUT SHARE CAPITAL

117 Public company share capital requirements.
118 The authorised minimum.
119 Provision for different amounts to be paid on shares.
120 Reserve liability of limited company.
121* Alteration of share capital (limited companies).
122 Notice to registrar of alteration.
123 Notice to registrar of increased share capital.
124* Reserve capital of unlimited company.

CHAPTER II CLASS RIGHTS

125 Variation of class rights.
126 Saving for court's powers under other provisions.
127 Shareholders' right to object to variation.
128 Registration of particulars of special rights.
129 Registration of newly created class rights.

CHAPTER III SHARE PREMIUMS

130 Application of share premiums.
131 Merger relief.
132 Relief in respect of group reconstructions.
133 Provisions supplementing ss 131, 132.
134 Provision for extending or restricting relief from s 130.

CHAPTER IV REDUCTION OF SHARE CAPITAL

135* Special resolution for reduction of share capital.
136 Application to court for order of confirmation.
137 Court order confirming reduction.
138 Registration of order and minute of reduction.
139 Public company reducing capital below authorised minimum.
140 Liability of members on reduced shares.
141 Penalty for concealing name of creditor, etc.

CHAPTER V MAINTENANCE OF CAPITAL

142 Duty of directors on serious loss of capital.
143* General rule against company acquiring own shares.
144 Acquisition of shares by company's nominee.
145 Exceptions from s 144.
146 Treatment of shares held by or for public company.
147 Matters arising out of compliance with s 146(2).
148 Further provisions supplementing ss 146, 147.
149 Sanctions for non-compliance.
150 Charges of public companies on own shares.

CHAPTER VIII MISCELLANEOUS PROVISIONS ABOUT SHARES AND DEBENTURES

Share and debenture certificates, transfers and warrants

182 Nature, transfer and numbering of shares.
183 Transfer and registration.
184 Certification of transfers.
185 Duty of company as to issue of certificates.
186 Certificate to be evidence of title.
187 Evidence of grant of probate or confirmation as executor.
188 Issue and effect of share warrant to bearer.
189 Offences in connection with share warrants (Scotland).

Debentures

190 Register of debenture holders.
191 Right to inspect register.
192 Liability of trustees of debentures.
193 Perpetual debentures.
194 Power to re-issue redeemed debentures.
195 Contract to subscribe for debentures.
196 Payment of debts out of assets subject to floating charge (England and Wales).
197 Debentures to bearer (Scotland).

Part VI Disclosure of Interests in Shares

Individual and group acquisitions

198 Obligation of disclosure: the cases in which it may arise and "the relevant time".
199 Interests to be disclosed.
200 "Percentage level" in relation to notifiable interests.
201 The notifiable percentage [repealed].
202 Particulars to be contained in notification.
203 Notification of family and corporate interests.
204 Agreement to acquire interests in a particular company.
205 Obligation of disclosure arising under s 204.
206 Obligation of persons acting together to keep each other informed.
207 Interests in shares by attribution.
208 Interests in shares which are to be notified.
209* Interests to be disregarded.
210 Other provisions about notification under this Part.
210A Power to make further provision by regulations.

Registration and investigation of share acquisitions and disposals

211 Register of interests in shares.
212 Company investigations.
213 Registration of interests disclosed under s 212.
214 Company investigation on requisition by members.
215 Company report to members.
216 Penalty for failure to provide information.
217 Removal of entries from register.

240 Requirements in connection with publication of accounts.

Laying and delivering of accounts and reports

241 Accounts and reports to be laid before company in general meeting.
242 Accounts and reports to be delivered to the registrar.
242A Civil penalty for failure to deliver accounts.
243 Accounts of subsidiary undertakings to be appended in certain cases.
244 Period allowed for laying and delivering accounts and reports.

Revision of defective accounts and reports

245 Voluntary revision of annual accounts or directors' report.
245A Secretary of State's notice in respect of annual accounts.
245B Application to court in respect of defective accounts.
245C Other persons authorised to apply to court.

CHAPTER II EXEMPTIONS, EXCEPTIONS AND SPECIAL PROVISIONS

Small and medium-sized companies and groups

246* Exemptions for small and medium-sized companies.
247 Qualification of company as small or medium-sized.
248* Exemption for small and medium-sized groups.
249 Qualification of group as small or medium-sized.

Dormant companies

250* Resolution not to appoint auditors.

Listed public companies

251 Provision of summary financial statement to shareholders.

Private companies

252 Election to dispense with laying of accounts and reports before general meeting.
253 Right of shareholder to require laying of accounts.

Unlimited companies

254* Exemption from requirement to deliver accounts and reports.

Banking and insurance companies and groups

255* Special provisions for banking and insurance companies.
255A* Special provisions for banking and insurance groups.
255B* Modification of disclosure requirements in relation to banking company or group.
255C* Directors' report where accounts prepared in accordance with special provisions.
255D* Power to apply provisions to banking partnerships.

CHAPTER III SUPPLEMENTARY PROVISIONS

Accounting standards

256 Accounting standards.

Power to alter accounting requirements

257 Power of Secretary of State to alter accounting requirements.

Parent and subsidiary undertakings

258 Parent and subsidiary undertakings.

Other interpretation provisions

259* Meaning of "undertaking" and related expressions.
260 Participating interests.
261 Notes to the accounts.
262* Minor definitions.
262A* Index of defined expressions.

Part VIII Distribution of Profits and Assets

Limits of company's power of distribution

263* Certain distributions prohibited.
264* Restriction on distribution of assets.
265* Other distributions by investment companies.
266* Meaning of "investment company".
267* Extension of ss 265, 266 to other companies.
268* Realised profits of insurance company with long term business.
269* Treatment of development costs.

Relevant accounts

270 Distribution to be justified by reference to company's accounts.
271 Requirements for last annual accounts.
272 Requirements for interim accounts.
273 Requirements for initial accounts.
274 Method of applying s 270 to successive distributions.
275 Treatment of assets in the relevant accounts.
276 Distributions in kind.

Supplementary

277 Consequences of unlawful distribution.
278 Saving for provision in articles operative before Act of 1980.
279* Distributions by banking or insurance companies.
280 Definitions for Part VIII.
281 Saving for other restraints on distribution.

Part IX A Company's Management; Directors and Secretaries; their Qualifications, Duties and Responsibilities

Officers and registered office

282 Directors.
283 Secretary.
284 Acts done by person in dual capacity.
285 Validity of acts of directors.
286 Qualifications of company secretaries.
287 Registered office.
288 Register of directors and secretaries.
289 Particulars of directors to be registered under s 288.
290 Particulars of secretaries to be registered under s 288.

Provisions governing appointment of directors

291 Share qualification of directors.
292 Appointment of directors to be voted on individually.
293 Age limit for directors.
294 Duty of director to disclose his age.

Disqualification

295-302 [Repealed].

Removal of directors

303 Resolution to remove director.
304 Director's right to protest removal.

Other provisions about directors and officers

305 Directors' names on company correspondence, etc.
306 Limited company may have directors with unlimited liability.
307 Special resolution making liability of directors unlimited.
308 Assignment of office by directors.
309 Directors to have regard to interests of employees.
310 Provisions exempting officers and auditors from liability.

Part X Enforcement of Fair Dealing by Directors

Restrictions on directors taking financial advantage

311 Prohibition on tax-free payments to directors.
312 Payment to director for loss of office, etc.
313 Company approval for property transfer.
314 Director's duty of disclosure on takeover, etc.
315 Consequences of non-compliance with s 314.
316 Provisions supplementing ss 312-315.
317 Directors to disclose interest in contracts.
318 Directors' service contracts to be open to inspection.
319 Director's contract of employment for more than 5 years.
320 Substantial property transactions involving directors, etc.
321 Exceptions from s 320.

322 Liabilities arising from contravention of s 320.
322A Invalidity of certain transactions involving directors, etc.

Share dealings by directors and their families

323 Prohibition on directors dealing in share options.
324 Duty of director to disclose shareholdings in own company.
325 Register of directors' interests notified under s 324.
326 Sanctions for non-compliance.
327 Extension of s 323 to spouses and children.
328 Extension of s 324 to spouses and children.
329 Duty to notify stock exchange of matters notified under preceding sections.

Restrictions on a company's power to make loans etc. to directors and persons connected with them

330* General restriction on loans etc. to directors and persons connected with them.
331 Definitions for ss 330 ff.
332 Short-term quasi-loans.
333 Inter-company loans in same group.
334 Loans of small amounts.
335 Minor and business transactions.
336 Transactions at behest of holding company.
337 Funding of director's expenditure on duty to company.
338* Loan or quasi-loan by money-lending company.
339* "Relevant amounts" for purposes of ss 334 ff.
340 "Value" of transactions and arrangements.
341 Civil remedies for breach of s 330.
342 Criminal penalties for breach of s 330.
343* Record of transactions not disclosed in company accounts.
344* Exceptions from s 343.

Supplementary

345 Power to increase financial limits.
346 "Connected persons", etc.
347 Transactions under foreign law.

Part XI Company Administration and Procedure

CHAPTER I COMPANY IDENTIFICATION

348 Company name to appear outside place of business.
349 Company's name to appear in its correspondence, etc.
350 Company seal.
351* Particulars in correspondence, etc.

CHAPTER II REGISTER OF MEMBERS

352 Obligation to keep and enter up register.
353 Location of register.
354 Index of members.
355 Entries in register in relation to share warrants.
356 Inspection of register and index.

CHAPTER V AUDITORS

Appointment of auditors

384 Duty to appoint auditors.
385 Appointment at general meeting at which accounts laid.
385A Appointment by private company which is not obliged to lay accounts.
386 Election by private company to dispense with annual appointment.
387 Appointment by Secretary of State in default of appointment by company.
388 Filling of casual vacancy.
388A Dormant company exempt from obligation to appoint auditors.
389 Qualification for appointment as auditors [repealed].

Rights of auditors

389A Rights to information.
390 Right to attend company meetings, etc.

Remuneration of auditors

390A Remuneration of auditors.
390B Remuneration of auditors or their associates for non-audit work.

Removal, resignation, etc. of auditors

391 Removal of auditors.
391A Rights of auditors who are removed or not re-appointed.
392 Resignation of auditors.
392A Rights of resigning auditors.
393 Termination of appointment of auditors not appointed annually.
394 Statement by person ceasing to hold office as auditor.
394A Offences of failing to comply with s 394.

Part XII Registration of Charges

Registration in the companies charges register

395 Introductory provisions.
396 Charges requiring registration.
397 The companies charges register.
398 Company's duty to deliver particulars of charge for registration.
399 Effect of failure to deliver particulars for registration.
400 Late delivery of particulars.
401 Delivery of further particulars.
402 Effect of omissions and errors in registered particulars.
403 Memorandum of charge ceasing to affect company's property.
404 Exclusion of voidness as against unregistered charges.
405 Restrictions on voidness by virtue of this Part.
406 Effect of exercise of power of sale.
407 Effect of voidness on obligation secured.

Additional information to be registered

408 Particulars of taking up of issue of debentures.
409 Notice of appointment of receiver or manager, etc.
410 Notice of crystallisation of floating charge, etc.

445 Power to impose restrictions on shares and debentures.
446 Investigation of share dealings.

Requisition and seizure of books and papers

447 Secretary of State's power to require production of documents.
448 Entry and search of premises.
449* Provision for security of information obtained.
450* Punishment for destroying, mutilating etc. company documents.
451* Punishment for furnishing false information.
451A* Disclosure of information by Secretary of State or inspector.

Supplementary

452* Privileged information.
453* Investigation of oversea companies.

Part XV Orders Imposing Restrictions on Shares (sections 210, 216, 445)

454 Consequence of order imposing restrictions.
455 Punishment for attempted evasion of restrictions.
456 Relaxation and removal of restrictions.
457 Further provisions on sale by court order of restricted shares.

Part XVI Fraudulent Trading by a Company

458 Punishment for fraudulent trading.

Part XVII Protection of Company's Members against Unfair Prejudice

459 Order on application of company member.
460* Order on application of Secretary of State.
461 Provisions as to petitions and orders under this Part.

Part XVIII Floating Charges and Receivers (Scotland)

CHAPTER I FLOATING CHARGES

462 Power of incorporated company to create floating charge.
463 Effect of floating charge on winding up.
464 Ranking of floating charges.
465 Continued effect of certain charges validated by Act of 1972.
466 Alteration of floating charges.

CHAPTER II RECEIVERS

467-485 [Repealed].

CHAPTER III GENERAL

486 Interpretation for Part XVIII generally.
487 Extent of Part XVIII.

Part XIX Receivers and Managers (England and Wales)

488-500 [Repealed].

Part XX Winding Up of Companies Registered under this Act or the former Companies Acts

CHAPTERS I-V

501-650 [Repealed].

CHAPTER VI MATTERS ARISING SUBSEQUENT TO WINDING UP

651 Power of court to declare dissolution of company void.
652 Registrar may strike defunct company off register.
653 Objection to striking off by person aggrieved.
654 Property of dissolved company to be bona vacantia.
655 Effect on s 654 of company's revival after dissolution.
656 Crown disclaimer of property vesting as bona vacantia.
657 Effect of Crown disclaimer under s 656.
658 Liability for rentcharge on company's land after dissolution.

CHAPTER VII

659-664 [Repealed].

Part XXI Winding Up of Unregistered Companies

665-674 [Repealed].

Part XXII Bodies Corporate subject, or becoming subject, to this Act (otherwise than by original formation under Part I)

CHAPTER I COMPANIES FORMED OR REGISTERED UNDER FORMER COMPANIES ACTS

675* Companies formed and registered under former Companies Acts.
676* Companies registered but not formed under former Companies Acts.
677* Companies re-registered with altered status under former Companies Acts.
678* Companies registered under Joint Stock Companies Acts.
679* Northern Ireland and Irish companies.

CHAPTER II COMPANIES NOT FORMED UNDER COMPANIES LEGISLATION, BUT AUTHORISED TO REGISTER

680* Companies capable of being registered under this Chapter.
681* Procedural requirements for registration.
682* Change of name on registration.
683* Definition of "joint stock company".
684* Requirements for registration by joint stock companies.
685* Registration of joint stock company as public company.
686* Other requirements for registration.
687* Name of company registering.
688* Certificate of registration under this Chapter.
689* Effect of registration.

Companies Act 1985

SCHEDULES

1	Particulars of directors etc. to be contained in statement under section 10.
2	Interpretation of references to "beneficial interest".
3	Mandatory contents of prospectus.
4*	Form and content of company accounts (paras 71-73).
4A*	Form and content of group accounts (para 1).
5	Disclosure of information: related undertakings.
6	Disclosure of information: emoluments and other benefits of directors and others.
7	Matters to be dealt with in directors' report.
8	Exemptions for small and medium-sized companies.
9*	Special provisions for banking and insurance companies and groups.
10*	Directors' report where accounts prepared in accordance with special provisions for banking or insurance companies or groups.
10A	Parent and subsidiary undertakings: supplementary provisions.
11*	Modification of Part VIII where company's accounts prepared in accordance with special provisions for banking or insurance companies.
12	Supplementary provisions in connection with disqualification orders [repealed].
13*	Provisions supplementing and interpreting ss 324-328.
14*	Overseas branch registers.
15	Contents of annual return of a company having a share capital [repealed].
15A	Written resolutions of private companies.
15B	Provisions subject to which ss 425-427 have effect in their application to mergers and divisions of public companies.
16-19	[Repealed].
20	Vesting of disclaimed property: protection of third parties.
21*	Effect of registration under section 680.
22*	Provisions of this Act applying to unregistered companies.
23*	Form of statement to be published by certain companies under s 720.
24*	Punishment of offences under this Act.
25	Companies Act 1981, section 38, as originally enacted.

PART I FORMATION AND REGISTRATION OF COMPANIES; JURIDICAL STATUS AND MEMBERSHIP

CHAPTER I COMPANY FORMATION

Memorandum of association

1 Mode of forming incorporated company

(1) Any two or more persons associated for a lawful purpose may, by subscribing their names to a memorandum of association and otherwise complying with the requirements of this Act in respect of registration, form an incorporated company, with or without limited liability.

(2) A company so formed may be either—

(a) a company having the liability of its members limited by the memorandum to the amount, if any, unpaid on the shares respectively held by them ("a company limited by shares");
(b) a company having the liability of its members limited by the memorandum to such amount as the members may respectively thereby undertake to contribute to the assets of the company in the event of its being wound up ("a company limited by guarantee"); or
(c) a company not having any limit on the liability of its members ("an unlimited company").

(3) A "public company" is a company limited by shares or limited by guarantee and having a share capital, being a company—

(a) the memorandum of which states that it is to be a public company, and
(b) in relation to which the provisions of this Act or the former Companies Acts as to the registration or re-registration of a company as a public company have been complied with on or after 22nd December 1980;

and a "private company" is a company that is not a public company.

(4) With effect from 22nd December 1980, a company cannot be formed as, or become, a company limited by guarantee with a share capital.

Cross references. See Sec 15(2) (memorandum and articles of company limited by guarantee).

---

2 Requirements with respect to memorandum

(1) The memorandum of every company must state—

(a) the name of the company;
(b) whether the registered office of the company is to be situated in England and Wales, or in Scotland;
(c) the objects of the company.

(2) Alternatively to subsection (1)(b), the memorandum may contain a statement that the company's registered office is to be situated in Wales; and a company whose registered office is situated in Wales may by special resolution alter its memorandum so as to provide that its registered office is to be so situated.

(3) The memorandum of a company limited by shares or by guarantee must also state that the liability of its members is limited.

(4) The memorandum of a company limited by guarantee must also state that each member undertakes to contribute to the assets of the company if it should be wound up while he is a member, or within one year after he ceases to be a member, for payment of the debts and liabilities of the company contracted before he ceases to be a member, and of the costs, charges and expenses of winding up, and for adjustment of the rights of the contributories among themselves, such amount as may be required, not exceeding a specified amount.

(5) In the case of a company having a share capital—

(a) the memorandum must also (unless it is an unlimited company) state the amount of the share capital with which the company proposes to be registered and the division of the share capital into shares of a fixed amount;
(b) no subscriber of the memorandum may take less than one share; and
(c) there must be shown in the memorandum against the name of each subscriber the number of shares he takes.

(6) The memorandum must be signed by each subscriber in the presence of at least one witness, who must attest the signature; and that attestation is sufficient in Scotland as well as in England and Wales.

(7) A company may not alter the conditions contained in its memorandum except in the cases, in the mode and to the extent, for which express provision is made by this Act.

3 Forms of memorandum

(1) Subject to the provisions of sections 1 and 2, the form of the memorandum of association of—

(a) a public company, being a company limited by shares,
(b) a public company, being a company limited by guarantee and having a share capital,
(c) a private company limited by shares,
(d) a private company limited by guarantee and not having a share capital,
(e) a private company limited by guarantee and having a share capital, and
(f) an unlimited company having a share capital,

shall be as specified respectively for such companies by regulations made by the Secretary of State, or as near to that form as circumstances admit.

(2) Regulations under this section shall be made by statutory instrument subject to annulment in pursuance of a resolution of either House of Parliament.

Regulations. The Companies (Tables A to F) Regulations 1985 (SI 1985 No 805).

Articles of association

7 Articles prescribing regulations for companies

(1) There may in the case of a company limited by shares, and there shall in the case of a company limited by guarantee or unlimited, be registered with the memorandum articles of association signed by the subscribers to the memorandum and prescribing regulations for the company.

(2) In the case of an unlimited company having a share capital, the articles must state the amount of share capital with which the company proposes to be registered.

(3) Articles must—

(a) be printed,
(b) be divided into paragraphs numbered consecutively, and
(c) be signed by each subscriber of the memorandum in the presence of at least one witness who must attest the signature (which attestation is sufficient in Scotland as well as in England and Wales).

8 Tables A, C, D and E

(1) Table A is as prescribed by regulations made by the Secretary of State; and a company may for its articles adopt the whole or any part of that Table.

(2) In the case of a company limited by shares, if articles are not registered or, if articles are registered, in so far as they do not exclude or modify Table A, that Table (so far as applicable, and as in force at the date of the company's registration) constitutes the company's articles, in the same manner and to the same extent as if articles in the form of that Table had been duly registered.

(3) If in consequence of regulations under this section Table A is altered, the alteration does not affect a company registered before the alteration takes effect, or repeal as respects that company any portion of the Table.

(4) The form of the articles of association of—

(a) a company limited by guarantee and not having a share capital,
(b) a company limited by guarantee and having a share capital, and
(c) an unlimited company having a share capital,

shall be respectively in accordance with Table C, D or E prescribed by regulations made by the Secretary of State, or as near to that form as circumstances admit.

(5) Regulations under this section shall be made by statutory instrument subject to annulment in pursuance of a resolution of either House of Parliament.

Regulations. The Companies (Tables A to F) Regulations 1985 (SI 1985 No 805).

[8A Table G

(1) The Secretary of State may by regulations prescribe a Table G containing articles of association appropriate for a partnership company, that is, a company limited by shares whose shares are intended to be held to a substantial extent by or on behalf of its employees.

(2) A company limited by shares may for its articles adopt the whole or any part of that Table.

(3) If in consequence of regulations under this section Table G is altered, the alteration does not affect a company registered before the alteration takes effect, or repeal as respects that company any portion of the Table.

(4) Regulations under this section shall be made by statutory instrument which shall be subject to annulment in pursuance of a resolution of either House of Parliament.][1]

---

1 Inserted by CA 1989, s 128 with effect from a date to be appointed.

Registration and its consequences

15 Memorandum and articles of company limited by guarantee

(1) In the case of a company limited by guarantee and not having a share capital, every provision in the memorandum or articles, or in any resolution of the company purporting to give any person a right to participate in the divisible profits of the company otherwise than as a member, is void.

(2) For purposes of provisions of this Act relating to the memorandum of a company limited by guarantee, and for those of section 1(4) and this section, every provision in the memorandum or articles, or in any resolution, of a company so limited purporting to divide the company's undertaking into shares or interests is to be treated as a provision for a share capital, notwithstanding that the nominal amount or number of the shares or interests is not specified by the provision.

Cross references. See CC(CP)A 1985, s 10 (pre-1901 companies).

CHAPTER II COMPANY NAMES

25 Name as stated in memorandum

(1) The name of a public company must end with the words "public limited company" or, if the memorandum states that the company's registered office is to be situated in Wales, those words or their equivalent in Welsh ("cwmni cyfyngedig cyhoeddus"); and those words or that equivalent may not be preceded by the word "limited" or its equivalent in Welsh ("cyfyngedig").

(2) In the case of a company limited by shares or by guarantee (not being a public company), the name must have "limited" as its last word, except that—

(a) this is subject to section 30 (exempting, in certain circumstances, a company from the requirement to have "limited" as part of the name), and

(b) if the company is to be registered with a memorandum stating that its registered office is to be situated in Wales, the name may have "cyfyngedig" as its last word.

30 Exemption from requirement of "limited" as part of the name

(1) Certain companies are exempt from requirements of this Act relating to the use of "limited" as part of the company name.

(2) A private company limited by guarantee is exempt from those requirements, and so too is a company which on 25th February 1982 was a private company limited by shares with a name which, by virtue of a licence under section 19 of the Companies Act 1948, did not include "limited"; but in either case the company must, to have the exemption, comply with the requirements of the following subsection.

(3) Those requirements are that—

(a) the objects of the company are (or, in the case of a company about to be registered, are to be) the promotion of commerce, art, science, education, religion, charity or any profession, and anything incidental or conducive to any of those objects; and

(b) the company's memorandum or articles—

(i) require its profits (if any) or other income to be applied in promoting its objects,

(ii) prohibit the payment of dividends to its members, and

(iii) require all the assets which would otherwise be available to its members generally to be transferred on its winding up either to another body with objects similar to its own or to another body the objects of which are the promotion of charity and anything incidental or conducive thereto (whether or not the body is a member of the company).

(4) A statutory declaration that a company complies with the requirements of subsection (3) may be delivered to the registrar of companies, who may accept the declaration as sufficient evidence of the matters stated in it; and the registrar may refuse to register a company by a name which does not include the word "limited" unless such a declaration has been delivered to him.

(5) The statutory declaration must be in the prescribed form and be made—

(a) in the case of a company to be formed, by a solicitor engaged in its formation or by a person named as director or secretary in the statement delivered under section 10(2);

(b) in the case of a company to be registered in pursuance of section 680, by two or more directors or other principal officers of the company; and

(c) in the case of a company proposing to change its name so that it ceases to have the word "limited" as part of its name, by a director or secretary of the company.

(6) References in this section to the word "limited" include (in an appropriate case) its Welsh equivalent ("cyfyngedig"), and the appropriate alternative ("ltd." or "cyf.", as the case may be).

(7) A company which is exempt from requirements relating to the use of "limited" and does not include that word as part of its name, is also exempt from the requirements of this Act relating to the publication of its name and the sending of lists of members to the registrar of companies.

Cross references. See Sec 31.

31 Provisions applying to company exempt under s 30

(1) A company which is exempt under section 30 and whose name does not include "limited" shall not alter its memorandum or articles of association so that it ceases to comply with the requirements of subsection (3) of that section.

(2) If it appears to the Secretary of State that such a company—

(a) has carried on any business other than the promotion of any of the objects mentioned in that subsection, or

(b) has applied any of its profits or other income otherwise than in promoting such objects, or

(c) has paid a dividend to any of its members,

he may, in writing, direct the company to change its name by resolution of the directors within such period as may be specified in the direction, so that its name ends with "limited".

A resolution passed by the directors in compliance with a direction under this subsection is subject to section 380 of this Act (copy to be forwarded to the registrar of companies within 15 days).

(3) A company which has received a direction under subsection (2) shall not thereafter be registered by a name which does not include "limited", without the approval of the Secretary of State.

(4) References in this section to the word "limited" include (in an appropriate case) its Welsh equivalent ("cyfyngedig"), and the appropriate alternative ("ltd." or "cyf.", as the case may be).

(5) A company which contravenes subsection (1), and any officer of it who is in default, is liable to a fine and, for continued contravention, to a daily default fine.

(6) A company which fails to comply with a direction by the Secretary of State under subsection (2), and any officer of the company who is in default, is liable to a fine and, for continued contravention, to a daily default fine.

Cross references. See 24 Sch (punishment of offences).

CHAPTER III A COMPANY'S CAPACITY; FORMALITIES OF CARRYING ON BUSINESS

[35 A company's capacity not limited by its memorandum

(1) The validity of an act done by a company shall not be called into question on the ground of lack of capacity by reason of anything in the company's memorandum.

(2) A member of a company may bring proceedings to restrain the doing of an act which but for subsection (1) would be beyond the company's capacity; but no such proceedings shall lie in respect of an act to be done in fulfilment of a legal obligation arising from a previous act of the company.

(3) It remains the duty of the directors to observe any limitations on their powers flowing from the company's memorandum; and action by the directors which but for subsection (1) would be beyond the company's capacity may only be ratified by the company by special resolution.

A resolution ratifying such action shall not affect any liability incurred by the directors or any other person; relief from any such liability must be agreed to separately by special resolution.

(4) The operation of this section is restricted by section 30B(1) of the Charities Act 1960 and section 112(3) of the Companies Act 1989 in relation to companies which are charities; and section 322A below (invalidity of certain transactions to which directors or their associates are parties) has effect notwithstanding this section.][1]

---

1 Substituted by CA 1989, s 108 with effect from a date to be appointed.

Cross references. See also Secs 35A and 35B for revised provisions applying after the substitution made by CA 1989, s 108; CA 1989, s 112 (charitable companies (Scotland)).

[35A Power of directors to bind the company

(1) In favour of a person dealing with a company in good faith, the power of the board of directors to bind the company, or authorise others to do so, shall be deemed to be free of any limitation under the company's constitution.

(2) For this purpose—

(a) a person "deals with" a company if he is a party to any transaction or other act to which the company is a party;
(b) a person shall not be regarded as acting in bad faith by reason only of his knowing that an act is beyond the powers of the directors under the company's constitution; and
(c) a person shall be presumed to have acted in good faith unless the contrary is proved.

(3) The references above to limitations on the directors' powers under the company's constitution include limitations deriving—

(a) from a resolution of the company in general meeting or a meeting of any class of shareholders, or
(b) from any agreement between the members of the company or of any class of shareholders.

(4) Subsection (1) does not affect any right of a member of the company to bring proceedings to restrain the doing of an act which is beyond the powers of the directors; but no such proceedings shall lie in respect of an act to be done in fulfilment of a legal obligation arising from a previous act of the company.

(5) Nor does that subsection affect any liability incurred by the directors, or any other person, by reason of the directors' exceeding their powers.

(6) The operation of this section is restricted by section 30B(1) of the Charities Act 1960 and section 112(3) of the Companies Act 1989 in relation to companies which are charities; and section 322A below (invalidity of certain transactions to which directors or their associates are parties) has effect notwithstanding this section.][1]

---

1 Inserted by CA 1989, s 108 with effect from a date to be appointed.

Cross references. See Sec 35 above for provisions applying before Sec 35A inserted; Sec 322A (invalidity of certain transactions involving directors); CA 1989, s 112(3) (charitable companies (Scotland)).

[35B No duty to enquire as to capacity of company or authority of directors

A party to a transaction with a company is not bound to enquire as to whether it is permitted by the company's memorandum or as to any limitation on the powers of the board of directors to bind the company or authorise others to do so.][1]

---

1 Inserted by CA 1989, s 108 with effect from a date to be appointed.

Cross references. See Sec 35 above for provisions applying before Sec 35B inserted.

PART II RE-REGISTRATION AS A MEANS OF ALTERING A COMPANY'S STATUS

Private company becoming public

43 Re-registration of private company as public

(1) Subject to this and the following five sections, a private company (other than a company not having a share capital) may be re-registered as a public company if—

(a) a special resolution that it should be so re-registered is passed; and
(b) an application for re-registration is delivered to the registrar of companies, together with the necessary documents.

A company cannot be re-registered under this section if it has previously been re-registered as unlimited.

(2) The special resolution must—

(a) alter the company's memorandum so that it states that the company is to be a public company; and
(b) make such other alterations in the memorandum as are necessary to bring it (in substance and in form) into conformity with the requirements of this Act with respect to the memorandum of a public company (the alterations to include compliance with section 25(1) as regards the company's name); and
(c) make such alterations in the company's articles as are requisite in the circumstances.

(3) The application must be in the prescribed form and be signed by a director or secretary of the company; and the documents to be delivered with it are the following—

(a) a printed copy of the memorandum and articles as altered in pursuance of the resolution;
(b) a copy of a written statement by the company's auditors that in their opinion the relevant balance sheet shows that at the balance sheet date the amount of the company's net assets (within the meaning given to that expression by section 264(2)) was not less than the aggregate of its called-up share capital and undistributable reserves;
(c) a copy of the relevant balance sheet, together with a copy of an unqualified report (defined in section 46) by the company's auditors in relation to that balance sheet;
(d) if section 44 applies, a copy of the valuation report under subsection (2)(b) of that section; and
(e) a statutory declaration in the prescribed form by a director or secretary of the company—
  (i) that the special resolution required by this section has been passed and that the conditions of the following two sections (so far as applicable) have been satisfied, and
  (ii) that, between the balance sheet date and the application for re-registration, there has been no change in the company's financial position that has resulted in the amount of its net assets becoming less than the aggregate of its called-up share capital and undistributable reserves.

(4) "Relevant balance sheet" means a balance sheet prepared as at a date not more than 7 months before the company's application under this section.

(5) A resolution that a company be re-registered as a public company may change the company name by deleting the word "company" or the words "and company", or its or their equivalent in Welsh ("cwmni", "a'r cwmni"), including any abbreviation of them.

48 Modification for unlimited company re-registering

(1) In their application to unlimited companies, sections 43 to 47 are modified as follows.

(2) The special resolution required by section 43(1) must, in addition to the matters mentioned in subsection (2) of that section—

(a) state that the liability of the members is to be limited by shares, and what the company's share capital is to be; and

(b) make such alterations in the company's memorandum as are necessary to bring it in substance and in form into conformity with the requirements of this Act with respect to the memorandum of a company limited by shares.

(3) The certificate of incorporation issued under section 47(1) shall, in addition to containing the statement required by paragraph (b) of that subsection, state that the company has been incorporated as a company limited by shares; and—

(a) the company by virtue of the issue of the certificate becomes a public company so limited; and

(b) the certificate is conclusive evidence of the fact that it is such a company.

Limited company becoming unlimited

49 Re-registration of limited company as unlimited

(1) Subject as follows, a company which is registered as limited may be re-registered as unlimited in pursuance of an application in that behalf complying with the requirements of this section.

(2) A company is excluded from re-registering under this section if it is limited by virtue of re-registration under section 44 of the Companies Act 1967 or section 51 of this Act.

(3) A public company cannot be re-registered under this section; nor can a company which has previously been re-registered as unlimited.

(4) An application under this section must be in the prescribed form and be signed by a director or the secretary of the company, and be lodged with the registrar of companies, together with the documents specified in subsection (8) below.

(5) The application must set out such alterations in the company's memorandum as—

(a) if it is to have a share capital, are requisite to bring it (in substance and in form) into conformity with the requirements of this Act with respect to the memorandum of a company to be formed as an unlimited company having a share capital; or

(b) if it is not to have a share capital, are requisite in the circumstances.

(6) If articles have been registered, the application must set out such alterations in them as—

(a) if the company is to have a share capital, are requisite to bring the articles (in substance and in form) into conformity with the requirements of this Act with respect to the articles of a company to be formed as an unlimited company having a share capital; or
(b) if the company is not to have a share capital, are requisite in the circumstances.

(7) If articles have not been registered, the application must have annexed to it, and request the registration of, printed articles; and these must, if the company is to have a share capital, comply with the requirements mentioned in subsection (6)(a) and, if not, be articles appropriate to the circumstances.

(8) The documents to be lodged with the registrar are—

(a) the prescribed form of assent to the company's being registered as unlimited, subscribed by or on behalf of all the members of the company;
(b) a statutory declaration made by the directors of the company—
 (i) that the persons by whom or on whose behalf the form of assent is subscribed constitute the whole membership of the company, and
 (ii) if any of the members have not subscribed that form themselves, that the directors have taken all reasonable steps to satisfy themselves that each person who subscribed it on behalf of a member was lawfully empowered to do so;
(c) a printed copy of the memorandum incorporating the alterations in it set out in the application; and
(d) if articles have been registered, a printed copy of them incorporating the alterations set out in the application.

(9) For purposes of this section—

(a) subscription to a form of assent by the legal personal representative of a deceased member of a company is deemed subscription by him; and
(b) a trustee in bankruptcy of a member of a company is, to the exclusion of the latter, deemed a member of the company.

50 Certificate of re-registration under s 49

(1) The registrar of companies shall retain the application and other documents lodged with him under section 49 and shall—

(a) if articles are annexed to the application, register them; and
(b) issue to the company a certificate of incorporation appropriate to the status to be assumed by it by virtue of that section.

(2) On the issue of the certificate—

(a) the status of the company, by virtue of the issue, is changed from limited to unlimited; and
(b) the alterations in the memorandum set out in the application and (if articles have been previously registered) any alterations to the articles so set out take effect as if duly made by resolution of the company; and
(c) the provisions of this Act apply accordingly to the memorandum and articles as altered.

(3) The certificate is conclusive evidence that the requirements of section 49 in respect of re-registration and of matters precedent and incidental to it have been complied with, and that the company was authorised to be re-registered under this Act in pursuance of that section and was duly so re-registered.

Unlimited company becoming limited

51 Re-registration of unlimited company as limited

(1) Subject as follows, a company which is registered as unlimited may be re-registered as limited if a special resolution that it should be so re-registered is passed, and the requirements of this section are complied with in respect of the resolution and otherwise.

(2) A company cannot under this section be re-registered as a public company; and a company is excluded from re-registering under it if it is unlimited by virtue of re-registration under section 43 of the Companies Act 1967 or section 49 of this Act.

(3) The special resolution must state whether the company is to be limited by shares or by guarantee and—

(a) if it is to be limited by shares, must state what the share capital is to be and provide for the making of such alterations in the memorandum as are necessary to bring it (in substance and in form) into conformity with the requirements of this Act with respect to the memorandum of a company so limited, and such alterations in the articles as are requisite in the circumstances;

(b) if it is to be limited by guarantee, must provide for the making of such alterations in its memorandum and articles as are necessary to bring them (in substance and in form) into conformity with the requirements of this Act with respect to the memorandum and articles of a company so limited.

(4) The special resolution is subject to section 380 of this Act (copy to be forwarded to registrar within 15 days); and an application for the company to be re-registered as limited, framed in the prescribed form and signed by a director or by the secretary of the company, must be lodged with the registrar of companies, together with the necessary documents, not earlier than the day on which the copy of the resolution forwarded under section 380 is received by him.

(5) The documents to be lodged with the registrar are—

(a) a printed copy of the memorandum as altered in pursuance of the resolution; and

(b) a printed copy of the articles as so altered.

(6) This section does not apply in relation to the re-registration of an unlimited company as a public company under section 43.

52 Certification of re-registration under s 51

(1) The registrar shall retain the application and other documents lodged with him under section 51, and shall issue to the company a certificate of incorporation appropriate to the status to be assumed by the company by virtue of that section.

(2) On the issue of the certificate—

(a) the status of the company is, by virtue of the issue, changed from unlimited to limited; and

(b) the alterations in the memorandum specified in the resolution and the alterations in, and additions to, the articles so specified take effect.

(3) The certificate is conclusive evidence that the requirements of section 51 in respect of re-registration and of matters precedent and incidental to it have been complied with, and that the company was authorised to be re-registered in pursuance of that section and was duly so re-registered.

Public company becoming private

53 Re-registration of public company as private

(1) A public company may be re-registered as a private company if—

(a) a special resolution complying with subsection (2) below that it should be so re-registered is passed and has not been cancelled by the court under the following section;

(b) an application for the purpose in the prescribed form and signed by a director or the secretary of the company is delivered to the registrar of companies, together with a printed copy of the memorandum and articles of the company as altered by the resolution; and

(c) the period during which an application for the cancellation of the resolution under the following section may be made has expired without any such application having been made; or

(d) where such an application has been made, the application has been withdrawn or an order has been made under section 54(5) confirming the resolution and a copy of that order has been delivered to the registrar.

(2) The special resolution must alter the company's memorandum so that it no longer states that the company is to be a public company and must make such other alterations in the company's memorandum and articles as are requisite in the circumstances.

(3) A company cannot under this section be re-registered otherwise than as a company limited by shares or by guarantee.

54 Litigated objection to resolution under s 53

(1) Where a special resolution by a public company to be re-registered under section 53 as a private company has been passed, an application may be made to the court for the cancellation of that resolution.

(2) The application may be made—

(a) by the holders of not less in the aggregate than 5 per cent. in nominal value of the company's issued share captial or any class thereof;

(b) if the company is not limited by shares, by not less than 5 per cent. of its members; or

(c) by not less than 50 of the company's members;

but not by a person who has consented to or voted in favour of the resolution.

(3) The application must be made within 28 days after the passing of the resolution and may be made on behalf of the persons entitled to make the application by such one or more of their number as they may appoint in writing for the purpose.

(4) If such an application is made, the company shall forthwith give notice in the prescribed form of that fact to the registrar of companies.

(5) On the hearing of the application, the court shall make an order either cancelling or confirming the resolution and—

(a) may make that order on such terms and conditions as it thinks fit, and may (if it thinks fit) adjourn the proceedings in order that an agreement may be made to the satisfaction of the court for the purchase of the interests of dissentient members; and
(b) may give such directions and make such orders as it thinks expedient for facilitating or carrying into effect any such arrangement.

(6) The court's order may, if the court thinks fit, provide for the purchase by the company of the shares of any of its members and for the reduction accordingly of the company's capital, and may make such alterations in the company's memorandum and articles as may be required in consequence of that provision.

(7) The company shall, within 15 days from the making of the court's order, or within such longer period as the court may at any time by order direct, deliver to the registrar of companies an office copy of the order.

(8) If the court's order requires the company not to make any, or any specified, alteration in its memorandum or articles, the company has not then power without the leave of the court to make any such alteration in breach of the requirement.

(9) An alteration in the memorandum or articles made by virtue of an order under this section, if not made by resolution of the company, is of the same effect as if duly made by resolution; and this Act applies accordingly to the memorandum of articles as so altered.

(10) A company which fails to comply with subsection (4) or subsection (7), and any officer of it who is in default, is liable to a fine and, for continued contravention, to a daily default fine.

Cross references. See 24 Sch (punishment of offences).

---

55 Certification of re-registration under s 53

(1) If the registrar of companies is satisfied that a company may be re-registered under section 53, he shall—

(a) retain the application and other documents delivered to him under that section; and
(b) issue the company with a certificate of incorporation appropriate to a private company.

(2) On the issue of the certificate—

(a) the company by virtue of the issue becomes a private company; and
(b) the alterations in the memorandum and articles set out in the resolution under section 53 take effect accordingly.

(3) The certificate is conclusive evidence—

(a) that the requirements of section 53 in respect of re-registration and of matters precedent and incidental to it have been complied with; and
(b) that the company is a private company.

PART III CAPITAL ISSUES

CHAPTER II ISSUES BY COMPANIES INCORPORATED, OR TO BE INCORPORATED, OUTSIDE GREAT BRITAIN

72 Prospectus of oversea company

(1) It is unlawful for a person to issue, circulate or distribute in Great Britain any prospectus offering for subscription shares in or debentures of a company incorporated or to be incorporated outside Great Britain (whether the company has or has not established, or when formed will or will not establish, a place of business in Great Britain) unless the prospectus complies with the requirements of the next two subsections.

(2) The prospectus must be dated and contain particulars with respect to the following matters—

(a) the instrument constituting or defining the constitution of the company;
(b) the enactments, or provisions having the force of an enactment, by or under which the incorporation of the company was effected;
(c) an address in Great Britain where that instrument, and those enactments or provisions, or copies of them (and, if they are in a foreign language, a translation of them certified in the prescribed manner), can be inspected;
(d) the date on which, and the country in which, the company was incorporated; and
(e) whether the company has established a place of business in Great Britain and, if so, the address of its principal office in Great Britain.

(3) Subject to the following provisions, the prospectus must comply—

(a) with Part I of Schedule 3, as respects the matters to be stated in the prospectus, and
(b) with Part II of that Schedule, as respects the reports to be set out.

(4) Paragraphs (a) to (c) of subsection (2) do not apply in the case of a prospectus issued more than 2 years after the company is entitled to commence business.

(5) It is unlawful for a person to issue to any person in Great Britain a form of application for shares in or debentures of such a company or intended company as is mentioned in subsection (1) unless the form is issued with a prospectus which complies with this Chapter and the issue of which in Great Britain does not contravene section 74 or 75 below.

This subsection does not apply if it is shown that the form of application was issued in connection with a bona fide invitation to a person to enter into an underwriting agreement with respect to the shares or debentures.

(6) This section—

(a) does not apply to the issue to a company's existing members or debenture holders of a prospectus or form of application relating to shares in or debentures of the company, whether an applicant for shares or debentures will or will not have the right to renounce in favour of other persons; and
(b) except in so far as it requires a prospectus to be dated, does not apply to the issue of a prospectus relating to shares or debentures which are or are to be in all respects uniform with shares or debentures previously issued and for the time being listed on a prescribed stock exchange;

but subject to this, it applies to a prospectus or form of application whether issued on or with reference to the formation of a company or subsequently.

77 Registration of oversea prospectus before issue

(1) It is unlawful for a person to issue, circulate or distribute in Great Britain a prospectus offering for subscription shares in or debentures of a company incorporated or to be incorporated outside Great Britain (whether the company has or has not established, or when formed will or will not establish, a place of business in Great Britain), unless before the issue, circulation or distribution the requirements of this section have been complied with.

(2) A copy of the prospectus, certified by the chairman and two other directors of the company as having been approved by resolution of the managing body, must have been delivered for registration to the registrar of companies.

(3) The prospectus must state on the face of it that a copy has been so delivered to the registrar of companies; and the following must be endorsed on or attached to that copy of the prospectus—

(a) any consent to the issue of the prospectus which is required by section 74;

(b) a copy of any contract required by paragraph 11 of Schedule 3 to be stated in the prospectus or, in the case of a contract not reduced into writing, a memorandum giving full particulars of it; and

(c) where the persons making any report required by Part II of Schedule 3 have made in it or have, without giving the reasons, indicated in it any such adjustments as are mentioned in paragraph 21 of the Schedule, a written statement signed by those persons setting out the adjustments and giving the reasons for them.

(4) If in the case of a prospectus deemed by virtue of a certificate under section 76 to comply with Schedule 3, a contract or a copy of it, or a memorandum of a contract, is required to be available for inspection in connection with application under that section to the stock exchange, a copy or (as the case may be) a memorandum of the contract must be endorsed on or attached to the copy of the prospectus delivered to the registrar for registration.

(5) References in subsections (3)(b) and (4) to the copy of a contract are, in the case of a contract wholly or partly in a foreign language, to a copy of a translation of the contract into English, or a copy embodying a translation into English of the parts in a foreign language (as the case may be); and—

(a) the translation must in either case be certified in the prescribed manner to be a correct translation, and

(b) the reference in subsection (4) to a copy of a contract required to be available for inspection includes a copy of a translation of it or a copy embodying a translation of parts of it.

PART IV ALLOTMENT OF SHARES AND DEBENTURES

General provisions as to allotment

81 Restriction on public offers by private company

(1) A private limited company (other than a company limited by guarantee and not having a share capital) commits an offence if it—

(a) offers to the public (whether for cash or otherwise) any shares in or debentures of the company; or

(b) allots or agrees to allot (whether for cash or otherwise) any shares in or debentures of the company with a view to all or any of those shares or debentures being offered for sale to the public (within the meaning given to that expression by sections 58 to 60).

(2) A company guilty of an offence under this section, and any officer of it who is in default, is liable to a fine.

(3) Nothing in this section affects the validity of any allotment or sale of shares or debentures, or of any agreement to allot or sell shares or debentures.

Notes

(a) Companies Act 1985, ss 81-83, 86, 87 are repealed by FSA 1986, s 212(3), 17 Sch Part I from a date or dates to be appointed by statutory instrument (see FSA 1986, s 211(1)).
To date the provisions have been repealed as follows.

(i) To the extent to which they would apply in relation to any investment which is listed or the subject of an application for listing in accordance with FSA 1986, Part IV (official listing of securities)

(A) with effect from 12 January 1987 for all purposes relating to the admission of securities offered by or on behalf of a Minister of the Crown or a body corporate controlled by a Minister of the Crown or a subsidiary of such a body to the Official List in respect of which an application is made after that date; and

(B) with effect from 16 February 1987 for purposes relating to the admission of securities in respect of which an application is made after that date other than those referred to in (A) above and otherwise for all purposes.

[SI 1986 No 2246].

(ii) With effect from 29 April 1988 in respect of a prospectus offering for subscription, or to any form of application for, units in a body corporate which is a recognised scheme. [SI 1988 No 740].

Cross references. See 24 Sch (punishment of offences); CC(CP)A 1985, s 7.

---

88 Return as to allotments, etc.

(1) This section applies to a company limited by shares and to a company limited by guarantee and having a share capital.

(2) When such a company makes an allotment of its shares, the company shall within one month thereafter deliver to the registrar of companies for registration—

(a) a return of the allotments (in the prescribed form) stating the number and nominal amount of the shares comprised in the allotment, the names and addresses of the allottees, and the amount (if any) paid or due and payable on each share, whether on account of the nominal value of the share or by way of premium; and

(b) in the case of shares allotted as fully or partly paid up otherwise than in cash—

(i) a contract in writing constituting the title of the allottee to the allotment together with any contract of sale, or for services or other consideration in respect of which that allotment was made (such contracts being duly stamped), and

(ii) a return stating the number and nominal amount of shares so allotted, the extent to which they are to be treated as paid up, and the consideration for which they have been allotted.

(3) Where such a contract as above mentioned is not reduced to writing, the company shall within one month after the allotment deliver to the registrar of companies for registration the prescribed particulars of the contract stamped with the same stamp duty as would have been payable if the contract had been reduced to writing.

(4) Those particulars are deemed an instrument within the meaning of the Stamp Act 1891; and the registrar may, as a condition of filing the particulars, require that the duty payable on them be adjudicated under section 12 of that Act.

(5) If default is made in complying with this section, every officer of the company who is in default is liable to a fine and, for continued contravention, to a daily default fine, but subject as follows.

(6) In the case of default in delivering to the registrar within one month after the allotment any document required by this section to be delivered, the company, or any officer liable for the default, may apply to the court for relief; and the court, if satisfied that the omission to deliver the document was accidental or due to inadvertence, or that it is just and equitable to grant relief, may make an order extending the time for the delivery of the document for such period as the court thinks proper.

Cross references. See 24 Sch (punishment of offences).

PART V SHARE CAPITAL, ITS INCREASE, MAINTENANCE AND REDUCTION

CHAPTER I GENERAL PROVISIONS ABOUT SHARE CAPITAL

121 Alteration of share capital (limited companies)

(1) A company limited by shares or a company limited by guarantee and having a share capital, if so authorised by its articles, may alter the conditions of its memorandum in any of the following ways.

(2) The company may—

(a) increase its share capital by new shares of such amount as it thinks expedient;

(b) consolidate and divide all or any of its share capital into shares of larger amount than its existing shares;

(c) convert all or any of its paid-up shares into stock, and re-convert that stock into paid-up shares of any denomination;

(d) sub-divide its shares, or any of them, into shares of smaller amount than is fixed by the memorandum (but subject to the following subsection);

(e) cancel shares which, at the date of the passing of the resolution to cancel them, have not been taken or agreed to be taken by any person, and diminish the amount of the company's share capital by the amount of the shares so cancelled.

(3) In any sub-division under subsection (2)(d) the proportion between the amount paid and the amount, if any, unpaid on each reduced share must be the same as it was in the case of the share from which the reduced share is derived.

(4) The powers conferred by this section must be exercised by the company in general meeting.

(5) A cancellation of shares under this section does not for purposes of this Act constitute a reduction of share capital.

124 Reserve capital of unlimited company

An unlimited company having a share capital may by its resolution for re-registration as a public company under section 43, or as a limited company under section 51—

(a) increase the nominal amount of its share capital by increasing the nominal amount of each of its shares (but subject to the condition that no part of the increased capital is to be capable of being called up except in the event and for the purpose of the company being wound up), and

(b) alternatively or in addition, provide that a specified portion of its uncalled share capital is not to be capable of being called up except in that event and for that purpose.

CHAPTER IV REDUCTION OF SHARE CAPITAL

135 Special resolution for reduction of share capital

(1) Subject to confirmation by the court, a company limited by shares or a company limited by guarantee and having a share capital may, if so authorised by its articles, by special resolution reduce its share capital in any way.

(2) In particular, and without prejudice to subsection (1), the company may—

(a) extinguish or reduce the liability on any of its shares in respect of share capital not paid up; or

(b) either with or without extinguishing or reducing liability on any of its shares, cancel any paid-up share capital which is lost or unrepresented by available assets; or

(c) either with or without extinguishing or reducing liability on any of its shares, pay off any paid-up share capital which is in excess of the company's wants;

and the company may, if and so far as is necessary, alter its memorandum by reducing the amount of its share capital and of its shares accordingly.

(3) A special resolution under this section is in this Act referred to as "a resolution for reducing share capital".

CHAPTER V MAINTENANCE OF CAPITAL

143 General rule against company acquiring own shares

(1) Subject to the following provisions, a company limited by shares or limited by guarantee and having a share capital shall not acquire its own shares, whether by purchase, subscription or otherwise.

(2) If a company purports to act in contravention of this section, the company is liable to a fine, and every officer of the company who is in default is liable to imprisonment or a fine, or both; and the purported acquisition is void.

(3) A company limited by shares may acquire any of its own fully paid shares otherwise than for valuable consideration; and subsection (1) does not apply in relation to—

(a) the redemption or purchase of shares in accordance with Chapter VII of this Part,
(b) the acquisition of shares in a reduction of capital duly made,
(c) the purchase of shares in pursuance of an order of the court under section 5 (alteration of objects), section 54 (litigated objection to resolution for company to be re-registered as private) or Part XVII (relief to members unfairly prejudiced), or
(d) the forfeiture of shares, or the acceptance of shares surrendered in lieu, in pursuance of the articles, for failure to pay any sum payable in respect of the shares.

Cross references. See 24 Sch (punishment of offences).

CHAPTER VII REDEEMABLE SHARES; PURCHASE BY A COMPANY OF ITS OWN SHARES

Redemption and purchase generally

159 Power to issue redeemable shares

(1) Subject to the provisions of this Chapter, a company limited by shares or limited by guarantee and having a share capital may, if authorised to do so by its articles, issue shares which are to be redeemed or are liable to be redeemed at the option of the company or the shareholder.

(2) No redeemable shares may be issued at a time when there are no issued shares of the company which are not redeemable.

(3) Redeemable shares may not be redeemed unless they are fully paid; and the terms of redemption must provide for payment on redemption.

162 Power of company to purchase own shares

(1) Subject to the following provisions of this Chapter, a company limited by shares or limited by guarantee and having a share capital may, if authorised to do so by its articles, purchase its own shares (including any redeemable shares).

(2) [Sections 159, 160 and 161 apply to the purchase by a company under this section of its own shares as they apply to the redemption of redeemable shares.][1]

(3) A company may not under this section purchase its shares if as a result of the purchase there would no longer be any member of the company holding shares other than redeemable shares.

---

1 Substituted by CA 1989, s 133 with effect from a date to be appointed.

Cross references. See Sec 171 (private companies).

Redemption or purchase of own shares out of capital (private companies only)

171 Power of private companies to redeem or purchase own shares out of capital

(1) Subject to the following provisions of this Chapter, a private company limited by shares or limited by guarantee and having a share capital may, if so authorised by its articles, make a payment in respect of the redemption or purchase under section 160 or (as the case may be) section 162, of its own shares otherwise than out of its distributable profits or the proceeds of a fresh issue of shares.

(2) References below in this Chapter to payment out of capital are (subject to subsection (6)) to any payment so made, whether or not it would be regarded apart from this section as a payment out of capital.

(3) The payment which may (if authorised in accordance with the following provisions of this Chapter) be made by a company out of capital in respect of the redemption or purchase of its own shares is such an amount as, taken together with—

(a) any available profits of the company, and
(b) the proceeds of any fresh issue of shares made for the purposes of the redemption or purchase,

is equal to the price of redemption or purchase; and the payment permissible under this subsection is referred to below in this Chapter as the permissible capital payment for the shares.

(4) Subject to subsection (6), if the permissible capital payment for shares redeemed or purchased is less than their nominal amount, the amount of the difference shall be transferred to the company's capital redemption reserve.

(5) Subject to subsection (6), if the permissible capital payment is greater than the nominal amount of the shares redeemed or purchased—

(a) the amount of any capital redemption reserve, share premium account or fully paid share capital of the company, and

(b) any amount representing unrealised profits of the company for the time being standing to the credit of any reserve maintained by the company in accordance with paragraph 34 of Schedule 4 (revaluation reserve),

may be reduced by a sum not exceeding (or by sums not in the aggregate exceeding) the amount by which the permissible capital payment exceeds the nominal amount of the shares.

(6) Where the proceeds of a fresh issue are applied by a company in making any redemption or purchase of its own shares in addition to a payment out of capital under this section, the references in subsections (4) and (5) to the permissible capital payment are to be read as referring to the aggregate of that payment and those proceeds.

Cross references. See Sec 172(1); Sec 179(2) (power of Secretary of State to modify provisions).

CHAPTER VIII MISCELLANEOUS PROVISIONS ABOUT SHARES AND DEBENTURES

PART VI DISCLOSURE OF INTERESTS IN SHARES

Individual and group acquisitions

209 Interests to be disregarded

(1) The following interests in shares are disregarded for purposes of sections 198 to 202—

(a) where property is held on trust according to the law of England and Wales and an interest in shares is comprised in that property, an interest in reversion or remainder or of a bare trustee or a custodian trustee, and any discretionary interest;

(b) where property is held on trust according to the law of Scotland and an interest in shares is comprised in that property, an interest in fee or of a simple trustee and any discretionary interest;

(c) an interest which subsists by virtue of an authorised unit trust scheme within the meaning of the [Financial Services Act 1986][2], a scheme made under section 22 of the Charities Act 1960, section 11 of the Trustee Investments Act 1961 or section 1 of the Administration of Justice Act 1965 or the scheme set out in the Schedule to the Church Funds Investment Measure 1958;

(d) an interest of the Church of Scotland General Trustees or of the Church of Scotland Trust in shares held by them or of any other person in shares held by those Trustees or that Trust otherwise than as simple trustees;

(e) an interest for the life of himself or another of a person under a settlement in the case of which the property comprised in the settlement consists of or includes shares, and the conditions mentioned in subsection (3) below are satisfied;

(f) an exempt interest held by a recognised jobber [or market maker][1];

(g) an exempt security interest;

(h) an interest of the President of the Family Division of the High Court subsisting by virtue of section 9 of the Administration of Estates Act 1925;

(i) an interest of the Accountant General of the Supreme Court in shares held by him;

(2) A person is not by virtue of section 208(4)(b) taken to be interested in shares by reason only that he has been appointed a proxy to vote at a specified meeting of a company or of any class of its members and at any adjournment of that meeting, or has been appointed by a corporation to act as its representative at any meeting of a company or of any class of its members.

(3) The conditions referred to in subsection (1)(e) are, in relation to a settlement—

(a) that it is irrevocable, and

(b) that the settlor (within the meaning of section [670 of the Income and Corporation Taxes Act 1988][3]) has no interest in any income arising under, or property comprised in, the settlement.

(4) A person is a recognised jobber for purposes of subsection (1)(f) if he is a member of The Stock Exchange recognised by the Council of The Stock Exchange as carrying on the business of a jobber; and an interest of such a person in shares is an exempt interest for those purposes if—

(a) he carries on that business in the United Kingdom, and
(b) he holds the interest for the purposes of that business.

[(4A) A person is a market maker for the purposes of subsection (1)(f) if—

(a) he holds himself out at all normal times in compliance with the rules of a recognised investment exchange other than an overseas investment exchange (within the meaning of the Financial Services Act 1986) as willing to buy and sell securities at prices specified by him; and
(b) is recognised as doing so by that investment exchange;

and an interest of such a person in shares is an exempt interest if he carries on business as a market maker in the United Kingdom, is subject to such rules in the carrying on of that business and holds the interest for the purposes of that business.][1]

(5) An interest in shares is an exempt security interest for purposes of subsection (1)(g) if—

(a) it is held by a person who is—
   (i) [a banking company], or an insurance company to which Part II of the Insurance Companies Act 1982 applies, or
   (ii) a trustee savings bank (within the Trustee Savings Banks Act 1981), or
   (iii) a member of The Stock Exchange carrying on business in the United Kingdom as a stockbroker, and
(b) it is held by way of security only for the purposes of a transaction entered into in the ordinary course of his business as such a person,

or if it is held by way of security only either by the Bank of England or by the Post Office for the purposes of a transaction entered into in the ordinary course of that part of the business of the Post Office which consists of the provision of banking services.

---

1 Inserted by FSA 1986, s 197 with effect from 29 April 1988 (see SI 1988 No 740).

2 Substituted by FSA 1986, s 212(2), 16 Sch 18 with effect from 29 April 1988 (see SI 1988 No 740). Previously 'Prevention of Fraud (Investments) Act 1958'.

3 Substituted by ICTA 1988, s 844, 29 Sch 32 for company accounting periods ending after 5 April 1988. Previously '444 of the Income and Corporation Taxes Act 1970'.

Regulations. The Public Companies (Disclosure of Interests in Shares) (Investment Management Exclusion) Regulations 1988 (SI 1988 No 706).

PART VII ACCOUNTS AND AUDIT

[CHAPTER II EXEMPTIONS, EXCEPTIONS AND SPECIAL PROVISIONS

Small and medium-sized companies and groups

246 Exemptions for small and medium-sized companies

(1) A company which qualifies as a small or medium-sized company in relation to a financial year—

(a) is exempt from the requirements of paragraph 36A of Schedule 4 (disclosure with respect to compliance with accounting standards), and
(b) is entitled to the exemptions provided by Schedule 8 with respect to the delivery to the registrar under section 242 of individual accounts and other documents for that financial year.

(2) In that Schedule—

Part I relates to small companies,

Part II relates to medium-sized companies, and

Part III contains supplementary provisions.

(3) A company is not entitled to the exemptions mentioned in subsection (1) if it is, or was at any time within the financial year to which the accounts relate—

(a) a public company,
(b) a banking or insurance company, or
(c) an authorised person under the Financial Services Act 1986,

or if it is or was at any time during that year a member of an ineligible group.

(4) A group is ineligible if any of its members is—

(a) a public company or a body corporate which (not being a company) has power under its constitution to offer its shares or debentures to the public and may lawfully exercise that power,
(b) an authorised institution under the Banking Act 1987,
(c) an insurance company to which Part II of the Insurance Companies Act 1982 applies, or
(d) an authorised person under the Financial Services Act 1986.

(5) A parent company shall not be treated as qualifying as a small company in relation to a financial year unless the group headed by it qualifies as a small group, and shall not be treated as qualifying as a medium-sized company in relation to a financial year unless that group qualifies as a medium-sized group (see section 249).][1]

---

1 Inserted by CA 1989, s 13 with effect from 1 April 1990 (SI 1990 No 355) subject to the transitional and saving provisions in Arts 6 to 9 of that Order.

[248 Exemption for small and medium-sized groups

(1) A parent company need not prepare group accounts for a financial year in relation to which the group headed by that company qualifies as a small or medium-sized group and is not an ineligible group.

(2) A group is ineligible if any of its members is—

(a) a public company or a body corporate which (not being a company) has power under its constitution to offer its shares or debentures to the public and may lawfully exercise that power,
(b) an authorised institution under the Banking Act 1987,
(c) an insurance company to which Part II of the Insurance Companies Act 1982 applies, or
(d) an authorised person under the Financial Services Act 1986.

(3) If the directors of a company propose to take advantage of the exemption conferred by this section, it is the auditors' duty to provide them with a report stating whether in their opinion the company is entitled to the exemption.

(4) The exemption does not apply unless—

(a) the auditors' report states that in their opinion the company is so entitled, and
(b) that report is attached to the individual accounts of the company.][1]

---

1 Inserted by CA 1989, s 13 with effect from 1 April 1990 (SI 1990 No 355) subject to the transitional and saving provisions in Arts 6 to 9 of that Order.

[*Dormant companies*

250 Resolution not to appoint auditors

(1) A company may by special resolution make itself exempt from the provisions of this Part relating to the audit of accounts in the following cases—

(a) if the company has been dormant from the time of its formation, by a special resolution passed before the first general meeting of the company at which annual accounts are laid;
(b) if the company has been dormant since the end of the previous financial year and—
  (i) is entitled in respect of its individual accounts for that year to the exemptions conferred by section 246 on a small company, or would be so entitled but for being a member of an ineligible group, and
  (ii) is not required to prepare group accounts for that year,

  by a special resolution passed at a general meeting of the company at which the annual accounts for that year are laid.

(2) A company may not pass such a resolution if it is—

(a) a public company,
(b) a banking or insurance company, or
(c) an authorised person under the Financial Services Act 1986.

(3) A company is "dormant" during a period in which no significant accounting transaction occurs, that is, no transaction which is required by section 221 to be entered in the company's accounting records; and a company ceases to be dormant on the occurrence of such a transaction.

For this purpose there shall be disregarded any transaction arising from the taking of shares in the company by a subscriber to the memorandum in pursuance of an undertaking of his in the memorandum.

(4) Where a company is, at the end of a financial year, exempt by virtue of this section from the provisions of this Part relating to the audit of accounts—

(a) sections 238 and 239 (right to receive or demand copies of accounts and reports) have effect with the omission of references to the auditors' report;

(b) no copies of an auditors' report need be laid before the company in general meeting;

(c) no copy of an auditors' report need be delivered to the registrar, and if none is delivered, the copy of the balance sheet so delivered shall contain a statement by the directors, in a position immediately above the signature required by section 233(4), that the company was dormant throughout the financial year; and

(d) the company shall be treated as entitled in respect of its individual accounts for that year to the exemptions conferred by section 246 on a small company notwithstanding that it is a member of an ineligible group.

(5) Where a company which is exempt by virtue of this section from the provisions of this Part relating to the audit of accounts—

(a) ceases to be dormant, or

(b) would no longer qualify (for any other reason) to make itself exempt by passing a resolution under this section,

it shall thereupon cease to be so exempt.][1]

---

1 Inserted by CA 1989, s 14 with effect from 1 April 1990 (SI 1990 No 355) subject to the transitional and saving provisions in Arts 6 to 9 of that Order.

[*Unlimited companies*

254 Exemption from requirement to deliver accounts and reports

(1) The directors of an unlimited company are not required to deliver accounts and reports to the registrar in respect of a financial year if the following conditions are met.

(2) The conditions are that at no time during the relevant accounting reference period—

(a) has the company been, to its knowledge, a subsidiary undertaking of an undertaking which was then limited, or

(b) have there been, to its knowledge, exercisable by or on behalf of two or more undertakings which were then limited, rights which if exercisable by one of them would have made the company a subsidiary undertaking of it, or

(c) has the company been a parent company of an undertaking which was then limited.

The references above to an undertaking being limited at a particular time are to an undertaking (under whatever law established) the liability of whose members is at that time limited.

(3) The exemption conferred by this section does not apply if at any time during the relevant accounting period the company carried on business as the promoter of a trading stamp scheme within the Trading Stamps Act 1964.

(4) Where a company is exempt by virtue of this section from the obligation to deliver accounts, section 240 (requirements in connection with publication of accounts) has effect with the following modifications—

(a) in subsection (3)(b) for the words from 'whether statutory accounts' to 'have been delivered to the registrar' substitute 'that the company is exempt from the requirement to deliver statutory accounts', and

(b) in subsection (5) for 'as required to be delivered to the registrar under section 242' substitute 'as prepared in accordance with this Part and approved by the board of directors'.][1]

---

1 Inserted by CA 1989, s 17 with effect from 1 April 1990 (SI 1990 No 355) subject to the transitional and saving provisions in Arts 6 to 9 of that Order.

[*Banking and insurance companies and groups*

255 Special provisions for banking and insurance companies

(1) A banking or insurance company may prepare its individual accounts in accordance with Part I of Schedule 9 rather than Schedule 4.

(2) Accounts so prepared shall contain a statement that they are prepared in accordance with the special provisions of this Part relating to banking companies or insurance companies, as the case may be.

(3) In relation to the preparation of individual accounts in accordance with the special provisions of this Part relating to banking or insurance companies, the references to the provisions of Schedule 4 in section 226(4) and (5) (relationship between specific requirements and duty to give true and fair view) shall be read as references to the provisions of Part I of Schedule 9.

(4) The Secretary of State may, on the application or with the consent of the directors of a company which prepares individual accounts in accordance with the special provisions of this Part relating to banking or insurance companies, modify in relation to the company any of the requirements of this Part for the purpose of adapting them to the circumstances of the company.

This does not affect the duty to give a true and fair view.][1]

---

1 Inserted by CA 1989, s 18 with effect from 1 April 1990 (SI 1990 No 355) subject to the transitional and saving provisions in Arts 6 to 9 of that Order.

[255A Special provisions for banking and insurance groups

(1) The parent company of a banking or insurance group may prepare group accounts in accordance with the provisions of this Part as modified by Part II of Schedule 9.

(2) Accounts so prepared shall contain a statement that they are prepared in accordance with the special provisions of this Part relating to banking groups or insurance groups, as the case may be.

(3) References in this Part to a banking group are to a group where—

(a) the parent company is a banking company, or
(b) at least one of the undertakings in the group is an authorised institution under the Banking Act 1987 and the predominant activities of the group are such as to make it inappropriate to prepare group accounts in accordance with the formats in Part I of Schedule 4.

(4) References in this Part to an insurance group are to a group where—

(a) the parent company is an insurance company, or
(b) the predominant activity of the group is insurance business and activities which are a direct extension of or ancillary to insurance business.

(5) In relation to the preparation of group accounts in accordance with the special provisions of this Part relating to banking or insurance groups, the references to the provisions of Schedule 4A in section 227(5) and (6) (relationship between specific requirements and duty to give true and fair view) shall be read as references to those provisions as modified by Part II of Schedule 9.

(6) The Secretary of State may, on the application or with the consent of the directors of a company which prepares group accounts in accordance with the special provisions of this Part relating to banking or insurance groups, modify in relation to the company any of the requirements of this Part for the purpose of adapting them to the circumstances of the company.][1]

---

1 Inserted by CA 1989, s 18 with effect from 1 April 1990 (SI 1990 No 355) subject to the transitional and saving provisions in Arts 6 to 9 of that Order.

[255B Modification of disclosure requirements in relation to banking company or group

(1) In relation to a company which prepares accounts in accordance with the special provisions of this Part relating to banking companies or groups, the provisions of Schedule 5 (additional disclosure: related undertakings) have effect subject to Part III of Schedule 9.

(2) In relation to a banking company, or the parent company of a banking company, the provisions of Schedule 6 (disclosure: emoluments and other benefits of directors and others) have effect subject to Part IV of Schedule 9.][1]

---

1 Inserted by CA 1989, s 18 with effect from 1 April 1990 (SI 1990 No 355) subject to the transitional and saving provisions in Arts 6 to 9 of that Order.

[255C Directors' report where accounts prepared in accordance with special provisions

(1) The following provisions apply in relation to the directors' report of a company for a financial year in respect of which it prepares accounts in accordance with the special provisions of this Part relating to banking or insurance companies or groups.

(2) The information required to be given by paragraph 6, 8 or 13 of Part I of Schedule 9 (which is allowed to be given in a statement or report annexed to the accounts), may be given in the directors' report instead.

Information so given shall be treated for the purposes of audit as forming part of the accounts.

(3) The reference in section 234(1)(b) to the amount proposed to be carried to reserves shall be construed as a reference to the amount proposed to be carried to reserves within the meaning of Part I of Schedule 9.

(4) If the company takes advantage, in relation to its individual or group accounts, of the exemptions conferred by paragraph 27 or 28 of Part I of Schedule 9, paragraph 1 of Schedule 7 (disclosure of asset values) does not apply.

(5) The directors' report shall, in addition to complying with Schedule 7, also comply with Schedule 10 (which specifies additional matters to be disclosed).][1]

---

1 Inserted by CA 1989, s 18 with effect from 1 April 1990 (SI 1990 No 355) subject to the transitional and saving provisions in Arts 6 to 9 of that Order.

[255D Power to apply provisions to banking partnerships

(1) The Secretary of State may by regulations apply to banking partnerships, subject to such exceptions, adaptations and modifications as he considers appropriate, the provisions of this Part applying to banking companies.

(2) A "banking partnership" means a partnership which is an authorised institution under the Banking Act 1987.

(3) Regulations under this section shall be made by statutory instrument.

(4) No regulations under this section shall be made unless a draft of the instrument containing the regulations has been laid before Parliament and approved by a resolution of each House.][1]

---

1 Inserted by CA 1989, s 18 with effect from 1 April 1990 (SI 1990 No 355) subject to the transitional and saving provisions in Arts 6 to 9 of that Order.

[CHAPTER III SUPPLEMENTARY PROVISIONS

[*Other interpretation provisions*

259 Meaning of "undertaking" and related expressions

(1) In this Part "undertaking" means—

(a) a body corporate or partnership, or
(b) an unincorporated association carrying on a trade or business, with or without a view to profit.

(2) In this Part references to shares—

(a) in relation to an undertaking with a share capital, are to allotted shares;
(b) in relation to an undertaking with capital but no share capital, are to rights to share in the capital of the undertaking; and
(c) in relation to an undertaking without capital, are to interests—
   (i) conferring any right to share in the profits or liability to contribute to the losses of the undertaking, or
   (ii) giving rise to an obligation to contribute to the debts or expenses of the undertaking in the event of a winding up.

(3) Other expressions appropriate to companies shall be construed, in relation to an undertaking which is not a company, as references to the corresponding persons, officers, documents or organs, as the case may be, appropriate to undertakings of that description.

This is subject to provision in any specific context providing for the translation of such expressions.

(4) References in this Part to "fellow subsidiary undertakings" are to undertakings which are subsidiary undertakings of the same parent undertaking but are not parent undertakings or subsidiary undertakings of each other.

(5) In this Part "group undertaking", in relation to an undertaking, means an undertaking which is—

(a) a parent undertaking or subsidiary undertaking of that undertaking, or
(b) a subsidiary undertaking of any parent undertaking of that undertaking.][1]

1 Inserted by CA 1989, s 22 with effect from 1 April 1990 (SI 1990 No 355) subject to the transitional and saving provisions in Arts 6 to 9 of that Order.

[262 Minor definitions

(1) In this Part—

"annual accounts" means—

(a) the individual accounts required by section 226, and
(b) any group accounts required by section 227,

(but see also section 230 (treatment of individual profit and loss account where group accounts prepared));

"annual report", in relation to a company, means the directors' report required by section 234;

"balance sheet date" means the date as at which the balance sheet was made up;

"capitalisation", in relation to work or costs, means treating that work or those costs as a fixed asset;

"credit institution" means an undertaking carrying on a deposit-taking business within the meaning of the Banking Act 1987;

"fixed assets" means assets of a company which are intended for use on a continuing basis in the company's activities, and "current assets" means assets not intended for such use;

"group" means a parent undertaking and its subsidiary undertakings;

"included in the consolidation", in relation to group accounts, or "included in consolidated group accounts", means that the undertaking is included in the accounts by the method of full (and not proportional) consolidation, and references to an undertaking excluded from consolidation shall be construed accordingly;

"purchase price", in relation to an asset of a company or any raw materials or consumables used in the production of such an asset, includes any consideration (whether in cash or otherwise) given by the company in respect of that asset or those materials or consumables, as the case may be;

"qualified", in relation to an auditors' report, means that the report does not state the auditors' unqualified opinion that the accounts have been properly prepared in accordance with this Act or, in the case of an undertaking not required to prepare accounts in accordance with this Act, under any corresponding legislation under which it is required to prepare accounts;

"true and fair view" refers—

(a) in the case of individual accounts, to the requirement of section 226(2), and
(b) in the case of group accounts, to the requirement of section 227(3);

"turnover", in relation to a company, means the amounts derived from the provision of goods and services falling within the company's ordinary activities, after deduction of—

(i) trade discounts,
(ii) value added tax, and

(iii) any other taxes based on the amounts so derived.

(2) In the case of an undertaking not trading for profit, any reference in this Part to a profit and loss account is to an income and expenditure account; and references to profit and loss and, in relation to group accounts, to a consolidated profit and loss account shall be construed accordingly.

(3) References in this Part to "realised profits" and "realised losses", in relation to a company's accounts, are to such profits or losses of the company as fall to be treated as realised in accordance with principles generally accepted, at the time when the accounts are prepared, with respect to the determination for accounting purposes of realised profits or losses.

This is without prejudice to—

(a) the construction of any other expression (where appropriate) by reference to accepted accounting principles or practice, or
(b) any specific provision for the treatment of profits or losses of any description as realised.][1]

---

1 Inserted by CA 1989, s 22 with effect from 1 April 1990 (SI 1990 No 355) subject to the transitional and saving provisions in Arts 6 to 9 of that Order.

[262A Index of defined expressions

The following Table shows the provisions of this Part defining or otherwise explaining expressions used in this Part (other than expressions used only in the same section or paragraph)—

accounting reference date and accounting reference period	section 224
accounting standards and applicable accounting standards	section 256
annual accounts	
(generally)	section 262(1)
(includes notes to the accounts)	section 261(2)
annual report	section 262(1)
associated undertaking (in Schedule 4A)	paragraph 20 of that Schedule
balance sheet (includes notes)	section 261(2)
balance sheet date	section 262(1)
banking group	section 255A(3)
capitalisation (in relation to work or costs)	section 262(1)
credit institution	section 262(1)
current assets	section 262(1)
fellow subsidiary undertaking	section 259(4)
financial year	section 223
fixed assets	section 262(1)
group	section 262(1)
group undertaking	section 259(5)
historical cost accounting rules (in Schedule 4)	paragraph 29 of that Schedule
included in the consolidation and related expressions	section 262(1)
individual accounts	section 262(1)
insurance group	section 255A(4)
land of freehold tenure and land of leasehold tenure (in relation to Scotland)	

—in Schedule 4	paragraph 93 of that Schedule
—in Schedule 9	paragraph 36 of that Schedule
lease, long lease and short lease	
—in Schedule 4	paragraph 83 of that Schedule
—in Schedule 9	paragraph 34 of that Schedule
listed investment	
—in Schedule 4	paragraph 84 of that Schedule
—in Schedule 9	paragraph 33 of that Schedule
notes to the accounts	section 261(1)
parent undertaking (and parent company)	section 258 and Schedule 10A
participating interest	section 260
pension costs (in Schedule 4)	paragraph 94(2) and (3) of that Schedule
period allowed for laying and delivering accounts and reports	section 244
profit and loss account	
(includes notes)	section 261(2)
(in relation to a company not trading for profit)	section 262(2)
provision	
—in Schedule 4	paragraphs 88 and 89 of that Schedule
—in Schedule 9	paragraph 32 of that Schedule
purchase price	section 262(1)
qualified	section 262(1)
realised losses and realised profits	section 262(3)
reserve (in Schedule 9)	paragraph 32 of that Schedule
shares	section 259(2)
social security costs (in Schedule 4)	paragraph 94(1) and (3) of that Schedule
special provisions for banking and insurance companies and groups	sections 255 and 255A
subsidiary undertaking	section 258 and Schedule 10A
true and fair view	section 262(1)
turnover	section 262(1)
undertaking and related expressions	section 259(1) to (3).][1]

[1] Inserted by CA 1989, s 22 with effect from 1 April 1990 (SI 1990 No 355) subject to the transitional and saving provisions in Arts 6 to 9 of that Order.

PART VIII DISTRIBUTION OF PROFITS AND ASSETS

Limits of company's power of distribution

263 Certain distributions prohibited

(1) A company shall not make a distribution except out of profits available for the purpose.

(2) In this Part, "distribution" means every description of distribution of a company's assets to its members, whether in cash or otherwise, except distribution by way of—

(a) an issue of shares as fully or partly paid bonus shares,
(b) the redemption or purchase of any of the company's own shares out of capital (including the proceeds of any fresh issue of shares) or out of unrealised profits in accordance with Chapter VII of Part V,
(c) the reduction of share capital by extinguishing or reducing the liability of any of the members on any of the company's shares in respect of share capital not paid up, or by paying off paid up share capital, and
(d) a distribution of assets to members of the company on its winding up.

(3) For purposes of this Part, a company's profits available for distribution are its accumulated, realised profits, so far as not previously utilised by distribution or capitalisation, less its accumulated, realised losses, so far as not previously written off in a reduction or reorganisation of capital duly made.

This is subject to the provision made by sections 265 and 266 for investment and other companies.

(4) A company shall not apply an unrealised profit in paying up debentures, or any amounts unpaid on its issued shares.

(5) Where the directors of a company are, after making all reasonable enquiries, unable to determine whether a particular profit made before 22nd December 1980 is realised or unrealised, they may treat the profit as realised; and where after making such enquiries they are unable to determine whether a particular loss so made is realised or unrealised, they may treat the loss as unrealised.

Cross references. See Secs 270–276 (distributions not contravening provisions).

---

264 Restriction on distribution of assets

(1) A public company may only make a distribution at any time—

(a) if at that time the amount of its net assets is not less than the aggregate of its called-up share capital and undistributable reserves, and
(b) if, and to the extent that, the distribution does not reduce the amount of those assets to less than that aggregate.

This is subject to the provision made by sections 265 and 266 for investment and other companies.

(2) In subsection (1), "net assets" means the aggregate of the company's assets less the aggregate of its liabilities ("liabilities" to include any provision for liabilities or charges within paragraph 89 of Schedule 4).

(3) A company's undistributable reserves are—

(a) the share premium account,

(b) the capital redemption reserve,

(c) the amount by which the company's accumulated, unrealised profits, so far as not previously utilised by capitalisation of a description to which this paragraph applies, exceed its accumulated, unrealised losses (so far as not previously written off in a reduction or reorganisation of capital duly made), and

(d) any other reserve which the company is prohibited from distributing by any enactment (other than one contained in this Part) or by its memorandum or articles;

and paragraph (c) applies to every description of capitalisation except a transfer of profits of the company to its capital redemption reserve on or after 22nd December 1980.

(4) A public company shall not include any uncalled share capital as an asset in any accounts relevant for purposes of this section.

Cross references. See Secs 270–276 (distributions not contravening provisions).

---

265 Other distributions by investment companies

(1) Subject to the following provisions of this section, an investment company (defined in section 266) may also make a distribution at any time out of its accumulated, realised revenue profits, so far as not previously utilised by distribution or capitalisation, less its accumulated revenue losses (whether realised or unrealised), so far as not previously written off in a reduction or reorganisation of capital duly made—

(a) if at that time the amount of its assets is at least equal to one and a half times the aggregate of its liabilities, and

(b) if, and to the extent that, the distribution does not reduce that amount to less than one and a half times that aggregate.

(2) In subsection (1)(a), "liabilities" includes any provision for liabilities or charges (within the meaning of paragraph 89 of Schedule 4).

(3) The company shall not include any uncalled share capital as an asset in any accounts relevant for purposes of this section.

(4) An investment company may not make a distribution by virtue of subsection (1) unless—

(a) its shares are listed on a [recognised investment exchange other than an overseas investment exchange within the meaning of the Financial Services Act 1986][1], and

(b) during the relevant period it has not—

(i) distributed any of its capital profits, or

(ii) applied any unrealised profits or any capital profits (realised or unrealised) in paying up debentures or amounts unpaid on its issued shares.

(5) The "relevant period" under subsection (4) is the period beginning with—

(a) the first day of the accounting reference period immediately preceding that in which the proposed distribution is to be made, or

(b) where the distribution is to be made in the company's first accounting reference period, the first day of that period, and ending with the date of the distribution.

(6) An investment company may not make a distribution by virtue of subsection (1) unless the company gave to the registrar of companies the requisite notice (that is, notice under section 266(1)) of the company's intention to carry on business as an investment company—

(a) before the beginning of the relevant period under subsection (4), or
(b) in the case of a company incorporated on or after 22nd December 1980, as soon as may have been reasonably practicable after the date of its incorporation.

---

1 Substituted by FSA 1986, s 212(2), 16 Sch 19 with effect from 29 April 1988 (see SI 1988 No 740). Previously 'recognised stock exchange'.

Cross references. See Sec 266; Secs 270–276 (distributions not contravening provisions).

---

266 Meaning of "investment company"

(1) In section 265 "investment company" means a public company which has given notice in the prescribed form (which has not been revoked) to the registrar of companies of its intention to carry on business as an investment company, and has since the date of that notice complied with the requirements specified below.

(2) Those requirements are—

(a) that the business of the company consists of investing its funds mainly in securities, with the aim of spreading investment risk and giving members of the company the benefit of the results of the management of its funds,
(b) that none of the company's holdings in companies (other than those which are for the time being in investment companies) represents more than 15 per cent. by value of the investing company's investments,
(c) that distribution of the company's capital profits is prohibited by its memorandum or articles of association,
(d) that the company has not retained, otherwise than in compliance with this Part, in respect of any accounting reference period more than 15 per cent. of the income it derives from securities.

(3) Notice to the registrar of companies under subsection (1) may be revoked at any time by the company on giving notice in the prescribed form to the registrar that it no longer wishes to be an investment company within the meaning of this section; and, on giving such notice, the company ceases to be such a company.

(4) [Subsections (1A) to (3) of section 842 of the Income and Corporation Taxes Act 1988 apply for the purposes of subsection (2)(b) above as for those of subsection (1)(b) of that section.][1]

---

1 Substituted by FA 1988, s 117(3) with effect for companies' accounting periods ending after 5 April 1988.

---

267 Extension of ss 265, 266 to other companies

(1) The Secretary of State may by regulations in a statutory instrument extend the provisions of sections 265 and 266 (with or without modifications) to companies whose principal business consists of investing their funds in securities, land or other assets with the aim of spreading investment risk and giving their members the benefit of the results of the management of the assets.

(2) Regulations under this section—

(a) may make different provision for different classes of companies and may contain such transitional and supplemental provisions as the Secretary of State considers necessary, and
(b) shall not be made unless a draft of the statutory instrument containing them has been laid before Parliament and approved by a resolution of each House.

268 Realised profits of insurance company with long term business

(1) Where an insurance company to which Part II of the Insurance Companies Act 1982 applies carries on long term business—

(a) any amount properly transferred to the profit and loss account of the company from a surplus in the fund or funds maintained by it in respect of that business, and
(b) any deficit in that fund or those funds,

are to be (respectively) treated, for purposes of this Part, as a realised profit and a realised loss; and, subject to this, any profit or loss arising in that business is to be left out of account for those purposes.

(2) In subsection (1)—

(a) the reference to a surplus in any fund or funds of an insurance company is to an excess of the assets representing that fund or those funds over the liabilities of the company attributable to its long term business, as shown by an actuarial investigation, and
(b) the reference to a deficit in any such fund or funds is to the excess of those liabilities over those assets, as so shown.

(3) In this section—

(a) "actuarial investigation" means an investigation to which section 18 of the Insurance Companies Act 1982 (periodic actuarial investigation of company with long term business) applies or which is made in pursuance of a requirement imposed by section 42 of that Act (actuarial investigation required by Secretary of State); and
(b) "long term business" has the same meaning as in that Act.

269 Treatment of development costs

(1) Subject as follows, where development costs are shown as an asset in a company's accounts, any amount shown in respect of those costs is to be treated—

(a) under section 263, as a realised loss, and
(b) under section 265, as a realised revenue loss.

(2) This does not apply to any part of that amount representing an unrealised profit made on revaluation of those costs; nor does it apply if—

(a) there are special circumstances in the company's case justifying the directors in deciding that the amount there mentioned is not to be treated as required by subsection (1), and
(b) the note to the accounts required by paragraph 20 of Schedule 4 (reasons for showing development costs as an asset) states that the amount is not to be so treated and explains the circumstances relied upon to justify the decision of the directors to that effect.

Supplementary

279 [Distributions by banking or insurance companies

Where a company's accounts relevant for the purposes of this Part are prepared in accordance with the special provisions of Part VII relating to banking or insurance companies, sections 264 to 275 apply with the modifications shown in Schedule 11.][1]

---

1 Substituted by CA 1989, 10 Sch 8 with effect from 1 April 1990 (SI 1990 No 355) subject to the transitional and saving provisions in Arts 6 to 9 of that Order.

PART X ENFORCEMENT OF FAIR DEALING BY DIRECTORS

Restrictions on a company's power to make loans, etc., to directors and persons connected with them

330 General restriction on loans etc. to directors and persons connected with them

(1) The prohibitions listed below in this section are subject to the exceptions in sections 332 to 338.

(2) A company shall not—

(a) make a loan to a director of the company or of its holding company;
(b) enter into any guarantee or provide any security in connection with a loan made by any person to such a director.

(3) A relevant company shall not—

(a) make a quasi-loan to a director of the company or of its holding company;
(b) make a loan or a quasi-loan to a person connected with such a director;
(c) enter into a guarantee or provide any security in connection with a loan or quasi-loan made by any other person for such a director or a person so connected.

(4) A relevant company shall not—

(a) enter into a credit transaction as creditor for such a director or a person so connected;
(b) enter into any guarantee or provide any security in connection with a credit transaction made by any other person for such a director or a person so connected.

(5) For purposes of sections 330 to 346, a shadow director is treated as a director.

(6) A company shall not arrange for the assignment to it, or the assumption by it, of any rights, obligations or liabilities under a transaction which, if it had been entered into by the company, would have contravened subsection (2), (3) or (4); but for the purposes of sections 330 to 347 the transaction is to be treated as having been entered into on the date of the arrangement.

(7) A company shall not take part in any arrangement whereby—

(a) another person enters into a transaction which, if it had been entered into by the company, would have contravened any of subsections (2), (3), (4) or (6); and
(b) that other person, in pursuance of the arrangement, has obtained or is to obtain any benefit from the company or its holding company or a subsidiary of the company or its holding company.

Cross references. See Sec 340 (value of transactions); Sec 341 (civil remedies for breach of Sec 330); Sec 342 (criminal penalties); Sec 347 (transactions under foreign law); Sec 741 (shadow directors).

---

338 Loan or quasi-loan by money-lending company

(1) There is excepted from the prohibitions in section 330—

(a) a loan or quasi-loan made by a money-lending company to any person; or
(b) a money-lending company entering into a guarantee in connection with any other loan or quasi-loan.

(2) "Money-lending company" means a company whose ordinary business includes the making of loans or quasi-loans, or the giving of guarantees in connection with loans or quasi-loans.

(3) Subsection (1) applies only if both the following conditions are satisfied—

(a) the loan or quasi-loan in question is made by the company, or it enters into the guarantee, in the ordinary course of the company's business; and
(b) the amount of the loan or quasi-loan, or the amount guaranteed, is not greater, and the terms of the loan, quasi-loan or guarantee are not more favourable, in the case of the person to whom the loan or quasi-loan is made or in respect of whom the guarantee is entered into, than that or those which it is reasonable to expect that company to have offered to or in respect of a person of the same financial standing but unconnected with the company.

(4) But subsection (1) does not authorise a relevant company (unless it is [a banking company][1]) to enter into any transaction if the aggregate of the relevant amounts exceeds [£100,000][2].

(5) In determining that aggregate, a company which a director does not control is deemed not to be connected with him.

(6) The condition specified in subsection (3)(b) does not of itself prevent a company from making a loan to one of its directors or a director of its holding company—

(a) for the purpose of facilitating the purchase, for use as that director's only or main residence, of the whole or part of any dwelling-house together with any land to be occupied and enjoyed with it;
(b) for the purpose of improving a dwelling-house or part of a dwelling-house so used or any land occupied and enjoyed with it;
(c) in substitution for any loan made by any person and falling within paragraph (a) or (b) of this subsection,

if loans of that description are ordinarily made by the company to its employees and on terms no less favourable than those on which the transaction in question is made, and the aggregate of the relevant amounts does not exceed [£100,000][2].

---

1 Substituted by CA 1989, 10 Sch 10 with effect from 1 April 1990 (SI 1990 No 355) subject to the transitional and saving provisions in Arts 6 to 9 of that Order.

2 Substituted by CA 1989, s 138 with effect from a date to be appointed.

Cross references. See Sec 330(5)(6).

---

339 "Relevant amounts" for purposes of ss 334 ff

(1) This section has effect for defining the "relevant amounts" to be aggregated under sections 334, 335(1), 337(3) and 338(4); and in relation to any proposed transaction or arrangement and the question whether it falls within one or other of the exceptions provided by those sections, "the relevant exception" is that exception; but where the relevant exception is the one provided by section 334 (loan of small amount), references in this section to a person connected with a director are to be disregarded.

(2) Subject as follows, the relevant amounts in relation to a proposed transaction or arrangement are—

(a) the value of the proposed transaction or arrangement,
(b) the value of any existing arrangement which—

(i) falls within subsection (6) or (7) of section 330, and
(ii) also falls within subsection (3) of this section, and
(iii) was entered into by virtue of the relevant exception by the company or by a subsidiary of the company or, where the proposed transaction or arrangement is to be made for a director of its holding company or a person connected with such a director, by that holding company or any of its subsidiaries;

(c) the amount outstanding under any other transaction—
(i) falling within subsection (3) below, and
(ii) made by virtue of the relevant exception, and
(iii) made by the company or by a subsidiary of the company or, where the proposed transaction or arrangement is to be made for a director of its holding company or a person connected with such a director, by that holding company or any of its subsidiaries.

(3) A transaction falls within this subsection if it was made—

(a) for the director for whom the proposed transaction or arrangement is to be made, or for any person connected with that director; or
(b) where the proposed transaction or arrangement is to be made for a person connected with a director of a company, for that director or any person connected with him;

and an arrangement also falls within this subsection if it relates to a transaction which does so.

(4) But where the proposed transaction falls within section 338 and is one which [a banking company][1] proposes to enter into under subsection (6) of that section (housing loans, etc.), any other transaction or arrangement which apart from this subsection would fall within subsection (3) of this section does not do so unless it was entered into in pursuance of section 338(6).

(5) A transaction entered into by a company which is (at the time of that transaction being entered into) a subsidiary of the company which is to make the proposed transaction, or is a subsidiary of that company's holding company, does not fall within subsection (3) if at the time when the question arises (that is to say, the question whether the proposed transaction or arrangement falls within any relevant exception), it no longer is such a subsidiary.

(6) Values for purposes of subsection (2) of this section are to be determined in accordance with the section next following; and "the amount outstanding" for purposes of subsection (2)(c) above is the value of the transaction less any amount by which that value has been reduced.

---

1 Substituted by CA 1989, 10 Sch 10 with effect from 1 April 1990 (SI 1990 No 355) subject to the transitional and saving provisions in Arts 6 to 9 of that Order.

Cross references. See Sec 330(5)(6); Sec 331.

---

343 Record of transactions not disclosed in company accounts

(1) The following provisions of this section—

(a) apply in the case of a company which is, or is the holding company of, [a banking company][1], and
(b) are subject to the exceptions provided by section 344.

(2) Such a company shall maintain a register containing a copy of every transaction, arrangement or agreement of which particulars would, but for [paragraph 2 of Part IV of Schedule 9, be required][2] to be disclosed in the company's accounts or group accounts for the current financial year and for each of the preceding 10 financial years.

(3) In the case of a transaction, arrangement or agreement which is not in writing, there shall be contained in the register a written memorandum setting out its terms.

(4) Such a company shall before its annual general meeting make available at its registered office for not less than 15 days ending with the date of the meeting a statement containing the particulars of transactions, arrangements and agreements which the company would, but for [paragraph 2 of Part IV of Schedule 9, be required][2] to disclose in its accounts or group accounts for the last complete financial year preceding that meeting.

(5) The statement shall be so made available for inspection by members of the company; and such a statement shall also be made available for their inspection at the annual general meeting.

(6) It is the duty of the company's auditors to examine the statement before it is made available to members of the company and to make a report to the members on it; and the report shall be annexed to the statement before it is made so available.

(7) The auditors' report shall state whether in their opinion the statement contains the particulars required by subsection (4); and, where their opinion is that it does not, they shall include in the report, so far as they are reasonably able to do so, a statement giving the required particulars.

(8) If a company fails to comply with any provision of subsections (2) to (5), every person who at the time of the failure is a director of it is guilty of an offence and liable to a fine; but—

(a) it is a defence in proceedings against a person for this offence to prove that he took all reasonable steps for securing compliance with the subsection concerned, and

(b) a person is not guilty of the offence by virtue only of being a shadow director of the company.

(9) For purposes of the application of this section to loans and quasi-loans made by a company to persons connected with a person who at any time is a director of the company or of its holding company, a company which a person does not control is not connected with him.

---

1 Substituted by CA 1989, 10 Sch 10 with effect from 1 April 1990 (SI 1990 No 355) subject to the transitional and saving provisions in Arts 6 to 9 of that Order.

2 Substituted by CA 1989, 10 Sch 11 with effect as in [1] above.

Cross references. See Sec 330(5)(6); Sec 344; 24 Sch (punishment of offences).

---

344 Exceptions from s 343

(1) Section 343 does not apply in relation to—

(a) transactions or arrangements made or subsisting during a financial year by a company or by a subsidiary of a company for a person who was at any time during that year a director of the company or of its holding company or was connected with such a director, or

(b) an agreement made or subsisting during that year to enter into such a transaction or arrangement,

if the aggregate of the values of each transaction or arrangement made for that person, and of each agreement for such a transaction or arrangement, less the amount (if any) by which the value of those transactions, arrangements and agreements has been reduced, did not exceed £1,000 at any time during the financial year.

For purposes of this subsection, values are to be determined as under section 340.

(2) Section 343(4) and (5) do not apply to [a banking company][1] which is the wholly-owned subsidiary of a company incorporated in the United Kingdom.

---

1 Substituted by CA 1989, 10 Sch 10 with effect from 1 April 1990 (SI 1990 No 355) subject to the transitional and saving provisions in Arts 6 to 9 of that Order.

Cross references. See Sec 330(5)(6); Sec 741 (shadow directors).

PART XI COMPANY ADMINISTRATION AND PROCEDURE

CHAPTER I COMPANY IDENTIFICATION

351 Particulars in correspondence, etc.

(1) Every company shall have the following particulars mentioned in legible characters in all business letters and order forms of the company, that is to say—

(a) the company's place of registration and the number with which it is registered,
(b) the address of its registered office,
(c) in the case of an investment company (as defined in section 266), the fact that it is such a company, and
(d) in the case of a limited company exempt from the obligation to use the word "limited" as part of its name, the fact that it is a limited company.

(2) If in the case of a company having a share capital there is on the stationery used for any such letters, or on the company's order forms, a reference to the amount of share capital, the reference must be to paid-up share capital.

(3) Where the name of a public company includes, as its last part, the equivalent in Welsh of the words "public limited company" ("cwmni cyfyngedig cyhoeddus"), the fact that the company is a public limited company shall be stated in English and in legible characters—

(a) in all prospectuses, bill-heads, letter paper, notices and other official publications of the company, and
(b) in a notice conspicuously displayed in every place in which the company's business is carried on.

(4) Where the name of a limited company has "cyfyngedig" as the last word, the fact that the company is a limited company shall be stated in English and in legible characters—

(a) in all prospectuses, bill-heads, letter paper, notices and other official publications of the company, and
(b) in a notice conspicuously displayed in every place in which the company's business is carried on.

(5) As to contraventions of this section, the following applies—

(a) if a company fails to comply with subsection (1) or (2), it is liable to a fine,
(b) if an officer of a company or a person on its behalf issues or authorises the issue of any business letter or order form not complying with those subsections, he is liable to a fine, and
(c) if subsection (3) or (4) is contravened, the company and every officer of it who is in default is liable to a fine and, in the case of subsection (3), to a daily default fine for continued contravention.

Cross references. See 24 Sch (punishment of offences).

CHAPTER IV MEETINGS AND RESOLUTIONS

Meetings

369 Length of notice for calling meetings

(1) A provision of a company's articles is void in so far as it provides for the calling of a meeting of the company (other than an adjourned meeting) by a shorter notice than—

(a) in the case of the annual general meeting, 21 days' notice in writing; and
(b) in the case of a meeting other than an annual general meeting or a meeting for the passing of a special resolution—
 (i) 7 days' notice in writing in the case of an unlimited company, and
 (ii) otherwise, 14 days' notice in writing.

(2) Save in so far as the articles of a company make other provision in that behalf (not being a provision avoided by subsection (1)), a meeting of the company (other than an adjourned meeting) may be called—

(a) in the case of the annual general meeting, by 21 days' notice in writing; and
(b) in the case of a meeting other than an annual general meeting or a meeting for the passing of a special resolution—
 (i) by 7 days' notice in writing in the case of an unlimited company, and
 (ii) otherwise, 14 days' notice in writing.

(3) Notwithstanding that a meeting is called by shorter notice than that specified in subsection (2) or in the company's articles (as the case may be), it is deemed to have been duly called if it is so agreed—

(a) in the case of a meeting called as the annual general meeting, by all the members entitled to attend and vote at it; and
(b) otherwise, by the requisite majority.

(4) The requisite majority for this purpose is a majority in number of the members having a right to attend and vote at the meeting, being a majority—

(a) together holding not less than 95 per cent. in nominal value of the shares giving a right to attend and vote at the meeting; or
(b) in the case of a company not having a share capital, together representing not less than 95 per cent. of the total voting rights at that meeting of all the members.

[A private company may elect (by elective resolution in accordance with section 379A) that the above provisions shall have effect in relation to the company as if for the references to 95 per cent. there were substituted references to such lesser percentage, but not less than 90 per cent., as may be specified in the resolution or subsequently determined by the company in general meeting.][1]

---

[1] Inserted by CA 1989, s 115 with effect from 1 April 1990 (SI 1990 No 355) subject to the transitional and saving provisions in Schedule 4 of that Order.

Requisition and seizure of books and papers

449 Provision for security of information obtained

(1) No information or document relating to a [company][18] which has been obtained under section 447 [. . .][19] shall, without the previous consent in writing of that [company][18], be published or disclosed, except to a competent authority, unless the publication or disclosure is required—

[(a) with a view to the institution of or otherwise for the purposes of criminal proceedings;][2]

[(ba) with a view to the institution of, or otherwise for the purposes of, any proceedings on an application under [section 6, 7 or 8 of the Company Directors Disqualification Act 1986][5],][1]

(c) [for the purposes of enabling or assisting any inspector appointed under this Part, or under section 94 or 177 of the Financial Services Act 1986, to discharge his functions;][7]

[(cc) for the purpose of enabling or assisting any person authorised to exercise powers under section 44 of the Insurance Companies Act 1982, section 447 of this Act, section 106 of the Financial Services Act 1986 or section 84 of the Companies Act 1989 to discharge his functions;][8]

[(d) for the purpose of enabling or assisting the Secretary of State to exercise any of his functions under this Act, the Insider Dealing Act, the Prevention of Fraud (Investments) Act 1958, the Insurance Companies Act 1982, the Insolvency Act 1986, the Company Directors Disqualification Act 1986 [the Financial Services Act 1986 or Part II, III or VII of the Companies Act 1989][9],

(dd) for the purpose of enabling or assisting the Department of Economic Development for Northern Ireland to exercise any powers conferred on it by the enactments relating to companies or insolvency or for the purpose of enabling or assisting any inspector appointed by it under the enactments relating to companies to discharge his functions,][3]

(e) [. . .][10]

[(f) for the purpose of enabling or assisting the Bank of England to discharge its functions under the Banking Act [1987][6] or any other functions,

(g) for the purpose of enabling or assisting the Deposit Protection Board to discharge its functions under that Act,

(h) for any purpose mentioned in section 180(1)(b), (e), (h), [or (n)][11] of the Financial Services Act 1986,

[(hh) for the purpose of enabling or assisting a body established by order under section 46 of the Companies Act 1989 to discharge its functions under Part II of that Act, or of enabling or assisting a recognised supervisory or qualifying body within the meaning of that Part to discharge its functions as such;][8]

(i) for the purpose of enabling or assisting the Industrial Assurance Commissioner or the Industrial Assurance Commissioner for Northern Ireland to discharge his functions under the enactments relating to industrial assurance,

(j) for the purpose of enabling or assisting the Insurance Brokers Registration Council to discharge its functions under the Insurance Brokers (Registration) Act 1977,

(k) for the purpose of enabling or assisting an official receiver to discharge his functions under the enactments relating to insolvency or for the purpose of enabling or assisting a body which is for the time being a recognised professional body for the purposes of section 391 of the Insolvency Act 1986 to discharge its functions as such,

(l) with a view to the institution of, or otherwise for the purposes of, any disciplinary proceedings relating to the exercise by a solicitor, auditor, accountant, valuer or actuary of his professional duties,

[(ll) with a view to the institution of, or otherwise for the purposes of, any disciplinary proceedings relating to the discharge by a public servant of his duties;][8]

(m) [for the purpose of enabling or assisting an overseas regulatory authority to exercise its regulatory functions.][12][4]

[(1A) In subsection (1)—

(a) in paragraph (ll) "public servant" means an officer or servant of the Crown or of any public or other authority for the time being designated for the purposes of that paragraph by the Secretary of State by order made by statutory instrument; and

(b) in paragraph (m) "overseas regulatory authority" and "regulatory functions" have the same meaning as in section 82 of the Companies Act 1989.][13]

[(1B) Subject to subsection (1C), subsection (1) shall not preclude publication or disclosure for the purpose of enabling or assisting any public or other authority for the time being designated for the purposes of this [subsection][14] by the Secretary of State by an order in a statutory instrument to discharge any functions which are specified in the order.

(1C) An order under subsection (1B) designating an authority for the purpose of that subsection may—

(a) impose conditions subject to which the publication or disclosure of any information or document is permitted by that subsection; and

(b) otherwise restrict the circumstances in which that subsection permits publication or disclosure.

(1D) Subsection (1) shall not preclude the publication or disclosure of any such information as is mentioned in section 180(5) of the Financial Services Act 1986 by any person who by virtue of that section is not precluded by section 179 of that Act from disclosing it.][4]

(2) A person who publishes or discloses any information or document in contravention of this section is guilty of an offence and liable to imprisonment or a fine, or both.

[Sections 732 (restriction on prosecutions), 733 (liability of individuals for corporate default) and 734 (criminal proceedings against unincorporated bodies) apply to this offence.][15]

[(3) For the purposes of this section each of the following is a competent authority—

(a) the Secretary of State,

(b) an inspector appointed under this Part or under section 94 or 177 of the Financial Services Act 1986,

(c) any person authorised to exercise powers under section 44 of the Insurance Companies Act 1982, section 447 of this Act, section 106 of the Financial Services Act 1986 or section 84 of the Companies Act 1989,

(d) the Department of Economic Development in Northern Ireland,
(e) the Treasury,
(f) the Bank of England,
(g) the Lord Advocate,
(h) the Director of Public Prosecutions, and the Director of Public Prosecutions for Northern Ireland,
(i) any designated agency or transferee body within the meaning of the Financial Services Act 1986, and any body administering a scheme under section 54 of or paragraph 18 of Schedule 11 to that Act (schemes for compensation of investors),
(j) the Chief Registrar of friendly societies and the Registrar of Friendly Societies for Northern Ireland,
(k) the Industrial Assurance Commissioner and the Industrial Assurance Commissioner for Northern Ireland,
(l) any constable,
(m) any procurator fiscal.

(3A) Any information which may by virtue of this section be disclosed to a competent authority may be disclosed to any officer or servant of the authority.][16]

[(4) A statutory instrument containing an order under [subsection (1A)(a) or (1B)][17] is subject to annulment in pursuance of a resolution of either House of Parliament.][4]

---

1 Inserted by IA 1985, s 109, 6 Sch 4 with effect from 28 April 1986 (see SI 1986 No 463).

2 Substituted by FSA 1986, s 182, 13 Sch 9 with effect from
(a) 15 November 1986 for purposes of anything done or which may be done under or by virtue of any provision brought into operation by SI 1986 No 1940; and
(b) 27 November 1986, for all other purposes (see SI 1987 No 2031).

3 Substituted by FSA 1986, s 182, 13 Sch 9 with effect as for [2] above.

4 Inserted by FSA 1986, s 182, 13 Sch 9 with effect as for [2] above.

5 Substituted by IA 1986, s 439(1), 13 Sch Part I with effect from 29 December 1986 (see IA 1986, s 443 and SI 1986 No 1924).

6 Substituted by Banking Act 1987, s 108(1), 6 Sch 18(7) with effect from 1 October 1987 (see SI 1987 No 1664).

7 Substituted by CA 1989, s 65 with effect from 21 February 1990 (SI 1990 No 142).

8 Inserted by CA 1989, s 65 with effect from 21 February 1990 (SI 1990 No 142) except to the extent that the insert refers to a body established by order under CA 1989, s 46.

9 Substituted by CA 1989, s 65 with effect from 21 February 1990 (SI 1990 No 142) except to the extent that the substitution refers to CA 1989, Part VII.

10 Deleted by CA 1989, s 65 with effect as in [7] above.

11 Substituted by CA 1989, s 65 with effect as in [7] above.

12 Substituted by CA 1989, s 65 with effect as in [7] above.

13 Substituted by CA 1989, s 65 with effect as in [7] above.

14 Substituted by CA 1989, s 65 with effect as in [7] above.

15 Substituted by CA 1989, s 65 with effect as in [7] above.

16 Substituted by CA 1989, s 65 with effect as in [7] above.

17 Substituted by CA 1989, s 65 with effect as in [7] above.

18 Substituted by CA 1989, s 65 with effect as in [7] above.

19 Repealed by CA 1989, 24 Sch with effect as in [7] above.

Notes

(a) In subsection (1)(d) above the words 'the Prevention of Fraud (Investments) Act 1958' are repealed by FSA 1986, s 212(3), 17 Sch Part I with effect from 29 April 1988 in respect of a prospectus offering for subscription, or to any form of application for, units in a body corporate which is a recognised scheme. [SI 1988 No 740].

Cross references. See Sec 452 (privileged information); Sec 734 (offences); 24 Sch (punishment of offences).

Regulations. The Financial Services (Disclosure of Information) (Designated Authorities) Order 1986 (SI 1986 No 2046); (No 2) Order 1987 (SI 1987 No 859); (No 3) Order 1987 (SI 1987 No 1141); (No 4) Order 1988 (SI 1988 No 1058); The Companies (Disclosure of Information) (Designated Authorities) Order 1988 (SI 1988 No 1334).

450 Punishment for destroying, mutilating etc. company documents

(1) [An officer of a company, or of an insurance company][1] to which Part II of the Insurance Companies Act 1982 applies, who—

(a) destroys, mutilates or falsifies, or is privy to the destruction, mutilation or falsification of a document affecting or relating to the [company's][2] property or affairs, or

(b) makes, or is privy to the making of, a false entry in such a document,

is guilty of an offence, unless he proves that he had no intention to conceal the state of affairs of [the company][3] or to defeat the law.

(2) Such a person as above mentioned who fraudulently either parts with, alters or makes an omission in any such document or is privy to fraudulent parting with, fraudulent altering or fraudulent making of an omission in, any such document, is guilty of an offence.

(3) A person guilty of an offence under this section is liable to imprisonment or a fine, or both.

(4) [Sections 732 (restriction on prosecutions), 733 (liability of individuals for corporate default) and 734 (criminal proceedings against unincorporated bodies) apply to an offence under this section.][4]

[(5) In this section "document" includes information recorded in any form.][5]

1 Substituted by CA 1989, s 66 with effect from 21 February 1990 (SI 1990 No 142).

2 Substituted by CA 1989, s 66 with effect as in 1 above.

3 Substituted by CA 1989, s 66 with effect as in 1 above.

4 Substituted by CA 1989, s 66 with effect as in 1 above.

5 Inserted by CA 1989, s 66 with effect as in 1 above.

Cross references. See Sec 452 (privileged information); Sec 734 (offences); 24 Sch (punishment of offences).

451 Punishment for furnishing false information

A person who, in purported compliance with a requirement imposed under section 447 to provide an explanation or make a statement, provides or makes an explanation or statement which he knows to be false in a material particular or recklessly provides or makes an explanation or statement which is so false, is guilty of an offence and liable to imprisonment or a fine, or both.

[Sections 732 (restriction on prosecutions), 733 (liability of individuals for corporate default) and 734 (criminal proceedings against unincorporated bodies) apply to this offence.][1]

1 Substituted by CA 1989, s 67 with effect from 21 February 1990 (SI 1990 No 142).

Cross references. See Sec 452 (privileged information); Sec 734 (offences); 24 Sch (punishment of offences).

[451A Disclosure of information by Secretary of State or inspector

(1) This section applies to information obtained under sections 434 to 446.

(2) The Secretary of State may, if he thinks fit—

(a) disclose any information to which this section applies to any person to whom, or for any purpose for which, disclosure is permitted under section 449, or
(b) authorise or require an inspector appointed under this Part to disclose such information to any such person or for any such purpose.

(3) Information to which this section applies may also be disclosed by an inspector appointed under this Part to—

(a) another inspector appointed under this Part or an inspector appointed under section 94 or 177 of the Financial Services Act 1986, or
(b) a person authorised to exercise powers under section 44 of the Insurance Companies Act 1982, section 447 of this Act, section 106 of the Financial Services Act 1986 or section 84 of the Companies Act 1989.

(4) Any information which may by virtue of subsection (3) be disclosed to any person may be disclosed to any officer or servant of that person.

(5) The Secretary of State may, if he thinks fit, disclose any information obtained under section 444 to—

(a) the company whose ownership was the subject of the investigation,
(b) any member of the company,
(c) any person whose conduct was investigated in the course of the investigation,
(d) the auditors of the company, or
(e) any person whose financial interests appear to the Secretary of State to be affected by matters covered by the investigation.][1]

---

1 Inserted by CA 1989, s 68 with effect from 21 February 1990 (SI 1990 No 142).

Supplementary

452 Privileged information

(1) Nothing in sections 431 to 446 requires the disclosure to the Secretary of State or to an inspector appointed by him—

(a) by any person of information which he would in an action in the High Court or the Court of Session be entitled to refuse to disclose on grounds of legal professional privilege except, if he is a lawyer, the name and address of his client,
(b) [. . .][1]

[(1A) Nothing in section 434, 443 or 446 requires a person (except as mentioned in subsection (1B) below) to disclose information or produce documents in respect of which he owes an obligation of confidence by virtue of carrying on the business of banking unless—

(a) the person to whom the obligation of confidence is owed is the company or other body corporate under investigation,
(b) the person to whom the obligation of confidence is owed consents to the disclosure or production, or

(c) the making of the requirement is authorised by the Secretary of State.

(1B) Subsection (1A) does not apply where the person owing the obligation of confidence is the company or other body corporate under investigation under section 431, 432 or 433.][2]

(2) Nothing in sections 447 to 451 compels the production by any person of a document which he would in an action in the High Court or the Court of Session be entitled to refuse to produce on grounds of legal professional privilege, or authorises the taking of possession of any such document which is in the person's possession.

(3) The Secretary of State shall not under section 447 require, or authorise an officer of his [or other person][2] to require, the production by a person carrying on the business of banking of a document relating to the affairs of a customer of his unless either it appears to the Secretary of State that it is necessary to do so for the purpose of investigating the affairs of the first-mentioned person, or the customer is a person on whom a requirement has been imposed under that section, or under section 44(2) to (4) of the Insurance Companies Act 1982 (provision corresponding to section 447).

---

1 Deleted by CA 1989, s 69 with effect from 21 February 1990 (SI 1990 No 142).

2 Inserted by CA 1989, s 69 with effect as in [1] above.

Cross references. See Sec 453 (investigation of oversea companies).

---

453 Investigation of oversea companies

[(1) The provisions of this Part apply to bodies corporate incorporated outside Great Britain which are carrying on business in Great Britain, or have at any time carried on business there, as they apply to companies under this Act; but subject to the following exceptions, adaptations and modifications.

(1A) The following provisions do not apply to such bodies—

(a) section 431 (investigation on application of company or its members),
(b) section 438 (power to bring civil proceedings on the company's behalf),
(c) sections 442 to 445 (investigation of company ownership and power to obtain information as to those interested in shares, etc.), and
(d) section 446 (investigation of share dealings).

(1B) The other provisions of this Part apply to such bodies subject to such adaptations and modifications as may be specified by regulations made by the Secretary of State.][1]

(2) Regulations under this section shall be made by statutory instrument subject to annulment in pursuance of a resolution of either House of Parliament.

---

1 Substituted by CA 1989, s 70 with effect from 21 February 1990 (SI 1990 No 142).

PART XVII PROTECTION OF COMPANY'S MEMBERS AGAINST UNFAIR PREJUDICE

460 Order on application of Secretary of State

(1) If in the case of any company—

(a) the Secretary of State has received a report under section 437, or exercised his powers under section 447 or 448 of this Act or section 44(2) to (6) of the Insurance Companies Act 1982 [. . .][2], and

(b) it appears to him that the company's affairs are being or have been conducted in a manner which is [unfairly prejudicial to the interests of its members generally or of some part of its members][1], or that any actual or proposed act or omission of the company (including an act or omission on its behalf is or would be so prejudicial,

he may himself (in addition to or instead of presenting a petition [. . .][3] for the winding up of the company) apply to the court by petition for an order under this Part.

(2) In this section (and, so far as applicable for its purposes, in the section next following) "company" means any body corporate which is liable to be wound up under this Act.

---

1 Substituted by CA 1989, 19 Sch 11 with effect from a date to be appointed.

2 Repealed by CA 1989, 24 Sch with effect from a date to be appointed.

3 Repealed by CA 1989, 24 Sch with effect from a date to be appointed.

PART XXII BODIES CORPORATE SUBJECT, OR BECOMING SUBJECT, TO THIS ACT (OTHERWISE THAN BY ORIGINAL FORMATION UNDER PART I)

CHAPTER I COMPANIES FORMED OR REGISTERED UNDER FORMER COMPANIES ACTS

675 Companies formed and registered under former Companies Acts

(1) In its application to existing companies, this Act applies in the same manner—

(a) in the case of a limited company (other than a company limited by guarantee), as if the company had been formed and registered under Part I of this Act as a company limited by shares,

(b) in the case of a company limited by guarantee, as if the company had been formed and registered under that Part as a company limited by guarantee, and

(c) in the case of a company other than a limited company, as if the company had been formed and registered under that Part as an unlimited company.

(2) But reference, express or implied, to the date of registration is to be read as the date at which the company was registered under the Joint Stock Companies Acts, the Companies Act 1862, the Companies (Consolidation) Act 1908, the Companies Act 1929, or the Companies Act 1948.

Cross references. See Sec 679 (Irish companies).

676 Companies registered but not formed under former Companies Acts

(1) This Act applies to every company registered but not formed under the Joint Stock Companies Acts, the Companies Act 1862, the Companies (Consolidation) Act 1908, the Companies Act 1929, or the Companies Act 1948, in the same manner as it is in Chapter II of this Part declared to apply to companies registered but not formed under this Act.

(2) But reference, express or implied, to the date of registration is to be read as referring to the date at which the company was registered under the Joint Stock Companies Acts, the Companies Act 1862, the Companies (Consolidation) Act 1908, the Companies Act 1929, or the Companies Act 1948.

Cross references. See Sec 679 (Irish companies).

677 Companies re-registered with altered status under former Companies Acts

(1) This Act applies to every unlimited company registered or re-registered as limited in pursuance of the Companies Act 1879, section 57 of the Companies (Consolidation) Act 1908, section 16 of the Companies Act 1929, section 16 of the Companies Act 1948 or section 44 of the Companies Act 1967 as it (this Act) applies to an unlimited company re-registered as limited in pursuance of Part II of this Act.

(2) But reference, express or implied, to the date of registration or re-registration is to be read as referring to the date at which the company was registered or re-registered as a limited company under the relevant enactment.

Cross references. See Sec 679.

678 Companies registered under Joint Stock Companies Acts

(1) A company registered under the Joint Stock Companies Acts may cause its shares to be transferred in manner hitherto in use, or in such other manner as the company may direct.

(2) The power of altering articles under section 9 of this Act extends, in the case of an unlimited company formed and registered under the Joint Stock Companies Acts, to altering any regulations relating to the amount of capital or to its distribution into shares, notwithstanding that those regulations are contained in the memorandum.

Cross references. See Sec 679.

679 Northern Ireland and Irish companies

Nothing in sections 675 to 678 applies to companies registered in Northern Ireland or the Republic of Ireland.

CHAPTER II COMPANIES NOT FORMED UNDER COMPANIES LEGISLATION, BUT AUTHORISED TO REGISTER

680 Companies capable of being registered under this Chapter

(1) With the exceptions and subject to the provisions contained in this section and the next—

(a) any company consisting of two or more members, which was in existence on 2nd November 1862, including any company registered under the Joint Stock Companies Acts, and

(b) any company formed after that date (whether before or after the commencement of this Act), in pursuance of any Act of Parliament (other than this Act), or of letters patent, or being otherwise duly constituted according to law, and consisting of two or more members,

may at any time, on making application in the prescribed form, register under this Act as an unlimited company, or as a company limited by shares, or as a company limited by guarantee; and the registration is not invalid by reason that it has taken place with a view to the company's being wound up.

(2) A company registered in any part of the United Kingdom under the Companies Act 1862, the Companies (Consolidation) Act 1908, the Companies Act 1929 or the Companies Act 1948 shall not register under this section.

(3) A company having the liability of its members limited by Act of Parliament or letters patent, and not being a joint stock company, shall not register under this section.

(4) A company having the liability of its members limited by Act of Parliament or letters patent shall not register in pursuance of this section as an unlimited company or as a company limited by guarantee.

(5) A company that is not a joint stock company shall not register under this section as a company limited by shares.

Cross references. See Sec 681; 21 Sch.

---

681 Procedural requirements for registration

(1) A company shall not register under section 680 without the assent of a majority of such of its members as are present in person or by proxy (in cases where proxies are allowed) at a general meeting summoned for the purpose.

(2) Where a company not having the liability of its members limited by Act of Parliament or letters patent is about to register as a limited company, the majority required to assent as required by subsection (1) shall consist of not less than three-fourths of the members present in person or by proxy at the meeting.

(3) In computing any majority under this section when a poll is demanded, regard is to be had to the number of votes to which each member is entitled according to the company's regulations.

(4) Where a company is about to register (under section 680) as a company limited by guarantee, the assent to its being so registered shall be accompanied by a resolution declaring that each member undertakes to contribute to the company's assets, in the event of its being wound up while he is a member, or within one year after he ceases to be a member, for payment of the company's debts and liabilities contracted before he ceased to be a member, and of the costs and expenses of winding up and for the adjustment of the rights of the contributories among themselves, such amount as may be required, not exceeding a specified amount.

(5) Before a company is registered under section 680, it shall deliver to the registrar of companies—

(a) a statement that the registered office of the company is to be situated in England and Wales, or in Wales, or in Scotland (as the case may be),
(b) a statement specifying the intended situation of the company's registered office after registration, and
(c) in an appropriate case, if the company wishes to be registered with the Welsh equivalent of "public limited company" or, as the case may be, "limited" as the last words or word of its name, a statement to that effect.

(6) Any statement delivered to the registrar under subsection (5) shall be made in the prescribed form.

682 Change of name on registration

(1) Where the name of a company seeking registration under section 680 is a name by which it is precluded from registration by section 26 of this Act, either because it falls within subsection (1) of that section or, if it falls within subsection (2), because the Secretary of State would not approve the company's being registered with that name, the company may change its name with effect from the date on which it is registered under this Chapter.

(2) A change of name under this section requires the like assent of the company's members as is required by section 681 for registration.

683 Definition of "joint stock company"

(1) For purposes of this Chapter, as far as relates to registration of companies as companies limited by shares, "joint stock company" means a company—

(a) having a permanent paid-up or nominal share capital of fixed amount divided into shares, also of fixed amount, or held and transferable as stock, or divided and held partly in one way and partly in the other, and
(b) formed on the principle of having for its members the holders of those shares or that stock, and no other persons.

(2) Such a company when registered with limited liability under this Act is deemed a company limited by shares.

684 Requirements for registration by joint stock companies

(1) Before the registration under section 680 of a joint stock company, there shall be delivered to the registrar of companies the following documents—

(a) a statement in the prescribed form specifying the name with which the company is proposed to be registered,

(b) a list in the prescribed form showing the names and addresses of all persons who on a day named in the list [(not more than 28 clear days before the day of registration)][1] were members of the company, with the addition of the shares or stock held by them respectively (distinguishing, in cases where the shares are numbered, each share by its number), and

(c) a copy of any Act of Parliament, royal charter, letters patent, deed of settlement, contract of copartnery or other instrument constituting or regulating the company.

(2) If the company is intended to be registered as a limited company, there shall also be delivered to the registrar of companies a statement in the prescribed form specifying the following particulars—

(a) the nominal share capital of the company and the number of shares into which it is divided, or the amount of stock of which it consists, and

(b) the number of shares taken and the amount paid on each share.

---

1 Substituted by CA 1989, 19 Sch 12 with effect from 1 March 1990 (SI 1990 No 142).

---

685 Registration of joint stock company as public company

(1) A joint stock company applying to be registered under section 680 as a company limited by shares may, subject to—

(a) satisfying the conditions set out in section 44(2)(a) and (b) (where applicable) and section 45(2) to (4) as applied by this section, and

(b) complying with subsection (4) below,

apply to be so registered as a public company.

(2) Sections 44 and 45 apply for this purpose as in the case of a private company applying to be re-registered under section 43, but as if a reference to the special resolution required by section 43 were to the joint stock company's resolution that it be a public company.

(3) The resolution may change the company's name by deleting the word "company" or the words "and company", or its or their equivalent in Welsh ("cwmni", "a'r cwmni"), including any abbreviation of them.

(4) The joint stock company's application shall be made in the form prescribed for the purpose, and shall be delivered to the registrar of companies together with the following documents (as well as those required by section 684), namely—

(a) a copy of the resolution that the company be a public company,

(b) a copy of a written statement by an accountant with the appropriate qualifications that in his opinion a relevant balance sheet shows that at the balance sheet date the amount of the company's net assets was not less than the aggregate of its called up share capital and undistributable reserves;

(c) a copy of the relevant balance sheet, together with a copy of an unqualified report (by an accountant with such qualifications) in relation to that balance sheet,

(d) a copy of any valuation report prepared under section 44(2)(b) as applied by this section, and

(e) a statutory declaration in the prescribed form by a director or secretary of the company—

(i) that the conditions set out in section 44(2)(a) and (b) (where applicable) and section 45(2) to (4) have been satisfied, and

(ii) that, between the balance sheet date referred to in paragraph (b) of this subsection and the joint stock company's application, there has been no change in the company's financial position that has resulted in the amount of its net assets becoming less than the aggregate of its called up share capital and undistributable reserves.

(5) The registrar may accept a declaration under subsection (4)(e) as sufficient evidence that the conditions referred to in that paragraph have been satisfied.

(6) In this section—

"accountant with the appropriate qualifications" means a person who would be qualified under section 389(1) for appointment as the company's auditor, if it were a company registered under this Act,

"relevant balance sheet" means a balance sheet prepared as at a date not more than 7 months before the joint stock company's application to be registered as a public company limited by shares, and

"undistributable reserves" has the meaning given by section 264(3);

and section 46 applies (with necessary modifications) for the interpretation of the reference in subsection (4)(c) above to an unqualified report by the accountant.

Cross references. See Sec 104(5) (transfer to public company of non-cash asset in initial period).

---

686 Other requirements for registration

(1) Before the registration in pursuance of this Chapter of any company (not being a joint stock company), there shall be delivered to the registrar of companies—

(a) a statement in the prescribed form specifying the name with which the company is proposed to be registered,

(b) [a list showing with respect to each director or manager of the company—

(i) in the case of an individual, his name, address, occupation and date of birth,

(ii) in the case of a corporation or Scottish firm, its corporate or firm name and registered or principal office,][1]

(c) a copy of any Act of Parliament, letters patent, deed of settlement, contract of copartnery or other instrument constituting or regulating the company, and

(d) in the case of a company intended to be registered as a company limited by guarantee, a copy of the resolution declaring the amount of the guarantee.

[(1A) For the purposes of subsection (1)(b)(i) a person's "name" means his Christian name (or other forename) and surname, except that in the case of a peer, or an individual usually known by a title, the title may be stated instead of his Christian name (or other forename) and surname or in addition to either or both of them.][2]

(2) The lists of members and directors and any other particulars relating to the company which are required by this Chapter to be delivered to the registrar shall be verified by a statutory declaration in the prescribed form made by any two or more directors or other principal officers of the company.

(3) The registrar may require such evidence as he thinks necessary for the purpose of satisfying himself whether a company proposing to be registered is or is not a joint stock company as defined by section 683.

1 Substituted by CA 1989, 19 Sch 5 with effect from a date to be appointed.

2 Inserted by CA 1989, 19 Sch 5 with effect from a date to be appointed.

687 Name of company registering

(1) The following applies with respect to the name of a company registering under this Chapter (whether a joint stock company or not).

(2) If the company is to be registered as a public company, its name must end with the words "public limited company" or, if it is stated that the company's registered office is to be situated in Wales, with those words or their equivalent in Welsh ("cwmni cyfyngedig cyhoeddus"); and those words or that equivalent may not be preceded by the word "limited" or its equivalent in Welsh ("cyfyngedig").

(3) In the case of a company limited by shares or by guarantee (not being a public company), the name must have "limited" as its last word (or, if the company's registered office is to be situated in Wales, "cyfyngedig"); but this is subject to section 30 (exempting a company, in certain circumstances, from having "limited" as part of the name).

(4) If the company is registered with limited liability, then any additions to the company's name set out in the statements delivered under section 684(1)(a) or 686(1)(a) shall form and be registered as the last part of the company's name.

688 Certificate of registration under this Chapter

(1) On compliance with the requirements of this Chapter with respect to registration, the registrar of companies shall give a certificate (which may be signed by him, or authenticated by his official seal) that the company applying for registration is incorporated as a company under this Act and, in the case of a limited company, that it is limited.

(2) On the issue of the certificate, the company shall be so incorporated; and a banking company in Scotland so incorporated is deemed a bank incorporated, constituted or established by or under Act of Parliament.

(3) The certificate is conclusive evidence that the requirements of this Chapter in respect of registration, and of matters precedent and incidental to it, have been complied with.

(4) Where on an application by a joint stock company to register as a public company limited by shares the registrar of companies is satisfied that the company may be registered as a public company so limited, the certificate of incorporation given under this section shall state that the company is a public company; and that statement is conclusive evidence that the requirements of section 685 have been complied with and that the company is a public company so limited.

689 Effect of registration

Schedule 21 to this Act has effect with respect to the consequences of registration under this Chapter, the vesting of property, savings for existing liabilities, continuation of existing actions, status of the company following registration, and other connected matters.

690 Power to substitute memorandum and articles for deed of settlement

(1) Subject as follows, a company registered in pursuance of this Chapter may by special resolution alter the form of its constitution by substituting a memorandum and articles for a deed of settlement.

(2) The provisions of sections 4 to 6 of this Act with respect to applications to the court for cancellation of alterations of the objects of a company and matters consequential on the passing of resolutions for such alterations (so far as applicable) apply, but with the following modifications—

(a) there is substituted for the printed copy of the altered memorandum required to be delivered to the registrar of companies a printed copy of the substituted memorandum and articles, and

(b) on the delivery to the registrar of the substituted memorandum and articles or the date when the alteration is no longer liable to be cancelled by order of the court (whichever is the later)—

(i) the substituted memorandum and articles apply to the company in the same manner as if it were a company registered under Part I with that memorandum and those articles, and

(ii) the company's deed of settlement ceases to apply to the company.

(3) An alteration under this section may be made either with or without alteration of the company's objects.

(4) In this section "deed of settlement" includes any contract of copartnery or other instrument constituting or regulating the company, not being an Act of Parliament, a royal charter or letters patent.

PART XXIII OVERSEA COMPANIES

CHAPTER I REGISTRATION, ETC.

691 Documents to be delivered to registrar

(1) When a company incorporated outside Great Britain establishes a place of business in Great Britain, it shall within one month of doing so deliver to the registrar of companies for registration—

(a) a certified copy of the charter, statutes or memorandum and articles of the company or other instrument constituting or defining the company's constitution, and, if the instrument is not written in the English language, a certified translation of it; and

(b) a return in the prescribed form containing—

(i) a list of the company's directors and secretary, containing the particulars specified in the next subsection,

(ii) a list of the names and addresses of some one or more persons resident in Great Britain authorised to accept on the company's behalf service of process and any notices required to be served on it,

(iii) a list of the documents delivered in compliance with paragraph (a) of this subsection, and

(iv) a statutory declaration (made by a director or secretary of the company or by any person whose name and address are given in the list required by sub-paragraph (ii)), stating the date on which the company's place of business in Great Britain was established.

[(2) The list referred to in subsection (1)(b)(i) shall contain the following particulars with respect to each director—

(a) in the case of an individual—

(i) his name,

(ii) any former name,

(iii) his usual residential address,

(iv) his nationality,

(v) his business occupation (if any),

(vi) if he has no business occupation but holds other directorships, particulars of them, and

(vii) his date of birth;

(b) in the case of a corporation or Scottish firm, its corporate or firm name and registered or principal office.

(3) The list referred to in subsection (1)(b)(i) shall contain the following particulars with respect to the secretary (or, where there are joint secretaries, with respect to each of them)—

(a) in the case of an individual, his name, any former name and his usual residential address;

(b) in the case of a corporation or Scottish firm, its corporate or firm name and registered or principal office.

Where all the partners in a firm are joint secretaries of the company, the name and principal office of the firm may be stated instead of the particulars required by paragraph (a).

(4) In subsections (2)(a) and (3)(a) above—

(a) "name" means a person's Christian name (or other forename) and surname, except that in the case of a peer, or an individual usually known by a title, the title may be stated instead of his Christian name (or other forename) and surname, or in addition to either or both of them; and

(b) the reference to a former name does not include—

(i) in the case of a peer, or an individual normally known by a British title, the name by which he was known previous to the adoption of or succession to the title, or

(ii) in the case of any person, a former name which was changed or disused before he attained the age of 18 years or which has been changed or disused for 20 years or more, or

(iii) in the case of a married woman, the name by which she was known previous to the marriage.][1]

---

[1] Substituted by CA 1989, 19 Sch 6 with effect from a date to be appointed.

Cross references. See Sec 697 (penalties); SI 1985 No 854, Reg 6 (translation of document into English).

---

692 Registration of altered particulars

(1) If any alteration is made in—

(a) the charter, statutes, or memorandum and articles of an oversea company or any such instrument as is mentioned above, or

(b) the directors or secretary of an oversea company or the particulars contained in the list of the directors and secretary, or

(c) the names or addresses of the persons authorised to accept service on behalf of an oversea company,

the company shall, within the time specified below, deliver to the registrar of companies for registration a return containing the prescribed particulars of the alteration.

(2) If any change is made in the corporate name of an oversea company, the company shall, within the time specified below, deliver to the registrar of companies for registration a return containing the prescribed particulars of the change.

(3) The time for delivery of the returns required by subsections (1) and (2) is—

(a) in the case of an alteration to which subsection (1)(c) applies, 21 days after the making of the alteration, and

(b) otherwise, 21 days after the date on which notice of the alteration or change in question could have been received in Great Britain in due course of post (if despatched with due diligence).

Cross references. See Sec 697 (penalties); SI 1985 No 854, Reg 7 (certification of constitution).

---

693 Obligation to state name and other particulars

Every oversea company shall—

(a) in every prospectus inviting subscriptions for its shares or debentures in Great Britain, state the country in which the company is incorporated,

(b) conspicuously exhibit on every place where it carries on business in Great Britain the company's name and the country in which it is incorporated,

(c) cause the company's name and the country in which it is incorporated to be stated in legible characters in all bill-heads and letter paper, and in all notices and other official publications of the company, and

(d) if the liability of the members of the company is limited, cause notice of that fact to be stated in legible characters in every such prospectus as above mentioned and in all bill-heads, letter paper, notices and other official publications of the company in Great Britain, and to be affixed on every place where it carries on its business.

Notes

(a) Paragraph (a) above and in paragraph (d) the words 'in every such prospectus as above-mentioned and' are repealed by FSA 1986, s 212(3), 17 Sch Part I from a date or dates to be appointed by statutory instrument (see FSA 1986, s 211(1)). To date the provisions have been repealed as follows.

(i) To the extent to which they would apply in relation to any investment which is listed or the subject of an application for listing in accordance with FSA 1986, Part IV (official listing of securities)

(A) with effect from 12 January 1987 for all purposes relating to the admission of securities offered by or on behalf of a Minister of the Crown or a body corporate controlled by a Minister of the Crown or a subsidiary of such a body to the Official List in respect of which an application is made after that date; and

(B) with effect from 16 February 1987 for purposes relating to the admission of securities in respect of which an application is made after that date other than those referred to in (A) above and otherwise for all purposes.

[SI 1986 No 2246].

(ii) With effect from 29 April 1988 in respect of a prospectus offering for subscription, or to any form of application for, units in a body corporate which is a recognised scheme. [SI 1988 No 740].

(iii) With effect from 1 December 1988 in respect of a prospectus offering for subscription, or to any application form for, units in a body which is an open-ended investment company. [SI 1988 No 740 as amended by SI 1988 No 995].

Cross references. See Sec 697 (penalties).

694 Regulation of oversea companies in respect of their names

(1) If it appears to the Secretary of State that the corporate name of an oversea company is a name by which the company, had it been formed under this Act, would on the relevant date (defined below in subsection (3)) have been precluded from being registered by section 26 either—

(a) because it falls within subsection (1) of that section, or

(b) if it falls within subsection (2) of that section, because the Secretary of State would not approve the company's being registered with that name,

the Secretary of State may serve a notice on the company, stating why the name would not have been registered.

(2) If the corporate name of an oversea company is in the Secretary of State's opinion too like a name appearing on the relevant date in the index of names kept by the registrar of companies under section 714 or which should have appeared in that index on that date, or is the same as a name which should have so appeared, the Secretary of State may serve a notice on the company specifying the name in the index which the company's name is too like or which is the same as the company's name.

(3) No notice shall be served on a company under subsection (1) or (2) later than 12 months after the relevant date, being the date on which the company has complied with—

(a) section 691 in this Part, or

(b) if there has been a change in the company's corporate name, section 692(2).

(4) An oversea company on which a notice is served under subsection (1) or (2)—

(a) may deliver to the registrar of companies for registration a statement in the prescribed form specifying a name approved by the Secretary of State other than its corporate name under which it proposes to carry on business in Great Britain, and

(b) may, after that name has been registered, at any time deliver to the registrar for registration a statement in the prescribed form specifying a name approved by the Secretary of State (other than its corporate name) in substitution for the name previously registered.

(5) The name by which an oversea company is for the time being registered under subsection (4) is, for all purposes of the law applying in Great Britain (including this Act and the Business Names Act 1985), deemed to be the company's corporate name; but—

(a) this does not affect references to the corporate name in this section, or any rights or obligations of the company, or render defective any legal proceedings by or against the company, and

(b) any legal proceedings that might have been continued or commenced against the company by its corporate name or its name previously registered under this section may be continued or commenced against it by its name for the time being so registered.

(6) An oversea company on which a notice is served under subsection (1) or (2) shall not at any time after the expiration of 2 months from the service of that notice (or such longer period as may be specified in that notice) carry on business in Great Britain under its corporate name.

Nothing in this subsection, or in section 697(2) (which imposes penalties for its contravention) invalidates any transaction entered into by the company.

(7) The Secretary of State may withdraw a notice served under subsection (1) or (2) at any time before the end of the period mentioned in subsection (6); and that subsection does not apply to a company served with a notice which has been withdrawn.

695 Service of documents on oversea company

(1) Any process or notice required to be served on an oversea company is sufficiently served if addressed to any person whose name has been delivered to the registrar under preceding sections in this Part and left at or sent by post to the address which has been so delivered.

(2) However—

(a) where such a company makes default in delivering to the registrar the name and address of a person resident in Great Britain who is authorised to accept on behalf of the company service of process or notices, or

(b) if at any time all the persons whose names and addresses have been so delivered are dead or have ceased so to reside, or refuse to accept service on the company's behalf, or for any reason cannot be served,

a document may be served on the company by leaving it at, or sending it by post to, any place of business established by the company in Great Britain.

696 [Registrar to whom documents to be delivered

(1) References to the registrar in relation to an oversea company (except references in Chapter III of this Part (registration of charges): see section 703E), shall be construed in accordance with the following provisions.

(2) The documents which an oversea company is required to deliver to the registrar shall be delivered—

(a) to the registrar for England and Wales if the company has established a place of business in England and Wales, and

(b) to the registrar for Scotland if the company has established a place of business in Scotland;

and if the company has an established place of business in both parts of Great Britain, the documents shall be delivered to both registrars.

(3) If a company ceases to have a place of business in either part of Great Britain, it shall forthwith give notice of that fact to the registrar for that part; and from the date on which notice is so given it is no longer obliged to deliver documents to that registrar.][1]

---

1 Substituted by CA 1989, 19 Sch 13 with effect from a date to be appointed.

Cross references. See Sec 697; Sec 703D(4) (charges over property).

---

697 Penalties for non-compliance

(1) If an oversea company fails to comply with any of sections 691 to 693 and 696, the company, and every officer or agent of the company who knowingly and wilfully authorises or permits the default, is liable to a fine and, in the case of a continuing offence, to a daily default fine for continued contravention.

(2) If an oversea company contravenes section 694(6), the company and every officer or agent of it who knowingly and wilfully authorises or permits the contravention is guilty of an offence and liable to a fine and, for continued contravention, to a daily default fine.

Cross references. See 24 Sch (punishment of offences).

---

698 Definitions for this Chapter

For purposes of this Chapter—

"certified" means certified in the prescribed manner to be a true copy or a correct translation;

"director", in relation to an oversea company, includes shadow director; and

"secretary" includes any person occupying the position of secretary by whatever name called.

Cross references. See SI 1985 No 854, Reg 6 (translation of document into English).

---

699 Channel Islands and Isle of Man companies

(1) With the exceptions specified in subsection (3) below, the provisions of this Act requiring documents to be forwarded or delivered to or filed with the registrar of companies and applying to companies formed and registered under Part I apply also (if they would not otherwise) to an oversea company incorporated in the Channel Islands or the Isle of Man.

(2) Those provisions apply to such a company—

(a) if it has established a place of business in England and Wales, as if it were registered in England and Wales,

(b) if it has established a place of business in Scotland, as if it were registered in Scotland, and

(c) if it has established a place of business both in England and Wales and in Scotland, as if it were registered in both England and Wales and Scotland,

with such modifications as may be necessary and, in particular, apply in a similar way to documents relating to things done outside Great Britain as if they had been done in Great Britain.

(3) The exceptions are—

section 6(1) (resolution altering company's objects),

section 18 (alteration of memorandum or articles by statute or statutory instrument),

[section 242(1)][1] (directors' duty to file accounts),

section 288(2) (notice to registrar of change of directors or secretary), and

section 380 (copies of certain resolutions and agreements to be sent to registrar within 15 days), so far as applicable to a resolution altering a company's memorandum or articles.

---

1 Substituted by CA 1989, 10 Sch 12 with effect from 1 April 1990 (SI 1990 No 355) subject to the transitional and saving provisions in Arts 6 to 9 of that Order.

[CHAPTER II DELIVERY OF ACCOUNTS AND REPORTS][1]

[1] Substituted by CA 1989, 10 Sch 13 with effect from a date to be appointed. Previously 'CHAPTER II DELIVERY OF ACCOUNTS'.

Note. The original provisions of this Chapter are substituted by CA 1989, 10 Sch 13 with effect from a date to be appointed.

[700 Preparation of accounts and reports by oversea companies

(1) Every oversea company shall in respect of each financial year of the company prepare the like accounts and directors' report, and cause to be prepared such an auditors' report, as would be required if the company were formed and registered under this Act.

(2) The Secretary of State may by order—

(a) modify the requirements referred to in subsection (1) for the purpose of their application to oversea companies;

(b) exempt an oversea company from those requirements or from such of them as may be specified in the order.

(3) An order may make different provision for different cases or classes of case and may contain such incidental and supplementary provisions as the Secretary of State thinks fit.

(4) An order under this section shall be made by statutory instrument which shall be subject to annulment in pursuance of a resolution of either House of Parliament.][1]

[1] Inserted by CA 1989, 10 Sch 13 with effect from 1 April 1990 (SI 1990 No 355) subject to the transitional and saving provisions in Arts 6 to 9 of that Order.

Cross references. See SI 1985 No 854, Reg 6 (translation of document into English).

[701 Oversea company's financial year and accounting reference periods

(1) Sections 223 to 225 (financial year and accounting reference periods) apply to an oversea company, subject to the following modifications.

(2) For the references to the incorporation of the company substitute references to the company establishing a place of business in Great Britain.

(3) Omit section 225(4) (restriction on frequency with which current accounting reference period may be extended).][1]

[1] Inserted by CA 1989, 10 Sch 13 with effect from 1 April 1990 (SI 1990 No 355) subject to the transitional and saving provisions in Arts 6 to 9 of that Order.

[702 Delivery to registrar of accounts and reports of oversea company

(1) An oversea company shall in respect of each financial year of the company deliver to the registrar copies of the accounts and reports prepared in accordance with section 700.

If any document comprised in those accounts or reports is in a language other than English, the directors shall annex to the copy delivered a translation of it into English, certified in the prescribed manner to be a correct translation.

(2) In relation to an oversea company the period allowed for delivering accounts and reports is 13 months after the end of the relevant accounting reference period.

This is subject to the following provisions of this section.

(3) If the relevant accounting reference period is the company's first and is a period of more than 12 months, the period allowed is 13 months from the first anniversary of the company's establishing a place of business in Great Britain.

(4) If the relevant accounting period is treated as shortened by virtue of a notice given by the company under section 225 (alteration of accounting reference date), the period allowed is that applicable in accordance with the above provisions or three months from the date of the notice under that section, whichever last expires.

(5) If for any special reason the Secretary of State thinks fit he may, on an application made before the expiry of the period otherwise allowed, by notice in writing to an oversea company extend that period by such further period as may be specified in the notice.

(6) In this section "the relevant accounting reference period" means the accounting reference period by reference to which the financial year for the accounts in question was determined.][1]

---

1 Inserted by CA 1989, 10 Sch 13 with effect from 1 April 1990 (SI 1990 No 355) subject to the transitional and saving provisions in Arts 6 to 9 of that Order.

[703 Penalty for non-compliance

(1) If the requirements of section 702(1) are not complied with before the end of the period allowed for delivering accounts and reports, or if the accounts and reports delivered do not comply with the requirements of this Act, the company and every person who immediately before the end of that period was a director of the company is guilty of an offence and liable to a fine and, for continued contravention, to a daily default fine.

(2) It is a defence for a person charged with such an offence to prove that he took all reasonable steps for securing that the requirements in question would be complied with.

(3) It is not a defence in relation to a failure to deliver copies to the registrar to prove that the documents in question were not in fact prepared as required by this Act.][1]

---

1 Inserted by CA 1989, 10 Sch 13 with effect from 1 April 1990 (SI 1990 No 355) subject to the transitional and saving provisions in Arts 6 to 9 of that Order.

Cross references. See 24 Sch (punishment of offences).

[CHAPTER III REGISTRATION OF CHARGES

Note. This chapter is inserted by CA 1989, 15 Sch and replaced the original provisions of Secs 409 and 424.

[703A Introductory provisions

(1) The provisions of this Chapter have effect for securing the registration in Great Britain of charges on the property of a registered oversea company.

(2) Section 395(2) and (3) (meaning of "charge" and "property") have effect for the purposes of this Chapter.

(3) A "registered oversea company", in relation to England and Wales or Scotland, means an oversea company which has duly delivered documents to the registrar for that part of Great Britain under section 691 and has not subsequently given notice to him under section 696(4) that it has ceased to have an established place of business in that part.

(4) References in this Chapter to the registrar shall be construed in accordance with section 703E below and references to registration, in relation to a charge, are to registration in the register kept by him under this Chapter.][1]

1 Inserted by CA 1989, 15 Sch with effect from a date to be appointed.

[703B Charges requiring registration

(1) The charges requiring registration under this Chapter are those which if created by a company registered in Great Britain would require registration under Part XII of this Act.

(2) Whether a charge is one requiring registration under this Chapter shall be determined—

- (a) in the case of a charge over property of a company at the date it delivers documents for registration under section 691, as at that date,
- (b) in the case of a charge created by a registered oversea company, as at the date the charge is created, and
- (c) in the case of a charge over property acquired by a registered oversea company, as at the date of the acquisition.

(3) In the following provisions of this Chapter references to a charge are, unless the context otherwise requires, to a charge requiring registration under this Chapter.

Where a charge not otherwise requiring registration relates to property by virtue of which it requires to be registered and to other property, the references are to the charge so far as it relates to property of the former description.][1]

1 Inserted by CA 1989, 15 Sch with effect from a date to be appointed.

[703C The register

(1) The registrar shall keep for each registered oversea company a register, in such form as he thinks fit, of charges on property of the company.

(2) The register shall consist of a file containing with respect to each such charge the particulars and other information delivered to the registrar under or by virtue of the following provisions of this Chapter.

(3) Section 397(3) to (5) (registrar's certificate as to date of delivery of particulars) applies in relation to the delivery of any particulars or other information under this Chapter.][1]

---

1 Inserted by CA 1989, 15 Sch with effect from a date to be appointed.

[703D Company's duty to deliver particulars of charges for registration

(1) If when an oversea company delivers documents for registration under section 691 any of its property is situated in Great Britain and subject to a charge, it is the company's duty at the same time to deliver the prescribed particulars of the charge, in the prescribed form, to the registrar for registration.

(2) Where a registered oversea company—

(a) creates a charge on property situated in Great Britain, or

(b) acquires property which is situated in Great Britain and subject to a charge,

it is the company's duty to deliver the prescribed particulars of the charge, in the prescribed form, to the registrar for registration within 21 days after the date of the charge's creation or, as the case may be, the date of the acquisition.

This subsection does not apply if the property subject to the charge is at the end of that period no longer situated in Great Britain.

(3) Where the preceding subsections do not apply and property of a registered oversea company is for a continuous period of four months situated in Great Britain and subject to a charge, it is the company's duty before the end of that period to deliver the prescribed particulars of the charge, in the prescribed form, to the registrar for registration.

(4) Particulars of a charge required to be delivered under subsections (1), (2) or (3) may be delivered for registration by any person interested in the charge.

(5) If a company fails to comply with subsection (1), (2) or (3), then, unless particulars of the charge have been delivered for registration by another person, the company and every officer of it who is in default is liable to a fine.

(6) Section 398(2), (4) and (5) (recovery of fees paid in connection with registration, filing of particulars in register and sending of copy of particulars filed and note as to date) apply in relation to particulars delivered under this Chapter.][1]

---

1 Inserted by CA 1989, 15 Sch with effect from a date to be appointed.

[703E Registrar to whom particulars, etc. to be delivered

(1) The particulars required to be delivered by section 703D(1) (charges over property of oversea company becoming registered in a part of Great Britain) shall be delivered to the registrar to whom the documents are delivered under section 691.

(2) The particulars required to be delivered by section 703D(2) or (3) (charges over property of registered oversea company) shall be delivered—

(a) if the company is registered in one part of Great Britain and not in the other, to the registrar for the part in which it is registered, and

(b) if the company is registered in both parts of Great Britain but the property subject to the charge is situated in one part of Great Britain only, to the registrar for that part;

and in any other case the particulars shall be delivered to the registrars for both parts of Great Britain.

(3) Other documents required or authorised by virtue of this Chapter to be delivered to the registrar shall be delivered to the registrar or registrars to whom particulars of the charge to which they relate have been, or ought to have been, delivered.

(4) If a company gives notice under section 696(4) that it has ceased to have an established place of business in either part of Great Britain, charges over property of the company shall cease to be subject to the provisions of this Chapter, as regards registration in that part of Great Britain, as from the date on which notice is so given.

This is without prejudice to rights arising by reason of events occurring before that date.][1]

[1] Inserted by CA 1989, 15 Sch with effect from a date to be appointed.

[703F Effect of failure to deliver particulars, late delivery and effect of errors and omissions

(1) The following provisions of Part XII—

(a) section 399 (effect of failure to deliver particulars),
(b) section 400 (late delivery of particulars), and
(c) section 402 (effect of errors and omissions in particulars delivered),

apply, with the following modifications, in relation to a charge created by a registered oversea company of which particulars are required to be delivered under this Chapter.

(2) Those provisions do not apply to a charge of which particulars are required to be delivered under section 703D(1) (charges existing when company delivers documents under section 691).

(3) In relation to a charge of which particulars are required to be delivered under section 703D(3) (charges registrable by virtue of property being within Great Britain for requisite period), the references to the period of 21 days after the charge's creation shall be construed as references to the period of four months referred to in that subsection.][1]

[1] Inserted by CA 1989, 15 Sch with effect from a date to be appointed.

[703G Delivery of further particulars or memorandum

Sections 401 and 403 (delivery of further particulars and memorandum of charge ceasing to affect company's property) apply in relation to a charge of which particulars have been delivered under this Chapter.][1]

[1] Inserted by CA 1989, 15 Sch with effect from a date to be appointed.

[703H Further provisions with respect to voidness of charges

(1) The following provisions of Part XII apply in relation to the voidness of a charge by virtue of this Chapter—

(a) section 404 (exclusion of voidness as against unregistered charges),
(b) section 405 (restrictions on cases in which charge is void),

(c) section 406 (effect of exercise of power of sale), and
(d) section 407 (effect of voidness on obligation secured).

(2) In relation to a charge of which particulars are required to be delivered under section 703D(3) (charges registrable by virtue of property being within Great Britain for requisite period), the reference in section 404 to the period of 21 days after the charge's creation shall be construed as a reference to the period of four months referred to in that subsection.][1]

---

1 Inserted by CA 1989, 15 Sch with effect from a date to be appointed.

[703I Additional information to be registered

(1) Section 408 (particulars of taking up of issue of debentures) applies in relation to a charge of which particulars have been delivered under this Chapter.

(2) Section 409 (notice of appointment of receiver or manager) applies in relation to the appointment of a receiver or manager of property of a registered oversea company.

(3) Regulations under section 410 (notice of crystallisation of floating charge, etc.) may apply in relation to a charge of which particulars have been delivered under this Chapter; but subject to such exceptions, adaptations and modifications as may be specified in the regulations.][1]

---

1 Inserted by CA 1989, 15 Sch with effect from a date to be appointed.

[703J Copies of instruments and register to be kept by company

(1) Sections 411 and 412 (copies of instruments and register to be kept by company) apply in relation to a registered oversea company and any charge over property of the company situated in Great Britain.

(2) They apply to any charge, whether or not particulars are required to be delivered to the registrar.

(3) In relation to such a company the references to the company's registered office shall be construed as references to its principal place of business in Great Britain.][1]

---

1 Inserted by CA 1989, 15 Sch with effect from a date to be appointed.

[703K Power to make further provision by regulations

(1) The Secretary of State may by regulations make further provision as to the application of the provisions of this Chapter, or the provisions of Part XII applied by this Chapter, in relation to charges of any description specified in the regulations.

(2) The regulations may apply any provisions of regulations made under section 413 (power to make further provision with respect to application of Part XII) or make any provision which may be made under that section with respect to the application of provisions of Part XII.][1]

---

1 Inserted by CA 1989, 15 Sch with effect from a date to be appointed.

[703L Provisions as to situation of property

(1) The following provisions apply for determining for the purposes of this Chapter whether a vehicle which is the property of an oversea company is situated in Great Britain—

(a) a ship, aircraft or hovercraft shall be regarded as situated in Great Britain if, and only if, it is registered in Great Britain;

(b) any other description of vehicle shall be regarded as situated in Great Britain on a day if, and only if, at any time on that day the management of the vehicle is directed from a place of business of the company in Great Britain;

and for the purposes of this Chapter a vehicle shall not be regarded as situated in one part of Great Britain only.

(2) For the purposes of this Chapter as it applies to a charge on future property, the subject-matter of the charge shall be treated as situated in Great Britain unless it relates exclusively to property of a kind which cannot, after being acquired or coming into existence, be situated in Great Britain; and references to property situated in a part of Great Britain shall be similarly construed.][1]

1 Inserted by CA 1989, 15 Sch with effect from a date to be appointed.

[703M Other supplementary provisions

The following provisions of Part XII apply for the purposes of this Chapter—

(a) section 414 (construction of references to date of creation of charge),
(b) section 415 (prescribed particulars and related expressions),
(c) section 416 (notice of matters disclosed on the register),
(d) section 417 (power of court to dispense with signature),
(e) section 418 (regulations) and
(f) section 419 (minor definitions).][1]

1 Inserted by CA 1989, 15 Sch with effect from a date to be appointed.

[703N Index of defined expressions

The following Table shows the provisions of this Chapter and Part XII defining or otherwise explaining expressions used in this Chapter (other than expressions used only in the same section)—

charge	sections 703A(2), 703B(3) and 395(2)
charge requiring registration	sections 703B(1) and 396
creation of charge	sections 703M(f) and 419(2)
date of acquisition (of property by a company)	sections 703M(f) and 419(3)
date of creation of charge	sections 703M(a) and 414
property	sections 703A(2) and 395(2)
registered oversea company	section 703A(3)
registrar and registration in relation to a charge	sections 703A(4) and 703E
situated in Great Britain	
in relation to vehicles	section 703L(1)
in relation to future property	section 703L(2)][1]

1 Inserted by CA 1989, 15 Sch with effect from a date to be appointed.

PART XXIV THE REGISTRAR OF COMPANIES, HIS FUNCTIONS AND OFFICES

705 [Companies' registered numbers

(1) The registrar shall allocate to every company a number, which shall be known as the company's registered number.

(2) Companies' registered numbers shall be in such form, consisting of one or more sequences of figures or letters, as the registrar may from time to time determine.

(3) The registrar may upon adopting a new form of registered number make such changes of existing registered numbers as appear to him necessary.

(4) A change of a company's registered number has effect from the date on which the company is notified by the registrar of the change; but for a period of three years beginning with the date on which that notification is sent by the registrar the requirement of section 351(1)(a) as to the use of the company's registered number on business letters and order forms is satisfied by the use of either the old number or the new.

(5) In this section "company" includes—

(a) any oversea company which has complied with section 691 (delivery of statutes to registrar, &c.), other than a company which appears to the registrar not to have a place of business in Great Britain; and
(b) any body to which any provision of this Act applies by virtue of section 718 (unregistered companies).][1]

---

1 Substituted by CA 1989, 19 Sch 14 with effect from a date to be appointed.

---

714 Registrar's index of company and corporate names

(1) The registrar of companies shall keep an index of the names of the following bodies—

(a) companies as defined by this Act,
(b) companies incorporated outside Great Britain which have complied with section 691 and which do not appear to the registrar of companies not to have a place of business in Great Britain,
(c) incorporated and unincorporated bodies to which any provision of this Act applies by virtue of section 718 (unregistered companies),
(d) limited partnerships registered under the Limited Partnerships Act 1907,
(e) companies within the meaning of the Companies Act (Northern Ireland) 1960,
(f) companies incorporated outside Northern Ireland which have complied with section 356 of that Act (which corresponds with section 691 of this Act), and which do not appear to the registrar not to have a place of business in Northern Ireland, and
(g) societies registered under the Industrial and Provident Societies Act 1965 or the Industrial and Provident Societies Act (Northern Ireland) 1969.

(2) The Secretary of State may by order in a statutory instrument vary subsection (1) by the addition or deletion of any class of body, except any within paragraph (a) or (b) of the subsection, whether incorporated or unincorporated; and any such statutory instrument is subject to annulment in pursuance of a resolution of either House of Parliament.

PART XXV MISCELLANEOUS AND SUPPLEMENTARY PROVISIONS

716 Prohibition of partnerships with more than 20 members

(1) No company, association or partnership consisting of more than 20 persons shall be formed for the purpose of carrying on any business that has for its object the acquisition of gain by the company, association or partnership, or by its individual members, unless it is registered as a company under this Act, or is formed in pursuance of some other Act of Parliament, or of letters patent.

(2) However, this does not prohibit the formation—

(a) for the purpose of carrying on practice as solicitors, of a partnership consisting of persons each of whom is a solicitor;
(b) for the purpose of carrying on practice as accountants, of a partnership consisting of persons each of whom falls within either paragraph (a) or (b) of section 389(1) (qualifications of company auditors);
(c) for the purpose of carrying on business as members of a recognised stock exchange, of a partnership consisting of persons each of whom is a member of that stock exchange;
[(d) for any purpose prescribed by regulations (which may include a purpose mentioned above), of a partnership of a description so prescribed.][1]

[. . .][2]

[(3) In subsection (2)(a) "solicitor"—

(a) in relation to England and Wales, means solicitor of the Supreme Court, and
(b) in relation to Scotland, means a person enrolled or deemed enrolled as a solicitor in pursuance of the Solicitors (Scotland) Act 1980.

(4) In subsection (2)(c) "recognised stock exchange" means—

(a) The International Stock Exchange of the United Kingdom and the Republic of Ireland Limited, and
(b) any other stock exchange for the time being recognised for the purposes of this section by the Secretary of State by order made by statutory instrument.][3]

(5) Subsection (1) does not apply in relation to any body of persons for the time being approved for the purposes of the Marine and Aviation Insurance (War Risks) Act 1952 by the Secretary of State, being a body the objects of which are or include the carrying on of business by way of the re-insurance of risks which may be re-insured under any agreement for the purpose mentioned in section 1(1)(b) of that Act.

---

1 Inserted by CA 1989, 19 Sch 15 with effect from 1 April 1990 (SI 1990 No 355).

2 Deleted by CA 1989, 19 Sch 15 with effect as in [1] above.

3 Substituted by CA 1989, 19 Sch 15 with effect as in [1] above.

---

717 Limited partnerships: limit on number of members

(1) So much of the Limited Partnerships Act 1907 as provides that a limited partnership shall not consist of more than 20 persons does not apply—

(a) to a partnership carrying on practice as solicitors and consisting of persons each of whom is a solicitor,

(b) to a partnership carrying on practice as accountants and consisting of persons each of whom falls within either paragraph (a) or (b) of section 389(1) of this Act (qualification of company auditors),

(c) to a partnership carrying on business as members of a recognised stock exchange and consisting of persons each of whom is a member of that exchange,

[(d) to a partnership carrying on business of any description prescribed by regulations (which may include a business of any description mentioned above), of a partnership of a description so prescribed.][1]

[...][2]

[(2) In subsection (1)(a) "solicitor"—

(a) in relation to England and Wales, means solicitor of the Supreme Court, and

(b) in relation to Scotland, means a person enrolled or deemed enrolled as a solicitor in pursuance of the Solicitors (Scotland) Act 1980.

(3) In subsection (1)(c) "recognised stock exchange" means—

(a) The International Stock Exchange of the United Kingdom and the Republic of Ireland Limited, and

(b) any other stock exchange for the time being recognised for the purposes of this section by the Secretary of State by order made by statutory instrument.][3]

---

1 Inserted by CA 1989, 19 Sch 16 with effect from 1 April 1990 (SI 1990 No 355).

2 Deleted by CA 1989, 19 Sch 16 with effect as in [1] above.

3 Substituted by CA 1989, 19 Sch 16 with effect as in [1] above.

---

718 Unregistered companies

(1) The provisions of this Act specified in the first column of Schedule 22 (relating respectively to the matters specified in the second column of the Schedule) apply to all bodies corporate incorporated in and having a principal place of business in Great Britain, other than those mentioned in subsection (2) below, as if they were companies registered under this Act, but subject to any limitations mentioned in relation to those provisions respectively in the third column and to such adaptations and modifications (if any) as may be specified by regulations made by the Secretary of State.

(2) Those provisions of this Act do not apply by virtue of this section to any of the following—

(a) any body incorporated by or registered under any public general Act of Parliament,

(b) any body not formed for the purpose of carrying on a business which has for its object the acquisition of gain by the body or its individual members,

(c) any body for the time being exempted by direction of the Secretary of State (or before him by the Board of Trade).

(3) Where against any provision of this Act specified in the first column of Schedule 22 there appears in the third column the entry "Subject to section 718(3)", it means that the provision is to apply by virtue of this section so far only as may be specified by regulations made by the Secretary of State and to such bodies corporate as may be so specified.

(4) The provisions specified in the first column of the Schedule also apply in like manner in relation to any unincorporated body of persons entitled by virtue of letters patent to any of the privileges conferred by the Chartered Companies Act 1837 and not registered under any other public general Act of Parliament, but subject to the like exceptions as are provided for in the case of bodies corporate by paragraphs (b) and (c) of subsection (2).

(5) This section does not repeal or revoke in whole or in part any enactment, royal charter or other instrument constituting or regulating any body in relation to which those provisions are applied by virtue of this section, or restrict the power of Her Majesty to grant a charter in lieu of or supplementary to any such charter as above mentioned; but, in relation to any such body, the operation of any such enactment, charter or instrument is suspended in so far as it is inconsistent with any of those provisions as they apply for the time being to that body.

(6) The power to make regulations conferred by this section (whether regulations under subsection (1) or subsection (3)) is exercisable by statutory instrument subject to annulment in pursuance of a resolution of either House of Parliament.

Regulations. The Companies (Unregistered Companies) Regulations 1985 (SI 1985 No 680).

719 Power of company to provide for employees on cessation or transfer of business

(1) The powers of a company include (if they would not otherwise do so apart from this section) power to make the following provision for the benefit of persons employed or formerly employed by the company or any of its subsidiaries, that is to say, provision in connection with the cessation or the transfer to any person of the whole or part of the undertaking of the company or that subsidiary.

(2) The power conferred by subsection (1) is exercisable notwithstanding that its exercise is not in the best interests of the company.

(3) The power which a company may exercise by virtue only of subsection (1) shall only be exercised by the company if sanctioned—

(a) in a case not falling within paragraph (b) or (c) below, by an ordinary resolution of the company, or
(b) if so authorised by the memorandum or articles, a resolution of the directors, or
(c) if the memorandum or articles require the exercise of the power to be sanctioned by a resolution of the company of some other description for which more than a simple majority of the members voting is necessary, with the sanction of a resolution of that description;

and in any case after compliance with any other requirements of the memorandum or articles applicable to its exercise.

(4) Any payment which may be made by a company under this section may, if made before the commencement of any winding up of the company, be made out of profits of the company which are available for dividend.

Cross references. See CA 1989, 18 Sch 36.

720 Certain companies to publish periodical statement

(1) Every company, being an insurance company or a deposit, provident or benefit society, shall before it commences business, and also on the first Monday in February and the first Tuesday in August in every year during which it carries on business, make a statement in the form set out in Schedule 23, or as near to it as circumstances admit.

(2) A copy of the statement shall be put up in a conspicuous place in the company's registered office, and in every branch office or place where the business of the company is carried on.

(3) Every member and every creditor of the company is entitled to a copy of the statement, on payment of a sum not exceeding 2½ pence.

(4) If default is made in complying with this section, the company and every officer of it who is in default is liable to a fine and, for continued contravention, to a daily default fine.

(5) For purposes of this Act, a company which carries on the business of insurance in common with any other business or businesses is deemed an insurance company.

(6) In the case of an insurance company to which Part II of the Insurance Companies Act 1982 applies, this section does not apply if the company complies with provisions of that Act as to the accounts and balance sheet to be prepared annually and deposited by such a company.

(7) The Secretary of State may, by regulations in a statutory instrument (subject to annulment in pursuance of a resolution of either House of Parliament), alter the form in Schedule 23.

Cross references. See 24 Sch (punishment of offences).

---

721 Production and inspection of books where offence suspected

(1) The following applies if on an application made—

(a) in England and Wales, to a judge of the High Court by the Director of Public Prosecutions, the Secretary of State or a chief officer of police, or
(b) in Scotland, to one of the Lords Commissioners of Justiciary by the Lord Advocate,

there is shown to be reasonable cause to believe that any person has, while an officer of a company, committed an offence in connection with the management of the company's affairs and that evidence of the commission of the offence is to be found in any books or papers of or under the control of the company.

(2) An order may be made—

(a) authorising any person named in it to inspect the books or papers in question, or any of them, for the purpose of investigating and obtaining evidence of the offence, or
(b) requiring the secretary of the company or such other officer of it as may be named in the order to produce the books or papers (or any of them) to a person named in the order at a place so named.

(3) The above applies also in relation to any books or papers of a person carrying on the business of banking so far as they relate to the company's affairs, as it applies to any books or papers of or under the control of the company, except that no such order as is referred to in subsection (2)(b) shall be made by virtue of this subsection.

(4) The decision of a judge of the High Court or of any of the Lords Commissioners of Justiciary on an application under this section is not appealable.

734 Criminal proceedings against unincorporated bodies

(1) Proceedings for an offence alleged to have been committed under [section 389A(3) or][1] [section 394A(1) or][2] any of sections 447 to 451 by an unincorporated body shall be brought in the name of that body (and not in that of any of its members), and for the purposes of any such proceedings, any rules of court relating to the service of documents apply as if that body were a corporation.

(2) A fine imposed on an unincorporated body on its conviction of such an offence shall be paid out of the funds of that body.

(3) In a case in which an unincorporated body is charged in England and Wales with such an offence, section 33 of the Criminal Justice Act 1925 and Schedule 3 to the Magistrates' Courts Act 1980 (procedure on charge of an offence against a corporation) have effect in like manner as in the case of a corporation so charged.

(4) In relation to proceedings on indictment in Scotland for such an offence alleged to have been committed by an unincorporated body, section 74 of the Criminal Procedure (Scotland) Act 1975 (proceedings on indictment against bodies corporate) has effect as if that body were a body corporate.

[(5) Where such an offence committed by a partnership is proved to have been committed with the consent or connivance of, or to be attributable to any neglect on the part of, a partner, he as well as the partnership is guilty of the offence and liable to be proceeded against and punished accordingly.

(6) Where such an offence committed by an unincorporated body (other than a partnership) is proved to have been committed with the consent or connivance of, or to be attributable to any neglect on the part of, any officer of the body or any member of its governing body, he as well as the body is guilty of the offence and liable to be proceeded against and punished accordingly.][3]

---

1 Inserted by CA 1989, s 120 with effect from 1 April 1990 (SI 1990 No 355) subject to the transitional and saving provisions in Schedule 4 of that Order.

2 Inserted by CA 1989, s 123 with effect as in [1] above.

3 Inserted by CA 1989, 19 Sch 18 with effect from 1 April 1990 (SI 1990 No 355).

PART XXVI INTERPRETATION

735 "Company", etc

(1) In this Act—

(a) "company" means a company formed and registered under this Act, or an existing company;

(b) "existing company" means a company formed and registered under the former Companies Acts, but does not include a company registered under the Joint Stock Companies Acts, the Companies Act 1862 or the Companies (Consolidation) Act 1908 in what was then Ireland;

(c) "the former Companies Acts" means the Joint Stock Companies Acts, the Companies Act 1862, the Companies (Consolidation) Act 1908, the Companies Act 1929 and the Companies Acts 1948 to 1983.

(2) "Public company" and "private company" have the meanings given by section 1(3).

(3) "The Joint Stock Companies Acts" means the Joint Stock Companies Act 1856, the Joint Stock Companies Acts 1856, 1857, the Joint Stock Banking Companies Act 1857 and the Act to enable Joint Stock Banking Companies to be formed on the principle of limited liability, or any one or more of those Acts (as the case may require), but does not include the Joint Stock Companies Act 1844.

(4) The definitions in this section apply unless the contrary intention appears.

740 "Body corporate" and "corporation"

References in this Act to a body corporate or to a corporation do not include a corporation sole, but include a company incorporated elsewhere than in Great Britain.

Such references to a body corporate do not include a Scottish firm.

PART XXVI INTERPRETATION

744 Expressions used generally in this Act

In this Act, unless the contrary intention appears, the following definitions apply—

"agent" does not include a person's counsel acting as such;

[. . .][7]

"articles" means, in relation to a company, its articles of association, as originally framed or as altered by resolution, including (so far as applicable to the company) regulations contained in or annexed to any enactment relating to companies passed before this Act, as altered by or under any such enactment;

[. . .][5]

[. . .][8]

"bank holiday" means a holiday under the Banking and Financial Dealings Act 1971;

["banking company" means a company which is authorised under the Banking Act 1987;][6]

"books and papers" and "books or papers" include accounts, deeds, writings and documents;

"the Companies Acts" means this Act, the Insider Dealing Act and the Consequential Provisions Act;

"the Consequential Provisions Act" means the Companies Consolidation (Consequential Provisions) Act 1985;

"the court", in relation to a company, means the court having jurisdiction to wind up the company;

"debenture" includes debenture stock, bonds and any other securities of a company, whether constituting a charge on the assets of the company or not;

"document" includes summons, notice, order, and other legal process, and registers;

"equity share capital" means, in relation to a company, its issued share capital excluding any part of that capital which, neither as respects dividends nor as respects capital, carries any right to participate beyond a specified amount in a distribution;

[. . .][9]

"the Gazette" means, as respects companies registered in England and Wales, the London Gazette and, as respects companies registered in Scotland, the Edinburgh Gazette;

[. . .][1]

"hire-purchase agreement" has the same meaning as in the Consumer Credit Act 1974;

"the Insider Dealing Act" means the Company Securities (Insider Dealing) Act 1985;

"insurance company" means the same as in the Insurance Companies Act 1982;

[. . .][10]

"memorandum", in relation to a company, means its memorandum of association, as originally framed or as altered in pursuance of any enactment;

"number", in relation to shares, includes amount, where the context admits of the reference to shares being construed to include stock;

"officer", in relation to a body corporate, includes a director, manager or secretary;

"official seal", in relation to the registrar of companies, means a seal prepared under section 704(4) for the authentication of documents required for or in connection with the registration of companies;

"oversea company" means—

(a) a company incorporated elsewhere than in Great Britain which, after the commencement of this Act, establishes a place of business in Great Britain, and

(b) a company so incorporated which has, before that commencement, established a place of business and continues to have an established place of business in Great Britain at that commencement;

"place of business" includes a share transfer or share registration office;

"prescribed" means—

(a) as respects provisions of this Act relating to winding up, prescribed by general rules [. . .][2], and

(b) otherwise, prescribed by statutory instrument made by the Secretary of State;

"prospectus" means any prospectus, notice, circular, advertisement, or other invitation, offering to the public for subscription or purchase any shares in or debentures of a company;

"prospectus issued generally" means a prospectus issued to persons who are not existing members of the company or holders of its debentures;

[. . .][3]

[. . .][4]

"the registrar of companies" and "the registrar" mean the registrar or other officer performing under this Act the duty of registration of companies in England and Wales or in Scotland, as the case may require;

"share" means share in the share capital of a company, and includes stock (except where a distinction between shares and stock is express or implied); and

[. . .][11].

---

1 Repealed by IA 1985, s 235(3), 10 Sch Part II with effect from 1 March 1986 in so far as relating to the making of general rules in England and Wales (SI 1986 No 185) and otherwise as from 29 December 1986 (SI 1986 No 1924).

2 Repealed by IA 1985, s 235(3), 10 Sch Part II as [1] above.

3 Repealed by Banking Act 1987, s 108(1), 6 Sch 18(8), 7 Sch Part I with effect from 1 October 1987 (see SI 1987 No 1664).

4 Repealed by FSA 1986, s 212(3), 17 Sch Part I with effect from 29 April 1988 (see SI 1988 No 740).

5 Deleted by CA 1989, 10 Sch 16 with effect from 1 April 1990 (SI 1990 No 355) subject to the transitional and saving provisions in Arts 6 to 9 of that Order reproduced above Sec 221 above.

6 Inserted by CA 1989, 10 Sch 16 with effect as in [5] above.

7 Repealed by CA 1989, 24 Sch with effect from a date to be appointed.

8 Repealed by CA 1989, 24 Sch with effect from a date to be appointed.

9 Repealed by CA 1989, 24 Sch with effect from a date to be appointed.

10 Repealed by CA 1989, 24 Sch with effect from a date to be appointed.

[11] Repealed by CA 1989, 24 Sch with effect from a date to be appointed.

Notes

(a) The definition of "prospectus issued generally" is repealed by FSA 1986, s 212(3), 17 Sch Part I with effect from 29 April 1988 to the extent that it applies to a prospectus offering for subscription, or to any form of application for, units in a body corporate which is a recognised scheme (SI 1988 No 740).

[744A Index of defined expressions

The following Table shows provisions defining or otherwise explaining expressions for the purposes of this Act generally—

Expression	Provision
accounting reference date, accounting reference period	sections 224 and 742(1)
acquisition (in relation to a non-cash asset)	section 739(2)
agent	section 744
allotment (and related expressions)	section 738
annual accounts	sections 261(2), 262(1) and 742(1)
annual general meeting	section 366
annual return	section 363
articles	section 744
authorised minimum	section 118
balance sheet and balance sheet date	sections 261(2), 262(1) and 742(1)
bank holiday	section 744
banking company	section 744
body corporate	section 740
books and papers, books or papers	section 744
called-up share capital	section 737(1)
capital redemption reserve	section 170(1)
the Companies Acts	section 744
companies charges register	section 397
company	section 735(1)
the Consequential Provisions Act	section 744
corporation	section 740
the court (in relation to a company)	section 744
current assets	sections 262(1) and 742(1)
debenture	section 744
director	section 741(1)
document	section 744
elective resolution	section 379A
employees' share scheme	section 743
equity share capital	section 744
existing company	section 735(1)
extraordinary general meeting	section 368
extraordinary resolution	section 378(1)
financial year (of a company)	sections 223 and 742(1)
fixed assets	sections 262(1) and 742(1)
floating charge (in Scotland)	section 462
the former Companies Acts	section 735(1)
the Gazette	section 744
hire-purchase agreement	section 744
holding company	section 736
the Insider Dealing Act	section 744

the Insolvency Act	section 735A(1)
insurance company	section 744
the Joint Stock Companies Acts	section 735(3)
limited company	section 1(2)
member (of a company)	section 22
memorandum (in relation to a company)	section 744
non-cash asset	section 739(1)
number (in relation to shares)	section 744
office copy (in relation to a court order in Scotland)	section 743A
officer (in relation to a body corporate)	section 744
official seal (in relation to the registrar of companies)	section 744
oversea company	section 744
overseas branch register	section 362
paid up (and related expressions)	section 738
parent company and parent undertaking	sections 258 and 742(1)
place of business	section 744
prescribed	section 744
private company	section 1(3)
profit and loss account	sections 261(2), 262(1) and 742(1)
prospectus	section 744
public company	section 1(3)
realised profits or losses	sections 262(3) and 742(2)
registered number (of a company)	section 705(1)
registered office (of a company)	section 287
registrar and registrar of companies	section 744
resolution for reducing share capital	section 135(3)
shadow director	section 741(2) and (3)
share	section 744
share premium account	section 130(1)
share warrant	section 188
special notice (in relation to a resolution)	section 379
special resolution	section 378(2)
subsidiary	section 736
subsidiary undertaking	sections 258 and 742(1)
transfer (in relation to a non-cash asset)	section 739(2)
uncalled share capital	section 737(2)
undistributable reserves	section 264(3)
unlimited company	section 1(2)
unregistered company	section 718
wholly-owned subsidiary	section 736(2)][1]

[1] Inserted by CA 1989, 19 Sch 20 with effect from a date to be appointed.

SCHEDULE 4
(Sections 228, 230 and as amended by CA 1989, s 4(2), 1 Sch)

FORM AND CONTENT OF COMPANY ACCOUNTS

PART V SPECIAL PROVISIONS WHERE THE COMPANY IS AN INVESTMENT COMPANY

71 (1) Paragraph 34 does not apply to the amount of any profit or loss arising from a determination of the value of any investments of an investment company on any basis mentioned in paragraph 31(3).

(2) Any provisions made by virtue of paragraph 19(1) or (2) in the case of an investment company in respect of any fixed asset investments need not be charged to the company's profit and loss account provided they are either—

(a) charged against any reserve account to which any amount excluded by sub-paragraph (1) from the requirements of paragraph 34 has been credited; or

(b) shown as a separate item in the company's balance sheet under the sub-heading "other reserves".

(3) For the purposes of this paragraph, as it applies in relation to any company, "fixed asset investment" means any asset falling to be included under any item shown in the company's balance sheet under the subdivision "investments" under the general item "fixed assets".

72 (1) Any distribution made by an investment company which reduces the amount of its net assets to less than the aggregate of its called-up share capital and undistributable reserves shall be disclosed in a note to the company's accounts.

(2) For purposes of this paragraph, a company's net assets are the aggregate of its assets less the aggregate of its liabilities (including any provision for liabilities or charges within paragraph 89); and "undistributable reserves" has the meaning given by section 264(3) of this Act.

73 A company shall be treated as an investment company for the purposes of this Part of this Schedule in relation to any financial year of the company if—

(a) during the whole of that year it was an investment company as defined by section 266 of this Act, and

(b) it was not at any time during that year prohibited under section 265(4) of this Act (no distribution where capital profits have been distributed, etc.) from making a distribution by virtue of that section.

SCHEDULE 4A
(Sections 5(2), CA 1989)

FORM AND CONTENT OF GROUP ACCOUNTS

Note. This Schedule inserted by CA 1989, 2 Sch with effect from 1 April 1990 (SI 1990 No 355) subject to the transitional and saving provisions in Arts 6 to 9 of that Order.

General rules

1 (1) Group accounts shall comply so far as practicable with the provisions of Schedule 4 as if the undertakings included in the consolidation ("the group") were a single company.

(2) In particular, for the purposes of paragraph 59 of that Schedule (dealings with or interests in group undertakings) as it applies to group accounts—

(a) any subsidiary undertakings of the parent company not included in the consolidation shall be treated as subsidiary undertakings of the group, and

(b) if the parent company is itself a subsidiary undertaking, the group shall be treated as a subsidiary undertaking of any parent undertaking of that company, and the reference to fellow-subsidiary undertakings shall be construed accordingly.

(3) Where the parent company is treated as an investment company for the purposes of Part V of that Schedule (special provisions for investment companies) the group shall be similarly treated.

SCHEDULE 9
(Section 255 inserted by CA 1989, s18(3)(4),7 Sch)

[SPECIAL PROVISIONS FOR BANKING AND INSURANCE COMPANIES AND GROUPS][1]

[1] Substituted by CA 1989, 7 Sch with effect from 1 April 1990 (SI 1990 No 355) subject to the transitional and saving provisions in Arts 6 to 9 of that Order.

[. . .][1]

[1] Deleted by CA 1989, 7 Sch with effect from 1 April 1990 (SI 1990 No 355) subject to the transitional and saving provisions in Arts 6 to 9 of that Order.

[PART I FORM AND CONTENT OF ACCOUNTS][1]

[1] Substituted by CA 1989, 7 Sch with effect from 1 April 1990 (SI 1990 No 355) subject to the transitional and saving provisions in Arts 6 to 9 of that Order.

Balance sheet

2 The authorised share capital, issued share capital, liabilities and assets shall be summarised, with such particulars as are necessary to disclose the general nature of the assets and liabilities, and there shall be specified—

(a) any part of the issued capital that consists of redeemable shares, the earliest and latest dates on which the company has power to redeem those shares, whether those shares must be redeemed in any event or are liable to be redeemed at the option of the company or of the shareholder and whether any (and, if so, what) premium is payable on redemption;
(b) so far as the information is not given in the profit and loss account, any share capital on which interest has been paid out of capital during the financial year, and the rate at which interest has been so paid;
(c) the amount of the share premium account;
(d) particulars of any redeemed debentures which the company has power to re-issue.

3 There shall be stated under separate headings, so far as they are not written off,—

(a) the preliminary expenses;
(b) any expenses incurred in connection with any issue of share capital or debentures;
(c) any sums paid by way of commission in respect of any shares or debentures;
(d) any sums allowed by way of discount in respect of any debentures; and
(e) the amount of the discount allowed on any issue of shares at a discount.

4 (1) The reserves, provisions, liabilities and assets shall be classified under headings appropriate to the company's business:

Provided that—

(a) where the amount of any class is not material, it may be included under the same heading as some other class; and
(b) where any assets of one class are not separable from assets of another class, those assets may be included under the same heading.

(2) Fixed assets, current assets and assets that are neither fixed nor current shall be separately identified.

(3) The method or methods used to arrive at the amount of the fixed assets under each heading shall be stated.

5 (1) The method of arriving at the amount of any fixed asset shall, subject to the next following sub-paragraph, be to take the difference between—

(a) its cost or, if it stands in the company's books at a valuation, the amount of the valuation; and
(b) the aggregate amount provided or written off since the date of acquisition or valuation, as the case may be, for depreciation or diminution in value;

and for the purposes of this paragraph the net amount at which any assets stood in the company's books on 1st July 1948 (after deduction of the amounts previously provided or written off for depreciation or diminution in value) shall, if the figures relating to the period before that date cannot be obtained without unreasonable expense or delay, be treated as if it were the amount of a valuation of those assets made at that date and, where any of those assets are sold, the said net amount less the amount of the sales shall be treated as if it were the amount of a valuation so made of the remaining assets.

(2) The foregoing sub-paragraph shall not apply—

(a) to assets for which the figures relating to the period beginning with 1st July 1948 cannot be obtained without unreasonable expense or delay; or
(b) to assets the replacement of which is provided for wholly or partly—
 (i) by making provision for renewals and charging the cost of replacement against the provision so made; or
 (ii) by charging the cost of replacement direct to revenue; or
(c) to any listed investments or to any unlisted investments of which the value as estimated by the directors is shown either as the amount of the investments or by way of note; or
(d) to goodwill, patents or trade marks.

(3) For the assets under each heading whose amount is arrived at in accordance with sub-paragraph (1) of this paragraph, there shall be shown—

(a) the aggregate of the amounts referred to in paragraph (a) of that sub-paragraph; and
(b) the aggregate of the amounts referred to in paragraph (b) thereof.

(4) As respects the assets under each heading whose amount is not arrived at in accordance with the said sub-paragraph (1) because their replacement is provided for as mentioned in sub-paragraph (2)(b) of this paragraph, there shall be stated—

(a) the means by which their replacement is provided for; and
(b) the aggregate amount of the provision (if any) made for renewals and not used.

6 In the case of unlisted investments consisting in equity share capital of other bodies corporate (other than any whose values as estimated by the directors are separately shown, either individually or collectively or as to some individually and as to the rest collectively, and are so shown either as the amount thereof, or by way of note), the matters referred to in the following heads shall, if not otherwise shown, be stated by way of note or in a statement or report annexed:—

(a) the aggregate amount of the company's income for the financial year that is ascribable to the investments;
(b) the amount of the company's share before taxation, and the amount of that share after taxation, of the net aggregate amount of the profits of the bodies in which the investments are held, being profits for the several periods to which accounts sent by them during the financial year to the company related, after deducting those bodies' losses for those periods (or vice versa);
(c) the amount of the company's share of the net aggregate amount of the undistributed profits accumulated by the bodies in which the investments are held since the time when the investments were acquired after deducting the losses accumulated by them since that time (or vice versa);
(d) the manner in which any losses incurred by the said bodies have been dealt with in the company's accounts.

7 The aggregate amounts respectively of reserves and provisions (other than provisions for depreciation, renewals or diminution in value of assets) shall be stated under separate headings;

Provided that—

(a) this paragraph shall not require a separate statement of either of the said amounts which is not material; and
(b) the Secretary of State may direct that a separate statement shall not be required of the amount of provisions where he is satisfied that that is not required in the public interest and would prejudice the company, but subject to the condition that any heading stating an amount arrived at after taking into account a provision (other than as aforesaid) shall be so framed or marked as to indicate that fact.

8 (1) There shall also be shown (unless it is shown in the profit and loss account or a statement or report annexed thereto, or the amount involved is not material)—

(a) where the amount of the reserves or of the provisions (other than provisions for depreciation, renewals or diminution in value of assets) shows an increase as compared with the amount at the end of the immediately preceding financial year, the source from which the amount of the increase has been derived; and
(b) where—
  (i) the amount of the reserves shows a decrease as compared with the amount at the end of the immediately preceding financial year; or
  (ii) the amount at the end of the immediately preceding financial year of the provisions (other than provisions for depreciation, renewals or diminution in value of assets) exceeded the aggregate of the sums since applied and amounts still retained for the purposes thereof;

the application of the amounts derived from the difference.

(2) Where the heading showing the reserves or any of the provisions aforesaid is divided into sub-headings, this paragraph shall apply to each of the separate amounts shown in the sub-headings instead of applying to the aggregate amount thereof.

9 If an amount is set aside for the purpose of its being used to prevent undue fluctuations in charges for taxation, it shall be stated.

10 (1) There shall be shown under separate headings—

(a) the aggregate amounts respectively of the company's listed investments and unlisted investments;

(b) if the amount of the goodwill and of any patents and trade marks or part of that amount is shown as a separate item in or is otherwise ascertainable from the books of the company, or from any contract for the sale or purchase of any property to be acquired by the company, or from any documents in the possession of the company relating to the stamp duty payable in respect of any such contract or the conveyance of any such property, the said amount so shown or ascertained as far as not written off or, as the case may be, the said amount so far as it is so shown or ascertainable and as so shown or ascertained, as the case may be;

(c) the aggregate amount of any outstanding loans made under the authority of section 153(4)(b) [, (b)(b)][2] or (c) or 155 of this Act;

(d) the aggregate amount of bank loans and overdrafts and the aggregate amount of loans made to the company which—

(i) are repayable otherwise than by instalments and fall due for repayment after the expiration of the period of five years beginning with the day next following the expiration of the financial year; or

(ii) are repayable by instalments any of which fall due for payment after the expiration of that period;

not being, in either case, bank loans or overdrafts;

(e) the aggregate amount which is recommended for distribution by way of dividend.

(2) Nothing in head (b) of the foregoing sub-paragraph shall be taken as requiring the amount of the goodwill, patents and trade marks to be stated otherwise than as a single item.

(3) The heading showing the amount of the listed investments shall be subdivided, where necessary, to distinguish the investments as respects which there has, and those as respects which there has not, been granted a listing on a [recognised investment exchange other than an overseas investment exchange within the meaning of the Financial Services Act 1986][1].

(4) In relation to each loan falling within head (d) of sub-paragraph (1) of this paragraph (other than a bank loan or overdraft), there shall be stated by way of note (if not otherwise stated) the terms on which it is repayable and the rate at which interest is payable thereon:

Provided that if the number of loans is such that, in the opinion of the directors, compliance with the foregoing requirement would result in a statement of excessive length, it shall be sufficient to give a general indication of the terms on which the loans are repayable and the rates at which interest is payable thereon.

---

1 Substituted by FSA 1986, s 212(2), 16 Sch 24 with effect from 29 April 1988 (see SI 1988 No 740).

2 Inserted by CA 1989, 7 Sch 1 with effect from 1 April 1990 (SI 1990 No 355) subject to the transitional and saving provisions in Arts 6 to 9 of that Order.

---

11 Where any liability of the company is secured otherwise than by operation of law on any assets of the company, the fact that that liability is so secured shall be stated, but it shall not be necessary to specify the assets on which the liability is secured.

12 Where any of the company's debentures are held by a nominee of or trustee for the company, the nominal amount of the debentures and the amount at which they are stated in the books of the company shall be stated.

13 (1) The matters referred to in the following sub-paragraphs shall be stated by way of note, or in a statement or report annexed, if not otherwise shown.

(2) The number, description and amount of any shares in the company which any person has an option to subscribe for, together with the following particulars of the option, that is to say—

(a) the period during which it is exercisable;
(b) the price to be paid for shares subscribed for under it.

(3) [. . .][1]

(4) Any distribution made by an investment company within the meaning of Part VIII of this Act which reduces the amount of its net assets to less than the aggregate of its called-up share capital and undistributable reserves.

For purposes of this sub-paragraph, a company's net assets are the aggregate of its assets less the aggregate of its liabilities; and "undistributable reserves" has the meaning given by section 264(3).

(5) The amount of any arrears of fixed cumulative dividends on the company's shares and the period for which the dividends or, if there is more than one class, each class of them are in arrear.

(6) Particulars of any charge on the assets of the company to secure the liabilities of any other person, including, where practicable, the amount secured.

(7) The general nature of any other contingent liabilities not provided for and, where practicable, the aggregate amount or estimated amount of those liabilities, if it is material.

(8) Where practicable the aggregate amount or estimated amount, if it is material, of contracts for capital expenditure, so far as not provided for and, where practicable, the aggregate amount or estimated amount, if it is material, of capital expenditure authorised by the directors which has not been contracted for.

(9) In the case of fixed assets under any heading whose amount is required to be arrived at in accordance with paragraph 5(1) of this Schedule (other than unlisted investments) and is so arrived at by reference to a valuation, the years (so far as they are known to the directors) in which the assets were severally valued and the several values, and, in the case of assets that have been valued during the financial year, the names of the persons who valued them or particulars of their qualifications for doing so and (whichever is stated) the bases of valuation used by them.

(10) If there are included amongst fixed assets under any heading (other than investments) assets that have been acquired during the financial year, the aggregate amount of the assets acquired as determined for the purpose of making up the balance sheet, and if during that year any fixed assets included under a heading in the balance sheet made up with respect to the immediately preceding financial year (other than investments) have been disposed of or destroyed, the aggregate amount thereof as determined for the purpose of making up that balance sheet.

(11) Of the amount of fixed assets consisting of land, how much is ascribable to land of freehold tenure and how much to land of leasehold tenure, and, of the latter, how much is ascribable to land held on long lease and how much to land held on short lease.

(12) If in the opinion of the directors any of the current assets have not a value, on realisation in the ordinary course of the company's business, at least equal to the amount at which they are stated, the fact that the directors are of that opinion.

(13) The aggregate market value of the company's listed investments where it differs from the amount of the investments as stated and the stock exchange value of any investments of which the market value is shown (whether separately or not) and is taken as being higher than their stock exchange value.

(14) If a sum set aside for the purpose of its being used to prevent undue fluctuations in charges for taxation has been used during the financial year for another purpose, the amount thereof and the fact that it has been so used.

(15) If the amount carried forward for stock in trade or work in progress is material for the appreciation by its members of the company's state of affairs or of its profit or loss for the financial year, the manner in which that amount has been computed.

(16) The basis on which foreign currencies have been converted into sterling, where the amount of the assets or liabilities affected is material.

(17) The basis on which the amount, if any, set aside for United Kingdom corporation tax is computed.

(18) [. . .][2]

---

1 Deleted by CA 1989, 7 Sch 2 with effect from 1 April 1990 (SI 1990 No 355) subject to the transitional and saving provisions in Arts 6 to 9 of that Order.

2 Repealed by CA 1989, 24 Sch with effect from a date to be appointed.

Profit and loss account

14 (1) There shall be shown—

(a) the amount charged to revenue by way of provision for depreciation, renewals or diminution in value of fixed assets;

(b) the amount of the interest on loans of the following kinds made to the company (whether on the security of debentures or not), namely, bank loans, overdrafts and loans which, not being bank loans or overdrafts,—

(i) are repayable otherwise than by instalments and fall due for repayment before the expiration of the period of five years beginning with the day next following the expiration of the financial year; or

(ii) are repayable by instalments the last of which falls due for payment before the expiration of that period;

and the amount of the interest on loans of other kinds so made (whether on the security of debentures or not);

(c) the amount of the charge to revenue for United Kingdom corporation tax and, if that amount would have been greater but for relief from double taxation, the amount which it would have been but for such relief, the amount of the charge for United Kingdom income tax, and the amount of the charge for taxation imposed outside the United Kingdom of profits, income and (so far as charged to revenue) capital gains;

(d) the amounts respectively set aside for redemption of share capital and for redemption of loans;

(e) the amount, if material, set aside or proposed to be set aside to, or withdrawn from, reserves;

(f) subject to sub-paragraph (2) of this paragraph, the amount, if material, set aside to provisions other than provisions for depreciation, renewals, or diminution in value of assets or, as the case may be, the amount, if material, withdrawn from such provisions and not applied for the purposes thereof;

(g) the amounts respectively of income from listed investments and income from unlisted investments;

(h) if a substantial part of the company's revenue for the financial year consists in rents from land, the amount thereof (after deduction of ground-rents, rates and other outgoings);

(j) the amount, if material, charged to revenue in respect of sums payable in respect of the hire of plant and machinery;

(k) the aggregate amount of the dividends paid and proposed.

(2) The Secretary of State may direct that a company shall not be obliged to show an amount set aside to provisions in accordance with sub-paragraph (1)(f) of this paragraph, if he is satisfied that that is not required in the public interest and would prejudice the company, but subject to the condition that any heading stating an amount arrived at after taking into account the amount set aside as aforesaid shall be so framed or marked as to indicate that fact.

(3) If, in the case of any assets in whose case an amount is charged to revenue by way of provision for depreciation or diminution in value, an amount is also so charged by way of provision for renewal thereof, the last-mentioned amount shall be shown separately.

(4) If the amount charged to revenue by way of provision for depreciation or diminution in value of any fixed assets (other than investments) has been determined otherwise than by reference to the amount of those assets as determined for the purpose of making up the balance sheet, that fact shall be stated.

15 The amount of any charge arising in consequence of the occurrence of an event in a preceding financial year and of any credit so arising shall, if not included in a heading relating to other matters, be stated under a separate heading.

16 [...][1]

[1] Repealed by CA 1989, 24 Sch with effect from 1 April 1990 (SI 1990 No 355) subject to the transitional and saving provisions in Arts 6 to 9 of that Order.

17 (1) The following matters shall be stated by way of note, if not otherwise shown.

(2) The turnover for the financial year, except in so far as it is attributable to the business of banking or discounting or to business of such other class as may be prescribed for the purposes of this sub-paragraph.

(3) If some or all of the turnover is omitted by reason of its being attributable as aforesaid, the fact that it is so omitted.

(4) The method by which turnover stated is arrived at.

(5) A company shall not be subject to the requirements of this paragraph if it is [neither a parent company nor a subsidiary undertaking][1] and the turnover which, apart from this sub-paragraph, would be required to be stated does not exceed £1 million.

---

1 Substituted by CA 1989, 7 Sch 3 with effect from 1 April 1990 (SI 1990 No 355) subject to the transitional and saving provisions in Arts 6 to 9 of that Order.

---

18 (1) The following matters shall be stated by way of note, if not otherwise shown.

(2) If depreciation or replacement of fixed assets is provided for by some method other than a depreciation charge or provision for renewals, or is not provided for, the method by which it is provided for or the fact that it is not provided for, as the case may be.

(3) The basis on which the charge for United Kingdom corporation tax and United Kingdom income tax is computed.

(4) Any special circumstances which affect liability in respect of taxation of profits, income or capital gains for the financial year or liability in respect of taxation of profits, income or capital gains for succeeding financial years.

(5) [. . .][1]

(6) Any material respects in which items shown in the profit and loss account are affected—

(a) by transactions of a sort not usually undertaken by the company or otherwise by circumstances of an exceptional or non-recurrent nature; or

(b) by any change in the basis of accounting.

---

1 Repealed by CA 1989, 24 Sch with effect from 1 April 1990 (SI 1990 No 355) subject to the transitional and saving provisions in Arts 6 to 9 of that Order.

[Supplementary provisions

18A (1) Accounting policies shall be applied consistently within the same accounts and from one financial year to the next.

(2) If it appears to the directors of a company that there are special reasons for departing from the principle stated in sub-paragraph (1) in preparing the company's accounts in respect of any financial year, they may do so; but particulars of the departure, the reasons for it and its effect shall be given in a note to the accounts.][1]

---

1 Inserted by CA 1989, 7 Sch 4 with effect from 1 April 1990 (SI 1990 No 355) subject to the transitional and saving provisions in Arts 6 to 9 of that Order.

[18B It shall be stated whether the accounts have been prepared in accordance with applicable accounting standards, and particulars of any material departure from those standards and the reasons for it shall be given.][1]

1 Inserted by CA 1989, 7 Sch 4 with effect from 1 April 1990 (SI 1990 No 355) subject to the transitional and saving provisions in Arts 6 to 9 of that Order.

[18C (1) In respect of every item shown in the balance sheet or profit and loss account, or stated in a note to the accounts, there shall be shown or stated the corresponding amount for the financial year immediately preceding that to which the accounts relate, subject to sub-paragraph (3).

(2) Where the corresponding amount is not comparable, it shall be adjusted and particulars of the adjustment and the reasons for it shall be given in a note to the accounts.

(3) Sub-paragraph (1) does not apply in relation to an amount shown—

(a) as an amount the source or application of which is required by paragraph 8 above (reserves and provisions),
(b) in pursuance of paragraph 13(10) above (acquisitions and disposals of fixed assets),
(c) by virtue of paragraph 13 of Schedule 4A (details of accounting treatment of acquisitions),
(d) by virtue of paragraph 2, 8(3), 16, 21(1)(d), 22(4) or (5), 24(3) or (4) or 27(3) or (4) of Schedule 5 (shareholdings in other undertakings), or
(e) by virtue of Part II or III of Schedule 6 (loans and other dealings in favour of directors and others).][1]

1 Inserted by CA 1989, 7 Sch 4 with effect from 1 April 1990 (SI 1990 No 355) subject to the transitional and saving provisions in Arts 6 to 9 of that Order.

[Provisions where company is a parent company or subsidiary undertaking][1]

1 Substituted by CA 1989, 7 Sch 5 with effect from 1 April 1990 (SI 1990 No 355) subject to the transitional and saving provisions in Arts 6 to 9 of that Order.

19 (1) This paragraph applies where the company [is a parent company][1].

(2) The aggregate amount of assets consisting of shares in, or amounts owing (whether on account of a loan or otherwise) from, the company's [subsidiary undertakings][2], distinguishing shares from indebtedness, shall be set out in the balance sheet separately from all the other assets of the company, and the aggregate amount of indebtedness (whether on account of a loan or otherwise) to the company's [subsidiary undertakings][2] shall be so set out separately from all its other liabilities and—

(a) the references in [paragraphs 5, 6, 10, 13 and 14][3] of this Schedule to the company's investments (except those in paragraphs 13(10) and 14(4)) shall not include investments in its [subsidiary undertakings][2] required by this paragraph to be separately set out; and
(b) paragraph 5, sub-paragraph (1)(a) of paragraph 14, and sub-paragraph (2) of paragraph 18 of this Schedule shall not apply in relation to fixed assets consisting of interests in the company's [subsidiary undertakings][2].

(3)-(7) [. . .][4]

1 Substituted by CA 1989, 7 Sch 5 with effect from 1 April 1990 (SI 1990 No 355) subject to the transitional and saving provisions in Arts 6 to 9 of that Order.

2 Substituted by CA 1989, 7 Sch 5 with effect as in [1] above.

3 Substituted by CA 1989, 7 Sch 5 with effect as in [1] above.

4 Deleted by CA 1989, 7 Sch 5 with effect as in [1] above.

20 [(1) This paragraph applies where the company is a subsidiary undertaking.

(2) The balance sheet of the company shall show—

(a) the aggregate amount of its indebtedness to undertakings of which it is a subsidiary undertaking or which are fellow subsidiary undertakings, and

(b) the aggregate amount of the indebtedness of all such undertakings to it,

distinguishing in each case between indebtedness in respect of debentures and otherwise.

(3) The balance sheet shall also show the aggregate amount of assets consisting of shares in fellow subsidiary undertakings.][1]

1 Substituted by CA 1989, 7 Sch 6 with effect from 1 April 1990 (SI 1990 No 355) subject to the transitional and saving provisions in Arts 6 to 9 of that Order.

21-26 [. . .][1]

1 Deleted by CA 1989, 7 Sch 7 with effect from 1 April 1990 (SI 1990 No 355) subject to the transitional and saving provisions in Arts 6 to 9 of that Order,

[Exceptions for certain companies][1]

1 Substituted by CA 1989, 7 Sch 8 with effect from 1 April 1990 (SI 1990 No 355) subject to the transitional and saving provisions in Arts 6 to 9 of that Order.

27 (1) The following applies to a banking company (if not subject to the Banking Companies (Accounts) Regulations 1970) which satisfies the Secretary of State that it ought to have the benefit of this paragraph.

(2) The company shall not be subject to the requirements of [paragraphs 2 to 18 of this Schedule][1] other than—

(a) as respects its balance sheet, those of paragraphs 2 and 3, paragraph 4 (so far as it relates to assets), paragraph 10 (except sub-paragraphs (1)(d) and (4)), paragraphs 11 and 12 and paragraph 13 (except sub-paragraphs (9), (10), (11), (13) and (14)); and

(b) as respects its profit and loss account, those of sub-paragraph (1)(h) and (k) of paragraph 14 [and paragraph 15][2].

(3) But, where in the company's balance sheet reserves or provisions (other than provisions for depreciation, renewals or diminution in value of assets) are not stated separately, any heading stating an amount arrived at after taking into account a reserve or such a provision shall be so framed or marked as to indicate that fact, and its profit and loss account shall indicate by appropriate words the manner in which the amount stated for the company's profit or loss has been arrived at.

(4) The company's accounts shall not be deemed, by reason only of the fact that they do not comply with any requirements [. . .][3] from which the company is exempt by virtue of this paragraph, not to give the true and fair view required by this Act.

---

1 Substituted by CA 1989, 7 Sch 8 with effect from 1 April 1990 (SI 1990 No 355) subject to the transitional and saving provisions in Arts 6 to 9 of that Order.

2 Substituted by CA 1989, 7 Sch 8 with effect as in [1] above.

3 Deleted by CA 1989, 7 Sch 8 with effect as in [1] above.

---

28 (1) An insurance company [. . .][2] shall not be subject to the following requirements of [paragraphs 2 to 18][1] of this Schedule, that is to say—

(a) as respects its balance sheet, those of paragraphs 4 to 8 (both inclusive), sub-paragraphs (1)(a) and (3) of paragraph 10 and sub-paragraphs (6), (7) and (9) to (13) (both inclusive) of paragraph 13;

(b) as respects its profit and loss account, those of paragraph 14 (except sub-paragraph (1)(b), (c), (d) and (k)) and paragraph 18(2);

but, where in its balance sheet reserves or provisions (other than provisions for depreciation, renewals or diminution in value of assets) are not stated separately, any heading stating an amount arrived at after taking into account a reserve or such a provision shall be so framed or marked as to indicate that fact, and its profit and loss account shall indicate by appropriate words the manner in which the amount stated for the company's profit or loss has been arrived at:

Provided that the Secretary of State may direct that any such insurance company whose business includes to a substantial extent business other than insurance business shall comply with all the requirements of the said [paragraphs 2 to 18][1] or such of them as may be specified in the direction and shall comply therewith as respects either the whole of its business or such part thereof as may be so specified.

(2) The accounts of a company shall not be deemed, by reason only of the fact that they do not comply with any requirement of [paragraphs 2 to 18][1] of this Schedule from which the company is exempt by virtue of this paragraph, not to give the true and fair view required by this Act.

---

1 Substituted by CA 1989, 7 Sch 9 with effect from 1 April 1990 (SI 1990 No 355) subject to the transitional and saving provisions in Arts 6 to 9 of that Order.

2 Repealed by CA 1989, 24 Sch with effect as in [1] above.

[28A Where a company is entitled to, and has availed itself of, any of the provisions of paragraph 27 or 28 of this Schedule, section 235(2) only requires the auditors to state whether in their opinion the accounts have been properly prepared in accordance with this Act.][1]

---

1 Inserted by CA 1989, 7 Sch 10 with effect from 1 April 1990 (SI 1990 No 355) subject to the transitional and saving provisions in Arts 6 to 9 of that Order.

29-31 [. . .][1]

---

1 Deleted by CA 1989, 7 Sch 11 with effect from 1 April 1990 (SI 1990 No 355) subject to the transitional and saving provisions in Arts 6 to 9 of that Order.

[Interpretation][1]

1 Substituted by CA 1989, 7 Sch 12 with effect from 1 April 1990 (SI 1990 No 355) subject to the transitional and saving provisions in Arts 6 to 9 of that Order.

32 (1) For the purposes of [this Part of this Schedule][1], unless the context otherwise requires,—

(a) the expression "provision" shall, subject to sub-paragraph (2) of this paragraph, mean any amount written off or retained by way of providing for depreciation, renewals or diminution in value of assets or retained by way of providing for any known liability of which the amount cannot be determined with substantial accuracy;

(b) the expression "reserve" shall not, subject as aforesaid, include any amount written off or retained by way of providing for depreciation, renewals or diminution in value of assets or retained by way of providing for any known liability or any sum set aside for the purpose of its being used to prevent undue fluctuations in charges for taxation;

and in this paragraph the expression "liability" shall include all liabilities in respect of expenditure contracted for and all disputed or contingent liabilities.

(2) Where—

(a) any amount written off or retained by way of providing for depreciation, renewals or diminution in value of assets; or

(b) any amount retained by way of providing for any known liability;

is in excess of that which in the opinion of the directors is reasonably necessary for the purpose, the excess shall be treated for the purposes of [this Part of this Schedule][1] as a reserve and not as a provision.

1 Substituted by CA 1989, 7 Sch 12 with effect from 1 April 1990 (SI 1990 No 355) subject to the transitional and saving provisions in Arts 6 to 9 of that Order.

33 For the purposes aforesaid, the expression "listed investment" means an investment as respects which there has been granted a listing on a [recognised investment exchange other than an overseas exchange within the meaning of the Financial Services Act 1986][1], or on any stock exchange of repute outside Great Britain and the expression "unlisted investment" shall be construed accordingly.

1 Substituted by FSA 1986, s 212(2), 16 Sch 24 with effect from 29 April 1988 (see SI 1988 No 740). Previously 'recognised stock exchange'.

34 For the purposes aforesaid, the expression "long lease" means a lease in the case of which the portion of the term for which it was granted remaining unexpired at the end of the financial year is not less than fifty years, the expression "short lease" means a lease which is not a long lease and the expression "lease" includes an agreement for a lease.

35 For the purposes aforesaid, a loan shall be deemed to fall due for repayment, and an instalment of a loan shall be deemed to fall due for payment, on the earliest date on which the lender could require repayment or, as the case may be, payment if he exercised all options and rights available to him.

36 In the application of [this Part of this Schedule][1] to Scotland, "land of freehold tenure" means land in respect of which the company is the proprietor of the dominium utile or, in the case of land not held on feudal tenure, is the owner; "land of leasehold tenure" means land of which the company is the tenant under a lease; and the reference to ground-rents, rates and other outgoings includes a reference to feu-duty and ground annual.

1 Substituted by CA 1989, 7 Sch 13 with effect from 1 April 1990 (SI 1990 No 355) subject to the transitional and saving provisions in Arts 6 to 9 of that Order.

[PART II ACCOUNTS OF BANKING OR INSURANCE GROUP][1]

1 Inserted by CA 1989, 7 Sch 13 with effect from 1 April 1990 (SI 1990 No 355) subject to the transitional and saving provisions in Arts 6 to 9 of that Order.

Note. See paragraphs 19-26 of Part I above for what was Part II of this Schedule before the amendments made by CA 1989.

[1 **Undertakings to be included in consolidation**

The following descriptions of undertaking shall not be excluded from consolidation under section 229(4) (exclusion of undertakings whose activities are different from those of the undertakings consolidated)—

(a) in the case of a banking group, an undertaking (other than a credit institution) whose activities are a direct extension of or ancillary to banking business;

(b) in the case of an insurance group, an undertaking (other than one carrying on insurance business) whose activities are a direct extension of or ancillary to insurance business.

For the purposes of paragraph (a) "banking" means the carrying on of a deposit-taking business within the meaning of the Banking Act 1987.][1]

1 Inserted by CA 1989, 7 Sch 13 with effect from 1 April 1990 (SI 1990 No 355) subject to the transitional and saving provisions in Arts 6 to 9 of that Order.

[2 **General application of provisions applicable to individual accounts**

(1) In paragraph 1 of Schedule 4A (application to group accounts of provisions applicable to individual accounts), the reference in sub-paragraph (1) to the provisions of Schedule 4 shall be construed as a reference to the provisions of Part I of this Schedule; and accordingly—

(a) the reference in sub-paragraph (2) to paragraph 59 of Schedule 4 shall be construed as a reference to paragraphs 19(2) and 20 of Part I of this Schedule; and

(b) sub-paragraph (3) shall be omitted.

(2) The general application of the provisions of Part I of this Schedule in place of those of Schedule 4 is subject to the following provisions.][1]

1 Inserted by CA 1989, 7 Sch 13 with effect from 1 April 1990 (SI 1990 No 355) subject to the transitional and saving provisions in Arts 6 to 9 of that Order.

[3 **Treatment of goodwill**

(1) The rules in paragraph 21 of Schedule 4 relating to the treatment of goodwill, and the rules in paragraphs 17 to 19 of that Schedule (valuation of fixed assets) so far as they relate to goodwill, apply for the purpose of dealing with any goodwill arising on consolidation.

(2) Goodwill shall be shown as a separate item in the balance sheet under an appropriate heading; and this applies notwithstanding anything in paragraph 10(1)(b) or (2) of Part I of this Schedule (under which goodwill, patents and trade marks may be stated in the company's individual accounts as a single item).][1]

1 Inserted by CA 1989, 7 Sch 13 with effect from 1 April 1990 (SI 1990 No 355) subject to the transitional and saving provisions in Arts 6 to 9 of that Order.

[4 **Minority interests and associated undertakings**

The information required by paragraphs 17 and 20 to 22 of Schedule 4A (minority interests and associated undertakings) to be shown under separate items in the formats set out in Part I of Schedule 4 shall be shown separately in the balance sheet and profit and loss account under appropriate headings.][1]

1 Inserted by CA 1989, 7 Sch 13 with effect from 1 April 1990 (SI 1990 No 355) subject to the transitional and saving provisions in Arts 6 to 9 of that Order.

[5 **Companies entitled to benefit of exemptions**

(1) Where a banking or insurance company is entitled to the exemptions conferred by paragraph 27 or 28 of Part I of this Schedule, a group headed by that company is similarly entitled.

(2) Paragraphs 27(4), 28(2) and 28A (accounts not to be taken to be other than true and fair; duty of auditors) apply accordingly where advantage is taken of those exemptions in relation to group accounts.][1]

1 Inserted by CA 1989, 7 Sch 13 with effect from 1 April 1990 (SI 1990 No 355) subject to the transitional and saving provisions in Arts 6 to 9 of that Order.

[6 **Information as to undertaking in which shares held as result of financial assistance operation**

(1) The following provisions apply where the parent company of a banking group has a subsidiary undertaking which—

(a) is a credit institution of which shares are held as a result of a financial assistance operation with a view to its reorganisation or rescue, and

(b) is excluded from consolidation under section 229(3)(c) (interest held with a view to resale).

(2) Information as to the nature and terms of the operation shall be given in a note to the group accounts and there shall be appended to the copy of the group accounts delivered to the registrar in accordance with section 242 a copy of the undertaking's latest individual accounts and, if it is a parent undertaking, its latest group accounts.

If the accounts appended are required by law to be audited, a copy of the auditors' report shall also be appended.

(3) If any document required to be appended is in a language other than English, the directors shall annex to the copy of that document delivered a translation of it into English, certified in the prescribed manner to be a correct translation.

(4) The above requirements are subject to the following qualifications—

(a) an undertaking is not required to prepare for the purposes of this paragraph accounts which would not otherwise be prepared, and if no accounts satisfying the above requirements are prepared none need be appended;

(b) the accounts of an undertaking need not be appended if they would not otherwise be required to be published, or made available for public inspection, anywhere in the world, but in that case the reason for not appending the accounts shall be stated in a note to the consolidated accounts.

(5) Where a copy of an undertaking's accounts is required to be appended to the copy of the group accounts delivered to the registrar, that fact shall be stated in a note to the group accounts.

(6) Subsections (2) to (4) of section 242 (penalties, etc. in case of default) apply in relation to the requirements of this paragraph as regards the delivery of documents to the registrar as they apply in relation to the requirements of subsection (1) of that section.][1]

---

1 Inserted by CA 1989, 7 Sch 13 with effect from 1 April 1990 (SI 1990 No 355) subject to the transitional and saving provisions in Arts 6 to 9 of that Order.

[PART III ADDITIONAL DISCLOSURE: RELATED UNDERTAKINGS][1]

---

1 Inserted by CA 1989, 7 Sch 13 with effect from 1 April 1990 (SI 1990 No 355) subject to the transitional and saving provisions in Arts 6 to 9 of that Order.

[1 Where accounts are prepared in accordance with the special provisions of this Part relating to banking companies or groups, there shall be disregarded for the purposes of—

(a) paragraphs 7(2)(a), 23(2)(a) and 26(2)(a) of Schedule 5 (information about significant holdings in undertakings other than subsidiary undertakings: definition of 10 per cent. holding), and

(b) paragraphs 9(1), 25(1) and 28(1) of that Schedule (additional information in case of 20 per cent. holding),

any holding of shares not comprised in the equity share capital of the undertaking in question.][1]

---

1 Inserted by CA 1989, 7 Sch 13 with effect from 1 April 1990 (SI 1990 No 355) subject to the transitional and saving provisions in Arts 6 to 9 of that Order.

[PART IV ADDITIONAL DISCLOSURE: EMOLUMENTS AND OTHER BENEFITS OF DIRECTORS AND OTHERS][1]

---

1 Inserted by CA 1989, 7 Sch 13 with effect from 1 April 1990 (SI 1990 No 355) subject to the transitional and saving provisions in Arts 6 to 9 of that Order.

[1 The provisions of this Part of this Schedule have effect with respect to the application of Schedule 6 (additional disclosure: emoluments and other benefits of directors and others) to a banking company or the holding company of such a company.][1]

---

1 Inserted by CA 1989, 7 Sch 13 with effect from 1 April 1990 (SI 1990 No 355) subject to the transitional and saving provisions in Arts 6 to 9 of that Order.

[2 **Loans, quasi-loans and other dealings**

Part II of Schedule 6 (loans, quasi-loans and other dealings) does not apply for the purposes of accounts prepared by a banking company, or a company which is the holding company of a banking company, in relation to a transaction or arrangement of a kind mentioned in section 330, or an agreement to enter into such a transaction or arrangement, to which that banking company is a party.][1]

---

1 Inserted by CA 1989, 7 Sch 13 with effect from 1 April 1990 (SI 1990 No 355) subject to the transitional and saving provisions in Arts 6 to 9 of that Order.

[3 **Other transactions, arrangements and agreements**

(1) Part III of Schedule 6 (other transactions, arrangements and agreements) applies for the purposes of accounts prepared by a banking company, or a company which is the holding company of a banking company, only in relation to a transaction, arrangement or agreement made by that banking company for—

(a) a person who was a director of the company preparing the accounts, or who was connected with such a director, or

(b) a person who was a chief executive or manager (within the meaning of the Banking Act 1987) of that company or its holding company.

(2) References in that Part to officers of the company shall be construed accordingly as including references to such persons.

(3) In this paragraph "director" includes a shadow director.

(4) For the purposes of that Part as it applies by virtue of this paragraph, a company which a person does not control shall not be treated as connected with him.

(5) Section 346 of this Act applies for the purposes of this paragraph as regards the interpretation of references to a person being connected with a director or controlling a company.][1]

---

1 Inserted by CA 1989, 7 Sch 13 with effect from 1 April 1990 (SI 1990 No 355) subject to the transitional and saving provisions in Arts 6 to 9 of that Order.

SCHEDULE 10
(As substituted by CA 1989, s 18(5), 8 Sch)

DIRECTORS' REPORT WHERE ACCOUNTS PREPARED IN ACCORDANCE WITH SPECIAL PROVISIONS FOR BANKING OR INSURANCE COMPANIES OR GROUPS

Note. This Schedule is substituted by CA 1989, 8 Sch with effect from 1 April 1990 (SI 1990 No 355) subject to the transitional and saving provisions in Arts 6 to 9 of that Order.

1 Recent issues

(1) This paragraph applies where a company prepares individual accounts in accordance with the special provisions of this Part relating to banking or insurance companies.

(2) If in the financial year to which the accounts relate the company has issued any shares or debentures, the directors' report shall state the reason for making the issue, the classes of shares or debentures issued and, as respects each class, the number of shares or amount of debentures issued and the consideration received by the company for the issue.

2 Turnover and profitability

(1) This paragraph applies where a company prepares group accounts in accordance with the special provisions of this Part relating to banking or insurance groups.

(2) If in the course of the financial year to which the accounts relate the group carried on business of two or more classes (other than banking or discounting or a class prescribed for the purposes of paragraph 17(2) of Part I of Schedule 9) that in the opinion of the directors differ substantially from each other, there shall be contained in the directors' report a statement of—

(a) the proportions in which the turnover for the financial year (so far as stated in the consolidated accounts) is divided amongst those classes (describing them), and

(b) as regards business of each class, the extent or approximate extent (expressed in money terms) to which, in the opinion of the directors, the carrying on of business of that class contributed to or restricted the profit or loss of the group for that year (before taxation).

(3) In sub-paragraph (2) "the group" means the undertakings included in the consolidation.

(4) For the purposes of this paragraph classes of business which in the opinion of the directors do not differ substantially from each other shall be treated as one class.

3 Labour force and wages paid

(1) This paragraph applies where a company prepares individual or group accounts in accordance with the special provisions of this Part relating to banking or insurance companies or groups.

(2) There shall be stated in the directors' report—

(a) the average number of persons employed by the company or, if the company prepares group accounts, by the company and its subsidiary undertakings, and

(b) the aggregate amount of the remuneration paid or payable to persons so employed.

(3) The average number of persons employed shall be determined by adding together the number of persons employed (whether throughout the week or not) in each week of the financial year and dividing that total by the number of weeks in the financial year.

(4) The aggregate amount of the remuneration paid or payable means the total amount of remuneration paid or payable in respect of the financial year; and for this purpose remuneration means gross remuneration and includes bonuses, whether payable under contract or not.

(5) The information required by this paragraph need not be given if the average number of persons employed is less than 100.

(6) No account shall be taken for the purposes of this paragraph of persons who worked wholly or mainly outside the United Kingdom.

(7) This paragraph does not apply to a company which is a wholly-owned subsidiary of a company incorporated in Great Britain.

Note. The above Schedule is substituted by CA 1989, 8 Sch.

SCHEDULE 11
(Section 279 and as amended by CA 1989, s 23, 10 Sch 21)

[MODIFICATIONS OF PART VIII WHERE COMPANY'S ACCOUNTS PREPARED IN ACCORDANCE WITH SPECIAL PROVISIONS FOR BANKING OR INSURANCE COMPANIES][1]

1 Substituted by CA 1989, 10 Sch 21 with effect from 1 April 1990 (SI 1990 No 355) subject to the transitional and saving provisions in Arts 6 to 9 of that Order.

1 Section 264 applies as if in subsection (2) for the words following "the aggregate of its liabilities" there were substituted "("liabilities" to include any provision within the meaning of [Part I of Schedule 9][1], except to the extent that that provision is taken into account in calculating the value of any asset of the company)".

1 Substituted by CA 1989, 10 Sch 21 with effect from 1 April 1990 (SI 1990 No 355) subject to the transitional and saving provisions in Arts 6 to 9 of that Order.

2 Section 265 applies as if—

(a) for subsection (2) there were substituted—

"(2) In subsection (1)(a), "liabilities" includes any provision (within the meaning of [Part I of Schedule 9][1]) except to the extent that that provision is taken into account for the purposes of that subsection in calculating the value of any asset of the company", and

(b) there were added at the end of the section—

"(7) In determining capital and revenue profits and losses, an asset which is not a fixed asset or a current asset is treated as a fixed asset".

1 Substituted by CA 1989, 10 Sch 21 with effect from 1 April 1990 (SI 1990 No 355) subject to the transitional and saving provisions in Arts 6 to 9 of that Order.

3 Section 269 does not apply.

4 Section 270 applies as if—

(a) in subsection (2) the following were substituted for paragraph (b)—

"(b) provisions (within the meaning of [Part I of Schedule 9][1])";

(b) [. . .][2]

(c) [. . .][3]

1 Substituted by CA 1989, 10 Sch 21 with effect from 1 April 1990 (SI 1990 No 355) subject to the transitional and saving provisions in Arts 6 to 9 of that Order.

2 Deleted by CA 1989, 10 Sch 21 with effect as in [1] above.

3 Deleted by CA 1989, 10 Sch 21 with effect from a date to be appointed.

5 Section 271 applies as if—

(a) in subsection (2), immediately before paragraph (a) there were inserted "except where the company is entitled to avail itself, and has availed itself, of any of the provisions of [paragraph 27 or 28][1] of Schedule 9", and

(b) [. . .][2]

1 Substituted by CA 1989, 10 Sch 21 with effect from 1 April 1990 (SI 1990 No 355) subject to the transitional and saving provisions in Arts 6 to 9 of that Order.

2 Deleted by CA 1989, 10 Sch 21 with effect as in [1] above.

6 Sections 272 and 273 apply as if in section 272(3)—

(a) for the references to [section 226][1] and Schedule 4 there were substituted references to [section 225 and Part I of Schedule 9][2], and

(b) immediately before paragraph (a) there were inserted "except where the company is entitled to avail itself, and has availed itself, of any of the provisions of [paragraph 27 or 28 of Schedule 9][3]".

1 Substituted by CA 1989, 10 Sch 21 with effect from 1 April 1990 (SI 1990 No 355) subject to the transitional and saving provisions in Arts 6 to 9 of that Order.

2 Substituted by CA 1989, 10 Sch 21 with effect as in [1] above.

3 Substituted by CA 1989, 10 Sch 21 with effect as in [1]above

7 Section 275 applies as if—

(a) for subsection (1) there were substituted—

"(1) For purposes of section 263, any provision (within the meaning of [Part I of Schedule 9][1]), other than one in respect of any diminution of value of a fixed asset appearing on a revaluation of all the fixed assets of the company, or of all its fixed assets other than goodwill, is to be treated as a realised loss"; and

(b) "fixed assets" were defined to include any other asset which is not a current asset.

1 Substituted by CA 1989, 10 Sch 21 with effect from 1 April 1990 (SI 1990 No 355) subject to the transitional and saving provisions in Arts 6 to 9 of that Order.

SCHEDULE 13

(Sections 324-326, 328, 346 and as amended by CA 1989, s 143)

PROVISIONS SUPPLEMENTING AND INTERPRETING SECTIONS 324 TO 328

PART I RULES FOR INTERPRETATION OF THE SECTIONS AND ALSO SECTION 346(4) AND (5)

1 (1) A reference to an interest in shares or debentures is to be read as including any interest of any kind whatsoever in shares or debentures.

(2) Accordingly, there are to be disregarded any restraints or restrictions to which the exercise of any right attached to the interest is or may be subject.

2 Where property is held on trust and any interest in shares or debentures is comprised in the property, any beneficiary of the trust who (apart from this paragraph) does not have an interest in the shares or debentures is to be taken as having such an interest; but this paragraph is without prejudice to the following provisions of this Part of this Schedule.

3 (1) A person is taken to have an interest in shares or debentures if—

(a) he enters into a contract for their purchase by him (whether for cash or other consideration), or

(b) not being the registered holder, he is entitled to exercise any right conferred by the holding of the shares or debentures, or is entitled to control the exercise of any such right.

(2) For purposes of sub-paragraph (1)(b), a person is taken to be entitled to exercise or control the exercise of a right conferred by the holding of shares or debentures if he—

(a) has a right (whether subject to conditions or not) the exercise of which would make him so entitled, or

(b) is under an obligation (whether or not so subject) the fulfilment of which would make him so entitled.

(3) A person is not by virtue of sub-paragraph (1)(b) taken to be interested in shares or debentures by reason only that he—

(a) has been appointed a proxy to vote at a specified meeting of a company or of any class of its members and at any adjournment of that meeting, or

(b) has been appointed by a corporation to act as its representative at any meeting of a company or of any class of its members.

4 A person is taken to be interested in shares or debentures if a body corporate is interested in them and—

(a) that body corporate or its directors are accustomed to act in accordance with his directions or instructions, or

(b) he is entitled to exercise or control the exercise of one-third or more of the voting power at general meetings of that body corporate.

As this paragraph applies for the purposes of section 346(4) and (5), "more than one-half" is substituted for "one-third or more".

5 Where a person is entitled to exercise or control the exercise of one-third or more of the voting power at general meetings of a body corporate, and that body corporate is entitled to exercise or control the exercise of any of the voting power at general meetings of another body corporate ("the effective voting power"), then, for purposes of paragraph 4(b), the effective voting power is taken to be exercisable by that person.

As this paragraph applies for the purposes of section 346(4) and (5), "more than one-half" is substituted for "one-third or more".

6 (1) A person is taken to have an interest in shares or debentures if, otherwise than by virtue of having an interest under a trust—

(a) he has a right to call for delivery of the shares or debentures to himself or to his order, or

(b) he has a right to acquire an interest in shares or debentures or is under an obligation to take an interest in shares or debentures;

whether in any case the right or obligation is conditional or absolute.

(2) Rights or obligations to subscribe for shares or debentures are not to be taken, for purposes of sub-paragraph (1), to be rights to acquire, or obligations to take, an interest in shares or debentures.

This is without prejudice to paragraph 1.

7 Persons having a joint interest are deemed each of them to have that interest.

8 It is immaterial that shares or debentures in which a person has an interest are unidentifiable.

9 So long as a person is entitled to receive, during the lifetime of himself or another, income from trust property comprising shares or debentures, an interest in the shares or debentures in reversion or remainder or (as regards Scotland) in fee, are to be disregarded.

10 A person is to be treated as uninterested in shares or debentures if, and so long as, he holds them under the law in force in England and Wales as a bare trustee or as a custodian trustee, or under the law in force in Scotland, as a simple trustee.

11 There is to be disregarded an interest of a person subsisting by virtue of—

(a) [any unit trust scheme which is an authorised unit trust scheme within the meaning of the Financial Services Act 1986][1];

(b) a scheme made under section 22 of the Charities Act 1960, section 11 of the Trustee Investments Act 1961 or section 1 of the Administration of Justice Act 1965; or

(c) the scheme set out in the Schedule to the Church Funds Investment Measure 1958.

---

1 Substituted by FSA 1986, s 212(2), 16 Sch 25 with effect from 29 April 1988 (see SI 1988 No 740).

---

12 There is to be disregarded any interest—

(a) of the Church of Scotland General Trustees or of the Church of Scotland Trust in shares or debentures held by them;

(b) of any other person in shares or debentures held by those Trustees or that Trust otherwise than as simple trustees.

"The Church of Scotland General Trustees" are the body incorporated by the order confirmed by the Church of Scotland (General Trustees) Order Confirmation Act 1921; and "the Church of Scotland Trust" is the body incorporated by the order confirmed by the Church of Scotland Trust Order Confirmation Act 1932.

13 Delivery to a person's order of shares or debentures in fulfilment of a contract for the purchase of them by him or in satisfaction of a right of his to call for their delivery, or failure to deliver shares or debentures in accordance with the terms of such a contract or on which such a right falls to be satisfied, is deemed to constitute an event in consequence of the occurrence of which he ceases to be interested in them, and so is the lapse of a person's right to call for delivery of shares or debentures.

PART II PERIODS WITHIN WHICH OBLIGATIONS IMPOSED BY SECTION 324 MUST BE FULFILLED

14 (1) An obligation imposed on a person by section 324(1) to notify an interest must, if he knows of the existence of the interest on the day on which he becomes a director, be fulfilled before the expiration of the period of 5 days beginning with the day following that day.

(2) Otherwise, the obligation must be fulfilled before the expiration of the period of 5 days beginning with the day following that on which the existence of the interest comes to his knowledge.

15 (1) An obligation imposed on a person by section 324(2) to notify the occurrence of an event must, if at the time at which the event occurs he knows of its occurrence and of the fact that its occurrence gives rise to the obligation, be fulfilled before the expiration of the period of 5 days beginning with the day following that on which the event occurs.

(2) Otherwise, the obligation must be fulfilled before the expiration of a period of 5 days beginning with the day following that on which the fact that the occurrence of the event gives rise to the obligation comes to his knowledge.

16 In reckoning, for purposes of paragraphs 14 and 15, any period of days, a day that is a Saturday or Sunday, or a bank holiday in any part of Great Britain, is to be disregarded.

PART III CIRCUMSTANCES IN WHICH OBLIGATION IMPOSED BY SECTION 324 IS NOT DISCHARGED

17 (1) Where an event of whose occurrence a director is, by virtue of section 324(2)(a), under obligation to notify a company consists of his entering into a contract for the purchase by him of shares or debentures, the obligation is not discharged in the absence of inclusion in the notice of a statement of the price to be paid by him under the contract.

(2) An obligation imposed on a director by section 324(2)(b) is not discharged in the absence of inclusion in the notice of the price to be received by him under the contract.

18 (1) An obligation imposed on a director by virtue of section 324(2)(c) to notify a company is not discharged in the absence of inclusion in the notice of a statement of the consideration for the assignment (or, if it be the case that there is no consideration, that fact).

(2) Where an event of whose occurrence a director is, by virtue of section 324(2)(d), under obligation to notify a company consists in his assigning a right, the obligation is not discharged in the absence of inclusion in the notice of a similar statement.

19 (1) Where an event of whose occurrence a director is, by virtue of section 324(2)(d), under obligation to notify a company consists in the grant to him of a right to subscribe for shares or debentures, the obligation is not discharged in the absence of inclusion in the notice of a statement of—

(a) the date on which the right was granted,
(b) the period during which or the time at which the right is exercisable,
(c) the consideration for the grant (or, if it be the case that there is no consideration, that fact), and
(d) the price to be paid for the shares or debentures.

(2) Where an event of whose occurrence a director is, by section 324(2)(d), under obligation to notify a company consists in the exercise of a right granted to him to subscribe for shares or debentures, the obligation is not discharged in the absence of inclusion in the notice of a statement of—

(a) the number of shares or amount of debentures in respect of which the right was exercised, and
(b) if it be the case that they were registered in his name, that fact, and, if not, the name or names of the person or persons in whose name or names they were registered, together (if they were registered in the names of 2 persons or more) with the number or amount registered in the name of each of them.

20 In this Part, a reference to price paid or received includes any consideration other than money.

PART IV PROVISIONS WITH RESPECT TO REGISTER OF DIRECTORS' INTERESTS TO BE KEPT UNDER SECTION 325

21 The register must be so made up that the entries in it against the several names appear in chronological order.

22 An obligation imposed by section 325(2) to (4) must be fulfilled before the expiration of the period of 3 days beginning with the day after that on which the obligation arises; but in reckoning that period, a day which is a Saturday or Sunday or a bank holiday in any part of Great Britain is to be disregarded.

23 The nature and extent of an interest recorded in the register of a director in any shares or debentures shall, if he so requires, be recorded in the register.

24 The company is not, by virtue of anything done for the purposes of section 325 or this Part of this Schedule, affected with notice of, or put upon enquiry as to, the rights of any person in relation to any shares or debentures.

25 The register shall—

(a) if the company's register of members is kept at its registered office, be kept there;
(b) if the company's register of members is not so kept, be kept at the company's registered office or at the place where its register of members is kept;

and shall [. . .][1] be open to the inspection of any member of the company without charge and of any other person on payment of [such fee as may be prescribed][2].

1 Deleted by CA 1989, s 143 with effect from a date to be appointed.

2 Substituted by CA 1989, s 143 with effect from a date to be appointed.

26 (1) Any member of the company or other person may require a copy of the register, or of any part of it, on payment of [such fee as may be prescribed][1].

(2) The company shall cause any copy so required by a person to be sent to him within the period of 10 days beginning with the day after that on which the requirement is received by the company.

1 Substituted by CA 1989, s 143 with effect from a date to be appointed.

27 The company shall send notice in the prescribed form to the registrar of companies of the place where the register is kept and of any change in that place, save in a case in which it has at all times been kept at its registered office.

28 Unless the register is in such a form as to constitute in itself an index, the company shall keep an index of the names inscribed in it, which shall—

(a) in respect of each name, contain a sufficient indication to enable the information entered against it to be readily found; and
(b) be kept at the same place as the register;

and the company shall, within 14 days after the date on which a name is entered in the register, make any necessary alteration in the index.

29 The register shall be produced at the commencement of the company's annual general meeting and remain open and accessible during the continuance of the meeting to any person attending the meeting.

SCHEDULE 14
(Section 362)

OVERSEAS BRANCH REGISTERS

PART I COUNTRIES AND TERRITORIES IN WHICH OVERSEAS BRANCH REGISTER MAY BE KEPT

Northern Ireland
Any part of Her Majesty's dominions outside the United Kingdom, the Channel Islands or the Isle of Man
Bangladesh
Cyprus
Dominica
The Gambia
Ghana
Guyana
India
Kenya
Kiribati
Lesotho
Malawi
Malaysia
Malta
Nigeria
Pakistan
Republic of Ireland
Seychelles
Sierra Leone
Singapore
South Africa
Sri Lanka
Swaziland
Trinidad and Tobago
Uganda
Zimbabwe

PART II GENERAL PROVISIONS WITH RESPECT TO OVERSEAS BRANCH REGISTERS

1 (1) A company keeping an overseas branch register shall give to the registrar of companies notice in the prescribed form of the situation of the office where any overseas branch register is kept and of any change in its situation, and, if it is discontinued, of its discontinuance.

(2) Any such notice shall be given within 14 days of the opening of the office or of the change or discontinuance, as the case may be.

(3) If default is made in complying with this paragraph, the company and every officer of it who is in default is liable to a fine and, for continued contravention, to a daily default fine.

Cross references. See 24 Sch (punishment of offences).

---

2 (1) An overseas branch register is deemed to be part of the company's register of members ("the principal register").

(2) It shall be kept in the same manner in which the principal register is by this Act required to be kept, except that the advertisement before closing the register shall be inserted in a newspaper circulating in the district where the overseas branch register is kept.

3 (1) A competent court in a country or territory where an overseas branch register is kept may exercise the same jurisdiction of rectifying the register as is under this Act exercisable by the court in Great Britain; and the offences of refusing inspection or copies of the register, and of authorising or permitting the refusal, may be prosecuted summarily before any tribunal having summary criminal jurisdiction.

(2) This paragraph extends only to those countries and territories where, immediately before the coming into force of this Act, provision to the same effect made by section 120(2) of the Companies Act 1948 had effect as part of the local law.

4 (1) The company shall—

(a) transmit to its registered office a copy of every entry in its overseas branch register as soon as may be after the entry is made, and
(b) cause to be kept at the place where the company's principal register is kept a duplicate of its overseas branch register duly entered up from time to time.

Every such duplicate is deemed for all purposes of this Act to be part of the principal register.

(2) If default is made in complying with sub-paragraph (1), the company and every officer of it who is in default is liable to a fine and, for continued contravention, to a daily default fine.

(3) Where, by virtue of section 353(1)(b), the principal register is kept at the office of some person other than the company, and by reason of any default of his the company fails to comply with sub-paragraph (1)(b) above he is liable to the same penalty as if he were an officer of the company who was in default.

Cross references. See 24 Sch (punishment of offences).

---

5 Subject to the above provisions with respect to the duplicate register, the shares registered in an overseas branch register shall be distinguished from those registered in the principal register; and no transaction with respect to any shares registered in an overseas branch register shall, during the continuance of that registration, be registered in any other register.

6 A company may discontinue to keep an overseas branch register, and thereupon all entries in that register shall be transferred to some other overseas branch register kept by the company in the same country or territory, or to the principal register.

7 Subject to the provisions of this Act, any company may, by its articles, make such provisions as it thinks fit respecting the keeping of overseas branch registers.

8 An instrument of transfer of a share registered in an overseas branch register (other than such a register kept in Northern Ireland) is deemed a transfer of property situated outside the United Kingdom and, unless executed in a part of the United Kingdom, is exempt from stamp duty chargeable in Great Britain.

PART III PROVISIONS FOR BRANCH REGISTERS OF OVERSEA COMPANIES TO BE KEPT IN GREAT BRITAIN

9 (1) If by virtue of the law in force in any country or territory to which this paragraph applies companies incorporated under that law have power to keep in Great Britain branch registers of their members resident in Great Britain, Her Majesty may by Order in Council direct that—

(a) so much of section 353 as requires a company's register of members to be kept at its registered office,
(b) section 356 (register to be open to inspection by members), and
(c) section 359 (power of court to rectify),

shall, subject to any modifications and adaptations specified in the Order, apply to and in relation to any such branch registers kept in Great Britain as they apply to and in relation to the registers of companies subject to those sections.

(2) The countries and territories to which this paragraph applies are—

(a) all those specified in Part I of this Schedule, plus the Channel Islands and the Isle of Man,
(b) Botswana, Zambia and Tonga, and
(c) any territory for the time being under Her Majesty's protection or administered by the Government of the United Kingdom under the Trusteeship System of the United Nations.

SCHEDULE 21

(Section 689 and as amended by CA 1989, s 108(2))

EFFECT OF REGISTRATION UNDER SECTION 680

1 Interpretation

In this Schedule—

"registration" means registration in pursuance of section 680 in Chapter II of Part XXII of this Act, and "registered" has the corresponding meaning, and

"instrument" includes deed of settlement, contract of copartnery and letters patent.

2 Vesting of property

All property belonging to or vested in the company at the date of its registration passes to and vests in the company on registration for all the estate and interest of the company in the property.

3 Existing liabilities

Registration does not affect the company's rights or liabilities in respect of any debt or obligation incurred, or contract entered into, by, to, with or on behalf of the company before registration.

4 Pending actions at law

(1) All actions and other legal proceedings which at the time of the company's registration are pending by or against the company, or the public officer or any member of it, may be continued in the same manner as if the registration had not taken place.

(2) However, execution shall not issue against the effects of any individual member of the company on any judgment, decree or order obtained in such an action or proceeding; but in the event of the company's property and effects being insufficient to satisfy the judgment, decree or order, an order may be obtained for winding up the company.

The company's constitution

5 (1) All provisions contained in any Act of Parliament or other instrument constituting or regulating the company are deemed to be conditions and regulations of the company, in the same manner and with the same incidents as if so much of them as would, if the company had been formed under this Act, have been required to be inserted in the memorandum, were contained in a registered memorandum, and the residue were contained in registered articles.

(2) The provisions brought in under this paragraph include, in the case of a company registered as a company limited by guarantee, those of the resolution declaring the amount of the guarantee; and they include also the statement under section 681(5)(a), and any statement under section 684(2).

6 (1) All the provisions of this Act apply to the company, and to its members, contributories and creditors, in the same manner in all respects as if it had been formed under this Act, subject as follows.

(2) Table A does not apply unless adopted by special resolution.

(3) Provisions relating to the numbering of shares do not apply to any joint stock company whose shares are not numbered.

(4) Subject to the provisions of this Schedule, the company does not have power—

(a) to alter any provision contained in an Act of Parliament relating to the company,
(b) without the sanction of the Secretary of State, to alter any provision contained in letters patent relating to the company.

(5) The company does not have power to alter any provision contained in a royal charter or letters patent with respect to the company's objects.

[(6) Where by virtue of sub-paragraph (4) or (5) a company does not have power to alter a provision, it does not have power to ratify acts of the directors in contravention of the provision.][1]

1 Inserted by CA 1989, s 108(2) with effect from a date to be appointed.

7 Capital structure

Provisions of this Act with respect to—

(a) the registration of an unlimited company as limited,
(b) the powers of an unlimited company on registration as a limited company to increase the nominal amount of its share capital and to provide that a portion of its share capital shall not be capable of being called up except in the event of winding up, and
(c) the power of a limited company to determine that a portion of its share capital shall not be capable of being called up except in that event,

apply, notwithstanding any provisions contained in an Act of Parliament, royal charter or other instrument constituting or regulating the company.

Supplementary

8 Nothing in paragraphs 5 to 7 authorises a company to alter any such provisions contained in an instrument constituting or regulating the company as would, if the company had originally been formed under this Act, have been required to be contained in the memorandum and are not authorised to be altered by this Act.

9 None of the provisions of this Act (except section 461(3)) derogate from any power of altering the company's constitution or regulations which may, by virtue of any Act of Parliament or other instrument constituting or regulating it, be vested in the company.

SCHEDULE 22

(Section 718 and as amended by CA 1989, ss 71, 106, 108(3), 109(2), 123(5), 127(7), 130, 142(2), 143(11), 19 Sch 21, 10 Sch 23, 24 Sch and FSA 1986, s 212(2), 16 Sch 26 and 17 Sch Pt I)

PROVISIONS OF THIS ACT APPLYING TO UNREGISTERED COMPANIES

Provisions of this Act applied	Subject matter	Limitations and exceptions (if any)
In Part I—		
section 18	Statutory and other amendments of memorandum and articles to be registered.	Subject to section 718(3).
[sections 35 to 35B][3]	Company's capacity; power of directors to bind it.	Subject to section 718(3).
[. . .][11]		
[section 36	Company contracts.	Subject to section 718(3).
sections 36A and 36B	Execution of documents.	Subject to section 718(3).
section 36C	Pre-incorporation contracts, deeds and obligations.][15]	Subject to section 718(3).
section 40	Official seal for share certificates, etc.	Subject to section 718(3).
section 42	Events affecting a company's status to be officially notified.	Subject to section 718(3).
In Part III, Chapter I (with Schedule 3)	Prospectus and requirements in connection with it.	Subject to section 718(3).
In Part IV, sections 82, 86 and 87	Allotments.	Subject to section 718(3).
In Part V—		
section 185(4)	Exemption from duty to prepare certificates where shares etc. issued to [clearing house or][1] nominee.	Subject to section 718(3).
section 186	Certificate as evidence of title.	Subject to section 718(3).
Part VII, with— Schedules 4 to 8 Schedule 9 (except sub-paragraphs (a) to (d) of paragraph 2, sub-paragraphs (c), (d) and (e) of paragraph 3 and sub-paragraph (1)(c) of paragraph 10), and [Schedules 10 and 10A][6]	Accounts and audit.	Subject to section 718(3).

In Part IX—		
section 287	Registered office.	Subject to section 718(3).
sections 288 to 290	Register of directors and secretaries.	—
In Part X—		
[section 322A	Invalidity of certain transactions involving directors, etc.	Subject to section 718(3)][4].
sections 343 to 347	Register to be kept of certain transactions not disclosed in accounts; other related matters.	Subject to section 718(3).
In Part XI—		
section 351(1), (2) and (5)(a)	Particulars of company to be given in correspondence.	Subject to section 718(3).
sections 363 [. . .][12] to 365	Annual return.	Subject to section 718(3).
sections 384 to [394A][7]	Appointment, [. . .][13] etc., of auditors.	Subject to section 718(3).
[Part XII	Registration of company charges; copies of instruments and register to be kept by company.	Subject to section 718(3).][2]
[Part XIV (except section 446)	Investigation of companies and their affairs; requisition of documents.	—][14].
Part XV	Effect of order imposing restrictions on shares.	To apply so far only as relates to orders under section 445.
[Part XVI	Fraudulent trading by a company.	—][5].
In Part XXIV—		
sections [706-710A, 713 and 715A][8]	Miscellaneous provisions about registration.	—
section 711	Public notice by registrar of companies with respect to certain documents.	Subject to section 718(3).
[section 711A	Abolition of doctrine of deemed notice.	Subject to section 718(3).][9]
In Part XXV—		
section 720	Companies to publish periodical statement.	Subject to section 718(3).

section 721	Production and inspection of company's books.	To apply so far only as these provisions have effect in relation to provisions applying by virtue of the foregoing provisions of this Schedule.
section 722	Form of company registers, etc.	
section 723	Use of computers for company records.	
[section 723A	Rights of inspection and related matters.][10]	
section 725	Service of documents.	
section 730, with Schedule 24	Punishment of offences; meaning of "officer in default".	
section 731	Summary proceedings.	
section 732	Prosecution by public authorities.	
Part XXVI	Interpretation.	To apply so far as requisite for the interpretation of other provisions applied by section 718 and this Schedule.

1 Substituted by FSA 1986, s 212(2), 16 Sch 26 with effect from 29 April 1988 (see SI 1988 No 740).

2 Inserted by CA 1989, s 106 with effect from a date to be appointed.

3 Substituted by CA 1989, s 108(3) with effect from a date to be appointed.

4 Inserted by CA 1989, s 109(2) with effect from a date to be appointed.

5 Inserted by CA 1989, 19 Sch 21 with effect from 1 March 1990 (SI 1990 No 142).

6 Substituted by CA 1989, 10 Sch 23 with effect from 1 April 1990 (SI 1990 No 355) subject to the transitional and saving provisions in Arts 6 to 9 of that Order reproduced above Sec 221 above.

7 Substituted by CA 1989, s 123(5) with effect from 1 April 1990 (SI 1990 No 355) subject to the transitional and saving provisions in Schedule 4 of that Order reproduced in the notes to CA 1989, s 118.

8 Substituted by CA 1989, s 127(7) with effect from a date to be appointed.

9 Inserted by CA 1989, s 142(2) with effect from a date to be appointed.

10 Inserted by CA 1989, s 143(11) with effect from a date to be appointed.

11 Deleted by CA 1989, 24 Sch with effect from a date to be appointed.

12 Deleted by CA 1989, 24 Sch with effect from a date to be appointed.

13 Deleted by CA 1989, 24 Sch with effect from 1 April 1990 (SI 1990 No 355) subject to the transitional and saving provisions in Arts 6 to 9 of that Order reproduced above Sec 221 above.

14 Substituted by CA 1989, s 71 with effect from 21 February 1990 (SI 1990 No 142).

15 Inserted by CA 1989, s 130 with effect from a date to be appointed.

Notes

(a) The entries in CA 1985, 22 Sch relating to Parts III and IV are repealed by FSA 1986, s 212(3), 17 Sch Part I from a date or dates to be appointed by statutory instrument (see FSA 1986, s 211(1)).
To date the entries have been repealed as follows.
- (i) To the extent to which they would apply in relation to any investment which is listed or the subject of an application for listing in accordance with FSA 1986, Part IV (official listing of securities)
  - (A) with effect from 12 January 1987 for all purposes relating to the admission of securities offered by or on behalf of a Minister of the Crown or a body corporate controlled by a Minister of the Crown or a subsidiary of such a body to the Official List in respect of which an application is made after that date; and
  - (B) with effect from 16 February 1987 for purposes relating to the admission of securities in respect of which an application is made after that date other than those referred to in (A) above and otherwise for all purposes.

  [SI 1986 No 2246].
- (ii) With effect from 29 April 1988 in respect of a prospectus offering for subscription, or to any form of application for, units in a body corporate which is a recognised scheme. [SI 1988 No 740].

SCHEDULE 23
(Section 720)

FORM OF STATEMENT TO BE PUBLISHED BY CERTAIN COMPANIES UNDER SECTION 720

*The share capital of the company is , divided into shares of each.

The number of shares issued is

Calls to the amount of pounds per share have been made, under which the sum of pounds has been received.

The liabilities of the company on the first day of January (*or* July) were—

Debts owing to sundry persons by the company.
On judgment (in Scotland, in respect of which decree has been granted), £
On specialty, £
On notes or bills, £
On simple contracts, £
On estimated liabilities, £

The assets of the company on that day were—

Government securities [*stating them*]
Bills of exchange and promissory notes, £
Cash at the bankers, £
Other securities, £

*If the company has no share capital the portion of the statement relating to capital and shares must be omitted.

SCHEDULE 24

(Section 730 and as amended by CA 1989, ss 63, 64, 119, 120, 122, 123, 139, 10 Sch 24, 16 Sch 2, 10 Sch 24, 24 Sch and 1A 1986, s 438, 12 Sch, FSA 1986, s 212(2) and 16 Sch 27)

PUNISHMENT OF OFFENCES UNDER THIS ACT

Note: In the fourth and fifth columns of this Schedule, "the statutory maximum" means—
(a) in England and Wales, the prescribed sum under section 32 of the Magistrates' Courts Act 1980 (c. 43), and
(b) in Scotland, the prescribed sum under section 289B of the Criminal Procedure (Scotland) Act 1975 (c. 21).

Section of Act creating offence	General nature of offence	Mode of prosecution	Punishment	Daily default fine (where applicable)
6(3)	Company failing to deliver to registrar notice or other document, following alteration of its objects.	Summary.	One-fifth of the statutory maximum.	One-fiftieth of the statutory maximum.
18(3)	Company failing to register change in memorandum or articles.	Summary.	One-fifth of the statutory maximum.	One-fiftieth of the statutory maximum.
19(2)	Company failing to send to one of its members a copy of the memorandum or articles, when so required by the member.	Summary.	One-fifth of the statutory maximum.	
20(2)	Where company's memorandum altered, company issuing copy of the memorandum without the alteration.	Summary.	One-fifth of the statutory maximum for each occasion on which copies are so issued after the date of the alteration.	
28(5)	Company failing to change name on direction of Secretary of State.	Summary.	One-fifth of the statutory maximum.	One-fiftieth of the statutory maximum.
31(5)	Company altering its memorandum or articles, so ceasing to be exempt from having "limited" as part of its name.	Summary.	The statutory maximum.	One-tenth of the statutory maximum.
31(6)	Company failing to change name, on Secretary of State's direction, so as to have "limited" (or Welsh equivalent) at the end.	Summary.	One-fifth of the statutory maximum.	One-fiftieth of the statutory maximum.

32(4)	Company failing to comply with Secretary of State's direction to change its name, on grounds that the name is misleading.	Summary.	One-fifth of the statutory maximum.	One-fiftieth of the statutory maximum.
33	Trading under misleading name (use of "public limited company" or Welsh equivalent when not so entitled); purporting to be a private company.	Summary.	One-fifth of the statutory maximum.	One-fiftieth of the statutory maximum.
34	Trading or carrying on business with improper use of "limited" or "cyfyngedig".	Summary.	One-fifth of the statutory maximum.	One-fiftieth of the statutory maximum.
54(10)	Public company failing to give notice, or copy of court order, to registrar, concerning application to re-register as private company.	Summary.	One-fifth of the statutory maximum.	One-fiftieth of the statutory maximum.
56(4)	Issuing form of application for shares or debentures without accompanying prospectus.	1. On indictment. 2. Summary.	A fine. The statutory maximum.	
61	Issuing prospectus with expert's statement in it, he not having given his consent; omission to state in prospectus that expert has consented.	1. On indictment. 2. Summary.	A fine. The statutory maximum.	
64(5)	Issuing company prospectus without copy being delivered to registrar of companies, or without requisite documents endorsed or attached.	Summary.	One-fifth of the statutory maximum.	One-fiftieth of the statutory maximum.
70(1)	Authorising issue of prospectus with untrue statement.	1. On indictment. 2. Summary.	2 years or a fine; or both. 6 months or the statutory maximum; or both.	
78(1)	Being responsible for issue, circulation of prospectus, etc. contrary to Part III, Chapter II (oversea companies).	1. On indictment. 2. Summary.	A fine. The statutory maximum.	
80(9)	Directors exercising company's power of allotment without the authority required by section 80(1).	1. On indictment. 2. Summary.	A fine. The statutory maximum.	

81(2)	Private limited company offering shares to the public, or allotting shares with a view to their being so offered.	1. On indictment. 2. Summary.	A fine. The statutory maximum.	
82(5)	Allotting shares or debentures before third day after issue of prospectus.	1. On indictment. 2. Summary.	A fine. The statutory maximum.	
86(6)	Company failing to keep money in separate bank account, where received in pursuance of prospectus stating that stock exchange listing is to be applied for.	1. On indictment. 2. Summary.	A fine. The statutory maximum.	
87(4)	Offeror of shares for sale failing to keep proceeds in separate bank account.	1. On indictment. 2. Summary.	A fine. The statutory maximum.	
88(5)	Officer of company failing to deliver return of allotments, etc., to registrar.	1. On indictment. 2. Summary.	A fine. The statutory maximum.	One-tenth of the statutory maximum.
95(6)	Knowingly or recklessly authorising or permitting misleading, false or deceptive material in statement by directors under section 95(5).	1. On indictment. 2. Summary.	2 years or a fine; or both. 6 months or the statutory maximum; or both.	
97(4)	Company failing to deliver to registrar the prescribed form disclosing amount or rate of share commission.	Summary.	One-fifth of the statutory maximum.	
110(2)	Making misleading, false or deceptive statement in connection with valuation under section 103 or 104.	1. On indictment. 2. Summary.	2 years or a fine; or both. 6 months or the statutory maximum; or both.	
111(3)	Officer of company failing to deliver copy of asset valuation report to registrar.	1. On indictment. 2. Summary.	A fine. The statutory maximum.	One-tenth of the statutory maximum.
111(4)	Company failing to deliver to registrar copy of resolution under section 104(4), with respect to transfer of an asset as consideration for allotment.	Summary.	One-fifth of the statutory maximum.	One-fiftieth of the statutory maximum.
114	Contravention of any of the provisions of sections 99 to 104, 106.	1. On indictment. 2. Summary.	A fine. The statutory maximum.	

117(7)	Company doing business or exercising borrowing powers contrary to section 117.	1. On indictment. 2. Summary.	A fine. The statutory maximum.	
122(2)	Company failing to give notice to registrar of re-organisation of share capital.	Summary.	One-fifth of the statutory maximum.	One-fiftieth of the statutory maximum.
123(4)	Company failing to give notice to registrar of increase of share capital.	Summary.	One-fifth of the statutory maximum.	One-fiftieth of the statutory maximum.
127(5)	Company failing to forward to registrar copy of court order, when application made to cancel resolution varying shareholders' rights.	Summary.	One-fifth of the statutory maximum.	One-fiftieth of the statutory maximum.
128(5)	Company failing to send to registrar statement or notice required by section 128 (particulars of shares carrying special rights).	Summary.	One-fifth of the statutory maximum.	One-fiftieth of the statutory maximum.
129(4)	Company failing to deliver to registrar statement or notice required by section 129 (registration of newly created class rights).	Summary.	One-fifth of the statutory maximum.	One-fiftieth of the statutory maximum.
141	Officer of company concealing name of creditor entitled to object to reduction of capital, or wilfully misrepresenting nature or amount of debt or claim, etc.	1. On indictment. 2. Summary.	A fine. The statutory maximum.	
142(2)	Director authorising or permitting non-compliance with section 142 (requirement to convene company meeting to consider serious loss of capital).	1. On indictment. 2. Summary.	A fine. The statutory maximum.	
143(2)	Company acquiring its own shares in breach of section 143.	1. On indictment.	In the case of the company, a fine. In the case of an officer of the company who is in default, 2 years or a fine; or both.	
		2. Summary.	In the case of the company, the statutory maximum.	

			In the case of an officer of the company who is in default, 6 months or the statutory maximum; or both.	
149(2)	Company failing to cancel its own shares, acquired by itself, as required by section 146(2); or failing to apply for re-registration as private company as so required in the case there mentioned.	Summary.	One-fifth of the statutory maximum.	One-fiftieth of the statutory maximum.
151(3)	Company giving financial assistance towards acquisition of its own shares.	1. On indictment.	Where the company is convicted, a fine. Where an officer of the company is convicted, 2 years or a fine; or both.	
		2. Summary.	Where the company is convicted, the statutory maximum. Where an officer of the company is convicted, 6 months or the statutory maximum; or both.	
156(6)	Company failing to register statutory declaration under section 155.	Summary.	The statutory maximum.	One-fiftieth of the statutory maximum.
156(7)	Director making statutory declaration under section 155, without having reasonable grounds for opinion expressed in it.	1. On indictment. 2. Summary.	2 years or a fine; or both. 6 months or the statutory maximum; or both.	
169(6)	Default by company's officer in delivering to registrar the return required by section 169 (disclosure by company of purchase of own shares).	1. On indictment. 2. Summary.	A fine. The statutory maximum.	One-tenth of the statutory maximum.
169(7)	Company failing to keep copy of contract, etc., at registered office; refusal of inspection to person demanding it.	Summary.	One-fifth of the statutory maximum.	One-fiftieth of the statutory maximum.

173(6)	Director making statutory declaration under section 173 without having reasonable grounds for the opinion expressed in the declaration.	1. On indictment. 2. Summary.	2 years or a fine; or both. 6 months or the statutory maximum; or both.	
175(7)	Refusal of inspection of statutory declaration and auditors' report under section 173, etc.	Summary.	One-fifth of the statutory maximum.	One-fiftieth of the statutory maximum.
176(4)	Company failing to give notice to registrar of application to court under section 176, or to register court order.	Summary.	One-fifth of the statutory maximum.	One-fiftieth of the statutory maximum.
183(6)	Company failing to send notice of refusal to register a transfer of shares or debentures.	Summary.	One-fifth of the statutory maximum.	One-fiftieth of the statutory maximum.
185(5)	Company default in compliance with section 185(1) (certificates to be made ready following allotment or transfer of shares, etc.).	Summary.	One-fifth of the statutory maximum.	One-fiftieth of the statutory maximum.
189(1)	Offences of fraud and forgery in connection with share warrants in Scotland.	1. On indictment. 2. Summary.	7 years or a fine; or both. 6 months or the statutory maximum; or both.	
189(2)	Unauthorised making of, or using or possessing apparatus for making, share warrants in Scotland.	1. On indictment. 2. Summary.	7 years or a fine; or both. 6 months or the statutory maximum; or both.	
191(4)	Refusal of inspection or copy of register of debenture-holders, etc.	Summary.	One-fifth of the statutory maximum.	One-fiftieth of the statutory maximum.
210(3)	Failure to discharge obligation of disclosure under Part VI; other forms of non-compliance with that Part.	1. On indictment. 2. Summary.	2 years or a fine; or both. 6 months or the statutory maximum; or both.	
211(10)	Company failing to keep register of interests disclosed under Part VI; other contraventions of section 211.	Summary.	One-fifth of the statutory maximum.	One-fiftieth of the statutory maximum.
214(5)	Company failing to exercise powers under section 212, when so required by the members.	1. On indictment. 2. Summary.	A fine. The statutory maximum.	

215(8)	Company default in compliance with section 215 (company report of investigation of shareholdings on members' requisition).	1. On indictment. 2. Summary.	A fine. The statutory maximum.	
216(3)	Failure to comply with company notice under section 212; making false statement in response, etc.	1. On indictment. 2. Summary.	2 years or a fine; or both. 6 months or the statutory maximum; or both.	
217(7)	Company failing to notify a person that he has been named as a shareholder; on removal of name from register, failing to alter associated index.	Summary.	One-fifth of the statutory maximum.	One-fiftieth of the statutory maximum.
218(3)	Improper removal of entry from register of interests disclosed; company failing to restore entry improperly removed.	Summary.	One-fifth of the statutory maximum.	For continued contravention of section 218(2) one-fiftieth of the statutory maximum.
219(3)	Refusal of inspection of register or report under Part VI; failure to send copy when required.	Summary.	One-fifth of the statutory maximum.	One-fiftieth of the statutory maximum.
[221(5) or 222(4)][12]	Company failing to keep accounting records (liability of officers).	1. On indictment. 2. Summary.	2 years or a fine; or both. 6 months or the statutory maximum; or both.	
[222(6)][12]	Officer of company failing to secure compliance with, or intentionally causing default under, section [222(5)][12] (preservation of accounting records for requisite number of years).	1. On indictment. 2. Summary.	2 years or a fine; or both. 6 months or the statutory maximum; or both.	
[231(6)][12]	Company failing to annex to its annual return certain particulars required by Schedule 5 and not included in annual accounts.	Summary.	One-fifth of the statutory maximum.	One-fiftieth of the statutory maximum.
[232(4)][12]	Default by director or officer of a company in giving notice of matters relating to himself for purposes of [Schedule 6, Part I][13].	Summary.	One-fifth of the statutory maximum.	
[233(5)	Approving defective accounts.	1. On indictment. 2. Summary.	A fine. The statutory maximum.][18]	

[233(6)][12]	Laying or delivery of unsigned balance sheet; circulating copies of balance sheet without signatures.	Summary.	One-fifth of the statutory maximum.	
[234(5)][12]	Non-compliance with [Part VII][14], as to directors' report and its content; directors individually liable.	1. On indictment. 2. Summary.	A fine. The statutory maximum.	
[234A(4)	Laying, circulating or delivering directors' report without required signature.	Summary.	One-fifth of the statutory maximum.][18]	
[236(4)	Laying, circulating or delivering auditors' report without required signature.	Summary.	One-fifth of the statutory maximum.][18]	
[238(5)][12]	Failing to send [company's annual accounts][15], directors' report and auditors' report to those entitled to receive them.	1. On indictment. 2. Summary.	A fine. The statutory maximum.	
[. . .][19]				
[239(3)][12]	Company failing to supply copy of accounts [and reports][18] to shareholder on his demand.	Summary.	One-fifth of the statutory maximum.	One-fiftieth of the statutory maximum.
[240(6)][12]	[Failure to comply with requirements in connection with publication of accounts][17].	Summary.	One-fifth of the statutory maximum.	
[241(2) or 242(2)][12]	Director in default as regards duty to lay and deliver [company's annual accounts, directors' report and auditors' report][16].	Summary.	The statutory maximum.	One-tenth of the statutory maximum.
[. . .][19]				
[251(6)	Failure to comply with requirements in relation to summary financial statements.	Summary.	One-fifth of the statutory maximum.][18]	
[. . .][23]				
288(4)	Default in complying with section 288 (keeping register of directors and secretaries, refusal of inspection).	Summary.	The statutory maximum.	One-tenth of the statutory maximum.

291(5)	Acting as director of a company without having the requisite share qualification.	Summary.	One-fifth of the statutory maximum.	One-fiftieth of the statutory maximum.
294(3)	Director failing to give notice of his attaining retirement age; acting as director under appointment invalid due to his attaining it.	Summary.	One-fifth of the statutory maximum.	One-fiftieth of the statutory maximum.
[. . .][2]				
305(3)	Company default in complying with section 305 (directors' names to appear on company correspondence, etc.).	Summary.	One-fifth of the statutory maximum.	
306(4)	Failure to state that liability of proposed director or manager is unlimited; failure to give notice of that fact to person accepting office.	1. On indictment. 2. Summary.	A fine. The statutory maximum.	
314(3)	Director failing to comply with section 314 (duty to disclose compensation payable on takeover, etc.); a person's failure to include required particulars in a notice he has to give of such matters.	Summary.	One-fifth of the statutory maximum.	
317(7)	Director failing to disclose interest in contract.	1. On indictment. 2. Summary.	A fine. The statutory maximum.	
318(8)	Company default in complying with section 318(1) or (5) (directors' service contracts to be open to inspection); 14 days' default in complying with section 318(4) (notice to registrar as to where copies of contracts and memoranda are kept); refusal of inspection required under section 318(7).	Summary.	One-fifth of the statutory maximum.	One-fiftieth of the statutory maximum.
323(2)	Director dealing in options to buy or sell company's listed shares or debentures.	1. On indictment. 2. Summary.	2 years or a fine; or both. 6 months or the statutory maximum; or both.	

324(7)	Director failing to notify interest in company's shares; making false statement in purported notification.	1. On indictment. 2. Summary.	2 years or a fine; or both. 6 months or the statutory maximum; or both.	
326(2), (3), (4), (5)	Various defaults in connection with company register of directors' interests.	Summary.	One-fifth of the statutory maximum.	Except in the case of section 326(5), one-fiftieth of the statutory maximum.
328(6)	Director failing to notify company that members of his family have, or have exercised, options to buy shares or debentures; making false statement in purported notification.	1. On indictment. 2. Summary.	2 years or a fine; or both. 6 months or the statutory maximum; or both.	
329(3)	Company failing to notify [investment exchange][3] of acquisition of its securities by a director.	Summary.	One-fifth of the statutory maximum.	One-fiftieth of the statutory maximum.
342(1)	Director of relevant company authorising or permitting company to enter into transaction or arrangement, knowing or suspecting it to contravene section 330.	1. On indictment. 2. Summary.	2 years or a fine; or both. 6 months or the statutory maximum; or both.	
342(2)	Relevant company entering into transaction or arrangement for a director in contravention of section 330.	1. On indictment. 2. Summary.	2 years or a fine; or both. 6 months or the statutory maximum; or both.	
342(3)	Procuring a relevant company to enter into transaction or arrangement known to be contrary to section 330.	1. On indictment. 2. Summary.	2 years or a fine; or both. 6 months or the statutory maximum; or both.	
343(8)	Company failing to maintain register of transactions, etc., made with and for directors and not disclosed in company accounts; failing to make register available at registered office or at company meeting.	1. On indictment. 2. Summary.	A fine. The statutory maximum.	
348(2)	Company failing to paint or affix name; failing to keep it painted or affixed.	Summary.	One-fifth of the statutory maximum.	In the case of failure to keep the name painted or affixed, one-fiftieth of the statutory maximum.

349(2)	Company failing to have name on business correspondence, invoices, etc.	Summary.	One-fifth of the statutory maximum.	
349(3)	Officer of company issuing business letter or document not bearing company's name.	Summary.	One-fifth of the statutory maximum.	
349(4)	Officer of company signing cheque, bill of exchange, etc. on which company's name not mentioned.	Summary.	One-fifth of the statutory maximum.	
350(1)	Company failing to have its name engraved on company seal.	Summary.	One-fifth of the statutory maximum.	
350(2)	Officer of company, etc., using company seal without name engraved on it.	Summary.	One-fifth of the statutory maximum.	
351(5)(a)	Company failing to comply with section 351(1) or (2) (matters to be stated on business correspondence, etc.).	Summary.	One-fifth of the statutory maximum.	
351(5)(b)	Officer or agent of company issuing, or authorising issue of, business document not complying with those subsections.	Summary.	One-fifth of the statutory maximum.	
351(5)(c)	Contravention of section 351(3) or (4) (information in English to be stated on Welsh company's business correspondence, etc.).	Summary.	One-fifth of the statutory maximum.	For contravention of section 351(3), one-fiftieth of the statutory maximum.
352(5)	Company default in complying with section 352 (requirement to keep register of members and their particulars).	Summary.	One-fifth of the statutory maximum.	One-fiftieth of the statutory maximum.
353(4)	Company failing to send notice to registrar as to place where register of members is kept.	Summary.	One-fifth of the statutory maximum.	One-fiftieth of the statutory maximum.
354(4)	Company failing to keep index of members.	Summary.	One-fifth of the statutory maximum.	One-fiftieth of the statutory maximum.
356(5)	Refusal of inspection of members' register; failure to send copy on requisition.	Summary.	One-fifth of the statutory maximum.	
[363(3)][11]	Company with share capital failing to make annual return.	Summary.	The statutory maximum.	One-tenth of the statutory maximum.

364(4)	Company without share capital failing to complete and register annual return in due time.	Summary.	The statutory maximum.	One-tenth of the statutory maximum.
[. . .][25]				
366(4)	Company default in holding annual general meeting.	1. On indictment. 2. Summary.	A fine. The statutory maximum.	
367(3)	Company default in complying with Secretary of State's direction to hold company meeting.	1. On indictment. 2. Summary.	A fine. The statutory maximum.	
367(5)	Company failing to register resolution that meeting held under section 367 is to be its annual general meeting.	Summary.	One-fifth of the statutory maximum.	One-fiftieth of the statutory maximum.
372(4)	Failure to give notice, to member entitled to vote at company meeting, that he may do so by proxy.	Summary.	One-fifth of the statutory maximum.	
372(6)	Officer of company authorising or permitting issue of irregular invitations to appoint proxies.	Summary.	One-fifth of the statutory maximum.	
376(7)	Officer of company in default as to circulation of members' resolutions for company meeting.	1. On indictment. 2. Summary.	A fine. The statutory maximum.	
380(5)	Company failing to comply with section 380 (copies of certain resolutions etc. to be sent to registrar of companies).	Summary.	One-fifth of the statutory maximum.	One-fiftieth of the statutory maximum.
380(6)	Company failing to include copy of resolution to which section 380 applies in articles; failing to forward copy to member on request.	Summary.	One-fifth of the statutory maximum for each occasion on which copies are issued or, as the case may be, requested.	
382(5)	Company failing to keep minutes of proceedings at company and board meetings, etc.	Summary.	One-fifth of the statutory maximum.	One-fiftieth of the statutory maximum.
383(4)	Refusal of inspection of minutes of general meeting; failure to send copy of minutes on member's request.	Summary.	One-fifth of the statutory maximum.	

[. . .][23]				
[. . .][26]				
[387(2)	Company failing to give Secretary of State notice of non-appointment of auditors.	Summary.	One-fifth of the statutory maximum.	One-fiftieth of the statutory maximum.][8]
[. . .][23]				
[389A(2)	Officer of company making false, misleading or deceptive statement to auditors.	1. On indictment. 2. Summary.	2 years or a fine; or both. 6 months or the statutory maximum; or both.	
389A(3)	Subsidiary undertaking or its auditor failing to give information to auditors of parent company.	Summary.	One-fifth of the statutory maximum.	
389A(4)	Parent company failing to obtain from subsidiary undertaking information for purposes of audit.	Summary.	One-fifth of the statutory maximum.][24]	
[391(2)	Failing to give notice to registrar of removal of auditor.	Summary.	One-fifth of the statutory maximum.	One-fiftieth of the statutory maximum.][9]
[. . .][23]				
[392(3)	Company failing to forward notice of auditor's resignation to registrar.	1. On indictment. 2. Summary.	A fine. The statutory maximum.	One-tenth of the statutory maximum.
392A(5)	Directors failing to convene meeting requisitioned by resigning auditor.	1. On indictment. 2. Summary.	A fine. The statutory maximum.][9]	
[. . .][23]				
[394A(1)	Person ceasing to hold office as auditor failing to deposit statement as to circumstances.	1. On indictment. 2. Summary.	A fine. The statutory maximum.	
394A(4)	Company failing to comply with requirements as to statement of person ceasing to hold office as auditor.	1. On indictment. 2. Summary.	A fine. The statutory maximum.	One-tenth of the statutory maximum.][10]
[398(3)	Company failing to deliver particulars of charge to registrar.	1. On indictment. 2. Summary.	A fine. The statutory maximum.][20]	
[408(3)	Company failing to deliver particulars of taking up of issue of debentures.	Summary.	One-fifth of the statutory maximum.][20]	

[409(4)	Failure to give notice to registrar of appointment of receiver or manager, or of his ceasing to act.	Summary.	One-fifth of the statutory maximum.][20]	
[410(4)	Failure to comply with requirements of regulations under s.410.	Summary.	One-fifth of the statutory maximum.][20]	
[411(4)	Failure to keep copies of charging instruments or register at registered office.	1. On indictment. 2. Summary.	A fine. The statutory maximum.][20]	
[412(4)	Refusing inspection of charging instrument or register or failing to supply copies.	Summary.	One-fifth of the statutory maximum.][20]	
423(3)	Officer of Scottish company refusing inspection of charging instrument, or of register of charges.	Summary.	One-fifth of the statutory maximum.	One-fiftieth of the statutory maximum.
425(4)	Company failing to annex to memorandum court order sanctioning compromise or arrangement with creditors.	Summary.	One-fifth of the statutory maximum.	
426(6)	Company failing to comply with requirements of section 426 (information to members and creditors about compromise or arrangement.)	1. On indictment. 2. Summary.	A fine. The statutory maximum.	
426(7)	Director or trustee for debenture holders failing to give notice to company of matters necessary for purposes of section 426.	Summary.	One-fifth of the statutory maximum.	
427(5)	Failure to deliver to registrar office copy of court order under section 427 (company reconstruction or amalgamation).	Summary.	One-fifth of the statutory maximum.	One-fiftieth of the statutory maximum.
[429(6)	Offeror failing to send copy of notice or making statutory declaration knowing it to be false, etc.	1. On indictment. 2. Summary.	2 years or a fine; or both. 6 months or the statutory maximum; or both.	 One-fiftieth of the statutory maximum.
430A(6)	Offeror failing to give notice of rights to minority shareholder.	1. On indictment. 2. Summary.	A fine. The statutory maximum.	 One-fiftieth of the statutory maximum][4].

444(3)	Failing to give Secretary of State, when required to do so, information about interests in shares, etc.; giving false information.	1. On indictment. 2. Summary.	2 years or a fine; or both. 6 months or the statutory maximum; or both.	
447(6)	Failure to comply with requirement to produce [documents][5] imposed by Secretary of State under section 447.	1. On indictment. 2. Summary.	A fine. The statutory maximum.	
[448(7)][6]	[Obstructing the exercise of any right conferred by a warrant or failing to comply with a requirement imposed under subsection (3)(d).][7]	1. On indictment. 2. Summary.	A fine. The statutory maximum.	
449(2)	Wrongful disclosure of information or document obtained under section 447 or 448.	1. On indictment. 2. Summary.	2 years or a fine; or both. 6 months or the statutory maximum; or both.	
450	Destroying or mutilating company documents; falsifying such documents or making false entries; parting with such documents or altering them or making omissions.	1. On indictment. 2. Summary.	7 years or a fine; or both. 6 months or the statutory maximum; or both.	
451	Making false statement or explanation in purported compliance with section 447.	1. On indictment. 2. Summary.	2 years or a fine; or both. 6 months or the statutory maximum; or both.	
455(1)	Exercising a right to dispose of, or vote in respect of, shares which are subject to restrictions under Part XV; failing to give notice in respect of shares so subject; entering into agreement void under section 454(2), (3).	1. On indictment. 2. Summary.	A fine. The statutory maximum.	
455(2)	Issuing shares in contravention of restrictions of Part XV.	1. On indictment. 2. Summary.	A fine. The statutory maximum.	
458	Being a party to carrying on company's business with intent to defraud creditors, or for any fraudulent purpose.	1. On indictment. 2. Summary.	7 years or a fine; or both. 6 months or the statutory maximum; or both.	

461(5)	Failure to register office copy of court order under Part XVII altering, or giving leave to alter, company's memorandum.	Summary.	One-fifth of the statutory maximum.	One-fiftieth of the statutory maximum.
[. . .][1]				
651(3)	Person obtaining court order to declare company's dissolution void, then failing to register the order.	Summary.	One-fifth of the statutory maximum.	One-fiftieth of the statutory maximum.
697(1)	Oversea company failing to comply with any of sections 691 to 693 or 696.	Summary.	For an offence which is not a continuing offence, one-fifth of the statutory maximum. For an offence which is a continuing offence, one-fifth of the statutory maximum.	One-fiftieth of the statutory maximum.
697(2)	Oversea company contravening section 694(6) (carrying on business under its corporate name after Secretary of State's direction).	1. On indictment. 2. Summary.	A fine. The statutory maximum.	 One-tenth of the statutory maximum
703(1)	Oversea company failing to comply with [requirements as to accounts and reports][22].	1. On indictment. 2. Summary.	A fine. The statutory maximum.	 One-tenth of the statutory maximum.
[703D(5)	Oversea company failing to deliver particulars of charge to registrar.	1. On indictment. 2. Summary.	A fine. The statutory maximum.][21]	
[. . .][1]				
720(4)	Insurance company etc. failing to send twice-yearly statement in form of Schedule 23.	Summary.	One-fifth of the statutory maximum.	One-fiftieth of the statutory maximum.
722(3)	Company failing to comply with section 722(2), as regards the manner of keeping registers, minute books and accounting records.	Summary.	One-fifth of the statutory maximum.	One-fiftieth of the statutory maximum.

Sch. 14, Pt. II, para. 1(3)	Company failing to give notice of location of overseas branch register, etc.	Summary.	One-fifth of the statutory maximum.	One-fiftieth of the statutory maximum.
Sch. 14, Pt. II, para. 4(2)	Company failing to transmit to its registered office in Great Britain copies of entries in overseas branch register, or to keep a duplicate of overseas branch register.	Summary.	One-fifth of the statutory maximum.	One-fiftieth of the statutory maximum.

[1] Repealed by IA 1986, s 438, 12 Sch with effect from 29 December 1986 (see IA 1986, s 443 and SI 1986 No 1924).

[2] Repealed by CDDA 1986, s 23(2), 4 Sch with effect from 29 December 1986 (see CDDA 1986, s 25; IA 1986, s 443 and SI 1986 No 1924).

[3] Substituted by FSA 1986, s 212(2), 16 Sch 27 with effect from 29 April 1988 (see SI 1988 No 740).

[4] Inserted by FSA 1986, s 212(2), 16 Sch 27 with effect from 4 June 1987 (see SI 1987 No 907).

[5] Substituted by CA 1989, s 63 with effect from 21 February 1990 (SI 1990 No 142).

[6] Substituted by CA 1989, s 64 with effect from 21 February 1990 (SI 1990 No 142).

[7] Substituted by CA 1989, s 64 with effect from 21 February 1990 (SI 1990 No 142).

[8] Inserted by CA 1989, s 119 with effect from 1 April 1990 (SI 1990 No 355) subject to the transitional and savings provisions in Schedule 4 of that Order reproduced in the notes to CA 1989, s 118.

[9] Inserted by CA 1989, s 122 with effect as in [8] above.

[10] Inserted by CA 1989, s 123 with effect as in [8] above.

[11] Substituted by CA 1989, s 139 with effect from a date to be appointed.

[12] Substituted by CA 1989, 10 Sch 24 with effect from 1 April 1990 (SI 1990 No 355) subject to the transitional and saving provisions in Acts 6 to 9 of that Order reproduced above s 221 above.

[13] Substituted by CA 1989, 10 Sch 24 with effect as in [12] above.

[14] Substituted by CA 1989, 10 Sch 24 with effect as in [12] above.

[15] Substituted by CA 1989, 10 Sch 24 with effect as in [12] above.

[16] Substituted by CA 1989, 10 Sch 24 with effect as in [12] above.

[17] Substituted by CA 1989, 10 Sch 24 with effect as in [12] above.

[18] Inserted by CA 1989, 10 Sch 24 with effect as in [12] above.

[19] Deleted by CA 1989, 10 Sch 24 with effect from a date to be appointed.

[20] Substituted by CA 1989, 16 Sch 2 with effect from a date to be appointed.

[21] Inserted by CA 1989, 16 Sch 2 with effect from a date to be appointed.

[22] Substituted by CA 1989, 10 Sch 24 with effect as in [12] above.

[23] Repealed by CA 1989, 24 Sch with effect as in [12] above.

[24] Inserted by CA 1989, s 120 with effect as in [8] above.

[25] Repealed by CA 1989, 24 Sch with effect from a date to be appointed.

[26] Repealed by CA 1989, 24 Sch with effect from a date to be appointed.

Notes

(a) The entries in CA 1985, 24 Sch relating to ss 56(4), 61, 64(5), 70(1), 78(1), 81(2), 82(5), 86(6), 87(4) and 97(4) are repealed by FSA 1986, s 212(3), 17 Sch Part I from a date or dates to be appointed by statutory instrument (see FSA 1986, s 211(1)).
To date the entries have been repealed as follows.
- (i) To the extent to which they would apply in relation to any investment which is listed or the subject of an application for listing in accordance with FSA 1986, Part IV (official listing of securities)
  - (A) with effect from 12 January 1987 for all purposes relating to the admission of securities offered by or on behalf of a Minister of the Crown or a body corporate controlled by a Minister of the Crown or a subsidiary of such a body to the Official List in respect of which an application is made after that date; and
  - (B) with effect from 16 February 1987 for purposes relating to the admission of securities in respect of which an application is made after that date other than those referred to in (A) above and otherwise for all purposes.

  [SI 1986 No 2246].
- (ii) With effect from 29 April 1988 in respect of a prospectus offering for subscription, or to any form of application for, units in a body corporate which is a recognised scheme. [SI 1988 No 740].

TABLE OF LEGISLATION AND OF OTHER REGULATIONS

STATUTORY INSTRUMENTS

EC LEGISLATION

ACCOUNTING STANDARDS

ACCOUNTING RECOMMENDATIONS

AUDITING GUIDELINES

ICAEW MEMBERS HANDBOOK

LAW SOCIETY RULES

ACCOUNTANT'S REPORT AMENDMENT RULES 1988

ACCOUNTANT'S REPORT RULES 1986

SOLICITORS' ACCOUNTS (DEPOSIT INTEREST) RULES 1988

SOLICITORS' ACCOUNTS RULES 1986

SOLICITORS' INVESTMENT BUSINESS RULES 1990

SOLICITORS' TRUST ACCOUNT RULES 1986

SIB RULES

FINANCIAL SERVICES (CLIENTS' MONEY) REGULATIONS 1987

FINANCIAL SERVICES (CONDUCT OF BUSINESS) RULES 1987

TABLE OF CASES

TABLE OF COMPANIES/ENTITIES

References are to paragraph numbers of this book where extracts from the financial statements of these companies/entities are reproduced.

INDEX

References are to paragraph numbers of this book

Index

Age - Aud

B

Index

Ban - Ban

Index

U

V

W